"This is the American history that Abraham Lincoln has long awaited."

— **Harry V. Jaffa**
author, *Crisis of the House Divided*

"[A] worthy and necessary book for our time."

— **Michael J. Lewis**
Commentary

"For too long Americans have been looking for a history of our country that tells the story of America's triumphs as well as its tragedies. Now Bill Bennett has come forward with *America: The Last Best Hope*, which tells the story—fairly and fully—from 1492 to 1914. Americans who have been reading recent biographies of the Founding Fathers will love this book."

— **Michael Barone**
US News & World Report

"The role of history is to inform, inspire, and sometimes provoke us, which is why Bill Bennett's wonderfully readable book is so important. He puts our nation's triumphs, along with its lapses, into the context of a narrative about the progress of freedom."

— **Walter Isaacson**
author, *Benjamin Franklin: An American Life*

"Bennett . . . has a strong sense of narrative, a flair for anecdote and a lively style. And the American story really is a remarkable one, filled with its share of brilliant leaders and tragic mistakes. Bennett brings that story to life."

— **Alan Wolfe**
The Washington Post

"[T]he importance of *America: The Last Best Hope* probably exceeds anything Dr. Bennett has ever written, and it is more elegantly crafted and eminently readable than any comprehensive work of history I've read in a very long time."

— **Brad Miner**
American Compass

"This lively book acknowledges mistakes and shortcomings, yet patriotically asserts that the American experiment in democracy is still a success story."

— *School Library Journal*

"Bennett offers to Americans young and old an exciting and enjoyable history of what makes America the greatest nation on earth."

— **Brian Kennedy**
The Claremont Institute

AMERICA

The Last Best Hope

Volume 1:
From *the* Age *of* Discovery
To *a* World *at* War
1492–1914

William J. Bennett

Thomas Nelson
Since 1798

thomasnelson.com

Published in Nashville, Tennessee, by Thomas Nelson, Inc.

Thomas Nelson, Inc. titles may be purchased in bulk for educational, business, fundraising, or sales promotional use. For information, please e-mail SpecialMarkets@ThomasNelson.com.

All interior images: Getty Images.

Library of Congress Cataloging-in-Publication Data on file with the Library of Congress.

Bennett, William J. (William John), 1943–
America : the last best hope / William J. Bennett.
p. cm.
ISBN-10: 1-59555-055-0 (hardcover)
ISBN-13: 978-1-59555-055-2 (hardcover)
ISBN-10: 1-59555-111-5 (trade paper)
ISBN-13: 978-1-59555-111-5 (trade paper)
1. United States—History. I. Title.
E178.B46 2006
973—dc22 2006006611

Printed in the United States of America

07 08 09 10 11 RRD 5 4 3 2 1

To the American soldier,
whose fidelity, patriotism, and valor
have made this land
the last best hope of earth.

Contents

Acknowledgments

This book has been a labor of love. My love for our country has been deepened and made more intense by this project. I could not have completed this task without the help and encouragement of friends and colleagues.

Bob Morrison, my former colleague at the Department of Education, has been with the project from the beginning. He has been of immense help. His effort has been exemplary and his love of the project has been contagious. With William Faulkner, Bob believes "the past isn't dead—it isn't even past."

Seth Leibsohn, my producer on *Morning in America* and a true friend, has graciously given his time and his thoughts to this book. Seth's wisdom about, and enthusiasm for, this project have been indispensable.

Noreen Burns has been smart about this book as she is about many things.

Steve Ochs is a great teacher. My sons and many others have benefited from his scholarship and his devotion to his students and this nation's past. I am grateful for his selfless contributions to the early chapters of this work.

Vin Cannato read this book and provided many helpful suggestions. A distinguished author and professor in his own right, Vin provided countless insights and helped me fact-check the thousands of facts herein.

Max Schulz and Ken Watson read key portions of this book and provided solid recommendations. I thank each for his friendship and valuable help.

John Cribb had good suggestions. I took them.

Brian Kennedy and the Claremont Institute and Lawrence and Susan Kadish encouraged and supported me and this project. They all think and encourage "big." I thank them.

Bob Barnett as usual counseled, advised, and made the deal that made the book possible.

I thank publisher David Dunham for his warm welcome to Thomas Nelson, Inc. He is accessible and responsive. My editor Joel Miller is painstakingly careful and helpful; I am grateful.

I want to thank my listeners. The callers to my radio talk show have encouraged me mightily by their love for and dedication to this country. They deserve our best efforts.

Finally, Elayne encouraged, read, and offered her always probing commentary and judgment. I am grateful to her and to my sons for their love and support.

Introduction

I wrote this book for many reasons. The first and most important is the need for hope. When President Lincoln wrote to Congress in December 1862, shortly after he issued the preliminary Emancipation Proclamation, he wrote, "We shall nobly save or meanly lose this last best hope of earth." For nearly a century before that message—and easily for a century afterward—Americans would not have doubted that this country was indeed that last best hope. In a speech scheduled for delivery in Dallas on 22 November 1963, President John F. Kennedy's text read, "We in this country are the watchmen on the walls of world freedom." Kennedy's view was Lincoln's before him and Jefferson's before Lincoln. Later it was Reagan's. Democrat, Republican, Federalist, Antifederalist . . . it hardly mattered. An abiding sense of American greatness, of American purpose, of American exceptionalism has long characterized many of our leaders and tens of millions of the rest of us as well. We have long had hope.

I believe America is still that hope, but I also believe that our conviction about American greatness and purpose is not as strong today. Newspaper columns and television reports are full of cynicism. Many express doubts about American motives on the world stage. Some Americans seem ready to believe the worst about our leaders and our country. Thinking and believing the worst certainly is not hopeful. It is my humble wish that those who read this book will find reason to reclaim some of the hope and conviction we have lost.

The second reason I wrote this book is to give Americans an opportunity to enjoy the story of their country, to take pleasure and pride in what we have done and become. Many books about America not only fail to counter cynicism and hopelessness, they don't encourage anything positive in their place. Some do not engage, entertain, educate, or encourage. History textbooks are often the worst in this regard. National tests repeatedly show that many high school (and college) students know little about their country's past. Dull histories drive young people away—away from serious study, away from reading history as adults, away from a reasoned, thoughtful, and heartfelt embrace of their country. Dumbed-down history, civics, and—worst of all—social studies textbooks may be one cause of voter and citizen apathy. An encouraging countertrend is the huge popularity of a few histories and biographies. David McCullough's *1776* and Walter Isaacson's *Benjamin Franklin* come to mind. The success of these books is much deserved: they give pleasure, they educate, and they entertain. But few such books have attempted to tell the *whole* American story. I hope this will be one.

The third reason I wrote this book is to give thanks and to remind my fellow citizens of their obligation of gratitude to those who made it possible for us to lead free and happy lives. To Lincoln and the Founders before him, and to many historical figures afterward, much is due. Obscurity and oblivion are not what they deserve.

Americans can be grateful that time and again, our ancestors and our contemporaries have chosen wisely and have by their demeanors defined us as a people. Over and over again we have shown the almost uniquely American capacity for self-renewal. And over and over again in our story, intelligence and leadership have counted in the nick of time. Think of those Americans at Philadelphia in 1787 who devised the most miraculous political document in history just as the young nation seemed to be falling apart.

Or Americans coming together to rebuild this nation after the long and devastating Civil War.

Or Americans standing fast against totalitarianism during the Cold War.

At the same time, it is regrettable but true that any number of American choices were not wise. For example, we failed to eliminate slavery when this nation was founded. For too long we failed to uphold our stated principles in the face of Jim Crow segregation laws.

We can be grateful that leaders like Frederick Douglass and Dr. Martin Luther King Jr. rose to prod our consciences and to force us to look into the mirror of our own souls, however belatedly. We needed them to help us right those wrongs. It is important to note that when such leaders stepped forward, they acknowledged a debt of gratitude: both Frederick Douglass and Dr. King appealed to the ideals of America's Founding Fathers. They reminded Americans that this country, in order to be true to itself, had to attend to the business of "establishing justice" and respecting the inalienable right to life, liberty, and the pursuit of happiness. To deny some people these universal rights because of the color of their skin, these reformers pointed out, was to deny the essence of what America was to the world. Those who would deny fundamental rights were, as Lincoln said, "blowing out the moral lights around us" and dishonoring our Fathers. We need to remember the Fathers and the lights that showed them the way.

The fourth reason I wrote this book is to tell the truth, get the facts out, correct the record, and put forward a reasoned, balanced presentation of the American story. In this work, I will not try to cover up great wrongs. Injustices need sunlight—always, as Justice Brandeis said, the best disinfectant. I will try to paint America as Oliver Cromwell asked to be painted: warts and all. But I will not follow the fashion of some today who see America as nothing *but* warts.

We must remember that America is still a great success story. When we criticize—as criticize we must—we should play the part of what James Madison called a "loving critic." Former Democratic Senator Daniel Patrick Moynihan put it best: "Am I embarrassed to speak for a less than perfect democracy? Not one bit. Find me a better one. Do I suppose there are societies that are free of sin? No, I don't. Do I think ours is on balance incomparably the most hopeful set of human relations the world has? Yes, I do. Have we done obscene things? Yes, we have. How did our people learn about them? They learned about them on television and in the newspapers."

The fifth reason I wrote this book to encourage a new patriotism—a new reflective, reasoned form of patriotism.

Ronald Reagan was especially proud of the new patriotism he had helped to spark during his two terms. It was something even his opponent Fritz Mondale was gracious enough to praise him for. But Reagan recognized that this spirit would not last unless it was an *informed* patriotism. Interestingly, the Old Man who dreamed dreams—and lived to see those dreams become reality—looked backward in his Farewell Address to the American people. It was something he rarely did:

> [T]here is a great tradition of warnings in Presidential farewells, and I've got one that's been on my mind for some time. But oddly enough it starts with one of the things I'm proudest of in the past 8 years: the resurgence of national pride that I called the new patriotism. This national feeling is good, but it won't count for much and it won't last unless it's grounded in thoughtfulness and knowledge.
>
> An informed patriotism is what we want. And are we doing a good enough job teaching our children what America is and what she represents in the long history of the world? Those of us who are over thirty-five or so years of age grew up in a different America. We were taught, very directly, what it means to be an American. And we absorbed, almost in the air, a love of country and an appreciation of its institutions. If you didn't get these things from your family you got them from the neighborhood, from the father down the street who fought in Korea or the family who lost someone at Anzio. Or you could get a sense of patriotism from school. And if all else failed you could get a sense of patriotism from the popular culture. The movies celebrated democratic values and implicitly reinforced the idea that America was special. TV was like that, too, through the mid-sixties.
>
> But now, we're about to enter the nineties, and some things have changed. Younger parents aren't sure that an unambivalent appreciation of America is the right thing to teach modern children. And as for those who create the popular culture, well-grounded patriotism is no longer the style. Our spirit is back, but we haven't reinstitutionalized it. We've got to do a better job of getting across that America is freedom—

> freedom of speech, freedom of religion, freedom of enterprise. And freedom is special and rare. It's fragile; it needs [protection].
>
> So we've got to teach history based not on what's in fashion but what's important—why the Pilgrims came here, who Jimmy Doolittle was, and what those thirty seconds over Tokyo meant. You know, four years ago on the fortieth anniversary of D-Day, I read a letter from a young woman writing to her late father, who'd fought on Omaha Beach. Her name was Lisa Zanatta Henn, and she said, "We will always remember, we will never forget what the boys of Normandy did." Well, let's help her keep her word.
>
> If we forget what we did, we won't know who we are. I'm warning of an eradication of the American memory that could result, ultimately, in an erosion of the American spirit. Let's start with some basics: more attention to American history and a greater emphasis on civic ritual.

Finally, I write this story to kindle romance, to encourage Americans to fall in love with this country, again or for the first time. Not unreflectively, not blindly, but with eyes wide open.

The great writer, adventurer, and map enthusiast Bernard DeVoto once had good reason to write to his friend Catherine Drinker Bowen, the wonderful historian whose works *Miracle at Philadelphia* and *Yankee from Olympus* made history come to life to a wide audience. She was losing heart, getting discouraged in her history writing craft. Were her stories of America important? Was her celebration of her country and its achievements right? Where was the romance? DeVoto wrote this to her:

> If the mad, impossible voyage of Columbus or Cartier or La Salle or Coronado or John Ledyard is not romantic, if the stars did not dance in the sky when our Constitutional Convention met, if Atlantis has any landscape stranger or the other side of the moon any lights or colors or shapes more unearthly than the customary homespun of Lincoln and the morning coat of Jackson, well, I don't know what romance is. Ours is a story mad with the impossible, it is by chaos out

> of dream, it began as dream and it has continued as dream down to the last headlines you read in a newspaper. . . . The simplest truth you can ever write about our history will be charged and surcharged with romanticism.

The dream of which DeVoto writes is, of course, the American dream, and as he reminds us, despite obstacles, setbacks, stupidities, and atrocities, there is an unparalleled and *documented* record of this dream's being real. America was, is, and—we pray—will continue to be the place where more than anyplace else, dreams actually do come true.

One

Westward the Course
(1492–1607)

America comes into view slowly for Europeans, just beyond the western horizon. Led by Christopher Columbus, a series of brave and ruthless explorers race to make new discoveries and lay claim to vast regions. Spain seeks empire, as does Portugal. Having freed the Iberian Peninsula from seven hundred years of Muslim rule, they nonetheless retain a dread practice of the Moors—human slavery. France and England come later, settling respectively in Canada and along the Atlantic seaboard. These latecomers, the English, challenge Spain's far-flung empire, eventually seizing control of the seas from their former Iberian masters. Despite fears of the unknown—disease, privations, wild animals, and sometimes hostile natives—the Europeans are irresistibly drawn to the possibilities of new life in the New World.

I. Columbus: "The Christ Bearer"

Bartholomeu Dias's two sailing ships limped back into Lisbon harbor in December 1488, bringing startling news: he had succeeded in rounding the Cape of Good Hope at the southern tip of Africa. The sea route to the riches of India and the Spice Islands of Asia lay open to the seafaring Portuguese. Among those waiting in Lisbon for Dias to bring his report to his king, John II, was a tall, red-haired sea captain from Genoa, Italy, named Christopher Columbus. Dias's triumph would mean more years of disappointment for the Italian mariner. If India could be reached by going *east,* the king would have little interest in financing Columbus's great enterprise—a *westward* voyage to the Indies.[1]

The Portuguese had been inching along the coast of Africa for a century. Unlike their neighbors in Spain, who spent most of the fifteenth century fighting to rid their country of the Muslim Moors, Portugal had been united, seeking. Prince Henry the Navigator had established a world famous school at Sagres to bring together all the elements of seamanship, mapmaking, piloting, and navigation.[2] Prince Henry sent out as many as fifteen expeditions to Africa's Cape Bojador, just south of the Canary Islands. His captains all returned claiming that the shallow waters and fierce currents made that point impassable. Finally, Prince Henry *ordered* Gil Eannes to sail beyond the cape. Eannes did so in 1434 by sailing *west* into the Atlantic before heading back to Africa's coast. He had at last passed the dreaded cape.[3] This same Eannes ten years later would bring back the first shipload of two hundred African slaves. Gomes Eanes de Zurara, a Portuguese contemporary of Eannes, writes that desperate African mothers would "clasp their infants in their arms, and throw themselves on the ground to cover them with their bodies, disregarding any injury to their own persons so that they could prevent their children from being separated from them."[4] Zurara tried to lessen the horror of these scenes by assuring readers that the slaves were "treated with kindness and no difference was made between them and free-born servants of Portugal." He said they were taught trades, converted to Christianity, and intermarried with the Portuguese.[5] Still, he gives us insight when he writes: "What heart could be so hard as not to be pierced by piteous feeling to see that company?"[6] And the presence of light-skinned Africans among them suggested that some, at least, had been bought in markets from "the ubiquitous Muslim salesmen."[7]

Slavery was an inescapable part of African life. Mansa Musa, a devout Muslim, was the king of Mali (currently part of Niger). He sold fourteen thousand female slaves to finance his journey to Cairo in 1324.[8] The Arabs were always "seizing our people as merchandise," complained the black king of Bornu (in present-day Nigeria) to the sultan of Egypt in the 1390s.[9] With the extension of Islam into West Africa's "Gold Coast" came an increasingly vigorous trade in black slaves.[10] The Christian Portuguese emulated this practice. Three hundred years before adoption of the U.S. Constitution, decisions made in Europe and Africa would have great and terrible consequences for a nation as yet unimagined and a people still unnamed.

Portugal's efforts gained momentum when the Muslim Ottoman Turks finally conquered Constantinople in 1453. This meant that city-states like Genoa and Venice would have to deal with the Turks for such prized goods as pepper, ginger, cinnamon, nutmeg, and cloves. And it would drive the Atlantic kingdoms *outward.*

Columbus had had to plead for King John II to give him a safe passage to Lisbon because he feared arrest for his debts. Columbus was surely capable of directing such a venture as he proposed. He had traveled as far away as Iceland and Britain and throughout the Mediterranean at a time when most mariners never ventured outside the sight of land. Still, Columbus spent years unsuccessfully appealing for support for his great project.

One thing Columbus did *not* have to contend with was any notion that the earth was flat. Although a popular misconception, in truth all scholars at that time knew the earth was a sphere. What they did *not* know was the circumference of the earth. Here, Columbus radically miscalculated. He thought that Japan lay only 2,400 to 2,500 miles west of the Canary Islands.[11]

Columbus heard Dias make his report to Portugal's king and returned, empty-handed, to Spain. These were years of great frustration for Columbus as Spain's monarchs—Ferdinand and Isabella—concentrated their attention on driving the Moors out of the Iberian peninsula. Finally, in 1492, the Spanish rulers succeeded in freeing their country of seven hundred years of Moorish domination. Ferdinand and Isabella saw their victory as a gift from God. They styled themselves "their most Catholic majesties." Columbus's devout religious faith clearly helped him in his appeals to them for aid. He took seriously his first name, which means "bearer of Christ." He pleaded for the chance to carry Christianity to the lands beyond the sea.[12]

With three small ships, called *caravels*, Columbus set sail from the port of Palos on 2 August 1492. Favored by fair winds and clear skies, the *Niña*, the *Pinta*, and his flagship, the *Santa Maria*, made excellent time. Even under such favorable conditions, Columbus's Spanish sailors soon began to grumble. With steady winds carrying them west, how would they return to Spain? And when the little flotilla entered a dense patch of *sargassum* (gulf weed), the men fretted about getting stuck in the thickening growths. Most troubling of all, perhaps, was the fact that they were Spaniards and the *Capitán General* was not. Columbus was Genoese, and centuries of foreign occupation had led these sons of Spain to be deeply suspicious of outsiders. Columbus had to deceive his sailors by keeping double logs of the ships' daily distance covered. Even by his false account, however, the men could tell that they had gone farther west than anyone had ever gone before, and farther west than they had been led to believe they would have to go in order to make a landfall.

Threatened with mutiny by his crew, Columbus was forced to promise his captains on October 9 that if they failed to sight land within *three days,* they would all turn about and head back to Spain. The captains were Martin Alonso Pinzon, commander of the *Pinta,* and his brother, Vicente Yanez Pinzon, who led the *Niña.* They were Spaniards, from a Palos shipping family, and gave Columbus help without which he could never have succeeded. Fortunately for Columbus, stiff breezes sped his ships' way and his crew began to see clear signs of land ahead. Flights of migrating birds covered the moon. Tree branches with still-green leaves floated by, giving assurances of land just over the horizon.[13]

Suddenly, gale winds and rough seas confronted the expectant mariners on the night of October 11. Determined, Columbus refused to shorten sail. Early in the morning of the twelfth, the cry came from Rodrigo de Triana, the lookout on the *Pinta*—"*Tierra! Tierra!*" Columbus gave orders to stand off the shore to avoid reefs and shoals and, finally, to shorten sail. At dawn, they began their search for a safe place to land.[14]

Columbus, the "admiral" as he was now called, put out in a longboat from the *Santa Maria* and headed into shore. It carried the royal flag of Castile (a great province of Spain) and the banner of the expedition, which was a cross of green surmounted by a crown, all on a white field. The brothers Pinzon joined the shore party in their own ships' boats. The men knelt in the sand, prayed, and gave thanks to God for their safe passage. Then Columbus named the island—a part of today's Bahamas—*San Salvador*, Holy Savior.[15]

Soon, Columbus and his men were exploring—and naming and claiming—other islands in the Caribbean. When natives appeared, docile, nearly naked, and eager to trade with the Europeans, Columbus named them *Indians*. If not India proper, he was certain he had landed somewhere in Asia—though the language and manners of the people did not correspond with anything travelers since Marco Polo had reported of the Orient.

Significantly, many of the Indians wore small, gold nose rings. Columbus had had to assure his seamen that the voyage would be worth their while. They were not the ones who would receive the glory, they knew. Nor would they achieve high office or status for the great discovery. Gold would have to suffice, and Columbus soon felt the pressure to find suitable quantities of the precious metal.

Equally significant, natives also introduced Columbus's men to tobacco and taught them to inhale its smoke. Tobacco use was ubiquitous throughout the Americas, and the Spaniards found smoking pleasurable. Here, in the earliest hours of the encounter between Europeans and native peoples, the exotic leaf loomed large. It would eventually become the cash crop for a number of American states and a major financial interest for more than five hundred years.[16]

On an island he would name *La Isla Española*—The Spanish Island (or Hispaniola), Columbus found more Indians eager to trade. Importantly, these Indians seemed to have plenty of gold.[17]

So willing, so easily plied with cheap trinkets—like little brass hawk's bells worth only pennies in Spain—these Indians were vulnerable to the Spaniards in many ways. They could be dominated as slaves and put to work mining gold. What's more, the native women seemed sexually open. To sailors who had had no contact with the opposite sex for months at a time and who had little fear of venereal disease, the sensual enticements proved irresistible. Syphilis has been traced to this first encounter of Columbus's men and the aboriginal peoples of the Caribbean. A contemporary of Columbus, Bishop Las Casas, thinks Indians who came back to Barcelona from the first voyage gave the disease to "women of the town," a euphemism for prostitutes, who then gave it to Spanish soldiers. From there, it spread throughout Europe and the world.[18] The Indians, on the other hand, contracted smallpox and measles from the Spaniards; these diseases devastated populations with no previous exposure and built-up immunity.

When the *Santa Maria* wrecked on a coral reef off Hispaniola on Christmas Day 1492, Columbus's men offloaded supplies, trading truck and food. A local chieftain, or *cacique*, named Guacanagari ordered his people to help retrieve the cargo of the stricken flagship. Columbus noted in his journal that the Indians guarded his supplies, taking not so much as "a lace point."[19] From the timbers of the wrecked vessel, Columbus built a fortress he named *La Navidad*—Christmas—that became the first European habitation in America. And when he prepared to return to Spain, he had little trouble recruiting volunteers to stay behind. The prospect of gold proved a powerful incentive.

The *Niña* and the *Pinta* departed 18 January 1493 from Samana Bay for the return trip. Columbus was not what we would call a capable *navigator*. The sextant and accurate chronometers were still centuries away. But he was an extraordinarily good *mariner*, with a keen sense of water and wind. He knew how to recognize currents and signs of land. His early calculations had placed Cuba at the same latitude as Cape Cod. Fortunately, he knew enough to correct that. Most of the return voyage passed uneventfully until, on February 12, the two ships sailed into a fierce winter gale. The admiral and Vicente Pinzon took turns guiding the *Niña's* helmsman. Each wave threatened to capsize the little vessel. There was no hope of rescue in such seas.[20] Columbus's men vowed to make a pilgrimage to the nearest shrine of the Virgin Mary if they survived the storm.

When they sighted land in the Portuguese Azores, it took three days before Columbus could come to a safe anchorage near a village called *Nossa Senhora dos Anjos* (Our Lady of the Angels). True to their vow, Columbus's men hurried to the local church, but while praying at the altar in their nightshirts as a sign of penitence, they were arrested! Portuguese authorities suspected the Spanish seamen had been sailing to prohibited parts of the African coast.[21] With his crewmen in jail, Columbus—still aboard ship—threatened to bombard the town if they were not freed. Fortunately, the captain of the port finally arrived after being delayed by yet another storm and was sufficiently persuaded that Columbus and his men had indeed come back from the *otro mundo*—the other world—and had not been poaching on Portugal's rich African preserves.[22] He generously provided them with supplies before their departure. The incident—almost a farce—nonetheless shows the extreme lengths to which the Portuguese were willing to go to protect their monopoly on the growing slave trade.

Setting out for the mainland in the *Niña*, Columbus again encountered severe storms. When he finally saw land again, it was at the mouth of Portugal's Tagus River. Menaced by a Portuguese warship, he applied for permission from the king to land. King João II—who had twice refused to support Columbus's great enterprise—not only granted the permission and ordered the ship's resupply, but he summoned the admiral to report to him at a monastery thirty miles away. Some of the king's jealous courtiers, realizing at last what Spain would gain from this amazing discovery, secretly advised him to have Columbus assassinated. When the Indians who had joined the crew showed the king a crude map of their islands made from beans, João cried out, "Why did I let slip such a wonderful chance?"[23] Despite the king's disappointment, no attempt was made on Columbus's life.

Even on leaving Portugal, Columbus's claim to be the discoverer of the New World was not secure. Martin Alonso Pinzon, captain of the *Pinta*, had missed most of the storms west of the Azores and thus the delays they caused in Columbus's return. Having arrived first, he sent word across Spain of his coming and asked Ferdinand and Isabella for permission to report directly to them. But the monarchs replied that they would hear the news first from their Admiral of the Ocean Sea. Meanwhile, Columbus made up for lost time and docked in Palos harbor shortly before the *Pinta* arrived. Columbus would not be robbed of the credit by his Spanish sea captain. Within a month, a broken Pinzon died at his country house near Palos.[24]

In April 1493, Columbus came to the Alcazar, the royal palace, to formally make his report to Ferdinand and Isabella. He knelt before the king and queen, but they arose and gave him the honor of a seat at Isabella's side. The Indians were presented and the assembly was awed not only by gold jewelry, but also by such oddities as the parrots that had never been seen in

Europe. Less impressive were the "spices" Columbus presented, for the fabled riches of the Indies were not to be seen in his collection of common American plants. Then the company adjourned for a *Te Deum* at the chapel royal. The last line—*O Lord, in Thee have I trusted, let me never be confounded*—moved the brave mariner to tears.[25]

If only Columbus had stopped there, at that chapel! Nothing that would happen in the remaining thirteen years of his life would add to his fame. Much that he did detracted from it. He proceeded to lead a second, third, and fourth voyage to the New World. The second voyage—the largest—proceeded with seventeen ships. Although he would continue to explore and claim rich islands in the Caribbean, and to range as far as modern-day Panama on the North American mainland, his record as an administrator was a dismal one. After the third voyage, he had even been arrested and returned to Spain in chains! Columbus added immeasurably to mankind's store of knowledge. Yet he never quite realized that his *otro mundo* was not, in fact, a part of Asia, but an entirely new continent.

The tragic turn in his relations with the Indians cannot be avoided. More importantly, the relations of the Indians with the Spanish settlers for whom Columbus opened the way would turn vicious. The gentle Tainos were not the only new people Columbus encountered. The fierce Caribs—whose warlike ways included cannibalism—presented a challenge to the benign intentions with which Columbus had set forth. Soon, the failure to produce a rich trove of spices reduced the Spanish colonial enterprise to grubbing for gold and enslaving Indians in order to get it. Columbus appealed, vainly, for a better quality of settler. After the initial voyage, in which only three crewmen had been recruited from Spain's prisons, many of those who came to the New World were criminals. Who else could be recruited? When tales of the Indians' wiping out the first settlement at Navidad came back to Spain, the initial enthusiasm for conversion of the Indians cooled.

The results of Columbus's voyages of discovery are truly incalculable. From this new land, Europe received maize, tomatoes, peppers, peanuts, yams, and turkeys. The introduction of the potato, alone, revolutionized European agriculture. Millions were fed from these new crops of the New World. This ironically fueled European dominance. Europeans introduced into the New World wheat, apples, grapes, as well as pigs and horses. Horses, in particular, became the basis for an entire hunting culture among the Indians of the Great Plains.[26] The courageous and incredibly skilled Plains Indians rode mounts that were all descended from those brought over by the Spaniards.

Columbus's discoveries opened the way for a "triangle trade" that would develop over the centuries. Ships from England and Europe would travel to the "Gold Coast" of Africa to pick up slaves for the dreaded, deadly "Middle Passage" westward across the Atlantic to the Caribbean and, in time, to the English colonies on the Atlantic seaboard of North America. American colonists would then exchange raw materials—tobacco, cotton, and timber—for slaves—and the ships would return eastward across the Atlantic.

To the modern complaint that Columbus brought slavery to the New World and that the Europeans' diseases wiped out indigenous peoples, a response is due. Slavery was a pervasive fact of life among the Europeans, but also particularly among the Arabs, the Africans, and the Indians themselves. In Asia, slavery had always existed. It seems hard to credit an attack on Columbus that singles him out for what was then a fairly universal practice. As much as we deplore slavery today, we cannot ignore the moral development of the West from our present vantage point outside the context of history. It was from the very experience of administering a far-flung empire that Spanish scholars began to elaborate universal doctrines of human rights that led, eventually, to the abolition of slavery in the West.[27] A counter-challenge might be offered: Who, in Columbus's time, did *not* practice slavery? One might conclude that far from being slavery's *worst* practitioners, westerners led the world to end the practice.

The very frightful consequences of smallpox and measles—which would continue to take their toll among Indians well into the nineteenth century—could hardly have been known by the European explorers of Columbus's day. Very little of the germ theory of disease was then known. And when it did become known, vaccines to protect against them were the product of that European culture—that same exploring, seeking spirit of Columbus—that is now so widely attacked. Even if Europeans of Columbus's time had had the scientific knowledge to test for diseases, the only way to have avoided infecting innocent aboriginal peoples would have been to have stayed at home in Spain.

Critics also seem to have discounted the devastation of Europe in the previous century brought on by the Plague. Estimates are that *one third* of Europeans died as a result of this epidemic that scholars believe originated in the Gobi Desert in the early 1300s.[28] The Black Death, as bubonic plague was known, had been brought to Europe from Asia. Much less *fashionable* than the moral indictment against Western nations for carrying disease to the New World is the counterclaim against Asia—and equally absurd.

No small part of the denunciation of Columbus and his successors in our times is an update of the *leyenda negra*—the Black Legend—that Protestant countries applied to the Catholic Spaniards. As the gifted writer G. K. Chesterton put it, many of the English histories of Spanish exploration and conquest reflected "the desire of the white man to despise the Red Indian and the flatly contradictory desire of the Englishman to despise the Spaniard for despising the Red Indian."[29]

Not all the Spaniards despised. Father Antonio de Montesinos addressed outraged settlers on the island of Hispaniola in 1511, barely a decade after Columbus's last voyage:

> I am the voice of one crying in the wilderness. This voice says that you are in mortal sin and live and die in it because of the cruelty and tyranny that you use against these innocent peoples. Tell me, by what right or justice do you hold these Indians in such cruel and horrible slavery? By what authority do you wage such detestable wars on these peoples who lived mildly and peacefully in their own lands, in which you have destroyed countless numbers of them with unheard of murder and ruin? . . . Are these Indians not men? Do they not have rational souls? Are you not obliged to love them as you love yourselves?[30]

And Montesinos was not as alone as his words would indicate.

Bartolome de Las Casas became the leading Spanish cleric *opposing* harsh measures against the Indians. He even went so far, in his famous *Confesionario,* to advise priests to deny absolution to any settlers who owned or abused aboriginal peoples. Las Casas engaged in a lengthy debate with the leading scholar of his day, Aristotle scholar Juan Gines de Sepulveda of Vallodolid. Sepulveda argued that the Indians were what the great philosopher had termed "slaves by nature." Las Casas disputed this and argued that the Indians, because they had been denied access to the Scriptures, were not fully morally culpable for the horrors of cannibalism and human sacrifice.[31] For his unwavering advocacy of the cause of the Indians, Las Casas was called *defensor de los indios.*[32]

Montesinos and Las Casas were not entirely voices crying in the wilderness. Both were active in pressing the Spanish monarchs to approve measures to help the Indians. But it was a long way from Spain to the New World. Speculation about the nature of the Indians—were they fully human?—led such Spanish thinkers as the Dominican friar Francisco de Vitoria to write extensively on the nature of human rights. He deserves to be ranked along with Suarez and Grotius as founders of modern international law.[33] Among Vitoria's firm principles were these:

> *Every Indian is a man and thus capable of attaining salvation or damnation.*
> *The Indians may not be deprived of their goods or power on account of their social backwardness.*
> *Every man has the right to the truth, to education . . .*
> *By natural law, every man has the right to his own life and to physical and mental integrity.*
> *The Indians have the right* not *to be baptized and not to be forced to convert against their will.*[34]

Critics have pointed out that these morally sophisticated principles were rarely honored in Latin America. That may be true, but where else were such principles even enunciated and defended? And it should be remembered that these leading thinkers were churchmen, not governors. Few of today's critics would argue for the state to be run by the church. Still, might the criticism of Spanish conduct in Latin America be not that it was too Catholic, but that it was not Catholic enough?

We can see in these impassioned writings and sermons by Spanish Christians the same moral earnestness and reasoned appeals that would be echoed by American evangelicals three hundred years later in their crusade against Negro slavery in the South. We shouldn't be surprised. They read the same Bible.

Rare is the European and virtually nonexistent is the Asian, African, or Arab writer who can be found to anguish about the condition and treatment of subject peoples. Is it possible that the Spaniards are being pilloried in history not because they were without conscience but because their consciences led them to cry out against the conduct of their own countrymen? The most stinging indictments of Spanish conduct remain those written in Spanish by Spanish witnesses.

The treatment of criminals and heretics at the time gives some idea of the level of public sensibility. In most of the kingdoms of Europe, a convicted traitor would be sentenced to be hanged, drawn, and quartered. This process involved hanging the unfortunate man until he was nearly unconscious. Pulled down, the victim would be disemboweled and his entrails burned before him. Finally, his body would then be pulled apart by four horses hitched to his extremities. Heretics fared little better. Burned at the stake, a slow and excruciating process of execution, they could consider themselves blessed if friends had secreted bags of gunpowder beneath their death robes to hasten their tortured end.

These medieval practices show a civilization that had not yet developed the sense of justice and mercy that was to come later. It is anachronistic and vindictively selective to indict European explorers and colonizers for failing to meet our modern standards of human rights.

II. The Scramble for Empire

Pope Alexander VI, a member of the notorious Borgia clan, had been supported for election as pontiff by Ferdinand and Isabella. Not surprisingly, therefore, the bull he promptly issued 4 May 1493 divided the world between Spain and Portugal on terms highly favorable to Spain. Prompted by Portuguese protests, and eager to keep their lines of communication with their newfound lands clear, the Spanish agreed to push the line of demarcation 1,175 miles *west* in the Treaty of Tordesillas of 1494. Thus, Portugal would be able to claim Brazil as well as vast territories in Africa, India, and the East Indies.[35] This might have ended contention in Catholic Europe had other strong-willed monarchs not seen their opportunities.

France's King Francis I was unimpressed. He noted that the "sun shone for him as for others," and he wittily replied to the pope's carving up by saying he would like to see Adam's will, "to learn how *he* had divided up the world!"[36] (Cenu Indians in the Americas were even less reverent. Their reaction to the news that the pope had divided up the world: "The Pope must have been drunk!"[37])

But that very sober decision by the pope had vast ramifications for Americans hundreds of years later. It meant, among other things, that Spain and Portugal would not contend for mastery of the North American continent.

As news of Columbus's discoveries sped throughout Europe—aided by the recent invention of the printing press—rulers realized that they would also have to seek new trading routes to the Indies or be forced to see that lucrative traffic monopolized by Spain and Portugal. Continuing their drive *eastward,* the Portuguese succeeded in 1498 in reaching India by an all-water route. The voyage of Vasco da Gama returned to Lisbon in 1499 with the true spices and real contact with the rulers of India that Columbus had markedly failed to achieve. Only two of da Gama's four ships—the *San Gabriel* and the *Berrio*—made it back, and only 55 of 170 seamen survived the arduous trip, but the foundations of Portugal's empire—the first and the last of European states to rule beyond the waves—were laid.[38]

John Cabot tried to do for England's Henry VII what Columbus had done for Spain's monarchs. Cabot—like Columbus a native of Genoa—persuaded the notoriously stingy first Tudor king to back his attempt to find a Northwest Passage to the Indies. In 1497, Cabot's little ship *Matthew* landed in North America at what he called the New Found Land. Although he stayed less than a month, established no permanent settlements, and brought back no riches, Cabot's claim would form the basis of later English dominance of the continent. Attempting for a second time in 1498 to reach the fabled Indies via North America, Cabot and all hands disappeared.[39]

Gradually, Europeans realized that the New World was not a part of Asia at all, but an entirely new land mass, two new continents. What should it be called? An Italian adventurer provided the answer. Amerigo Vespucci was the son of a wealthy family from Florence. The Vespuccis were connected to the powerful Medici family that produced rulers of the Florentine Republic and popes. Amerigo wrote lurid reports of his voyages to South America. "I was more skilled than all the shipmasters of the world," Vespucci boasted shamelessly.[40] He vastly exaggerated the full extent of his travels, conveniently leaving out of his accounts any reference to the brave captains under whom he sailed.

But Amerigo could spin a tale. One of his stories told of a band of native women and girls who came down to the shore, along the coast of today's Brazil. Amerigo's captain decided to charm these naked women by sending his handsomest young sailor onto the beach to talk to them and offer them gifts. Charmed they may have been, but Amerigo related in vivid terms how one large female suddenly clubbed the young sailor to death and how the Portuguese crew watched in horror as these *Amazons** proceeded to roast and eat the young sailor's body![41] Amerigo was the first European writer since Columbus to describe the plants and animals *and people* of the New World in such vibrant and unforgettable detail.[42] Europe was both horrified and fascinated by such stories. Small wonder that when a German mapmaker, Martin Waldseemüller, decided to publish a book of engravings in 1507, he placed a large AMERICA on his map of the southern continent.[43] Very quickly the name of this adventurous scamp was taken up as the name for both new continents.

France was not to be left out. In 1524, the cultured Italian Giovanni da Verrazano succeeded in getting backing from King Francis I and a consortium of bankers to seek a passageway to *Cathay*—as China was then known—by sailing west. Verrazano sailed the little *Dauphine* (Princess) up

---

* *Amazons* were a race of female warriors identified in Greek mythology. Thus, the name came to be applied to these natives of Brazil and, in time, to the great Amazon River.

the coast of North America identifying the broad outlines of the continent. Although he failed to penetrate the natural harbors—Chesapeake Bay, Delaware Bay, and New York—he confirmed that the North American continent was a *new world* and not just a promontory of Asia. He did, however, sail around New York's Staten Island, describing the narrows that today bear his name. He misidentified the Outer Banks of North Carolina as an isthmus leading to the Pacific, but he kept detailed navigational records that aided significantly in mapmaking.

Verrazano hoped to establish a New France in this New World, a colonial empire that would stretch from Florida to Newfoundland. He braved a mutiny on his second voyage to the Americas, fooling his men into going the distance to Brazil. There, he was able to obtain a valuable cargo of rare woods to compensate his backers for the lack of Chinese goods. His final voyage, in 1528, ended in tragedy as he came ashore on an island we presume to be Guadeloupe. He was set upon by warlike Caribs in sight of his brother, Girolamo, and his boat crew. The Caribs promptly hacked him to pieces and ate him. His early death and his failure to locate any sea route to China caused Francis I and the French to lose interest for a time. But his explorations did have the effect of turning English and French attentions once again toward a Northwest Passage to the Orient.[44]

More than merely unimpressed, Francis I was also distracted. At one point, he was even imprisoned. Still, he was able to give his support to the vitally important voyages of Jacques Cartier. The father of New France took a northerly course of discovery toward North America in 1534, in his flagship *La Grande Hermine* (The Big Weasel) after an Atlantic crossing of barely three weeks. He spent his days exploring Newfoundland, the Labrador, and Prince Edward Island. The great Gulf of St. Lawrence—the gateway to Canada—he named for the Roman Christian martyr. His men deftly avoided icebergs and feasted on polar bear.[45]

Cartier's skill as a mariner is unsurpassed. He never lost a ship. He never lost a sailor at sea. In his three visits to North America, he entered and left fifty uncharted harbors without incident.[46] His title was *Capitaine et Pilote de Roy.* King Francis could make him a captain, but it was this hardy

Breton sailor's own skill that made him a *pilot.* As a tribute to Cartier's seamanship and his fairness as a skipper, sailors from St. Malo (a seaport in Brittany, in Northwest France) were eager to ship with him.[47] Although Cartier's discoveries—including the fur-rich interior of Québec (from the Huron word for "narrowing of the river")—would form the solid basis for the French empire in America, the immediate results of his voyages were meager. He brought back cargoes of pyrite—fool's gold—and quartz, hardly the diamonds he had hoped for. He fell for tall tales of fabulous riches in a kingdom of the Saguenay told him by Donnaconna, a chieftain of the Hurons (and he kidnapped the unfortunate Indian to let him tell his story to the king). Soon, France would be embroiled in religious warfare. Francis I's successor, Henry II, had no interest in a Canadian venture—despite the fact that furs and fish could have vastly enriched his realm. And, for a century, cynical Frenchmen dismissed anything phony as a *diamant de Canada* ("a diamond from Canada").[48]

Meanwhile, Spain quickly followed up Columbus's discoveries with major action on land and sea early in the sixteenth century. From their base on the island of Hispaniola that Columbus discovered, Spanish ships ranged throughout the Caribbean. Explorer Ponce de León (called an *adelantado*—advancer) sought out new lands, sailing along the peninsula he named *Florida* (actually, *Pascua Florida*—flowery Easter) in 1513. From there, he advanced to the Florida Keys and to Yucatan, in Mexico. When Vasco Nunez de Balboa crossed the Isthmus of Panama, also in 1513, he was the first European to see the Pacific Ocean.

A generation after Columbus, another foreign mariner was about to add luster to the annals of Spanish exploration and discovery. Ferdinand Magellan was a Portuguese. "God gave the Portuguese a small country to live in but a wide world to die in" goes the old adage, and Magellan was to dramatize it by sailing around the world.[49] His great voyage of *circumnavigation* almost ended before it began. Rebuffed by the king of Portugal, just as Columbus had been, Magellan sought and received support from Spain's ruler, Emperor Charles V. As his ships were being outfitted for the journey in a shipyard in Seville, he made the mistake of leaving his family banners flying from the stern of his ship while it was being overhauled.

The Spanish flags had been taken down for repainting. Magellan was a nobleman whose family flag clearly showed his Portuguese origins. This was taken as a great affront by the fiercely proud people of Seville. A mob rushed in, threatening to lynch Magellan on the spot. With sword points at his throat, he coolly informed the leaders of the mob that the incoming tide threatened to swamp his ship—a vessel owned by Charles V. If the emperor's ship was lost, *they* would be held responsible. Finally, the mob retreated.[50] Magellan would show this courage and self-command time and again throughout his voyage.

Setting out in 1519 with a flotilla of five creaking ships with crews numbering 250, Magellan was bound for the Spice Islands (modern-day Indonesia) by going west. There he expected to find supplies of clove, peppercorn, and nutmeg. Virtually unavailable any other place on earth, their scarcity made their trade highly lucrative.

Magellan planned to find a strait at the extreme southern tip of South America.[51] But soon, he was in danger. Wintering over on the coast of Argentina, the men began to grumble. Three of his ships mutinied in Port San Julian.[52] He had received word warning him that the Spanish captains, who hated him, planned to kill him. Captains Cartagena, Mendoza, and Quesada accused Magellan of violating royal instructions in taking them so far south. Magellan had told them he would rather die than turn back. He sent his man Espinosa to the *Victoria* with a message to Captain Mendoza ordering him to cease his defiance and obey orders. Mendoza laughed when he read the letter, which proved a mistake. Espinosa immediately grabbed Mendoza by the beard and stabbed him to death—exactly as Magellan had commanded him. Magellan then subdued another mutinous ship, the *Concepcion*, with naval gunfire and boarded her, taking Captain Quesada as prisoner. The revolt soon collapsed.

Magellan had Mendoza's body quartered—gruesomely cut into four parts—and "cried" (exhibited) through the fleet as a warning to everyone against mutiny. Quesada was hanged and Cartagena was spared—for the moment. Soon, however, Captain Cartagena was found to be stirring up new discontent, along with a priest. Magellan had the two men tried and marooned. Abandoned on the shores of Argentina, they would die of exposure, starvation, or Indian attack.[53] They were last seen "kneeling at the water's edge, bawling for mercy."[54]

Pressing on, after the loss of one of his ships, Magellan finally entered "the strait that shall forever bear his name."[55] In October and November of 1520, Magellan carefully made his way through the hazards of these uncharted waters. Strong currents and sudden storms make it one of the most dangerous passages on earth, even today. The Strait is anything but *straight;* it is a maze of treacherous waters and dangerous rocks. Magellan's task was like the threading of a dozen needles. Magellan had to retrace his steps, searching in vain for one of his four remaining ships. He did not know that the *San Antonio* had headed back to Spain.

His fleet now reduced to three ships, Magellan headed out into the sea he named *Pacific.* Ahead of him lay open waters. Magellan and his men prayed regularly and well they might. Though they did not realize it, they faced a journey more than twice the distance faced by Columbus. Here, Magellan proved his mettle. Antonio Pigafetta, an Italian member of the crew, kept a detailed journal and wrote of him: "He endured hunger better than all the rest . . . and more accurately than any man in the world, he understood dead reckoning and celestial navigation."[56]

Pigafetta tells us of the privations of the voyage to Guam:

> We were three months and twenty days without any kind of fresh food. We ate biscuit which was no longer biscuit but powder of biscuit swarming with worms. It stank strongly of the urine of rats. We also ate some ox hides that covered the top of the mainyard to prevent the yard from chafing the shrouds. Rats were sold for one-half ducado [about $1.16 in gold] apiece and even then we could not get them.[57]

The expedition would not have survived at all had Magellan not first hugged the coast of Chile before striking out across the Pacific. Pigafetta realized this: "Had not God and his blessed mother given us so good weather, we would all have died of hunger."[58] The trip was three times longer than anyone could have expected. No reliable charts or maps existed.

Finally landing on Guam 6 March 1521, Magellan found his three ships overwhelmed by swarms of natives who, though friendly, carried off much of the cargo of trade. The ships stayed only long enough to resupply and then made for the Spice Islands. Within a week, Magellan had reached the Philippines in the region of Leyte Gulf.* The king of Cebu persuaded Magellan that he had converted from Islam to Christianity and sought the aid of the Spaniards in a battle with a neighboring island of Mactan. Magellan's men pleaded with him not to go, but he felt a duty to aid a fellow Christian. When he came ashore, he left his three ships anchored too far out to give him assistance. He and a small, loyal party, including Pigafetta, were soon overwhelmed by Mactanese warriors using poisoned arrows and scimitars. Magellan covered the retreat of his men, but was cut down, pitching face down in the sand. Pigafetta faithfully records:

> When they wounded him, he turned back many times to see whether we were all in the boats. Then, seeing him dead, we wounded made the best of our way to the boats, which were already pulling away. But for him, not one of us . . . would have been saved.[59]

Magellan was mourned by Pigafetta as "our mirror, our light, our comfort and our true guide."[60] But his mission had not ended. Captain Juan Sebastian del Cano took command of the *Victoria,* abandoning both the *Concepcion* and the *Trinidad.* Sailing ever westward, del Cano cleared the Cape of Good Hope, only to face on the homeward leg the imprisonment of nearly half his crew by the Portuguese at the Cape Verde Islands. Limping back into Seville on 8 September 1522, Captain del Cano commanded only eighteen sea-weary men of the *Victoria.* As they had promised, the men immediately walked barefoot to the cathedral, clad only in long shirts and each one bearing a candle to do penance and to give thanks for their survival.[61] Thus ended, nearly three years after they set sail, the first voyage of circumnavigation of the earth. Spain was unchallenged as the leading sea power of the world. Magellan's historic voyage coincided with, even as it symbolized, Spain's new command of the seas.

---

* In 1944, Leyte Gulf would see one of the greatest sea battles in history.

Christopher Columbus. *As Admiral of the Ocean Sea, this Italian explorer showed courage, skill, and zeal in his great enterprise. He sought a westward route to the Indies. Instead, he discovered a New World. He gave his Spanish sponsors the chance to rule a vast empire in the Americas. Newly freed from seven hundred years of Muslim rule, the Spaniards seized the opportunity. Despite early conflicts with native peoples, disease, and exploitation, Hispanic culture continues to thrive in Latin America to this day.*

Ferdinand Magellan. *The first man to circumnavigate the earth, Magellan gave his name to the strait at the tip of South America. His voyage across the vast Pacific Ocean brought his men to the brink of starvation. He ruthlessly enforced discipline and braved plots against his life. When he fell victim to natives in the Philippines, he may have been abandoned by envious Spanish subordinates. Magellan's global voyage underscored Spain's dominion over the seas—for a time.*

Jacques Cartier. *A hardy French sailor from coastal Brittany, Cartier explored the fur-rich interior of Canada. Québec is the Huron word for "a narrowing of the river." Despite the often treacherous and uncharted waters of the St. Lawrence River, Cartier never ran his ship aground. His voyages in his flagship,* La Grande Hermine, *or "Big Weasel," laid the basis for New France, an empire based on trade. Cartier disappointed his grasping king, Francis I, however, by bringing back only quartz, not the promised diamonds.*

Sir Francis Drake. *Drake was the most famous of all the English "sea dogs." He challenged Spanish rule of the seas. Drake could be personally courteous even as he burned towns and looted churches in Spain's New World colonies. The emeralds he seized from the Spanish treasure ship* Cacafuego *would appear in the State Crown of England—where they remain to this day. When he returned from his own voyage around the world, he was knighted on the deck of the* Golden Hind *by Queen Elizabeth I. Soon, he would join in the fight against Spain's Armada.*

Her ability to exercise control over her American empire depended entirely on *admiralty*—the ability to control the sea.

There followed, quickly, the incredible Spanish military campaigns against the Aztecs in Mexico by Hernán Cortés (1521) and the Incas of Peru by Francisco Pizarro (1535). These *conquistadors* (conquerors) used methods of cruelty and deception to bring down the two great native empires. The advanced cultures dwarfed in numbers the tiny expeditionary forces of Spanish warriors who boldly advanced on their capitals. But the native rulers were seemingly unprepared for the determination and ruthlessness of their conquerors.

The Aztec practice of human sacrifice stunned the conquerors. Each year, thousands of victims would be taken to the top of magnificent pyramids and their hearts would be cut out and offered up to the Aztec gods. In the case of the Aztecs, Cortés appeared to many of the tribes they held in bondage as one of their deities, *Quetzalcoatl.* Cortés shrewdly took advantage of this to lead a revolt against the imperial Aztecs.[62] The Spaniards, mounted on horseback and armored, could attack native forces almost with impunity, but even with this advantage they might have been swallowed up by the sheer number of their foes. That these tiny forces could impose their will on such cultures can only be attributed to their nerve and will.

Pizarro will forever be remembered as the man who took the Inca emperor Atahualpa hostage, demanding roomfuls of gold and silver in ransom. When the ransom was paid in full, Pizarro accused Atahaulpa of fomenting a revolt and had him garroted.* History records the image of the "weeping Inca" against the name of Francisco Pizarro. That Atahualpa had recently killed his own brother in a civil war hardly mitigates the evil of Pizarro's deed. Few could have mourned when Pizarro was himself murdered in 1541.

In a period of less than twenty years, the shocking brutality of Cortés and Pizarro added vast regions of Central and South America to the burgeoning Spanish empire. Soon, however, a new Latin American civilization

* To garrote is to kill by slow strangulation.

would arise on the ashes of the old. This new culture would grow and enrich and ennoble the world into our own time.

But Spain would soon see a potent rival. Cold, remote, and small in territory, population, and resources, England was vastly overshadowed by Spain and the other continental powers in the 1500s. In a matter of decades, all that would change.

III. The Rise of England

Just as Spain's war with the Moors had caused her to fall behind Portugal in the fifteenth century, England in the *sixteenth* century found domestic affairs a barrier to effective exploration and colonization. King Henry VIII succeeded to his father Henry VII's throne in 1509. Henry VIII was young, athletic, well-educated, and charming. Soon he married his brother Arthur's widow, the Spanish princess Catherine of Aragon. Catherine was deeply religious, like her parents, the famed *reyes católicos* Ferdinand and Isabella.

With such a connection, Henry VIII might have been expected to lead a bold, adventurous program of exploration. But it was not so. It was matters at home that occupied him. In twenty years of marriage, Queen Catherine gave the king no sons and only one daughter, Mary. Although a woman could legally inherit England's throne, it was thought to be a dangerous prospect.

Desperate for a male heir to steady his insecure Tudor family dynasty, Henry began to cast about for a way to end his marriage. He appealed to the pope to grant him an *annulment.* An annulment would mean that the marriage of King Henry and Queen Catherine had never been valid. It was awkward, to say the least, because Henry had had to ask the pope for a special dispensation to marry his brother's widow in the first place. The pope, who refused Henry's increasingly urgent pleas, may have been influenced by the threats made against him and church lands in Italy by the Holy Roman Emperor, Charles V, who just happened to be Queen Catherine's *nephew.*

Henry knew that *two* could play that game. He seized Catholic Church lands in England and redistributed them to his nobles to buy their support. He broke with Rome and created his own national church, which he called the Church of England—*Anglican.* Henry's obedient parliament soon confirmed him as "Supreme Head of the Church in England." Boldly, he retained the title "Defender of the Faith" that the pope had given him a few years before when he violently, even obscenely, attacked the Reformer Martin Luther in a widely read pamphlet.*

King Henry brooked no interference. He sent the famous Sir Thomas More and John Cardinal Fisher—both highly revered Catholics—to the block. More, author of *Utopia*, was a leading humanist scholar. In an act of little more than judicial murder, the two were beheaded for opposing the king's divorce and remarriage to Lady Anne Boleyn.**

But Henry was soon disappointed by his new wife. Their marriage lasted only three years and produced yet another daughter. He soon had Queen Anne framed, tried, and sent to the Tower of London on a charge of adultery with five different men, including her own brother. Henry's only mercy was to import from France an executioner who used a supposedly painless silver sword to sever the beautifully thin neck of Anne Boleyn. Her death left young Princess Elizabeth without a mother.

Desperate for an heir, the king was to wed again—the very moment the Tower's cannon boomed the signal that Anne's head was off. The third wife proved the charm. Jane Seymour provided the frantic king with his long-sought boy.

Henry was devastated when Queen Jane died, mere weeks after their son's birth. He was to marry *three more wives*, but the increasingly diseased, indulgent king sired no more children.

Europe was in the throes of the Protestant Reformation when King Henry VIII died in 1547. His son, Edward VI, always sickly, was only nine when his father died. Edward VI reigned only for six years but he never ruled. His arch-Protestant Privy Council—a body of powerful nobles—suppressed the Catholic Church in England. The famous Anglican *Book of Common Prayer* was issued in the young king's name.

King Edward VI died in 1553 at age fifteen. Now, the devoutly Catholic

---

* British monarchs are, to this day, called "The Defender of the Faith," despite the curious origins of this title.

** Both men were made saints in the Catholic Church by Pope Pius XI in 1935, four hundred years after their martyrdom.

daughter of King Henry VIII and Catherine of Aragon, Mary Tudor, came to the throne. Queen Mary I attempted to bring England back into the Catholic fold. When her attempts at persuasion failed, she resorted to force. She began to burn "heretics" at the stake. Archbishop of Canterbury Thomas Cranmer was sent to the Tower of London. His "sonorous phrases" had formed the basis for the *Book of Common Prayer*. He had written the Anglican Church's statement of belief, the *Thirty-Nine Articles.* Now, in 1556, he was tortured and forced to recant his Protestant beliefs. Queen Mary was not satisfied that Cranmer had returned to the Catholic Church. She condemned him to death by burning. Cranmer was executed at Oxford. There, he cast the hand that had signed the recantation into the flames first, dramatically saying: "This is that hand that hath offended."

Other leading Anglicans were executed during the brief, increasingly stormy reign of the queen who came to be known as Bloody Mary. Queen Mary was hated by the people of England. Her marriage to Spain's King Philip II only deepened their suspicion of her, even though the deeply Catholic Philip tried to persuade Mary to end her bloody persecutions of Protestants. Philip knew they were only turning the English people against their queen. Philip did succeed in having the Princess Elizabeth released from the Tower of London, where she was in grave danger of being murdered. When Philip left England to return home to Spain, Mary thought she was pregnant. Mary *prayed* she was pregnant. But it was only a cancerous tumor that caused her belly to swell. She died, childless, friendless, alone, and unmourned, in 1558 at age forty-two.

When she received word of her half-sister's death, twenty-five-year-old Princess Elizabeth fell to her knees and recited in Latin the words of the Psalm: "This is the Lord's doing. It is *marvelous* in our eyes."

Although she suppressed the public celebration of the Catholic Mass, Queen Elizabeth was unwilling to search out secret Catholics. "I have no window to look into men's souls," she famously said. Despite a number of plots against her life—encouraged by the pope and framed by Jesuit priests—Elizabeth continued to rely on the loyalty of her subjects, including not a few great Catholic noble families. In turn, Elizabeth wanted no religious turmoil in England. She ran the Church of England as a Protestant monarch, but she wanted to stop arguments *among* the fractious Protestants. After breaking from the Catholic Church, Lutherans and Calvinists disputed with Baptists and with each other over the meaning of communion and baptism. Elizabeth cleverly glossed over such theological disputes. About the Lord's Supper, she said:

Christ was the word that spake it.
He took the bread and break it;
And what his words did make it
That I believe and take it.

Elizabeth had an amazing knack for politics and public relations. She turned her greatest liabilities—that she was a woman and unmarried—into her great strengths. She cultivated her image as "the virgin Queen," and fostered a cult of personality that dubbed her "Gloriana." English arts and letters flourished under her rule. Shakespeare, Marlowe, and Spenser made everlasting contributions of world literature. Elizabeth created a heightened sense of English nationalism and remained highly popular throughout her long reign (1558–1603). She looked and acted the part, dressing extravagantly and displaying herself before the people as she went forward on as many as twenty-five "royal progresses"—visits to great estates around the country.[63] These visits served a dual purpose; they were also a shrewd way of avoiding the cost of maintaining a splendid court, since her hosts were expected to feed and house Elizabeth and her hundreds of nobles and retainers. To keep France and Spain at bay, she held out for nearly twenty years the prospect of her hand in marriage. To undermine their power, she financed rebellions against Spanish rule in the Netherlands and gave aid to the French Protestants, the Huguenots. One of the most remarkable personalities in history, Elizabeth relied on her people's affection to secure her throne: "There is no jewel, be it of never so high a price, which I set before this jewel; I mean your love," she told Parliament.

Queen Elizabeth encouraged the explorations of Sir Humphrey Gilbert (Newfoundland) and the colonization schemes of Sir Walter Raleigh (in the land he named *Virginia* in her honor). After the pope issued a decree absolving English Catholics from obedience to her in 1570 (thus inviting her overthrow or assassination), Elizabeth waged a cold war against Spain. Excitement over the discoveries in the northern voyages of Sir Martin Frobisher faded when the ore he brought back from Canada proved to be, like that of Cartier, worthless.

Still, the *idea* of an English greatness at home as well as beyond the seas would not die. Shakespeare's immortal writings fired men's imagination:

This royal throne of kings, this sceptred isle,
This earth of majesty, this seat of Mars,
This other Eden, demi-paradise,
This fortress built by Nature for herself
Against infection and the hand of war,
This happy breed of men, this little world,
This precious stone set in the silver sea,
Which serves it in the office of a wall
Or as a moat defensive to a house,
Against the envy of less happier lands,—
This blessed plot, this earth, this realm, this England.

Francis Drake resolved to equal Magellan's great feat and challenge Spain's rule of the seas in the process. Sailing in his flagship, the *Golden Hind,* he led his flotilla southwest to the coast of Argentina. Drake had to contend, as Magellan had, with mutiny. Master Doughty, who had soldiered with Drake in Ireland, was convicted and executed at Puerto San Julian—the same place Magellan had suppressed his mutineers.[64] Drake continued on through the Strait and then headed north. He raided the Chilean coast, seizing silver and gold and capturing Spanish vessels laden with rich cargoes.

Drake led his "sea dogs" on a merry adventure. Spanish writers long considered him no more than a pirate, Spanish grandees (the noblemen) called him *El Draque* (The Dragon), but documents unveiled in the last century from Spanish archives showed that his prisoners uniformly praised his humanity and good nature.[65] He did not, however, hesitate to burn Spanish towns and loot magnificent Catholic churches. Chasing the Spanish treasure ship *Cacafuego,* he took time to grab another prize that yielded a golden crucifix and a clutch of emeralds that would later appear in Queen Elizabeth's crown.[66] A Spanish prisoner wrote sympathetically of Drake that "he has a fine countenance, ruddy of complexion and fair beard. He has the mark of an arrow wound in his right cheek . . . in one leg he had the ball of an arquebus. . . . He read the Psalms and preached. . . ."[67] (Apparently not dwelling long on that part of the Good Book that says, "Thou shalt not steal.")

Drake explored the coast of California before setting off across the Pacific. By duplicating Magellan's feat, Drake gave a great boost to English self-confidence. The *Golden Hind* returned to London in November 1580, following three years at sea. She off-loaded silver into the Tower of London by night. Queen Elizabeth showed her great favor by knighting Drake on the deck of his flagship, in 1581. This act of open defiance of Spain's Philip II prompted the king to commence plans for an invasion of England.

Drake was to play a crucial role in his famous raid on Cadiz in 1587. He burned the city and the fleet that Philip II was then preparing for his invasion, a daring exploit known to history as "singeing the beard of the king of Spain." He delayed for a year the fateful clash. The decade of mounting tension between England and Spain came to a head when Elizabeth's ministers lured her captive cousin, Mary, Queen of Scots, into a plot against the queen's life. Brought to trial and beheaded, Mary Stuart became in death what she never was in life, a martyr to the Catholic cause. Elizabeth spat defiance. She played the part of warrior queen to the hilt:

> I know I have but the body of a weak and feeble woman; but I have the heart of a king, and of a king of England, too; and think foul scorn that Parma or Spain, or any prince of Europe, should dare to invade the borders of my realms: to which, rather than any dishonor should grow by me, I myself will take up arms.

Supported by Pope Sixtus V, who renewed the excommunication of Elizabeth and subsidized his costs, Spain's King Philip II in 1588 assembled the greatest war fleet in history—the Armada. One hundred thirty ships—

great galleons, galleasses, galleys, and merchant ships—and thirty thousand men (of whom three-quarters were soldiers primed for the invasion) proceeded up the English Channel. They were set upon by the English sea dogs—Drake, Hawkins, and Frobisher. The Armada was greatly hampered by ineffective leadership. Philip II had insisted that the duke of Medina Sidonia assume command. Brave and honest as he was, the duke was a soldier, completely inexperienced in the ways of the sea. The duke could not rely on the support of English Catholics who, in the main, were energetic in their defense of their island *against* their fellow Catholics from Spain.

Drake and his fellows set upon the great and ponderous ships of the Armada with fire ships. Less maneuverable, burdened by horses and cattle and great masses of supply, the Spanish ships were almost helpless against the fierce English warships. When a great storm came up, the Spanish Armada was dispersed. Many of the ships were wrecked on the forbidding coasts of Scotland and Ireland.

The victory of the English against the Armada broke the back of Spain's sea power, and the empire began its centuries-long decline. This clash marked the transfer of admiralty from great Spain to little England. English sea dogs could go where they wished with confidence. From this time until 1941—with one important local exception—it was England that "ruled the waves." That temporary exception—in the waters off Yorktown, Virginia, in 1781—would have the greatest consequences for America.

Dominance over the seas assured that England in the next century would be able to send more and more colonists to North America without fear of Spanish interference. It gave the English a sense of national destiny. They knew the battering storm had as much to do with the wreck of the Armada as did English fighting skill. "God blew and they were dispersed," read the official medallion Elizabeth ordered struck to commemorate England's great victory.

And the English believed it.

Two

A City Upon a Hill

(1607–1765)

Spain and Portugal create a distinctive civilization in Latin America. England and France vie for control of North America. Added to national and commercial rivalries are religious antagonisms between Protestant New England and Catholic New France. Following a promising start, relationships with the Indians strain, worsened by old European struggles. Unique experiments in religious and political toleration emerge as Dutch, Swedish, and German Protestants, Catholics, and a small number of Jews flock to English colonies to escape the Old World strife. Thirteen self-governing colonies along the Atlantic grow rapidly in population, wealth, and self-awareness. Along with their first legislature, however, the Virginia colony also tragically opens the way to slaves from Africa. The English finally rid North America of French political control. But even as England triumphs, the American colonists' need for English protection is eliminated as well. Coupled with increased taxation, this drives the thirteen colonies to revolution. The political ideas developed by American colonists—drawn from Locke and Montesquieu and from biblical and classical sources—create an American Enlightenment to rival that of Europe.

I. Coming to America

"Come over and help us," pleads the nearly naked Indian on the first Great Seal of the Massachusetts Bay Colony.[1] He is beckoning those Protestants remaining in England to brave the perils of an Atlantic crossing—as stormy then as it is now. What the Indian is asking for is the Christian gospel. It was a powerful communications tool, some would say a sly piece of propaganda. For this appealing seal was, of course, engraved by Englishmen and addressed to other Englishmen. As we shall see, within the span of a few years, the Pilgrims and Puritans of Massachusetts, and the other English settlers of Virginia, will go from a welcoming acceptance by the native peoples to a pitiless warfare with many of the indigenous tribes. After roasting wild turkeys together for the first Thanksgiving, the English and some warring Indian tribes will soon be putting the torch to each others' dwellings. In this, the Protestant English encounter with the tribes of North America almost echoes that of the Catholic Spaniards and Portuguese in Central and South America. The French, although generally more successful with the aboriginal peoples, would also suffer the loss of many brave Jesuit priests to cruel torture and death.

Following England's defeat of their Armada in 1588, the Spanish found it harder to protect their rich colonies in the New World. Menendez de Aviles had founded St. Augustine in East Florida in 1566 with a view to safeguarding the treasure-laden galleons that regularly plied their way between Mexico, the Caribbean, and Spain. Now, English sea dogs posed a constant threat. These hardy sea captains viewed Spanish ships as rich prizes—and easy pickings.

But the English were up to more than piracy. They were setting down roots. England's first effort at colonization was promoted by the energetic Sir Walter Raleigh. A prime example of the Elizabethan era and all the pomp, exuberance, and newfound confidence it entailed, Raleigh was a man as capable of writing poetry, playing musical instruments, and dancing a galliard as he was of fighting a duel with his sword. Raleigh, according to historian David Hackett Fischer, cut quite a figure:

> [He] walked, or rather teetered, through a world of filth and woe in a costume that consisted of red high heels, white silk hose, a white satin doublet [vest] embroidered with pearls, a necklace of great pearls, a starched ruff [worn about the neck], and lace cuffs so broad as to bury his hands in fluffy clouds of extravagant finery. His outfit was completed by a jaunty plume of ostrich feathers that bobbed above his beaver hat, and precious stones in high profusion. The jewels that Raleigh wore on one occasion were said to be worth £30,000—more than the capital assets of some American colonies.[2]

And remember, *he* wasn't the queen.

The English called the coast of America between Newfoundland and Florida *Virginia*, in tribute to Elizabeth I, the Virgin Queen. Virgin though she was, Queen Elizabeth yet had an eye for handsome and dashing young men like Raleigh. And she positively abhorred ugly men. She banned from her royal court those who were disfigured by pockmarks or who had bad breath—which were common enough in those days before inoculations and toothbrushes. Elizabeth herself bore scars from smallpox but skillfully covered these with heavy makeup made of eggshells. As she aged, putting on her red wigs, her thick mask of makeup, her many strings of pearls and other precious jewels, and especially making her daily selection of more than one thousand gowns consumed more and more of her waking hours. She labored to create a fantastic image of "Gloriana"—ever youthful, ever desirable, ever dazzling—provided you didn't look too closely. Raleigh and other ambitious young courtiers were more than happy to collaborate with "Good Queen Bess" in this charade.

Bold and enterprising as he was, Sir Walter did not go to America. He led the company of investors who sought to pay for all their court finery by making a profit from the New World. Returns on investment were anything but certain, and loss could result in impoverishment and imprisonment for debt. Roanoke, Raleigh's settlement off the coast of present-day North Carolina, vanished entirely after only five years. The colony was cut off from home by the constant threat of Spain's invasion of *Merrie* England. The Roanoke colony could not survive. When an English relief ship finally arrived in 1590, sailors found the entire settlement—including the first English child born in the New World, Virginia Dare—had disappeared. Only the word "Croatoan" carved in a tree trunk gave evidence that Europeans had ever set foot on the site. Its meaning is a mystery to this day.

Despite these discouraging beginnings, the English persisted. Following the death of Queen Elizabeth in 1603, the king of Scotland, James Stuart, came to the throne. His reign would begin a century of division and instability in England, during which England would fight a civil war, see one king beheaded, his first son restored to the throne, and his second son dethroned and banished. The effects of these tumultuous years of the Stuart kings would be felt in America.

By 1607, the Virginia Company of London had cobbled together enough investors who would risk the overwhelming odds in hopes of reaping profits from new settlements in America. They financed three small ships—*Susan Constant, Godspeed*, and *Discovery* to make the dangerous passage across the Atlantic in midwinter. Under the command of Captain Christopher Newport, with a crew of 120 men, the English ships sailed west.

They made land, but the start was inauspicious. Naming their first settlement after their king, in the spring of 1607 the Jamestown settlers began building a village that could be defended against both Spanish raiders and Indians. Few of the first settlers in this stronghold on the James River had any knowledge of farming, and the first attempts at communal sharing of all food and supplies resulted in near starvation. Diseases—malaria, typhoid, dysentery, and yellow fever—were the direct result of locating the settlement on marshy, swampy land. With many deaths and with discipline breaking down, it seemed this attempt, too, would fail.[3] These early years were to be known as the Jamestown colony's "Starving Time."

Then came Captain John Smith. He quickly imposed firm discipline on the colony, discarding the ineffectual sharing system and replacing it with incentives for hard work. He persuaded the colonists to raise maize, which went a long way toward solving the food shortages; acre for acre, Indian corn produces more grain than any other cereal crop.[4] The young and daring Smith was an English patriot: "Why should the brave Spanish soldier brag the sun never sets in the Spanish dominions, but ever shineth on one part or other we have conquered for our king?"[5] Smith was determined to succeed for his king. He favorably negotiated with Chief Powhatan, leader of the Algonquian Indians. In 1608, according to legend, Smith was even saved from death by the chief's young daughter, Pocahontas, when he had displeased her father.[6]

Her name means "little wanton," and it well describes the high-spirited young girl who would frolic, doing cartwheels naked among the stunned soldiers of the English camp at Jamestown.[7] But it wasn't Smith she fell for. Pocahontas set her cap, or feather, for the Englishman John Rolfe. It was Rolfe whom she married, after she converted to Christianity and was baptized. And it was with Rolfe she sailed off to England. There, she was presented to King James and the Royal Court.[8] When she died there in 1617 and was buried in Gravesend, she was genuinely mourned on both sides of the Atlantic. Captain Smith may have left the best tribute when he said she was "the instrument to [preserve] this colonie from death, famine, and utter confusion."[9] Even today, we can see the sprightly, highly intelligent girl behind the façade of the Elizabethan lady of fashion who stares out at us from her stiff official portrait.

When Captain Smith returned to England because of an injury, he was succeeded by less able men. In short order, the Jamestown colony sank into near collapse. It was Rolfe who saved the colony this time—by introducing yet another important New World crop in 1612: tobacco.[10] Reputedly, he introduced a milder tasting variety, *Nicotina tobaccum*, which he brought in seed form from the West Indies.[11] The natives near Virginia cultivated *Nicotina rustica*, a much coarser variety. Rolfe hardly could have pleased the king. James famously hated tobacco. He even wrote a pamphlet titled *A Counterblaste to Tobacco* condemning its use: "a custome lothsome to the eye, hatefull to the Nose, harmefull to the braine, dangerous to the Lungs." Thus, James became one of history's first antismoking crusaders. But money is money, and King James's unyielding opposition appears to have had no impact on the thriving tobacco trade. Within a decade, the Virginia colonists were exporting as much as forty thousand pounds of broadleaf back to England.[12]

Tobacco culture would have a profound influence on the development of Virginia and the South. Younger men and women from the British Isles and Europe were so eager to get a new start in America, they would sign up for a period of five or seven years' labor as indentured servants in the New World, in return for their passage across the ocean. The vast majority of early settlers in Virginia in the 1600s were white indentured servants. But tobacco requires intensive cultivation. Once their indebtedness was over, these indentured servants were eager to escape the intense heat and the backbreaking labor. The turnover would increase the desire for a more permanent sort of labor—slaves from Africa. In 1671, Sir William Berkeley listed the number of indentured servants as about eight thousand, slaves at two thousand, and freemen at forty-five thousand.[13] Within a few decades, slaves would begin to outnumber the indentured servants from England. This is the heart of the American paradox. Better conditions and greater liberty for indentured servants would come only at the expense of the unoffending Africans.

Tobacco farming would also lead to "land hunger" as the crop seriously depleted the soil. Virginians would constantly be searching for new lands to expand their holdings. This incessant grasping for new lands would be the source of many conflicts with the Indian tribes.

Captain John Smith's attempts to establish good relations with the tribes were successful at the start. Smith showed a genuine interest in Indian culture, commenting respectfully in his 1616 book, *A Description of New England*.[14] But these good relations were not to last. Just as the Europeans were divided into fiercely competitive nations, with rivalries between Spain, France, and England being exported to America, so were the Indian tribes set against each other. All too often, attempts to befriend one tribe would be taken as a warlike gesture by that tribe's Indian enemies.[15]

In 1619, three events occurred that would shape the future of Virginia. (1) English women arrived at Jamestown to begin the transition from mere trading outpost to a genuinely self-sustaining community. (2) Twenty black Africans debarked from a Dutch vessel to begin their people's long years of "unrequited toil" in America. And, (3) on instructions from the Virginia Company in London, the colonists elected representatives for the first colonial assembly in the New World. The Virginia

House of Burgesses met on 30 July 1619. The twenty-two members had been elected by all the free male colonists aged seventeen and older. For its time, this was an extraordinarily democratic procedure. From this point, Virginians would be governed under English common law largely by lawmakers of their own choosing.[16]

The Virginia Company of London's reforming leaders showed serious concern with the colony's heavy reliance on tobacco. They encouraged colonists to grow more and varied crops and to begin to diversify local industry. When in 1622, however, Indians attacked a local ironworks, war spread throughout the far-flung colony. More than three hundred settlers—men, women, and children—were slaughtered. This Great Massacre led to the assumption of direct royal control over the colony.[17] The king appointed a royal governor. Still, he did not dissolve the House of Burgesses or even reverse the process of colonial self-government.

Even in these first conflicts with the Indian tribes, the English held three distinct advantages. They were politically unified, they had greater numbers, and they were experienced in the use of firearms. Again and again, these advantages would prevail over the Indians' greater familiarity with the forests and rivers, their warrior culture, and their typical surprise tactic of strike and disappear.

II. The Great Migration

When Captain John Smith visited the uninhabited northern regions of Virginia in 1614, his reports to England were glowing. Though he could not interest the merchant adventurers of the London Company, that did not mean his reports went unread. When English Separatists and Puritans began to cast about for a religious refuge, they naturally looked west to America.

Queen Elizabeth's long reign (1558–1603) had meant that England would be Protestant. Her success in holding the Catholic powers of Europe at bay—aiding the Protestant Huguenots in France, financing Dutch Protestants' rebellion against their Spanish overlords—gave her an unchallenged standing at home. Her defeat of the Armada was Protestantism's greatest worldly victory. When the great wind blew and scattered the Spanish war fleet, Englishmen saw the hand of Providence in it.

With James I's accession, divisions within the English Protestant community began to shake the unity of the realm. The Scottish king had gained little personal respect or loyalty among many English believers. He lacked Elizabeth's charm and grace and wit. He was learned without being able to apply his learning. Given to long, tedious lectures, he was called by some "the wisest fool in Christendom." Even his sponsorship of the great King James Version of the Bible—one of the masterpieces of world literature and, along with Shakespeare, the greatest achievement of English letters—bought him little credit with the more rigorously Protestant people of England. James attempted to bring all Protestants under the "big tent" of the Church of England. He threatened those who dissented. They will conform, he said, "or I will harry them out of the land."

Harry them he did. Puritans were those members of the Anglican Church who sought to remain within the state church while "purifying" it of what they saw as its corruptions. Separatists were Protestants who wanted to make a clean break with the king's church. They saw the Church of England as hopelessly corrupt and viewed the whole structure of bishops and archbishops controlled by the king with deep suspicion.

Puritans tended to be more highly educated. They were especially strong in the universities of Oxford and Cambridge, more successful as merchants in the City of London, and had, in general, a greater stake in English society. Separatists recruited their members from the farmers, artisans, and lower ranks of society. It would not be uncommon for Puritan leaders to be able to read and write Latin and Greek, but both groups had extremely high levels of literacy in English, absolutely necessary for Bible reading.

Harassed by the king's forces, a group of Separatists departed England for Holland in 1609. Settling in the university city of Leiden, they took advantage of the Netherlands' greater tolerance for dissent. After a decade, however, these English exiles began to fear that they were losing their identity. They began to consider the possibility of founding a holy commonwealth of their own in the New World. The small Separatist community, who now called themselves Pilgrims, set sail for America on the tiny English ship *Mayflower.**

Blown off course by fierce storms, they landed south of present-day Boston on the coast of Massachusetts. Soon, this region would be called New England. Anchoring offshore on 11 November 1620, the small company took care before disembarking to sign a document known to history as *The Mayflower Compact.* In it, the Pilgrims agreed on how they would govern themselves. Forty-one of the *Mayflower*'s 102 passengers affixed their signatures to this document.[18] In it, they announced their purpose in founding a colony in the New World—"for the Glory of God, and Advancement of the Christian faith, and the Honour of our King and Country." By signing the compact they pledged to *covenant* together to establish the rules under which they would live. This was the first effort at self-government in New England.

The compact's text contains references to "our dread Sovereign Lord King James" and describes him as king "by the Grace of God," even calling him by his title "Defender of the Faith." The Pilgrims describe themselves as loyal subjects of this king. They apparently saw no inconsistency in the fact that they had removed themselves across a wide ocean in winter expressly to avoid persecution by this same "dread Sovereign Lord." They might have stayed at home in England, quietly conformed by attending the king's church and convincing themselves it was for the greater good. Fully *half* of those who made the voyage would die in the next year of starvation and disease. Yet how strong must have been their determination and their consciences to take such risks. When, in the following spring, the *Mayflower* prepared to return to England, not a single Pilgrim would return with her.[19]

Calling their settlement Plymouth, the name Captain John Smith had earlier given it, the Pilgrims proceeded in the spring to plant for a fall harvest. They were helped by an English-speaking Indian, Squanto, who taught

---

* How tiny was the *Mayflower*? She was a 4-masted, square rigger mounting six sails, 106 feet long, 25 feet wide and displacing 236 tons. Online source: www.plimoth.org/visit/what/mayflower2.asp#5.

them how to plant corn and to catch fish.[20] Without Squanto's generous help, all the Pilgrims might have died.*

Soon, in March of 1621, the Pilgrims signed a treaty with Massasoit, the chief of the Wampanoag tribe. This treaty lasted. In it, the settlers and the Indians pledged mutual friendship and support.[21] It would later prove essential to the survival of the young colony when, in 1636, the settlers fought the Pequot War. Because of the treaty, the Wampanoags stayed out of the conflict.

By autumn of 1621, a successful harvest was crowned by a three-day feast. Chief Massasoit of the Wampanoags brought ninety of his braves for a festival of foot races, wrestling matches, and eating. Deer, turkey, ducks, game birds, rabbits, fish, and other rich foods—many new to the English pilgrims—formed the fare of this first Thanksgiving holiday. Imagine the trust and friendship that had been built up in just a few months. What courage to invite into their settlement ninety strong warriors who might easily have overpowered and wiped out this little community. Small wonder the Pilgrims gave credit to God for the survival of their little band. And little wonder, too, that Americans ever after found in these Pilgrim fathers' setting foot on Plymouth Rock a source of inspiration. As Alexis de Tocqueville wrote in 1835: "Here is a stone which the feet of a few outcasts pressed for an instant; and the stone becomes famous; it is treasured by a great nation; its very dust is shared as a relic."[22]

Within a year, the Pilgrims had elected William Bradford as governor. This young man, only thirty-one, had lost his wife on the *Mayflower*. His remarriage in 1623 was the occasion of another great feast, like the early Thanksgiving, in which the Indians took part. He was reelected yearly after that and governed the little colony until his death in 1657. Bradford had earned his living in Holland as a silk weaver and had learned to speak Dutch and French. These language skills he put to good use in representing

* How could Squanto speak English? He had been captured and taken to Spain by John Smith's rebellious lieutenant Thomas Hunt, who intended to sell him into slavery at Málaga. Rescued by Spanish priests, he later made his way to England, where he lived in London with a shipbuilder who taught him the language. Eventually, he returned to North America. He was abroad about five years. See: Charles C. Mann, *1491* (Knopf, 2005), pp. 49, 53, 54.

the colony. When a French Catholic priest came to Plymouth from Canada seeking help in defending against the Iroquois, he was amazed at the welcome he received from Bradford, who showed remarkable deference and consideration to his guest:

> The governor of the place, named Jehan Brentford [William Bradford], received me with courtesy, and appointed me an audience for the next day; and he invited me to a dinner of fish, which he prepared on my account, knowing that it was Friday.* I found considerable favor in this settlement, for the farmers—and among others the captain, Thomas Willets [Thomas Willett]—spoke to the governor in advocacy of my negotiation. . . . [23]

Soon, the Pilgrims were joined in Massachusetts by a much larger body of immigrants. The new king of England, Charles I, had intensified the persecutions of all dissenters, especially the Puritans. In 1630, seventeen ships and a thousand men, women, and children set sail for America.[24] This would become known as The Great Migration. Led by lawyer John Winthrop aboard the *Arbella,* this group not only brought educated dissenters together, but Winthrop knew his errand into the wilderness would have world significance. "We shall be as a city upon a hill. The eyes of all people are upon us," he said in one of the most destiny-laden sermons ever preached in America.[25] Before they had even set foot in the New World, these Puritans were being assured that their new "Bible Commonwealth" would make them the center of attention for the world.[26] They applied Jesus's words from the Sermon on the Mount to themselves.

In their typically self-critical fashion, however, this was no vain boast. These Puritans wrestled daily with their consciences, with their profound sense of their own sinfulness. Winthrop's conclusion makes this clear. He warned them that if they failed to uphold God's law, they would become "a byword among the nations." The Puritans knew well what that meant. They knew by heart not just the hopeful promises of the New Testament but

* At that time, Catholics were not permitted to eat meat on Fridays.

equally the stern warnings of the Old. In Deuteronomy, Moses warned the children of Israel they could be outcasts if they turned their backs on the living God.[27] Thus, from the earliest moments, America held out her promises and her perils.

The *Arbella* was no humble, fragile little *Mayflower*. She was a rich, proud ship of the line. She mounted twenty-eight cannons with which she rendered and received naval gun salutes.[28] Perhaps prophetically, *Arbella's* figurehead—that great carved image on the vessel's prow—was a huge eagle.[29]

We will have many occasions to comment on the ironies of American history.[30] Here is one: These Puritans wanted to *purify* their own Protestant Church of England, to rid it of every "trapping" of Roman Catholicism. No laced robes for their priests. No elaborate gold crosses. Above all, no crucifixes showing Christ in his passion, no *graven images* of the Blessed Virgin Mary and all the saints. Yet here we have these saints sailing off across the Atlantic with the graven figure of an eagle leading their way.

Soon after landing in 1630, the Puritans transferred the charter of their Massachusetts Bay Company across the sea to their new home. This was an early move toward independence. By 1634, Governor Winthrop had broadened the numbers of those who could vote for the General Court—legislature—to include virtually all adult male church members. Thus, from the start, Americans were developing the habits and experience of self-government.

Boston soon became the largest city in America, large enough to support a university. Harvard, founded in 1636, was expected to prepare young men for the ministry, schooling them in Latin and Greek and making sure that the Puritan ideals were upheld. The Puritans knew that their highly intellectual form of Protestantism needed a strong scholarly foundation. Reading and understanding and explaining the Bible, which they held to be the Word of God, required intense preparation. It would be Harvard's responsibility to transmit these holy truths to the rising generation. Thus, Harvard's motto—*Veritas* (Truth)—meant the truth of salvation that sets men free.

"The Old Deluder" was how the Puritans referred to Satan. And it was to keep their children safe from his snares that the Massachusetts General Court passed the Old Deluder Law in 1647. This law required townships of fifty or more families to hire a tutor to make sure the children learned to read and write; towns of one hundred families or larger were required to support a grammar school.[31] Thus, from the earliest days, Massachusetts set a high standard for literacy and learning. *The New England Primer,* a popular teaching tool, continued to be used well into the nineteenth century.[32] From its stern admonitions, we gain an impression of the moral earnestness and sober realism of these Puritans:

> A *In Adam's Fall*
> *We sinned all.*
> B *Thy Life to Mend*
> *This Book Attend.*
> C *The Cat doth play*
> *And after slay.*
> D *A Dog will bite*
> *A Thief at night.*
> E *An Eagle's flight*
> *Is Out of sight.*
> F *The Idle Fool*
> *Is Whipt at School.*[33]

Serious study of the Bible did not eliminate conflict. These very ideals brought conflict early. Disagreements over doctrine led Puritan leaders to banish such dissenters as Reverend Roger Williams and, later, Mistress Anne Hutchinson. Williams set up another colony on Narragansett Bay in Rhode Island in 1644. *Providence* was to become a haven for dissenters such as Hutchinson fleeing from strict Puritan rule in Boston. "Forced worship," Williams said, "stinks in God's nostrils."[34] His bold stand would inspire lovers of religious liberty in the coming centuries.

III. Expanding English Rule

Massachusetts Bay was not the only colony to banish religious dissenters. When Sir George Calvert, the first Lord Baltimore, converted to Catholicism, the Virginia authorities ordered him to leave. He appealed to King Charles I for a charter for a colony on the north shore of Chesapeake Bay. Although Lord Baltimore died before the charter for Maryland could be approved, it was finally granted to his son, Cecilius, in 1634.* Planned as a profit-making enterprise, Maryland was also intended as a refuge for Catholics. Despite this, however, the majority of Maryland colonists were Protestants. Early attempts by the Calverts to assure religious liberty in the form of an Act of Toleration—a measure that granted religious freedom to all Christians—had only limited results.** Protestant small landholders rebelled against the rule of Catholic lords and repealed the act.[35]

Between these English-dominated coastal regions, the Dutch and the Swedes planted two small colonies. New Netherlands was located along the banks of the Hudson River with a capital on Manhattan Island, which they called New Amsterdam. Peter Minuit, on authority from the Dutch West India Company, had bought Manhattan Island from the Canarsie Indians for sixty *guilders*—the equivalent of $23.70. (This real estate is today worth $60 billion.) The Dutch were drawn to the New World by the prospects of rich profits in fur trading.[36] Their settlements hugged the banks of the river named for the famed explorer, Henry Hudson, an Englishman who had sailed for the Netherlands. (Hudson gave his name to the majestic river. In another attempt to find a Northwest Passage to India, he discovered Hudson's Bay. He met a cruel death when his men mutinied and marooned him in a small boat.) Soon, the Dutch merchants of New Netherlands were squeezing out English traders, outbidding them and underselling them.[37]

When the autocratic, peg-legged Peter Stuyvesant took over as governor of New Netherlands, he ordered in 1657 the erection of a nine-foot wall in lower Manhattan to defend the settlement. The street that ran along these defenses would later become world famous as Wall Street. Stuyvesant

* To mistrustful English Protestants, Maryland's Catholic founders could say they named their colony after the queen, Henrietta *Maria,* but among themselves it was understood that Maryland was dedicated to the Blessed Virgin Mary.

** Clearly, it was in the Catholics' *self-interest* to seek toleration for all Christians. They saw they would soon be outnumbered. But this is often the beginning of wisdom as well as liberty—an *enlightened* self-interest.

was a no-nonsense figure who forcibly took over the little Swedish settlement near present-day Wilmington, Delaware.

The English, who had protested the first Dutch settlements in the lands they claimed, were distracted during the middle decades of the seventeenth century by the Puritan rebellion and their own civil war. King Charles I's attempts to force uniformity of religious worship and to rule without Parliament led to violence. Oliver Cromwell, a local, landed leader, led an army against the king. From 1642 to 1648, the parliamentary army—known as *Roundheads* for their close-cropped haircuts—battled the royal forces called *Cavaliers*.* When the king was finally defeated, Cromwell and his fellow Puritan leaders vowed to bring him to trial for treason. Not all Puritans agreed with this unprecedented action. King Charles's constant attempts to break out of captivity, his alliances with foreign kings, and his untrustworthiness led Cromwell to declare: "We intend to cut off the king's head *with his crown on*." Thus, in January 1649, England became, for a brief period, a republic. The Puritan leaders called it a *commonwealth*.**

Parliament had triumphed over the forces of royal despotism. But when Parliament itself became unruly, splintered into bitter factions, Cromwell dispersed it and ruled as a military dictator. He called himself the Lord Protector. With Cromwell's death in 1658, the attempt to install his son Richard as protector soon collapsed. The English people, weary of the Puritans' severity, welcomed back the exiled Charles II. In 1660, England became a monarchy once again. England would never again have a republican government, but from this point on, the kings and queens were forced to take Parliament's role seriously.

After the restoration of the monarchy in Britain, the English moved quickly to reestablish their authority along the Atlantic coast from Newfoundland to Florida. They sent a small fleet against New Amsterdam in 1664. Peter Stuyvesant had little choice but to surrender when the English sails appeared off Manhattan. Theodore Roosevelt's family had been among

* Cromwell's New Model Army, which he completely dominated, was never defeated in battle.

** "No King but Jesus," the more radical Commonwealth men cried. These Levelers, as they were called, believed that any form of monarchy or nobility was against God's law. In a *republic*, all citizens are equal before the law.

the Dutch *patroons*—rich farmers of the Hudson Valley—who continued to hold sway under both Dutch and English rule. Roosevelt writes:

> The expedition against New Amsterdam had been organized with the Duke of York, afterward King James II, as its special patron, and the city was re-christened in his honor. To this day its name perpetuates the memory of the dull, cruel bigot with whose short reign came to a close the ignoble line of the Stuart kings.

Roosevelt didn't mince words. Actually, the Duke of York's government of New York was fairly enlightened. The Dutch had permitted English immigrants and French Huguenots to settle in their colony while they retained overall political control. As many as a third of the 1,500 colonists were non-Dutch. Under the new English colonial rule, freedom of religion and language were maintained. The patroons had little cause for discontent. When, briefly, the Dutch recaptured the colony in 1673, their rule lasted only one year. They willingly gave up New York for English concessions in the Caribbean, for those colonies were then considered far richer prizes. The great New York Dutch families—Van Rensselaers, Schuylers, and Roosevelts—would continue to play an important role in the life of the state and nation.

The importance of the English takeover of New York, however, cannot be overestimated. New England had already formed a confederation, uniting for external purposes the English colonies north and east of the Hudson River. Without New York, English colonial rule would have been broken, with Virginia and Maryland being cut off from New England. With New York firmly under English government, a continental union came closer to reality.

A new religious sect arose in England after the restoration of the monarchy: the Society of Friends, known as *Quakers* because some of its members felt such religious intensity that they actually quaked during worship services. Quakers faced persecution from the Church of England authorities. Quakers were pacifists, refusing to bear arms or support wars. They declined to take oaths, citing Jesus's words, and thus ran afoul of the court system. Despite, or perhaps because of oppression (thousands had been jailed), the Quaker movement spread. When the son of the famous Admiral Sir William Penn converted to the new faith, his father was furious. But the two reconciled, and the younger William Penn applied for a charter for a *proprietary* colony in America. A proprietary colony was one in which the Crown granted power to a rich individual or family to establish a settlement for profit. The younger William Penn applied in 1682 to the Duke of York, who owed his father sixteen thousand pounds, for a charter. Penn intended his land grant to be a refuge for his fellow Quakers. Penn had visited Germany and appealed to other pacifist Christian sects there to emigrate and join in his Holy Experiment.[38]

Pennsylvania ("Penn's Forest") was an immediate success. Penn's guarantee of religious freedom was then one of the most comprehensive in the world. Catholics, Lutherans, Baptists, Presbyterians, and even Anglicans (Church of England members) rushed to settle the rich lands. By 1700, Pennsylvania had as many as twenty-one thousand settlers.[39] Despite growing pains, the colony was the first community specifically planned to include diverse populations and extending a broad measure of religious and political equality. The capital—Philadelphia ("City of Brotherly Love")—became a thriving metropolis, soon the largest of colonial cities. The example of such a community—living peacefully without absolute royal authority or an established religion—inspired the French philosopher Voltaire.[40]

Although Voltaire had only a fuzzy idea of Philadelphia, he was correct in seeing a thriving colony that attracted Scots-Irish and Germans in vast numbers. Add to these the Dutch, the Swedes, and the Jews, and America begins to "look like America."

IV. Britain and France: Conflict for a Continent

Parliament's Act of Union of 1707 formally joined Scotland and England as one United Kingdom. Thus, thousands of Scots now joined their countrymen in the *British* colonies of the New World. While English colonies were expanding rapidly along the Atlantic seaboard, France was penetrating deep into the interior of Canada. Under the leadership of the courageous Samuel de Champlain, French objectives were the rich fur trade and the conversion of the Indians. Champlain made the hazardous passage across the Atlantic no less than *twenty times* between 1603 and 1633.[41] He founded Quebec City in 1608. From this outpost, trappers and traders—known as *coureurs de bois* (forest runners)—traveled to the innermost sections of the continent. These adventurous French Canadians traveled as far as the Dakotas before the English had advanced to the crest of the Appalachians.[42]

Far ahead of his time, Champlain saw Canada as an ideal location for New France, for the building up of a distinct society in the New World. But the royal government at Versailles was unwilling to send political or religious dissidents, or even criminals, to populate New France. Thus, French colonization never achieved the impact that massive English emigration did in the Atlantic colonies. This fact also contributed to the generally more favorable relations the French enjoyed with the Indian tribes. Their settlements, largely trading posts, intruded less on the Indian way of life. Unlike the English, where the marriage of John Rolfe and Pocahontas was an exception, the French *coureurs* were more likely to take Indian wives.

French missionary efforts saw notable success among the Huron Indians but met the hostility of the Iroquois Confederation. Young, zealous Catholic priests of the Society of Jesus—the Jesuits—were especially active among the tribes. Father Isaac Jogues ventured from Quebec City in 1636. He preached the gospel a thousand miles in the interior, as the historian George Bancroft noted, "five years before [Protestant missionary] John Eliot addressed the Indians six miles from Boston Harbour."[43] He proposed to convert the Indians of Lake Superior and even to send missionaries to the Sioux in the distant Dakotas.

But Isaac Jogues's bold vision was not realized. He was taken captive in 1642 by Mohawks, members of the Iroquois Confederation. He was seized some forty miles from the Dutch settlement at Fort Orange, present-day Albany. Tortured and held in slavery for months, Jogues finally escaped. He made his way to New Amsterdam, where he was kindly treated by the Dutch. Making his way back to France, Jogues was treated as a virtual

Lazarus, a man returned from the dead. He created a sensation in France. Despite the fact that several of his fingers had been eaten by his captors, he was allowed by the pope to celebrate Mass.*

Disregarding his wounds, Father Jogues returned to Canada and set out once again in 1646 as a missionary to the Mohawks. As a result of his ordeal, he had learned several Indian languages. At first, he was well received by his former captors. Soon, however, disease broke out among the tribes and their crops failed. Some among the Mohawks blamed this on the "black robes"—as the Jesuits were known to the Indians. Jogues and a companion were recaptured. Stripped naked, beaten, slashed with knives, Jogues was led into the Indian village. As he entered a cabin, he was killed with a tomahawk. This, and the very similar fate of Jean de Brebeuf and several other young Jesuits, led the Catholic Church to declare Isaac Jogues and his brothers martyrs and saints.[44]

The French mastered the internal waterways of the North American continent. *Voyageurs*—who succeeded the *coureurs*—set forth in birch bark canoes with nearly the same skill as the Indians. In 1682, the Sieur de La Salle managed an incredible feat: he sailed and rowed down the Mississippi River to a point below the site of present-day New Orleans. La Salle claimed the whole region for France and named it for King Louis XIV—*Louisiana.*[45] (On a second voyage, this time to the Texas coast, La Salle was murdered by his own men. They were themselves then massacred by the Comanche tribe—a testament to the continued dangers of exploration.[46])

The French sought control of the Ohio River, a major tributary of the Mississippi. The region was rich in furs. To get them, they had to ward off the English. With the aid of Indian allies, the French staged raids against the neighboring colonies. The governor of New France was the fierce Louis de Bouade, the comte de Frontenac. He used his Indian forces to terrorize the English settlements on the frontiers of New York and New England in 1690–92. Frontenac reasoned if he could terrorize the English in their home colonies, they would not move west into the Ohio Valley. Massacres

* Catholic priests must raise the communion wafer between the thumb and forefinger. Thus, it required a special *dispensation* from the pope to allow Father Jogues to celebrate Mass.

of women and children, accompanied by scalping and the torture of victims, embittered the two nations against one another—and their colonists were especially hostile.[47]

The early harmony that characterized the relations between colonists like Captain John Smith, Governor William Bradford, and William Penn the proprietor and their Indian neighbors did not long prevail. Here, less than half a century after the English had first come to America with such high hopes, we see growing resistance by the native peoples to the steady, irresistible influx of Europeans. The Puritans of New England fought a war against the Pequots in 1636–37. In one jarring episode, Puritan warriors burned a tribe that had taken refuge in a stockade—*and sang hymns while applying the torch.* Significantly, King Philip, grandson of Massasoit, was defeated when *other* Indians combined with the settlers against him. This was part of a pattern of Indians clashing with Indians that should not be forgotten. Iroquois warriors destroyed the Hurons, and attacked the Susquehannocks, the Nipissings, the Potawatomi, and the Delawares in the period 1649–84, failing only against the Illinois.[48] No wonder the warlike Iroquois were referred to as the "Romans of the West."

Wars between the British and the French in Europe necessarily spilled over into America. King Philip's War (1675–76) brought terror to the New England frontier and devastation to the Wampanoags. One-fourth of New England villages were destroyed; one of every sixteen male settlers was killed. King William's War (1689–97) in the colonies was a mere continuation of the conflict that had been going on between William and Louis XIV when William was still a *stadtholder* in Holland. He and his English wife, Mary, had taken over the thrones of England in 1688 when Mary's father, James II, was exiled in the near bloodless Glorious Revolution. "I will maintain the liberties of England and the Protestant Religion," read William's banners as he came ashore.

The French in Canada tried to secure the mouth of the St. Lawrence with a great fortress on Cape Breton Island, called Louisbourg, "the Gibraltar of America." Despite its defenses, it fell to English raids repeatedly. Massive walls and quarters for six armed regiments only added to the expense of the failure. Begun in 1721, construction of Louisbourg proceeded for years. It was a huge and impractical French prestige project. Louis XV is said to have thrown back the heavily embroidered drapes at his grand Palace of Versailles—telling courtiers he wanted to see the spires of Louisbourg rising above the western horizon. Boston men attacking Louisbourg found they could cut the great fort off and fire down on it from higher ground.[49]

V. Religious and Intellectual Awakenings

Against this backdrop of fear and danger came one of the most bizarre and discreditable episodes in American history. In the Massachusetts village of Salem in 1692, a young woman named Tituba, of mixed black and Indian heritage, was accused of witchcraft. Understandably alarmed, she accused several leading members of the village of being in league with the devil. Her words were given more weight because she confessed to being allied to Satan herself. Soon, teenagers were offering "spectral" evidence in court. Far from the kind of evidence acceptable in a modern court of law, it consisted of claims of hostile and ungodly actions by the *specters,* or spirits, of accused men and women. The authorities accepted the testimony of obviously hysterical teens and condemned some twenty villagers, including a congregational minister, to death by hanging—and, in one case, by pressing with heavy stones.

Compounding the tragedy was the intervention of the great Cotton Mather. Reverend Mather was the leading man of learning and piety in the English colonies. His writings and sermons carried enormous influence. Mather's writings on science and nature were so highly regarded that he was the first American elected into membership in the Royal Society in London. But in Salem, Cotton Mather argued that spectral evidence should be accepted. Because of his weighty influence, innocent people died.

English colonists in the eighteenth century were a religiously diverse people. While dissenters had been deliberately kept out of Spanish and French colonies, England welcomed many kinds of Protestants—Presbyterians, Lutherans, Baptists, Dutch Reformed, Quakers, Mennonites, Moravians, Anglicans—and also increasing numbers of Catholics and Jews in settling their New World colonies.

Following the revered Cotton Mather, the next most important figure in colonial America was Jonathan Edwards. Born in Connecticut in 1703, he was highly educated. He came to believe in a far more demanding, more intense religious experience of conversion of the heart. Most famous for his sermon *Sinners in the Hands of an Angry God*, which held out the horrors of hellfire for the unrepentant, he nonetheless gave equal emphasis to the transforming power of the love of Christ. When his search for greater conviction in himself and others led him into conflict with his congregational church in 1750, he left prosperous Connecticut for Stockbridge, Massachusetts. In that frontier community, Edwards preached for seven years to the Mohawks and Mohegans. His ministry met with mixed success, but his influential writings became a source of inspiration to thousands. He composed *The Nature of True Virtue*, *Original Sin*, and *Freedom of the Will*—some of the most profound theological works ever written in America. Edwards left Stockbridge to assume the presidency of the College of New Jersey at Princeton, but he died soon afterward of complications from a smallpox inoculation.[50] In addition to Princeton, Dartmouth and Brown trace their origins to the powerful religious movements of this time.

Although Edwards delivered his powerful sermons in a quiet, conversational tone, his preaching is nonetheless seen as one of the first evidences of the religious revival in America known as the Great Awakening. Many Protestant denominations were affected by the fervor of this movement, especially among frontier communities. There, daily life was threatened not only by Indian raids but also by the ravages of disease, wild animals, and crop failures.

While rejected by many of the established religious authorities of the time, the Great Awakening was powerfully expressed in the mass outdoor gatherings that heard the English preacher George Whitefield. In Philadelphia, when the older churches shut their doors to the "enthusiastic" Whitefield, Benjamin Franklin arranged to have a hall built to accommodate the great evangelist. (Later, the hall would serve the University of Pennsylvania, a nonsectarian institution.) Whitefield's preaching was a marvel—an excited, animated presentation that could be heard by as many as twenty thousand people at a time. Beginning in Philadelphia in 1739,

Whitefield continued on to New England in 1740, preaching 130 sermons in 73 days.[51] Soon, his earnest, emotion-filled style of preaching was styled *Methodist.* The process of cleaving yet another new denomination continued. The Methodist movement began in England within the Anglican Church and was led by reformer John Wesley. In Protestant North America, this process of churches dividing was to prove nearly endless.

But while factions and splits abounded, Whitefield became a strangely unifying figure for the colonies. When high-ranking figures of the "established" Church of England seemed to look down their well-bred noses at his earnest, emotional, *powerful* preaching style, Whitefield only became more popular in America. At home in England, he was the favorite preacher of coal miners and London roughnecks.[52] But he crossed the Atlantic *thirteen times* to hold thousands of Americans spellbound. Even Benjamin Franklin, that genial skeptic, was moved. With typical wit, Franklin wrote:

> I happened soon after to attend one of his sermons, in the course of which I perceived he intended to finish with a collection, and I silently resolved he should get nothing from me. I had in my pocket a handful of copper money, three or four silver dollars, and five pistoles in gold. As he proceeded I began to soften, and concluded to give the coppers. Another stroke of his oratory made me ashamed of that, and determined me to give the silver, and he finished so admirably, that I emptied my pocket wholly into the collector's dish, gold and all.[53]

Of course, what Whitefield wanted was his hearers' hearts. A later preacher, the great evangelist Charles Haddon Spurgeon, described the impact of Whitefield's ministry in America: "He *lived.* Other men seemed to be only half-alive; but Whitefield was all life, fire, wing, force."[54]

The Great Awakening was a phenomenon played out over twenty to thirty years throughout America. It was the first truly *mass* movement in America. Although it was a powerful *religious* movement and not a political event, its influence was to be felt in the politics of the era. People who had already rejected the authority of powerful clergy tied to the British monarchy were more likely to reject as well the power of royal officials.

Benjamin Franklin had his first contact with Cotton Mather while still an apprentice in his brother James's Boston print shop. The Franklin brothers in 1721 were waging a strong campaign *against* smallpox inoculations in the pages of their newspaper, the *New England Courant.* Ben was only sixteen at the time, but it was an unpromising start for the man who would become the leading scientific mind in America. Cotton Mather was backed by his respected father, Increase Mather. The Mathers denounced the Franklins' newspaper as a scandal sheet. The Mathers were ultimately successful in persuading their fellow colonists of the effectiveness of inoculation. The learned Cotton had read of the procedure in the journal of the Royal Society of London.[55] Soon, young Ben would run away from his older brother's harsh apprenticeship, leaving Boston for a freer Philadelphia. Years later, when Ben Franklin returned from Philadelphia for a visit, he met with the aged Cotton Mather. Mather received him cordially, never mentioning the clash over inoculation. As Franklin was leaving, Mather called after him: "Stoop! Stoop!" But it was too late. Franklin bumped his head on a low hanging beam. Mather could not resist a moralizing tale: he told the young Franklin that he had the world before him. "Stoop as you go through it and you will miss many hard thumps."[56] Franklin never forgot.*

Franklin's success as a Philadelphia printer enabled him to publish his newspaper, the *Pennsylvania Gazette,* beginning in 1729. Four years later, he expanded his output to include *Poor Richard's Almanack.* In addition to the usual fare offered to farmers and rural townsmen, Franklin's witty, worldly advice from Poor Richard gained him a following throughout the colonies. Franklin also actively pursued voluntary associations for the betterment of Philadelphia—including paving, lighting, and cleaning the streets—which helped Franklin's adopted hometown surpass his native Boston as the leading city in America. Franklin was the organizing spirit behind the volunteer fire company, the lending library, and the fire insurance company. In 1743,

* Franklin might have agreed, too, with Cotton Mather's famous observation about the thrift and industry of the New England Puritans: "Religion begat prosperity, and the daughter devoured the mother." As the New Englanders got richer, they tended to fall away from their faith. Such statements are reflected in contemporary concerns about affluence and decadence in America.

the man who never attended university himself helped found the American Philosophical Society, one of the oldest of learned organizations. His was the guidance behind the hospital and the college that was to become the University of Pennsylvania.

Franklin's success as a businessman gave him the income and the leisure time to pursue his genius for practical invention. In addition to the revolutionary Franklin stove—which brought comfort to millions—he invented swim fins used by today's scuba divers and experimented with stilling the waves by applying oil. Most remarkable of all were Franklin's 1749 experiments with electricity. By flying a kite into thunder clouds and letting lightning travel along a wire to a key, Franklin demonstrated that lightning was, in fact, an electrical phenomenon. Ever practical, Franklin devised the lightning rod to safely convey the bolts of electricity to the ground, thus saving innumerable church steeples and public buildings as well as houses and barns.

Nor did Franklin neglect his role as citizen. He first began attending meetings of the Pennsylvania Assembly to make official records of its proceedings. In time, he was elected to the assembly in his own right, and his fellow legislators looked to him for leadership. The majority moved steadily into opposition to the colony's proprietors.

William Penn's descendants lacked his diplomatic skills and his commitment to the welfare of the colony. The assembly chafed at the proprietors' petulant demand that their extensive lands in Pennsylvania not be taxed. By this time, the proprietors lived in London and could not be expected to share the Pennsylvanians' concerns about colonial defense. Legislators from the frontier protested loudly when Philadelphia Quakers and absentee proprietors turned a deaf ear to their reports of Indian atrocities. Because he took the lead in organizing defense in Pennsylvania, Benjamin Franklin soon became the popular leader of the colony.

VI. Britain and France: The Final Conflict

Britain and France had been at war intermittently for nearly a hundred years. Most of these quarrels had started in Europe, but by 1754, America would become the flash point for a final contest for control of the continent. Because of their home country's restrictive emigration policies, British command of the seas, and French trading policies, New France numbered only 60,000 at midcentury. The British colonies, by contrast, had 1.25 million people living along the Atlantic.[57]

Seeing the threat of a war on the American frontier, London prodded the colonies to unite under a single royal administration. Franklin, the acknowledged leader of Pennsylvania, was chosen in 1754 to go to Albany, New York, to present a plan for colonial union under British administration. To gain popular support, Franklin's *Pennsylvania Gazette* published his own drawing of a snake cut in parts labeled "N[ew] E[ngland], N.Y., N.J., P[ennsylvania], D[elaware], M[aryland], V[irginia], N[orth] C[arolina] and S[outh] C[arolina]." Beneath this early political cartoon was printed the legend: "Join or Die." The jealousies of colonial legislatures prevented the Albany Plan of Union from coming to fruition, but Franklin was not embittered. He had played a key role on a national stage as an advocate of American union.

Meanwhile, in Virginia, Governor Robert Dinwiddie also saw war clouds on the western horizon. He knew that the French disputed Virginia's claim to the Ohio Country, the region west of the confluence of the Monongahela, Allegheny, and Ohio Rivers. He had heard of the French building a fort there that they called Fort Duquesne on the site of present-day Pittsburgh. The governor needed a Virginian to warn the French to leave the disputed territory. He chose a young planter, a lieutenant colonel of militia, from Fairfax County. The twenty-two-year-old George Washington was tall, strong, and able to face the trials of the wilderness because of his years surveying western lands. Reputed to be the best rider in Virginia, young Washington conducted himself as a gentleman and was eager to advance his military career.

Washington set out at the end of October 1753 with a party of six, including his friend Christopher Gist, who would serve as guide. A month out of Virginia, the Washington party met Half King, an emissary from the Iroquois. Half King told Washington he had met up with French forces and had ordered them to leave the Ohio Country. When Washington finally arrived at Fort LeBoeuf, one hundred miles north of the three rivers, he changed from his buckskins to a dress uniform and enjoyed the gracious hospitality of the French garrison. He delivered his governor's stern message and was met with steely cordiality in response. The French would not leave what they clearly regarded as their own lands, and they would resist anyone, British or Indian, who tried to remove them.[58]

Washington nearly lost his life on his return voyage. First, an Indian guide turned on him and Gist and, without warning, fired a single-shot pistol at Washington. It missed. Then Washington was pitched from his raft into the freezing Allegheny River. He barely escaped drowning and death from hypothermia.[59] Washington published an account of this action that made his name a household word throughout the colonies. People were amazed that he survived. Already, they began to think of him as invincible.

When he reported the French intransigence to Governor Dinwiddie, the governor quickly assembled a military expedition to expel them by force. Washington soon became the leader. Approaching the Ohio River, Washington learned that a French party was moving through the forest. Taking forty men, including Half King and a number of Iroquois, Washington soon overtook the French force. He ordered an attack. When the stunned Frenchmen surrendered, Washington was unable to prevent several of the French party from being massacred by his Indian allies. The French leader, Ensign Jumonville, was tomahawked by Half King, who showed Washington the poor man's still-warm brains.[60]

The French survivors waved papers at Washington—shouting in their outrage that they were a peaceful diplomatic mission.[61] Why then was the French company moving quietly and stealthily through the forest, just like a war party? When Washington had approached the French Fort LeBoeuf, near Lake Erie, the previous year, hadn't he come openly, marching in broad daylight with his Indian allies? The French answer could well have been that hostile Indian warriors like Half King would show no mercy to a diplomatic party, however peaceful its intent. The tragic loss of life can now be seen as a terrible misunderstanding.

On the return trip to Virginia, Washington stopped to build a small stockade he named Fort Necessity. Half King, unimpressed, called it "that little thing in the meadow."[62] It failed to impress the French as well. When a larger force of French and Indians surrounded the fort, Washington had little choice but to surrender. The French commander turned out to be the slaughtered Jumonville's brother![63] He forced Washington to sign a document on 4 July 1754, in which Washington confessed to the "assassination" of the emissary Jumonville.

Washington was nonetheless treated as a hero back in Virginia. He wrote to his brother that he "heard the bullets whistle, and believe me there is something charming in the sound."[64] When King George II (that "snuffy old drone from the German hive"*) heard that, he said Washington could not have heard very many bullets if he found them "charming." The young Virginia colonel's bold challenge to the French was just what colonists wanted. His name was known throughout the colonies—as indeed it was carried to London and Versailles. The French regarded his actions on the Ohio as a *casus belli*—cause of war.

When a regular British force of two regiments under General Edward Braddock was assembled in Virginia the next year, it was only natural that Colonel Washington would accompany them to Fort Duquesne. Franklin actively aided Braddock's force by rounding up supply wagons for the British troops.[65] Although Braddock was very friendly to young Washington, he did not take the Virginia militia seriously. Nor did he take seriously Washington's warnings about "the *Canadian* French" and their Indian allies.[66]

Barely a year after Washington's humiliating surrender of Fort Necessity, Braddock's large force was ambushed on 9 July 1755, just twelve miles from Fort Duquesne. Washington was barely able to ride, suffering from crippling dysentery, but he rallied when the attack came. General Braddock contemptuously refused Washington's plea to lead the Virginians in an Indian-style counterattack and soon paid for that mistake with his life.[67]

With five hundred dead, including the commander, it was the worst military defeat the British had ever suffered in North America. Others who were among the defeated ranks that streamed in panic back to Philadelphia included Thomas Gage, who would later command British troops at Bunker

* "Seventeen hundred and fifty-five, Georgius Secundus was then alive, Snuffy old drone from the German hive . . ."—from "The Deacon's Masterpiece," by Oliver Wendell Holmes Sr.

Hill; Horatio Gates, the American victor at Saratoga; and Daniel Boone, the pioneer and founder of Kentucky.[68] Franklin would later write that the sight of the defeated British ranks straggling back to Philadelphia—and their abusive treatment of the American farmers on their way—would have a deep impact on colonial sentiment. Once again, though, Washington was regarded as the hero who tried to warn his British superiors and who, when his advice was spurned, was able to bring the survivors safely home. Washington was one of the few officers untouched in the fatal encounter.

Louisbourg, as we have seen, was not the Gibraltar of North America, but Quebec City was. The British had failed repeatedly to take this redoubt. To commemorate French successes, the cathedral church in the Old City was named *Notre Dame des Victoires* (Our Lady of Victories). But when, in December 1756, William Pitt became prime minister, Britain determined to strike at the heart of New France. Pitt recognized that continued frontier warfare risked more disasters like the one that overtook Braddock. To lay siege to the fortress city would force the brave French commander, the Marquis de Montcalm, to withdraw his overextended forces from the Ohio, thus relieving the settlers of New York and New England. It would also minimize the French advantage of Indian allies. Pitt was the first British prime minister to recognize the strategic importance of North America.

General Montcalm, father of ten, was a skilled leader. In 1757, he defeated the British at Fort William Henry (later Ticonderoga) in northern New York. When the British garrison marched out of the fort, under a flag of surrender, Montcalm's Abenaki allies massacred many of them. Only with difficulty did the general restore order.[69] This was precisely the kind of outrage the French had charged against Washington. Montcalm's successful attack on the British fortress would later provide the historical setting for James Fenimore Cooper's classic novel *Last of the Mohicans.* This early literary masterpiece would give America the frontier hero Natty Bumppo—*Hawkeye*—and a compelling portrait of the Indian guide Chingachgook.

The success of Pitt's strategy showed when the French were forced to abandon Fort Duquesne in the face of a large force of Pennsylvania and Virginia troops. George Washington was among the victors in November

1758 as overwhelming numbers began to work against the French.[70] They renamed it Fort Pitt (and it was soon to become known as Pittsburgh).

Tall, lanky, red-haired James Wolfe was the British commander at the siege of Quebec. He occupied the beautiful Isle d'Orleans, just downstream from Quebec City. From there, he put gunners ashore at Pointe Levis to bombard the city.[71] Wolfe, a major general at thirty-two, was fifteen years younger than the aristocratic General Montcalm. Unlike Montcalm, who had to contend with a troublesome and cowardly Governor Rigaud de Vaudreuil, Wolfe enjoyed excellent relations with British Admiral Charles Saunders, who commanded forty-nine vessels.[72]

General Wolfe disguised himself as a common soldier to reconnoiter the fortress city. He wanted to find the ideal place for his troops to mount the Plains of Abraham and assault the town. When, in shock, General Montcalm said he saw the British "where they have no business to be"—advancing toward the unprotected side of the city—he firmly resolved to go out and meet the enemy. Cringing Governor Vaudreuil refused to commit the city garrison, which meant Montcalm would be outnumbered. Bravely, Montcalm met the enemy. General Wolfe, at the moment of victory, was mortally wounded. So, in the same engagement, was Montcalm.[73] It was 13 September 1759. The battle had lasted less than an hour.

With the fall of Quebec City, Americans celebrated up and down the Atlantic seaboard. Within a year, Montreal, too, would fall and 150 years of French rule in North America would end. The French threat would be removed—and with it the Americans' need for British protection. Benjamin Franklin, by this time living in London as Pennsylvania's unofficial agent, had high hopes for an Anglo-American empire expanding into the Ohio Country, extending all the way to the Mississippi. Incredibly, Franklin heard rumors that the British peace negotiators might *not* demand all of Canada in the extended talks in Paris. Guadeloupe, the French island colony in the Caribbean, seemed to some a richer prize.

Prime Minister Pitt's strategy was successful not only in North America but around the world. Britain and Prussia defeated France in Europe. Britain defeated France in India and on the high seas. Under Pitt's direction,

Britain's power even extended into West Africa. William Pitt was rightly seen as the father of the British Empire.[74] These victories made him extremely popular with the British people. Dr. Samuel Johnson, that great man of letters, reportedly said, "Walpole was a [prime] minister given by the king to the people, but Pitt was a [prime] minister given by the people to the king."[75] Although the beloved Pitt, "the great Commoner," enjoyed the support of the people, it was not enough to keep him in King George III's good graces. He was dismissed as prime minister in 1761 as the king sought men more subservient to his will.

Pitt thought it was a mistake for the British not to press on to a final victory over France.[76] Some influential Britons thought it might be better to keep a French presence in Canada so that the Americans did not unite and demand independence from Great Britain. Franklin had to counter that view. He published a pamphlet in London, *The Interest of Great Britain Considered, With Regard to her Colonies, And the Acquisitions of Canada and Guadeloupe.* In it, he argued strongly for keeping Canada, for the security it would bring to the English colonies in America.[77]

The treaty that ended the Seven Years War in Europe—called the French and Indian War in America—was titled the Peace of Paris. It was signed in 1763. Pitt thought the Peace of Paris was "too lenient," and he denounced the ministry's policy toward the Americans.[78] Gone was New France, but not the rich French-speaking culture that flourishes in Canada to this day.* As always, Benjamin Franklin took the long view. In a letter to an English friend after the treaty, he wrote, "No one can rejoice more sincerely than I do on the Reduction of Canada; and this, not merely as I am a Colonist, but as I am a Briton. I have long been of Opinion that the Foundations of the future Grandeur and Stability of the British Empire lie in America."[79]

In saying this, Franklin personified the attitude of the Americans. They were proud of being Britons. They were proud of themselves and what they had accomplished *within the British Empire*. They expected greater respect and greater autonomy as a result of their exertions during

* When people in Quebec say, "Je me reviens"—*I remember*—it is the hope and the glory of a "French fact" in North America that they recall. For some it is even more militant and defiant; Quebec separatists have blown up the statue of Wolfe on the Plains of Abraham.

the French and Indian War. They were determined to claim these as their part of the fruits of victory.

With the removal of the French danger, would the colonies now unite in *opposition* to Britain? Franklin had seen the failure of the Albany Plan of Union. At this point in his career, he sincerely believed in a Grand Union of Britain *and* America—united by the British Crown. Franklin thought an American union against the Mother Country impossible. *Or, nearly so.* He did not rule it out completely. The ever-practical Franklin knew that in politics as in the atmosphere, storm clouds could blow up suddenly and unexpectedly. "When I say such an union is impossible, I mean without the most grievous tyranny and oppression."[80] Over the next twenty years, Americans would be faced by a succession of British ministries that engaged in precisely such tyranny and oppression.

Three

THE GREATEST REVOLUTION (1765–1783)

Parliament passes the Stamp Act. This notorious act of taxation without representation sows the seeds of revolution and sparks an earthshaking shift in colonial political allegiances. Undergirding the practical concerns of British policies, the colonies catch fire with stirring talk about equality, the consent of the governed, and the importance of ancient rights and newly asserted liberties. Thomas Jefferson pens an immortal Declaration of Independence. The War for Independence, grim and bloody, claims the lives of twenty-five thousand American Patriots. George Washington proves himself as invaluable on the field as Benjamin Franklin in his diplomatic capacities and John Adams in leading Congress. Benedict Arnold, suffering from wounded pride, betrays his countrymen, but the colonies rally and are victorious. The Revolution frees Americans from the bondage of Britain's colonial rule, but the liberation is not complete. Chattel slavery continues, though the ideals that inspired the Revolution lead to the emancipation of slaves in many states in the early years after peace—and to the whole country in time.

I. STAMPING OUT UNFAIR TAXES

Deborah Franklin had just begun to enjoy her new home on Philadelphia's Market Street. She missed her husband, who was in London as an agent for the colony's assembly. Her fear of sailing had prevented her from going to England to be with him. Fearing water, she by no means feared fire. In late September 1765, when some Philadelphians spread the rumor that Benjamin Franklin had consented to the hated Stamp Tax, a mob gathered to set fire to the Franklin home. Franklin's business partner, David Hall, had warned him in a letter. "The spirit of the people is so violently against anyone they think has the least concern with the Stamp Law," he wrote, telling his friend they had "imbibed the notion that you had a hand in framing it, which has occasioned you many enemies."[1]

Deborah reacted like a lioness to the threat of having her house torched. She sent her daughter to New Jersey but summoned her cousin and his friends to help defend the home. "Fetch a gun or two," she said defiantly.[2] Her wits and resolve saved the home.

Franklin had been in London as a colonial agent since 1759 and, although he corresponded regularly with friends in Pennsylvania and other colonies, it took at least six weeks for a letter to go from America to England. Franklin was woefully behind recent developments. While he sternly opposed the new tax, Franklin did not know just how hostile the colonists were toward it. Passed in Parliament with neither representation nor consent, George Grenville, the British chancellor of the exchequer, sought to make the pill more palatable by having *Americans* do the tax collecting.[3] Franklin went along with the idea and nominated his friend John Hughes for the job in Pennsylvania.[4] Misreading the political pulse at home, neither man realized that the act was so hated that Hughes's appointment would destroy his political career.[5] It would not take long for everyone on both sides of the Atlantic to judge America's true feelings about the Stamp Act.

The tax was intended to raise revenue in the colonies to cover the huge debts Britain had incurred during the French and Indian War. Grenville believed that taxing the colonies for the expense of their defense was only right and just. After all, the costs of maintaining military defense and civilian administration in the colonies had jumped from £70,000 in 1748 to £350,000 in 1764.[6] Under his Stamp Act, colonists would pay a tax on almost anything written or printed. This would include licenses, contracts, commissions, mortgages, wills, deeds, newspapers, advertisements, calendars, and almanacs—even dice and playing cards.[7]

Passed in February 1765, the act was to go into effect in America on November 1. Details of the act began to appear in colonial newspapers—as yet untaxed—in May. Ominously, those accused of violating the act would not be tried in their own communities by juries of their peers, but taken to far-off Halifax, Nova Scotia, and tried before special Admiralty courts.[8] The reaction was immediate—and hostile.

The Virginia House of Burgesses was sitting in Williamsburg when word came. As young member Patrick Henry took his seat for the first time on 20 May 1765, older, more seasoned members waited for the fiery orator to respond. They did not have to wait long. On May 29, Colonel George Washington was almost surely in his accustomed place.[9] Young Thomas Jefferson, not yet a member of the Burgesses but already a leading graduate of the College of William and Mary, stood in the assembly's doorway. Everyone listened intently as the new member from Louisa County rose to speak.

Henry introduced a series of five resolutions. He had hastily jotted them down on a blank page of an old law book.[10] The resolutions supported the idea that only the people's elected representatives could lawfully tax them. The resolutions were mildly phrased and offered little more than what John Locke, the philosopher of England's Glorious Revolution of 1688, had written—to general approval. But it was his speech, not his resolutions, that caused a stir. Henry's words stunned the crowded, hushed legislative hall.

"Caesar had his Brutus, Charles the First his Cromwell," he said, citing the two most famous cases of rulers whose actions had led to their own deaths, "and George the Third . . ." Members were shocked that a British colonist would name the ruling sovereign in such company. "Treason!" roared the Speaker. "*Treason!*" echoed some other members. But the famous courtroom advocate neatly avoided their charge by concluding cleverly: ". . . and George the Third may profit from their example." He then added cockily: "If *this* be treason, make the most of it!"[11] Jefferson would later say that Henry spoke as the Greek poet Homer wrote.[12]

The Burgesses quickly adopted the Virginia Resolves denouncing the Stamp Act as unconstitutional. They knew their rights as Englishmen. They had studied the Magna Carta and the Petition of Right from the English civil war of the previous century.

In Boston that August, a mob trashed the fine home of Andrew Oliver, a rich but unpopular royal official. Oliver had suffered because a newspaper had erroneously named him as one of those designated to collect the revenue from the stamps.[13] Samuel Adams took the lead in organizing resistance among the Sons of Liberty. A failure at various businesses, this brewery owner showed a real knack for political organization. He pulled together the Sons of Liberty and declared their intention to resist the Stamp Tax "to the last extremity."[14]

Resistance flared up throughout the colonies. In Charleston, South Carolina, Christopher Gadsden led protests. There, a mob tore up the homes of two "stampmen."[15] Gadsden said, "There ought to be no New England man, no New Yorkers known on this continent, but all of us Americans."[16] Annapolis, Maryland, was a scene of destruction as a crowd pulled down a warehouse owned by a tax collector.[17] In New York City, the royal governor's coach was attacked. Rhode Island stamp protesters hanged tax collectors in effigy. In Newport, their signs accused one collector of being an infamous *Jacobite*—a charge that meant he was a supporter of the deposed Stuart monarch James II, a Catholic.[18]

Grenville was desperate to raise revenue. He reasoned that the recent war had removed the French from America. With such a threat to their safety and livelihoods gone, it was only fair for Americans now to help pay the costs of the eviction. Most of Parliament agreed.

Undeterred by the hostility of American critics, Grenville directed his secretary, Thomas Whately, to answer the growing number of pamphlets from colonists that argued for the right of Englishmen not to be taxed except by their own representatives. That was true, Whately wrote, but colonists *were* represented in the British Parliament. Just as most Englishmen could not vote in parliamentary elections, they and their colonial countrymen were *virtually* represented in the House of Commons by members who considered the needs of the entire empire whenever they debated and voted. Whately was a close friend of Lord Grenville, but his pamphlet (*Regulations Lately Made Concerning the Colonies*, 1765) gained him no friends in America.

To colonists accustomed to choosing their own legislators, such ideas were nonsense. In New York, where resistance to the Stamp Act burned brightly, the assembly boldly claimed a complete freedom from taxation by Parliament.[19] New York's merchants unleashed a powerful weapon—a complete boycott of British goods.

Following the lead of Massachusetts's brilliant James Otis, nine colonies agreed to send delegates to a *congress* in New York in October 1765. Virginia, whose royal governor had dismissed the House of Burgesses, could send no delegates. New Hampshire, Georgia, and South Carolina were also unrepresented, but Nova Scotia was.[20] The Stamp Act Congress met and issued a Declaration of Rights on October 19. Despite their professions of loyalty to the king and to his royal family, the delegates took a firm line *against* the claims of the Grenville government. They approved Patrick Henry's resolution that only the colonial legislatures had the right to tax colonists. Five of the key resolutions passed by the delegates were:

> *1st. That His Majesty's subjects in these colonies owe the same allegiance to the crown of Great Britain that is owing from his subjects born within the realm, and all due subordination to that august body, the Parliament of Great Britain.*
>
> *2d. That His Majesty's liege subjects in these colonies are entitled to all the inherent rights and privileges of his natural born subjects within the kingdom of Great Britain.*
>
> *3d. That it is inseparably essential to the freedom of a people, and the undoubted rights of Englishmen, that no taxes should be imposed on them, but with their own consent, given personally, or by their representatives.*
>
> *4th. That the people of these colonies are not, and from their local circumstances cannot be, represented in the House of Commons in Great Britain.*
>
> *5th. That the only representatives of the people of these colonies are persons chosen therein, by themselves; and that no taxes ever have been or can be constitutionally imposed on them but by their respective legislatures.*

Because of the delay in trans-Atlantic travel, the delegates to the Stamp Act Congress did not know that Grenville's government had already fallen.* Grenville had unwisely tried to pare down even the king's allowance. Wrong move. The king had used those funds to bribe members of Parliament into supporting his policies.

Grenville was nothing if not conscientious. He was said to be the first British minister who actually read the colonial dispatches.[21] His ill-fated attempts to impose fiscal discipline on the colonies prompted the first serious, continent-wide resistance to royal authority. Grenville had ended the policy of a century and a half of what the great parliamentarian Edmund Burke would call "a wise and salutary neglect."

In the face of such united opposition, the Stamp Tax simply could not be collected. By autumn of 1765, no Americans could be found to serve as "Stampmen." They all had been co-opted or scared away.[22] The crisis had made thousands of Americans acutely aware of their rights. As John Adams wrote, the people were "more attentive to their liberties, more inquisitive about them, and more determined to defend them."[23] They were still loyal to the king, however. Even at the height of the crisis, children would dance around Boston's Liberty Tree with a flag that read, "King, Pitt, and Liberty." Thus, colonists showed their continued allegiance to the crown, while openly favoring the return to power of William Pitt, the respected wartime prime minister.[24] Sons of Liberty were not willing to break with all royal authority. By adopting that name, colonists showed themselves aware of having been "born free," and willing to stand up for their rights as Americans *and as Englishmen.*[25]

Reflecting on the Stamp Act crisis that December, Adams would say 1765 was "the most remarkable year of my life. The enormous engine fabricated by the British Parliament for battering down all the rights and liberties of America . . . has raised through the whole continent a spirit that will be recorded to our honor with all future generations."[26]

Prior to this, America was governed at only the cost of paper and ink; Americans were "led by a thread," as Franklin said.[27] Afterward, the stub-

* When a parliamentary ministry loses, it is described as "falling."

bornness and stupidity of the British Crown and Parliament made America increasingly *ungovernable*.[28] John Adams would later write that it was during James Otis' legal struggle against the overreacting Writs of Assistance in 1761 that 'the child Independence' was born in American's minds. By the time of the Stamp Act Crisis of 1765, that child could walk and talk.[29]

When, in the spring of 1766, Parliament repealed the Stamp Act, the colonies exploded with joy. There were bonfires and fireworks—*illuminations* in the language of the day. Americans credited the king with this turnabout (even though his dismissal of Grenville hinged on totally different issues). In New York City, the people put up a statue of King George III mounted on a horse. It was happily paid for by public subscription.[30] They did not protest, either, when Parliament passed the Declaratory Act that reasserted its right to legislate for Americans on all matters whatsoever.

For a brief season, Americans seemed content to live under what they readily acknowledged was the freest government on earth. There were other sources of transatlantic tension, to be sure. Parliament had recently begun to enforce the Navigation Acts that had lain dormant for more than a century. These would have an impact especially on New England merchants.

Americans did not take too seriously the Royal Proclamation of 1763, which, issued at the close of the French and Indian War, had tried to limit colonial settlement beyond the crest of the Appalachian mountains. Frontiersman Daniel Boone was one who was undeterred. He led parties of settlers into Kentucky's "dark and bloody" ground. George Washington initially thought the proclamation would be only temporary, but became more concerned when, after five years, London continued to "hold the line."[31] These were years of rapid population growth in the colonies, much of it coming from the British Isles, and there were pressures to open western lands to settlement. Washington and his Virginia militia felt that they had won the right to expand westward through their blood and sacrifice against the French and Indians.[32]

The ministry in London feared antagonizing further the Indians who hunted the lands of the Ohio and the trans-Appalachian territories that today form Kentucky and Tennessee. Putting down Chief Pontiac's rebellion in the Ohio Valley in 1763 had been a bloody and expensive affair. Pontiac, like many of the Indians, had been a natural ally of the French.* The removal of the French, whose empire was based primarily on fur trading, alarmed the Indians. Royal authorities were eager to befriend them. But this led to tension with the colonists. Benjamin Franklin and George Washington were only two of the thousands of Americans who had staked their careers and their livelihoods on westward expansion.[33] They expected that would be one of the major gains in defeating France.

Americans were overjoyed when their friend William Pitt returned to power as the king's first minister in 1766. But their celebrations proved to be premature. Pitt was ailing, and the dominant personality in his government was Charles Townsend. Townsend understood that Americans objected only to "internal taxes" like the Stamp Tax. Internal taxes were levied on items produced and sold *within* the colonies. So he decided to lay "external" duties on items imported to America, such as glass, paint, lead, paper, and tea. The Townsend Acts went into effect 1 January 1767.[34] They were supposed to raise as much as £400,000 a year to contribute to the cost of administering the colonies.

Townsend might have been forgiven for his mistake. Franklin, as colonial agent in London, had argued against *internal* taxes. It was a fair inference by the British ministry that other duties might have been less objectionable. Franklin's advocacy may be attributed less to a desire to deceive as to the problem of his having been so long away from home. (This shows why even the best of colonial delegates could not successfully have represented their distant constituents, even if they had been admitted to the British Parliament.)

Parliament had also passed the Quartering Act of 1766 that required colonists to provide British soldiers—*redcoats* as they were soon called—with barracks, bedding, fuel, candles, and even beer, cider, and rum.[35] Americans saw that the great increase in the number of British troops in the colonies—greater than they had seen in wartime—was not being directed to the frontier, where they might have been expected to defend against such dangers as Pontiac had posed. Instead, the redcoats were seen in growing numbers in major colonial cities—especially Boston.

---

* Pontiac's name lives on as a speedy American "muscle" car. The Pontiac logo is a stylized arrowhead.

Americans began to suspect that the redcoats were being sent to control *them.* This suspicion grew when the royal authorities began to issue "Writs of Assistance" to customs officials. These writs were generalized search warrants. They did not have to specify a specific good to be searched for. They allowed the customs officers to *break into* ships, warehouses, even private homes! The heavy import taxes had encouraged smuggling by colonial merchants; the writs were an attempt to stop their tax evasion. Anytime any royal official merely suspected smuggled goods, he had the power to search.[36] What's more, Admiralty courts and Boards of Customs commissioners had the power to try those who sought to evade the king's duties.[37] Americans soon saw that their cherished right to trial by jury was in jeopardy.

John Dickinson spoke for many Americans when he wrote a series of articles in 1767–68, *Letters from a Farmer in Pennsylvania.* Dickinson attacked the "excesses and outrages" of the British ministry. He urged his fellow colonists to resist. But he was careful to assert his loyalty to the king and to channel the opposition into "constitutional methods of seeking redress," such as continued petitions to the government and even resuming the costly *nonimportation* policy that had proved so successful against the Stamp Tax.[38] Dickinson, who had been an opponent of Franklin in Philadelphia politics, completely *rejected* the use of force "as much out of the way."[39]

For now, colonists were inclined to follow Dickinson's lead. But some leaders, such as Washington, were beginning to think that force might be necessary for Americans to preserve their freedom.[40] As early as 1769, Washington was telling his neighbor George Mason that America must arm to resist British tyranny.[41] In saying this, Washington had many reasons, some high-minded; some less so. He was particularly upset about the financial drain he was suffering because of the duties levied on his expensive tastes. But luxury and concern for liberty are not mutually exclusive, and Washington was fully in the tradition of John Locke, who had laid down the philosophical basis for the English constitution. Locke had specified the resort to force—"the appeal to heaven" as he called it—as the final *but legitimate* course of action when a ruler refused to listen to reason. The growing restiveness of the Virginia landed gentry—especially influential men like Washington—led the noble Lord Fairfax to return to England.

Virginians were increasingly hostile to royal authority. Washington regretted the loss of these dear friends, but he did not change his views.

Boston soon became the center of unrest. In June 1768, the royal governor disbanded the Massachusetts Assembly. Almost at the same time, the sailing sloop called *Liberty*—owned by the rich and popular merchant John Hancock—was seized by customs officials. They charged Hancock with smuggling Madeira wine and imposed a fine. A city mob soon spilled into the town's narrow streets and chased the customs officials. They escaped with their lives, but their houses were trashed.[42] Sam Adams made sure that colonists up and down the eastern seaboard were fully informed of the Boston outrages. Adams was able to make excellent use of the efficient colonial postal system that Benjamin Franklin had established. Franklin's efforts had cut the time for a letter to travel up and down the coast from six weeks to three.[43]*

By 1770, tensions were rising between the people of Boston and the British troops whom they saw as occupiers. In March, following a winter of sporadic incidents, a mob of boys and young men began to taunt British soldiers, calling them *lobsters* and pelting them with trash, oyster shells, and snowballs. With their backs to the royal Customs House, and feeling hemmed in, the frightened soldiers opened fire on the mob. Crispus Attucks, a free black man and a whaler, was one of the first to fall. In all, five colonists were killed in what instantly became known as "the Boston Massacre."[44]

Realizing the explosive situation he had on hand, Governor Thomas Hutchinson had the Customs House guards arrested on a charge of murder and ordered the rest of the British garrison to return to Castle William, a fort in the harbor.[45] Quickly, the colonists had taken up the cry of murder. Boston's Paul Revere, a silversmith, soon engraved a powerful—but *exaggerated*—depiction of the killings. In Revere's rendering, the number of fallen is greater and the redcoats fire a volley on the order of their officer. The truth was much more complicated than that.

Surprisingly, or perhaps not so surprisingly, young John Adams,

* For example, Franklin published in his and other newspapers the names of those with letters in the post office. This speeded up delivery.

Samuel's cousin, and *his* cousin Josiah Quincy, took responsibility for the legal defense of the accused British soldiers. Determined to prove that British soldiers could be fairly tried in an American courtroom, John Adams demonstrated that most of the soldiers fired in self-defense, that no order to fire on the crowd had ever been given, and that the unruly colonials had provoked the soldiers. Adams argued persuasively that hanging the redcoats for murder would disgrace Massachusetts's name in history. It would be worse than the blot of the Salem witch trials and the hanging of the Quakers.[46] John Adams made a name for himself when the jury found all but two of the accused not guilty and convicted those two of lesser charges. Their punishment, an odd one, was the branding of their thumbs.

Cousin Sam, however, was not dismayed. For the next five years, he and the Sons of Liberty organized mass demonstrations on the anniversary of the Boston Massacre.[47]

II. A Total Separation

After a decade of political upheaval in London and in the colonies, a new ministry was finally installed in Parliament. King George found in Lord North a man after his own mind. In an attempt to reconcile with the colonies, the North administration persuaded Parliament to repeal all of the objectionable Townsend duties *except* the tax on tea.[48]

While they attempted to bring the colonists to order, Parliament was determined *not* to recognize Americans' rights to rule themselves in a union of equals under the same crown. Franklin could see this as he wrote, from London, to James Otis and Samuel Adams: "I think one may clearly see, in the system of customs to be exacted in America, by act of Parliament, the seeds sown of a total disunion of the two countries."[49] This is significant because Franklin was already referring to America as a different country.

In the spring of 1772, Rhode Islanders had a chance to take out their resentments of British high-handedness. The HMS ("His Majesty's Ship") *Gaspée* had been particularly active as a customs ship in the Narragansett Bay, roughly handling fishermen and small boats. The officers of the *Gaspée* applied the laws strictly in a region that previously had seen little or no enforcement. When the ship ran aground chasing smugglers, boatloads of Patriots rowed out, surrounded the ship, and forced the crew ashore. Then they gleefully burned to the waterline this symbol of British misrule.[50]

The entire conduct of the royal authorities in America smacked of a lordly disdain for the colonists. All Americans became aware of how they were looked down upon by the English. *Yankee* was a well-known term of contempt for all Americans. For a time, Americans lived in the hope that it was only certain British *ministers* who were responsible for tormenting them. They held on to the belief that the king and the British people were in sympathy with them. But Franklin knew better. As early as 1769, he was writing that the British people were "in full cry against America."[51]

Despite Samuel Adams's continual agitation, the period of 1771–73 saw a lessening of tensions between colonial subjects and the mother country. Then, without explanation, Lord North committed "a fatal blunder." He passed through Parliament a Tea Act that would have allowed the nearly bankrupt East India Company to claim a monopoly on tea in the colonies.[52]

Americans instantly recognized that if Britain could monopolize the importation of this important staple, there was no place they might stop. They could strangle American commerce and industry. Once again, resistance to British taxation was *continental.* It flamed up between Maine and Georgia. In Charleston, ship owners were allowed to unload their tea, but it was kept under guard in a warehouse. Philadelphia and New York refused to allow the tea to be off-loaded at all. Everyone waited for Boston's reaction.

On 16 December 1773, under cover of darkness, some two thousand Boston men went down to Griffin's Wharf. There, a smaller party of thirty men disguised as Mohawk Indians boarded three vessels and dumped their cargoes of tea into the harbor. "Boston harbor a tea-pot tonight!" cried one of the supporters. Samuel Adams had planned the whole raid with great care.[53] The damage to property was extensive. In today's terms, the losses to the East India Company would be valued at $1 million.[54] A British admiral, who watched the entire episode from a house near the wharf, called out good naturedly to the "Mohawks": "Well, boys, you have had a fine pleasant evening for your Indian caper, haven't you? But mind, you have got to pay the fiddler yet."[55]

By now, John Adams had cast his lot with his cousin, Sam, and the Patriots. He wrote in his diary: "This destruction of the tea is so bold, so daring, so firm, intrepid and inflexible, and it must have so important consequences . . . that I cannot but consider it as an epoch in history."[56]

Indeed, Boston would be made to pay the fiddler. Outraged by this act of colonial defiance, King George III appeared the following spring in person before Parliament, demanding harsh reprisal. "We must master them or totally leave them alone," he said.[57] Lord North was in full accord with his royal master. He was determined to show the colonies who was boss.

Parliament's answer in 1774 to floating tea was the speedy passage of five *coercive* acts. Patriots in America quickly dubbed them the "Intolerable Acts."[58] The first of these closed the Port of Boston and removed the Customs House. Another act changed Massachusetts's revered charter, stripping colonists of the right to elect members of the Upper House of their assembly. The Quartering Act allowed royal officials to place soldiers in colonists' homes at the colonists' expense. Still another act provided that royal officers indicted for murder while suppressing riots should be tried in London rather than where the offense occurred. This act, despite John Adams's proof that British soldiers could get a fair trial in America, was a calculated insult.

Finally, Parliament passed the Quebec Act. The new law extended the southern border of Quebec to the Ohio River, thus effectively closing off the Ohio Country to American expansion. It did much more. For the French Canadians, it laid down an enlightened basis for British rule of a conquered people. The *Quebecois* would be allowed to retain their language, their customs, and continue to worship freely in their ancient Catholic faith. Their system of laws and land tenure would continue essentially as they had been under New France.

To the American colonists, however, this was not tolerance but menace. As Englishmen, they had always feared France as an absolute monarchy, a country where the people enjoyed no liberties. The Catholic Church was seen as a support for that absolutist idea of monarchy. By enlarging the Province of Quebec to border on Virginia and Pennsylvania, the king was saying to them:

"I can take away *your* liberties, too." That seemed exactly what he was doing to Boston. The great William Pitt had warned Parliament not to treat Americans as "the bastards of England," but as true sons.[59] From this point on, however, the English government treated the colonists' cause as illegitimate.

George Washington also reacted sharply to Parliament's Intolerable Acts. The North ministry was setting up "the most despotic system of tyranny that was ever practiced in a free government," he charged.[60] He rallied to the plight of his Massachusetts countrymen: "The cause of Boston . . . is the cause of America," he said.[61]

Back in London, Franklin became the center of a raging controversy. He had received copies of letters written by the royal governor of Massachusetts, letters in which Thomas Hutchinson called for stronger measures *against his fellow Americans.* The letters had shown Patriot leaders that their royal officials were conspiring against their liberties. British opinion, however, was outraged at the violation of the governor's privacy. They charged that Franklin, the colonial postmaster, had somehow *stolen* Governor Hutchinson's letters.

Doctor Franklin had received that honorary title from St. Andrew's University in Scotland for his discoveries in electricity. Now, he was summoned on 11 January 1774 to a meeting of the Privy Council. They met in a room notorious for its fierce debate—the Cockpit. There, for more than an hour, the British solicitor general verbally abused Franklin. Impassive throughout the lawyer's vicious harangue, Franklin remained silent. Alexander Wedderburn had a reputation for slashing sarcasm and personal attacks. He lived up—or down—to that reputation in his snarling assault on the most famous man in the world. He sneeringly called Dr. Franklin "a man of letters," twisting that admiring title into a slur.[62]

This startling scene could have represented the entire relationship between the British monarchy and the American colonies. It did not matter that Franklin was the world's most illustrious common man. It did not matter that Franklin had served his colony, several neighbor colonies, and the British Empire with true genius and genuine loyalty. It did not matter that Franklin's natural son served as New Jersey's royal governor. Benjamin Franklin had dared to think for himself and had dared to speak his mind. That was enough to earn him the hatred of lesser men.

Unwilling to take the Intolerable Acts lying down, Patriot leaders in the colonies elected delegates to attend the first Continental Congress in Philadelphia in the fall of 1774. As they assembled, Philadelphia merchants were determined not to get burned again. If there was to be a renewal of the nonimportation, nonexport pledges that had proved so successful at the time of the Stamp Act crisis, Philadelphia's men of commerce demanded that this time the entire continent must take part. They had lost precious business when Baltimore merchants failed to support previous embargoes. This time, it must be all or nothing.

In this way, a continental *union* was being forged. The first Continental Congress quickly adopted the radical "Suffolk Resolves" that rider Paul Revere had brought to them from Massachusetts. Those resolves, drafted by the Patriot leader Dr. Joseph Warren, declared the Intolerable Acts null and void. Congress urged Massachusetts to form a free government and, ominously, advised Massachusetts's citizens to arm themselves.[63]

This last word from Congress was hardly necessary. Colonists in Massachusetts—and every other colony—had developed a militia system from their first days of settlement. Dangers of Spanish coastal raids, French and Indian attacks on the frontiers, fears of slave revolts—all these threats combined to make colonial Americans an armed people.

When Congress adjourned in October 1774, delegates pledged to reassemble the following May if Parliament failed to repeal the Intolerable Acts. Early in 1775, William Pitt arose in Parliament and tried to persuade Parliament to do just that. Now known as Lord Chatham, Pitt tried to make his fellow lords see reason. Franklin was in the gallery as this last attempt at avoiding a clash was made. Once again, Franklin was the target of a speaker's attack. This time, the dissolute Lord Sandwich pointed him out and claimed, untruly, that no English lord could have written such a thing, that the American was the *real* author of Chatham's motion.[64]* Chatham bravely responded that he would consider it an *honor* if he had had the

* The Earl of Sandwich can at least claim this much comparison to the great inventor from America: he was the inventor of the bread-and-meat meal that bears his name. The sandwich continues to be popular in America even if his lordship is not.

assistance of Dr. Franklin, a man who was esteemed by all of Europe. But he was hooted down. So were others who rose to plead for moderation. The Chatham motion was overwhelmingly rejected.[65]

When the brilliant Edmund Burke rose in the House of Commons on 22 March 1775 to plead for *conciliation*, the eloquent Irishman warned that America could never be subdued by force. He urged Britons to change their course, to adopt mild measures for dealing with the colonies. For more than a century, American high school students were required to memorize portions of Burke's magnificent speech. "Great empires and little minds," he cried, "go ill together." Burke, too, went unheeded. Thus did the British Parliament arrogantly and stupidly throw away the lifeline that alone could have tied them to their empire in America.

Burke's eloquence found an answer the very next day in Virginia, 23 March 1775. Patrick Henry appealed to his fellow Virginians to take up arms and stand with imperiled Boston. "I know not what course others may take," Henry cried, "but as for me, *give me liberty or give me death!*"

III. "The Shot Heard 'Round the World"

In Boston, the British general Thomas Gage had been named royal governor. He was determined not to let colonists arm. On the night of 18 April 1775, he ordered his troops to seize the militia's military stores at Concord and to arrest Patriot leaders Samuel Adams and John Hancock.

Hoping to catch the colonists unaware, Gage's troops moved out of their barracks by night, by boat. But there was a spy under Gage's roof. The general's American wife, Margaret, got word to Dr. Warren who passed it on to Paul Revere.[66]

Revere had arranged a signal—two lanterns—to be placed in the tower of Old North Church to let the Patriots know the regulars were moving out. Revere himself was rowed past HMS *Somerset*, a British warship. The low hanging moon behind Boston's buildings cast a shadow that concealed Revere's movements.[67] Once mounted on horseback, Revere and William Dawes managed to evade British patrols and brought the warning to Lexington. There at the home of Reverend Jonas Clarke, where the Patriot leaders were sleeping, Revere was challenged by Sergeant William Munroe. Munroe shushed him for making too much noise. "Noise!" Revere shouted "You'll have noise enough before long. The regulars are coming out!" (Revere would only have confused colonists if he had yelled: "The British are coming," since Massachusetts people still thought of themselves as British.)[68]

At five o'clock the next morning, the Minutemen (so called because they could be ready for military duty in a minute) were drawn up on the village green in Lexington as the British regulars came marching up. Captain Jonas Parker ordered the Minutemen to stand their ground. "Don't fire unless fired upon," he said, "but if they mean to have a war, let it begin here!"[69] British Major of Marines John Pitcairn ordered the Americans to lay down their arms. "You damned rebels, disperse!" he cried.[70] The Americans were beginning to disperse when a shot rang out. In a flash, there were competing volleys that left eight Americans dead in the spring sunlight. Three British soldiers were wounded.[71] In vain, Major Pitcairn had tried to stop his men from shooting.

The British column marched on to Concord, where another force of colonials met them. There the British destroyed militia stores and turned back toward Boston, mission accomplished. The road back became a highway of death, with Minutemen firing from behind walls and trees. Many of the regulars, who had been marching for more than twenty-four hours carrying heavy packs on their backs, fell out, exhausted. By the time they got back to Boston, they had lost 73 dead, 174 wounded, and 26 missing. The Americans suffered 49 dead, 39 wounded, and 5 taken prisoner.[72] These were little more than skirmishes as the world measures warfare, but the American farmers had indeed "fired the shot heard 'round the world."*

---

* In 1836, New Englander Ralph Waldo Emerson would immortalize the "embattled farmers" of the Revolution with his poem "Concord Hymn":

By the rude bridge that arched the flood,
Their flag to April's breeze unfurled,
Here once the embattled farmers stood,
And fired the shot heard round the world,

The foe long since in silence slept,
Alike the Conqueror silent sleeps,
And Time the ruined bridge has swept
Down the dark stream which seaward creeps.

On this green bank, by this soft stream,
We set to-day a votive stone,
That memory may their deed redeem,
When like our sires our sons are gone.

Spirit! who made those freemen dare
To die, or leave their children free,
Bid time and nature gently spare
The shaft we raise to them and Thee.

Less than a month later, the second Continental Congress assembled in Philadelphia. One of its first acts was to authorize a Continental Army. This army pledged its loyalty to Congress, and not to the individual colonies, as was the practice in the militia.[73] John Adams and other Massachusetts men worried that Boston might be abandoned by other colonies. To prevent this from ever happening, Adams nominated Colonel George Washington of Virginia to command all American forces, with the rank of general. Congress knew it needed a leader it could trust. The delegates recalled Oliver Cromwell, who had fought King Charles I in the name of Parliament only to wind up using the force he had been given to purge Parliament itself.[74] George Washington not only had more military experience than any other colonist, he had been a reliable member of the House of Burgesses since 1759. Washington, resplendent in his full dress military uniform, humbly accepted Congress's call and left immediately for embattled Boston. Congress also named as postmaster general Benjamin Franklin, recently returned from London.[75]

En route to Boston, Washington received word of a battle that was no skirmish. Stung by his earlier losses to ragtag colonials, General Gage was determined to overawe the rebels by a show of military force in clear view of all of Boston. He ordered General William Howe to take Bunker Hill.* On 17 June 1775, Howe led his disciplined regulars up the slope, vowing never to order them to go where he was unwilling to lead. When they neared the American lines, they were cut down by a fierce musket volley. "Don't fire until you see the whites of their eyes," was the order given all along the line of determined American defenders.

In his blood-spattered white silk breeches, General Howe rallied his men and finally drove the Americans off the hill. British losses—including Major Pitcairn—were tremendous—nearly 1,000 out of 2,000 in action.[76] American losses were far fewer—about 440 out of 3,200 defenders. Among the Patriot dead, though, was the revered Dr. Joseph Warren. Although the Americans were driven back, they had inflicted major casualties on the most professional and well-trained army in the world, an impossible accomplishment that imbued them with a swelling sense of confidence and pride.

---

* A historical misnomer, the battle was actually fought on nearby Breed's Hill.

When Washington arrived a week later to take command of American forces surrounding Boston, he had another advantage. He had amassed considerable artillery. These cannon had been captured from the British at Fort Ticonderoga in upper New York. Colonel Ethan Allen, supported by his Vermont "Green Mountain Boys" and ably aided by the courageous Benedict Arnold, had taken the defenders by surprise. Allen demanded surrender from the started British commander "in the name of the great Jehovah and the Continental Congress." A young Boston bookseller, the energetic, three hundred-pound Henry Knox, was put in charge of the cannon, dragging them across mountains and valleys to the aid of Boston Patriots. His patriotism and zeal impressed General Washington.[77] With the addition of the captured artillery, Washington was able to force the evacuation of the British from Boston. This was another great boost to American morale.* And it helped establish the Continental Army as an effective force.

Congress sent General Richard Montgomery and Benedict Arnold to take on the British in Canada in the summer of 1775. Montgomery succeeded in taking Montreal, but was stopped in Quebec City at year's end, where he lost his life. The ragged American force soon bogged down and was driven out. Arnold was wounded, but won praise for bringing order to the retreat.

Against this background, Washington's actions in camp have special significance. In November 1775, he learned that New England soldiers were preparing their annual celebration of Pope's Day, during which effigies of the pope were burned to the amusement of their Protestant neighbors. New England had been celebrating this holiday for more than a century. Washington issued an order sternly forbidding this "ridiculous and childish" display. He explained that the aid of French Catholics in Canada and across the sea was important to the American cause. He also wanted help from Catholics throughout the colonies. Washington's firmness ended a New England tradition and marked a major step forward in religious tolerance and national unity.

---

* Evacuation Day, 17 March 1776, is commemorated in Boston to this day. And it does not hurt that Beantown revelers can mix their celebrations with St. Patrick's Day festivities!

Congress needed help. Without Canada's support, Congress felt that the British would always threaten invasion from the north. So in March 1776 they named a diplomatic delegation including Benjamin Franklin, Samuel Chase of Maryland, and Charles and John Carroll, two prominent Catholic Patriots from Maryland (the Carrolls were cousins; John was a priest).

Franklin, who had just turned seventy, thought the northern trip might kill him, but he actually weathered the strain better than some of the younger men.[78] The delegation's reception in Canada was not favorable, however. French Canadians appreciated the tolerance of their language and religion shown by King George's Parliament—and they resented the anti-Catholicism that they sensed was a part of some of the colonial petitions and pamphlets.

While Franklin and his compatriots were in Canada, events were moving quickly in America. Thomas Paine, whom Franklin had met in London and given letters of recommendation just two years previously, came out with the most influential pamphlet of all: *Common Sense.* Published in January 1776, and selling for a mere eighteen pence, *Common Sense* sold more than 150,000 copies. Americans had heard the case for their rights put with great legal expertise and scholarship from men such as John Adams and John Dickinson, but Paine had a flair for colorful writing and he surely had the common touch. As a recent immigrant from England, his fierce writing against this king—*and against all kings*—struck a responsive chord. As soon as it came off the presses, New Hampshire delegate Josiah Bartlett noted, *Common Sense* was "greedily bought up and read by all ranks of people."[79] John Adams was probably more influential than any other American in moving Congress, but it was Paine who moved the people.[80] Of all the arguments Paine made, his charges against the king were most devastating. He attacked the pretended "FATHER OF HIS PEOPLE [who] can unfeelingly hear of their slaughter, and composedly sleep with their blood upon his soul."[81]

Paine knew the religious beliefs of his readers. He used the Bible to hammer home his points: "[T]he children of Israel in their request for a king urged this plea, 'that he may judge us, and go out before us and fight our battles.' But in countries where he is neither a judge nor a general, as in

England, a man would be puzzled to know what *is* his business."[82] This was amazingly bold. Paine might have been making a personal appeal with this powerful and emotional plea: "O! ye that love mankind! Ye that dare oppose not only the tyranny, but the tyrant, stand forth! Every spot of the old world is overrun with oppression. Freedom hath been haunted round the globe. Asia, and Africa, have long expelled her. Europe regards her like a stranger, and England hath given her warning to depart. [America] receive the fugitive, and prepare in time an asylum for mankind."[83]*

The Americans, recalling how grasping Parliament had been for their taxes, were shocked to see Lord North's ministry hiring German and Scottish mercenaries to make war on them (although the *need* to do so betrayed the war's deep unpopularity in Britain). News that the king would send to America twelve thousand *Hessian* troops (hired from the German state of Hesse) reached America in May.[84] Every American coffin seemed to bring death, as well, to the idea of reconciliation with England.

In addition to their increasing bitterness caused by British warfare against their colonies, Americans were facing the practical problem that no European state would support them while they were still formally members of the British Empire. They were still rebels. And there was a danger to the French, the Dutch, and the Spanish that the Americans might make peace with the mother country and leave them to fight a vengeful England by themselves. Independence would help Americans gain European recognition and practical help.

Finally, on 7 June 1776, Virginia's Richard Henry Lee introduced before Congress his motion "that these United Colonies are, and of right ought to be, Free and Independent States."[85] Congress then named a committee to draft a declaration of causes for independence: John Adams (Massachusetts), Benjamin Franklin (Pennsylvania), Thomas Jefferson (Virginia), Robert Livingston (New York), and Roger Sherman (Connecticut). Adams was keenly aware that there were four Northerners and only one Southerner on the drafting committee.

Once again, Adams made a fateful decision. He was desperate to have

* What better example of "American exceptionalism" can we find?

Virginia's support. He knew that Virginia led the South. And with Virginia's help, Massachusetts would never have to stand alone. Again, he opted for a Virginian to take the lead for the sake of national unity. He nominated Jefferson to draft the Declaration of Independence. Later, Adams would recall the reasons why he did so:

> 1. That [Jefferson] was a Virginian and I a Massachusettensian. 2. That he was a southern Man and I a northern one. 3. That I had become so obnoxious for my early and constant Zeal in promoting [Independence] that any [draft] of mine would undergo more severe Scrutiny and Criticism in Congress than one of his composition. 4thly and lastly that would be reason enough if there were no other, I had a great Opinion of the Elegance of his pen and none at all of my own. . . . He accordingly took the Minutes and in a day or two produced to me his [draft].[86]

In this passage—wordy, stuffy, but brutally honest—we see the best of John Adams. He was acutely conscious of his own role, undeniably ambitious to make his mark, but he constantly put his country first. Seldom could such a world-changing event be described in such spare terms—"in a day or two produced to me his draft."

And what a draft! Jefferson's "peculiar felicity of expression" (another Adams phrase) gave America a founding document that surpasses any other in the world for beauty, logic, and inspirational power. About the *philosophy* of the Declaration of Independence, there was no debate in Congress. It was what the Founders believed. Jefferson's immortal words were conventional wisdom of the time.[87] And the words of the Declaration became the greatest, most consequential statement of political philosophy of all time:

> We hold these truths to be self-evident, that all men are created equal, that they are endowed by their Creator with certain unalienable Rights, that among these are Life, Liberty and the pursuit of Happiness—That to secure these rights, governments are instituted among Men, deriving their just powers from the consent of the governed. . . .[88]

Franklin in Paris. *Franklin created a sensation in Paris. When he and Voltaire embraced, a throng of Parisian intellectuals wept for joy. King Louis XVI poked fun—crudely— at the Franklin craze by giving a lady courtier a porcelain chamber pot with the electrifying doctor's face emblazoned in it. Franklin's diplomatic finesse resulted in the Treaty of Alliance and Friendship with France in 1778. Without French help, America's cause might well have failed.*

George Washington as commanding general. *He risked his life, his fortune, and his sacred honor for American independence.*

Jefferson as author of the Declaration. *John Adams nominated the thirty-three-year-old Thomas Jefferson to draft the Declaration of Independence because of his "peculiar felicity of expression." Jefferson could "calculate an eclipse, survey an estate, tie an artery, plan an edifice, try a cause, break a horse, dance a minuet, and play the violin." Forever in debt, he could not free himself from reliance on slave labor, but the principles he enunciated in the Declaration would inspire Lincoln, Douglass, and every friend of freedom.*

Independence Hall. *Nineteenth century view of Independence Hall, Philadelphia. Here the Declaration of Independence was signed in 1776 and the Constitution was framed in 1787.*

This is America's political creed in a nutshell. Yes, they meant *all* men, regardless of race, religion, sex, or riches. They imposed no religious test for adherence to these ideals except belief in a creator God who *endows* us with our inalienable rights. They defined the purpose of all government. And they laid down the requirement that governments must rule by consent if they were to rule with justice at all. We will return to the philosophy of this Declaration in future chapters. Suffice for now, the Founders did not immediately free the slaves, give votes to their wives, or invite the Indian tribes to sign the Declaration with them. But we must realize that *all* the greatest advocates for human equality in America—Abraham Lincoln and Frederick Douglass, Elizabeth Cady Stanton and the Suffragettes, Martin Luther King Jr.—pointed to this passage in the Declaration to give force to their demands for justice.

The philosophical sentiment was near universal, but the practical matter of voting for independence was less so. The final tally was close. Congress had to wait for uninstructed delegates to return to Philadelphia. Caesar Rodney, suffering from asthma and cancer, rode eighty miles from his Delaware home to the sweltering capital on the night of 1 July 1776 in order to break a tie in his state's delegation and carry the motion for independence.

The men who signed the Declaration knew this was no casual debating society resolution. They acknowledged this as they pledged "our lives, our fortunes and our sacred honor" to support independence. When John Hancock summoned the delegates to sign the parchment "fair" copy of the Declaration, he wrote his own signature in large, bold strokes so that King George (legend has it) could read his name without his glasses.

He urged them to make it unanimous. "There must be no pulling different ways," he said. "We must all hang together." To that, Franklin, ever the wit, reportedly responded: "Yes, we must indeed all hang together, or most assuredly, we shall all hang separately."[89] Though none of the signers was hanged, seventeen served in the military, and five were captured by the British during the war. Richard Stockton, a New Jersey signer, never recovered from slow torture during captivity and died in 1781.[90]

IV. A Continental War

While Congress made its fateful move, General Washington was facing the danger of entrapment by the British army in New York. It was there that he had the Declaration of Independence read to his troops. There, the famous statue of George III was pulled down and its lead melted into bullets. Washington had been widely acclaimed when the British withdrew from Boston in March, but a string of defeats followed. Boston was to be his last victory for almost a year. Washington knew that no one who did not control the sea could hold waterborne Manhattan Island. Congress did not want to abandon the new nation's second largest city to the enemy.

Colonel John Glover's Marblehead men from Massachusetts were sailors and fishermen, more at home on the water than on dry land.[91] The night of 29 August 1776, their seagoing ways would prove vital to the Patriot cause.

The Continental Army had initially held firm under murderous British fire on Long Island, but the redcoats marched through the night, in perfect military order, to take the Americans by surprise.[92] Hessian soldiers took no prisoners. They stabbed the surrendering Americans with their bayonets, the blades of which were seventeen inches long.

Washington knew he had to withdraw from Brooklyn on Long Island and escape with his army to Manhattan. Five British warships were prepared to sail up the East River to block Washington's retreat, but the wind "miraculously" shifted and the British squadron was unable to come upriver.[93] Then, when Washington ordered Glover's Marblehead men to man the boats, he evacuated the bulk of the army from Brooklyn. Only a portion of the army was able to escape under the cover of darkness the night of August 29, but then a thick fog rolled in to hide the action as the remainder of the army entered the boats. One Connecticut officer claimed he made eleven crossings of the East River that night.[94] Author David McCullough called that covering fog incredible—an unlikely turn of fate. Believers in Providence called it the Hand of God.[95]*

* When the British Expeditionary Force was similarly evacuated from Dunkirk in 1940, thus saving England and the cause of freedom from the Nazi menace, Winston Churchill called it "a miracle of deliverance."

Washington felt the disappointment personally when his men ran before the advancing Hessians and Scots Highlanders. In anguish, he threw his hat to the ground and cried out: "Are *these* the men with whom I am to defend America?"[96] But he could also point with pride at troops who stood their ground and did their duty, as when 250 Marylanders attacked General Cornwallis's forces to cover the army's retreat, risking death or capture. "Good God, what brave fellows I must lose this day," Washington said. He then gave Maryland troops the name by which the state is known to this day—The Old Line.

The city could not be held. In September, as Washington withdrew to Harlem Heights, the city of New York caught fire. No one knows how it started. Loyalists—called Tories—who supported the Crown naturally blamed the rebels. Angered, British General William Howe seized a young American officer whom he accused of spying for Washington. Nathan Hale, of Connecticut, was about twenty-four. Howe gave him no trial. Hale was in civilian clothes, so he was treated as a spy. Shocking Americans, Howe denied the young man's last request for a pastor, or even a Bible. As Howe prepared to hang him, the fearless Patriot recited words from the popular play *Cato:*

> *How beautiful is death, when earned by virtue!*
> *Who would not be that youth? What pity is it*
> *That we can die but once to serve our country.*[97]

The quote has come down to us, in paraphrase, as "I regret I have but one life to give for my country." The Revolution had its first martyr.

Despite failure of his diplomatic mission to Canada, Benjamin Franklin agreed to go to France in the fall of 1776 to plead the American cause. Franklin embarked on a ship named *Reprisal.* It was a very rough crossing, with many seasick. It was also dangerous, too, as Franklin was the most recognizable of all the rebels and the British still held mastery of the seas. Even when he disembarked in France, he found himself on a country road where a gang of thieves had only recently murdered a party of twelve travelers. Happily, Franklin entered Paris safely in December 1776.[98]

Throughout that fall, General Howe and his lieutenant, Lord Cornwallis, pushed Washington south through New Jersey. The military position was helped when Benedict Arnold delayed a British thrust down from Canada and Patriots defending Charleston, South Carolina, repelled a British assault. Although Washington had kept his army together and with it the Revolution, retreat was still dispiriting. Throughout New Jersey, farmers were tacking red ribbons to their doors to show sympathy with the king. By December 1776, with enlistments running out for many militia forces, Washington's Continental Army was dwindling.

At Christmastime, most armies went into winter quarters. Washington had retreated across the Delaware River into Pennsylvania, chopping down bridges and taking boats with him. Washington knew that as soon as the river froze solid, Lord Cornwallis's superior numbers could cross over on the ice. Washington was running out of money and supplies. He appealed to Pennsylvania's master of finance, Robert Morris, to raise hard cash to pay bonuses to his soldiers. Only when they had been paid did some of his ragged, starving soldiers agree to extend their enlistments into the new year.

So, on Christmas night, in foul weather, General Washington prepared a sudden assault on Trenton, New Jersey. Once again, Washington relied on Colonel John Glover's seasoned Marblehead, Massachusetts troops. They were all excellent sailors and boat handlers. They had already saved the Continental Army by ferrying it from Brooklyn to Manhattan. Now, Glover's men carried the entire army—with horses and cannon—across the ice-choked Delaware. The little band of ragged men took the Hessian defenders by surprise. In a short, sharp action, Washington's men killed the Hessian commander, Colonel Johann Rall, and took nearly a thousand prisoners. Only two Americans were wounded, one of them Lieutenant James Monroe, the future president. Captain Alexander Hamilton's cannon, whose touch holes had been kept dry on the boat trip over, were used to devastating effect. Another in the boats that night was young John Marshall, the future chief justice of the United States. America in 1776 could have fielded an army of 280,000 men,[99] but that Christmas night, just 2,400 held the fate of a continent in their hands.

Washington's attack had been a great success. He quickly put into practice the "policy of humanity" that John Adams and others in Congress had urged upon him. Instead of bayoneting the surrendering Hessians—as the Hessians had done to Americans who gave up on Long Island—Washington treated them with compassion. As a result of this enlightened policy, thousands of Hessian Germans would later settle in the backcountry of Pennsylvania and Virginia.

American Patriots rejoiced with the retaking of Trenton and were overjoyed when, just two weeks later, Washington followed up his victory with another successful attack on Princeton. In this battle, Washington galloped directly into the smoke of British cannon fire. One of his young aides, Colonel John Fitzgerald, covered his eyes with his hat, certain the commander in chief would be killed. Washington came riding out of the smoke, eyes ablaze with victory. "Thank God your Excellency is safe," Fitzgerald cried out, offering his hand. Washington grasped it with enthusiasm, perhaps realizing how close to death he had come. "It's a fine fox chase, my boys," Washington cried, as his men sent the British defenders of Princeton into headlong retreat.[100]

Independence did not bring French help immediately, at least not openly. But one man was to be a harbinger of things to come. In July 1777, a tall, nineteen-year-old French aristocrat named Marie Joseph Paul Yves Roch Gilbert du Motier, better known to history as the Marquis de Lafayette, arrived in Philadelphia. Congress was embarrassed when the eager young nobleman—who had already seen plenty of military action—showed up to present his credentials from the American minister in Paris, Silas Deane. They had no money to pay him, members explained, and Deane had exceeded his authority in promising commissions. Lafayette could not return home. He had defied King Louis XVI in sailing to America. Instead, he offered to serve *without pay* as a volunteer in the ranks.[101] By August, he was riding by Washington's side as a major general—at age twenty! Lafayette would soon see action in September 1777, at the Battle of Brandywine in Pennsylvania. There, he was wounded as he gallantly led American troops. Although Washington's forces fought bravely, they lost and the road to Philadelphia lay open to the British.

Washington was hundreds of miles away when America's greatest military victory was achieved. Americans waited expectantly as Patriot forces faced British General John Burgoyne at Saratoga, New York, in October 1777. Burgoyne, "Gentleman Johnny" to London society, was a member of Parliament, a playwright, and flamboyant figure. He had bet parliamentary leader Charles James Fox a substantial wager that he would come home from America victorious by Christmas Day 1777. His task was to come down from Canada and link up with General Howe, leading a British force north from New York. But Howe was headed for Philadelphia—trying to catch Washington. Burgoyne let it be known his Indian soldiers had permission to scalp any British deserters. Initially crowned with success, Burgoyne had retaken Fort Ticonderoga and had burned the fine Albany home of American General Philip Schuyler.[102]

But Burgoyne's army moved too slowly—burdened by a huge baggage train—and he was trapped by the Americans. The sound of turkey gobble calls—Americans signaling each other before the attack—spooked the British troops. Gunfire erupted, and Dan Morgan's riflemen, who could drop a redcoat a mile away, quickly cut down Burgoyne's men.[103]

Surrendering his entire force of more than six thousand at Saratoga on 17 October 1777, Burgoyne was amazed by the merciful response he received from General Schuyler. "Is it to *me,* who have done you so much injury, that you show so much kindness?"[104]

Gentleman Johnny had lost his big wager. Fox, who predicted his friend would return a prisoner on parole, had won.[105] Saratoga was America's greatest victory to this point. American General Horatio Gates was quick to claim the victor's laurels, but as before, much of the credit for victory goes to General Benedict Arnold. Although seriously wounded, Arnold had nonetheless rallied American soldiers for action. The French foreign minister, Charles Gravier, the Comte de Vergennes, would see in Saratoga evidence of the Americans' ability to outlast the English.

General Washington's position was not improved as he moved into winter quarters at Valley Forge. With General Howe's British forces firmly in control of Philadelphia, Washington could only watch and wait. This was the worst winter of the war. Once again, he desperately appealed to Congress for aid. He wrote that you could trace his men's tracks by the bloody footprints in the snow. When he said his men were naked and starving, that was not an exaggeration. Some Continental soldiers had to borrow pants just to go out to stand watch.

Fortunately, another foreign addition to America's army arrived on the scene at this moment. A Prussian officer, Baron von Steuben, had met Benjamin Franklin in Paris and was recommended to Congress. Von Steuben, who spoke no English, was a colorful figure who had inflated his credentials—an eighteenth-century résumé padder. Still, he knew the art of drill, and he knew the importance of discipline and training to turn a rabble into a fighting force. Von Steuben began whipping the ragged, dispirited men of Valley Forge into shape. He comically employed an interpreter to translate his French and German curses into English the men could understand. (Every drill instructor in the American military since is a spiritual descendant of the outlandish Prussian.)

General Anthony Wayne, a thirty-two-year-old Pennsylvania surveyor and legislator, needed no translator. He was known for his violent oaths. One lieutenant complained that Wayne had "damned all our souls to hell" when he found no sentry posted outside an American camp.[106] Washington was known to hate profanity,[107] still Washington wisely chose Anthony Wayne to help straighten out the problems of supply. Without "Mad Anthony" Wayne's raids on Tory farms, the army might have starved.

V. The French Alliance

Thomas Paine's anguished cry "These are the times that try men's souls" had rallied Americans in that dark December of 1776. Now, a year later, his words echoed through the soldiers' huts at Valley Forge: "The summer soldier and the sunshine patriot will, in this crisis, shrink from the service of his country; but he that stands it now, deserves the love and thanks of man and woman." Summer soldiers and sunshine patriots *did* in fact drift away from Washington's camp. But many would return. And with the spring of 1778 came the news that changed everything. Benjamin Franklin had succeeded in securing the French Alliance. After years of secret aid, France now would openly recognize the United States and take her side in the war with England. The Dutch and Spaniards would also now begin to help. This meant, among other things, that Britain would have to bring ships back to home waters to guard against French raids and would also have to reinforce the garrison at Gibraltar in case of Spanish attack.

Meanwhile, the American frontier was ablaze. In the Wyoming Valley of Pennsylvania, Sir John Butler and his Indian allies struck on 4 July 1778, killing hundreds. Farmers were burned at the stake, thrown on beds of burning coals, and held down with pitchforks as their horrified families watched.[108] Virginia sent native son George Rogers Clark to reestablish her claims to the old Northwest Territory across the Ohio River. British Colonel Henry Hamilton, known as "Hair Buyer" because he paid Indians to bring in American scalps, holed up at a fort at Vincennes (in present-day Indiana). Clark marched his small force of 130 Americans and French for days through chest-deep waters in midwinter to get at his enemy.[109] Surrounding "Hair Buyer" and marching his men back and forth outside the British encampment, Clark gave the illusion of thousands. Most of Henry Hamilton's Indians took flight. Then, when Clark captured five Indians with scalps on their belts, he had them tomahawked to death in front of the British fort. Henry Hamilton immediately surrendered. He would later describe the big Virginian, speaking "with rapture of his late achievements while he washed the blood from his hands."[110] With this victory and his success at Kaskaskia (near present-day East Saint Louis, Illinois), George Rogers Clark laid the basis for America's claim to the entire Northwest Territory (Ohio, Indiana, Michigan, Illinois, Wisconsin, and part of Minnesota).*

Franklin's diplomatic skills were the key to another great coup for the American cause. Captain John Paul Jones had been living in Virginia when the war broke out. He went to France seeking Dr. Franklin's help in outfitting ships. He had a bold plan. He wanted to attack the British in their home waters. Jones, born in Scotland, had served on ships from his boyhood. He had even served for a time on slave ships. John Paul Jones's appearance deceived. Abigail Adams would write of him that he was nothing like the

---

* George Rogers Clark richly deserves his title, *Conqueror of the Northwest.* His exploits would add vastly to America's territory—an area *twice* the size of Great Britain and larger than France. And his record would spur on his younger brother, William Clark of the Lewis and Clark Expedition, to match his deeds.

Crossing the Delaware. *Washington risked all on Christmas night, 1776. Joining him in the boats on the ice-choked river were 2,400 ragged continental soldiers, including Alexander Hamilton, Henry Knox, James Monroe, and John Marshall. American victories at Trenton and Princeton renewed flagging hopes for independence.*

HMS *Serapis* battles the USS *Bonhomme Richard* off Flambrough Head, England, 23 September 1779. *Captain John Paul Jones braves British cannonballs and "friendly fire" from a faithless French ally. He issued his legendary reply: "I have not yet begun to fight!" Jones's victories stirred American hearts and gave the U.S. Navy its first great hero in the Age of Fighting Sail.*

Surrender at Yorktown. *His Excellency General Washington invited his defeated enemy, General Lord Cornwallis, to dinner at his headquarters outside Yorktown, Virginia. The Battle of Yorktown marked the end of the War of Independence. The British army band played "The World Turned Upside Down"—and it was.*

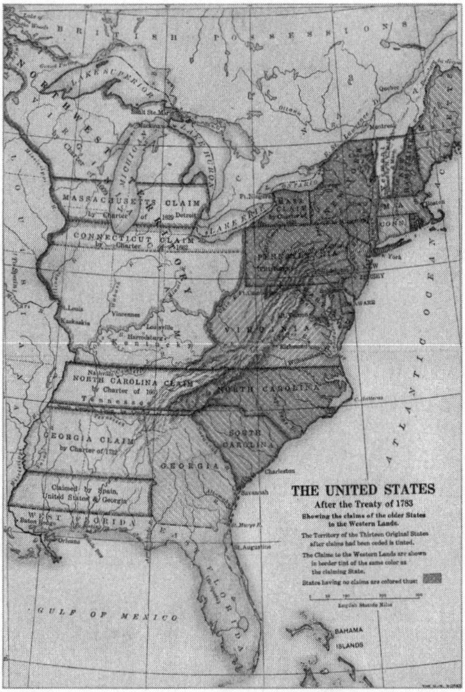

America in 1783. *By terms of the Treaty of Paris of 1783, Britain recognized American independence and ceded to the United States all lands up to the Mississippi River. Under Jefferson's plan, new states were admitted to the Union on an equal basis with the original thirteen. But Congress failed—by one vote—to adopt Jefferson's motion to ban slavery forever from the trans-Appalachian west. "And Heaven was silent in that awful moment," Jefferson mourned.*

"rough, stout, war-like Roman" she imagined. Instead, he was small, slight, soft-spoken: "I should sooner think of wrapping him up in cotton wool and putting him into my pocket, than sending him to contend with cannon ball," she wrote.[111]

Mrs. Adams could not have been more wrong. Jones was a fierce combatant. "I wish to have no connection with any ship that does not sail fast, for I intend to go in harm's way," he had written. Jones succeeded in spreading panic along the coast of England and Scotland in 1778, seizing British merchant ships and even raiding seaports. Commanding *Ranger,* Jones attacked the seaside town of Whitehaven, less than a hundred miles northwest of London.[112] Jones knew the harbor well. He had left England from that very port. His stunning raid sparked fear in London. All at once, the English realized they might be vulnerable in their home islands.

When Franklin persuaded the French to give Jones a ship, Jones gratefully christened her *Bonhomme Richard.* This was the French translation of Franklin's famous *Poor Richard.* Franklin had been upset upon hearing of the British fleet burning Fairfield and Norwalk and other towns along the Connecticut shore. He wanted a *reprisal.*

On 23 September 1779, Commodore Jones overtook a rich Baltic convoy off Flambrough Head, Yorkshire. The fearless British Captain Richard Pearson and his swift, copper-bottomed HMS *Serapis* shepherded the convoy. Pearson had nailed his blood-red British ensign to his mast that morning as he set out to search for Jones.[113] The other ships in his small squadron soon abandoned Jones, but he brought *Bonhomme Richard* in close with *Serapis.* At his first cannon volley, a gun exploded on Jones's ship, killing many of his own men. Jones's great skill in maneuver helped him come alongside *Serapis,* where he used his French Marine musketeers to devastating effect. *Bonhomme Richard* was on fire, taking on water and likely to sink, when Pearson called out to Jones, asking if he had "struck." To strike, or haul down your flag, meant you were surrendering. Jones's reply—that they had done but a little fighting and he was determined to fight on—has come down to us as "I have not yet begun to fight!"

Whether or not he said exactly those words, his actions followed them precisely. For hours the two ships were locked in a deadly embrace, "snug as two logs in a woodpile, guns muzzle to muzzle."[114] English farmers coming home from their fields watched, awestruck, under a harvest moon as the two ships lit up the night.[115] Both ships called for a temporary ceasefire, sending crews aloft to put out the flames that threatened to engulf them all.[116] *Serapis* tried to break from the clinch, to use her superior firepower to blast *Bonhomme Richard,* but Commodore Jones had ordered Sailing Master Stacey to use heavy hawsers to tie the ships securely together. When he heard Master Stacey cursing a blue streak, Jones reminded the salty sailor to watch his language because he might "in the next moment be in eternity."[117]

Unexpectedly, Jones faced "friendly fire" when the *Alliance,* commanded by French Captain Pierre Landais, suddenly reappeared. Twice, Landais's ship raked the *Bonhomme Richard* with deadly grapeshot. Despite this, Jones finally won a victory of the "tops" as his American and French marksmen high up in the masts completely cleared *Serapis*'s decks. Jones was able to board and capture the valuable prize. History offers no greater example of courage and determination. Americans—long sneered at as cowards by the British—could ever after answer *Bonhomme Richard.* Both ships had suffered terribly, nearly 50 percent casualty rates.[118] *Bonhomme Richard* could not be saved. (What must Alexander Wedderburn, by this time Britain's attorney general, have thought of his "man of letters" gibe now? Franklin's *Poor Richard* had leapt off his pages and spit fire at British arrogance.)

VI. "The World Turned Upside Down"

General Benedict Arnold, the hero of many battles, was unjustly treated by Congress. As lesser men like Horatio Gates received promotions and credit that rightly belonged to Arnold, he became embittered. His young wife, Peggy Shippen, came from a rich, Tory family. When Washington named Arnold as military commander of Philadelphia, Arnold clashed with the radical political leader, Joseph Reed. Because Arnold refused to hang five hundred Tories and seize their property, as Reed demanded, the Pennsylvanian spread rumors that Arnold was disloyal.[119] It became a self-fulfilling prophecy.

Arnold pleaded with Washington to make him commander of the American fortress at West Point, New York. Overlooking the Hudson River, sixty miles north of New York City, West Point was essential to preventing the British from cutting the United States in two. Arnold began to conspire with Sir Henry Clinton, General Howe's replacement in Manhattan. For £10,000, Arnold promised he would turn over West Point to the British. Arnold even plotted with Clinton's dashing young aide-de-camp, Major John André, how they might capture General Washington and turn him over to the British, but they soon dropped the idea as impractical.[120]

To capture or kill Washington had long been a British war aim.[121] Arnold and André met at a farmstead now known as Treason House. Sending the young man back to Clinton, Arnold persuaded André to change into civilian clothes. André carried papers in his boot that incriminated both Arnold and himself. When André was taken prisoner, Arnold escaped to a British warship anchored in the Hudson—the aptly named HMS *Vulture*.[122]

Washington had been meeting in Hartford, Connecticut, with General Jean Baptiste Donatien de Vimeur, comte de Rochambeau, the commander of the newly arrived army of five thousand French regulars. When he arrived at West Point, 25 September 1780, a seemingly insane Peggy Shippen Arnold confronted General Washington. Only partially clothed, she ranted that the general wanted to kill her baby. Washington, Henry Knox, Lafayette, Alexander Hamilton, and the other American officers felt pity for the beautiful young woman, who had seemingly been driven to madness by her husband's treachery. It was all an act. When Washington chivalrously allowed Peggy to rejoin her treasonous husband, it became clear that she had been plotting with Arnold from the outset. She would have richly merited hanging for treason.

Instead, that sad fate befell the talented, brave, young Major André. Court-martialed and sentenced to die, André did not plead for his life, but asked only to be shot as an officer and gentleman. Washington's officers recommended granting this plea. Stout-hearted Nathanael Greene, who had presided at the trial, dissented. André was either a spy or an innocent man, Greene reasoned. If innocent, he should be released, but if a spy, then the penalty for spying was death by hanging.[123] Perhaps remembering young Nathan Hale, Washington sternly sided with General Greene. With Americans weeping openly, Major John André, resplendent in his scarlet uniform, was hanged 2 October 1780.[124]

Arnold escaped, but died in poverty and disgrace in London twenty years later.[125] Benedict Arnold's name has ever after been a synonym for betrayal.

The British had shifted their major combat operations to the American South in 1780. Following the loss of Charleston, South Carolina, on 12 May 1780, Congress placed General Horatio Gates, the victor of Saratoga, in command of the Southern army. They rejected Washington's recommendation of General Nathanael Greene. (Gates still had support in Congress, despite the failure of a move two years prior to remove Washington and put Gates in his place.) Soon, however, Gates proved his unfitness to command.

In a battle at Camden, South Carolina, on 16 August 1780, General Cornwallis's troops scattered the Virginia and North Carolina militiamen. The rout was shameful, the worst American defeat of the war.[126] General Gates managed to arrive in Charlotte, North Carolina, sixty miles away, well *ahead* of his fleeing army. Alexander Hamilton expressed the views of most Americans when he asked: "Was there ever such an instance of a general running away . . . from his whole army?"[127] Behind him, Gates left the mortally wounded Baron de Kalb, another of the brave foreigners who had come to fight for America. By October, Congress agreed with Washington. Gates was out; Greene was in.

Lord Cornwallis had the help of Colonel Banastre Tarleton, a twenty-six-year-old dashing cavalry officer who specialized in raiding the coasts. Tarleton came within minutes of capturing Virginia's governor, Thomas Jefferson, as well as leaders of the Old Dominion's legislature, in June of 1781. Fortunately, Jefferson, Patrick Henry, and other Virginia Patriot leaders were warned in time. Jack Jouett rode all night, fifty miles through dense woodlands along Indian trails to carry the warning to Jefferson's home at Monticello. Captain Jouett is justly known as "the Paul Revere of the South."*

The South experienced the full rigors of war—actually civil war—as Loyalists clashed with Patriot forces for two years. Francis Marion, renowned as the "Swamp Fox," harassed the British and Tory forces in South

---

* Hearken good people: awhile abide
And hear of stout Jack Jouett's ride;
How he rushed his steed, nor stopped nor stayed
Till he warned the people of Tarleton's raid.
—*Charlottesville Daily Progress,* 1909

Carolina. General Marion's fearless raids saved South Carolina from being overrun by the British.[128] Neglected by a distracted Congress, Marion's contribution to the war effort was generously recognized by Virginia's "Lighthorse Harry" Lee.[129]* Cornwallis found he could win battles and take towns, but he could not get supplies or information from the people.

Nathanael Greene was the son of a Rhode Island farmer, a Quaker. His appointment to head the Southern army was very popular with the soldiers.

General Greene encouraged Dan Morgan to operate independently. The blunt-spoken Morgan, affectionately called "Old Wagoner" by his men because he had been a wagon driver in the French and Indian War, won a signal victory over British Major Patrick Ferguson and his American Loyalists at Kings Mountain, North Carolina, in October 1780. The intrepid Ferguson made a point of listening to his American Loyalists and not treating them with disdain, as so many regular British officers did. Major Ferguson had brought his troop to this high point, saying he could defend it against "God almighty and all the rebels out of hell." When Ferguson fell, at the head of his forces, he had taken seven rifle balls, and his hat and clothing were shot through.[130] Ferguson's defeated forces cried for "Quarter!"—a plea for mercy. But Morgan's soldiers answered back, "Tarleton's Quarter!" as they killed the desperate Tories. Tarleton had slaughtered surrendering Patriots at the Battle of Waxhaws the previous May.[131]

Dan Morgan won another great victory at Cowpens, South Carolina, on 17 January 1781. There, Morgan decisively defeated Tarleton's British regulars and sent Tarleton himself scurrying back to Cornwallis.[132]

Greene fought Cornwallis's force at Guilford Court House, near Greensboro, North Carolina, on 15 March 1781. Greene was defeated in the fierce battle, but his forces maintained order and so mauled Cornwallis's army that the British had no choice but to regroup and fall back for supplies. Greene had won no major battles, but he had forced Cornwallis to exhaust himself and his army, marching more than five hundred miles through the Virginia and North Carolina countryside.[133]

* South Carolinians long remembered General Lighthorse Harry Lee's enthusiasm for their hero, the Swamp Fox. They later rallied around General Lee's even more famous son—General Robert E. Lee.

Greene's success is shown by Cornwallis's letter to Sir Henry Clinton in New York: "I am quite tired of marching about the country. . . . If we mean an offensive war in America, we must abandon New York and bring our whole force into Virginia."[134] The wearing down of the British forces in the South is what led them to Yorktown. Nathanael Greene, Dan Morgan, and the guerilla leaders Swamp Fox Francis Marion and Thomas Sumter achieved this result.

General Washington, with the help of Rochambeau and seven thousand French soldiers, was preparing to lay siege to the British in New York City in the summer of 1781. Then stunning news came. On August 14, Washington received a message informing him that French Admiral Francois Joseph Paul, the comte de Grasse, was bringing twenty-eight warships to the Chesapeake Bay.[135] Leaving a portion of his army behind to deceive General Clinton, Washington and Rochambeau quickly departed for Virginia. His swift, bold move, taking the bulk of his forces away from their positions around British-occupied New York City and striking out for the South, may have been his greatest achievement of the war.[136]

Local command of the sea—critical to American success—was established thanks to the French. On September 5, Admiral de Grasse defeated a smaller British squadron in the Battle of the Capes.[137] The battle was fought between Virginia's Cape Henry and Cape Charles, and it prevented Cornwallis's force from being evacuated by sea—or even resupplied.

By 26 September 1781, Washington's combined American-French force of seventeen thousand—including Rochambeau's regulars, Lafayette's and Anthony Wayne's Virginians, and reinforcements from de Grasse—had Cornwallis's seven thousand British troops trapped on the York peninsula.[138] (The York peninsula is a spit of land that juts out into Chesapeake Bay.)

Lafayette had assured Washington that Cornwallis could not escape. When he and Washington met again, the enthusiastic young Frenchman grabbed Washington and smothered him with kisses. Washington, who had begun to look upon Lafayette as a son, did not object.[139] He quickly ordered a siege. Following the tactics taught by the great French military engineer Sébastien Le Prestre de Vauban, the allied force soon began to squeeze the life out of the encircled British. Lord Cornwallis used the Yorktown home of

Virginia's Governor Thomas Nelson as his headquarters—and the governor urged Washington to cannonade his own house.[140]

Within weeks, Cornwallis's men were reduced to eating their horses. Their attempts at answering the daily battering from Washington's artillery were feeble. Once, when a British cannonball landed in the American trenches, Colonel Alexander Hamilton jumped back and took shelter behind the ample Henry Knox. The normally genial Knox scolded Hamilton, warning him "not to make a breastwork of me again!"[141]

Finally, on 19 October 1781, Lord Cornwallis bowed to the inevitable and surrendered unconditionally. As his men marched out to lay down their weapons, they were surrounded by French hussars; Cornwallis was nowhere to be seen.[142] Claiming illness, he had sent his second-in-command, General Charles O'Hara, to offer his sword. First, the embarrassed O'Hara tried to give it to General Rochambeau, who nodded in the direction of General Washington. But Washington, standing on ceremony, indicated that only *his* second-in-command, General Benjamin Lincoln, could properly take the surrender.[143]

The common redcoat soldiers wept in frustration and smashed their muskets. British drummer boys bashed in their drumheads.[144] They were all headed for a prisoner-of-war camp. The British band played "The World Turned Upside Down." Indeed, it was.

VII. A Dangerous Peace

Washington returned to New York to keep General Clinton hemmed in. As long as the British controlled the seas, however, he had little hope of starving the British out. King George III, who had cried out, "Oh, God, it's all over!" when he received the news of Yorktown, faced the defeat in Parliament of Lord North's government in March 1782. The new British government determined to make peace.

Congress dispatched John Jay, the head of its committee on foreign affairs, to join Benjamin Franklin and John Adams in Paris. Henry Laurens, a distinguished South Carolinian who had been president of Congress, was released from captivity in the Tower of London to join the delegation.

Laurens had been taken captive by the British as he sailed to Holland to negotiate a loan for the American cause. Laurens, however, was shattered by the death in battle of his brilliant son, John, who had been an aide-de-camp to General Washington. The younger Laurens had been best friend to Alexander Hamilton, also a Washington aide. The young South Carolinian had advanced a plan to emancipate the slaves if they would join the fight for American independence. Hamilton eagerly embraced the idea. But the plan died with gallant young Laurens. His father, burdened by grief, took little part in the Paris peace talks. John Laurens's country and South Carolina would have reason to mourn the loss of this young visionary.

Those negotiations would drag on for many months. For a time, it seemed Franklin might succeed in winning all of Canada as well as all the territory up to the Mississippi River, but that project failed. John Adams, conscious of his New England roots, held out for fishing rights for his Gloucester and New Bedford neighbors of Massachusetts. The provisional treaty was signed on 30 November 1782, but the final document was not approved until almost a year later, 3 September 1783.[145]

While the Paris peace talks dragged on and on, Congress was sinking further into debt, and its inability to pay the army was creating a very dangerous situation. Washington knew this. In May 1782, he received a shocking letter from Colonel Lewis Nicola, an Irish immigrant and former commander of Fort Mifflin. Nicola, citing the rising disorder in the army and the country, urged Washington to *use* the army to set himself up as a king. Washington's response was short and sharp:

> No occurrence in the course of the war has given me more painful sensations than your information of there being such ideas existing in the army. . . . I must view with abhorrence and reprehend with severity [an idea that was] big with the greatest mischiefs that can befall my country.[146]

Always aware, painfully aware, of the impression he was making, Washington demanded to know what in his conduct could ever have given rise to such a notion. In forcefully putting down Nicola's suggestion,

Washington drove a stake through the heart of monarchy in America: if he would not be king, *nobody* could be king. And that was the end of kingship in America *forever.* America has had forty-three presidents—including some liars, "lemons," and losers—but we have never had a tyrant. For that we can thank George Washington.

An unpaid army that is unable to disband but not fully engaged against the enemy is a very dangerous instrument. Early in the next year, 1783, there were more rumblings of discontent. Anonymous pamphlets began to circulate in the camp around Newburgh, New York, urging the army to march on Congress to enforce its legitimate demands *at the point of a bayonet.* Washington summoned his officers to a meeting for March 15. He planned his address carefully. Appearing before a large, sullen gathering, Washington made a dramatic entrance. He urgently pleaded with his men to understand the slowness of deliberative bodies, to have patience. Do not, he pleaded, "open the flood gates of civil discord, and deluge our rising empire in blood."[147]

The officers' response to this powerful appeal was an angry silence. They remained unconvinced. They had heard all that before. Their families were hungry, and the Congress was doing nothing to honor its promises to those who had bled and died for independence.

Then Washington remembered a letter he'd received from a congressman. He rummaged through his pockets for an embarrassing few seconds. Opening the envelope, he realized he could not read the small handwriting. Slowly, deliberately, he went through his pockets again, this time bringing out his spectacles. Few of the officers present had ever seen their fifty-one-year-old commander in chief wearing eyeglasses. "Gentlemen," said Washington as he carefully put them on, "you will permit me to put on my spectacles, for I have not only grown gray but almost blind in the service of my country."[148] His soft words turned away wrath. Many of the battle-hardened veterans wept openly. The movement toward a military coup d'état collapsed at that moment.

When word came of the final ratification of the Treaty of Paris, a treaty in which American independence was fully recognized, the British agreed to evacuate New York and Charleston. In November 1783, the redcoats boarded their ships and sailed away from Manhattan. Washington invited his officers to dine with him at Fraunces Tavern, near Wall Street, in what is now the city's financial district. There, on 4 December 1783, another emotional scene occurred. Washington was no marble man, as his grim visage on the dollar bill would suggest. At the conclusion of the evening, when he invited his officers to come and take him by the hand, all of those present, including Washington, dissolved in tears. "With a heart full of love and gratitude, I now take leave of you," he told the assembled officers. "I most devoutly wish that your latter days will be as prosperous and happy as your former ones have been glorious and honorable."[149]

It remained for Washington to return to Congress—the source of all his authority—to close out his service in the war. Meeting in Annapolis, Maryland, Congress was eager to welcome him back. At noon, on 23 December 1783, Washington appeared in the Senate Chamber of the Old Maryland State House. The chamber was packed with members, visiting dignitaries, and ladies. Washington rose to congratulate Congress on the successful achievement of independence and peace. When he came to that part of his text that contained a tribute to his fellow officers, his hands shook, and he struggled to maintain his composure. Then he closed with these words: "And of presenting myself before them [Congress] to surrender into their hands the trust committed to me and to claim the indulgence of retiring from the service of my country."[150]

King George III had said if Washington voluntarily gave up power, then he truly *would* be the greatest man on earth. Cromwell hadn't done it. Napoleon would not do it. But Washington did it.

How great a general was Washington? Winners *always* seem like great generals. He lost more battles than any general in modern history, indeed. But he won some very big ones.

Washington had many superior qualities—bravery, self-control, administrative skill, strategic sense, tactical boldness—and an ability to learn from his mistakes. But most of all, he had *judgment.* He refused to burn American towns, and refused to take hostages or shoot collaborators. He kept the army under firm control. He *always* subordinated himself and his restive army to the authority of Congress. So despite shortcomings and defeats, he was greater than any other American general of the Revolution.

Congress's official response was delivered by its president, Thomas Mifflin. In an earlier day, Mifflin had conspired to replace Washington with Horatio Gates. Fortunately for Mifflin and for us, his text was prepared for him by Thomas Jefferson:

> You have conducted the great military contest with wisdom and fortitude, invariably regarding the rights of the civil power, through all the disasters and changes. . . . You have persevered until these United States have been enabled, under a just Providence, to close the war in freedom, safety and independence. . . . And for you, we address to Him our earnest prayers that a life so beloved may be fostered with all His care. . . .[151]

Freedom, safety, independence, and peace. By 1783, that was already George Washington's legacy to his country. Soon, he would give more.

Four

REFLECTION AND CHOICE: FRAMING THE CONSTITUTION (1783–1789)

The newly independent nation struggles to shape a durable form of government that maximizes every citizen's liberty and protects their unalienable rights. The Northwest Ordinance establishes enlightened policies about slavery and religious tolerance, but the Union under the Articles of Confederation begins to fray at the edges—too weak to hold itself together. Shays's Rebellion finally galvanizes James Madison to action. Teamed with Alexander Hamilton, backed by Washington and Franklin, he leads the fledgling nation on the path to a new Constitution. The two great points of dispute? The division of power between state and national governments and the question of slavery. Stark divisions give way to compromises, and a blueprint for republic emerges. "Little short of a miracle"—that's how George Washington describes the new Constitution to his French friend, Lafayette. Ratification takes all the skill, reason, and persuasion the Founders could muster.

I. A CRITICAL PERIOD

Fashionable French ladies fainted as the huge, hot-air balloon rose above the cheering crowd at the Palace of Versailles. People gasped as the balloon snagged on tree branches. Benjamin Franklin, the American minister to

Paris and one of the world's leading men of science, confessed in a letter to the Royal Society in London: "I was then in great pain for the men, thinking them in danger of being thrown out or burnt."[1] But the balloon soon cleared the obstructions and floated up and out over the River Seine. Fifty thousand spectators had witnessed the stunning achievement of the Montgolfier brothers—Joseph and Étienne—and the beginning of manned flight on 21 November 1783. Franklin had to watch from his carriage, so crippled was he with gout. One of the witnesses turned to Franklin to ask him what *practical* use it was. The most practical man on earth answered simply: "What is the use of a new-born baby?"[2]

Franklin was rapidly closing out his Paris days, planning to turn over the embassy to the new man Congress had sent over in 1784 to succeed him. When a Parisian asked Thomas Jefferson, the new American minister, if he had come to *replace* Dr. Franklin, Jefferson replied diplomatically: "No one can replace him. I am only his successor."[3]

The irreplaceable Dr. Franklin would himself soon have reason to wonder what is the use of a newborn republic. Many of the leaders of the Revolution began to see difficulties ahead for the infant United States as the Congress repeatedly failed to meet its financial obligations. We have already seen the dangers of mutiny and military insurrection within the Continental Army. Peacetime would show further defects of the Confederation government.

The Articles of Confederation had been drafted in 1777, but had not been ratified until four long, war-filled years later, in 1781. The primary purpose of the Confederation government was the successful prosecution of the War of Independence. That was achieved with the leadership of General Washington and the aid of the French alliance. Although the Articles committed the states to a "perpetual Union," the states still jealously guarded their prerogatives. Article II stated clearly that "each State retains its sovereignty, freedom and independence, and every power, jurisdiction, and right, which is not by this confederation expressly granted to the United States, in Congress assembled."[4] In those days, and for years thereafter, it was common to refer to *these* United States, not *the* United States.

Congress, under the Articles, had power to wage war, conduct foreign affairs, borrow money, deal with the Indians, and settle disputes among the states.[5] But, in order to raise an army or cover its bills, Congress could only *requisition* men and money from the state governments. If the states complied fully, so much the better. But if states failed to meet their obligations to the Union, Congress could not compel them.

Each state was represented equally in Congress. Although each state might send several members to comprise its delegation, those members had to agree among themselves how their state's one vote should be cast. For routine matters, the votes of a majority of states—seven out of thirteen—was sufficient. But for major issues, it took nine states to render a decision. And for any changes in the Articles, or for disputed matters that seemed to call for a change in the Articles, total unanimity was required—a *de facto* veto that little Rhode Island would repeatedly use to threaten disruption of Congress's business.

The Articles instituted neither an executive branch, nor a judiciary. For the first eight years of independence, of course, the most important "executive" work to be accomplished was victory in the war. For that, General Washington was commander in chief.

Despite these drawbacks, the Congress under the Articles of Confederation did boast some remarkable talents. John Adams, before he left for France, and Thomas Jefferson were leading members. James Madison and Alexander Hamilton soon joined older members. Robert Morris, Pennsylvania's brilliant financier of the Revolution, and John Jay, a New Yorker skilled at diplomacy, brought needed talents. As the years wore on, however, Congress's prestige and reservoir of skilled members sank.

Maryland's stubbornness had actually helped Confederation government resolve a thorny issue—the western lands. A number of states claimed vast tracts beyond the Appalachians. Virginia, New York, even Connecticut, held titles from the colonial era. Maryland refused to ratify the Articles of Confederation *until* these state land claims were ceded to the Union. Thus, the territories became a source of *national* unity (and, ironically, later the source as well of the greatest national conflict, the Civil War).

After independence and peace, the greatest achievement of the Confederation government was the Northwest Ordinance of 1787. From the old Northwest Territory would be carved a huge region—the modern states of Ohio, Indiana, Michigan, Illinois, Wisconsin, and part of Minnesota. It was the culmination of a series of land measures that began as early as 1780.[6] Under that wise, far-seeing measure, slavery was forever banned in those lands.[7] Further, the lands were divided into townships six miles square, and subdivided into thirty-six sections of 640 acres each. One of these sections was to be donated for the purposes of public education. "Religion, morality and knowledge being necessary to government and the happiness of mankind, schools and the means of education shall be forever encouraged," Congress said.[8] Thus, even from the beginning of the republic, the focus of attention in education was on the moral as well as the intellectual development of youth.

The Northwest Ordinance continued Congress's plan to treat each new territory as a state-in-embryo. Settlers in the territories could establish free governments and write constitutions, and once they had achieved sixty thousand inhabitants, they could apply for admission to the Union as new states. Each new state would be admitted on an equal basis with all previous states. Thomas Jefferson had set the pattern for this unprecedented treatment of new states with his plans for Kentucky and fourteen other new states.[9]*

This was the first time in the history of the world that the principle of equality was so recognized. American territories would not be colonies, held in perpetual subordination to the "mother" country. We had learned that from the failure of the British Empire.

A critically important feature of the Northwest Ordinance was its treatment of religion. The first article stated: "No person, demeaning himself in a peaceable and orderly manner shall ever be molested on account of his mode of worship, or religious sentiments, in the said territory." This enlightened principle was little short of revolutionary for its time. No other government had ever laid out such a principle for administering newly acquired territories. In setting up this rule, Congress was clearly drawing on the recently passed Virginia Statute for Religious Freedom.[10]

Originally introduced in 1779 by Thomas Jefferson, the Virginia statute

---

* But for Jefferson's visionary plan, author Christopher Hitchens says, the United States might have been confined to a long narrow strip along the Atlantic Seaboard—a North American Chile!

had failed to win majority support in wartime Virginia. When Mr. Jefferson left America in 1784 for Paris, he arranged to stay in the closest possible contact with his good friend and neighbor, James Madison. They exchanged letters, news, books, and pamphlets regularly. Jefferson especially wanted to be kept informed of events in the Virginia Assembly.[11]

Patrick Henry introduced a bill in 1785 to provide state support for "Teachers of the Christian Religion." Many people saw it as a step *forward* for religious tolerance. After all, Virginia had previously required all its citizens to support the Anglican (now Episcopal) church. Under Henry's bill, government support would be given to a wide variety of Christian sects. James Madison, however, immediately stepped forward with his famous *Memorial and Remonstrance.* In it, Madison showed how government support for *only some* churches violated the essential religious liberty of all. Madison showed that allowing the government to set terms for the support of the Christian religion would also permit the same government to control it. Madison's *Remonstrance* argued persuasively:

> Who does not see that the same authority which can establish Christianity, in exclusion of all other Religions, may establish with the same ease any particular sect of Christians, in exclusion of all other Sects? that the same authority which can force a citizen to contribute three pence only of his property for the support of any one establishment, may force him to conform to any other establishment in all cases whatsoever?

So successful was Madison's argument that many of the Christian denominations saw the force of his reason and petitioned the Virginia Assembly to vote down the Henry bill. The new consensus broke the logjam of resistance to Jefferson's Virginia Statute for Religious Freedom, which Madison ably guided through the assembly.

Thus, in the midst of a seemingly local legislative contest, a principle was established that has worldwide significance to this day. Madison, characteristically a modest man, nonetheless boasted of the achievement. In a letter to Jefferson, he wrote the Richmond lawmakers had "in this country

[Virginia] extinguished forever the ambitious hope of making laws for the human mind."[12] Less than a year later, Jefferson could write to his friend that "the Virginia Act for Religious Freedom has been received with infinite approbation in Europe and propagated with enthusiasm."[13] Jefferson meant, of course, the statute had been approved by continental thinkers, *philosophes,* activists; certainly, it was *not* welcomed by those in power.

Despite these advances for civil and religious liberty, the *financial* situation of the new United States was spinning out of control. Rhode Island, little *Rhody,* led the way in financial irresponsibility. Debtors had dominated the little state's legislature and had pushed through a program of debt relief. Flooding the Ocean State with paper currency, they demanded that creditors accept the worthless bills. If creditors refused, the legislature provided that debtors could deposit the funny money with a nearby state judge.[14] In Charleston, South Carolina, the radicals' program turned ugly. The Hint Club made a practice of sending a section of rope—like a hangman's—to rich planters who had refused to take the "hint" and accept devalued paper money. Thomas Jefferson worried about the "pride of independence" he saw that had taken a "deep and dangerous hold on the hearts" of many of the state politicians.[15]

The Union also showed signs of coming unglued over foreign affairs. John Jay was the highly capable secretary of foreign affairs under the Confederation. Descended from French Huguenots, his family had prospered in colonial New York. When Jay prepared to negotiate with Spain's ambassador, Don Diego de Gardoqui, he sought instructions from Congress. The Confederation Congress—with Southern members especially vehement—told Jay under no circumstances to bargain away America's appeal for the "right of deposit" at New Orleans. Southerners and westerners needed an outlet for their goods. The Ohio, the Missouri, and the Mississippi Rivers all flowed into the Gulf through New Orleans. John Jay, however, was concerned about a too-rapid growth of the American republic in the Southwest. Many other Northern delegates even favored trading away Mississippi River navigation rights in return for Spanish concessions on fisheries off Newfoundland and opening Spanish ports to American merchant seamen. Gardoqui was a smooth operator. He gave George Washington a pair of Spanish jackasses for breeding mules at Mount Vernon.[16] While this "Royal Gift" represented King Carlos III's sincere admiration for General Washington, many other "gifts" from Gardoqui were more questionable. Members of the Confederation Congress enjoyed the Havana *segars* he provided. He "loaned" one member $5,000—an ill-disguised bribe. He escorted the beautiful Mrs. Jay to New York social events. "I am acting the gallant and accompanying Madame to the official entertainments and dances, because she likes it and I will do everything which appeals to me for the king's best interest," Gardoqui wrote home to Madrid.[17]

Jay's head was turned, but probably most by the arguments of northeastern merchants. He appealed to Congress to let him give up Americans' right to navigate the Mississippi. The first serious split in the Union occurred over this issue, with seven Northern states voting to drop the demand and five Southern states vigorously protesting. Under the formula then in effect, it mattered little that the Northern states had a majority. Nine votes would be needed to ratify a new treaty with Spain, and they weren't there.[18] Gardoqui, nonetheless, knew that the Americans, divided among themselves, could not apply pressure on Spain for the Mississippi. "I believe without vanity to have squeezed this orange to the last drop," he wrote his king.[19] His actions had led Massachusetts's Rufus King and other Northern delegates to the brink of disunion in the summer of 1786.[20]

Strains on the Union continued to grow. Most alarming of all was the armed uprising in Massachusetts. Revolutionary War veteran Captain Daniel Shays led an "army" of desperate farmers who tried to close down the courts to prevent foreclosures and imprisonment for debt. When Shays's ragged forces tried to seize a federal arsenal, they were repulsed with cannon fire.[21] The state organized the militia with funding from major merchants and soon put down Shays's Rebellion. Those captured rebels who were sentenced to death, however, were soon pardoned.[22]

Shays's Rebellion alarmed most of the responsible leaders of the Revolution. George Washington was especially upset. "I feel . . . infinitely more than I can express . . . for the disorders that have arisen. Good God! Who besides a Tory could have foreseen, or a Briton predicted them!"[23] Franklin, recently returned from France, was one of the mildest. He said,

"Having dreaded giving too much power to our governors, now we are faced with the danger of too little obedience in the subjects."[24]

To Thomas Jefferson, faraway in France, too much was being made of Shays's Rebellion. Jefferson wrote to Madison and famously put the case for periodic uprisings:

> I hold it that a little rebellion now and then is a good thing, and as necessary in the political world as storms in the physical. Unsuccessful rebellions, indeed, generally establish the encroachments on the rights of the people which have produced them. An observation of this truth should render honest republican governors so mild in their punishment of rebellions as not to discourage them too much. It is a medicine necessary for the sound health of government.[25]

His friend did not agree. Once again, this may have been an example of the distortions of distance. Paris was far from the disorders in Massachusetts. Madison was alarmed that the "seditious party have become formidable . . . and have opened a communication with the [British] viceroy of Canada."[26]

Madison had already begun his active cooperation with Alexander Hamilton the previous September at the Annapolis Convention. That meeting of delegates from a mere five states had accomplished one thing only: it called for a general convention for the following May in Philadelphia. In Hamilton's words, delegates were being summoned "to render the Constitution of the Federal Government adequate to the exigencies of the Union."[27] This was a bold move.

Madison thought such boldness was necessary. He warned of monarchists' maneuvers to capitalize on the discontent. "All the real friends of the Revolution" needed to come together "to perpetuate the Union and redeem the honor of the Republican name," he wrote.[28] Washington, too, worried that supporters of an American king would take advantage of the rising disorders. He could hardly believe what he was hearing: "Even respectable [citizens] speak of [monarchy] without horror."[29] Madison knew he had one important supporter for his and Hamilton's project—the *most* important one. George Washington prodded the younger man on. He wrote Madison in November 1786:

> No morn ever dawned more favorably than ours did; and no day was ever more clouded than the present! Wisdom and good examples are necessary to rescue the political machine from the impending storm.[30]

II. "The Great Little Madison"

James Madison, small and slight, usually wore black. He was no match in oratory for the powerful Patrick Henry or other strong speakers. Yet, if knowledge is power, Madison was a Titan. He had spent his days in the spring and summer of 1786 "boning up" on the history of every previous experiment with *republican* government. He knew the strengths and weaknesses of all those states in which the people governed. In his extensive reading, Madison had help from his friend Jefferson. The American minister in Paris had sent to Montpelier, Madison's country home, a "literary cargo" of books on history, politics, and economics.[31]

Madison's immediate concern in the upcoming convention in Philadelphia was whether General George Washington would attend. Washington fully supported Madison and Hamilton's efforts, but he hesitated about whether he could go. Washington's reasons for holding back were weighty. He had dramatically surrendered his commission in Annapolis less than four years before. For that selfless act, he was revered throughout the world.[32] Would plunging back into politics now sully his reputation? Also, he had told his friends in the Society of the Cincinnati—an honorary group of officers from the Continental Army—that he could *not* attend their meeting in Philadelphia.* Would his attendance at the federal convention in the same city at the same time now constitute a breach of his word to his dearest wartime friends? Then there was the very real danger that the convention

* Thomas Jefferson was among the critics of the Society of the Cincinnati who saw it as a budding aristocracy that threatened to bring hereditary privilege into the new republic. Washington took Jefferson's criticisms seriously and tried to reform the bylaws of the Society.

would fail.[33] In fact, Benjamin Franklin had warned of that possibility. In a letter to Thomas Jefferson in Paris, Franklin wrote:

> I hope Good from their Meeting [in Philadelphia]. Indeed, if it does not do good, it must do Harm, as it will show that we have not Wisdom enough among us to govern ourselves; and will strengthen the opinion of some Political writers that popular Governments cannot long support themselves.[34]

Finally, Washington bowed to the urgent pleas of Madison, Hamilton, Virginia's governor, Edmund Randolph, and his army colleague, Henry Knox, and agreed to attend.[35] Madison immediately sent the great news to Jefferson.

> To forsake the honorable retreat to which [General Washington] had retired and risk the reputation he had so deservedly acquired manifested a zeal for the public interest that could, after so many illustrious services, scarcely have been expected of him.[36]

Washington was greeted upon his arrival in Philadelphia by pealing church bells, booming cannon, cheering crowds, and a mounted troop of Pennsylvania cavalry. He went straight to the grand home of Robert Morris, where he would lodge throughout the summer. Morris, who had served as financial secretary under the Confederation, repeatedly saving the Patriot cause, was Philadelphia's richest merchant. As soon as he had settled in, Washington headed for Benjamin Franklin's home on Market Street. There, under his famous mulberry tree, the old sage was greeting arriving delegates. Franklin was president (in today's terms, governor) of Pennsylvania and the official host of the convention. Washington had not seen Franklin since 1775, but they had been friends since Franklin supplied Braddock's army in 1755.

By agreeing to attend, Washington and Franklin lent their enormous prestige to the project of Madison and Hamilton. Washington and Franklin also, interestingly, were two of the Founders who lacked a formal education. Many of the others among the fifty-five who framed the Constitution had received college education at such institutions as Princeton (9), Yale (4), William & Mary (4), Harvard (3), Columbia (2), University of Pennsylvania (2), and such British institutions as Oxford (1) and St. Andrews (1).

When the delegates assembled, tardily, on May 25, they unanimously elected General Washington president of the convention. They met in the old Pennsylvania State House, now known as Independence Hall. Their first decision—to conduct all their discussions secretly—was probably essential to completing their business, but it was not uncontroversial. When Jefferson learned of it, he wrote immediately to John Adams, who was serving as the American minister in London. Jefferson strongly disapproved, but the reputations of Washington and Franklin and many of the other delegates allayed the suspicions of most Americans:

> I am sorry [the delegates] began their deliberations by so abominable a precedent as that of tying up the tongues of their members. Nothing can justify this example but the innocence of their intentions and ignorance of the value of public discussions. I have no doubt that all their other measures will be good and wise. It is really an assembly of demigods.[37]

James Madison's first decision at the Constitutional Convention would echo down the centuries. He took up his seat near the presiding officer—Washington—and began taking copious notes of the proceedings.[38] He would later say that he was absent from the sessions for only a few minutes at a time, so that only the briefest of comments by a delegate would have gone unrecorded. Each evening, following the day's meeting, Madison would painstakingly write out his record from the shorthand notes he had taken that day. Thus we have the best record of the convention's proceedings from the man who was the main engine of the meeting.

Madison had crafted a plan of government based on his extensive studies. With typical tact, he asked Governor Randolph of Virginia to introduce the plan. Soon, it became known as the Virginia Plan. It was a breathtaking proposal because it went far beyond the Confederation Congress's instructions to the convention. Congress approved the Philadelphia meeting "for the sole and express purpose of revising the Articles of Confederation."[39] The Virginia

Plan—which called for a two-chamber national legislature based on population—was a bold departure. It represented the entering bid of the large states.*

Soon, William Paterson of New Jersey responded with his state's plan, the key element of which was equal representation of the states in a one-house legislature, just as it was under the Confederation Congress. The New Jersey Plan became the small states' response to the Virginia Plan. Both plans contained many specific details, which Pennsylvania's James Wilson—a key ally of Madison—compared and contrasted for the delegates. The Scottish-born Wilson had a powerful, organized mind and was a strong proponent of a federal union:

> *Virginia Plan proposes two branches in the legislature.*
> *Jersey, a single legislative body.*
> *Virginia, the legislative powers derived from the people.*
> *Jersey, from the states.*
> *Virginia, a single executive.*
> *Jersey, more than one.*
> *Virginia, a majority of the legislature can act.*
> *Jersey, a small minority can control.*
> *Virginia, the legislature can legislate on all national concerns.*
> *Jersey, only on limited objects.*
> *Virginia, the legislature can negative all state laws.*
> *Jersey, giving power to the executive to compel obedience by force.*
> *Virginia, to remove the executive by impeachment.*
> *Jersey, on application of a majority of states.*
> *Virginia, for the establishment of inferior judiciary tribunals.*
> *Jersey, no provision.*[40]

As temperatures outside the convention hall rose, tempers inside the crowded chamber rose, too. Delaware's Gunning Bedford—described as "fluent, fat, and angry"—arose to challenge the Virginia Plan. The large

* "Large," in this sense, meant greater in population, not necessarily in territory. Georgia, which was the second largest state after Virginia, was a decidedly small state in the Constitutional Convention because of its sparse population.

states "insist . . . they will never hurt or injure the lesser states. *I do not, gentlemen, trust you!*" Then Bedford shocked the delegates with this response to the threat of the large states to form a federal union *without* the small states: "The small states will find some foreign ally of more honor and good faith who will take them by the hand and do them justice!"[41]

The delegates knew this was no idle threat. Spain had been secretly dealing with settlers in the western territories. There was talk of disunion in the Mississippi Valley. British ministers had contemptuously told John Adams, our ambassador in London, that they would rather deal with *thirteen* state governments than with him.[42] And no one could be quite sure what part France or Holland might take if the Union fell apart.

Alexander Hamilton stunned many delegates when he arose to attack *both* plans. Both plans, he charged, gave too much power to the people. He thought the people were "turbulent and changing" and they "seldom judge or determine right."[43] Hamilton urged a purely *national* government, with states having no more authority than counties do in relation to the states. Hamilton argued for giving propertied men a larger share of authority and influence in the new government.[44]

Did Hamilton really believe this? Or was he skillfully laying out a case for a centralized government dominated by wealth that would make Madison's Virginia Plan look moderate by comparison?

With tensions building, the revered Benjamin Franklin made one of his rare speeches to the convention. He recalled that when the Continental Congress sat in days of great danger, they had asked God's help in prayer. "Have we forgotten our powerful Friend? Or do we imagine we no longer need its assistance?" Franklin said he had lived a long time—he was the oldest delegate—"And the longer I live the more convincing proofs I see of this truth, *that God governs in the affairs of men*. And if a sparrow cannot fall to the ground without his notice, is it probable than an empire can rise without his aid?" Franklin concluded, quoting the Bible: "Except the Lord build the house, they labor in vain that build it."[45] We know that the delegates did *not* follow Franklin's suggestion to begin their sessions with prayer—they had no funds to hire a clergyman! But they didn't break up, either, and that answered Franklin's fervent prayer.

To answer Gunning Bedford's furious assault, "the great little Madison" (his wife's charming description of him) responded with invincible logic: "If the large states possess the avarice and ambition with which they are charged, will the small ones in their neighborhood be more secure when all control of a general government is withdrawn?"[46] Who would really suffer more from *disunion,* he asked mildly.

Unless the deadlock could be broken, the convention would fail. George Washington had seen this danger before. It had nearly caused the Continental Army to collapse. Washington called this assertion of a veto power by the states the "monster sovereignty."[47]

Connecticut's Roger Sherman arose to break the deadlock. Sherman was a small, spare man, who dressed plainly and wore his hair straight back. Unadorned and simply spoken, Sherman had risen from humble beginnings to become a respected figure in his little state. Sherman—Madison called him "Mr. Sharman" in his notes—offered what became the Great Compromise: the national legislature would be comprised of *two* houses—a House of Representatives based on population and a Senate based on the principle of equality of the states. Madison bitterly regretted this compromise. He thought it violated the essential principle of republican government—the equality of citizens. Franklin, too, opposed it. Only when they saw it as the only way to save the Union did they accept it. This was a greater source of dissension than any other issue before the convention, Madison would later write.[48]

Now, curiously, once they found themselves protected by a federal Senate, many of the small state delegates began to support a *stronger* federal government. Other issues remained to be resolved. The executive would be single—a president. He would be elected not by the legislature, but by an electoral college specially chosen every four years for that purpose. The president would have a veto over legislation, but two-thirds of Congress could override his veto. He could negotiate treaties, but two-thirds of the Senate had to ratify. The president would serve a term of four years, but he would be eligible for reelection indefinitely.* A president who

* This was changed by the Twenty-second Amendment in 1951, which limited the president to two terms.

abused his powers could be impeached by a majority of the House of Representatives, but could only be removed from office following trial and conviction by two-thirds of the Senate. The president would be the commander in chief of the armed forces, but he would have to ask Congress for a declaration of war. And Congress always held the "power of the purse" to hold him in check.

Once it had been determined that the House of Representatives would represent the people directly, the delegates required that all bills for taxation must originate in the House. Nor could monies be appropriated unless they also originated in the House. The federal judiciary would try "real cases and controversies" arising out of the Constitution and laws. Although the Constitution does not say so, judicial review of federal and state laws was *presumed* when the Framers asserted that "this Constitution and all laws and treaties made pursuant thereto shall be *the supreme law of the land.*" This supremacy clause assured ours would be a federal union, that the states would no longer have power over the Union.

Most discussion of the Constitution and religion today focuses naturally on the First Amendment, but the original Constitution contained a powerful provision that receives less attention. Article VI, Section 3 states: "No religious Test shall ever be required as a Qualification to any Office or public Trust under the United States." This was a revolutionary breakthrough for religious liberty, one of the most advanced statements in the world—then or even now.

Maryland's John Carroll, a Catholic, had noted that "the American army swarmed with Roman Catholic soldiers." How could the new government justify denying them full civil rights? Similarly, Jewish Americans had participated in the struggle for independence, notably Hayim Solomon, who had arranged loans for the Continental Congress and helped save Washington's army from starvation. By banning religious tests for office, the Constitution assured that religion would never be a bar to any able American serving the new republic.

But what about *slavery*? "Persons held to service or labor." That is the awkward phrase the Constitution uses to describe slaves. After the fight over large state/small state representation, the treatment of slavery became the greatest source of conflict. Very early, a clash occurred over this "peculiar institution."* The Founders' reticence in dealing with this explosive topic came from their belief, as Madison pointed out, that it was "wrong to admit in the Constitution the idea that there could be property in men."[49] At the time of the Constitutional Convention, slavery existed in nearly all of the states—and had existed since they were founded. Massachusetts had abolished slavery and four states—New Hampshire, Rhode Island, Connecticut, and Pennsylvania—were in the process of doing so. Emancipation was advancing in New York and New Jersey. The Founders believed that slavery was on the path to extinction.[50] Ninety percent of slaves lived in the South.[51]

The Founders were born into a society that permitted slavery. Connecticut's Roger Sherman called the slave trade "iniquitous." New York's Gouverneur Morris, a brilliant orator and a representative of great wealth, stood stoutly on his wooden leg and denounced slavery in the harshest terms. This "nefarious institution" was "the curse of heaven in the states where it prevailed," he said, ignoring the fact that his own New York still permitted slavery.[52] He compared the slave states with the free regions. Slavery is characterized by misery and poverty, but the free regions (actually, states with relatively few slaves) were characterized by "rich and noble cultivation."[53]

This was brave talk from a man who was a close friend to George Washington. Sitting silently in the chair, Washington was America's most prominent slaveholder. But Morris was hardly alone in his disdain for slavery. Washington's good friend and neighbor, George Mason, was also a slaveholder. Still, Mason expressed the enlightened prevailing opinion of the Upper South: "Slavery discourages arts and manufactures. The poor despise labor when performed by slaves. Slavery prevents whites from immigrating and produces the most pernicious effects on manners." Those were the practical reasons. Mason went further: "Every master of slaves is born a petty tyrant. They bring the judgment of heaven on a country!" Mason passionately called for the general government to *prevent* the increase of slavery.[54]

---

* *Peculiar* in these times did not mean "odd" or "strange" as it does to us today. It meant "characteristic of" or "unique to."

High-minded as they were, these noble arguments ran into a stone wall of resistance. "Interest alone is the governing principle of nations," South Carolina's John Rutledge answered coolly.[55] Morris, Mason, and Madison did not move him with their moral case against slavery. Just as bluntly, Rutledge said that *any* attempt to interfere with slavery in the states would result in the South's refusing to ratify the Constitution.[56] Once, again, the threat of disunion loomed.

Faced with this impasse, the Founders carefully crafted a Constitution that avoided even mentioning *slavery*, Africans, or the slave trade. It dealt with slavery by talking *around* the subject. First, it based representation in the House of Representatives on a *three-fifths* formula carried over from the Articles of Confederation. The Constitution required a census to count the whole number of free persons, to exempt "Indians not taxed," and to count "three-fifths of all other Persons." Second, they compromised on abolishing the African slave trade by permitting Congress to outlaw it, but only twenty years after ratification of the Constitution. Third, the Constitution required states to return to their states of origin all "persons held to service or labor" in another state. In effect, this was a fugitive slave clause.

Volumes have been written about these *compromises* with the existence of slavery. Some have claimed that by compromising with this hated institution, the Founders surrendered all moral claims to being defenders of liberty and human rights. Foreigners laughed when England's Samuel Johnson asked: "How is it that we hear the loudest *yelps* for liberty among the drivers of Negroes?" Some even argue that they voided the philosophy of the declaration that "all men are created equal."[57]

It is clear that all but a tiny few of the delegates to the Constitutional Convention morally *disapproved* of slavery. It is equally clear that not a word of the Constitution would have to be changed if the states continued to emancipate the slaves on their own.

Even some of the compromises with slavery can be seen in this light. For example, the Three-Fifths Compromise was a mere mathematical formula, advanced by Northern delegates, and was never intended as a statement that the Founders thought slaves to be less than fully human. After all, they referred to slaves as *persons*. Who, after all, wanted slaves counted fully for purposes of representation? *Slaveholders.* This would artificially increase their representation in the House of Representatives and as well in the electoral college. Also, and this cannot be stressed enough, the Three-Fifths Compromise provided an *incentive* for states to continue the emancipation process. When a state freed its slaves, it would get *increased* representation in the House of Representatives. And, because each state's electoral vote was based on its number of representatives, the state that abolished slavery would also be *rewarded* in the selection of the president.

Madison, we know, was deeply downcast over the failure of the delegates to outlaw the African slave trade immediately. He thought it "dishonorable to the American character."[58] Yet the choice was not between ending or not ending the slave trade. If the Founders had not accepted a twenty-year delay in banning the trade, South Carolina and Georgia would have stayed out of the Union and there would have been *no ban at all* on this "execrable traffic." The virtue of this compromise was that it clearly and unequivocally spelled the end of the slave trade in the not too distant future.

The fugitive slave clause was a bitter pill Northern delegates had to swallow. They did so only because they sincerely believed the Constitution would not have been ratified without it.

In *A New Birth of Freedom*, Harry Jaffa explains some of the understanding that led even such antislavery men as Abraham Lincoln to accept, albeit grudgingly, the Constitution as it was originally written in 1787:

> Lincoln's reasons for fidelity to the fugitive slave clause of the Constitution resemble, but are not identical to, those for honoring the right of each state to order and control its own domestic institutions. In both instances it is the law of the Constitution, and fidelity to the Constitution is a *sine qua non* for the continued existence of the Union. . . . The general assumption, which Lincoln shared, was that a government as powerful as the one established in the Constitution would not have been ratified without the fugitive slave clause. . . . But Lincoln also believed that the strengthening of the government of the Union added enormously to the prosperity of the Union, which in turn strengthened the Union itself. . . . The concession to slavery in the

fugitive slave clause was ultimately, he thought, in the interest of the slaves themselves.[59]

Small wonder that no less a passionate advocate for freedom than ex-slave Frederick Douglass could later say of the Founders' handiwork in Philadelphia: "Now, take the [C]onstitution according to its plain reading, and I defy the presentation of a single proslavery clause in it. On the other hand it will be found to contain principles and purposes, entirely hostile to the existence of slavery."

Benjamin Franklin was also dissatisfied with the slavery compromises. He wasn't big on equal representation of the states either. But in the closing hours of the convention, he used his famous wit to try to soothe raw nerves. He quoted the highborn French lady who said: "I don't know how it is, sister, that I meet with nobody but myself that's always in the right."[60] He shared with his fellow delegates a British writer's description of the "only" difference between the Anglican and Roman Catholic churches: "The Church of Rome is infallible and the Church of England is never in the wrong."[61] Franklin went on to make the serious point that the older he grew, the more he doubted his own judgment and the more regard he had for the opinions of others.

That was a powerful statement coming from Franklin. Considered the greatest sage of the age, if even *he* could so humbly put aside his strongly held views, how could other delegates stubbornly persist in opposition? Yet some of them did just that. Two powerful Virginians, George Mason and Edmund Randolph, would refuse to sign. So would Maryland's Luther Martin, whose long-winded, rambling, sometimes boozy speeches against federal power had bored so many.[62] Massachusetts's Elbridge Gerry was the only Northern delegate who refused to sign. Most of these *nonsigners* argued that the Constitution created a federal government that was *too* powerful.

George Washington's influence is harder to find. He spoke very rarely. Once, when a delegate suggested limiting the standing army to five thousand, Washington dryly observed that it would be a good idea *provided that we could also require that no enemy would ever invade with more than five thousand troops.* Just before adjournment, he descended from the chair to encourage delegates to amend a provision for representation in the House of Representatives. By changing the formula from 40,000:1 to 30,000:1, he argued, the House would be closer to the people it represented. The change—toward a more *democratic* House—was adopted unanimously.

Washington may have had the least formal education of any member of the convention; still he was held in awe. Once, when he sternly rebuked members for leaving notes of the secret discussions where they could be picked up, the greatest men on the continent sat shamefaced like errant schoolboys.[63] Another incident showed Washington's famous reserve. When delegates were talking about it, Gouverneur Morris disagreed. He was sure he could approach his good friend quite familiarly, he said. Alexander Hamilton bet him a dinner he would not put his hand on the general's shoulder and greet him. When Morris said: "My dear general, how happy I am to see you look so well," Washington stepped back and froze Morris with a disapproving stare.[64] Happily, Washington did not hold a grudge, and within days he was seen laughing at the merry Morris's witticisms.

It was Morris who shared Washington's confidence in the constitutional project. He noted that Washington told him it was all too likely the people would reject *any* new Constitution. "If to please the people, we offer what we ourselves disapprove, how can we afterwards defend our work? Let us raise a standard to which the wise and honest can repair. The event is in the hand of God."[65]

At the last session, Franklin remarked that he had long watched the carving on the back of the presiding officer's chair. Was it, he asked himself, a rising or a setting sun? With the signing of the Constitution, Franklin said, he was now sure. "I have the happiness to know that it is a rising and not a setting sun."[66]

When a lady asked him what kind of government he and his fellow delegates had given them, Dr. Franklin replied: "A republic, if you can keep it."

III. The Struggle for Ratification

When the delegates left Philadelphia in September 1787, prospects for ratification of the new Constitution were by no means bright. Yes, they had not broken up in bitter disagreement. But of fifty-five who convened in May, only thirty-nine were willing to put their names to the final draft polished and refined by the expert penmanship of Gouverneur Morris. It must have taken courage for some of those who refused to face the stern, disapproving stare of George Washington.[67] They knew they well could be committing political suicide by their failure to support the Constitution.

Madison knew that key battleground states would be Massachusetts, New York, and his home state of Virginia. Rhode Island—"Rogue Island"—as some of the delegates called it, had refused to send representatives. The old Confederation Congress, then meeting in New York, helped immeasurably by accepting the draft of the Constitution and affirming its call for "nine necessary states" before it could take effect. Had they stuck to the Articles' *unanimity* requirement, Rhode Island, or any one recalcitrant state, could have doomed the entire project.

Even so, "the nine necessary states" to ratify would be hard to find. Madison hurried to New York and began to work for ratification with Alexander Hamilton and John Jay. Their joint efforts—a series of essays published in pamphlet form—became known as *The Federalist Papers* and the two parties that formed in favor of and in opposition to the new Constitution quickly adopted the names of *Federalist* and *Antifederalist*. The Antifederalists were formidable. In Massachusetts, they included (at least at the start) Sam Adams and John Hancock; in New York, the powerful Livingstons and the Clintons. In Virginia, Patrick Henry led the opposition. He had memorably refused to attend the Philadelphia convention ("I smelt a rat"). In addition, the Lees and George Mason spoke against ratification.

Hamilton began *The Federalist Papers* with an essay by "Publius," a name taken up by his fellow writers. They wrote anonymously, and it has taken extensive efforts by later scholars to determine which man wrote which essay. The essays—written at a feverish pace while the debates raged in the states—had a certain "slap-dash" quality to them.[68] Even so, *The Federalist Papers* has become a treasure of political theory and the most reliable source of information about the *intentions* of the Founders. George Washington praised the work and even paid to have it reprinted in Richmond. He wrote to Hamilton:

> That work will merit the Notice of Posterity; because in it are candidly and ably discussed the principles of freedom and the topics of government, which will always be interesting to mankind.[69]

Madison, who may have lacked Jefferson's winged prose, nonetheless laid out in compelling terms the case for the new government. As he had done with Gunning Bedford's furious attacks, he turned the arguments of the Antifederalists on their head. First, he argued, "If men were angels, no government would be necessary." Then he continued, laying out the best case for a system of checks and balances: "Ambition must be made to counteract ambition." He showed how the Constitution enabled each branch—executive, legislative, and judicial—to perform its assigned function while resisting power grabs by other branches. To critics who said that no republic—a government of the people—could exist over so vast a territory, Madison pointed out that previous failed attempts at republican government failed *because they were not extensive enough*! Here, in *Federalist* No. 10, he boldly argued that free people inevitably formed "factions." These factions corresponded to their economic, religious, and social interests. In a far-flung republic—like the expanding United States—no one faction, no one *coalition* of factions, could form that would oppress those in the minority. The larger the number of contending groups, therefore, the more likely freedom would be to prevail.

If Madison was especially concerned to make the case for *the preservation of liberty,* Hamilton argued passionately for "energy in the executive." Government under the Articles was dying away because it could not enforce its obligations—neither enforcing treaties with foreign powers, nor raising and equipping an army and a navy at home. Hamilton wanted a government that could defend the country, promote a strong economy, and create a stable future for investment. When writing of the judiciary in *Federalist* No. 78, Hamilton stated his belief that the courts would always be "the least dangerous branch" because judges possessed "neither the sword (executive) nor the purse (legislative)."

The Federalist Papers remains today the best source for explaining the ideas and principles that Americans held in the 1780s and which, to a great extent, Americans still hold. Although Hamilton is often seen as an antidemocratic figure, aligning himself with the rich and wellborn, he could write as memorably of natural law and human rights as any of the Founders:

> The sacred rights of mankind are not to be rummaged for among old parchments or musty records. They are written, as with a sunbeam, in the whole volume of human nature, by the hand of the Divinity itself and can never be erased or obscured by mortal power.[70]

In Massachusetts, Sam Adams was persuaded to drop his opposition when Boston merchants pledged to build new ships if the state would only ratify the Constitution. The shipwrights, caulkers, and chandlers—always Sam Adams's most loyal backers—pressed the old Patriot to come over to the Federalist side.[71] They needed the work! Sam Adams brought John Hancock around.

Massachusetts ratified by a close vote of 187–168 in February 1788. Maryland heard another interminable harangue from Luther Martin—and voted overwhelmingly to ratify in April 1788.[72]

Madison hastened back to Virginia in time to be elected to the state's ratifying convention. His election was by no means assured. Only after he met with the leader of Virginia's Baptists and gave him assurances that the new Congress would take up the pressing issue of a Bill of Rights did Elder John Leland give Madison his endorsement. Leland wanted the new federal government to provide the same kind of protections for religious liberty that Madison's sponsorship of Jefferson's Virginia Statute for Religious Freedom had assured them within the state.[73]

This may be the appropriate place to pause for a moment to discuss further James Madison's views on religious liberty. Few of the Founders have been so misunderstood. Even as the U.S. Supreme Court in the past sixty years has woefully misunderstood Madison's ideas, they have been taken up and defended by the Roman Catholic Church in the epochal Vatican II Council. Madison's beliefs, as reflected in his *Memorial and Remonstrance* of 1785, his fatherhood of the Constitution of 1787, and his authorship of the Bill of Rights of 1791, deserve to be considered among the greatest of American achievements. Religious liberty, as Madison said, "promised a lustre to our country."

Madison's achievement is America's achievement. As such, it stands as one of world historical importance. As Judge John Noonan has put it: "Free exercise—let us as Americans assert it—is an *American* invention. How foolish it would be to let a false modesty, a nervous fear of chauvinism, obscure the originality."[74] Perhaps it was Madison's very diffidence, his unwillingness to beat his own drum, that has caused us to fail to appreciate the greatness of his achievement. Noonan sees beyond Madison's modesty to his monumental inspiration:

> Modest in all things, including his Christian commitment, James Madison was, so far as I know, the first statesman who, himself a believer, and not knowing any persecution himself, had enough empathy with the victims of persecution to loathe the idea of enforced religious conformity and to work to produce law that would forever end it. It is easy to be tolerant if you don't believe. To believe and to champion freedom—that is Madison's accomplishment. Overshadowed by Jefferson, Madison was the better workman. In the phrase "free exercise" that the founder of seventeenth century Maryland had brought to America, Madison found the perfect expression, an expression that in his mind excluded the establishment of a church as well as the enforcing of religious opinion.[75]

Madison would not be alone in arguing the case for the new Constitution in Richmond. He would be supported by George Wythe (Jefferson's law professor at William & Mary) and by young John Marshall. Also, curiously, the state's governor, Edmund Randolph, one of the famous nonsigners in Philadelphia, now urged ratification.

Patrick Henry charged that the new Constitution "squints toward monarchy"[76] and condemned it. He charged a power grab. He even took issue with Gouverneur Morris's eloquent opening lines of the Constitution's Preamble, "We the People":

> I have the highest veneration for those Gentlemen,—but, Sir, give me leave to demand, what right had they to say, We, the People. My political curiosity, exclusive of my anxious solicitude for the public welfare, leads me to ask, who authorised them to speak the language of, We, the People, instead of We, the States? States are the characteristics, and the soul of a confederation. If the States be not the agents of this compact, it must be one great consolidated National Government of the people of all the States.

Debate continued for weeks through a sweltering June in Richmond. Madison patiently, quietly, answered Henry's objections. He rebutted point-by-point Henry's impassioned but ill-organized attack on the Constitution. Sometimes the gallery could hardly hear Madison's soft, almost inaudible voice. But the delegates listened intently. Yes, a Bill of Rights might be added, as Antifederalists demanded, but only *as amendments and only after the Constitution had been ratified.*

Finally, Henry rose dramatically at the end to say, "I see the awful immensity of the dangers" of the new Constitution, "I *feel* it." Then, as a summer storm shook the convention hall with violent thunder and lightning, Henry argued that heaven itself was watching the delegates' actions. Despite Henry's own flashes of eloquence and rhetorical thundering, the delegates voted with Madison—but barely: 89–79.[77]

Virginia was not the ninth "necessary state." New Hampshire's ratification had beaten the Old Dominion by mere days. But without Virginia's ratification, George Washington would have been *ineligible* to serve as the new government's first president. So, too, would Jefferson and Madison and all the distinguished Virginians have been disqualified.

The debate shifted to New York. Even though the Constitution could go into effect with only ten states, New York State, by staying out, would cut the Union in half. (Americans would have done to themselves what Gentleman Johnny Burgoyne had *failed* to do ten years earlier in the War for Independence.) During the ratification debate in Poughkeepsie, Hamilton's brilliant performance prompted one of the ablest of the Antifederalists, Melancthon Smith, to admit he was won over. Smith's change of heart was crucial.[78] George Washington, quite familiar with the contentious factions in New York from his war experiences there, found "more wickedness than ignorance" in the Empire State's Antifederalists.[79] As in all fiercely fought campaigns, not everything was left to debate and persuasion. When New York Antifederalists maneuvered to keep the state out of the new Union, Hamilton and Jay threatened *to take New York City out of the state*![80] In the end, New York ratified by the heart stopping close vote of 30–27.

Ratification was celebrated by a huge victory parade down Broadway in Manhattan. Thirty seamen and ten horses pulled a twenty-seven-foot model ship named *Hamilton*. Workers, artisans, and craftsmen joined merchants in celebration. The teamsters—called *cartmen*—carried a banner with this poem:

Behold the federal ship of fame;
The Hamilton *we call her name;*
To every craft she gives employ;
Sure cartmen have their share of joy.[81]

It was the first of many more tumultuous parades down Broadway under the new government. Later, they would add "ticker tape" to celebrate peace, victory, and—sweetest of all—liberty.

Five

The New Republic
(1789–1801)

Americans begin their experiment in republican self-government with many advantages, but the era is a time of barely restrained political passion. Strong central direction by Treasury Secretary Hamilton and President Washington's firm hand as an administrator enable the new government to develop the resources needed to grow and prosper. Americans split into two parties as they divide over friendship with Britain or friendship with revolutionary France. Through it all, strong institutions are established—the presidency, the cabinet, the Supreme Court, and, of course, Congress. A Bill of Rights is added to the new Constitution—as promised. Americans enjoy greater religious and press freedom than any other people on earth—and just as soon some Americans begin to abuse their new freedom guarantees. New states are added to the thirteen original states—on a completely equal basis. For all this, four presidential elections are held.

I. "The Sacred Fire of Liberty"

George Washington stood on the north portico of Mount Vernon, overlooking the majestic Potomac River, on 14 April 1789. There, he received word that the electoral college had met and *unanimously* chosen him to be the new republic's first president.

There was no cheering there. Washington knew that the new government was nearly bankrupt. The old government of the Articles of Confederation had quietly and peacefully expired, but deeply in debt. Like many planters, even the wealthy Washington was "cash poor." He had to borrow money to travel the 250 miles between Mount Vernon and New York City for the inauguration.[1] Washington was concerned that people might think he had gone back on his solemn promise to retire, assuaging concerns that he aimed to assume the mantle of king. He had given that promise to Congress in Annapolis, just before Christmas 1783. Now he was back—though under different circumstances and in a different capacity.

He need not have worried.

Jubilant crowds greeted his coach in every village and town on his way to the temporary capital in New York City. They shouted themselves hoarse in praise. But Washington was wise. He knew that the popular acclaim might not last. Such an emotional outpouring, he thought, might easily turn "into equally extravagant (though I will fondly hope unmerited) censures."[2]

Perhaps like the reluctant Moses, Washington often expressed doubts about his abilities to measure up to his appointed tasks. It was just what he had done in 1775 when the Continental Congress unanimously made him commander in chief of the army. Washington also knew that others might come to doubt his abilities. Good graces in politics are more like winds than mountains. Hadn't he seen some of those who cheered him in Congress conspire only a few years later to replace him? So it would be with those raucous citizens who hailed the conquering hero now.

The great Revolutionary leader had been the model for the presidency. He had presided with dignity, patience, and strength for five long, sultry months while delegates to the Constitutional Convention measured the constitutional fabric to his frame like so many tailors. Despite the delegates' heated arguments and occasional long-winded speeches, Washington had been an attentive student in the greatest graduate seminar in political science, history, and economics ever conducted on this continent. Not as bookish or brilliant as many, Washington could weigh each speaker's words against his own rich experience as farmer, surveyor, legislator, military commander, and diplomat.

Only Franklin could rival Washington's breadth of experience. Although he had never been to Europe, or even to Canada, George Washington had traveled more extensively throughout America than all but a few men of his day. If Washington was not prepared, then no one was. That was precisely what many of the world's most powerful thought; they did not believe *any* people were capable of self-government, least of all the Americans.

Washington arrived in the festive city and proceeded to Federal Hall, in Lower Manhattan, for the inaugural ceremonies. The building had been redesigned for the occasion by Major Pierre L'Enfant. Washington had known the talented French émigré since he arrived at Valley Forge as a member of Baron von Steuben's staff.

On 30 April 1789, before the assembled crowds, George Washington took the presidential oath from Chancellor Robert Livingston. (Yes, Livingston, the *Antifederalist*, now apparently reconciled to the new government.) Dressed in a homespun American-made brown suit with eagles on the buttons, he placed his hand on the Bible and recited the oath, adding, significantly, four words, repeated by every president since as a matter of tradition if not sincere belief: "So help me God." Then he kissed the Bible. In his brief inaugural address to members of Congress, he claimed that heaven itself seemed to have ordained that the republican model of government—indeed, "the sacred fire of liberty" itself—had been placed in the hands of the American people. It was, he said, an *experiment.*[3]

There were no proud boasts, no rah-rah claims of sure success. As an experiment, it might fail.

The odds were certainly not in the Founders' favor. Washington had listened carefully to the debates of the Constitutional Convention—as most of the members of the new government had. He heard, as they all did, the long and detailed descriptions offered by James Madison and other delegates of the failure of republican governments of the past. The track record was less than reassuring. Every effort would have to be made to see the experiment did not fail; if eternal *vigilance* was required to guard against tyranny, then eternal *diligence* was required to secure the success of the new nation.

Washington proceeded with dispatch to organize the executive branch of government. He chose Alexander Hamilton, just thirty-five years old, as his secretary of the Treasury. Hamilton had already served Washington as an aide-de-camp in the army. Washington knew his mercurial temper. He was a serious man with a habit of speaking his mind—bluntly. But the president also knew his young friend was brilliant and tireless. Add to that pair of highly desirable qualities Hamilton's undying realism, and he was perfect for the bill.

For secretary of state, Washington chose a fellow Virginian, Thomas Jefferson, forty-seven, still serving as ambassador in France. Jefferson would be uncharacteristically tardy in joining the new administration. As attorney general, Washington selected the charismatic but indecisive Edmund Randolph, just a year Hamilton's senior. This was a generous act on Washington's part, since Randolph had dithered about signing the Constitution, declined, but then lined up behind Madison at the Virginia ratifying convention. Rounding out the president's cabinet—although it was not yet called that—was the redoubtable Henry Knox, thirty-nine, now secretary of war. The former bookseller from Boston had served Washington faithfully throughout the war as chief of artillery.

An astute and natural manager, Washington had carefully balanced geographical sections and political points of view in selecting the heads of the executive departments. These were young men of the Revolution—their average age, including Washington himself at fifty-seven, was only forty-two years old. Other leading figures in the new government would be John Adams, fifty-four, the vice president; James Madison, thirty-eight, newly elected to the House of Representatives; and John Jay, forty-four, soon to become the nation's first chief justice.

The First Congress was to be a very productive one; some even called it a second constitutional convention. But it got off to a very rocky start. Meeting in temporary quarters in New York City, the House and Senate had to flesh out the new government. There were executive departments to be organized, a judiciary to be created, treaties to be considered, and pressing financial business.

And the difficulties didn't end with policy and procedure. Recently returned from five years as America's ambassador to the Court of Saint James's in London, John Adams stumbled in his new role as presiding officer of the Senate. He had faithfully and ably represented his country's cause abroad, but had also lost touch with many in the new Congress. In a routine discussion of titles for the new president, Adams weighed in, *disastrously*. He monopolized the debate for a full month with long and pedantic speeches. Completely missing the tenor of the times, Adams suggested the chief executive should be called "His Highness, the President of the United States and Protector of Their Liberties."

Some Senators were put off by the vice president's intruding so brusquely into what they saw as *their* role, debating the nation's laws and policies. Others were offended by the frankly *royalist* tone of Adams's suggestion. Had he spent too much time in a foreign court filled with the bowing and scraping lackeys of the king? When Adams spoke of President Washington's inaugural address, he called it "his most gracious speech." Critics were quick to point out that this was precisely the standard form for referring to the King's Speech from the Throne.[4] What had happened to Honest John Adams? *His Rotundity* was the snickering title his senatorial colleagues bestowed on poor Vice President Adams behind his back.[5]

One of his sharpest critics, Pennsylvania's Senator William Maclay, confided to his diary. Whenever he looked at Adams presiding in the chair, "I cannot help thinking of a monkey just put into britches." Cruel and unfair, to be sure, but Maclay's serious point on the Senate floor was undoubtedly correct: the Constitution specifically said, "No title of nobility shall be granted by the United States."[6] The suggestions for highfalutin titles all violated the spirit if not the letter of the Constitution.

Fortunately, the House of Representatives voted that the chief executive would be called, simply, "Mr. President," and the Senate concurred. John Adams, the bold Patriot of '76, was seriously misunderstood and deeply wounded by this affair. He never wished to give hereditary titles to officers of the new republic; he simply thought a *dignified* title would be some compensation for the times away from family and farm and for the many criticisms public officers had to endure. The incident was politically sticky enough that it caused George Washington to pull away from his vice president. He was advised that Adams's reputation in Virginia was *odious*.[7] Virginians were shocked to see Adams the Patriot assume what they saw as monarchical "airs." The vice president would not be included in discussions

President Washington. *"North and South will hang together if they have you to hang on," Jefferson told President Washington in 1792. Reluctantly, Washington agreed to serve a second term. He declared American neutrality in the war between France and Britain. He provided a firm hand at the tiller as dangerous political passions rose.*

Martha Washington. *The richest widow in colonial Virginia, Martha Dandridge Custis's marriage to the young colonel of the Virginia militia afforded him a devoted companion, a stable home life, and a dignified consort. Martha described herself as always "cheerful as a cricket, busy as a bee." During the general's long absences, she managed home affairs with skill and courage.*

John Adams as president. *John Adams's presidency was an unhappy one. He signed the disastrous Alien and Sedition Acts, but he split with his own Federalist Party to send a diplomatic mission to France. "I desire no other inscription over my gravestone than this: Here lies John Adams, who took upon himself the responsibility of peace with France in the year 1800." He was the first president to live in the newly constructed Executive Mansion. His prayer for it was "I pray Heaven to bestow the best of blessings on this house, and on all that shall hereafter inhabit it. May none but honest and wise men ever rule under this roof."*

Abigail Adams. *Smart, loyal, and passionately involved in the nation's founding, Abigail Adams endured long separations and family sorrows to give Honest John Adams the emotional and spiritual support he craved. When apart, they wrote long, loving letters to each other daily. Their correspondence, on microfilm, extends fully five miles. It gives us an incomparable view of this remarkable couple and the age they adorned.*

of Washington's official family,* a slight that greatly hurt the sensitive Adams.

The vice president did not fully realize that he had come home from London only to step into a conflict that would dominate the 1790s—between those who desired the style of monarchy if not the political system and those who favored a more egalitarian simplicity from their rulers. Few people criticized George Washington's elegant coach drawn by six matched greys, prancing smartly through Manhattan's narrow cobblestoned streets. People liked to have a president who was conscious of high fashion. But those who gathered around the new government went far beyond the requirements of style. Washington's birthday was celebrated as a national holiday—as King George's had been. And some wanted to see the president's face impressed on the coins.

Worse, according to Jefferson and Madison, was the growth of a "republican court" in always status-conscious New York.[8] Weekly *levies* were the Washingtons' way of officially entertaining guests. On a raised dais, President and *Lady* Washington would greet their guests, who bowed to the first couple and received stiff, formal bows in return. Sensitive even to the *appearance* of ascendant monarchy, Jefferson had inveighed often against such trappings in his many writings.

He did score some victories for republican simplicity, as when he persuaded American judges to discard the large, flowing wigs worn by English magistrates. Said Jefferson, "They look like *rats* peeping through bunches of oakum," the wooly wadding used for stuffing between the timbers of sailing ships.[9] His gibe was enough to pierce pomposity and overturn a centuries-old tradition. Madison spoke for Americans of the Jeffersonian bent when he told the House: "The more simple, the more republican we are in manners, the more national dignity we shall acquire."[10]

The Jeffersonians considered this a serious matter. The world was still dominated by monarchies. America was surrounded by them—in Canada, in Florida, in Louisiana. During the war years, Jefferson had not only worked to *disestablish* Virginia's official church—always a prop of monarchy—but he had also worked to abolish *primogeniture* and *entail*. Primogeniture was the

* Washington's appointed department heads were not yet called the cabinet, but Washington as general had always referred to his aides as his *military* family.

rule in Europe's monarchies that required all land be passed down from father to eldest son. Entail prescribed how property was to be inherited only by lineal descendents of the landowner. These measures, Jefferson's reforms, taken together, were *essential* for America to move from royal government to a truly *republican* system.

These were serious questions to Jefferson and Madison because creating a new republic required new ways of behaving. America, they believed, had to leave behind all the "trappings" of monarchy *and* an aristocratic social system. President Washington received many official greetings from voluntary associations and religious groups upon taking office. His formal response to one of these—the Hebrew Congregation in Newport, Rhode Island—made a contribution as significant as Jefferson's Virginia Statute for Religious Freedom. In 1790, he wrote:

> It is now no more that toleration is spoken of as if it were by the indulgence of one class of people that another enjoyed the exercise of their inherent natural rights, for, happily, the Government of the United States, which gives to bigotry no sanction, to persecution no assistance, requires only that they who live under its protection should demean themselves as good citizens in giving it on all occasions their effectual support.

As Claremont professor Harry Jaffa has pointed out, this was the first time in human history that any ruler addressed the Jews as *equals.*[11] President Washington closed his letter with these gentle words, taken from Scripture: "May the Children of the Stock of Abraham, who dwell in this land, continue to merit and enjoy the good will of the other inhabitants; while every one shall sit in safety under his own vine and fig tree, and there shall be none to make him afraid."[12]

II. Madison's Bill of Rights

When Congress turned to constitutional matters, they took up the question of amendments—what was to become known as a Bill of Rights. During the battle for ratification, promises were made to Antifederalists that the federal Congress would be open to suggestions for amendment. Madison, who had originally argued that a Bill of Rights was *unnecessary* because the new government had no power to violate the rights of citizens, now honored his commitment to his Virginia neighbors. As a leading member of the new House of Representatives, Madison became the author of the Bill of Rights. Only ten of the twelve amendments that passed Congress were ratified by the states, but they became justly famous as Americans' charter of freedom.*

To read the first ten amendments, we can read the history of the colonial struggle against British despotism. Freedom of speech, press, and religion were guaranteed by the First Amendment, as well as the right to assemble and to petition for "redress of grievances." These rights form the core of a free society, and they had been violated in one way or another by British misrule. The Second Amendment—still controversial in our day—meant what it said. Americans remembered that General Howe's redcoats marched out of Boston to seize the militia's gunpowder and weapons. An armed people remained a free people because they are the last redoubt against a hostile government's tyrannical advances. And, just as importantly, an armed people could resist the demands of militarists to *regiment* society. Americans would be free without ever resorting to the sort of goose-stepping mindlessness of Prussian (not to mention Soviet or North Korean) dictatorial states. The Third Amendment prevented government from stationing, or "quartering," troops in private homes in peacetime—a major abuse of the British in Boston.

The next *five* amendments, all relating to judicial procedures, each corresponded to very real British acts of tyranny, many of which are detailed in the Declaration of Independence. Those notorious "Writs of Assistance" were general warrants that allowed British colonial officials to rummage through Americans' homes, farms, and shops looking for incriminating evidence. The Fourth Amendment banned them, specifying

* Another amendment that required members of Congress to face the voters before receiving a pay increase they had voted for—surely a constitutional "little engine that could"—was also passed by the First Congress in 1789. It was ratified as Amendment XXVII only in 1992. It shows that good ideas have a long shelf life.

no "unreasonable searches or seizures." The Fifth protected Americans from having to testify against themselves or from being tried twice for the same offense. The Sixth Amendment called for a speedy public trial, with the right of the accused to confront witnesses, compel witnesses for the defense to testify, and to have the assistance of counsel. The Seventh Amendment guaranteed the right of trial by jury, while the Eighth outlawed "cruel and unusual punishment."

The final two amendments were the capstones—the bookends to the preamble's acknowledgement that the powers of government were delegated by the people. The Ninth Amendment recognized that rights enumerated in the Constitution were not the *only* rights the people enjoyed, and the Tenth assured that any powers *not* granted to the federal government or prohibited to the states were retained by the states or by the people.

Madison's careful drafting and skilled floor management of the Bill of Rights through Congress gives him just title to two great tributes—Father of the Constitution and Father of the Bill of Rights. The Founders deeply admired classical heroes. But no figure of antiquity—no Greek like Pericles or Solon, no Roman like Cicero or Cincinnatus—can claim an equal standing with Madison as lawgiver and champion of liberty. Madison told his fellow members of Congress, who exercised powers he had carefully crafted for them, why a Bill of Rights was necessary: "If we can make the Constitution better in the opinion of those who are opposed to it, without weakening its frame, or abridging its usefulness in the judgment of those who are attached to it, we act the part of wise and liberal men to make such alterations as shall produce the effect."[13]

Madison hoped the Bill of Rights would bring the Antifederalists around, especially those still holding out against ratification in North Carolina and Rhode Island.[14] In this, he was strongly supported by Jefferson, who generally supported the new Constitution, yet embodied so many of the Antifederalist concerns. While still in Paris, Jefferson spoke for many when he wrote to Madison: "A bill of rights is what the people are entitled to against every government on earth . . . and what no just government should refuse. . . ."[15]

Madison's rhetoric does not soar as Jefferson's does, but he keeps pace in the dignity, reason, and *force* of his arguments. In keeping his promises to Elder John Leland and the Virginia Baptists, and to a host of political allies and opponents, Madison's inspired draftsmanship helped dispel much of the lingering suspicion that had attended the work of the Philadelphia Convention.

III. "A Host in Himself": Hamilton's New System

When Hamilton wrote, in *The Federalist,* of the urgent need for "energy in the executive," he may not have had himself in mind. Yet Hamilton's incredible outpouring of energy, creativity, and purpose still stuns us. He knew that the new government would be judged in no small measure on how it managed the new republic's economy.

With the Constitution ratified, Hamilton quickly responded to Congress's call for a *Report on the Public Credit.* It was Hamilton's chance to exhibit his genius as well as to tutor men twice his age in the realities of modern finance. In this, Hamilton was as justified as Madison had been in making good the pledges made in the heated state contests. The new secretary of the Treasury, barely thirty-five, would call for two key moves by the new administration—*funding* the debt and *assuming* the debts of the states. "The only plan that can preserve the currency is one that will make it to the immediate interest of the monied men to cooperate with the government in its support," said Hamilton with his characteristic forthrightness. "No plan could succeed which does not unite the interest and credit of rich individuals with that of the state."[16]

Funding meant that the federal government would honor the obligations incurred under the Articles of Confederation—a sum of about $55 million. On the surface, this was an obvious move. Had the new government repudiated the debts of its predecessor, investors would have scattered like dry leaves before a gust of wind. The tricky question was *how* the debt should be funded. Should the federal government pay the holders of government bonds the full face value? Many of these bonds were originally issued to Patriots and their families in the first flush days of revolutionary enthusiasm. The Patriots had pledged their lives, their *fortunes,* and their sacred honor to the American cause. Over the years, however, the Confederation Congress had authorized worthless paper money (giving rise to the dread phrase "not worth a Continental" dollar). Seeing little chance their bonds would ever be redeemed, thousands of hard-pressed soldiers, farmers, and small merchants had sold their bonds for a fraction of their face value. Purchasers of these discounted bonds were highly unpopular, seen as trafficking in human misery. To fund the debt meant paying these "speculators" at par. Thus, a one-hundred-dollar bond would be redeemed at one hundred dollars face value.

Assumption meant that the federal government would pay off some $25 million in war debts incurred by the states. This would help bind the states to the new government. (It might be an incentive, as well, for Rhode Island to ratify the Constitution.) It would be an act of justice, since the war had been fought for the Union, not for any single state or group of states. The costs of the war were not equally distributed throughout the country, just as the battles were not evenly spread out over the extensive territory.

Madison was quick to respond to Hamilton's program—negatively. Madison thought it would be a travesty not to recognize the original holders of bonds—especially war widows and veterans—and to give, in effect, a windfall profit to the entire class of speculators in discounted bonds. He also pointed out that some of the states had met their obligations to creditors in a timely fashion, while other states had avoided prompt payments. (That these solvent states tended to be in the South was early evidence of a sectional split in Congress.)

When, after March 1790, Thomas Jefferson formally joined the Washington administration, a genuine clash over Hamilton's financial system seemed inevitable. This was avoided, however, by one of the earliest examples of a practice in Congress that came to be known as "logrolling," a less incendiary term for vote-swapping.

At the same time the new government had to decide on a financial system, it also had to determine where its permanent capital would be located—the *Residence* question. Hamilton's commercial allies wanted the capital to remain in New York City or, failing that, to be situated between New Jersey and Pennsylvania. They saw many advantages in keeping the capital close to the growing centers of finance and trade. Pennsylvanians knew that the return of the government to Philadelphia for ten years—a temporary move while the new capital was constructed—might in the end become permanent.

The Assumption and Residence questions, it would seem, could hardly become more complicated. And then they did. Benjamin Franklin, in his last public act, sent to Congress a petition from the Pennsylvania Society for Promoting the Abolition of Slavery. He had earlier accepted the presidency of the society. Unwilling to upset the delicate work of the Constitutional Convention with their appeals, Franklin now embraced the abolition cause wholeheartedly. The Franklin petition called for Congress "to promote mercy and justice towards this distressed race" by immediately ending the African slave trade and by working to end slavery in America.[17]

George Washington was known to favor placing the new capital between Virginia and Maryland. He had long had a keen interest in canal building on the Potomac River. Other Southerners began to see trouble ahead if the federal government were permanently located in Philadelphia. The prominent Quaker community there had long taken the lead in agitating for the abolition of slavery. Many Southerners condemned slavery and were willing to discuss *gradual* emancipation, but they were united in not wanting to be pushed into abolition.

Hamilton, desperate to create a solid foundation for the new government, agreed to compromise with Jefferson and Madison on the Assumption and Residence questions: in return for locating the new capital on the Potomac, Jefferson and Madison would enlist Southerners in Congress to support Hamilton's plans for Assumption.

It was a classic compromise. Few could have thought then that locating the nation's capital between *two* slave states would continue to rub salt into the nation's wound for another seventy-five years. The nation would be shamed by foreign diplomats seeing slave markets in the very heart of what Jefferson called this "empire for liberty." But a thorn in the side is not easily ignored; if the Residence question had been decided otherwise, it might have been possible to sweep the issue under the rug. By confronting Northern congressmen with the daily spectacle of human bondage, the slavery question was kept alive. Prior to the Civil War, it should be remembered, there were many Northern communities where few if any slaves or black freemen lived.

Hamilton built on his early success by proposing a national bank. Once again, Jefferson and Madison opposed him. It was necessary for credit and commerce, he argued, and besides, the Constitution's "elastic clause" permitted Congress to exercise those powers "necessary and proper" to carrying out its enumerated powers. Jefferson wrote to President Washington that a bank was not necessary. Madison argued that it was not even constitutional.

In each of these instances, President Washington welcomed advice and opinions from Jefferson and Madison, but he sided with Hamilton. This was not, as some have charged, because Washington favored the wealthy commercial class—Hamilton's strongest supporters. Washington was a farmer and a slaveholder. He knew that Jefferson's hopes of an *agrarian* republic sustained by the votes of small landowners rested, ultimately, unavoidably, on slavery. It was built into the very fabric of the agrarian economic model. And Washington was struggling to find a way *out* of the system into which he and so many others of the Founders' generation had been born. Washington leaned consciously in favor of Hamilton's system because he knew it had no need for slaves. "I clearly foresee," Washington told an English visitor to Mount Vernon, "that nothing but the rooting out of slavery can perpetuate the existence of our Union. . . ."[18] If the Union itself was split into Northern and Southern sections by the slavery question, even though he was a proud Virginian, Washington told Edmund Randolph, "he had made up his mind to move and be of the northern."[19]

To Jefferson and Madison, however, the system Hamilton was setting up went far beyond the slavery/free-labor question. Jefferson had elaborated his agrarian ideas in his famous *Notes on Virginia.*

> While we have land to labour then, let us never wish to see our citizens occupied at a work-bench, or twirling a distaff. Carpenters, masons, smiths, are wanting in husbandry [agriculture]: but, for the general operations of manufacture, let our work-shops remain in Europe. It is better to carry provisions and materials to workmen there, than bring them to the provisions and materials, and with them their manners and principles. The loss by the transportation of commodities across the Atlantic will be made up in happiness and permanence of government.

> The mobs of great cities add just so much to the support of pure government, as sores do to the strength of the human body. It is the manners and spirit of a people which preserve a republic in vigour. A degeneracy in these is a canker which soon eats to the heart of its laws and constitution.

No modern politician could survive by praising farmers so lavishly while condemning urban dwellers as "mobs" and comparing them to "sores" on the body. But America in 1790 was an overwhelmingly *rural* country, as the Census of 1790 would confirm. Of America's 3.9 million people, only 5 percent lived in towns or cities; the remaining 95 percent were rural. Jefferson's views made him highly popular with farmers, Northern and Southern.

Hamilton's financial system, enacted over the objections of Jefferson and Madison, soon bore fruit. The new republic thrived. The government's credit was "as good as gold." Small, swift cutters of Hamilton's Revenue Marine (today known as the Coast Guard) began immediately to enforce customs laws, helping to generate large import duties for the new government. The economic boom greatly increased revenues for the federal government, allowing it to strengthen its credit and meet its new obligations.

Meanwhile, President Washington began a series of presidential tours of the country. In the summer of 1790, he visited New England, traveling by carriage. Americans accustomed to presidential travel in the age of Air Force One can hardly imagine that the president of the United States would actually journey without guards, without a Secret Service, being jostled along deeply rutted and dusty roads in a single coach. Jefferson expressed concern for Washington's safety—not because of outlaws or Indian raids—but because of the incredibly bad roads.[20] Tiring and uncomfortable as it was, Washington knew that such visits helped the American people to feel the presence of their new government. Despite grousing by some that these trips seemed like royal *progresses,* Washington knew they served to unify the republic. In his first such trip to Connecticut and Massachusetts, he had carefully *avoided* going through Rhode Island, which had still not ratified the Constitution. Shortly after, little Rhody came in and was rewarded with a presidential visit to Newport.

On his southern tour in April 1791, President Washington would be completely out of contact with the government literally for weeks on end. Innkeepers would be stunned to see pulling up to their establishments "the greatest man in the world."[21] Washington endured the heat and dirt, but he positively beamed in the company of "fair compatriots," always enjoying the company of beautiful and intelligent women. In ever-fashionable Charleston, South Carolina, he reached the high point of his presidential tour. As he delighted in recording, he was flattered by "four hundred ladies, the number and appearance of which exceeded anything of the kind I had ever seen."[22]

When Washington fell ill, the country shuddered. In New York, he suffered through surgery without anesthesia to remove a carbuncle deeply imbedded in his thigh. While he recovered, the city fathers spread straw on the streets to quiet the clop-clop of horses and let the weary executive get his rest.

New York's leaders had more thought for Washington than did all too many of his colleagues. Hamilton reacted to increasing opposition to his program from Jefferson and Madison and their many allies in Congress. He appealed to Washington to dismiss Jefferson, saying that the divisions in his official family "must destroy the energy of the government."[23]

Not to be outdone, Jefferson and Madison took to calling themselves and their supporters *Republicans.** The clear implication was that Hamilton and his backers were *Monarchists.* Jefferson called them *Monocrats*, by which he presumably referred to Hamilton's known preference for a strong executive indefinitely eligible for reelection—essentially an elective monarchy.

At the close of his first term, Washington wanted to leave public office, to return to Mount Vernon. More frequently now, he would speak of having only a few years left of his life. He often said the time could not be far off when he would, in the words of the Bible, "sleep with my fathers." With Madison's help, he even prepared a Farewell Address to the nation for 1792. And he tried, without notable success, to keep *both* of his brilliant aides in his cabinet. Washington wrote to Jefferson: "I have a great, a sincere esteem

---

* Mr. Jefferson's Republicans are not to be confused with the Republican Party of today. Today's Republicans were not founded until 1854. The Jeffersonians were called first Republicans, then *Democratic*-Republicans, and finally, from Andrew Jackson's time onward, simply the Democrats.

Houdon sculpture of Washington. *"First in War, First in Peace, and First in the Hearts of his Countrymen," says "Lighthorse Harry" Lee of Washington in his eulogy. As president, Washington was keenly aware that his every action set a precedent for future American chief executives. "I walk on untrodden ground," he said. This 1785 bust by Jean-Antoine Houdon, commissioned by Jefferson when he was America's ambassador to France, is the best likeness we have of George Washington in his prime. It would be "right on the money."*

Houdon sculpture of Jefferson. *"No one can replace him," said Thomas Jefferson on his arrival in Paris, "I am only his successor." Still, Jefferson's years as Franklin's successor were to prove highly beneficial for the American ambassador and for his country. Jefferson negotiated treaties, studied architecture, and made friends with the philosophes. His intimate knowledge of France would help him as he later moved to buy Louisiana from Napoleon.*

James Madison. *Father of the Constitution, author of the Bill of Rights, and champion of religious liberty, "the great little Madison" was a giant of the American founding. Madison's close cooperation with Thomas Jefferson has no equal in American history. They are America's David and Jonathan. "Take care of me when dead," Jefferson asked of him at the end of his life. Madison's two terms as president were less than illustrious, but he continued to serve his country—and defend the Union—into his eighties.*

Alexander Hamilton as secretary of treasury. *Born out of wedlock on the British West Indian island of Nevis, Hamilton was managing a merchant fleet at thirteen years old. He served heroically as Washington's* aide de camp *during the war. With Madison, he spearheaded the move for the Constitutional Convention of 1787. Again with Madison, he co-wrote* The Federalist Papers. *As Washington's first secretary of the Treasury, his energy, knowledge, and boldness dominated the first term. He laid the foundations for a powerful national economy, but he alarmed Jefferson and Madison. They opposed his plans even as Jefferson called Hamilton a colossus—"Without numbers he is a host in himself." Hamilton died in a duel with Vice President Aaron Burr—the only Founder to die by the hand of violence.*

and regard for you both, and ardently wish that some line could be marked out by which both of you could walk."[24]

Hamilton's advantage over Jefferson cannot be traced only to Washington's support for his program. Hamilton headed up the Treasury. At this point, it was the *largest* of federal departments, with nearly five hundred full-time employees. The other departments had only twenty-two![25] Congress and the courts were in session for only a few months while Hamilton and his subordinates labored ceaselessly.[26] *Energy in the executive, indeed.*

Hamilton went out of his way to deflect criticism of his department. He insisted on keeping the Treasury clean and above corruption. His instructions to captains in the Revenue Marine—read by Coast Guard commanders to this day—show a keen appreciation for how to deal with Americans. Commanders should "always keep in mind that their Countrymen are Freemen. . . . They will therefore refrain with the most guarded circumspection from whatever has the semblance of haughtiness, rudeness or insult."[27]

As President Washington prepared for his southern tour in April 1791, he asked his cabinet to meet in his absence. Jefferson invited Henry Knox, John Adams, and Hamilton to join him for dinner. It was a friendly affair as after-dinner conversation turned to the British constitution.

Adams said, "Purge that constitution of its corruption . . . and it would be the most perfect constitution ever devised by the wit of man."[28]

To Jefferson, this was a shocking statement, coming as it did from "the Colossus of Independence." But what Hamilton said next was truly breathtaking: "Purge [the British constitution] of its corruption . . . and it would become an *impracticable* government: as it stands at present, with all its supposed defects, it is the most perfect government which ever existed."[29]

For Jefferson, such sentiments would be scandalous if expressed by *any* American. But coming from one man who stood "a heartbeat away" from the presidency and another who had just pushed through Congress his bill to create a national bank, the ideas were enough to make his head spin. All the Patriot leaders had denounced the corruption of the monarch during the Revolution. The king used the vast wealth brought into Crown revenues from India to bribe members of Parliament to support his policies. For twenty years, the eloquent Edmund Burke impeached Warren Hastings of the East

India Company and decried the corruption of the rich young "nabobs" who had fattened themselves on the riches of India.*

Could Jefferson really be exaggerating the dangers of monarchy in America if this is what the highest officials of the government said in their unguarded moments?

How could Britain have *any* admirers in this government after all she had done? Didn't these men believe what Jefferson had written in the Declaration? Those who governed under this same British constitution that Adams and Hamilton claimed to admire had, in fact, incited savage attacks on their countrymen and had "a design to reduce them under absolute Despotism."

This may have been the most important dinner party in American history. From this fateful encounter, we might date the beginning of America's two-party system. Jefferson certainly saw the significance of the evening in terms of the attitudes of Adams and Hamilton toward England. He wanted no part of their stated admiration for the British constitution.

IV. Hurricane Genet

Thomas Jefferson was preparing to leave Paris for home in July 1789 when the momentous news of the storming of the Bastille prison broke. He welcomed it. The Paris mob had broken its word. (Can a mob even *give* its word?) They had hacked to death the unfortunate Governor DeLaunay after promising him and his men safe conduct. They paraded through the streets with heads on pikes and pulled down the hated symbol of absolute monarchy brick by brick. Lafayette, America's most loved Frenchman, commanded royal troops, but gave his full support to the Revolution. He sent his "adoptive father," George Washington, the key to the Bastille (where it is exhibited to this day at Mount Vernon). Jefferson left a city in turmoil. Even in those early stages, when some deplored the rising level of violence, Jefferson waved away their concerns with one of his memorable

* In this context, Burke's *impeachment* of Hastings was a lengthy, public, denunciation of his conduct and character.

epigrams. He wrote to Lafayette: "We are not to expect to be translated from despotism to liberty in a feather-bed."[30]

Few who witnessed the French Revolution were neutral about it. "Bliss it was in that dawn to be alive; but to be young was very heaven!" enthused the English poet William Wordsworth. Edmund Burke, the great parliamentarian, had defended American liberty, cried out for the natural rights of the Indian people, and called for Catholic emancipation in Ireland. Surely, this friend of liberty, revered on three continents, would bless the French people's uprising. Not at all. Burke immediately dashed off his immortal *Reflections on the Revolution in France.* This great churning in Paris was nothing less, in Burke's unforgettable prose, than "the hot alembick of Hell."* Burke stunned many of the *enlightened* figures of his day with the fury of his assault on the French Revolution. He wrote: "[Am I] seriously to felicitate a madman who has escaped from the protecting restraint and wholesome darkness of his cell on his restoration of light and liberty? Am I to congratulate a highwayman and murderer who has broke prison upon the recovery of his natural rights?"[31]

Burke's assault at least arrested the wholesale embrace of the French Revolution by England's thinkers. In America, where he was held in highest regard, Burke's work circulated with approval among Hamilton's supporters, increasingly known as *Federalists*, in contradistinction to Jefferson's *Republicans.*

On the larger question, events would prove Burke correct. The French did *not* move closer to the ideal of ordered liberty that was the hallmark of the American Revolution. Instead, the world saw a *dégringolade*—a French word that describes a downward spiral of ever increasing destruction, bloodshed, and chaos.

Americans by and large did not see things that way. They believed that the French were moving toward establishment of another great republic. They hoped that movement would be the beginning of a *worldwide* revolution against monarchy and despotism and for liberty and constitutionalism. They flattered themselves that their own revolution would serve as the

* An alembick was a large pot, rather like a witch's kettle.

model for this world movement. They little knew how *unimpressed* the French had been with America's revolution. Maximilian Robespierre, leader of the radical *Jacobin* faction in the French National Assembly, put it bluntly: "America's example, as an argument for our success, is worthless, because the circumstances are different."[32] The Jacobins took their name from a convent in Paris where they met, and despite Wordsworth's poetic hopes, their unfolding Reign of Terror was to prove anything but *heavenly*!

Events spinning out of control in France did not affect America greatly in Washington's first term. Americans busied themselves in establishing their new government and enjoying "the blessings of liberty." All sides agreed that Washington's continued service was "indispensable." Though opposed to many of Washington's policies, Jefferson nonetheless told him he must serve a second term: "North and South will hang together if they have you to hang on," he told his chief.

Washington heeded his friend's words.

In 1792, the president was reelected by a unanimous vote in the electoral college—the first and only American president to be twice elected unanimously. The harmony at home was contrasted by the shocking discord across the Atlantic. Hardly had Washington been inaugurated for a second term in March 1793, when news reached America that King Louis XVI had been tried, convicted of treason, and put to death in Paris by the new and frighteningly efficient instrument of execution, the *guillotine.* With its monarch beheaded, France proclaimed itself a republic and promptly declared war on Britain.

Although they shuddered at the fate of King Louis XVI—fondly remembered for his timely help during the Revolution—many Americans nonetheless welcomed the news of the French republic.

At this yeasty moment, a new French ambassador arrived in America. Edmond Charles Genet—known to history as *Citizen Genet*—put to shore in Charleston, South Carolina. The new French republic was determined to eliminate *all* titles of distinction. So, even an *ambassador* would be known simply as "Citizen." His ship had set sail for Philadelphia, but had been blown off course by a severe storm.

Genet himself hit America's coastline like a hurricane. Charleston received him with rapturous applause. Governor William Moultrie and the cream of South Carolina society feted him. Governor Moultrie enthusiastically approved of Genet's plans.

And what plans! Citizen Genet set about recruiting American seamen and outfitting American ships to serve as privateers against British commerce. This was always a lucrative practice. The difference between privateering and piracy was simple: privateers could *legally* seize merchant ships and their cargoes if they had *letters of marque* issued by recognized governments; pirates were simply thieves—highwaymen of the seas—and could be hanged at the yardarm as soon as captured.

Citizen Genet also issued calls for his grandly named *Armée du Mississippe* and *Armée des Florides.*[33] With these forces, he would plan to attack Spanish holdings in Louisiana and Florida. How would he *pay* for all these ambitious plans? Genet was nothing if not imaginative. He issued *assignments.* In effect, these were promissory notes that he applied against the $5.6 million the United States owed France in war debts.

Further, Genet pushed America to *accelerate* repayment of that war debt. But, in order not to press his ally too hard, Citizen Genet helpfully suggested that France would accept repayment in the form of grain, timber, and other supplies that would help the French republic fight its enemies. This, Genet said, would give a stimulus to the American economy.[34] (About this, he was surely right, as the U.S. Marshall Plan would prove 150 years later.)

Citizen Genet swept up the eastern seaboard like a raging storm. All along his way, there were overjoyed receptions—church bells ringing, cannon salutes, laudatory speeches.[35] Arriving in Philadelphia after a leisurely twenty-eight-day journey, he presented the Washington administration with immediate problems. Should America even *recognize* the new French republic? Should we receive its ambassador?

Jefferson argued, persuasively, that America could not fail to recognize a government based on the same principle of the people's *consent* that underlay our own independence. Americans certainly could not appear to prefer a monarchy over a republic.[36] Hamilton was concerned that the chaotic situation in France might well lead to an overthrow of the shaky revolutionary government there. If we continued repayment of our debts, would a new French government credit our payments? What about the Treaty of Alliance of 1778? Hamilton said the treaty had been signed with Louis XVI, who was now dead. Jefferson responded that treaties are made between *nations,* not rulers.[37]

Jefferson believed the French Revolution to be a harbinger of world liberation. His young protégé, William Short, whom he had left behind in Paris, began writing him alarmed letters. Short included gruesome details of their own dear French friends who had been horribly butchered by revolutionary mobs of *sans culottes.** Jefferson sternly rebuked his friend:

> The liberty of the whole world was depending on the issue of the contest, and was ever a prize won with so little innocent blood?
>
> My own affections have been deeply wounded by some of the martyrs to this cause, but rather than it should have failed I would have seen half the earth desolated; were there an Adam and an Eve left in every country, and left free, it would be better than it now is.[38]

Thomas Jefferson wrote over seventy thousand letters in his lifetime. Surely, this was the *worst* thing he ever wrote—as myopic in its own way as Hamilton's waxing Tory at dinner with Jefferson, Knox, and Adams.

The violence was not all one-sided, however. For ten long years, the British had refused to leave their forts on the northwest frontier—as required by the Treaty of Paris. There, they supplied the Indians with weapons and whiskey. Americans believed "the hand that sells the whiskey rules the tomahawk."[39] Along the southwest border, too, Indian raids bore the mark of foreign, that is, Spanish assistance. Genet's plans could not be totally unwelcome to Americans facing slaughter on the borders.

Nor was Genet's outfitting of American ships with American crews in American harbors completely out of line. After all, France had equipped John Paul Jones's famous *Bonhomme Richard* for exactly the same purpose—raiding British commerce.[40]

---

* Poor men could not afford white silk stockings and britches (culottes) buttoned beneath the knee. Thus, the *sans culottes* became a symbol of revolution and marked the change in men's fashions to this day.

But France was then at war with Britain. As of April 1793 the United States was officially neutral. President Washington knew that the new nation could not afford to become entangled in war between the great powers of Europe. He issued the nation's first Proclamation of Neutrality.

In this, Thomas Jefferson supported him. How could he? Well, Jefferson was serving in Washington's cabinet. He also knew the United States was not *prepared* for war. And from his avid reading of newspapers, he had a keen sense of popular opinion. As he wrote Gouverneur Morris in Paris, "No country perhaps was ever so thoroughly against war as ours."[41] Madison did not agree. He thought we were dishonoring our Treaty of 1778 with France and that the president did not have constitutional authority to proclaim neutrality. After all, if the Constitution gave to Congress, not the executive, the power to declare war, was it not logical to infer that the power to declare *no war* also resided there?[42]

Washington might have been hard-pressed to steer a middle course between impassioned partisans of Britain and France had not Citizen Genet overplayed his hand. Great crowds had cheered Genet wherever he went. Francophiles even distributed a woodcut showing George Washington being guillotined.[43] The Neutrality Proclamation stirred violent passions. Genet thought he might appeal to the people *over Washington's head*. Surely these good republicans would support America's only true ally.

When the French warship *Embuscade* captured a British vessel, the *Little Sarah,* she brought her prize into Philadelphia, defying President Washington. Citizen Genet put the ship under a French flag and ordered her out to sea with a new name—the *Little Democrat*. Sailors believe it is bad luck to rename a ship, and so it was to prove for Citizen Genet. In ordering the ship to set sail, Genet had broken his word to Secretary of State Jefferson, who increasingly saw the Frenchman as a "Jonah."* He warned his chief lieutenant Madison that the impetuous French ambassador would "sink the Republican interest if they do not abandon him."[44]

George Washington rarely gave way to anger. When he did, it was terrible

* Jefferson used the Bible story of Jonah. It tells of frightened sailors who threw the prophet overboard to be swallowed by a whale because they feared he would cause God to sink their ship.

to behold. Citizen Genet provoked him, for it was not just Washington but the government of the United States that was being defied by the undiplomatic diplomat. "Is the minister of the French Republic to set the acts of this government at defiance with impunity?" Washington asked. "And then threaten the executive with an appeal to the people? What must the world think of such conduct, and of the government of the United States in submitting to it?"[45] Even in his rage, Washington was coolly logical. Even more than the insult to himself, he deplored the disrespect shown to his country. Jefferson could not disagree: Citizen Genet would have to go.

The Americans could not have known it, but the bloody wheel of revolution had already solved their problem for them. In June 1793, the radical Jacobins had taken full control of France and were already dispatching their rivals, the *Girondins,* to the guillotine. Genet was of the Girondin* Party. Almost before the Americans could demand his recall, the French Republic beckoned their errant minister home. Genet knew what that meant and so did the only sensible thing. He defected and begged for asylum.

When the new French minister arrived, he bore in his diplomatic pouch a warrant for the arrest of Citizen Genet. With perfect courtesy, President Washington received the new ambassador, and just as courteously, he brushed aside the demand to deliver up Edmond Charles Genet. Citizen Genet became *Mr.* Genet. He quickly took a wife, the daughter of New York's Governor George Clinton, and settled down to the life of a gentleman farmer in the Hudson Valley.

Genet had insulted George Washington. He had abused Washington's hospitality. He had even threatened him with a revolutionary appeal to the American people. Yet President Washington saved his life. Nothing in Washington's long career reflects more honorably on him than this singular act of mercy. Thanks to Washington and the new republic he helped create, Genet lived happily ever after.

Washington steered a steady course, with a strong hand on the tiller. In

---

* *Girondins,* or sometimes called Girondists, were more moderate French revolutionaries. Their leaders in the national assembly hailed from the Gironde region of France. Many of the Girondins had opposed the execution of the king and the queen. They would suffer the same fate as the monarchs, under the blade of the dreaded guillotine.

years to come, Americans would revere his role in this crisis. A century later, British poet Rudyard Kipling would write in *If*—"If you can keep your head / When all about you are losing theirs"—and he could well have been writing of George Washington in the crisis provoked by Hurricane Genet.[46]

One lasting effect of the storm over Genet was the solidifying of *party* differences in the American government. The Founders had rejected the very concept, but after Genet, party differences increased and took on a permanent cast—Federalists versus Republicans.

V. A Long and Difficult Farewell

If President Washington hoped for a more serene second term, he was to be sadly disappointed. No sooner had the Genet affair ended than trouble erupted on the Northwest Frontier. The British government had delayed and delayed leaving their forts.

In London, Lord Grenville told the American minister the forts would be held *indefinitely*. At the same time, the British began to step up efforts to choke off the French by seizing more and more ships on the high seas. They issued *Orders in Council* that gave Royal Navy captains greater powers to search and seize neutral ships and to *impress* their crews. *Impressment* was the process of taking sailors from their ships and *pressing* them into service on Royal Navy vessels.[47] This was supposed to be done only with sailors who were British subjects serving in foreign ships, but the Royal Navy was not overly careful about how it proved a man was really British. Sometimes, little more than an English-sounding accent would be enough; a few syllables could mean the difference between freedom and slavery.

President Washington had a hard time keeping Congress from declaring war on Britain, but he did send a force under General "Mad Anthony" Wayne to the Northwest. Wayne had earned his colorful nickname during the Revolution. He had, legend has it, responded to Washington's order to take the strongly held British fort at Stony Point, New York, with the famously warlike cry: "Give the order, sir, and I will lay siege to hell."[48]

Wayne defeated a threatening alliance of Indians at the Battle of the Fallen Timbers (near present-day Toledo, Ohio), in August 1794, thus erasing earlier humiliating defeats on the frontier. The Indians had been put up to it by the British, as always.[49] General Wayne next year signed the Treaty of Greenville by which America laid claim to the current sites of Detroit and Chicago. Fort Wayne was built on the forks of the Maumee River.[50]

Little did George Washington think, when he laid down his soldier's sword at Annapolis in 1783 that he would have to take it up again. Yet in 1794, that is what President Washington did. In western Pennsylvania, resistance to Secretary Hamilton's new taxes flared up. Farmers there needed to be able to convert corn and other grains into whiskey. This was because they lacked the means to preserve their crops for the long term. Hamilton's Excise Act of 1791—which placed a levy on liquor—hit them hard.

When resistance broke into open rebellion, the government was alarmed. Rebels overcame small numbers of federal troops, closed down courts, and vowed to march on Pittsburgh.[51] Hamilton urged Washington to act. The authority of the new government was in jeopardy. Supreme Court Justice James Wilson—himself a Pennsylvanian who had been instrumental in crafting the Constitution—certified that the laws were being opposed "*by combinations too powerful to be suppressed. . . .*"[52*]

Washington personally led twelve thousand heavily armed militiamen from four states—Pennsylvania, Virginia, Maryland, and New Jersey—across the Alleghenies. Washington wore the full uniform of a lieutenant general.

Attorney General William Bradford wrote that "the Presdt. means to convince these people & the World of the moderation & the firmness of the Gov."[53] Hamilton was all for overwhelming force. "Wherever the Government appears in arms it ought to appear like a *Hercules*," for it was dangerous for the authority of the United States to seem weak and irresolute. The Whiskey Rebellion was quickly put down. The more radical leaders of the rebellion immediately fled, others faded away, and two were brought back to Philadelphia for trial for treason. Convicted, they were soon pardoned by the gracious and understanding Washington.[54]

Washington blamed the rebellion on local "Democratic clubs," voluntary

* We will see this phrase again, in Lincoln's proclamation on the rebellion in the South. He will thus use the Whiskey Rebellion as a precedent for federal action.

associations generally loyal to Jefferson's Republicans. The president's vigorous action—and his merciful treatment of the defeated rebels—seemed exactly the right combination. The American people broadly supported him.[55] Some were still unconvinced that such a show of force was necessary. Thomas Jefferson—who had been fairly casual about Shays's Rebellion of 1786 from the distance of his Paris salon—wrote that "an insurrection was announced and proclaimed and armed against, but could never be found."[56]

The importance of the Whiskey Rebellion cannot be minimized. Washington knew he was walking "on untrodden ground." So many of his actions as president would become precedents for later leaders. This action showed the president willing to brook no unruly defiance of federal law. The place to change federal law was at the ballot box. Washington's spirited action in that beautiful autumn in the Pennsylvania mountains would form the basis for action by Presidents Jackson and Lincoln (as well as Presidents Eisenhower and Kennedy).*

Damn John Jay! Damn everyone who won't damn John Jay!! Damn everyone that won't put lights in his windows and sit up all night damning John Jay!!![57]

That was the sign on a Boston wall. Few Patriots ever suffered so much abuse from ungrateful countrymen as New Yorker John Jay. As chief justice of the United States Supreme Court, he might easily have declined President Washington's request to undertake the arduous journey to Britain to negotiate a treaty. But Washington felt a treaty was urgently necessary to prevent war.[58] Congress was restive. As mentioned, the British had refused to evacuate their forts in the Northwest. They claimed, not entirely unreasonably, that until Americans paid war claims of the Tories—as we had agreed to do

* In the movie *Gods and Generals*, produced by Ted Turner, Robert Duval plays the part of Robert E. Lee. Lee says he never thought he would live to see the day when an American president would "invade" an American state. In real life, Lee was the stepgrandson-in-law of George Washington. He surely would have known of President Washington's autumn campaign against rebels in the Pennsylvania mountains—and of his use of Maryland and Virginia troops to do it!

in the 1783 Treaty of Paris—they were justified in holding their forts. They continued to impress our seamen and to seize American ships trading with belligerent France.

Jay sailed for London with knowledge of "Mad Anthony" Wayne's great victory at the Battle of the Fallen Timbers. That should have strengthened his hand in negotiations. The final treaty he brought back, however, was a weak thing.

Washington knew that the United States was unprepared for war. He thought Jay's treaty would allow settlement of the Ohio Valley, end British attempts to incite the Indians against us (several white Canadians had been found among the dead at Fallen Timbers), and quiet the demands for war from those whose property had been seized under the Orders in Council. Jay's treaty provided for compensation.[59] Bracing for a storm of protest, Washington submitted the treaty to a Senate precariously divided between Federalists (20) and Republicans (10).[60] Washington would need the votes of every Federalist to achieve the necessary two-thirds for ratification of the treaty.

The public outcry was terrifying—the sign in Boston but a token of the animosity toward the administration. Virginia's Republican congressman, John Randolph, went so far as to raise a toast of "Damn George Washington!"[61] Jay was burned in effigy and mock guillotined. He was denounced as "Sir John Jay" and everywhere called "the arch traitor."[62]

Republican newspapers poured out torrents of abuse, not sparing George Washington. He wanted to be king, many of them claimed. Washington was deeply wounded by these irresponsible charges. As he had said during the Whiskey Rebellion, Washington only did his duty as he knew it—one of the reasons he led the troops himself, accepting responsibility for the action. "By God, I had rather be on my farm than be made emperor of the world!" he said.[63]

When the Senate ratified the treaty—just barely—in June 1795, the Republicans attempted another run at Jay's effort. They would use their strong position in the House of Representatives to cut off the funds needed to implement the treaty. The Constitution had clearly given to the president and the Senate the sole responsibility for negotiating and ratifying treaties, but it just as clearly gave the House of Representatives power over all appropriations. During the months-long debate, the British and French ministers wrestled with individual members, arguing for approval and rejection. Jay's treaty survived by a mere three votes when the House voted the necessary funds in April 1796.[64] The divisions were deep and bitter. And they were dangerous—Southerners angrily denouncing it, while Northerners—especially the mercantile interests of the Northeast—broadly favored it.

In the wake of this menacing and bruising fight, George Washington prepared to step down as president. He asked Hamilton to help him craft his final message to the American people.* It has come down to us as Washington's Farewell Address, even though it was published in a Philadelphia newspaper and never delivered as a speech.

Washington reminded Americans of those qualities necessary to maintain free government:

> Of all the dispositions and habits which lead to political prosperity, Religion and morality are indispensable supports. In vain would that man claim the tribute of Patriotism, who should labor to subvert these great Pillars of human happiness, these firmest props of the duties of Men and citizens.[65]

The heart of the address was his warning against twin evils—the spirit of party and "permanent" alliances with foreign states. Washington had just seen how the contention of political parties and the intrigues of foreign agents threatened the very unity of the country. Although the address could have been written with reference to the battle over Jay's treaty, it has taken on a timeless quality that contains wise counsel for us even today.

As the election of 1796 approached, Republicans and Federalists prepared to fight for the top prizes in government. Federalists had little choice

* The brilliant Hamilton might normally have been considered the likeliest successor to Washington as President. But Hamilton had effectively eliminated himself when he admitted to congressional investigators that he had paid blackmail to hush up an adulterous affair with Maria Reynolds. Hamilton's forthright confession is a model for political men—if rarely followed.

but to line up behind Vice President John Adams. The Republican choice was obvious. Thomas Jefferson had left the Washington administration in 1793, but he had kept in regular contact with James Madison, James Monroe, and other Republican leaders.

Adams received seventy-one electoral votes to Jefferson's sixty-eight. The Federalists had failed to deliver the votes necessary to elect Thomas Pinckney vice president so, under the Constitution as it was then written, Jefferson won the office. Since the Founders had not anticipated the creation of parties, they did not foresee the top two offices being held by men from different parties. It would prove an awkward arrangement for the next four years.

VI. War, Peace, and Honest John Adams

When, on 4 March 1797, George Washington attended the inauguration of his successor, he created yet another precedent. John Adams reflected on the scene in a letter to his beloved wife, Abigail: "It was made more affecting to me by the presence of the General, whose countenance was as serene and unclouded as the day. He seemed to me to enjoy a triumph over me. Methought I heard him say 'Ay! I am fairly out, and you fairly in. See which of us will be happiest.' When the ceremony was over, he came and made me a visit, and cordially congratulated me, and wished my administration might be happy, successful and honorable."[66]

As the new president left the hall where he had been sworn in, Vice President Jefferson waited for now *former* President Washington to precede him. Washington, with a firm gesture of command, indicated to Jefferson to go out before him. Washington was now a private citizen and was unwilling to hold on to any of the honors of office. Even in this, Washington was setting the standard for the government of a free people. Once again, the "greatest man in the world" was surrendering power and assuring a peaceful and orderly succession. President Adams was keenly aware of the *importance* of this first transition, but, as usual, his bluff exterior masked a tender heart. His acute sense of participating in an historic moment was all mixed up with his *personal* feelings. He could not resist telling Abigail about the reaction of the crowds at his inaugural.

> [T]here has been more weeping than there has ever been at the representation of any tragedy. But whether it was from grief or joy, whether from the loss of their beloved President, or from the accession of an unbeloved one, or from the pleasure of exchanging Presidents without tumult, or from the novelty of the thing, or from the sublimity of it arising out of the multitude present, or whatever other cause, I know not.[67]*

Adams's first task was to try to keep peace with the French. No greater contrast could be imagined than that between revolutionary France and the new American republic. During Washington's second term, France had lived under Maximilian Robespierre's Reign of Terror. The guillotine had claimed 16,600 victims nationwide in less than a year (1793–94).[68] As many as half a million languished in the prisons of the Revolution. Although the Terror would largely end with the death of Robespierre "the Incorruptible," the politics of France would be "poisoned" for centuries to come.[69]

Even trying to deal with such a government was hazardous. Hoping for a stable balance in foreign affairs, President Adams sent a delegation to negotiate a new treaty with France, just as President Washington had done with Jay's treaty with England. Adams was worried about the threat of a "Quasi-War" at sea because French frigates had begun to seize American ships—just as the British were doing.

The slippery French foreign minister Talleyrand refused even to see the American diplomats. He demanded a huge personal bribe just to talk to them. And he claimed France should be paid the staggering sum of $10 million to compensate France's honor for an insulting speech by President Adams. Talleyrand sent three agents to sound out the Americans and see if they would pay. One member of the American delegation, John Marshall, was a brave Revolutionary War veteran. He was a Virginian who had crossed the Delaware River with Washington in 1776, and he was having none of this French nonsense. Marshall labeled the three French agents

---

* Pulitzer Prize-winning author David McCullough says his biography of John Adams was helped immeasurably by transcripts of the letters of John and Abigail Adams. The microfiche record of this remarkable couple's letters to each other is five miles long!

"Messers X, Y, and Z" in his secret dispatches home. And he soon turned on his heels and set sail for America.

When word of the "XYZ Affair" reached America in April 1798, the country exploded in anti-French rage. "Millions for Defense, but not One Cent for Tribute" became the Federalists' rallying cry.[70] Once again, Jefferson's Republicans—known as "Gallomen" to their opponents—were deeply embarrassed by French conduct.

President Adams basked in his newfound popularity. In 1798, Congress readily agreed to his proposal to rebuild the navy. (The modern navy dates from Adams's administration.) Soon, Captain Thomas Truxton, commanding the powerful new USS *Constellation,* thrilled Americans with his daring capture of the French frigate *L'Insurgente* on 5 February 1799. Off the Caribbean island of Nevis, Captain Truxton's guns killed twenty-nine French sailors and wounded seventy-one, with the loss of only two dead and two wounded. The following year, his well-trained crew battled another French warship in the great Age of Fighting Sail. *La Vengeance* barely escaped sinking by *Constellation's* deadly accurate fire. These short, violent actions continued the navy's victorious traditions established by John Paul Jones. As Americans celebrated their independence from *both* great powers on the Fourth of July, they said they'd finally found in Captain Truxton an "envoy" whom the French would *have* to receive.[71]

John Adams might have been reelected handily in 1800 had he not been goaded into a disastrous misstep. Stung by truly vicious press criticism, and harassed in Congress by Jefferson's ally, Swiss immigrant Albert Gallatin, Adams agreed to two of the most ill-advised bills in American history—the Alien and Sedition Acts. The Alien Act lengthened from five to fourteen years the time necessary for an immigrant to become a naturalized U.S. citizen.[72] The Sedition Act was passed to permit prosecution of any person who published "false and defamatory" statements against the leaders of the government.

Neither Adams nor Hamilton *wanted* these bills. Hamilton realized they could be counterproductive. "Let us not establish a tyranny," he warned; "energy is very a different thing than violence."[73] But the ultra-Federalists in Congress pressed hard. They were certain that an invasion by France was imminent. Adams resisted panic—with humor: "There is no more prospect of seeing a French army *here* than there is in Heaven."[74] Nor were these Federalist leaders the only ones to oppose the extremely unwise measures. Running as a Federalist for election to Congress from Virginia, John Marshall said he "certainly would have opposed them" and that he thought they were only "calculated to create unnecessary discontents and jealousies."[75] Adams might have *vetoed* the Alien and Sedition Acts, but that would have opened a fatal division between him and the Federalist majority in Congress that was hell-bent on passing them. Soon, the Federalists would have cause to regret their haste. The Irish and the Germans were two large groups—especially numerous in critical Pennsylvania—who were *alienated* by this unwise legislation.

Jefferson and Madison responded to this challenge with their now famous "Virginia and Kentucky Resolutions." In 1798, the resolutions' authorship was unknown, but many of the ideas contained within them had been visible in the two men's response to Hamilton's national bank proposal of 1791. Madison's Virginia Resolutions were the more restrained, more tightly reasoned of the two state responses. Jefferson's Kentucky Resolutions, longer and bolder, attracted wide attention. The Jeffersonian style was recognizable:

> In questions of power, then, let no more be heard of confidence in man, but bind him down from mischief by the chains of the Constitution. That this commonwealth [Kentucky] does therefore call on its co-States for an expression of their sentiments on the acts concerning aliens, and for the punishment of certain crimes [sedition] . . . plainly declaring whether these acts are or are not authorized by the federal compact [Constitution].[76]

Jefferson scholar Merrill Peterson provides the linkages and underscores their importance: "The secession movement was a remarkable testament to the compact theory of government which Jefferson, more than anyone, had fixed upon the American mind."[77] If the American Union was a compact of the states, then might not any individual state *leave* the Union as it wished? Jefferson declined to spell that out. And, most importantly, he recognized that the American people would not permit *armed* resistance. Shays's Rebellion and the Whiskey Rebellion had taught him that. "Keep away from all use of force and [the American people] will bear down the evil propensities of the government by *election and petition*," he concluded.[78]

Nevertheless, it is possible to argue that Mr. Jefferson planted the seeds of secession with his anonymous Kentucky Resolutions. Jefferson comes perilously close to this. But Madison holds him back, by the coattails. The ever practical Madison *always* keeps Jefferson from going over the brink. (Madison will later *denounce* nullification.)

What Jefferson and Madison really sought was a *change in behavior* by Congress by this form of pressure from the state legislatures—or by electoral change.[79] If resistance to unconstitutional legislation was to be by election and petition, then what was called for was an organized appeal to voters. This was a major shift in party politics. Not only had Jefferson and Madison helped form a political party, their Virginia and Kentucky Resolutions offered, in effect, the first party platform and initiated a national political campaign.

The Undeclared Naval War with France (1798–1800) came closer and closer to declared war as former President Washington was called out of retirement to head up an army to meet a French invasion. Over President Adams's objections, Washington insisted on making Hamilton inspector general of the army. Many feared that Hamilton would create a power base for himself in the new army—much as Napoleon Bonaparte had done in France. American sailors, on a high state of alert, sang out their feelings in a sea chanty:

Now let each jolly tar [sailor], with one heart and one voice
Drink a can of good grog [rum] to the man of our choice;
Under John [Adams], the State pilot, and George's [Washington]
command,
There's a fig for the French and that sly Tallyrand.[80]

Despite Hamilton's agitation for war with France, despite the support given the idea by Federalists in Congress, President John Adams decided to make one last try for peace with France.

Surprisingly, the French were in a receptive mood. Napoleon, now clearly in charge, wanted no war with America. The Federalists exploded in rage—against their own president. They wanted to seize New Orleans and the Floridas. They wanted to further discredit the pro-French Jeffersonians. Adams's stubbornness, his *independent* streak, would be their undoing, they were sure.

After eight long months of negotiation, the French bluntly refused to pay $20 million in damages to the United States for shipping seized during the Quasi-War. But the two sides found room for agreement. The French let America out of her obligations under the Treaty of Alliance of 1778. In effect, we got a divorce from France for $20 million in alimony.[81]

The news of the Convention of 1800 between the United States and France came too late to affect the presidential election. History will always wonder what would have happened if voters had learned of Adams's diplomatic success before marking their ballots for president. One thing is sure: had Adams given in to Hamilton's war cry, there is no chance the French would have sold Louisiana to the United States three years later.[82] While Jefferson is rightly regarded as the father of the Louisiana Purchase, Adams was at least its godfather.[83]

Adams knew he was courting political disaster by sending his diplomatic mission to France: "I will defend my missions to France as long as I have an eye to direct my hand, or a finger to hold my pen," he said. "They were the most disinterested and meritorious actions of my life. I reflect on them with so much satisfaction that I desire no other inscription over my gravestone than: Here lies John Adams, who took upon himself the responsibility of peace with France in the year 1800."[84]

Americans were stunned by the news many received just before Christmas in 1799. George Washington had died at Mount Vernon after an illness that lasted barely thirty-six hours.

The Father of the Country gone!

And they felt like orphans for his passing. None more than Hamilton. "He was an *aegis* [protector] very essential to me," he would write. Stricken members of Congress gathered in Philadelphia's German Lutheran Church at a memorial service to hear Virginian Henry "Lighthorse Harry" Lee eulogize Washington as "first in war, first in peace, and first in the hearts of his countrymen."*

VII. The Revolution of 1800

Aaron Burr won election to the U.S. Senate from New York in 1790, defeating Alexander Hamilton's father-in-law, Philip Schuyler. Burr, a war hero, had to be a supreme political organizer to bring off that feat.[85] Under the original Constitution, senators were elected by the state legislatures.** Burr's power base in New York proved irresistible when Jefferson and Madison were looking for Northern allies to oppose Hamilton's centralizing plans. Their coalition became the basis for the Republican (that is, the modern *Democratic*) Party. Jefferson and Madison traveled north in 1791 to New York and New England on their famed "botanizing expedition." It was a real vacation for the Virginia farmers, who studied the plants and agricultural methods of the northern region. But it also provided them the occasion to meet with Burr and New York's powerful Chancellor Robert R. Livingston.[86]

As the 1800 election approached, Jefferson knew he would have to have Northern support to win. The alliance with Aaron Burr promised to bring New York's large bloc of electoral votes behind the Virginian.*** Nor would the Republicans want a replay of the election of 1796, where the victors for president and vice president represented different parties. Greater organization and party discipline would be required to avoid that outcome.

The campaign of 1800 was the first true presidential campaign in American history. Republicans fought Federalists in every state. Few elections since would match this one in the scurrilous attacks made on both candidates. The partisan newspapers called Adams "senile" and denounced him for his pride, vanity, and pig-headedness. This was mild, however, compared to the all-out assault on Thomas Jefferson. The soft-spoken,

* These words would long be remembered by Americans. Among those who knew them "by heart" were Henry Lee's son, Robert E. Lee.

** This was changed by Amendment XVII, which in 1914 provided for the direct election of U.S. Senators.

*** Virginia would cast twenty-one electoral votes, New York twelve, of a total of seventy needed for election in 1800.

philosophical Virginian was accused of atheism and of seeking to bring the bloodiest of French revolutionary violence to America's peaceful shores. "Mad Tom," "Jacobin," "apostle of the racetrack and cock-pit" were but some of the gibes of the Federalist press.[87] (The racetrack charge was particularly ridiculous since Mr. Jefferson *never* frequented them, but the Federalist icon, George Washington, clearly did!)

Jefferson was constantly compared, unfavorably, with Washington. The death in late 1799 of the nation's first president had plunged the country into deepest mourning. Logic is usually the first casualty in political campaigns. If Jefferson was, in truth, such a notorious radical, how loyal could Washington have been in choosing him as his first secretary of state?

Nothing, however, that the Republicans could say about the Federalists could compare with what the Federalists said about each other. In this most extraordinary of presidential campaigns, the Federalist Party literally fell apart. Personal rancor was its undoing. Without the unifying figure of Washington to hold them together, Federalists tore into one another.

In May of 1800, Adams had flown into a rage in a discussion with his secretary of war, James McHenry. He had learned that members of his cabinet were regularly reporting to Hamilton. He called Hamilton "the greatest intriguer in the world—a man devoid of every moral principle—a Bastard and as much a foreigner as Gallatin. Mr. Jefferson is an infinitely better man . . . you are subservient to Hamilton, who ruled Washington, and would still rule if he could."[88] Stunned, McHenry had little choice but to resign—and give a blow-by-blow description of Adams's tirade to Hamilton.

Alexander Hamilton, stung by the old man's denunciation, struck back. He wrote to Adams demanding an explanation. Receiving none, he produced a fifty-four-page pamphlet originally intended only for party leaders. The *Letter from Alexander Hamilton, Concerning the Public Conduct and Characters of John Adams, Esq., President of the United States*, of course, could not *stay* private. It was one of the most unbelievable documents in American history.

In the midst of a hotly contested presidential campaign, one in which President Adams was a strong candidate, Hamilton, the acknowledged leader of the Federalist Party, attacked his own team! Hamilton denounced Adams for his "great intrinsic defects of character," his "disgusting egotism," and his "ungovernable temper."[89] Hamilton did not quite call Adams insane, but he charged "it is a fact that he is often liable to paroxisms of anger which deprive him of self-command and produce very outrageous behavior."[90] Still, at the end of the tirade, Hamilton incredibly called for Adams's reelection!

No one has ever recorded Jefferson or Madison in a similar rant. Perhaps Jefferson got it all out of his system by means of letters, some of them unguarded and unwise. We also know that poor John Adams was suffering great heartache at this time. His son, Charles, was descending into the depths of alcoholism and insanity that would eventually claim his life. Abigail had written to her husband: "I am wounded to the soul by the consideration of what is to become of him. What will be his fate embitters every moment of my life."[91] Parents can suffer no greater pain.

The Hamilton pamphlet had done its damage. John Adams received sixty-five electoral votes and Charles Cotesworth Pinckney received sixty-four. The Federalists were narrowly defeated. That much was clear. But who had won?

Thomas Jefferson received seventy-three electoral votes, but so had Aaron Burr! The Republicans' party discipline had proven too disciplined. This tie in the electoral college meant that the House of Representatives would have to resolve the election. Worse, under the Constitution as then written, the election would be decided *not* by the House of Representatives just elected, but by the "lame duck" House that had been elected in 1798.* That House had a *Federalist* majority.

Some of these Federalists saw an opportunity to confound their opponents by elevating Aaron Burr to the presidency. They reasoned that the ambitious Burr would be indebted to them for letting him enter the newly completed president's house in the new city of Washington. They thought they could deal with Burr far more readily than with Jefferson.

When the House convened for the first time in the nation's new capitol, it began balloting to select the new president. When the House is

* The terms of the House of Representatives, the Senate, the president, and vice president were changed by Amendment XX in 1933 to *shorten* the length of time between election and taking office.

called upon to elect the president, it does so *by state*. That means that small states have an equal say with large states in the choice of the president. And when a state had only *one* representative, that congressman wielded great power.

The prospect of Burr's election as president shocked most Americans. Burr cagily resisted a clear, forthright statement of what everyone in America knew: that the Republican Party had intended Jefferson for president and Burr for vice president and that that is what its voters thought they were getting. Burr waited, in silence.[92]

Hamilton became alarmed after thirty-five ballots failed to produce a winner. There had even been talk of how the Federalist John Marshall might become president if the House could not resolve its deadlock. Virginia's Governor James Monroe, Jefferson's loyal friend, threatened the use of state troops if the defeated Federalists should steal the election.

In a feverish set of letters, Hamilton pleaded with Federalists to resolve the election in favor of his archrival Jefferson. "For heaven's sake, let not the Federal Party be responsible for the elevation of this man [Burr]," he wrote to one friend. To Gouverneur Morris, "[Burr] could be bound by no agreement—will listen to no monitor but his own ambition." To the thought that Burr might bargain for the office, Hamilton scoffed: "He will laugh in his sleeve when he makes them and he will break them the first moment it may serve his purpose."[93]

Hamilton had a point. Aaron Burr was the grandson of the great colonial preacher and writer Jonathan Edwards. But no one had ever found much holiness in Burr's career as womanizer, or as a man whose greatest skill seemed to be eluding creditors.[94] He was charming and intelligent, to be sure. But it is no accident we do not study the writings of Aaron Burr. He was all maneuver, all action, all ambition—little else than a gamesman. And the Republicans knew this when they selected him.

Finally, on the thirty-sixth ballot, Delaware's Federalist congressman, James A. Bayard, broke the deadlock by *casting a blank ballot*. He had previously agreed with several others in his party to do the same thing. This resolved the issue in Jefferson's favor.[95] It was 17 February 1801, just fifteen days before the scheduled inauguration.

Thomas Jefferson walked from his rooming house to the new Capitol, where he took the oath as president on 4 March 1801.

"We are all republicans: we are all federalists," he said in his inaugural address, "we have called by different names brethren of the same principle."[96] Jefferson extended the olive branch to his political opponents. He also took advantage of the general disgust many Americans felt at the dangerous wheeling and dealing of the lame-duck Federalists in Congress.[97]

Jefferson was no great orator, his voice was almost inaudible in public addresses. But his words on this occasion—in which our country was spared a civil war—bear study two hundred years later.

> All, too, will bear in mind this sacred principle, that though the will of the majority is in all cases to prevail, that will, to be rightful must be reasonable; that the minority possess their equal rights, which equal laws must protect, and to violate which would be oppression.

Here, he laid down the philosophical basis for free government, even as he took part in history's first peaceful transfer of political power from one ruling party to another. He went on to give a moving appeal for civil concord:

> Let us then, as fellow-citizens, unite with one heart and one mind. Let us restore to social intercourse that harmony and affection without which liberty and even life itself are but dreary things.
>
> And let us reflect that having banished from our land that religious intolerance under which mankind so long bled and suffered, we have yet gained little if we countenance a political intolerance as despotic, as wicked, and capable of as bitter and bloody persecutions.[98]

The next two hundred years would see such examples of both religious and political persecution. America would suffer from them, as well. We would have Jefferson's words to encourage us to redouble our efforts for "harmony and affection" in public life.

John Adams had left the Executive Mansion that morning. Not having been invited to witness his successor's inauguration, he took the early coach home to Braintree, Massachusetts. Before departing, he had left a benediction for the new house: "I pray Heaven to bestow the best of blessings on this house, and on all that shall hereafter inhabit it. May none but honest and wise men ever rule under this roof."

Six

The Jeffersonians (1801–1829)

No sooner has President Jefferson taken office, it seems, than the United States pulls off the greatest diplomatic coup in the history of the world. Two hundred years later, the Louisiana Purchase remains a stunning feat of inspired statesmanship. But the growing dissension over the expansion of slavery into the new territories will threaten the nation's life. And, following a decade of tension, America goes to war with Britain in 1812. Unprepared, almost unarmed, America faces defeat in Canada, defeat in the Northwest, and the humiliation of seeing Washington, D.C., burned by invaders. Only the brave resistance of Baltimore's Fort McHenry and some splendid victories at sea brighten the gloomy landscape. Then, in a thunder clap, news comes to the charred capital that General Andrew Jackson has miraculously turned back the British at the Battle of New Orleans. On the heels of Jackson's great victory comes word of the Treaty of Ghent, ending the War of 1812. Soon, America is exulting in the mere fact that she has withstood invasion by the greatest power in the world. To many, it seems a second War of Independence gloriously concluded. Jefferson's heirs—his political lieutenants Madison and Monroe—look south and west for territorial gains. Monroe presides, surprisingly, over "an era of good feeling."

I. "An Empire for Liberty"

Thomas Jefferson was fifty-seven years old when he entered the President's House. His public career had included service as a Virginia legislator, member of Congress, a highly successful term as America's minister to France (following a conspicuously unsuccessful term as Virginia's wartime governor), the first secretary of state, the second vice president, and now the third president of the United States. Author of the Declaration of Independence and of Virginia's Statute for Religious Freedom, he was described as a man who could "calculate an eclipse, survey an estate, tie an artery, plan an edifice, try a cause, break a horse, dance a minuet, and play the violin."[1]*

Not all of Jefferson's successors were so impressed. Young Theodore Roosevelt described Jefferson as "perhaps the most incapable Executive that ever filled the presidential chair . . . utterly unable to grapple with the slightest danger . . . it would be difficult to imagine a man less fit to guide the state. . . ."[2]

Impressions of Jefferson were no less divided during his lifetime. He began his presidential term determined to make a sharp change from the previous administrations. In part because he was a poor public speaker, in part because he wanted to do nothing that looked like delivering a king's "speech from the throne," Jefferson in 1801 began the practice of sending written messages to Congress on the state of the Union. That tradition lasted until 1913, when the polished orator Woodrow Wilson resumed the practice of delivering the address in person.

Jefferson dispensed with the levies that had been the Washingtons' preferred method of entertaining. These were stiffly formal affairs. Instead, the widower invited members of Congress regularly to small dinners in the President's House. In these small groups, the new president was able to exercise firm leadership. Political men were eager to dine with the man they knew as "Mr. Jefferson."

* Small wonder that President Kennedy would welcome forty-nine Nobel Prize winners to a 1962 White House dinner with these words: "I think this is the most extraordinary collection of talent, of human knowledge, that has ever been gathered at the White House—with the possible exception of when Thomas Jefferson dined alone."

One of the most colorful incidents of Jefferson's presidency was the arrival at the President's House of Elder John Leland and the "Mammoth Cheese." The Baptist leader Leland had been instrumental in supporting Jefferson and Madison in Virginia in the 1780s in their great efforts for establishing religious liberty. Leland had returned to his native New England in 1791 and continued his strong support of his famous Virginia friends. Unlike so many of the New England clergy, Leland loudly backed Jefferson for president in 1800. Now, he persuaded his western Massachusetts neighbors to honor their hero with a huge cheese. Weighing 1,235 pounds, the cheese was transported to Washington by Leland and fellow Baptists. The cheese bore Jefferson's personal motto: "Rebellion to Tyrants is Obedience to God."[3] Elder John took advantage of the curious crowds attracted by the cheese to preach the gospel all along his route.[4]

His journey took more than a month to complete. When he arrived at the President's House on New Year's Day 1802, Elder John found President Jefferson waiting for him with outstretched arms.[5] John Leland was not only invited to take part in the holiday reception but was also asked to preach two days later in the U.S. House of Representatives. President Jefferson joined in the religious service on federal property in the federal city.* In Virginia, John Leland had fought against the established Episcopal Church. With Jefferson and Madison's help, he succeeded in ending official discrimination against Baptists and all other sects there. In Massachusetts, Leland would also press against the established Congregational Church.

Jefferson continued to provide guidance by means of his letters. One of the first of these letters has had great influence on church-state relations in America. He had received a letter of congratulations on his election from the Danbury Baptist Association on 30 December 1801. He responded with astonishing speed. On 1 January 1802, President Jefferson wrote a letter that has become one of the most famous he ever wrote. It has also been one of his most misunderstood public acts.

* Jefferson attended this evangelical service in the House of Representatives barely hours after he wrote his oft-cited "Letter to the Danbury Baptists." That letter has been cited as requiring "a high wall of separation between church and state." But it didn't stop President Jefferson from giving his sanction to a religious service on federal property.

Jefferson thanked the Connecticut Baptists and took the opportunity to explain *why* he had declined to proclaim days of fasting and thanksgiving. Expressing his "strict constructionist" constitutional beliefs, he explained that the president is only empowered to execute the laws that Congress passes. The people have wisely approved the First Amendment to the Constitution, he wrote. Since the amendment specifically *prohibits* Congress from passing any law "respecting the establishment of religion or restricting the free exercise thereof," he believed he had no constitutional authority to proclaim days of fasting and thanksgiving.

We now know that Jefferson had gone further in his first draft of the letter. Proclaiming religious observances had been a standard practice of the *British* monarchy because the king was the head of the Church of England. Jefferson was striking out once again at his Federalist opponents. But his attorney general persuaded him that many good New England *Republicans* had always looked to their governors and legislatures to proclaim such important days.[6] In fact, Jefferson had fully supported a national day of fasting and prayer when he was a member of the Continental Congress.

Jefferson then used the phrase that has been associated with him ever since. He wrote there is "a wall of separation between Church & State."[7] This letter needs to be seen in the context of the still-bubbling controversy over Jefferson's election in 1800. Federalists and their supporters in many New England pulpits had denounced Jefferson as an atheist and "infidel." Yale University President Timothy Dwight, a Congregationalist minister, had warned that if the Jeffersonian Republicans were elected, "we might see the Bible cast into a bonfire." Worse, children would be taught to chant "mockeries against God."[8] Presbyterian pastor John Mitchell Mason assured his congregation that electing Jefferson would be "a crime never to be forgiven . . . a sin against God."[9] The Federalist *Gazette of the United States* had summed up the election as a choice between "God and a Religious President [Adams]" and "Jefferson—AND NO GOD!"[10]

Jefferson spoke out against such unreasoning hysteria and blatant abuse of religious authority for partisan politicking. "I have sworn upon the altar of God eternal hostility against every form of tyranny over the mind of man," penned Jefferson in a letter to Dr. Benjamin Rush.[11] He assured Rush he would *oppose* any attempt to establish one particular form of Christianity in America.[12] This stance made Jefferson highly popular among minority religious groups. In time, it would soon lead to the *disestablishment* of the Congregational Church in New England—just as Leland had desired.

As the elections of 1802 approached, the Federalist Party of Adams, Hamilton, and Jay grew more desperate. Jefferson had not pulled down church altars, nor seized Bibles, nor had he set up a guillotine on the National Mall. One Federalist leader, Fisher Ames, cried out, "Our country is too big for union, too sordid for patriotism, too democratic for liberty."[13] Even the energetic Alexander Hamilton seemed to despair. "Every day proves to me more and more that this American world was not made for me," he wrote.[14] Facing political disaster in the upcoming congressional elections, Federalists became even more strident than they had been in 1800. They seized upon a scandalous article written by James T. Callender. Callender charged that President Jefferson had fathered children by one of his Monticello slaves, Sally Hemings.

Jefferson had tried to help Callender with money and jobs, but he should have broken off all contact when the alcoholic Scottish refugee publicized Hamilton's adulterous affair with Maria Reynolds. Instead, Jefferson's help began to look like hush money. When Callender turned on him, Jefferson had no one to blame but himself. "The serpent you cherished and warmed," wrote Abigail Adams to Jefferson, "bit the hand that nourished him."[15] It was a deserved rebuke.*

Callender's revenge on Jefferson did him little good. He was found the next year face down in the James River in Virginia. He had gotten drunk and drowned.[16] Nor did the scandal raise the Federalists' fortunes. In the

---

* Jefferson's alleged liaison with Sally Hemings surfaced again in 1998, when it was claimed that DNA evidence now confirmed he was the father of some or all of her children. The Jefferson-Hemings Scholars Commission, however, considered the new findings and disagreed: "After a careful review of all of the evidence, the commission agrees unanimously that the allegation is by no means proven." The Scholars Commission does not deny that Sally Hemings's children were sired by *a* Jefferson, they simply maintain that it cannot be proven they were fathered by *Thomas* Jefferson. Most likely, according to Pulitzer Prize winning journalist Virginius Dabney, the real father of Sally Hemings's children was Jefferson's nephew, Peter Carr. (*The Jefferson Scandals*, Dodd, Mead, 1981)

midterm elections of 1802, Republicans triumphed. They won 102 seats in the House of Representatives to a mere 39 for the Federalists.

Jefferson faced a lingering foreign crisis early in his administration. For more than twenty years, he had been urging military action against Arab corsairs on the Barbary coast. These were fast, cheap warships that preyed upon merchant shipping along the northern shore of Africa. Various Arab rulers there would regularly declare war against European countries and then begin seizing their ships and men. The captured crews would be held for ransom or sold in the market as slaves. "Christians are cheap today!" was the auctioneer's cry.[17]

This practice had been going on for centuries. As many as a million and a quarter Europeans had been enslaved by Muslims operating out of North Africa.[18] When he served as America's minister to France in the mid-1780s, Jefferson had once confronted an Arab diplomat, demanding to know by what right his country attacked Americans in the Mediterranean:

> The Ambassador answered us that it was founded on the Laws of the Prophet, that it was written in their Koran, that all nations who should not have answered their authority were sinners, that it was their right and duty to make war upon them wherever they could be found, and to make slaves of all they could take as prisoners.[19]

Confronted by such obstinacy, Jefferson appealed to John Adams, who was then America's minister to England. But Adams was unwilling to fight. Jefferson resolved from those early days to fight the Muslim hostage-takers. "We ought to begin a naval power, if we mean to carry on our own commerce. Can we begin it on a more honourable occasions or with a weaker foe?" he wrote to James Madison in 1784.[20] The kidnapping and ransoming of American merchantmen continued for nearly twenty years.

The Washington and Adams administrations had gone along with the European practice of paying off the Barbary rulers. It was a protection racket, pure and simple. Adams believed paying tribute was cheaper than war. "We ought not to fight them at all unless we determine to fight them forever," he said.[21] Paying off the Barbary rulers was not cheap. When Jefferson came into office, the United States had already paid out nearly $2 million. This was nearly one fifth of the federal government's yearly income![22]

The Bashaw of Tripoli declared war on the United States in 1801. Jefferson was determined to fight rather than pay tribute. Jefferson sent Commodore Edward Preble in command of the USS *Constitution* to strengthen America's naval forces in the Mediterranean Sea. Preble stirred American hearts with his spirited reply to an arrogant British naval captain who had challenged him to identify himself when shrouded in fog. "This is His Britannic Majesty's ship *Donnegal,* 84 guns," the captain hailed, demanding Preble put over a boat and prepare to be searched. "This is the United States ship *Constitution,* Edward Preble, an American commodore, who will be *damned* before he sends his boat on board of any vessel. Strike your matches, boys!" Faced with this threat of cannon fire, the Royal Navy captain backed down.[23] Before Preble could arrive, however, the USS *Philadelphia* went aground off Tripoli harbor. The Bashaw took the crew captive.

Young Navy Lieutenant Stephen Decatur knew that he must not allow the Bashaw to convert the *Philadelphia* to his own use. He stole into the harbor by night and set the ship ablaze.[24] America's consul in Tunis, William Eaton, followed this daring exploit. He gathered a motley crew of U.S. Marines, sailors, Greek and Arab mercenaries and their camels. Eaton marched his men five hundred miles across the Libyan desert to take the coastal town of Derna. Three U.S. warships, in a coordinated attack, bombarded the town.[25] From this stunning victory, the Marine hymn takes the line "to the shores of Tripoli" and their officers still wear Mameluke swords shaped like Arab scimitars.[26] Stephen Decatur added to his reputation by offering this famous toast: "Our Country: In her intercourse with foreign nations, may she always be in the right; but our country right or wrong!"[27]

By 1805, the pirates had had enough. Jefferson's willingness to use force had triumphed in America's first war on terror in the Middle East.[28]

Another foreign danger loomed in Jefferson's first term. By means of a secret treaty, France's conqueror Napoleon Bonaparte had gained control of the vast expanse of North America known as Louisiana. France had given this tract over to Spain forty years before. Now she reclaimed it. Jefferson knew that New Orleans was vital. "There is on the globe one spot, the possessor of which is our natural and habitual enemy," he wrote. "It is New Orleans, through which the produce of three eighths of our territory must pass to market."[29] In 1803, Spain was weak. But France was the greatest military power in the world. Despite his long friendship with France, Jefferson sensed danger. "The day that France takes possession of New Orleans, we must marry ourselves to the British fleet and nation."[30] Jefferson knew that only the powerful British fleet could prevent Napoleon from bringing tens of thousands of soldiers to control the Mississippi.

Napoleon might have sent those troops, too, had it not been for the Haitian revolt. Inspired by the French Revolution, Toussaint L'Ouverture led a slave uprising on Haiti. A French army sent to put down the rebellion bogged down, with thousands dying of the dreaded yellow fever. Napoleon was planning to renew his war with England. But without an army, without superior naval power, Napoleon knew the British might seize Louisiana at the outbreak of war. Then he would have nothing. Better to sell it to the Americans.[31]

Still, America's minister in Paris was stunned when Napoleon offered to sell *all of Louisiana*—which was then a vast territory, much larger than the present-day state that bears its name. Robert Livingston had only been empowered to buy the City of New Orleans—and maybe small portions of Florida. Jefferson sent his good friend James Monroe to aid in the negotiations.

The French told the American that the Louisiana territory would be useless to them without New Orleans. Livingston found it hard to live in Paris under Napoleon's dictatorship. He was relieved when he was able to deal with Napoleon's finance minister, Francois Barbé-Marbois, instead of the bribe-taking Talleyrand. Barbé-Marbois was known for his honesty—and for his pro-American spirit.[32] Initially, Barbé-Marbois demanded $25 million, but he soon lowered the price to $15 million.[33]

At home in America, no one knew what Napoleon had in mind. Federalists in Congress attacked the Monroe mission. They wanted President Jefferson to threaten war over New Orleans. Some even wanted Alexander Hamilton to lead an army to capture the Crescent City.[34] Hamilton said there was "not the remotest chance" Napoleon would sell territory for money.[35]

Publicly, Jefferson talked peace. He let it be known that he was restraining the western governors from taking matters into their own hands. Privately, he let his loyal secretary of state, James Madison, talk tough to the French minister. Americans disliked the secrecy with which Napoleon had reclaimed Louisiana, Madison told Louis André Pichon. More to the point, Madison warned Pichon that "France cannot long preserve Louisiana against the United States."[36]

Few people in Napoleon's Paris knew what was happening. But his brothers—Joseph and Lucien—opposed the deal. The British had bribed both of them heavily. They confronted their brother while he was in the bathtub. "There will be no debate," Napoleon yelled. The sale of Louisiana would be arranged by a treaty with the Americans. And that treaty would be "negotiated, ratified and executed *by me alone*." With that, the first consul of France threw himself back in the tub and soaked his brothers with perfumed water.[37] As a virtual dictator, Napoleon knew he did not have to consult his "rubber stamp" legislature.

The Americans, fortunately, did *not* get soaked. When Monroe joined Livingston, he agreed that the offer was simply too good to pass up. Seizing the opportunity, they inked the treaty before Napoleon changed his mind. Monroe had dared to *exceed* his instructions because he knew Jefferson's mind. Monroe was Jefferson's intimate friend and neighbor and Livingston was not.

Thomas Jefferson had the pleasure of announcing the Louisiana Purchase in the President's House on 4 July 1803.[38] The nation had *more than doubled its size*. "It is something larger than the whole U.S.," Jefferson wrote, "probably containing 500 millions of acres, the U.S. containing 434 millions."[39] He couldn't resist adding that the purchase would make the new United States *sixteen and a half times larger* than Great Britain and Ireland.[40] This vast territory had been acquired for $12 million—or about four cents an acre![41]

Some of the Federalists still griped. "We are to give money of which we have too little for land of which we already have too much," groused one.[42] Proving once again how out of touch they were, the editors of Alexander Hamilton's *New York Post* condemned the treaty as "the greatest curse that ever befell this country."[43] Harvard president Josiah Quincy warned, "Thick skinned beasts will crowd Congress Hall, Buffaloes from the head of the Missouri and Alligators from the Red River."[44]

Jefferson welcomed the treaty, but asked his cabinet to consider whether the acquisition might require a constitutional amendment. Jeffersonians were for *strict construction* and the Constitution said nothing about land purchases. Madison strongly supported Gallatin's case that the purchase was covered by the treaty-making power of the president and the Senate.[45] Then came an alarming message from Robert Livingston: Napoleon "appears to wish the thing undone."[46] Worse, if war broke out any moment between England and France, England could seize New Orleans and permanently block America's westward expansion.[47]

With Madison at his side at Monticello urging him to jump on it, Jefferson dropped all hesitation. He rushed the treaty to the Senate for ratification.[48] The Senate quickly consented on 20 October 1803, by a vote of twenty-four to seven.[49] Napoleon may never really have had second thoughts. He knew that if the British didn't take Louisiana from him, the Americans could. With the treaty signed, he could pocket the sixty million *francs* and prepare for his war. Like the French bantam rooster he was, he crowed in triumph: "Sixty millions for an occupation that will not perhaps last a day! I have given England a rival who, sooner or later, will humble her pride."[50]

Some embittered Federalists feared that what they called "a Virginia dynasty" of Jefferson, Madison, and Monroe could never be beaten. They began to plot secession.[51] But the son of the Federalists' last president, John Quincy Adams, understood it best. The Louisiana Purchase would be "next in historical importance to the Declaration of Independence and the adoption of the Constitution," he said.[52]

II. Lewis & Clark: "The Corps of Discovery"

Thomas Jefferson had been planning an expedition to the Pacific for at least ten years. Statesmen had been seeking a Northwest Passage to the Orient for centuries. Jefferson thought there might be an all-water route across the continent. As early as 1792, Jefferson had persuaded the American Philosophical Society in Philadelphia to sponsor a party to explore the upper reaches of the Missouri

River and sail down the Columbia River to the sea. That effort got no further west than Kentucky.[53]

Now, President Jefferson chose a young man who was his neighbor, his personal secretary, and whom he treated like a son—Captain Meriwether Lewis. Lewis was the son of a deceased Revolutionary War soldier. He had not been formally educated, but he was bright and eager to learn. From youth, he had been an avid hunter and explorer. Service in the army added to his preparation.

Jefferson planned the expedition at Monticello, teaching Lewis himself, then sending him on to Philadelphia for further training. There, Captain Lewis was taught basic medical care by Dr. Benjamin Rush. Rush was Jefferson's close friend, a signer of the Declaration of Independence, and probably America's leading physician. Rush also supplied Lewis with *fifty dozen* of his famous pills. These were purgatives. Comprised of calomel, mercury, and chlorine, they were known as "Rush's Thunderclappers."[54] Jefferson's Philadelphia friends also taught Lewis such essentials as celestial navigation and how to preserve animal and plant specimens for transport back to Monticello.[55]

Lewis's choice of a partner was an inspired one. William Clark was a tall, powerfully built outdoorsman. Four years older than Lewis, he was the younger brother of General George Rogers Clark, "the conqueror of the Northwest." The general was a close friend of President Jefferson. Lewis then did something *very* unusual: he agreed to share command with Clark. Both would be captains. There is hardly an example before or since of such an arrangement's working, but here it served brilliantly.[56] Fittingly, they have been known to history as Lewis and Clark.

Lewis outfitted what Jefferson called "the Corps of Discovery" beginning with fifteen Kentucky rifles issued from the federal arsenal at Harper's Ferry. He bought a large boat and stocked it with trading goods for dealing with the Indians. A key item was a brass medallion with Jefferson's profile on it—a token of respect from the Great Chief to the Indian leaders. Jefferson gave Lewis a letter of credit that enabled him to obtain other supplies at government expense—perhaps the original American credit card.[57]

The Lewis and Clark Expedition comprised thirty-three individuals.

In addition to the captains, there were sergeants and privates—subject to strict military discipline. Then there was the famous French trapper Toussaint Charbonneau; his Shoshone Indian wife, Sacagawea; their infant son (nicknamed "Pomp" by Lewis); and York, the corps' only black man. York was a slave of William Clark. And Lewis also took "Seaman," his large Newfoundland dog.

Lewis and Clark set out from St. Louis in their fifty-five-foot keelboat in May 1804. They sailed up the Missouri River to Mandan, near present-day Bismarck, North Dakota.[58] Pressing on to the "Stony Mountains"—now the Rockies—they made contact with Shoshone tribesmen. Sacagawea was overcome with joy to see her long-lost brother as a chief. This helped greatly to resupply the corps with horses and helpers. Crossing the Bitterroot Mountains in September 1805, Lewis later reported, "We suffered all Cold, Hunger, and Fatigue could impart" during the eleven-day trek.[59]

Add to cold the bitter disappointment Lewis and Clark felt at realizing there was no easy all water route to the Pacific. The dream of centuries died on that trail.

President Jefferson had instructed the captains to take special care to make a favorable impression on the powerful Sioux nation.[60] This proved harder to do when several Sioux warriors seized the boat's lines and demanded "presents." Lewis trained the boat's cannon on the warriors and had his men ready to fire on them when a chief, Black Buffalo, intervened to keep the peace. Black Buffalo then invited the corps to attend the first "scalp dance" ever witnessed by travelers from the East. With some care, Lewis turned down the chief's offer of a young woman to share his bed.[61]

After nearly two years of grueling marches and boat voyages, the Corps of Discovery descended the Columbia River to the Pacific. Clark captured the excitement of the corps in this typical journal entry: "Ocian in view! O! the joy." They built Fort Clatsop on the Pacific shore and wintered over in 1805–06. They had hoped to find an American sailing ship to take them home. The local Indians' use of phrases like "son-of-a-pitch" told them that American sailors had been in the region.[62] When no ship appeared, Lewis and Clark decided to make the arduous return journey overland.

Once, when a critical decision had to be made, the captains put the measure up for a vote. It was the first *referendum* held by Americans in which voters included an Indian, a black man, and a woman. Sometimes, the clash of cultures produced humorous results. When an Indian chieftain expressed shock at the one hundred lashes Lewis had meted out to an enlisted man who had fallen asleep on watch, Lewis asked him how *he* would make an example of a disobedient warrior. He would *kill* him, the chief said, but he would never beat him. Lewis and Clark were equipped with many small gifts to give the Indians along the way, including tobacco and whiskey.[63] Once, a small tribal group asked the captains a hard question. If President Jefferson really was their great *father*, why would a father want them to lose their reason by getting them drunk? It remains an excellent question.

Jefferson and the country were delighted with Lewis and Clark's discoveries. The president praised their "undaunted courage" upon their return to St. Louis in September 1806. Their success remains heroic in the annals of discovery. Only one man—Sargeant Charles Floyd—died on the journey. Except for a brief clash over horse stealing, the Corps of Discovery maintained good relations with the Indians. Jefferson had instructed them to tell the Indians we wanted their commerce, not their lands. It would soon become apparent we wanted their commerce *and* their lands.*

III. Plots, Trials, and Treason

Stunning events were happening in the East as Lewis and Clark braved the wilds of Montana and Idaho. Vice President Aaron Burr was widely distrusted by the Jeffersonians. They suspected him of trying to slip past the party's presidential nominee by backroom dealings with the Federalists. Burr knew he would not be renominated for the job in 1804 so he decided to run for governor of New York. Backing Burr were certain

* Lewis's subsequent career was marked by tragedy. Appointed governor of Louisiana, he became depressed, took to drink, and eventually took his own life. William Clark served for more than thirty years as a respected Indian agent—"the red-haired chief." But he dishonored himself by brutally refusing brave York's request to be freed from slavery. York had trudged every step of the way to the Pacific and back, the first son of Africa to do so.

"High" Federalists who had given up hope of returning to power on the national stage. Men like Timothy Pickering of Massachusetts and Roger Griswold of Connecticut believed the only chance for cultured gentlemen like themselves to continue in office would be for New England to join New York in a Northern Confederacy. They needed Burr as governor to accomplish this.[64]

Federalists like Pickering and Griswold hated Jefferson. Jefferson's brilliant diplomatic stroke in the Louisiana Purchase convinced such men—correctly, as it turned out—that the Federalist Party would never win another national election. They could foresee new states being admitted from the vast expanse that would be carved out of the Louisiana Territory. These new states, they were sure, would support Jefferson's Republicans. Facing such a dismal prospect, these New England Yankees thought it was better to secede from the Union.

Alexander Hamilton was still respected by most Federalists. And Hamilton would have no part of secession. To Massachusetts Federalist Theodore Sedgwick, he wrote that secession would do no good because the real problem was *democracy* itself. And that "poison" was spreading through every state.[65]* Hamilton continued his bitterly anti-Burr campaign, denouncing the man as an unprincipled adventurer. Burr was defeated by Morgan Lewis, another Republican, but one who had the lion's share of Federalist backing. Burr naturally blamed Hamilton—and demanded satisfaction. In those times, that meant a duel.

Though dueling was illegal in New York and increasingly looked down upon throughout the North, Hamilton felt he could not refuse Burr's challenge without appearing cowardly. It could not have been an easy decision; Hamilton's eldest son, Phillip, had been killed in a duel just two and a half years earlier.[66] He said he would reserve his fire. He was resolved to "live

* Hamilton's reference to *democracy* as a "poison" spreading through all the states would not have been as shocking to the Founders' generation as it is to us. They tended to view democracy as direct rule, sometimes leading to mob action, such as Shays's Rebellion and the Whiskey Rebellion. Many of them equated democracy with the Paris mobs that cheered as heads fell from the guillotine. Hamilton clearly supported what we today know as democracy: regular elections, freedom of the press, and majority rule. He demonstrated this by backing Jefferson, clearly the people's choice, in the 1801 presidential decision.

innocent" rather than "die guilty" of shedding another man's blood.[67] Knowing he was very likely to die, Hamilton wrote to his wife the night before he met Burr. She had charitably forgiven him for his affair with Maria Reynolds. Now, hoping to console her, he wrote: "Remember, my Eliza, you are a Christian."

Hamilton and Burr were each rowed separately over to the New Jersey side because dueling was not yet illegal in that state. There, on an outcropping in Weehauken, the two men faced each other on the morning of 11 July 1804. True to his word, Hamilton held fire. Burr leveled his pistol and shot Hamilton, his bullet passing through his enemy's liver, diaphragm, and lodging in his spine. Hamilton knew the wound was mortal. Carried back to New York City by boat, he warned his friends to be careful of a still-loaded pistol. Friends fetched the Episcopal Bishop of New York, Benjamin Moore, to give the dying man communion. At first, the bishop hesitated, so strong was his revulsion at dueling. But when Hamilton pleaded, forgave Burr, and confessed his faith in Christ, Bishop Moore relented.[68]

Hamilton died after thirty hours of pain. His death was widely mourned. Even the Republican press took up the cry. He was the only one of the Founders to die a violent death. Now, he seemed a martyr to national unity. New York City hung out the crepe for Hamilton's funeral. Ships in the harbor boomed out a final salute. While dueling itself may not have been illegal in New Jersey, Burr was nonetheless indicted for murder in that state and pursued throughout New York—the fugitive vice president.

Fearing for his life, Burr fled to Philadelphia, where he found himself at reasonable enough distance from his troubles to court a lady friend.[69] From there he traveled to South Carolina and then Virginia, where his reception was much warmer. Hamilton had never been popular in the South and dueling was considered the ultimate way to preserve a gentleman's honor.[70]

Jeffersonian Republicans faced the 1804 elections that fall with confidence. They replaced Burr with the aged George Clinton, New York's long-time governor. Jefferson carried *every* state except Connecticut and Delaware. In Congress, the Republicans had an overwhelming majority—116–25 in the House, 27–7 in the Senate.[71]

In firm control of the two elective branches of the federal government, Republicans now prepared to bring the judiciary to heel. For years, Jefferson and his party had denounced the "midnight judges" appointed in the last days of the outgoing Adams administration. Foremost of these was Chief Justice John Marshall. Jefferson's Republican Party was even more outraged when Marshall gave his famous opinion in the case of *Marbury v. Madison* (1803).

In this landmark opinion, the chief justice led the Supreme Court in ruling *against* Federalist William Marbury. He could *not* force Secretary of State Madison to sign a commission so he could have the federal office to which the outgoing President Adams had appointed him. This part of the ruling seemed like a *surrender* by the Federalist Marshall to the powerful Jeffersonians.

But Marshall ruled that the *reason* Marbury could not have his commission was that a portion of the Judiciary Act of 1789 that gave the Supreme Court the power to issue such writs was *unconstitutional*. It was the first time the Supreme Court had exercised the power of judicial review. It was a bold stroke by Marshall. In *seeming* to give in to Jefferson and Madison on a minor point, he had assumed a great and powerful weapon to use against his fellow Virginians. Jefferson responded that "the doctrines of that case were given extra-judicially and against law, and . . . their reverse will be the rule of action with the Executive."[72]

Republicans were determined to rid themselves of a packed court. As Jefferson would later write in his autobiography, "As, for the safety of society, we commit honest maniacs to Bedlam, so judges should be withdrawn from their bench, whose erroneous biases are leading us to dissolution."[73] They would begin by impeaching and removing Justice Samuel Chase.

Jefferson's leader in the House was Virginia Congressman William Branch Giles. Bluntly, Giles announced that "high crimes and misdemeanors" were not necessary for removing a federal judge. Impeachment meant no more than this: "[Y]ou hold dangerous opinions, and if you are [permitted] to carry them into effect, you will work the destruction of the Union. We want your offices for the purpose of giving them to men who will fill them better." Even more boldly, Giles said Chase was only the Republicans' first target: "Not only Mr. Chase, but all the other Judges of the Supreme Court. . . ." He would spare only the justice Jefferson had named.[74]

This great Jeffersonian Court "unpacking" scheme seemed very promising. But the Republicans failed to take Vice President Burr into account. His last official act would be to preside over the Chase impeachment trial in the Senate. Rejecting Giles's matter-of-fact treatment of impeachment, Burr outfitted the Senate in red, green, and blue banners, just like the British House of Lords when it considered impeachment. Burr made it a very formal affair. He denied the old man a chair, treating Justice Chase like a man under indictment. One Federalist newspaper sneered at the spectacle: usually, it said, "the practice in courts of Justice [is] to arraign the *murderer* before the *Judge*, but now we behold the *Judge* arraigned before the *murderer*."[75]

Actually, Justice Chase was lucky that Burr was in the chair. Although he had been a signer of the Declaration, Chase's frequent outbursts on the bench made him obnoxious to many. "Our republican Constitution will sink into *mobocracy*—the worst of all possible governments," he had said.[76] Still, by treating the matter with all the formality of a criminal trial, Burr *saved* Justice Chase from conviction. This is because Chase could not have survived the purely *political* process Giles had planned. But Justice Chase was found *not guilty* on any article of impeachment.[77] The impeachment trial ended just days before Burr left office. It was to be Aaron Burr's last act as a public official.

No sooner had Burr left the vice presidential chair, however, than he began to conspire with the British minister in Washington. Burr was plotting to take the western states and the Louisiana territory *out* of the Union. He appealed for half a million dollars from the British to help him assemble a force to attack Spanish colonies.[78] In this plot, Burr involved his old friend, General James Wilkinson. Wilkinson was the military governor of the Louisiana Territory. More that that, he had been an agent of a foreign government for twenty years—*Agent 13* in the pay of the king of Spain.[79]*

Burr swept through the West, hailed as a hero. Dueling presented no problems for these rough-and-ready frontiersmen. Nor would they be put off by a plan to attack the Spaniards. Obviously, Burr would not have told

* Shockingly, General Wilkinson was then the most senior officer in the U.S. military, a position equivalent to chairman of the Joint Chiefs of Staff!

such new friends as General Andrew Jackson that he was plotting with the hated British to destroy the Union.[80] He wisely denied admitting any secessionist intent, as his conspiracy stirred throughout 1805 and 1806. But then, in December 1806, the plot unraveled. General Wilkinson betrayed his fellow plotter and wrote to President Jefferson, informing him of "a deep, dark, wicked, and widespread conspiracy" by Burr to destroy the Union.[81] Jefferson immediately ordered the arrest of his former vice president, and Burr was hauled back to Richmond for trial. The charge would be treason. The penalty: death by hanging.

Richmond was the center of Jefferson's power base. George Hay was to lead the prosecution. He was a zealous supporter of the president. Hay had once beaten James Callender with a club when Callender had charged Jefferson with having an affair with Sally Hemings.[82]

Jefferson reckoned without one major factor: presiding over this sensational trial would be Jefferson's cousin, Chief Justice John Marshall. Marshall did not forget that it was Burr who had saved the Federalist judges from Jeffersonian impeachments. Marshall summoned President Jefferson to testify at the trial. Citing the constitutional separation of powers, Jefferson declined. Marshall allowed Burr every protection of the law.

Luther Martin's long-winded speeches had irritated George Washington at the Constitutional Convention, but he spoke for *three full days* in defending Burr.[83] Here, he was effective. Marshall's final instruction to the jury construed treason *very narrowly*. In order to prove a charge of treason, the accused must not only have *conspired*, but there must also be two witnesses to some *overt* act.[84] As a result of this charge to the jury, Burr was "not proved to be guilty. . . ."[85] "Marshall has stepped in between Burr and death," said William Wirt, another prosecutor.[86]

As soon as the acquittal was announced, the Jeffersonians released to the press some of the incriminating documents that John Marshall had refused to admit as evidence. Burr escaped with his neck, but not his reputation. Once again fearing for his life, Burr this time fled to Europe. There, he continued his plotting. He sought money from Napoleon, and from Napoleon's enemies, the British, from *anyone* who might pay him to betray his country. He found no takers. Aaron Burr was a spent force.

Today, we can be grateful for Marshall's courage. Aaron Burr was surely guilty. But it would have been very dangerous to hang a former vice president of the United States on anything less than overwhelming evidence. As it happened, Burr was politically dead, and that was enough.

The summer of 1805 saw an epic sea battle beyond the eastern horizon that was to influence America's development throughout the nineteenth century. English Admiral Horatio Nelson chased a combined French-Spanish fleet across the Atlantic and back. At a time when nothing on land moved faster than a horse, the sailing ships manned by Nelson's sailors were the most complex man-made machines on earth.* French Admiral Pierre de Villeneuve was skilled and brave, but he had no chance against Nelson's fleet, and he knew it. The Royal Navy was disciplined. Press gangs made sure that the best sailors were dragged into service, including many unfortunate Americans. On the morning of 21 October 1805, Nelson sighted the French-Spanish fleet off Spain's Cape Trafalgar and hoisted his famous signal: "England expects every man will do his duty." Though fewer in numbers than the combined French-Spanish fleet, Nelson had superior firepower. English crews could fire more rapidly, more accurately. "Nelson's touch" destroyed the combined fleet and ended Napoleon's hopes of invading England. Nelson died heroically, shot down by a French sniper on the quarterdeck of HMS *Victory*. Nelson's victory at Trafalgar established England's naval supremacy *for a full century.*

And that meant England alone would have the power to threaten America's westward expansion.

IV. "A Splendid Misery": Jefferson's Last Years

Thomas Jefferson had described the presidency as "a splendid misery" when he saw the toll it took on George Washington's health and happiness. That was in 1797. Ten years later, he would experience this misery for himself.

* Some of Nelson's ships' speed could top twelve knots (or more than thirteen miles per hour). This was faster, over time, than teams of horses could run. And Nelson's ships—famously—could direct accurate cannon broadsides three times in less than five minutes—a lethal rate of fire.

Early in June 1807, HMS *Leopard* attacked the USS *Chesapeake* barely ten miles outside Chesapeake Bay.[87] The attack came because the American warship had refused to be boarded by Royal Navy press gangs. The British had for years resorted to impressment to man their ships. They would simply board American merchant ships and grab any man whom they thought was an English sailor. This time, they humiliated America by seizing crewmen right out from under the flag of the United States. Jefferson might have had a unanimous declaration of war had he called Congress into session at that moment.

Jefferson was desperate to avoid war. To do so, he resorted to two disastrous alternatives. First, he built more small, cheap gunboats. He wanted to avoid "the ruinous folly of a navy."[88] Next, he tried to pressure Britain by threatening a cutoff of trade. For years, he and Madison had hoped to pressure England by an *embargo* on their manufactured goods. They believed that mobs of unemployed English workers would march on London demanding action to save their jobs.[89] Soon, Jefferson prevailed upon the Republican majority in Congress to pass his embargo. Not only were Federalists almost unanimously opposed to it, even some of Jefferson's Republicans saw it as folly. Virginia Congressman John Randolph mocked Secretary of State Madison. He said Madison had pathetically thrown a sheaf of paper at Britain's *eight hundred warships.*[90]

"O Grab Me!"—*embargo* spelled backward—was the cartoon reproduced in Northern newspapers. It showed a snapping turtle labeled "embargo" tearing at President Jefferson's trousers. Jefferson was indeed *grabbed* by this ill-advised policy.

Nor was New England soothed when the president added France to the list of forbidden importers. Both Napoleon and the British had grossly interfered with American rights, seizing merchant ship cargoes, impressing our seamen. The obvious answer was to build more frigates like the USS *Constitution* and send American merchant ships abroad under armed escort. America needed to be ready to fight to protect her rights. The first flag of the U.S. Navy captured the right spirit: reminiscent of the Culpeper Minuteman flag, it depicted a rattlesnake on a field of red and white stripes with the legend: "Don't Tread on Me!" But building a first-class navy would have been very costly. Jeffersonians were committed to paying off the national debt and lowering taxes. They also had to pay off the loans that were required for the Louisiana Purchase.

Only one shining moment relieved the gloom of Jefferson's second term. In his annual Message to Congress in 1806, President Jefferson "congratulated" his fellow citizens on the approach of the year 1808, when they could legislate against the slave trade. In a compromise, the Constitution had permitted the outlawing of the importation of "such persons" as the states saw fit to receive. But Congress had to wait twenty years from the adoption of the Constitution to act. Now, Jefferson urged Congress to act *early* by passing a law to go into effect on 1 January 1808. He wanted to make sure no slave ships would even depart from the "Gold Coast" of Africa if they could not arrive here before the cutoff date. Jefferson's words were significant. He wanted "to withdraw the citizens of the United States from all further participation in those violations of human rights which have been so long continued on the unoffending inhabitants of Africa, and which the morality, the reputation, and the best interests of our country have long been eager to proscribe."[91] The great English evangelical, William Wilberforce, had been pleading for just such a measure in the British Parliament for a generation; his efforts would be crowned with success in March 1807. Jefferson wanted the United States similarly to reject this inhuman trafficking in human lives. His eloquent statement was the strongest *official* condemnation of slavery to be penned by a president before the election of Abraham Lincoln.*

Despite the economic downturn caused by the embargo, Jefferson was happy to see his chosen successor elected easily in 1808. Despite the unpopularity of Jefferson's embargo, James Madison trounced the unfortunate Federalist Charles Cotesworth Pinckney by 122 electoral votes to 47. Madison swept every region except New England and Delaware. After signing the repeal of the failed embargo, Jefferson rode simply to his successor's

* Jefferson's increasing indebtedness, and the hardening attitudes of his Virginia neighbors *against* manumission of slaves, would shackle the master of Monticello to the hated institution of slavery. But this should not blind us to many of his official words *and* deeds registered against it.

inauguration. He had no guard of honor. He hitched his own horse to the hitching post and joined the throng at the ceremony.

"Never did a prisoner, released from his chains, feel such relief as I shall on shaking off the shackles of power," he wrote to a friend.[92] We sense that he meant it.

V. "Mr. Madison's War"

President Madison should have known his term in office would be troubled when he tried to name his close friend, Albert Gallatin, as his secretary of state. Virginia's William Branch Giles bluntly told the new president that Republicans in the Senate would not accept the brilliant Swiss immigrant in that post.[93] Thus, very early, Madison lost control of events. One of the greatest of the Founders, he was not as well suited for governing what he had helped gather.

Madison eagerly sought peace with England. When he negotiated a treaty with the British minister in Washington, it seemed the English would withdraw their Orders in Council that had punished neutral shipping. Unfortunately, this chance to avert war was lost when Britain's foreign minister turned thumbs down on the treaty.[94]

In 1810, Republicans in Congress responded, incredibly, to the renewed threat by *slashing* appropriations for the army and navy.[95] Although Thomas Jefferson had approved the creation of West Point in 1802, it remained a Republican belief that a standing army and navy were dangerous and too expensive. They preferred to rely on militia forces and on the woefully inadequate fleet of little gunboats.

The northwest frontier grew restive. An astonishing leader arose among the Indians. Tecumseh was a powerful orator with an even more powerful message: "Where today are the Pequot? Where are the Narragansett, the Mohican, the Pokanoket, and many other once powerful tribes of our people? They have vanished before the avarice and oppression of the white man, as snow before a summer sun."[96]

Tecumseh traveled throughout the territory urging the tribes to form a confederation to resist the Americans' steady pressure. With his brother, known as the Prophet, Tecumseh sternly told the Indians to give up the white man's ways—and especially to avoid alcohol. Tecumseh had seen how other chiefs had been plied with whiskey during negotiations and had signed away some forty-eight million acres since the 1790s.[97] Carried away by this powerful rhetoric, the Prophet refused to be held back by Tecumseh. Instead, he attacked the American militia at a place called Tippecanoe, in modern-day Indiana.*

The Americans, led by General William Henry Harrison, fought off his attackers and claimed the victory on 11 November 1811 that would make him president thirty years later. All recognized Harrison's cool courage in fending off what was rare for the Indians, a night attack.[98]

Americans on the frontier naturally blamed the British for stirring up the Indians. The elections of 1810 had brought to Congress a powerful new group of young Republicans known as "the War Hawks."[99] These War Hawks installed Henry Clay of Kentucky as speaker of the House. South Carolina's John C. Calhoun joined the group that would shape America's destiny for the next forty years. Older Republicans like Virginia Congressman John Randolph ridiculed the war fever of the new members. He believed that men who had never smelled salt water cared little for "Free Trade and Sailor's Rights."[100] Randolph compared his new colleagues to the whippoorwill that calls "but one monotonous tone—Canada! Canada! Canada!"[101] It was true that the frontiersman wanted to take Canada and remove the British threat once and for all. In retirement, Thomas Jefferson even encouraged them, saying the conquest of Canada would be "a mere matter of marching."

The British government in London withdrew the Orders in Council on 16 June 1812. But the U.S. Congress did not know that and declared war just two days later. Then, in utter defiance of anything resembling sense, Congress adjourned without increasing the navy.[102] Soon, Americans would be stunned by the surrender of General William Hull at Detroit. The British commander in Canada, General Isaac Brock, had threatened Hull with an Indian massacre if he resisted.[103] Then, in Chicago, there occurred another of the horrors

* "Tippecanoe" would come to symbolize a heroic victory that secured the Old Northwest against a grave and growing threat.

Meriwether Lewis and William Clark. *Jefferson's team led a Corps of Discovery from St. Charles, Missouri, to the Pacific and back. The president praised them for their "undaunted courage." They led one of the greatest adventures of the age. Known to history as Lewis & Clark, their rare joint command succeeded brilliantly. These intrepid pioneers lost only one man on their three-year expedition.*

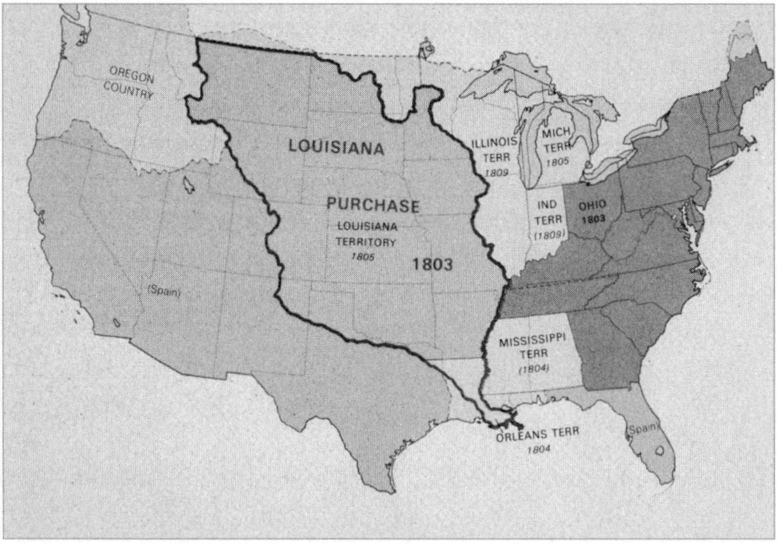

Louisiana Purchase (map of U.S. 1803). *While President Jefferson publicly spoke of peace and friendship with France, his loyal lieutenant Madison privately warned the French ambassador Napoleon might lose all if he did not go through with the sale of Louisiana. This greatest diplomatic stroke in history doubled the size of the United States—for just three cents an acre.*

Andrew Jackson, as officer of militia. *His men called him "Old Hickory"—not entirely affectionately. His iron will and steely courage marked him early for leadership. A harsh disciplinarian, he was nonetheless respected by his frontier troops because he brought victories. In his long military and political careers, he almost never tasted defeat.*

John Marshall, chief justice of the United States. *War hero, diplomat, skilled politician, John Marshall was the best of John Adams's "midnight judges." He presided over the Supreme Court with a commanding intellect legal acumen, and a rare gift for friendship. This great Virginian was also a great American, laying the foundation for the Constitution as truly "the supreme law of the land."*

that so inflamed the people of the American frontier. A Canadian writer tells the story of what happened when six hundred Pottawatomie Indians overwhelmed the Illinois militia:

> At the wagon train, the soldiers' wives, armed with their husbands' swords, fight as fiercely as the men. Two are hacked to pieces: a Mrs. Corbin, wife of a private, who has vowed never to be taken prisoner, and . . . Cicely [a black woman, and a slave] who is cut down with her infant son. Within the wagons, where the younger children [of the soldiers] are huddled, there is greater horror. One young Indian slips in and slaughters twelve single-handed, slicing their heads from their bodies in a fury of bloodlust.[104]

Black Bird, a Pottawatomie chieftain, does not keep his word to spare survivors in return for a ransom of one hundred dollars each:

> Sergeant Thomas Burns of the militia is killed almost immediately by the squaws. His is a more fortunate fate than that of five of his comrades who are tortured to death that night, their cries breaking the silence over the great lake and sending shivers through the survivors.[105]

Mrs. John Simmons survives the massacre in the wagons. Her husband died in a desperate charge. It is worth recounting her heroic and tragic story in full:

> Believing that the Indians delight in tormenting prisoners who show any emotion, this remarkable woman resolves to preserve the life of her six-month-old child by suppressing all outward manifestations of grief, even when she is led past a row of small, mutilated corpses which includes that of her two-year-old boy, David. Faced with this grisly spectacle, she neither blinks an eye nor sheds a tear, nor will she during the long months of her captivity.
>
> Her Indian [captors] set out for Green Bay on the western shore of

Lake Michigan. Mrs. Simmons, carrying her baby, trudges the entire distance working as a servant in the evenings, gathering wood and building fires. When the village is at last reached, she is insulted, kicked, and abused. The following day, she is forced to run the gauntlet between a double line of men and women wielding sticks and clubs. Wrapping her infant in a blanket and shielding it in her arms, she races down the long line, emerging bruised and bleeding but with her child unharmed.

She is given over to an Indian "mother," who feeds her, bathes her wounds, allows her to rest. She needs such sustenance, for a worse ordeal faces her—a long tribal [trek] back around the lake. Somehow, Mrs. Simmons, lightly clad, suffering from cold, fatigue, and malnutrition, manages to carry her child for the entire six hundred miles and survive. She has walked with the Indians from Green Bay back to Chicago, then around the entire eastern shore of the lake to Michilimackinac. But a second even more terrible trek faces her—a three-hundred-mile journey through the snow to Detroit, where the Indians intend to ransom her. Ragged and starving, she exists on roots and acorns found beneath the snows. Her child, now a year old, has grown much heavier. Her own strength is waning. Only the prospect of release sustains her.

. . . . [E]ven after her release, her ordeal is not over. The route to her home is long and hard. By March of 1813 she reaches Fort Meigs on the Maumee [in Indiana]. Here she manages to secure passage on a government wagon [that deposits her] in mid-April, four miles from her father's farm [near Piqua, Ohio].

Mother and child walk the remaining distance to find that the family, which has . . . given her up for dead, has taken refuge in a blockhouse against Indian marauders. Here, safe at last, she breaks down and for several months cannot contain her tears. In August, she has further reason to weep. Her sister and brother-in-law, working in a nearby flax field, are surprised by Indians, shot, tomahawked, and scalped in front of their four horrified children. Such . . . is the legacy of Tippecanoe and all that proceeded it.[106]

This extended passage helps us understand the intense hostility so many American settlers felt toward the Indians—and toward British officers like Isaac Brock in Canada whom they charged with using the Indians as a terror weapon against them.

Not only are Americans horrified by the terror on the burning frontier, they are deeply disappointed that Canada would be no easy conquest. Far from being "a mere matter of marching," Americans find that Canadians are determined to resist forcible incorporation into the Yankee republic.

Americans are shocked to find they are *not* welcomed by the vastly outnumbered Canadians. As in the Revolutionary War, the French in Canada remain loyal to the British Crown. Even American settlers here, who had been lured north by the promise of cheap land, proved unwilling to help their invading fellow countrymen.

When the slight, mud-stained figure of Laura Secord trudges nineteen miles on foot through a dreaded black swamp to carry a warning to the Canadian militia, a legend is born. This thirty-eight-year-old wife of a wounded Canadian alerts Lieutenant James Fitzgibbons and his "Bloody Boys" that the Americans are coming. Her brave exploit fires the Canadian imagination and inspires a new patriotism across the flaming border.[107] Laura Secord will become for Canadians what Paul Revere was to Americans. She quickly became a legendary figure representing courage and loyalty—to the British crown.

"Mr. Madison's War," as the War of 1812 was called throughout New England, proved to be highly unpopular. It is always trouble for a president when a war is identified with him—and not with the country's enemy. A number of state governments there refused to supply militia troops for the war effort.[108] Some Federalists who bitterly opposed the war were even accused of putting lights on the shore to signal British warships blockading their country. This charge of "blue light Federalist" would be hurled at them for a generation.

By 1814, America was exposed to invasion on three fronts at once: Niagara-Lake Champlain in the north, New Orleans in the south, and in the Chesapeake Bay.[109] On 11 September 1814, a British fleet on Lake Champlain tried to establish control of the area. They were met by Americans under

Captain Thomas McDonough in his flagship, the USS *Saratoga*. McDonough wound his badly battered ship around while still at anchor and forced the surrender of HMS *Confiance* and three other British vessels. British Captain George Downie was killed when one of his big guns was hit by one of McDonough's cannonballs.*

McDonough's great victory caused the British general, Sir George Prevost, to retreat. Thus, McDonough's ship *Saratoga* accomplished what the Battle of Saratoga had accomplished for the Americans in 1777. Britain's northern invasion of the United States was turned back.

Americans in the Chesapeake Bay region were not so fortunate. A powerful British fleet raided Maryland's coastal towns and landed a large force of veteran British soldiers.**

Led by General Robert Ross, British regulars met little opposition as they marched toward Washington, D.C. Winning victories at Bladensburg and Upper Marlboro, Maryland, the British force entered Washington on 24 August 1814. American Commodore Joshua Barney with only 400 sailors and 120 Marines bravely held the British off for two hours. But the bulk of American militia forces commanded by the grossly incompetent General William Winder broke and ran. They were put to flight by the new Congreve rockets the British employed. These rockets couldn't be aimed accurately. Few hit their targets. But despite the harmlessness of most of them, they made a lot of noise and scared the horses—and the militia.[110]

James Madison was doing his best to organize the resistance to the triumphant British forces. He rode out to the front, where he hastily penciled a note to his heroic wife, Dolley, warning her to flee the city. She and Paul Jennings, a fifteen-year-old black youth, cut the famous Gilbert Stuart portrait of George Washington from its frame so it could be carried off to safety. The government evacuated the capital before the advancing redcoats. Fortunately, Secretary of State James Monroe had ordered Stephen Pleasanton, a clerk, to

* The British gun, with the indentation made by McDonough's cannonball clearly visible, is on display to this day at the U.S. Naval Academy in Annapolis. It is in front of *McDonough* Hall.

** The little town of St. Michael's on Maryland's eastern shore staged the first blackout in history during the 1814 British assault. Residents hung lanterns in trees outside of the town and doused their candles. The British fleet shelled the stand of trees, leaving the town unharmed.

save such historic documents as George Washington's commission, the Declaration of Independence, and the Constitution.[111] Secured in a canvas sack, they were spirited away in a carriage.

British Marines entered the Executive Mansion unopposed. After eating the dinner that had been prepared for the Madisons, General Ross ordered his men to torch the President's House. The new Capitol building, too, was burned, as well the Library of Congress.

Dr. William Thornton, a brave local physician, saved the U.S. Patent Office by appealing to the British not to burn the hundreds of inventors' models. That would be as barbarous, he warned them, as the Turks' burning of the great Alexandria Library in Egypt.[112]

Nothing could save the offices of a leading newspaper, however. British Admiral George Cockburn had been irritated by the way the *National Intelligencer* published exaggerated accounts accusing him of cruelty. When British soldiers smashed the printing presses and threw the little blocks of type out of the window, Cockburn laughingly called out: "Be sure that all the c's are destroyed so the rascals can't abuse my name any more!"[113]

Another humorous incident occurred amidst the national shame. The city fathers of Alexandria, Virginia, and Georgetown finally succeeded after two days in tracking down Admiral Cockburn. They wanted to *surrender* to him even though not a single British soldier had come near their toney towns.[114]

Confident they could continue to rout the poorly led Americans, General Ross and Admiral Cockburn sailed up the Chesapeake to Baltimore. General Ross jauntily told a Maryland farmer in whose house he had breakfasted that he would not return for dinner. "I'll have supper tonight in Baltimore, or in hell."[115] He may have gotten his wish. Shortly afterward, two American sharpshooters fired on the advancing British column. One of them hit General Ross, mortally wounding him on 12 September 1814.[116]

Admiral Cockburn continued on toward Baltimore. First, he would have to get past the stout Fort McHenry. Again, he used the fearsome Congreve rockets. But the defenders of Baltimore were made of sterner stuff. The fort held.

During the nights of September 13–14, a young lawyer named Francis

Scott Key boarded a British warship. Key was determined to obtain the release of an elderly American doctor who had been caught taking British stragglers prisoner. Key persuaded the British that Dr. Beanes had actually treated his prisoners very humanely. The Americans could not be released, however, while the bombardment of Fort McHenry was in progress. Throughout the night, old Dr. Beanes asked Key if our flag was still there. Thus was born the inspiration for Francis Scott Key's poem, "The Defense of Fort M'Henry." The poem, later to become our national anthem as "The Star-Spangled Banner," lifted American spirits even as Baltimore was spared.[117]

The British invasion force then withdrew to the island of Jamaica to prepare their next assault on America. This time their target would be New Orleans. In the Southwest, Americans had already faced another Indian uprising. Upper Creeks, known as "Red Sticks," had overwhelmed Fort Mims on 30 August 1813. The fort was located forty miles from present-day Mobile, Alabama. There, the Red Sticks under Chief Red Eagle had massacred nearly 250 settlers. "The children were seized by the legs, and killed by batting their heads against the stockading. The women were scalped, and those who were pregnant were opened while they were still alive and the embryo infants were let out of the womb."[118] Red Eagle tried to stop these atrocities, but could not.

The news of the Fort Mims massacre electrified Tennessee. General Andrew Jackson was on a sickbed, recuperating from wounds he received in a barroom fight with Thomas Hart Benton and Jesse Benton. Despite the loss of blood and the bullet still lodged in his shoulder, the pale, gaunt Jackson got up to lead militia troops against the Creeks. When some of his men panicked and tried to escape duty, Jackson had six of them executed "to encourage the others" and quickly proceeded to defeat the Creeks.[119] Jackson's tall, lean, ramrod straight stance and his hard, unyielding discipline quickly gained him the nickname "Old Hickory." The Indians who felt his wrath called him "Sharp Knife."

The Upper Creeks had been inspired by Tecumseh's brave resistance. When Jackson killed nine hundred Creeks at the Battle of Horseshoe Bend, 27 March 1814, he broke the back of the uprising. He ordered the Creeks to meet him at Fort Jackson (present-day Jackson, Mississippi), where he forced them to cede some twenty-three million acres to the United States. Nearly three-fifths of Alabama and one-fifth of Georgia were obtained by the hard treaty Jackson demanded. "Until this is done, your nation cannot expect happiness or mine security," Jackson told the assembled Creeks on 10 July 1814.[120]

As President Madison's diplomatic representatives met their British counterparts for peace talks in Ghent, Belgium, the American position was weak, indeed. The British demanded large parts of Maine, which they then occupied, and the creation of a large Indian buffer state along the Ohio River. America's John Quincy Adams already had thirty years of experience in diplomacy. And Henry Clay had thirty years of experience playing poker. Both men's skills were to prove indispensable.[121]

VI. The Battle of New Orleans

The leader of the British invasion force was the brave young general, Sir Edward Pakenham. General Pakenham was the brother-in-law of the Duke of Wellington, England's greatest soldier. Among Sir Edward's 7,500 red-coats were many veterans of Wellington's successful campaigns against Napoleon's troops. The British intended to take the City of New Orleans and as much of Louisiana as possible. These would be valuable bargaining chips in the peace negotiations in Ghent. Pakenham was to encourage the people of Louisiana to secede from the United States and join either the Spanish empire or attach themselves to the British.[122] Some Americans worried that Louisiana, purchased a decade earlier and admitted as a state only in 1812, might be lured away.

As General Jackson prepared to meet the British invaders, he imposed strict martial law on the lively city. This was a very unpopular move. He also had to deal with the famed Baratarian pirates—led by Jean Lafitte. Seemingly loyal to no side but their own, Lafitte's pirates had turned down a British offer because it was too small. Jackson needed every man he could find to defend the besieged city. Although he had denounced Lafitte and his men as "hellish banditti," Jackson gave in to the pleas of Edward Livingston and other leaders of New Orleans and accepted Lafitte's help.

As the British advanced toward New Orleans, they were undetected until 23 December 1814, when they came to the plantation of Major Gabriel Villaré. Villaré had been sitting on his front porch, smoking a cigar, and talking to his brother. Suddenly, redcoats came crashing through the dense woods and seized both brothers. Gabriel jumped out an open window. "Catch him or kill him!" yelled the British colonel. Villaré was too fast for them. He jumped over a picket fence and ran into the underbrush. Legend has it he had to kill a favorite dog, "with tears in his eyes," to keep it from giving him away.[123]

Villaré's timely warning enabled Jackson to fortify his position in front of the Crescent City. Jackson had his men arrange themselves in front of the Rodriguez Canal, which ran perpendicular to the Mississippi River. With the river on his right and an impassable cypress wood on his left, Jackson's defensive position was a commanding one. He led an extraordinary group of some five thousand men. He had volunteers from New Orleans, including Creole aristocrats, tradesmen, and manual workers. He had Tennessee and Kentucky militia. Free Negroes formed a key element of his force. Also included were Spanish, French, Portuguese, Italians, and Indians. And, of course, he had the pirates.[124] It was just the kind of "rabble" the British had been taught to despise. They called the Americans "dirty shirts."[125] But high manners and neatly laundered tunics would not save the day.

On Christmas Day 1814, a number of fugitive slaves entered the British lines in front of New Orleans.[126] They would gladly work if they could only achieve their freedom. One of these poor men addressed a British officer in perfect French. He implored them to remove a horrible spiked collar. It had been fastened around his neck as punishment for his attempts at escape.[127] Freeing him from this torture, a British officer sneered at the Americans' claims. "This [is an] ingenious symbol of a land of liberty," he said.[128] Still, the British were no liberators for the oppressed slaves of Louisiana. Their agents posted notices throughout the bayou country: YOUR SLAVES SHALL BE PRESERVED TO YOU. They appealed to the formerly French plantation owners to forsake their new American identity.[129]

When the British commenced their attack on the morning of 8 January 1815, General Pakenham ordered a rocket fired off. Jackson's calm courage inspired his men. "Don't mind those rockets," he said, "they are mere toys to amuse children."[130] Pakenham's invaders included the famed Ninety-third Highland Regiment, the fierce, kilted Scots. Jackson's men took dead aim on the advancing redcoats and mowed them down. Described as "more a massacre than a battle," the redcoats could not overcome the murderously accurate rifle and artillery fire that Jackson poured into them.[131] General Pakenham himself was shot to death, along with several subordinate general officers. The British toll was devastating. In just minutes, they lost 291 dead, 1,262 wounded, and 484 captured or missing. The American toll, incredibly, was just 13 dead, 39 wounded, and 19 missing in action.[132]

It was a bitter blow to British pride. Who could believe the American "dirty shirts" could inflict such a defeat on His Majesty's best troops? When a Tennessee militiaman demanded the surrender of a wounded invader, the redcoat officer turned around and saw a wild-eyed, unshaven, unwashed American. He was appalled: "What a disgrace for a British officer to have to surrender to a chimney sweep!"[133]

One revealing incident suggests why the Americans were so formidable.

Immediately after the battle, three dead British soldiers' bodies were taken out of a ditch.[134] Several members of a New Orleans militia company were disputing among themselves about which one had killed the colonel. "If he isn't hit above the eyebrows," said a merchant named Withers, "it wasn't my shot." Sure enough, the colonel's body revealed Withers's shot—a testament to the deadly *withering* fire of the American line.[135]

Not all the invading troops were so eager to bring the Americans under the English heel, however. Some of the prisoners were Irishmen. Their homeland had risen up unsuccessfully against English rule as recently as 1798. They had not been told they would be fighting Americans when they were loaded onto British ships. Then why had they marched so courageously into the withering American fire, their captors asked them. "And faith were we not *obliged,* with officers behind sticking and stabbing us with their swords?" replied survivors with typical Gaelic wit.[136]

Jackson did not pursue the retreating British. Nor did he relax his strict military discipline over his men and the now saved city. Soon, however, the British withdrew, never to return. Jackson told the leading Catholic cleric in the city, Abbé Guillaume Dubourg, that the victory was the result of the "signal interposition of heaven."[137] Few Americans would disagree. The Abbé agreed and asked Jackson to join him in a *Te Deum*, a Mass of celebration in the cathedral.

Within weeks, news of the great victory came to Washington, D.C. Still depressed over the burning of the capital the previous August, Washingtonians now went wild with joy. "Incredible Victory!" read the headlines. Editors with a more literary bent quoted Shakespeare's *Henry VI*: "Advance our waving colors on the walls / Rescued is Orleans from the English wolves."[138]

Within days of Jackson's great victory the capital had further reason to rejoice. The Treaty of Ghent had been signed on Christmas Eve 1814. The news had taken almost six weeks to cross the Atlantic. Had there been a cable, the Battle of New Orleans might never have been fought. If Americans had known what this treaty would look like *before* they had gone to war, few would ever have approved the course. The Treaty of Ghent gave America no gains. The British had yielded not one inch on impressment. But neither had they insisted on territorial concessions.

It settled nothing, and yet it settled everything.

For, with the victory of New Orleans, Americans could be proud of themselves once more. They had taken on the greatest power in the world and survived with their independence intact. Even if they had not conquered Canada, they now had what Theodore Roosevelt would call "a hostage" for Britain's good behavior. They had a great naval tradition, a beloved new hero, Old Hickory, and a renewed sense of patriotism, as evidenced by "The Star-Spangled Banner." To this day, America has never enjoyed so stunning and spectacular a military triumph as Jackson gained at New Orleans. And the War of 1812 helped to form a new American consciousness. This American identity was fused in the crucible of battle.[139]

While General Jackson and his lady, the plump, lively Rachel, were dancing in New Orleans to the tune of "Possum up de Gum Tree," a delegation of gloomy Federalists had come to Washington in no party mood. With the spectacularly bad timing that had become the party's trademark, they had chosen this moment of national jubilation to report on their recently concluded Hartford Convention (1814). Fortunately for the many capable and loyal members of the Federalist Party, the convention had firmly *rejected* secession. Further, they suggested a number of constitutional amendments but did not threaten to make a separate peace with Britain if their proposals were not accepted by the Madison administration. Even so, the longtime opposition of so many leading Federalists to the war effort, the disloyalty of some of their governors in not providing needed troops and their fondness for the British tainted the Federalist Party.[140] Never again would they seriously contend for the presidency.

VII. "An Era of Good Feeling"

By 1816, the election of James Monroe to the presidency was a foregone conclusion. Monroe was one of the few of Madison's cabinet to come through the war with his reputation intact. Monroe won an astounding 183 electoral votes to Rufus King's mere 34. It was to be the Federalist Party's dying gasp. They had been fatally tainted with suspicion of secession and disloyalty during the War of 1812. Some of the Jeffersonian Republicans even taunted their opponents with an unsubstantiated charge of being "blue light Federalists."

General Andrew Jackson welcomed Monroe's election and looked forward to further territorial expansion. Jackson had his eye on Florida. The Spaniards had sided with England in the late war. Jackson saw Florida as a staging area for Indian raids against the settlers on the American side of the long border. Jackson was now ready to settle scores. But would President Monroe allow him?

When war broke out with the Seminoles of Florida in 1817, General Jackson was commander of the Southern Department of the U.S. Army. He did not hesitate to cross the border in hot pursuit of his enemies. After another Indian massacre of American settlers, Jackson captured two Seminole chieftains and hanged them. Then he found two British subjects whom he believed were aiding the Indians—Alexander Arbuthnot and Robert Ambrister. He turned them over to an American court-martial in the town of St. Mark's. Arbuthnot was hanged from the yardarm of his own ship. Ambrister died before a firing squad.[141] The two Britons died 29 April

1818. Jackson's fierce determination to deal with his country's enemies made him wildly popular on the frontier. He did not wait to see the unfortunate Britons executed. Instead, he marched west and seized the Spanish port of Pensacola on 24 May 1818.[142] Secretary of State John Quincy Adams tactfully brushed aside vehement Spanish protests over Jackson's bold moves. Realizing they could never hang on to Florida with such a determined leader as Jackson on the rampage, the Spaniards quickly agreed to Adams's proposed treaty. They sold Florida to the United States for $5 million on 22 February 1819.[143]

To most Americans, General Jackson's brilliant success at New Orleans, followed by his victories against the Indians and the Spaniards earned him the very simple title—the *Hero*. But Jackson's actions were not approved by all.

Speaker of the House Henry Clay of Kentucky was also a westerner. Clay announced that he would make a speech on the subject of Jackson's conquests. An electric current of excitement went through Washington. Clay was already one of the greatest figures in the young republic. What would he say? Suspense rose. The galleries were packed when Clay descended to the well of the House. For a man who had begun his career as a War Hawk, spoiling for a fight with Britain, how could Clay *not* applaud what Jackson had done? Not only did he not applaud General Jackson, Clay galvanized the packed galleries with his powerful and elegant arguments *against* what Jackson had done. Clay denounced Jackson's executions of the British subjects, he deplored Jackson's harsh treaty with the Indians, and he condemned Jackson's seizure of Pensacola.[144] Then, in a hushed and tense House, he warned what might happen if an infant republic let its military leaders run rampant. In words that echoed Patrick Henry's speech against King George III, Clay said: "Remember that Greece had her Alexander, Rome her Caesar, England her Cromwell, France her Bonaparte, and that if we would escape the rock on which they split, we must avoid their errors!"[145]

Clay assured his listeners again and again in the more than two hours that he spoke that he meant nothing *personal* in his criticisms of the general. He spoke only for the good of the republic, he said. Jackson and his supporters were having none of it. From that moment, 20 January 1819, there was between these two great leaders of the West an unbridgeable gap. Jackson reacted with cold fury, an enmity that he would carry to the grave a quarter of a century later.

VIII. The Missouri Compromise

Efforts to make states out of the vast lands conveyed in the Louisiana Purchase were bound to bring conflict. Louisiana had been admitted as a slave state in 1812. But slavery had already existed there under the French and the Spanish.

The Missouri Territory was different.

Northerners were concerned to see that slavery was not withering away, as so many of the Founders' generation thought it would. Instead, it seemed to be expanding. Alabama and Mississippi had been admitted as slave states, but they were in the Deep South. There, the strength of slavery seemed to be increasing. The cotton gin had been invented in 1793 by Eli Whitney of Connecticut. This device helped make cotton much more profitable. And cotton was the basis of slave agriculture. But with Missouri, slavery seemed to be pressing dangerously north and west.

Northern members of Congress managed to hold out for concessions. Missouri would be admitted as a slave state even as Maine, formerly a region of Massachusetts, was admitted as a free state. The *southern* boundary line of Missouri at 36°30' north latitude would be the dividing line. No slavery would be allowed *north* of that line. Both sides seemed satisfied.

Henry Clay was the moving force in crafting this legislative solution to a seemingly insoluble problem. His efforts to preserve the union earned him the admiration of thousands and the title "the Great Compromiser."*

But Thomas Jefferson was troubled. In retirement at Monticello, the former president wrote that "this momentous question, like a fire bell in the night, awakened and filled me with terror. I considered it the knell of the union."[146] Jefferson presciently saw that "a geographical line, coinciding with a

* The Missouri Compromise preserved the peace of the Union for forty years. It can be argued that the *repeal* of the Missouri Compromise in the 1850s led directly to civil war.

marked principle, moral and political, once conceived and held up to the angry passions of men, will never be obliterated; and every new irritation will mark it deeper and deeper."[147] Here, Jefferson forecast with astonishing precision the history of his country over the next forty years. At this point, Jefferson had changed his position on the expansion of slavery. He previously had *opposed* slavery's extension (and had fallen just one vote short of establishing that as national policy when he proposed it to the Confederation Congress in 1784). Now, perhaps influenced by Madison's writings in *Federalist* No. 10, Jefferson thought it might be easier to eradicate slavery if it were more *diluted* throughout the Union. Jefferson admitted his own paradox. "We have a wolf by the ears, and we can neither hold him, nor safely let him go."[148]

IX. The Monroe Doctrine

Aware that he was coming to the end of his second term with no major achievements to his credit, President Monroe began to cast about for a way to make his mark on history. When the British foreign secretary, George Canning, proposed a joint Anglo-American declaration on Latin America, Monroe was keenly interested. Relations had warmed with Britain since the end of the War of 1812. This would be a way to advance ties. Jefferson and Madison, both now retired, commended the idea of declaring the Western Hemisphere "off limits" to further colonization by the powers of Europe. Canning wanted to preserve Britain's strong commercial ties with the newly independent Latin American republics. America wanted to limit Russia's advance in the Pacific Northwest.[149]

It was Secretary of State Adams, however, who gave Monroe his great opening. Adams proposed that President Monroe issue the declaration *on his own*. "It would be more candid as well as more dignified to avow our principles explicitly to France and Russia than to come in as a cock-boat in the wake of a British man-of-war," Adams told Monroe's cabinet.[150]

And so it was decided that the document that bears his name would be announced in the president's annual Message to Congress in December 1823. President Monroe's message came to be known as the Monroe Doctrine. He offered it as the policy of the United States that the Western Hemisphere would not be open to further colonization by the Great Powers of Europe. The United States would not try to seize colonial possessions—a point welcomed by the British who still ruled Canada—but we would not permit any European nation to retake colonies that had already become independent—or that might *become* independent in the future.

The Monroe Doctrine has been a pillar of American foreign policy ever since. Surprisingly, the British did not react negatively to having been "left at the altar." The British *chargé* in Washington wrote home to London commending "the explicit and manly tone" of the declaration.[151] The truth, of course, was that it was the "oaken walls" of the British fleet that protected Latin America's independence at this point and not the "parchment picket fence" of Mr. Monroe's declaration. Still, this bold move showed that America intended to stand on her own two feet in the community of nations.

X. "A Corrupt Bargain": The Election of 1824

The collapse of the Federalist Party had meant that presidents were chosen by the caucus system. "King Caucus," as it was called, was a gathering of the dominant Jeffersonian Republican members of Congress that put forward names for selection by the electoral college. President Monroe was reelected in 1820 with virtually no opposition. He won every electoral vote except one (and that elector simply wanted to keep President Washington's record intact). This was the system the Founders had tried to avoid in Philadelphia. They had rejected selection of the president by Congress. But by 1824, no alternative could be found to this method.

With no *obvious* successor to the popular James Monroe, the system was breaking down. Andrew Jackson was nominated by the Tennessee legislature and Speaker of the House Henry Clay was put forward by his own Kentucky legislature. Some congressional Republicans favored Secretary of State Adams. Treasury Secretary Wiliam H. Crawford, an early favorite, suffered a paralyzing stroke. Still, he stubbornly remained in the race. Secretary of War John C. Calhoun was South Carolina's "favorite son." It soon became clear that Calhoun lacked sufficient support, so he agreed to serve as vice president.

When the electoral votes were counted, Jackson led all his rivals with 99. Adams was second with 84. Since there was no majority in the electoral college, the election was thrown into the House of Representatives. This was only the second time this had occurred. Since Henry Clay came in *fourth* in the electoral college voting, and the Constitution provided that only the top three electoral vote winners could be considered, Clay was eliminated. When the balloting began between Jackson, Crawford, and Adams, Clay threw his support to Adams. John Quincy Adams was thus chosen the sixth president of the United States. He was admirably qualified. He had served as a U.S. senator, a skilled diplomat, and a cabinet member.

His next move, however, showed that John Quincy Adams was as politically inept as his father had been. Adams named Henry Clay as his secretary of state. Jackson's supporters immediately set up a howl that lasted fully four years. "A corrupt bargain," they yelled. And so the campaign of 1828 began almost from the moment that John Quincy Adams had been sworn in.

Adams was a stubborn man. He now claimed the mantle of *national* Republican, a part of the *Jeffersonian* coalition. His first Message to Congress, however, laid out an ambitious plan for federal action that would have made Hamilton proud. Adams called for roads and canals, an increase in the navy, and efforts to improve scientific knowledge.[152] When he called for a national astronomical observatory, he poetically referred to observatories as "lighthouses of the sky."[153] Congressional reaction was to lampoon the president as an impractical dreamer, one whose head was in the clouds, and a wasteful one at that.

XI. "Is It the Fourth?": Adams and Jefferson Die

Thomas Jefferson had not rested in retirement. He maintained an active correspondence with hundreds of friends and political allies. He developed new strains of plants, saying, "I am an old man, but a *young* gardener." And he received hordes of visitors at Monticello.

In one of his famous letters, he wrote this advice to the son of a good friend, the young Thomas Jefferson Smith. It was to be shown to the lad when he was old enough to appreciate it:

> Few words will be necessary, with good dispositions on your part. Adore God. Reverence and cherish your parents. Love your neighbor as yourself, and your country more than yourself. Be just. Be true. Murmur not at the ways of Providence. So shall the life into which you have entered be the portal to one of eternal and ineffable bliss. And if to the dead it is permitted to care for the things of this world, every action of your life will be under my regard. Farewell.[154]

One of the most illustrious of his visitors was the aged Marquis de Lafayette. Three hundred people gathered at the entrance to Jefferson's mountaintop home when the aged French hero's coach arrived. "Ah, Jefferson!" cried the sixty-seven-year-old general. "Ah, Lafayette!" replied the declining eighty-one-year-old statesman. Both men broke into tears.[155] The next night, 5 November 1824, Jefferson hosted Lafayette at a grand dinner in the Dome Room of the not-yet-completed Rotunda of the University of Virginia. Among those in attendance were *former* Presidents James Madison and James Monroe.[156] Both of these Jefferson friends and intimates were involved in the project of his old age, the university.*

Jefferson and Madison had engaged in "a great collaboration" for nearly fifty years. Now, both retired to their farms in the rolling Piedmont country, they worked together to establish the University of Virginia. American history affords no better example of a friendship so true, so intimate, so filled with productive labors for their country. "To myself you have been a pillar of support through life. Take care of me when dead, and be assured that I shall leave you with my last affections," Jefferson wrote to the Great Little Madison in the last year of his life.[157]

There now occurred during John Quincy Adams's single term an event

* If Thomas Jefferson had done nothing else, he would still have gained distinction as an architect. In 1976, the American Institute of Architects selected Jefferson's designs for the University of Virginia—his "Academical Village"—as the greatest achievement of American architecture in two hundred years.

that even today astonishes. President Adams's father, John, had been reconciled to Thomas Jefferson in 1811 after nearly a decade of sullen silence between the two giants of the Revolution. Dr. Benjamin Rush brought about the end of their estrangement. It was one of Rush's innumerable services to America. "I have always loved Thomas Jefferson!" said Adams to two of Jefferson's young Virginia neighbors. They immediately resumed writing one another.[158] Although they would be no closer than Braintree, Massachusetts, is to Charlottesville, Virginia, they conducted a long, affectionate correspondence for the rest of their lives.

As the fiftieth anniversary of the Declaration of Independence approached, the country began to turn its eyes once again to these two revolutionary leaders. When the mayor of Washington, D.C., invited Mr. Jefferson to a celebration in the capital, the author of the Declaration had to decline. He was eighty-three years old and in failing health. But he sent a letter in which he said: "All eyes are opened or opening to the rights of man. The general spread of the light of science has already laid open to every view that the mass of mankind has not been born with saddles on their backs, nor a favored few booted and spurred ready to ride them legitimately by the grace of God. . . . Let the annual return to this day forever refresh our recollection of these rights, and an undiminished devotion to them."[159]

John Adams, at ninety, could no longer wield his pen. But he gave a visiting delegation on June 30 an eloquent answer to their request for a Fourth of July message. "Independence Forever!" the old patriot said.

As Jefferson lay dying at Monticello, he asked: "Is it the Fourth?" It was. Five hundred miles north, John Adams, unaware that Jefferson had died earlier that day, said: "Thomas Jefferson still survives." He then slipped away. His death was followed by a violent thunderstorm; it was called "the artillery of Heaven."[160] The simultaneous passing of the two heroes of the Revolution touched Americans as nothing had since New Orleans. Many saw the hand of Providence in the event. Many still do.

Seven

Jackson and Democracy (1829–1849)

Andrew Jackson's rough-shod practice of democracy dominates the period from the disputed election of 1824 until his death in 1845. Jackson's steely resolve faces down the greatest threat to the Union in the Nullification Crisis of 1832. Jackson's threat to "hang as high as Haman" any man who tries to obstruct federal law enforcement is matched with a shrewd and timely concession to South Carolina on the tariff issue. He defies courts and people of conscience with his policy of Indian removal. Following an era when Congress dominated presidents, Jackson will not be mastered. He wields the president's veto as a club, using it not simply for unconstitutional bills, but as a policy weapon. "The Federal Union—It Must Be Preserved," says Jackson in a legendary toast, as he helps create the world's first mass democracy.

I. From Caucus to Raucous: The Election of 1828

Strong men feared Andrew Jackson. A story from his past shows why. When Jackson was a judge in Tennessee in the 1790s, he sent a succession of bailiffs, sheriffs, and deputies to apprehend a huge, strong man who, in a drunken rage, had cut off his own child's ears. When all of these came back empty-handed, Judge Jackson himself went to seize the accused. Asked why he meekly surrendered to Jackson after resisting an entire posse, the man said: "Why, when he came up, I looked him in the eye, and I saw shoot. And there wasn't shoot in nary other eye in the crowd."[1] Stories like this made Jackson a legend in his own time.

As mentioned in the preceding chapter, the day the House of Representatives controversially chose John Quincy Adams as president following the election of 1824, the portentous election of 1828 began. Andrew Jackson's supporters cried "corrupt bargain" when President-elect Adams rewarded Kentuckian Henry Clay with the post of secretary of state. Every president since Thomas Jefferson had served in that key position before assuming the presidency. Surely, by accepting the offer of this post from Adams, the ambitious Clay thought his chances of becoming president after Adams would improve. It would prove to be a disastrous miscalculation for both men.*

Unjustly, the Jacksonians accused Adams of selling the secretaryship outright in return for Clay's support in the House of Representatives polling. This was almost surely untrue.[2] That did not stop Jacksonians from sneering that Adams was "our Clay President," suggesting he was putty in the hands of Harry of the West.[3]

The days of King Caucus were clearly over. The people were not going to accept a president who had been chosen by a small caucus of party leaders in the House and the Senate. They demanded a say in the selection of their chief magistrate. And no one believed they should have a say more strongly or more sincerely than Andrew Jackson.

The tradition of not campaigning openly for the presidency was well established by George Washington. But the practice of candidates' encouraging their supporters by means of their numerous *letters* was just as well entrenched. Jackson considered himself to be a Jeffersonian, and his letters from his Nashville home, the Hermitage, followed the well-worn paths laid out by "the sage of Monticello." The sources of Jackson's support for the

---

* When the House selects a president, each state's delegation of representatives casts only one vote. They choose among the top three vote-getters in the electoral college. That meant Jackson, J. Q. Adams, and Georgia's William Crawford were eligible. Henry Clay was eliminated from the balloting. He was courted by Jackson, Adams, *and* Crawford supporters, so the cry of "corrupt bargain" was never really based in fact.

much-anticipated election of 1828 were quite similar to those of the Jeffersonians. Strong in the South and West, he made a critical alliance with Senator Martin Van Buren of New York. Just as Jefferson's teaming up with Aaron Burr had provided his margin of victory, Jackson's support from Van Buren's political organization—the Albany Regency—made him unstoppable. Jackson was also backed more or less openly by Vice President John C. Calhoun and the Southern planters he represented.

President Adams, Jackson's opponent in 1828, fairly assured the Tennessee war hero's landslide election. Few American presidents could surpass the towering intellect, the capacity for hard work, the personal integrity, the religious faith, and the sincere devotion to his country that characterized John Quincy Adams. But it is also true that few men have reached the presidency without developing at least *some* skills as a politician. John Quincy Adams was one of them.

Adams knew that he was cold, austere, respected, but never much liked. Unlike his great father, he lacked any trace of humor. Even his most innocent diversions from the crushing burdens of office came back to haunt him. When he purchased a billiard table with his own money, he was loudly attacked for installing "gaming tables and gambling furniture" in the President's House.[4] He was an awkward and uninspiring speaker. So was Jefferson, but John Quincy Adams lacked the Virginian's "peculiar felicity of expression." Once, when called upon in Baltimore to celebrate the defense of the city in the War of 1812, President Adams was asked to propose a toast. "Ebony and Topaz," the scholarly president cried out, explaining it was British General Robert Ross's posthumous coat of arms, "and to the Republican militiamen who gave it." His hearers were stunned. You had to know about British heraldry. You had to know that Ross had been killed by American sharpshooters. The toast was so pedantic, so muddled that he might as well have spoken in the classical Greek in which he was so accomplished. The president was hooted at throughout the country. "Ebony and Topaz" became a rallying cry for the Jacksonians nationwide to show how out of touch with the rising democratic spirit of the age John Quincy Adams was.[5] It did not help that Adams spent much of his term in a blue funk, exuding the impression of a loser.

When Adams laid out his program in a Message to Congress, it bore strong resemblance to the "American System" advocated by Henry Clay. Adams supported tariffs and a national bank. He proposed a national university, a naval academy, further explorations on the model of Lewis and Clark, and an extensive system of roads, canals, and harbors. He knew such an ambitious program would meet with resistance from taxpayers, but he urged members of Congress not to let the world see that America's government was "palsied by the will of our constituents." British statesman Edmund Burke might have been proud of that statement, but it was political suicide for Adams to say it.

Jackson and his followers sincerely believed he represented the true Jeffersonian philosophy. To Jackson, Adams's frosty manner concealed a man of aristocratic pretensions. Was John Quincy Adams not, after all, the son of Jefferson's defeated rival?

The Jacksonians immediately seized upon Adams's *elitist* disdain for the common man. If the will of the people was not to govern in a *democratic* republic, whose will would rule?[6]

With the collapse of the Federalists after 1816, Jeffersonian Republicans dominated national politics. The Adams and Clay faction of this Jeffersonian party was known as National Republicans. Their leaders knew they were saddled with an unattractive candidate. They knew he lacked the fundamental skills of politics. So they did what today we would call "driving up the opponent's negatives." They began a vicious campaign of character assassination directed at Jackson.

Without authorization from President Adams, to be sure, they nonetheless accused Andrew Jackson of adultery. He had married his beloved Rachel, they charged, *before* she was divorced from her first husband, Lewis Robards. The accusation was true, but more complicated. Robards, an abusive and vindictive man, had filed for divorce before the Virginia legislature, *but had failed to complete the divorce proceedings.* Impetuous Andrew had married Rachel before seeing the documents that would prove she was finally free. When, in 1793, the couple learned that Robards had belatedly gone through with the process, they quickly *remarried*. The vast majority of people in Tennessee gave no more thought to the matter. Such irregularities were not uncommon on the frontier where communications were slow and law and custom more flexible.

What was less flexible was Jackson's temper when someone was foolish enough to impugn Rachel's honor. The fierce Jackson was fire-flash quick to call him to account—usually by pistol duel. People feared Jackson with good cause. He participated in more than a dozen recorded duels, many of them over his wife's besmirched name. Until his dying day, he bore in his chest a bullet from Charles Dickinson. He had met Dickinson, who had taken Rachel's "sacred name" in his "polluted mouth," for a duel on what frontiersmen called "the field of honor" in 1806.[7] Dickinson, a crack shot, had fired first at Jackson. Due to an ill-fitting suit on which the vest buttons were too far to the left, Jackson was hit two inches to the *right* of his heart. Jackson took deadly aim and killed the dashing young man. "I should have hit him if he had shot me through the brain," Jackson reportedly said.[8]

Not content with smearing Jackson's darling wife, opponents charged his mother had been a common prostitute. In an overt appeal to racism, they said his father was a mulatto, a man of mixed black and white racial background.

When it seemed the campaign of 1828 could not get uglier, it did with the "Coffin Handbill," a classic example of a *negative* ad. No obscure references to topaz and ebony here, this poster was as crude as it was effective. It depicted six black coffins with the names of the Tennessee militiamen whom General Jackson had ordered shot for desertion. The purpose of the Coffin Handbill was to tarnish the reputation of the Hero of New Orleans and show him up as a cruel and barbarous tyrant. It little mattered that even the revered Washington had had to execute mutinous soldiers in the Revolution. Or that *failure* to instill military discipline had opened up the nation's capital to the torches of British invaders in the same war Jackson was fighting.

Jackson's backers were hardly innocent in this first campaign of the new mass democracy. They charged President Adams with having pimped for the tsar when he was U.S. ambassador to Russia. There was no truth whatsoever to the malicious lie that Adams had provided an *American* girl to "the Autocrat of all the Russias," but the story fit in with Americans' rising suspicions of all haughty aristocrats.

Isn't this what the critics of democracy throughout the ages had warned of? Wasn't it *inevitable* that popular government would descend into the gutter? All this talk of pimps and prostitutes was just what the friends of aristocracy found so distasteful in democracy. Here, in the first truly mass contest in American history, the standards for decency and just plain truthfulness could hardly have been lower.

The vicious mudslinging barely slowed the Jackson juggernaut. Jackson swept most of the nation. Adams's support was confined to New England, New Jersey, and the old Federalist strongholds in New York, Maryland, and Delaware. With 178 electoral votes to 83, Jackson had also triumphed in the newly important *popular* vote. Carrying more than 56 percent of the people's votes, Jackson rode in on a tide of democracy. This was the first election in history in which more than one million votes were cast. Although women generally did not vote and very few black males were enfranchised, the election of 1828 is nonetheless important because it began an ongoing process of an ever-expanding electorate.* With 1,155,340 votes cast in a population of thirteen million,[9] American democracy in 1828 offered a broader franchise than any nation in history had ever enjoyed.

Following the vindication Jackson must have felt on election day, tragedy struck at the Hermitage. Just before Christmas 1828, Rachel Jackson suffered a massive heart attack and died suddenly. The grief-stricken Andrew Jackson knew his wife was a deeply religious woman. He believed the shame and stress of seeing her name dragged through the mud had killed her. He would never forgive his political enemies for this. At times, his vengeance would be self-defeating, but his enemies had good reason to fear his wrath.

"Jackson and Reform" had been the campaign cry of the Democrats. What the reform would be had been left purposely vague. One thing it meant to Jackson was "rotation in office." He intended to remove longtime officeholders from the federal payroll. "To the victor belong the spoils," one politico cried. The general's opponents denounced this as a "spoils system," but Jackson thought it was basic good government. No one was entitled by

* Some women *did* vote in early America, though it may not have been more than 1 percent. Women who voted were those who met the *property* qualification in their own right. Thus, they would most likely have been older women and widows.

birth or family connection to hold a paid position. Too many had seen their federal jobs as lifetime appointments. In the end it was more sound and fury than substance; the president replaced only about 10–20 percent of federal appointees during his two terms. Many of these were replacements for vacancies.[10]

As Jackson approached the Federal City by steamboat and by coach, there was a growing sense of excitement. President Adams, deeply hurt by Americans' rejection, noted that the general had failed even to call upon him after he arrived in Washington. Adams was stung by this incivility. He denied having anything to do with the scurrilous attacks on the Jacksons. He resolved to depart the President's House and break the tradition of attending his successor's inauguration. This decision was taken for the same reason his father had sullenly departed the city in 1801: no one had bothered to invite him to the ceremony. Even so, both Adamses looked like sore losers to their countrymen and to history.

Wearing a black mourning suit with a "weeper" wrapped around his tall hat, General Jackson stood erect and commanding as he approached the inaugural stand on 4 March 1829.* A huge crowd had come from all parts of the country to see the "Gin'ral" take the oath. Senator Daniel Webster marveled at the sight of fifteen to twenty thousand citizens who jostled one another for a better view: "Persons have come five hundred miles to General Jackson and they really seem to think that the country is rescued from some dreadful danger!"[11] Before letting Chief Justice John Marshall administer the oath, the general gave a sweeping and stately bow to the assembled multitude. *Democracy!*

All were impressed with Jackson's natural dignity. Although his sketchy education and his irregular spelling brought him contempt from Adams's Harvard friends, Jackson was well versed in the Bible. For his countrymen, this was enough. Following the inauguration at the Capitol,

* Although Queen Victoria would be seen as a model of devotion for wearing widow's weeds for forty years after the loss of her beloved Albert, Andrew Jackson set an earlier standard for the grieving spouse. Jackson wore funeral black from the day of Rachel's death in 1828 until his own in 1845. It was doubtless a sincere expression of his grief, but it was also a rebuke to the opponents he believed had hounded his beloved Rachel into her grave.

a huge mob arrived by cart and carriage, by horse and on foot at the White House.

There had been no planning for such a throng as that which invaded the Executive Mansion that inauguration day. President Jackson was nearly crushed as the crowd pressed in on him. Rough frontiersmen stood on elegant chairs wearing muddy boots, trying to see the Hero. The president had to be rescued by a "flying wedge" of friends as butlers carried buckets of liquor punch out on to the lawn. People jumped out of windows, breaking glass and tearing at curtains. To Washington's "cliff dwellers," the somewhat stuffy social elite, the scene looked like the Paris mob invading Versailles. One Unitarian minister, horrified by the scene, preached the next Sunday on Luke 19:41: Jesus "saw the city and wept over it."[12] Nothing like it had ever been seen before, and nothing since.

Criticism of the vulgarity of the mob cannot alter one fact: no one could imagine such a multitude even *wanting* to rub elbows with the frosty Adams. It was doubtless the most incredible inauguration party in our history. And Jackson, even more than Jefferson, was determined to be "the people's president."

II. The Peggy Eaton Affair

President Jackson's idea of reform included a change in the *social* ways of the nation as well as its political practices. He immediately installed the able Martin Van Buren as secretary of state. The rest of his cabinet he filled with mediocre men whose only distinction seemed to be unbending loyalty to Jackson. This would matter little, since over time Jackson would take his advice from an informal group of advisers known as "the Kitchen Cabinet." The press gave this group of Jackson's intimates this name because they met unofficially in the Executive Mansion's kitchen.[13]

One of the undistinguished choices Jackson made was to have great significance. Former Tennessee Senator John Eaton was named to be secretary of war. He had no particular experience or aptitude for the post. This came not to matter at all. Eaton had become involved with the daughter of the tavern keeper where he roomed. The lively and pretty Peggy O'Neale was the wife of a U.S. Navy lieutenant who either died or committed suicide when his accounts came up short. Gossiping Washington socialites believed that Peggy had been the senator's mistress for years. To put an end to it all, Jackson urged his new secretary of war to speedily marry the comely widow and "make an honest woman" of her. But the hasty marriage didn't solve the problem. Cabinet wives, led by the wife of Vice President John C. Calhoun, refused to receive Mrs. Eaton. Even Jackson's own niece refused to have anything to do with the unfortunate Peggy. All of social Washington, it seemed, had come down with a case of "Eaton malaria."[14]

Whether President Jackson thought Peggy Eaton was wronged as his precious Rachel had been wronged is not clear. He did believe that the rumors were being circulated by "the minions of Mr. Clay." By attacking the Eatons, Clay was really trying to get at the president, Jackson believed.[15]

Jackson may also have been announcing the arrival of the New Men in Washington. Jackson himself had a "past" to live down. And not just the untimely marriage to Rachel, the duels, the brawls, and the executions. As a young *blood* on the frontier, the high-spirited Jackson had been a definite rowdy. Card playing, horseracing, drinking, and crude jokes had marked the earliest years of this war orphan. One elderly North Carolina woman expressed her astonishment:

> What! Jackson up for President? Jackson? Andrew Jackson? The Jackson that used to live here in Salisbury? Why, when he was here, he was such a rake that my husband would not bring him into the house. It is true, he might have taken him out to the stable to weigh horses for a race, and might drink a glass of whiskey with him there. Well, if Andrew Jackson can be President, anybody can![16]

Once he even cruelly invited the town prostitute and her wayward daughters to a society ball in Salisbury, North Carolina. But ever since the day the thirteen-year-old Andrew had warded off the saber blow of a brutal British officer with his bare hand, no one doubted his courage.

It took courage to claim that Mrs. Eaton was "as chaste as a virgin," but President Jackson's steel blue eyes flashed as he told his cabinet she would be received socially. As secretary of state, Martin Van Buren had an advantage over all his colleagues. He was a widower. He could pay a respectful call on the embattled Peggy and not have to worry about the disapproval of the society ladies. When he heard about Jackson's staunch defense of Mrs. Eaton, Henry Clay sarcastically replied: "Age cannot wither nor time stale her infinite virginity!"[17]* Surely, Jackson learned of Clay's cruel gibe. It could only have confirmed in his mind Clay's involvement in the assault on the mourned Rachel.

There was, of course, another side to all this. Peggy O'Neale Eaton bore one of the most distinctive of *Irish* names. By sticking up for the shunned Peggy, the president was making a strong statement for inclusion in the new *democratic* America. The Irish were only now beginning to flood the cities of the East. They would become one of the most loyal of the groups devoted to Andrew Jackson.

Vice President John C. Calhoun was the great loser in this affair. He had made clear his opposition to President John Quincy Adams for the first four years he served in the vice presidency. Calhoun's support for Jackson in the 1828 contest helped line up the planters of the South for the Hero. He certainly could have looked to the aged Jackson to return the favor in 1832. It was not far-fetched for Calhoun to think *he* might be the next president of the United States.

But now Jackson blamed Calhoun's wife, Floride, for stirring up the cabinet wives against Peggy Eaton. From this point on, Jackson would show a clear preference for Martin Van Buren. Not for nothing was the clever New Yorker known as "the Magician." Peggy Eaton would prove worthy of Old Hickory's friendship. Once, when she attended a dinner at the Hermitage, Mrs. Eaton saw Jackson out in the garden, stretched out over Rachel's grave. "This great old hater was also a grand old lover," she said tenderly.[18]

Jackson would also learn that Calhoun had secretly sought to have him censured for his Florida exploits when the South Carolinian had served in the Monroe cabinet. Only Adams had defended the daring general behind those

* Clay was at least as clever as he was cruel. His jest was a turn on a phrase from Shakespeare's *Antony and Cleopatra*: "Age cannot wither her, nor custom stale/Her infinite *variety*" (Act II, Scene 2).

closed doors. While this belated truth did not bring Jackson to look more kindly on his defeated rival, it did sour his relations with his vice president.

III. John C. Calhoun: The Cast-Iron Man

South Carolina's champion had not always been a sectional man. John Caldwell Calhoun had been born in the upcountry region of the Palmetto State. In 1782, that inland area was still considered the western frontier. His hometown of Abbeville had been held against attack both by the marauding British *and* by the Cherokee.[19] Tories had murdered his uncle and namesake, John Caldwell, in the remorseless civil war that characterized the American Revolution in the Carolinas.[20] Young John C. Calhoun had chosen, surprisingly, to attend Yale University in New Haven, Connecticut. It was an unusual choice for a Southerner. Yale's president, the Reverend Timothy Dwight, was a High Federalist and an outspoken Christian. Neither his politics nor his religion appealed to the lanky young Carolinian. Calhoun stayed away from Dwight's sermons and avoided his anti-Jefferson polemics.

Young John Calhoun actually visited President Jefferson at Monticello during his student days. And Calhoun's supporters would ever after view that midnight meeting as a symbolic "passing of the torch."[21]* At six feet two inches, rangy, with a shock of dark hair and dark, penetrating eyes, Calhoun had no trouble attracting attention at Yale. Because he felt the views of his Connecticut neighbors uncongenial, Calhoun burrowed ever deeper into his books. He became an excellent student, soon selected for academic honors and membership in Phi Beta Kappa.[22]

Although Calhoun did not share Reverend Dwight's views, he could not avoid the university president's classes altogether. He sharpened his own opinions *in opposition* to the clergyman's views. One view the High Federalism of Timothy Dwight openly avowed was duly impressed on *all* his students. Rather than continue to live under the rule of the hated Jeffersonians, Dwight advocated *secession* of the Northern states.[23] Calhoun

---

* Americans of our day are familiar with this phenomenon. Who has not seen the photograph of the teenage Bill Clinton shaking hands with President John F. Kennedy in 1962?

graduated with honors from Yale and went to study law under the famous Tapping Reeve, in Litchfield, Connecticut. Here, he would find no greater political affinities—Judge Reeve would actually be indicted for libeling President Jefferson.[24]

Back in South Carolina, young Calhoun was both drawn to and repelled by his state's great seaport, Charleston. He compared it with the dour, serious ways of the upcountry: "It was Cavalier from the start; we were Puritan."* Charleston's merchant princes welcomed to their beautiful city French Huguenots, Irish Catholics, German Lutherans, and Sephardic Jews, creating a lively, cultured ambience. George Washington considered the comely women of Charleston the high point of his entire southern tour of 1791. Charlestonians were confident, capable, and proud. "Here, sir, the Ashley and Cooper Rivers join to form the Atlantic Ocean," they would tell visitors. It was said with a merry twinkle in their eyes.

Calhoun was put off by the city's worldly ways. At Yale he had been accused of Sabbath-breaking because he took long walks instead of attending church, but here in Charleston Sunday was given over to social visits and horse racing.[25] He thought the city corrupt and "inattentive to every call of religion."[26]

George Washington was not the only Southerner, however, to be captivated by Charleston's charms. John C. Calhoun soon courted and married the lovely Floride Calhoun. She was from the Charleston branch of his extended family. They would remain devoted to one another throughout their lives. And she would bring him wealth and social prominence.

Very soon, Calhoun entered Congress. He quickly joined the "War Hawks" in the House of Representatives who were banging the war drums, ready to fight England in 1812. Calhoun suddenly rose to the top rank and was called "the young Hercules" of the prowar party.[27]

Calhoun in Congress was respected more than he was loved. Kentucky's Henry Clay, also an avid War Hawk, described him thus: "[T]all, careworn, with furrowed brow, haggard and intensely gazing, looking as if

* The reference was to the English civil war of two centuries earlier. There, royalist Cavaliers sported long hair, feathered hats, elegant manners, and a fondness for high living. The serious, sober, pious Puritans fought for Parliament against the king in defense of their rights.

he were dissecting the last abstraction which sprung from the metaphysician's brain, and muttering to himself, in half-uttered tones, 'This is indeed a real crisis.'"[28]

Women in Washington followed politics avidly. They flocked to the House and Senate galleries to watch the members contend on the floor below. Harriet Martineau was an acute Englishwoman who reported on political economy for the *Washington Globe*. She offered this observation on the great figures of the Senate in her time:

> Mr. Clay, sitting upright on the sofa, with his snuffbox ever in his hand, would discourse for many an hour in his even, soft, deliberate tone, on any one of the great subjects of American policy which we might happen to start, always amazing us with the moderation of estimate and speech which so impetuous a nature has been able to attain. Mr. Webster, leaning back at his ease, telling stories, cracking jokes, shaking the sofa with burst after burst of laughter, or smoothly discoursing to the perfect felicity of the logical part of one's constitution, would illuminate an evening now and then.[29]

Miss Martineau perhaps saved her most penetrating portrait for South Carolina's Calhoun.

> Mr. Calhoun, the cast-iron man, who looks as if he had never been born and never could be extinguished, would come in sometimes to keep our understanding upon a painful stretch for a short while, and leave us to take to pieces his close, rapid, theoretical, illustrated talk, and see what we could make of it.[30]

Theoretical?

Yes, Varina Howell Davis, wife of Mississippi's Jefferson Davis, described Calhoun as "a mental and moral abstraction."[31] Women appreciated Calhoun's brilliance and his magnetism, but they noted his humorlessness. Calhoun could never write a love poem, they said of him, because he always began with "*Whereas. . . .*"[32]

Calhoun was twice Andrew Jackson's running mate, in 1824 and 1828. When the House chose Adams in 1824, the Senate selected Calhoun as vice president.* When the Hero was finally elected president in 1828, Calhoun succeeded in winning his second term in the position. By this time, however, Calhoun's early infatuation with Thomas Jefferson's natural rights philosophy had undergone a profound change. Boldly, bluntly, he *denied* Jefferson's Declaration of Independence. "Taking the proposition literally," Calhoun stated, "there is not a word of truth in it. It begins with 'all men are born,' which is utterly untrue. Men are not born. Infants are born. They grow to be men. . . . They are not born free. While infants, they are incapable of freedom. . . ."[33] Actually, Jefferson had said nothing about *born*. He said, of course, all men are *created*. And Calhoun's unimaginative logic-chopping would have gotten him short shrift at the Second Continental Congress.

The change in Calhoun's political stance came about as he recognized the need to defend slavery—the "peculiar institution." Unlike Jefferson, Washington, Franklin, and virtually every one of the Founders, Calhoun did not view slavery as a wrong. It guaranteed equality for whites and was a "positive good" for blacks, he argued.[34]

Calhoun thought he had no choice. He saw the Northern states expanding in population and wealth. He saw the immigrants flooding into Northern cities. He feared a future in which more and more *free* states would be admitted to the Union until such time as they comprised *three-fourths* of all the states. Then, they would simply pass a Constitutional amendment to emancipate the slaves. That was why he insisted that the territories remain open to slavery. South Carolina's slaves outnumbered her white citizens. Once free, black South Carolinians would first be made citizens, then voters, and finally masters. This was the fear that stalked John C. Calhoun's days and haunted his dreams.

Never conventionally religious, Calhoun nonetheless had a keen interest in theology. And part of this interest led him to biblical prophecy. One of the passages that troubled John C. Calhoun's sleep was from the eleventh

* This provision of the Constitution is still in force. If the House of Representatives had chosen George W. Bush as president in 2000, the Senate would have chosen Dick Cheney as vice president.

chapter of the book of Daniel: "So the king of the north shall come, and cast up a mount, and take the most fenced cities: and the arms of the south shall not withstand, neither his chosen people, neither shall there be any strength to withstand."[35] That was why he decided to support *nullification* of the Tariff of 1828. Just as abolition threatened the South's source of cheap labor, so the tariff was a tax on the *profit* from that cheap labor.[36]

IV. "Our Federal Union: It *Must* Be Preserved!"

South Carolina was in turmoil over what it called the Tariff of Abominations in 1828. The Constitution did not permit the federal government to tax exports. South Carolinians and other planter aristocrats would never have signed the document if it had. But tariffs—taxes on *imports*—could prove onerous for an agriculture-based economy. They had to import many of their machines and nearly all their luxuries.

As planters and slaveholders, they expected Jackson to side with them against the Tariff of Abominations in 1828 that Congress had approved that year. Vice President Calhoun had not-so-anonymously penned his famous Exposition and Protest of 1828. In that document, Calhoun went *beyond* the positions staked out by Madison and Jefferson in their Virginia and Kentucky Resolutions of 1798. Calhoun argued that when a state's rights were violated by the federal government, the state had a right to *nullify* the offending federal law and prevent its enforcement within the borders of the state. If that failed, Calhoun clearly implied, the state had a right to leave the Union. Thus, *secession,* the logical end result of *nullification,* began seriously to be argued by slaveholders. The South was, to be sure, not the only section that had argued for secession. High Federalists had toyed with it in New England during the War of 1812. Westerners had from time to time threatened it. But this was the first time *disunion* was incorporated into a serious political philosophy.

Calhoun's ideas were publicly defended by South Carolina's senior U.S. senator, Robert Y. Hayne. In January 1830, Hayne spoke at length on his "compact theory" of the Union. Under this theory, the Union was a league, or compact, of the states. They formed it; if it ever threatens their rights, they can dissolve it. Hayne's conclusions were carefully and closely reasoned and would have been persuasive—if the Union were a mere league or compact.

Massachusetts Senator Daniel Webster arose to dispute Hayne's interpretation of the Constitution. Vice President Calhoun presided over the Senate, adding to the drama of the clash. The "Godlike Daniel"—as his admirers called him—proceeded to shred the case made by Hayne. "I go for the Union as it is," he cried, flinging his words as a challenge to Calhoun. "It is, Sir, the people's Constitution, the people's government, made for the people, made by the people, and answerable to the people."[37]

The Senate galleries were packed to hear Webster's reply to Hayne. Webster thrilled his listeners with his emotional but reasoned defense of the Union. The conclusion of his two-day, six-hour address was so stirring that generations of American schoolchildren learned it by heart:

> I have not allowed myself, sir, to look beyond the Union, to see what might be hidden in the dark recess behind. I have not coolly weighed the chances of preserving liberty when the bonds that unite us together shall be broken asunder. I have not accustomed myself to hang over the precipice of disunion, to see whether, with my short sight, I can fathom the depth of the abyss below; *nor could I regard him as a safe counselor in the affairs in this government whose thoughts should be mainly bent on considering, not how the Union may be best preserved but how tolerable might be the condition of the people when it should be broken up and destroyed.* While the Union lasts, we have high, exciting, gratifying prospects spread out before us, for us and our children. Beyond that I seek not to penetrate the veil.
>
> God grant that in my day, at least, that curtain may not rise! God grant that on my vision never may be opened what lies behind! When my eyes shall be turned to behold for the last time the sun in heaven, may I not see him shining on the broken and dishonored fragments of a once glorious Union; on states dissevered, discordant, belligerent; on a land rent with civil feuds, or drenched, it may be, in fraternal blood! Let their last feeble and lingering glance rather behold the gorgeous

> ensign of the republic, now known and honored throughout the earth, still full high advanced, its arms and trophies streaming in their original luster, not a stripe erased or polluted, nor a single star obscured, bearing for its motto, no such miserable interrogatory as "What is all this worth?" nor those other words of delusion and folly, "Liberty first and Union afterwards"; but everywhere, spread all over in characters of living light, blazing on all its ample folds, as they float over the sea and over the land, and in every wind under the whole heavens, that other sentiment, dear to every true American heart—Liberty and Union, now and forever, one and inseparable!

Imagine the excitement of the people in the gallery as they watched Calhoun's expressive face when Webster hurled those stinging words—not a "safe counselor"—directly at him. Nicholas Trist was one of those who witnessed this drama. Grandson-in-law of Thomas Jefferson and an advisor to President Jackson, Trist wrote to James Madison that Webster's devastating reply to Hayne was like "the mammoth deliberately treading the canebrake."[38]

Attention soon focused on the Jefferson Day banquet—13 April 1830—at Washington's Indian Queen Hotel. Toasts and speeches by the leading Democrats praised the Sage of Monticello's commitment to states' rights. They implied he would favor nullification. Out of courtesy, President Jackson was asked to deliver a toast. No "Ebony and Topaz" on this occasion, Jackson looked directly at John C. Calhoun and vowed: "Our federal Union. It *must* be preserved!"

There was stunned silence. Little Van Buren stood on a chair to see the clash of wills. Pale and shaken, Calhoun raised his glass, even spilling some of his wine. Then he said: "The Union, next to our liberty, the most dear."[39]

President Jackson regarded himself as a sincere Jeffersonian. He believed in states' rights. But he was firmly opposed to nullification. Jackson could rely on the great prestige of James Madison, the Father of the Constitution and Jefferson's intimate friend of half a century. Former President Madison spoke out from his retirement home, Montpelier.

The *people,* not the states, had created the Union, Madison argued. The people had created the Union *and* the states. Still vigorous in his eightieth year, Madison in October 1830 denounced Calhoun's doctrine of nullification. The result of nullification must be "a final rupture and dissolution of the Union." Such an event "must be shuddered at by every friend to his country, to liberty, to the happiness of man," Madison wrote.[40]

Madison enjoyed enormous prestige as the last survivor of the Constitutional Convention and as Jefferson's political lieutenant, successor, and heir. He utterly rejected the "nullies'" (Jackson's name for them) propositions. If they did not yield to reason, he wrote, "the explanation will lie between an impenetrable stupidity and an incurable prejudice."[41]

As the crisis over nullification intensified, Calhoun cast his lot with South Carolina. When Jackson chose Van Buren as his running mate and was reelected in 1832, Calhoun knew he would never be president. He even resigned as vice president. South Carolina immediately sent him to represent her in the Senate (a seat he held until his death in 1850). Congress passed a new Tariff of 1832 designed to mollify South Carolina by removing some but not all of the offending portions of the Tariff of Abominations.

Urged on by Calhoun, South Carolina convened a Nullification Convention. South Carolina planters believed the tariff was responsible for their economic depression. They even spoke of it as a "forty bale" tariff. They charged the tariff with costing them forty of every one hundred bales of cotton they produced.[42] On 24 November 1832, this convention passed an Ordinance of Nullification. This ordinance said the Tariff of 1832 was "null and void" and would not be obeyed in South Carolina after 1 February 1833. Even more ominously, the ordinance declared that if Jackson attempted to use force, the state would secede from the Union.[43] Some "nullies" even struck medals bearing the inscription: "John C. Calhoun, First President of the Southern Confederacy."[44]

Jackson responded quickly with his own Proclamation to the People of South Carolina on 10 December 1832. The Union, he said, was not the creature of the states. The Union was older than the states, he said: "Perpetuity is stamped upon the Constitution by blood. . . ."[45]* "Those who told you," he

* On this point, even Ronald Reagan got it wrong. He told the crowds at his First Inaugural: "All of us need to be reminded that the Federal Government did not create the States; the States created the Federal Government."

wrote to the people of his native state, "that you might peacefully prevent . . . execution [of the laws] deceived you. . . . Their object is disunion. But be not deceived by names. Disunion by armed force is treason. Are you really ready to incur its guilt?"[46]

Jackson did not rule out compromise. He called for a *lowering* of the tariff to more acceptable levels. And he sought support from Unionists within South Carolina and other Southern states. He was not disappointed. Virginia, Georgia, and Alabama gave him support.[47] Leading South Carolina *opponents* of nullification took heart. "What have we to fear, we are right and God and Old Hickory are with us," they exulted.[48]

South Carolina had reason to fear. In many low country districts, slaves outnumbered freemen three and four to one.[49] The Denmark Vesey plan for a slave rebellion had been nipped in the bud in 1822, but white Carolinians read with horror the story of Nat Turner's 1831 rebellion in Virginia. Turner was a slave, a spellbinding preacher who believed he had a God-given mission to raise a band of slaves to slaughter remote farm families. He killed nearly a hundred whites before the militia subdued him and his small force. The retribution that was carried out chilled everyone's blood. South Carolinians had also rushed to beat Jefferson's 1808 deadline for cutting off the African slave trade. They hastily imported forty thousand slaves from the "Gold Coast" of Africa. Many of these, still speaking the *Gullah* dialect the planters could not understand, added to the South Carolinians' fears of being surrounded on their farms.[50]

With a 1 January 1831 editorial, a new paper appeared in America that would herald the birth of a powerful movement. Editor William Lloyd Garrison cast away the tact and moderation of the past. Inaugurating his journal, the *Liberator,* Garrison stated, "I do not wish to think, or speak, or write, with moderation. . . . I am in earnest—I will not equivocate—*I will not excuse—I will not retreat a single inch*—and *I WILL BE HEARD*." To Southerners, Garrison and his little newspaper seemed as reckless as a man smoking in a powder magazine. From the safe distance of Massachusetts, Garrison could demand immediate *abolition* of slavery. The planters of South Carolina felt they would be not only economically ruined, but perhaps even exterminated were they to relax their grip on their slaves. But Garrison was heard.

South Carolinians led the entire South in these days in taking care not to refer to slavery directly. They talked *around* the subject, using such terms as "our peculiar institution" and "our domestic policy." Southern slaveholders did not want Congress even to debate slavery. They feared that any open discussion of the topic would provide the "spark" that would ignite a full-scale revolt. They suppressed abolitionist newspapers as "incendiary." Even one of their favorite holidays—the Fourth of July—came to be a time of unbearable tension as planters feared their slaves would hear the inspiring words of Thomas Jefferson's Declaration of Independence and realize that their Creator intended that they, too, should be free.[51]

If the nullies carried out their plans, the Hero let it be known he would lead ten thousand volunteers into South Carolina to "crush and hang" all traitors.[52] He vowed to hold Fort Sumter, in Charleston harbor, "to the last extremity."[53]* He rammed a Force Bill through Congress, a measure that authorized him to coerce South Carolina into compliance with law.

Although the immediate cause of the controversy was the tariff, everyone knew that at the bottom of it all lay slavery. Calhoun acknowledged this. "I consider the Tariff but the occasion rather than the real cause of the present unhappy state of things. . . ." The states must be allowed to guard their "domestick institutions" or be forced to rebel, he said.[54]

Into this explosive mix stepped Kentucky Senator Henry Clay. Although recently defeated by Jackson for the presidency, Clay labored mightily to put together the Compromise Tariff of 1833. The bill met many of the demands of the nullifiers. This bill passed Congress and went to the president's desk on the same day that the Force Bill arrived there. This combination of firmness and flexibility proved successful.[55] Senator Calhoun's mind doubtless was concentrated by Jackson's threat to hang him "as high as Haman."** Calhoun accepted the Compromise Tariff and the crisis eased.

President Jackson had been born in South Carolina. He was himself a planter, a slaveholder. He had sympathy for the South Carolina

* Here, this Democratic president would set the bar for the first Republican president. Could Lincoln in 1861 surrender what Jackson had vowed never to give up?

** "So they hanged Haman on the gallows that he had prepared for Mordecai. Then the king's wrath subsided" (Esther 7:10).

planters. But on disunion, he would not budge. He was not called Old Hickory for nothing.

"Nullification is dead," Jackson pronounced, but he knew the long-term clash was not resolved. "The next pretext will be the Negro or slavery question," he accurately predicted.[56] Henry Clay here earned the title "the Great Compromiser." His unselfish and timely action helped save the Union. But it was the fearless Old Hickory who had "shoot" in his eyes. Even on his deathbed in 1845, Jackson admitted that he regretted only two things: that none of his race horses had ever beaten the famed Haynie's Maria—and that he had *not* hanged John C. Calhoun.[57]

V. The Tragedy of Indian Removal

During the same years that the nullification crisis was coming to a head, President Jackson had to contend with the question of Indian removal. "Sharp Knife" Jackson had gained much of his reputation and his immense popularity as an Indian fighter. Americans on the frontier looked to him for protection from the depredations of warlike tribes.

The greatest of the Indian warriors, Tecumseh, had planned a war of extermination against the settlers. Tecumseh rallied his powerful confederation with strong words. "Let the white race perish!" he said to his people. "They seize your land; they corrupt your women; they trample on the bones of your dead! Back—aye, back to the great water whose accursed waves brought them to our shores! Burn their dwellings—destroy their stock—slay their wives and children, that the very breed may perish! War now! War always! War on the living! War on the dead!"[58]

Congress had resolved to deal with the problem of Indians by *removing* them west of the Mississippi River. Ideally, they were to receive money and western lands to compensate them for their losses in the East. This policy was begun under President Monroe but had slowed during the administration of the humane John Quincy Adams.[59] When Jackson became president, Americans looked to him to speed up the removal of the Indians. Georgia, Alabama, and Mississippi were particularly impatient. They asserted that *state* laws would apply to all persons living within their borders.[60] This was a fundamental Jeffersonian principle, they argued.

But this abstract principle would have ominous consequences for the Indian tribes. It meant they would be at the mercy of hostile state legislatures—in which they would have no genuine representation. More outrageous, it meant they would not be able to claim the protection of treaties they had duly signed with the *federal* government.

Facing the mounting danger of nullification in South Carolina, Jackson could not afford to antagonize other Deep South states over the Indian question. Besides, Jackson *agreed* with the people of Georgia, Alabama, and Mississippi. His commitment to ending the bloody raids on the frontier was a major factor in his election as president. Jackson did not lose a single state in which Indian warfare was still a public concern.

Georgia tried to prevent whites from working with the Indians. Georgia's law might have been a wise one if it prevented whites from plying the Indians with liquor and defrauding them of their lands. But the state's law applied even to Christian missionaries. Vermonter Rev. Samuel Worcester brought suit in federal court. He wanted to continue his work among the Cherokee. Chief Justice John Marshall spoke for the majority of the U.S. Supreme Court when he ruled in the missionary's favor in the case of *Worcester v. Georgia* (1832): "The Cherokee nation, then, is a distinct community occupying its own territory in which the laws of Georgia can have no force. The whole intercourse between the United States and this nation, is, by our constitution and laws, vested in the government of the United States."*

Marshall thus found that Georgia's action was *unconstitutional.* Old Hickory is supposed to have responded: "John Marshall has made his decision. Now let him enforce it."[61] It sounds so much like Jackson. But it is more likely Jackson adopted a wait-and-see attitude toward the Court's ruling.[62] He disagreed that tribes were independent nations. He sincerely believed that unscrupulous chieftains had exploited their own people.[63] Although he never sought to extend democracy to the Indian tribes, he was

* The issue remains with us. In 2003, Arnold Schwarzenegger campaigned for governor of California, pledging to make casinos located on Indian tribal lands pay *state* taxes.

unwilling to consider them as privileged corporations exempt from the laws of the states.

In the spring of 1832, the Illinois frontier erupted in the Black Hawk War. Chief Black Hawk had been a British ally during the War of 1812. His Sac and Fox tribe had been resettled west of the Mississippi, but they were starving. They returned to their old homes when hostile Sioux forced them back into Illinois. The state's governor called out the militia—including company commander Abraham Lincoln. Black Hawk's vastly outnumbered Sac and Fox tribe chased Major Stillman's half-drunk volunteers twenty-five miles in what became known as "Stillman's Run."[64] Encouraged by this unexpected win, Black Hawk terrorized the frontier, burning farms and taking scalps. When a large force of 1,300 troops finally overtook Black Hawk's small force in August, the Indians tried to surrender. No quarter was given as the militiamen proceeded to massacre the remnant of the Sac and Fox tribe, including women and children. Black Hawk escaped to Wisconsin, where the Winnebagos turned him over to the army.[65] Here, at least, he received chivalrous treatment from West Pointer Jefferson Davis.[66] The courtly Davis would permit no humiliation of his Indian captive and, in fact, treated him with typical Southern courtesy.

President Jackson met with Black Hawk. He sternly told the chief: "You behaved very badly in raising the tomahawk against the white people, and killing men, women and children upon the frontier. . . ." Jackson sent Black Hawk on a tour of eastern cities. This was done not so much to humiliate the captive foe as to impress him with the overwhelming power of America. "You will see that our young men are as numerous as the leaves in the woods," Jackson told him.[67] While visiting the population centers of the East, Black Hawk was introduced at hotel dinners. Audiences applauded as the defeated warrior politely nodded and smiled.[68]

No case of Indian removal was more tragic than the fate that befell the Cherokee nation. The great Indian leader, Sequoia, developed a written language for the Cherokee. His people read the weekly *Cherokee Phoenix* in their own language, printed Bibles and other books, accepted Christian missionaries, organized a legislature, and settled into stable farming communities. None of this high civilization saved them from the depredations of their neighbors, however. When gold was discovered on Cherokee lands, President Jackson *removed* the federal troops that John Quincy Adams had sent into Georgia to protect them.[69] More than one-quarter of the Cherokee died on the long, heartbreaking "Trail of Tears" that they were forced to take to the Indian Territory, modern-day Oklahoma. Although the worst of the outrages against the Cherokee occurred in 1838, under the administration of President Martin Van Buren, Jackson ruthlessly pursued the removal policy and therefore bears the responsibility for it.[70] In this instance, too, Jackson had shoot in his eye, and the result is an indelible stain on America's reputation.

In Andrew Jackson's mind, his policy was the only humane one that could be pursued. From vast experience, he believed that the Indians could not survive if they remained within the eastern states. Hundreds of thousands of immigrants flooded into America in the 1830s, creating enormous pressure for more land. Immigrants and native-born citizens voted. Indians did not. Jacksonian democracy had proclaimed that the people shall rule. The American people, with few exceptions, not only supported but *demanded* Indian removal.[71]

Some of Jackson's Senate opponents, notably Kentucky's Henry Clay and New Jersey's Theodore Frelinghuysen, spoke out eloquently against Indian removal. Frelinghuysen was a devoutly religious man. His ancestor had founded the Dutch Reformed Church in America. Clay's opposition was perhaps even more remarkable since his Kentucky constituents had no sympathy for the Indians.[72]

Maverick Davy Crockett's lonely stand against Jackson's policy of removal finished his political career. The colorful Crockett, an Indian fighter and frontiersman, was defeated for reelection to Congress. He had opposed Indian removal on principle and on that principle his neighbors voted him out. "I'm going to Texas," he bluntly told his Tennessee constituents, "and you can go to hell."

Jackson is often portrayed as a semiliterate backwoodsman. That is certainly how his opponents saw him. And his Indian policy is cited as an example of ignorance and bigotry. Yet Jackson had the support of millions of Americans who agreed with his policy. The Indians were regarded

Jackson as president. *"Our Federal Union—It Must Be Preserved" was Jackson's famous toast. He threw it down as a challenge to the pale and trembling Vice President Calhoun at a Jefferson Day dinner in 1830. On nullification as on so much else, Jackson was unbending. Under Jackson, more Americans voted than any other people on earth. Alexis de Tocqueville came from France to analyze this new democracy in America. Jackson brandished the veto as a powerful new weapon in his battles with courts and Congress. He smashed the Second Bank of the United States and drove the Indians beyond the Mississippi. In doing so, he enjoyed overwhelming popular support in his day—and merited strong criticism from historians ever since.*

Henry Clay, U.S. senator. *Great Harry of the West, Clay began his career as a War Hawk and remained a staunch nationalist throughout his forty years in office. His patriotism, his charm, his well-reasoned arguments, and his constant appeals for peace among the sections earned him the admiration of ladies, the loyalty of men, and the title "The Great Compromiser." Three times a candidate, Clay said he would "rather be right than be president," and he was. He was first among the Great Triumvirate and towered above many lesser men who actually became chief executive in his time.*

President James Monroe. *As a young Virginia volunteer, he crossed the Delaware with George Washington and was wounded in battle. His diplomatic career was less than stellar, but his steadfast loyalty to Jefferson assured his ultimate success. Last of the Virginia Dynasty of Presidents, he presided, somewhat surprisingly, over an Era of Good Feeling. He gave his name to a message drafted by John Quincy Adams. It would become the cornerstone of U.S. foreign policy as the Monroe Doctrine.*

John Quincy Adams. *This son of a president should have been a success in politics. But he knew he was cold, remote, and unloved by the people. His single term as president was eclipsed by the inevitability of Jackson's triumph. He made a second career as a member of the House of Representatives, where his defense of free speech and the right of petition against "the slave power" earned him the sobriquet Old Man Eloquent.*

John C. Calhoun, U.S. senator. *South Carolina's Calhoun began his career as a Jeffersonian and a nationalist. A "War Hawk," he urged hostilities with Britain in 1812. He clashed with President Jackson over the doctrine of nullification in 1830—while he was serving as Old Hickory's vice president. Thereafter, Calhoun became "the Cast Iron Man." He was the acknowledged leader of pro-slavery forces in the U.S. Senate and the most important theorist of secession.*

Daniel Webster, U.S. senator. *The "God-like Daniel" to his many Northern admirers, Webster's Reply to Hayne in 1830 was memorized by schoolchildren in this country for more than a century: "Liberty and Union—now and forever, one and inseparable!" Webster's intellectual and oratorical fireworks provided a powerful rejoinder to the South's Calhoun. He broke the hearts of many of his supporters, however, when he joined with Calhoun and Clay in the Compromise of 1850.*

as *terrorists*—pure and simple. Terrorists were those who killed innocent men, women, and children. Jefferson was very pro-Indian, defending them to European philosophers who called them degenerate. President Jefferson gave Lewis and Clark orders to pursue a humane policy toward the Indians that they labored dutifully to carry out. Yet even the enlightened Jefferson in the Declaration of Independence as much as calls the Indians terrorists: "[The King] has excited domestic insurrections amongst us, and has endeavoured to bring on the inhabitants of our frontiers, the merciless Indian Savages, whose known rule of warfare is an undistinguished destruction of all ages, sexes and conditions."

The problem was that too many Americans made no distinctions; none between the ferocity of a Tecumseh and a peaceful Cherokee leader like Sequoia. Some Indians, certainly, behaved like terrorists. But Jackson's cruel policy made no allowances for the highly civilized tribes. And even the warlike Tecumseh was honored when he spared American prisoners taken in Canada during the War of 1812.

America in 1831 and 1832 was a field of dreams for a young French nobleman. Alexis de Tocqueville toured the United States, ostensibly to report on prison conditions. His *Democracy in America,* published in 1835 when he was just thirty, is an enduring classic of what he called "political science." Tocqueville believed in the inevitability of democracy's spreading throughout Europe, and he saw America as the world's leading democratic society. Tocqueville wrote about *everything* he observed, and he observed much. He wrote, for example, of the effect of the advance of settlement on the Indian tribes: "The approach of the whites was often felt at two hundred leagues from the frontier.* Thus their influence is exerted on tribes whose names they hardly know, and who suffer the evils of usurpation long before recognizing its authors."[73]

Tocqueville happened to see one episode of Indian removal that was less *impersonal,* less benign than the inexorable process he described above. It is worth quoting in full:

* A *league* as a traditional measure of distance was three miles long. Thus, the impact of settlement was felt by Indians as much as *six hundred miles* away.

> At the end of the year 1831, I found myself on the left bank of the Mississippi, at a place named Memphis by the Europeans. While I was at this place, a numerous troop of Choctaws came. . . . [T]he savages were leaving their country and sought to cross to the right bank of the Mississippi, where they flattered themselves they would find the refuge that the American government promised them. It was then in the heart of winter, and the cold ravaged that year with an unaccustomed violence; snow had hardened on the ground, and the river carried enormous pieces of ice. The Indians brought along their families with them; they dragged behind them the wounded, the ill, infants who had just been born, and the old who were going to die. They had neither tents nor carts, but only some provisions and arms. I saw them embark to cross the great river, and this solemn spectacle will never leave my memory. One heard neither tears nor complaints among this assembled crowd; they were silent. Their misfortunes were old, and they felt them to be irreparable. All the Indians had already entered the vessels that were to carry them; their dogs still remained on the shore; when the animals finally saw that they were going away forever, together they let out frightful howls, and dashing at once into the icy waters of the Mississippi, they followed their masters swimming.[74]

VI. Jackson's War on the Bank

Andrew Jackson had a lifelong hostility to what he regarded as aristocratic privilege. He believed passionately in *democracy* as he understood it. Therefore, when Senator Henry Clay in 1832 pushed through Congress a bill to recharter the Second Bank of the United States, the stage was set for a great contest. Jackson shared the prejudice of most frontiersmen against large and powerful central banks. Jackson hated the Bank of the United States for issuing what he regarded as unreliable paper currency—"rag money."* When the bill arrived at his desk, Jackson

* It's hard to know what Old Hickory would think of the fact that his stern image is one of the most familiar to Americans 170 years after his term. His face adorns the *paper* $20 bill, the one most often issued by automatic teller machines.

vigorously vetoed the recharter. He called the bank a "Monster." Jackson was particularly angered that the bank would give profit and privilege to those already wealthy. Some of those who benefited from its influential role were foreigners. This was entirely normal in banking, even necessary. But it struck Jackson as an outrage that American citizens' honest labors would serve to enrich aliens.

Senator Henry Clay was a dominant figure in the U.S. Senate. Nothing required the Senate to act on the Bank of the United States in 1832. The national charter of the bank ran until 1836. But Clay was running against Jackson for president, and he believed recharter would be a good issue for him to use against Jackson. Clay was confident of success. If Jackson were to veto the recharter, Clay said with a winning smile, "I will veto him!"[75]

All the powerful, moneyed men supported the bank. More than that, all the knowledgeable members of the financial elite understood and appreciated the need for a central bank. Because of this, even the Jeffersonians at the height of their power had not quite dared to kill the bank, the centerpiece of Hamilton's financial plan.

President Jackson's veto message was blunt. He looked to Maryland's Roger B. Taney and to members of his informal Kitchen Cabinet for their help in drafting a powerful and popular document:

> It is to be regretted that the rich and powerful too often bend the acts of government to their selfish purposes. Distinctions in society will always exist under every just government. Equality of talents, of education, or of wealth can not be produced by human institutions. In the full enjoyment of the gifts of Heaven and the fruits of superior industry, economy, and virtue, every man is equally entitled to protection by law; but when the laws undertake to add to these natural and just advantages artificial distinctions, to grant titles, gratuities, and exclusive privileges, to make the rich richer and the potent more powerful, the humble members of society—the farmers, mechanics, and laborers—who have neither the time nor the means of securing like favors to themselves, have a right to complain of the injustice of their Government.[76]

Nicholas Biddle, president of the bank, agreed with Clay. Nicknamed "Tsar Nicholas" for his highborn manner, Biddle thought the veto message would backfire on the president. Biddle even ordered thirty thousand copies of Jackson's veto message printed—to be distributed as a campaign document for Henry Clay![77] Biddle scorned Andrew Jackson: "This worthy President thinks that because he has scalped Indians and imprisoned judges he is to have his own way with the Bank. He is mistaken."[78] Biddle waded dangerously into the strong currents of presidential politics when he compared Jackson's veto message to "the fury of a caged panther biting at the bars of his cage."[79] Biddle totally identified himself with the Bank of the United States and the bank with himself. He even had his country home on the banks of the Delaware River, which he grandly named *Andalusia*, built as an exact replica of the Greek Revival architecture of the bank building in downtown Philadelphia![80]

Jackson was indeed plowing new ground. He boldly stated that the president had a duty, just as the Congress did, to consider questions of constitutionality of legislation. He was completely unwilling to *surrender* that power to the Supreme Court alone. The fact that Chief Justice Marshall and the Supreme Court majority had approved the bank in the famous case of *McCulloch v. Maryland* (1819) did not settle the issue as far as Jackson was concerned. Each branch was separate and independent, he believed.

Jackson went further. He would cast his vetoes not only on constitutional grounds, but whenever he thought good public policy required it. This was nearly a revolutionary doctrine. It meant that the president was vitally involved in all legislation. He could prevent *any* measure from becoming law if he had one-third plus one member of either House of Congress to support him. Little wonder his opponents called him King Andrew I and spoke of King Veto.

In the days before public opinion polling, it is perhaps not so surprising that candidate Henry Clay and the Whigs could have so badly miscalculated.*

* Jackson's opponents called themselves Whigs. It was a name taken from English politics of the previous century. Originally a term of abuse, "Whig" was taken up proudly by those who opposed the despotism and corruption of King George III. American Patriots in the Revolution, too, called themselves Whigs.

Political men tend to talk to their friends. Those who favored the policies of the bank thought Jackson had badly erred. But the voters thought differently. Jackson and Van Buren won a landslide victory, carrying 219 electoral votes to Clay's 49. In the popular vote, Jackson won an overwhelming 56 percent. The "farmers, mechanics, and laborers" who constituted the vast majority of the new American electorate saw Jackson as their friend, their unyielding champion. In the battle between "hickory and gold," hickory won.

Jackson succeeded in destroying the Bank of the United States. When his secretary of the Treasury refused to withdraw public funds from the bank, Jackson replaced him. His new secretary likewise refused, and Jackson again wielded the axe. Finally, with Roger B. Taney at Treasury, he had a willing partner. Jackson placed public funds instead in *state* banks. Jackson forced the Democratic Party to support him, even when the economy began to slide into recession. "The golden calf may be worshipped by others but as for myself, I serve the Lord," he said.[81]

Opponents soon labeled these institutions "pet banks." When they began to engage in unchecked land speculation, Jackson responded by issuing his Specie Circular in 1836. This document said that public lands could not be bought with unsecured paper currency, but that purchasers must pay *in gold*. This policy would soon have a disastrous effect on the economy. By the time that the Panic of 1837 struck, however, Jackson had returned to his beloved Hermitage. The roof fell in on his chosen successor, Martin Van Buren. And this time, "the Magician" had run out of tricks.

VII. "Old Man Eloquent"

When F. Scott Fitzgerald wrote that there are "no second acts" in America, he spoke in ignorance of the career of John Quincy Adams. Hurt and saddened by Americans' rejection of him as their president, Adams returned to Massachusetts in 1829. Personal tragedy haunted the famous family. Two of his brothers and two of his sons died of alcoholism. He might all too easily have slipped into despondency after his single presidential term. His four unhappy years had been served in anticipation of the inevitable Jackson tidal wave.

The times, however, gave John Quincy Adams a place to stand and a cause to defend. Throughout his long career, Adams had never been known as an antislavery man. Like his father, he disapproved of slavery. But he had also worked closely with many statesmen who were slaveholders. It would not have been prudent to offend these national figures by being too outspoken.

In 1830, all such hesitancy was cast to the winds. Without his seeking it, Adams was offered a seat in the U.S. House of Representatives. "My election as President of the United States was not half so gratifying to my inmost soul. No election or appointment conferred upon me ever gave me so much pleasure," he confided to his ever-present diary. He considered it in no way beneath his dignity to serve as a member of the House. At this time in our history, the House of Representatives was the only federal office chosen directly by the people.

Soon, he would be embroiled in the growing sectional conflict over slavery. The issue was first raised *indirectly*. The South was determined to fight "a battle of the outposts."

With "a dense slave population at our firesides," wrote one South Carolinian, the Northerners could never be allowed "to discuss the subject *here*."[82] And to prevent that happening, it shortly became necessary even to prevent a discussion of the subject *there*, in Congress. Virtually everyone acknowledged Congress had no right to interfere with slavery in the states. So slave-state congressmen argued that Congress had no right even to receive petitions from citizens demanding emancipation. They imposed a "gag rule" that consigned such petitions to a committee, where they were ignored.

Congressman John Quincy Adams believed that the "right of petition" was being unlawfully infringed by this process. He arose to defend the Constitution's guarantee.

Each year, his opposition to the gag rule grew louder, more insistent. There was no obscure "Ebony and Topaz" now. Adams was blunt, forceful, and passionate. He soon earned the nickname "Old Man Eloquent." He began to develop an idea that was to become widespread throughout the North. He argued that free men were being shackled by the "Slave Power." At the height of Adams's campaign against the gag rule, citizens flooded Congress with as many as one hundred thousand petitions.[83]

Adams was surely correct. While Congress did not have authority to interfere with slavery in the states, it *did* have power under the Constitution to propose amendments. Even this was denied by the Slave Power. One petition asked Congress to protect Northern citizens who traveled to the South. A North Carolina congressman had said that any abolitionist would be hanged in his state.

Adams rose to combat this idea. "[I]f a Northern abolitionist should go to North Carolina and utter a principle of the Declaration of Independence," Adams began. He was nearly shouted down with demands for "Order! Order!" But he braved the torrent of abuse and bulled his way forward.[84] In this struggle, Adams was no longer the remote, passionless scholar; he was a *brawler,* giving as good as he got. The sight of a former president of the United States hurling defiance at his attackers was both shocking and sublime.

Adams joined the new Whig Party of anti-Jackson men. Like his father, though, a party could not contain him. He supported Jackson on Nullification. He supported Jackson's vigorous and successful effort to force France to pay damages for American shipping seized during the Napoleonic wars. But he did not forget his ancient feud with Old Hickory. When his alma mater, Harvard College, voted to grant Andrew Jackson an honorary degree, he cried out in anguish: "I could not be present to see my Darling Harvard disgrace herself by conferring a Doctor's degree upon a barbarian and savage who could scarcely spell his own name."[85]

Adams reached the heights in 1839 when he was called upon to defend fifty-three Africans from the Spanish ship, *Amistad*. Under the powerful leadership of Cinque, they had killed the captain and most of the crew. When the *Amistad* was brought into New Haven, Connecticut, by a U.S. warship, Spain demanded that the mutineers be returned to Cuba. Spain wanted to try the Africans for piracy. Lewis Tappan and Roger Sherman Baldwin, a Connecticut abolitionist, appealed to Adams to argue the Africans' case before the U.S. Supreme Court.[86] Citing his age and the fact that he had not been in a courtroom in decades, Adams tried to beg off. His supporters persisted. Finally, he gave in. "By the blessing of God, I will argue the case before the Supreme Court," he said.[87]

The Van Buren administration provided an ingenious argument for the prosecution. According to the Transcontinental Treaty (1819) that John Quincy Adams himself had negotiated with Spain, each country pledged to return lost or stolen "property" of the other. Adams denied that the Africans were *property* in this sense. He pointed to a framed document on the wall. "The moment you come to the Declaration of Independence, that every man has a right to life and liberty, as an inalienable right, this case is decided. I ask nothing more on behalf of these unfortunate men than this Declaration."[88]

Adams won his case in 1841. Even Chief Justice Roger B. Taney, a slaveholder, joined the majority. Taney could so rule because the Court found that the Africans had not been slaves at all, but free Africans kidnapped and transported to Cuba.[89] At this point, the United States had banned the Transatlantic slave trade for more than three decades, originally at the urging of President Thomas Jefferson. John Quincy Adams did not receive a fee for his brilliant defense, but the Africans gave him a handsomely bound Bible in gratitude. Ironically, when Cinque returned to his African home, he immediately became a slave trader.[90] The defenders of slavery were quick to exploit the fact.

VIII. "Tippecanoe and Tyler, Too!"

Martin Van Buren had labored all his life to succeed in the game of politics. But when the Panic of 1837 struck shortly after his inauguration, the new president seemed incapable of rallying the country behind him as his mentor Andrew Jackson had done. To a very real extent, the severe economic depression was the result of Jackson's war on the bank. Determined to destroy the Second Bank of the United States as a citadel of privilege, an *undemocratic* institution in a rising democracy, Jackson and Van Buren failed to create any effective and responsive institution to replace it.

Good Jeffersonians that they were, Jackson and Van Buren were deeply suspicious of banks. They did not appreciate the need for a strong central bank to bring confidence and stability to the nation's financial institutions. Even though they had vigorously *opposed* Hamilton's plan for the first Bank of the United States, Jefferson and Madison had wisely avoided trying to smash it once it was in place.

Van Buren acted decisively in the Canadian crisis of 1837, however. When prodemocracy rebels tried to overthrow the aristocratic British colonial government in Ontario, many Americans saw this as the natural outgrowth of the Spirit of '76. In Quebec province, there was even a *Fils de la Liberte* (Sons of Liberty) group organized in open imitation of the American Patriots.[91] Canadian Loyalists pursuing rebels stormed across the Niagara River and sank an American vessel on the U.S. side of the border. Van Buren resisted demands for war with Britain. He was willing to lose popularity by jailing Canadian rebels, even while protesting to the combative British foreign minister, Henry John Temple, Lord Palmerston, about intrusions onto American soil.[92] When the rebels returned to Canada, many of them were hanged.

Texans, too, had rebellion in mind. They had captured many American hearts with their bold insurrection against Mexican authority. Soon after achieving independence from Spain, Mexico had fallen under military dictatorship. In 1836, General Lopez de Santa Anna abolished the Mexican constitution with its guarantees of "states' rights" to provinces like Texas. The Americans—many from Kentucky and Tennessee—who had flooded into Texas when Mexico ruled, revolted against the despotic Santa Anna. Frontier heroes Davy Crockett and Jim Bowie were among 183 defenders who held out against Santa Anna's overwhelming force at the Alamo in San Antonio. When Colonel William Travis drew his famous "line in the sand" with his sword, none of the defenders chose to leave the embattled old mission. On March 6, Santa Anna's Mexicans finally stormed the Alamo; cruelly, he ordered every one of the defenders killed.

The bravery of the fighters for Texas independence inspired General Sam Houston's army of volunteers. "*Remember the Alamo!*" was their battle cry. Houston was a devoted friend of Andrew Jackson and was cut from the same cloth. Houston overwhelmed the Mexicans on April 21 at the Battle of San Jacinto and took Santa Anna prisoner. Texas's independence was achieved. Sam Houston became president of the "Lone Star Republic."[93] The Texans appealed for admission to the Union.

Van Buren could not afford to be so decisive about Texas. Northerners were deeply suspicious of annexation attempts, viewing them as a bid by slaveholders to increase their power. Southern Democrats clamored for annexation. Calhoun even threatened to break up the Union if Texas was not admitted as a slave state.[94] Jackson knew that New England whaling interests might be more agreeable to Texas's annexation if California's rich coast could be added to the United States. Somewhat uncharacteristically, Jackson advised *patience.*[95] Resistance to Texas's "reannexation" did not disappear overnight, however. In 1838, John Quincy Adams spoke *for three weeks* on the House floor and defeated a move to annex Texas.[96]

With the approaching election of 1840, the opposing Whigs determined to do to Van Buren what Democrats had done to Adams in 1828. They nominated the aged hero of the War of 1812, William Henry Harrison. "Old Tippecanoe" took no public positions. The Whigs did not issue a party platform. Their campaign featured fierce attacks on Van Buren as a pampered aristocrat. "Van, Van, The Used-up Man!" They lampooned the New Yorker's elegant dress and manners, his taste for fine wines. Old Tippecanoe was born in a log cabin, Whigs claimed, and preferred hard cider. The old general's running mate was an anti-Jackson Democrat from Virginia, John Tyler. The ticket was immortalized as "Tippecanoe and Tyler, Too!" The campaign slogan was not as mindless as it seemed. It reminded voters that Whigs, too, had played their part in ending the threat of Indian attacks on the frontier. "Keep the ball rolling" was the Whig cry and, for once, this party of educated and refined men achieved real popular appeal. Harrison buried Van Buren by 234 electoral votes to 60. The popular vote was closer—1,275,016 to 1,129,102. This popular vote total—*nearly two and a half million*—reflected the enormous expansion of the electorate under Jackson.

Harrison at sixty-eight years was the oldest man elected president prior to Ronald Reagan. He wrote his own inaugural address, filled with classical allusions. Whig leaders had drafted Senator Daniel Webster to edit it down. Webster joked that he had killed "seventeen Roman proconsuls as dead as smelts, every one of them." Even so, Harrison's speech was the longest ever delivered. Speaking in a cold and driving rain, the aged general soon came down with pneumonia. He died after just a month in office, 4 April 1841. Vice President John Tyler moved with dispatch to claim the title deeds of office. He would not be "acting President," he informed Harrison's cabinet, but would function fully as the chief executive.* When he vetoed a bill for internal improvements, however, he seemed to Whig leaders no better than the strong-willed Jackson. Very shortly, President Tyler became a man without a party. Secretary of State Daniel Webster was the only Whig to stay in the Tyler cabinet—and that was only because he was negotiating a vitally important treaty with England. The Webster-Ashburton Treaty of 1842 resolved nearly all remaining disputes between England and America and formed the basis of an Anglo-American "special relationship" that exists to this day.

IX. Great Harry of the West

When Henry Clay visited New Orleans in 1844, a local newspaper, the *Tropic,* had great fun with the great Kentuckian. It published as a spoof a Dutch-accented verse about the Great Compromiser:

Vell, Henry you're in town at last,
Ve're wery glad to see you,
Ve'll breakfast and ve'll dine you,
And ve'll sup you and ve'll tea you
It's wery fortunate for us
That yu veren't born a Turk,
You might among the ladies here
Do so much orrid verk.
They think of you the blessed day
At night ven in their beds;
It's vell their politics to turn
But not to turn their heads![97]

Here we see Great Harry's famous appeal to the ladies. He was by far the least handsome of the three great senators of his day. Webster was "the

* Tyler's bold assertion set an important precedent for presidential succession and was formally agreed to when Congress passed and the states ratified Amendment XXV on presidential disability in 1967.

Godlike Daniel" and "Black Dan" to his women admirers. And Calhoun was a compelling figure in his younger days, tall and straight, with a shock of black hair and those dark piercing eyes.

Women liked Clay because he liked them. And he took them seriously. He was charming, soft-spoken, and *reasonable.* In an age of passionate intensity, Clay's efforts to preserve the Union—and peace—through reason and persuasion struck a responsive chord, especially with women. No one could imagine Clay's campaigning with such an idiot election slogan as "Rumsey, Dumsey / Rumsey, Dumsey / Colonel Johnson killed Tecumseh." He appealed to the reserved, the thoughtful, the serious. And yes, even in Andrew Jackson's rollicking America, there were still some of those.

Clay's *Ashland* was a stately, well-managed Kentucky plantation outside of Lexington. Its six hundred acres were given over to the planting of corn, wheat, rye, and hemp. It buzzed with efficiency. And it was said to inspire visitors with a vision of Clay's famous *American System.*[98] Clay had offered that view of an independent, self-sufficient republic, one at peace with its neighbors because it needed nothing from them.

But Ashland was a slave plantation. Henry Clay had some sixty slaves. To abolitionists, it was intolerable to associate a slave plantation with any *American* system. That was, they sincerely believed, the most wrong thing in America.

During the 1844 campaign, Clay was confronted as he was speaking from a public platform in Indiana. There, he was confronted by a Hiram Mendenhall who presented him with a petition that challenged him to free his slaves. Clay had for many years called slavery evil. He had been a leading backer of the American Colonization Society that aided emancipated slaves by booking them passage to Liberia, in Africa. That was then considered an *enlightened* position for slaveholders to take.

He did not like being set upon in public by people whom he thought were "monomaniacs," however.[99] And he turned on the petitioner. Mendenhall knew nothing of the condition of slaves at Ashland, he said. He pointed out his servant Charles, standing placidly at the side of the platform. Charles could leave him any time. But if he did, how would Charles and his other servants make a living for themselves? How could they manage on being turned out of their homes and their accustomed ways? To Clay and to millions of other Americans, simply *freeing* the slaves without providing for their training and employment was no solution at all.

With his practiced orator's skill, with his commanding dignity, Clay turned on the petitioner and said: "Go home, Mr. Mendenhall, and attend to your business, and I will endeavor to attend to mine."[100]

"*Go home, Mr. Mendenhall,*" was an effective rebuke from a powerful stump speaker, but it haunted Henry Clay for the rest of the campaign.

X. Reannexing Texas and Reoccupying Oregon

President Tyler proved no more popular with the party of Andrew Jackson than with the Whigs. As Democrats sought a standard-bearer for the election of 1844, former President Martin Van Buren seemed in the strongest position. Jackson was expected to support his loyal lieutenant. But Van Buren had unwisely agreed with Henry Clay about Texas. Both men had exchanged letters pledging *not* to make Texas an issue in the forthcoming campaign. Jackson was an ardent expansionist. He turned away from Van Buren to his fellow Tennessean, James Knox Polk.

"Who is Polk?" asked the Whigs derisively. Polk lacked the fame of Jackson and Clay, to be sure, but he was not a nobody. A faithful Jackson supporter, Polk had served as governor of Tennessee and speaker of the U.S. House of Representatives. Today, we would consider such qualifications more than sufficient for a presidential candidate. The Whigs were to learn soon enough who Polk was. Running on a platform that called for "Re-annexation of Texas and Re-occupation of Oregon," Polk won a narrow victory in 1844 over the great Henry Clay. Antislavery activists bitterly opposed acquiring Texas, where slavery was legal. Not only did they resent the idea of two more proslavery members of the U.S. Senate, they feared the possibility that Texas might be carved into as many as *five* new states! That would mean *ten more proslavery senators.*

Polk won 1,337,243 popular votes, a mere 38,181 more than Clay's

1,299,062. The electoral college tally was 170 for Polk and 105 for Clay.* The 1844 election was decided by the vote of New York State. James G. Birney was the nominee of the small, antislavery Liberty Party. Birney's 62,300 votes (2.3 percent) nationwide came disproportionately from New York and New England. Birney's vote in the Empire State pushed New York into Polk's column, guaranteeing him 36 additional electoral votes and the election. Thus, the slavery issue began to have a serious impact on presidential politics.

Whigs, of course, complained bitterly. Although a slaveholder himself, Clay had argued for gradual emancipation. Once again, this was a bold stand for a man who represented the slave state of Kentucky. Antislavery agitators, however, remembered Clay's stern rebuke, "Go home, Mr. Mendenhall." That retort, so effective on the stump in Indiana, cost Harry of the West dearly in New York and New England.

President Tyler took Polk's election as evidence of popular support for "Manifest Destiny" and quickly proposed admitting Texas to the Union by joint resolution. The reason Democrats spoke of "reannexation" of Texas is because they maintained Texas had been part of the original Louisiana Purchase and that John Quincy Adams had failed when he negotiated the Transcontinental Treaty with Spain in 1819. (The fact that the treaty was approved by President Monroe and ratified by a majority of Democratic-Republicans in the Senate did not seem to deter these eager expansionists.) Similarly, "reoccupation" of Oregon was intended to assert America's claim to all of the Pacific Northwest. Expansionists aggressively called for extending the border up 54°40' north latitude. This meant they wanted all of the Oregon territory up to the southern border of Russian Alaska. The claim to Oregon rested on the 1792 voyage of American Captain Robert Gray in his ship USS *Columbia.* Gray had anchored off Cape Disappointment, unable to enter the mouth of the raging river he named *Columbia*. Lewis and Clark had wintered over near this site on their famous expedition.

Democrats hoped that adding Oregon to their list of territorial ambitions

* Clay had been a candidate in 1824, 1832, and now 1844. Three losses for the nation's highest office had nonetheless won the great Kentuckian thousands of loyal followers, perhaps the most important of whom was young Abraham Lincoln of Illinois. Clay was the greatest of the "also rans."

would persuade Northerners to look more kindly on the admission of Texas.[101] Texas's annexation was rushed through Congress in the last days of the Tyler administration because Southerners feared that England might make a favorable treaty with the Republic of Texas that would call for emancipation of the slaves.

The British Hudson's Bay Company had been the power and the law in the Pacific Northwest for a generation. The company's influence was based on fur trapping and trading. When "Oregon Fever" struck the Midwest in 1842, thousands of Americans packed up and took their Conestoga wagons along the Oregon Trail. The rich farmland of the Willamette Valley beckoned. If the land was a *pull*, the rising agitation over slavery in the territories was surely a *push*. American missionaries—both Protestant and Catholic—had led the way.[102] In Massachusetts, Henry David Thoreau spoke for many when he wrote:

> *I must walk toward Oregon, and not toward Europe.**
> *And that way the nation is moving,*
> *And I may say that mankind progress from east to west.*

The trail had been blazed by twenty years of "Mountainy Men." Most of these rough trappers were Americans who lived beyond the settled frontiers and knew the land intimately.

Jim Clyman's life illustrated the Mountain Man restlessness. Clyman saw George Washington in Fauquier County, Virginia, where he was born in 1792. He "lit out for the territories" early. By the time he died, Chester Alan Arthur was president. Clyman died in 1881 on his Napa, California, ranch. His life had spanned the continent.[103] There were other Mountain Men whose lives were no less remarkable:

> The mountain man's eye had the Indian's alertness, forever watching for the movement of boughs or grasses, for the passage of wildlife

* It is perhaps not too unpoetic to point out that walking *eastward* would have required Thoreau to walk on water.

> downwind, something unexplained floating in a stream, dust stirring in a calm, or the configuration of mere scratches on a cottonwood. His ear would never again hear church bells or the noises of a farm but, like the Indian's, was tuned to catch any sound in a country where every sound was provisionally a death warning. He dressed like an Indian, in blankets, robes, buckskins, and mocasins, and it was sometimes his humor to grease his hair and stripe his face with vermilion. He lived like an Indian in bark huts or skin lodges, and married a succession of squaws. . . . He had a call on brutality as instant as the Indian's and rather more relentless. The Indians who had proved themselves his friends were his friends just so long as they seemed to be; all others were to be shot and scalped at sight. It was the Indian law, no violence to be left unavenged.[104]

However hard these Mountain Men were, Americans could not have crossed the Rockies or settled the fertile valleys of California and Oregon without them. They were the guides who led the wagon trains west. They were the hunters who staved off starvation when the wagons were hit by blizzards in the mountain passes. When they failed—as they did with the doomed Donner Party—the results would be catastrophic. In 1846, these inexperienced pioneers were trapped on the eastern slope of the Sierra Nevada Mountains. Of the eighty-seven members of the party, only forty-six survived the cold, hunger, and even horrors of cannibalism. But thousands more got through.

Another amazing westward trek was made by the Mormons. Led by the visionary and strong-willed Brigham Young, thousands of Mormons journeyed to the Great Salt Lake in 1847. Mormons were fleeing persecution in Missouri and Illinois where the man they regarded as their prophet, Joseph Smith, had been murdered by a mob. The Mormon practice of polygamy deeply offended their neighbors, as did the economic muscle they wielded through communal buying and selling. This tactic seemed a direct threat to the economic individualism of single-family farm homesteads that was seen as central to the American way. Brigham Young was determined to find a remote region in which to build his "Deseret."[105]

In just a few years, the thousands of Americans who went to Oregon created new realities "on the ground." By 1845, the bottoming out of the fur trade prompted the Hudson's Bay Company to abandon their trading post at Fort Vancouver, north of the Columbia River. Withdrawing to the outpost of Victoria on Vancouver Island, the British presence in the Pacific Northwest was melting away like snows receding up the side of the mountain.

"Fifty-four Forty or Fight!" became the rallying cry of Democrats bent on westward expansion. It meant we wanted all the territory in the Pacific Northwest up to 54°40' north latitude. Democratic editor John O'Sullivan saw heavenly approval for this policy. In his *New York Morning News,* he wrote it is "our *manifest destiny* to overspread and to possess the whole of the continent which Providence has given us for the development of the great experiment of liberty and federated self-government."[106] Some expansionists even bragged openly of extending American rule from sea to sea and from pole to pole.

Not all Americans were willing to fight for Oregon. *Niles' Weekly Register,* a Whig paper, poured cold water on all such wild talk. War with Britain over Oregon, the editor said, "would be one of the most reckless and insane exhibitions that the civilized world has ever witnessed."[107] President Polk did not want war with Britain. But he did not shrink from the possibility of war. "[T]he only way to treat John Bull [Great Britain] was to look him straight in the eye. . . . I considered a bold & firm course on our part the pacific one. . . ."[108]

Events proved "Young Hickory" correct. Britain was unwilling to fight a war over a remote territory whose fur trade was increasingly trapped out. We didn't get Fifty-four Forty. We didn't get the fight, either. Americans were fortunate in this, for by the time Britain agreed to compromise at the line of 49° north latitude we were already headed for war with Mexico. Missouri's Senator Thomas Hart Benton laughed at Polk: "Why not march up to 'Fifty-four Forty' as courageously as we march upon the Rio Grande? Because Great Britain is powerful and Mexico is weak. . . ."[109] Polk could take ridicule and resentment. He had pocketed the first of the great Pacific coast harbors. He now turned his attention to Mexico to secure the other two.

XI. "The Halls of Montezuma"

President Polk had instructed his envoy, John Slidell, to offer the Mexicans $4.5 million to settle claims for damages from the incessant Mexican civil wars if Mexico would recognize the Rio Grande as Texas's southern border. Slidell was also empowered to offer a further $5 million if the Mexicans would sell their province of New Mexico.[110] Slidell was even instructed to offer up to $25 million if California were thrown into the bargain. "Money would be no object," Secretary of State James Buchanan wrote to the American ambassador in Mexico City.[111]

Mexicans found the very offer insulting. They refused to receive Slidell. Another military uprising (*golpe*)—an increasingly familiar phenomenon in Latin America—ousted the moderate Herrera government and installed the militantly anti-American General Mariano Paredes in power. Paredes vowed to stand up to the pushy *Yanquis.*[112] By New Year's Day 1846, Paredes was eager for war with America.[113]

President Polk also feared rumored British attempts to buy California. The British Admiralty was said to covet the fine harbor of San Francisco Bay.[114] Polk reasserted the principles of the Monroe Doctrine. This hemisphere would be off-limits to European colonization. He said nothing about American expansion.

Polk ordered General Zachary Taylor to take an army into the disputed territory between the Nueces and Rio Grande Rivers. General Pedro de Ampudia warned Taylor that he was intruding on Mexican land and ordered him to leave. Taylor ignored Ampudia's warning, instead building an American fort.[115] On 25 April 1846, a Mexican force ambushed an American patrol, killing eleven. Polk had resolved to go to war even before this clash. Now, he told Congress, Mexico had "shed American blood on American soil."[116] Congress soon gave him his declaration of war, by a lopsided vote of 174–14 in the House and 40–2 in the Senate.[117]

Mexico was hardly blameless in all this. Contemptuous of the *Yanquis*, Mexicans remembered the American failure to conquer Canada and the humiliating British capture of Washington, D.C., in the War of 1812. A Mexican officer bragged that his cavalry could take care of American infantry by *lassoing* them.[118] Mexico was not alone in holding America in low regard. London's *Britannia* sneered that the United States "as an aggressive power is one of the weakest in the world . . . fit for nothing but to fight Indians."[119]

Although the war was very popular in the Mississippi Valley, and in the South, New England once again broadly opposed the war. The Whig Party questioned the war, but made sure to vote to supply the troops. Whigs remembered how Federalists had been tainted with disloyalty during the War of 1812.[120] Literary figures like James Russell Lowell saw only the designs of the Slave Power in the rush to war:

They just want this Californy
So's to lug new slave-states in
To abuse ye, an' to scorn ye,
An' to plunder ye like sin.[121]

Massachusetts's legislature denounced the war as an effort to strengthen the Slave Power. And his strong opposition led Henry David Thoreau to spend a night in jail for refusing to pay war taxes. Thoreau's *Essay on Civil Disobedience* became a classic of American literature.[122] Theodore Parker, a Unitarian minister, said that if the "war be right then Christianity is wrong, a falsehood, a lie." Abolitionist William Lloyd Garrison's militant newspaper, the *Liberator*, expressed open support for the Mexican people: "Every lover of Freedom and humanity throughout the world must wish them the most triumphant success."

Garrison went even further. His *Liberator* proclaimed: "Accursed be the American Union, as a stupendous republican imposture! Accursed be it, as the most frightful despotism, with regard to three millions of the people, ever exercised over any portion of the human family! NO UNION WITH SLAVEHOLDERS!"[123]

To men of Garrison's mind, O'Sullivan's concept of "Manifest Destiny" was the foulest hypocrisy. And Garrison's new, young ally would give them more reason to resist the Slave Power. A brilliant runaway slave in 1845 published the sensational autobiography, *Narrative of the Life of Frederick Douglass*. Now, thousands of Americans could read of the horrors of life under the lash in the compelling words of a polished writer and orator. Douglass appeared on the scene just in time to put flesh and blood onto the abstract idealism of Garrison and the abolitionists.

The campaign in Mexico, despite some early setbacks, proceeded swiftly. General Zachary Taylor, known as "Old Rough and Ready," gained a reputation for victory. President Polk feared his growing popularity, though, and was determined not to make another Whig a military hero. Polk ordered General Winfield Scott to take Mexico City. Scott fought a brilliant campaign, ably assisted by the first *amphibious* landing staged by the U.S. Navy.*

Army Captain Robert E. Lee moved around the main Mexican force to bring victory. Two of his subordinates who also won laurels in this operation were Lieutenants George B. McClellan and Ulysses S. Grant.[124]** U.S. Marines marched from Vera Cruz and earned their famous "blood stripe"—the crimson stripe that runs down their trouser leg—at the Battle of Chapultepec. They suffered heavy casualties in this action, but they reached the Halls of Montezuma in Mexico City.

The American assault on Mexico City took place over the bitter resistance of two amazing groups of fighters. The young cadets of the Mexican Military Academy, aged just thirteen to nineteen, fought with astonishing bravery against the grimly advancing "Gringos."*** These brave youngsters are known in Mexican history as *los Niños* (the boys). Many of them paid with their lives for every mile the Americans moved.[125] The other fighters were the *San Patricios* (Saint Patricks). These were mostly deserters—many of them Irish—from the American army. They fought valiantly against their former comrades. Twenty-nine captured Patricios were made to stand in wagons, condemned as traitors, in the broiling September sun. With nooses around their necks, they were forced to witness the final *yanqui*

---

* A greater awareness of the importance of sea power led President Polk to break from Jeffersonian tradition and found the U.S. Naval Academy at Annapolis (1845).

** Both Lee and Grant thought that the war against Mexico was unjust, but both nonetheless distinguished themselves in their military capacities.

*** *Gringo*—Mexican slang for an American—was long thought to have come from the song American troops sang as they marched through Mexico's parched, dusty valleys—"Green grow the lilacs. . . ." More likely, *Gringo* is a corruption of *griego*—to speak Spanish like a Greek.

attack on Mexico City. When the Stars and Stripes were raised on the heights above the city, the Patricios actually cheered their old flag! Then the wagons jolted forward, ending a sad but compelling little chapter in the history of American warfare.[126]

U.S. battle deaths in the Mexican War were not heavy by ancient or even modern standards. Killed in combat were 1,733, or 2 percent of 78,718 troops committed. But the greatest toll was taken by disease. Add to combat deaths the figure of 11,550 noncombat deaths, or 14 percent. This means fully 16 percent of those engaged died.[127] This was all too typical of warfare in the days before modern medicine.

In the Southwest, Americans moved swiftly to take New Mexico and move on to California. General Steven Kearny led a force that included the extraordinary Mormon Brigade in an easy conquest. Mormon leader Brigham Young made a crucial decision to *support* the United States in its war against Mexico. He sent hundreds of young recruits to aid the American forces in the Southwest. The army pay these clean-living young men tithed to the Mormon church helped the embattled colony to survive.

California's short-lived "Bear Flag Republic" was almost a comical affair. Meeting little resistance from the Mexican natives, Captain John Charles Frémont took action to detach the province from the mother country. But Frémont's reputation as "The Pathfinder" was largely the result of skillful public relations and family connections. (His father-in-law was the powerful Senator Thomas Hart Benton.) General Kearny generally found Frémont a nuisance. Despite Frémont's court-martial and his threats of a duel (his opponent proposed shotguns no less), a semblance of order was restored and California was soon incorporated into the Union.[128]

Meanwhile, Polk had to deal with opposition. His war aims were widely misunderstood, even in his own cabinet. When his secretary of state, the fussy James Buchanan, wrote to American diplomats informing them that the United States had no territorial ambitions in California, Polk overruled him. The humorless president ordered Buchanan to remove such a self-denying statement.[129]

Many Whigs called him "the mendacious Polk," rudely suggesting that the president was a *liar*. Congressman Abraham Lincoln of Illinois was more respectful, but no less pointed. Waiting until hostilities ended in September 1847, Lincoln offered his "Spot Resolution" in December. Lincoln's resolution asked President Polk to point out precisely the *spot* on which American blood had been shed on American soil. Lincoln could not deny American blood had been shed, but he wanted Polk to prove that it had been shed on *American* soil. Polk ignored him.

Less easy to ignore was the measure introduced by Pennsylvania Democratic Congressman David Wilmot. "Neither slavery nor involuntary servitude shall ever exist" in any territory we might take from Mexico, Wilmot's amendment read. This Wilmot *Proviso* passed the House in 1846, but the Senate failed to act on it. Wilmot introduced it again in 1847 and this time the Senate *rejected* it.[130] Senator John C. Calhoun had rightly feared that a war with Mexico would lead to just such antislavery agitation.

The war continued to drive Americans apart. When a resolution to praise the veterans of the war was offered in the House of Representatives on 21 February 1848, Old Man Eloquent rose to *oppose* it! John Quincy Adams was voted down, overwhelmingly. When the House clerk read a tribute to the soldiers, Adams struggled to his feet to object. He soon collapsed, felled by a stroke. He was carried off to the Speaker's office, where he died two days later.[131] Among those chosen by the House for the funeral committee was a one-termer from the prairies—Congressman Abraham Lincoln.

James Knox Polk received few thanks for adding vast territories to the American republic. He is the American Bismarck. Just as "the Iron Chancellor" is credited with creating the greater German empire in the 1860s and 1870s, James Knox Polk had three great objects in mind: the harbors of San Diego, San Francisco, and Puget Sound. Like Bismarck, Polk was willing to go to war to achieve his objects. But unlike Bismarck, Polk could rely on the sweep of thousands of settlers to achieve most of his goals without fighting. While the Mexicans in Mexico bravely resisted American invaders, the huge Southwest was seized almost bloodlessly.

Polk treated his envoy in Mexico City, Nicholas Trist, with shocking ingratitude. But he had the good sense to submit Trist's Treaty of Guadelupe-Hidalgo (1848) to the Senate. In doing so, he wisely rejected the demands of some ultra-nationalists here and some young reformers in Mexico that we incorporate the entire country into the United States.*

Mexico gave up California, Arizona, and New Mexico and recognized the Rio Grande as the southern border of the United States. America agreed to pay Mexico $15 million. The treaty was quickly ratified. The territory of what was called the Mexican Cession comprised 525,000 square miles. Of course, the Louisiana Purchase had brought 828,000 square miles of rich, well-watered lands into the American Union. Still, the great Southwest was a region of incomparable mineral wealth and natural beauty.

Did the $15 million payment represent an uneasy conscience on Polk's part? Or was it an astonishing act of compassion? One thing is clear: such an act is almost unimaginable by any other great power at the conclusion of a successful war with a weaker neighbor.

Polk kept his promise to serve only one term. Rigid and suspicious but brave and determined, he left the White House in March 1849, and died just three months later at the age of fifty-four. His labors had worn him out. "His administration has been a curse to the country," said William Lloyd Garrison, who found no reason to deplore the former president's death.[132]

Americans, reflecting on the contribution of these vast territories have made to the national life, and the hope and aspiration of many immigrants drawn to them, may think otherwise.

* The war also saved West Point. Although founded under Jefferson's administration in 1803, the military academy was viewed as an *unrepublican* institution by Jefferson's political heirs. The outstanding performance of so many well-trained West Point officers in the Mexican War, however, ended congressional attempts to close it down.

Eight

The Rising Storm
(1849–1861)

When sailors talk of "losing the bubble," they mean the ship's navigator has lost a clear sense of where he is and where he is bound. America in the 1850s very nearly loses the bubble. The nation that hailed its own birth as a "new order of the ages" (novus ordo seclorum) *had always identified itself with the cause of liberty. George Washington said Americans had been given custody of the "sacred fire of liberty." Americans took it for granted that the spread of our republican ideals and institutions would be a benefit to mankind. All the Founders had looked at slavery as an aberration. All of them deplored it and thought it unjust. All of them hoped that eventually it would be eradicated. In the 1850s, the Founders' vision is obscured. The expansion of slavery is the issue that drives John Brown to murder and a foredoomed rebellion, yet it is being pressed by respectable public men like John C. Calhoun, Jefferson Davis, and Albert Gallatin Brown. Abraham Lincoln will describe slavery as the rattlesnake that lay coiled beneath the table where the Founders debated America's future. In the 1840s, the rattler awakes. Throughout the 1850s, its menacing rattle can be heard, and its venom is felt. Can liberty itself survive?*

I. California and The Compromise of 1850

Grim, determined James Knox Polk had achieved his major territorial goals. He succeeded in expanding U.S. power to the Pacific. Polk single-mindedly pursued the goal of adding San Diego harbor and San Francisco Bay to the American Union. It was this presidential decisiveness—far more than the enthusiasm of newspapermen for "Manifest Destiny"—that accounted for the stunning expansion of U.S. power and influence in the late 1840s.[1] But Polk found he could not do all this without creating military heroes for his great political rivals—the Whigs. The Whig Party had led the opposition to the Mexican War. Now, ironically, the Whigs nominated General Zachary Taylor, a great hero of that war, as their presidential candidate in 1848.

"Old Rough and Ready" Taylor was a Louisiana slaveholder whose views on political issues were unknown. That's why the Whigs chose him. "Ask my arse," a crude but funny political cartoon of the day has Taylor telling nosy reporters. The Whig Party approved no platform and relied on the same formula that had elected "Tippecanoe and Tyler, Too" eight years earlier. But some "Conscience Whigs" like Massachusetts's Charles Sumner were unwilling to support Taylor because he refused to give them any assurances he would oppose the spread of slavery into the territories.[2]

A Whig congressman from Illinois who supported General Taylor poked fun at the Democratic nominee, the aged Lewis Cass. Democrats tried to inflate Cass's war record—from the War of 1812! General Cass, Abraham Lincoln teased, had "*in*vaded Canada without resistance and *out*-vaded without pursuit."[3] Lincoln further ridiculed the feckless Cass. Since General William Henry Harrison was picking huckleberries on the day of the Battle of the Thames, and since Cass boasted of being Harrison's aide, Lincoln said: "I suppose it is a just conclusion . . . to say Cass was aiding Harrison to pick huckleberries."[4]

Cass fared little better with the voters. Former President Martin Van Buren, who had been a Democrat, teamed up with Charles Francis Adams, the son and grandson of presidents, to lead the antislavery Free-Soil Party.

Unfortunately for Jackson's political heirs, James Knox Polk's ambitious program to acquire the great ports of the Pacific—Puget Sound, San Francisco Bay, and San Diego harbor—had split his own Democratic Party.

This new faction, the Free-Soil Party, was comprised of many ex-Democrats who were willing to tolerate slavery in the South, but were *unwilling* to see it expand into the territories won from Mexico. To keep peace with their Southern slaveholding allies, most Northern Democrats were willing to let slavery expand across the hot and sparsely populated Southwest.

Free-Soilers Van Buren and Adams actually ran ahead of the Democrat Cass in New York State (26.4 percent to 25.1 percent), throwing the vital Empire State and the election to Taylor and the Whigs. The Free-Soil ticket also made major inroads into Democratic Party strength in Connecticut, Massachusetts, and Vermont.[5] We saw in the previous chapter how James Birney and his Liberty Party had cost Henry Clay and the Whigs the election of 1844.

Now, four years later, the slavery issue broke the Democrats' unity. Van Buren was denounced by his former friends in the Democratic Party as a "barn burner."[6] The term referred to the old Dutch legend of the crazed farmer who burned down his own barn to get rid of the rats. The barb bore an especially sharp point for Van Buren—as his name suggests, his forebears *were* Dutch.

Zachary Taylor had not so much as cast a ballot for president in over forty years of army service.[7] As president, though, he would not be able to avoid the issues much longer. Events in California would astonish the world—and put pressure on Washington to keep pace. The peace had not even been signed with Mexico before gold was discovered at Sutter's Mill on the south fork of the American River, near Coloma, California. Word spread throughout the United States, speeded by means of the newly developed telegraph. The California Gold Rush began almost immediately. Tens of thousands of Americans from all regions and others from around the world struck out for the gold fields of the Sacramento Valley.

They came overland and by sea. As far away as China, California became known as *Gum Shan*—the Mountain of Gold.[8] Many of them entered by way of the *Golden Gate*. With a typical pitchman's flourish, U.S. Army Major John Charles Frémont, the Pathfinder, had named this entrance to San Francisco Bay.[9] These "Forty-niners" (1849) swelled the territory's population. As much as $30,000 to $50,000 in gold was being taken out of the mines *each day*! West Pointer William Tecumseh Sherman, serving with the army in California, thought the gold would be more than sufficient to pay for the entire Mexican War.[10]

Soon California would be pressing for statehood. And, to Taylor's chagrin, a decision about slavery in the territories could not be avoided. It was a decision that would split the nation.

California's fate would be decided in Washington. And there the slavery issue dominated. "If the South is to be saved," wrote an ailing John C. Calhoun, "now is the time."[11] Calhoun had originally been a nationalist, a rising member of the Jeffersonian Republican Party. After his clash with Jackson, however, the great South Carolinian increasingly saw himself as the leader of an embattled sectionalist South.

President Taylor stunned his Southern supporters by urging California's admission *without first organizing as a territory*. Although Taylor hailed from the South, he had developed a national outlook in his long years in the army. Defiantly, and near death, Calhoun arose in the Senate to demand "guarantees."[12] The federal republic of 1787, he argued, was being transformed into a great national *democracy*. The South must be assured that it would continue to have equal representation in the national government *or it would have to consider secession*. New York Senator William H. Seward matched Calhoun's militancy. Seward, a Whig, said the rise of the free states was irresistible. It was a law of nature. He said that Congress surely had the right under the Constitution to limit the expansion of slavery. Even so, he argued provocatively, there was a "higher law" than the Constitution—natural law.[13] Not only could slavery's expansion be limited, Seward said, but in time it could be abolished.[14]

Henry Clay of Kentucky arose on the Senate floor, determined to play the role of the Great Compromiser once again, as he had in 1820 and 1833. "I know no South, no North, no East, no West, to which I owe any allegiance.... My allegiance is to the American Union and to my state," he cried. He went further, stating that he would *never* pledge his allegiance to any form of Southern confederacy.[15] In this age of thrilling political oratory, the fame of

Clay's address spread from the packed Senate galleries throughout the Union.

Clay offered a bundle of legislative proposals that covered many aspects of the dispute over slavery in the territories. Whether it was *great* or not, it was aptly called a compromise. First, California was to be admitted as a free state. Second, New Mexico would be organized as a territory with no restrictions on slavery. Third, the slave trade in the District of Columbia would be abolished. But, fourth, Congress would pledge no further interference with the owning of slaves in the nation's capital. Fifth, Congress would refrain from using its great power under the Commerce Clause of the Constitution to regulate the slave trade *among* the states. Sixth and finally, Congress would pass a new, more stringent Fugitive Slave Act.[16] Southerners claimed that as many as thirty thousand slaves had run away from their masters. This *fugitive slave* problem, they claimed, had cost Southerners as much as $15 million.[17]

We must be guided by the wisdom of George Washington in his Farewell Address, Clay argued.[18] When someone suggested that this latest effort would prevent his ever becoming president, Clay memorably responded: "Sir, I had rather be *right* than be President!"[19]

Henry Clay's inspiring address prompted a patriotic Virginian, Edward Coles, to send the Great Compromiser the previously unpublished "Advice to my Country" that James Madison had written shortly before his death in 1836. Coles hoped Clay would use it in debate. As if from the grave, Madison argued forcefully *again*st disunion: "Let the Union of the States be cherished and perpetuated. Let the open enemy to it be regarded as a Pandora with her box opened; and the disguised one, as the Serpent creeping with his deadly wiles into paradise."[20]

All eyes now looked to Daniel Webster to respond to Calhoun and Clay. Would he help Clay to pass this controversial compromise? Or would he speak for the North and *reject* it? The "Godlike Daniel" rose by his desk, his voice filling the crowded chamber: "I wish to speak today not as a Massachusetts man, nor as a Northern man, but as an American, and a member of the Senate of the United States. . . . I speak today for the preservation of the Union. 'Hear me for my cause!'"*[21]

* From Brutus's speech in Shakespeare's *Julius Caesar*, act 3, scene 2.

Speaking for more than three hours on 7 March 1850, Webster kept his promise not to speak as a Northern man. He stunned his Massachusetts supporters by attacking the fanaticism of the abolitionists and by withdrawing his support for the Wilmot Proviso. The Wilmot Proviso had been offered by a Democratic congressman from Pennsylvania, David Wilmot. It said that slavery would be banned in any new territory acquired as a result of the war with Mexico. The Wilmot Proviso passed the House of Representatives repeatedly, but it was always bottled up in the Senate. The Proviso was not *necessary,* Webster now argued, since God himself had made the arid, barren territories of the Southwest inhospitable to slave agriculture. He endorsed Clay's compromise, giving it essential backing at a critical moment. Webster still had confidence that the preservation of the Union would in the end bring an expansion of liberty. He still hoped to see slavery wither away in the West.

John C. Calhoun sat in his seat, glowering, almost unable to speak. He was visibly failing. Calhoun and his followers insisted that California's admission be delayed until she was organized as a territory—as almost all other states had been admitted. Calhoun hoped to use that time to settle California's rich central valley with slave agriculture. A slaveholding California would have given Calhoun's "peculiar institution" a window on the Pacific.

Yet when Webster warned the Senate that *dissolution of the Union* could never be achieved peaceably, Calhoun cried out: "No sir! The Union *can* be broken."[22] If the North refused to respect Calhoun's "Platform of the South," Calhoun believed secession was the only answer. In that platform, Calhoun demanded the right of slaveholders to take their "property" with them anywhere in the Union. Slavery, he claimed, must follow the flag.[23] He was unyielding on California. "We have borne the wrongs and the insults of the North long enough," he wrote.[24]

By redefining liberty as the right of a dominant race to carry its own "peculiar institution" throughout the Union, Calhoun admitted that he disagreed with Jefferson. Jefferson's erroneous belief that "all men are created equal" had caused him, Calhoun argued, to "take an utterly false view of the subordinate relation of the black race to the white race in the South; and to hold . . . that the former . . . were as fully entitled to both liberty and equality as the latter; and that to deprive them of it was both unjust and immoral."[25]

What Calhoun treated as a thought unique to Thomas Jefferson was no such thing. John Adams had said there was not an idea in the Declaration of Independence that had not been "hackneyed about" in Congress for years. Jefferson himself disclaimed any originality, saying the Declaration was "an expression of the American mind."[26] Thus, Calhoun was not merely challenging Jefferson. He was rejecting the entire natural rights philosophy upon which the United States of America was based. His dissent could not have been more radical, even in a sense subversive. But despite his revolutionary proclamations, he could not stop the Compromise of 1850. Within a month of Webster's "Seventh of March" speech, Calhoun was dead.

While the Southern press praised Webster for his fair-mindedness, many of his own constituents reacted with horror at his embrace of compromise, especially the hated Fugitive Slave Act. Massachusetts poet John Greenleaf Whittier bitterly condemned Webster in his "Ichabod":*

Then, pay the reverence of old days
To his dead fame;
Walk backward, with averted gaze,
And hide the shame.[27]

Although Ralph Waldo Emerson had once urged his Massachusetts readers to "love their neighbors more and their colored brethren less," the philosopher-poet was now horrified by the Fugitive Slave Act. "This filthy enactment was made in the nineteenth century, by people who could read and write. I *will* not obey it, by God!"[28]

Another obstacle to passage of Clay's Compromise of 1850 was President Zachary Taylor. Old Rough and Ready saw no reason to make all these concessions to the South on California. Bluntly, directly, Taylor wanted to admit California as a free state without seeking approval from Calhoun or his allies

---

* Whittier drew on well-known sources. First, his style echoes the great Puritan poet, John Milton. In Milton's *Paradise Lost,* Satan laments the fall from heaven. Thus, Whittier in this poem likened Webster's fall to Lucifer's! He also drew on the Bible: "Then she named the child Ichabod, saying, 'The glory has departed from Israel!' because the ark of God had been captured . . ." (1 Samuel 4:21). For the highly literate Brahmins of Boston, Whittier's shaft was a doubly pointed one.

in the Senate. Taylor ridiculed Clay's bundle of legislative proposals as an "omnibus"—a horse-drawn city coach that everyone could board. Taylor thus unwittingly gave Clay's large and complex package of measures a name to what would become a standard legislative term to this day.

Calhoun's death, at the height of agitation over the Compromise of 1850, only increased tensions. The South was desperate for leadership. Many Southerners found cause for alarm in the Census of 1850.[29] The population of the free states had increased a full 20 percent in the previous decade. This growing strength was fueled by the fact that seven-eighths of all immigrants to the United States settled in the North.[30] These immigrants were attracted to the free-labor system in the North. As a result, Southerners worried that they were becoming a minority in the national government. The House of Representatives reflected population, so that popular branch of the legislature became more antislavery with each decennial census. The repeated attempts to pass the Wilmot Proviso banning slavery in the territories acquired from Mexico filled slave state representatives with foreboding. And admission of new free states threatened their stronghold in the Senate, where each state had equal representation. Hence the reason California's admission as a free state seemed so menacing.

President Taylor said he was ready to lead an army himself to "crush" secession, thus evoking memories of Old Hickory.[31] Taylor threatened to hang Robert Toombs and Alexander Hamilton Stephens, both from Georgia. They were ready to seize the fallen flags of Southern nationalism, to assume the mantle of Calhoun. The president even denounced his own former son-in-law, Mississippi's Jefferson Davis, as "the chief conspirator."[32] Instead of paying Texas for her claims against New Mexico, Taylor rattled his saber and threatened to resist Texas's demands *by force*![33]

But President Taylor had no chance to unsheathe his sword. In 1850, he was struck with "cholera morbus" after enduring hours of Fourth of July oratory. Consuming large quantities of ice milk and cucumbers, in the stifling heat of a Washington summer, Taylor quickly took to his sickbed in the White House.[34] There, the doctors invaded, and he was dead within the week.

The new president, Millard Fillmore of New York, was an anti-Seward Whig. He was more malleable than Taylor and quickly signaled his willingness to sign the Compromise of 1850. Fillmore seemed to hope that Calhoun's dying wish—the end of agitation over slavery—could be achieved.

A rising generation, represented by men like Stephen A. Douglas of Illinois, Jefferson Davis of Mississippi, William H. Seward of New York, and Charles Sumner of Massachusetts, now moved to center stage in the Senate. Douglas earned the nickname "the Little Giant" when he took up and passed Clay's compromise as individual bills. Douglas, too, hoped to end the growing controversy over slavery.

Such hopes were illusory, especially when the Fugitive Slave Act brought the long arm of slavery into Northern communities that had previously thought themselves "free." The sight of black people being pursued through Northern streets was a constant source of agitation. Bostonians rioted when Anthony Burns was hauled back into slavery after he had lived in freedom for many years.

A unique system of escape for runaway slaves was organized by former slaves with the help of sympathetic whites. The Underground Railroad was funded and supported largely by Quakers. It was neither underground nor really a railroad, but it nonetheless carried hundreds of fugitive slaves to freedom in the North or even in Canada. Former slave Harriet Tubman served as "conductor" on this railroad, and she reentered the South scores of times to help her brothers and sisters escape. Braving the hangman's noose if captured, Miss Tubman humorously said she never ran her railroad off the tracks.

Henry "Box" Brown relied on a real railroad when he had himself hidden in a packing crate and shipped north to freedom. Box Brown's daring escape made him an international celebrity. "Follow the Drinking Gourd" was the Negro spiritual that dates from this time. The song referred to the Big Dipper and the guiding North Star that must have been especially brilliant in the night sky before the advent of rural electrification. It's no wonder that Frederick Douglass would call his antislavery journal *The North Star*.

Calhoun's loss was deeply mourned by the people of the South. Even his frequent foe, Missouri's Thomas Hart Benton, said of him: "He is not dead, sir—he is not dead. There may be no vitality in his body, but there is in his doctrines."[35]

Those doctrines! Calhoun was important because he dared to contradict

Jefferson directly. Men were *not* born equal, he said, but *unequal.* He dared to say that slavery was *not* a necessary evil, but a positive good. He recognized that the "peculiar institution" could never be defended if men thought it was fundamentally wrong. For all the intellectual force of his ideas on the rights of political minorities within a genuinely federal government, it is also true that no man's *doctrines* did more to put his country on the road to civil war than did those of John C. Calhoun. At the end of the war, poet Walt Whitman reported a dispute between two battle-weary, wounded Union veterans. One said he had seen Calhoun's monument while marching through South Carolina. The other soldier disagreed, "*I* have seen Calhoun's monument. That you saw is not the real monument. It is the desolated, ruined South; nearly the whole generation of young men between seventeen and thirty used up: the rich impoverished; the plantations covered with weeds; the slaves unloosed and become the masters; and the name of Southerner blackened with every shame—all that is Calhoun's *real* monument."[36]

Somehow, Americans recognized, the second great generation of national leaders had passed from the scene. And the agitation over the meaning of slavery in a nation dedicated to freedom had not slackened. In fact, it had hardly begun.

II. Railroads and Reform

In a single generation, Americans had seen canals and steamboats revolutionize transport. Railroads revolutionized it yet again. Just as the nation's territory had expanded to the Pacific, the means for tying the country together physically were found in the railways.

Technical questions abounded: What should be the means of propulsion? Horses? Sails? Steam? *Steam*, emphatically, steam.

How should rails be constructed? Of steel? Of wood? Steel.

These decisions were not made by the government, but by rigorous experimentation by inventors, investors, and industrialists. The free enterprise system was proving to be the most creative and productive force in the world.

Americans understood that their national life was being transformed by the railroad and what Indians called the Iron Horse had profound implications for the spread of free institutions across the continent. When the Baltimore & Ohio Railroad (B&O) drove the first spike on 4 July 1828, Maryland leaders asked Charles Carroll, the oldest living signer of the Declaration of Independence, to preside over the ceremony.[37] South Carolina followed soon thereafter, building her first railroad in the critical year of 1833.[38] *DeBow's Register*, a Southern newspaper, boasted of the phenomenal growth of U.S. railroads. In just over a decade, the United States had created the world's *largest* railroad system. With 3,688 miles of track, America led Britain (2,069), Germany (1,997), and France (552).[39]

The development of American railroads was not uniform throughout the country, however. The rise of "King Cotton" in the South meant that transportation would be at the service of the slave-based plantation economy. In the North and West, rails often *led* the way in the development of the economy. Southern entrepreneurs were not encouraged to invest in railroads as they were in the North.[40] Most railroads ran east and west, especially those that carried the waves of new immigrants. Because so few immigrants wanted to go to the South—or were welcomed *in* the South—this east-west development of the rail lines further served to isolate and alienate the South from the rest of the country.

The first decades of development had shown that steam locomotives required single tracks, and the idea of competition over a single line of track would not work.[41] Soon, the railroads came to rely on long, single cars called "saloons" with an aisle running down the center.[42] "First-class" tickets provided more comfortable travel, but they also reinforced social divisions. This was an idea that ran counter to Jacksonian democracy. Many Americans came to have concerns about the rise of monopoly in the railroad industry. Vast fortunes were made in railroads. Some Americans worried about a class system based on wealth. They feared that the great disparities in wealth that characterized Europe would undermine the Jeffersonian ideal of yeoman farmers, independent and free.

---

* "Jim Crow" was a character created by a white man, "Daddy" Dan Rice, in 1832. Rice blackened his face with burnt cork and shucked and jived in a crude caricature of a black man. Jim Crow became synonymous with a Negro and lived a long and less-than-honorable life in American culture. (Online source: http://xroads.virginia.edu/~HYPER/JACOBS/hj-jcrow.htm)

Even in the North, however, racial prejudice dictated that segregation would prevail. "Jim Crow"* cars were put on behind other passenger cars to accommodate black passengers.[43] Frederick Douglass created a national stir when he *refused* to leave his seat in a first class railroad car in Massachusetts. Douglass challenged the enraged white conductor to give him "one good reason" why he should leave his seat. "Because you are black!" the conductor shouted as he summoned several muscular stevedores to eject the famous abolitionist. "Snake out the damned n——," the conductor yelled. Douglass, who had fought and floored a vicious "slave breaker" on Maryland's Eastern Shore, grabbed his seat tightly. By the time he was finally put off on the station platform, he had the seat he had paid for still held in his powerful grip. He had wrenched it from its mount. "They should at least have let me travel half way," Douglass later told an English audience, "after all, I'm only *half* a Negro!"[44] The "half a Negro" gibe referred to the fact that Frederick's father had been a white slaveholder on Maryland's Eastern Shore.

By the end of the 1850s, railroad construction had more than tripled. A government grant of twenty-two million acres of public lands provided a huge incentive for industry growth; though the rail system could not have been built as quickly or as efficiently by other means, this system was open to criticism for bringing corruption into state legislatures and Congress.[45] Despite these political challenges and the severe but temporary depression of 1857, America had clearly become a nation on wheels. In the North,* some 22,385 miles of track connected the major cities and provided railheads for an agricultural revolution that was keeping pace with rapid industrialization. The vast territory of the South was less well served. Even here, however, the 8,783 miles of track exceeded most other nations in the world.[46]

Paralleling the railroads came the development of Samuel F. B. Morse's telegraph. After he tapped out his first message—"What hath God wrought?"—in 1844, Morse would see his invention quickly spread. By 1850, telegraph lines stretched from Maine to Florida and soon spanned

---

* North and South. It should be noted that in this decade, the western states were increasingly tied to the East and Northeast by *railroad* connections. The fact that western states were free states also became critically important to the rising idea that the South meant only those states that held slaves—*and everything else was North.*

the continent.[47] Morse also developed for his invention the Morse Code, a system of dots and dashes memorized for a century by Boy Scouts and military recruits that was essential to communication.* At the same time, Cyrus McCormick's reaper did for wheat what Eli Whitney's cotton gin had done for cotton half a century before.[48]

The rush of immigrants into America's coastal cities and the spread of public education in the Northern states prompted the yearnings for reform. Emerson said that the young men of these days had been born "with knives in their brains."[49] Labor unions began to demand better conditions for urban workers. Southern writers were quick to point to the unhealthy conditions these "wage slaves" labored under. (Nonetheless, no Northern manufacturers ever sought a national Fugitive *Employees* Act. This truth was doubtless attributable in part to the tide of cheap labor from immigration.)

The 1850s saw such city-based labor federations as the National Typographic Union (1852), the United Hatters (1856), and the Iron Moulders' Union (1859).[50] Some of the German immigrants—radical refugees from the failed European Revolution of 1848—brought Marxist socialism in their steamer trunks.[51] By contrast, English writer Charles Dickens marveled at the clean and bright factories where Massachusetts's famous "Lowell Girls" worked.[52] Still, the model textile plants where these young women were employed were hardly representative of the rising new industrialism. The Democratic Party—known in these years simply as the Democracy—reached out to labor and to immigrants.

Women's rights groups began their long march toward freedom with the Seneca Falls, New York, convention in 1848. Elizabeth Cady Stanton and Lucretia Mott led the way in demanding votes (suffrage) for women.[53] This movement soon expressed itself in other ways, too. The dignified Mrs. Stanton—daughter of a distinguished judge and wife of a New York senator—shocked many when she discarded the familiar floor-length hooped skirt and adopted the newly fashionable "bloomers." This practical attire

* Morse was a virulent anti-Catholic. He shared this dubious distinction of inventive genius and religious bigotry with Henry Ford (except, in Ford's case, the objects of his contempt were Jews).

featured a short skirt and leggings. The respectable Mrs. Stanton and her fellow *suffragettes* faced the ridicule expressed in this doggerel verse:

Heigh! ho! Carrion crow,
Mrs. Stanton's all the go;
Twenty tailors take the stitches.
Mrs. Stanton wears the britches.[54]

Undeterred, women took the lead in such important social reform movements as Temperance (abstinence from alcoholic beverages), prison reform, and improvements in the treatment of the insane. "Cold Water Armies" formed to discourage drunkenness and saloons and to offer "the pledge" to young men. "Lips that touch liquor shall never touch mine," promised legions of virtuous young women.

Many hard-working, hard-drinking laborers not surprisingly took a dim view of these efforts from socially prominent "do-gooders." (Even in our own time, we've seen this superior and disdainful attitude of many reformers who look down their noses at hard hats and others who smoke and polish off a few beers after work.) As in England and Europe, the saloon often fulfilled an important social need for immigrants crammed into dark and unsanitary tenements. Party organizers often found in these taverns a ready audience for political recruitment.

Nor was the spirit of reform confined to dry land. Commodore Uriah Philips Levy finally succeeded in 1850 in banning *flogging* in the U.S. Navy. He had campaigned for decades against the inhuman practice. Now, neither black nor white American sailors could be beaten as a form of discipline. Although he may not have intended it as an abolition measure, the contrast with the treatment of slaves in the cotton fields could not have been more striking.*

Nativism—a political and social movement to restrict the flood of

* Levy (pronounced *LEV-ee*) was the first Jewish commodore in the U.S. Navy. He was also a leader in historic preservation. He purchased Thomas Jefferson's Monticello in 1836, thus saving this architectural jewel. Marc Leepson, author of *Saving Monticello,* says this was the first instance of historic preservation in America.

immigration—flared in the 1850s to challenge the two-party system. In a number of Northern states—including Massachusetts and New York—a new group virtually eclipsed the Whig Party. Calling themselves the American Party, movement leaders organized secretly to take over legislatures and prevent immigrants' voting. They answered all questions from outsiders: "I know nothing"; hence the name of derision history gives them—"Know-Nothings." In Baltimore, groups like the "Plug Uglies" used violence to prevent immigrants from voting.[55]

Much of this Nativism took on an anti-Catholic tone, with legislatures investigating Catholic parochial schools and convents. Requests for Catholic public school students to be allowed to read from their own *Douay* version of the Bible led to riots in Philadelphia. When Nativists elected a mayor in New York City, the legendary Catholic Archbishop John Hughes requested a meeting. If any of his houses of worship were attacked, he mildly informed His Honor, Catholics would "turn New York into a second Moscow." *Dagger John's* warning produced the desired effect: New York remained at peace.* It surely didn't help the abolitionist cause with Democrats that most Nativists were ardently antislavery.

The 1850s also gave America a literary treasure trove. Henry Wadsworth Longfellow published his immortal works—*The Golden Legend, Hiawatha,* and *The Courtship of Miles Standish.* Nathaniel Hawthorne wrote *The Scarlet Letter* and *The House of the Seven Gables.* Herman Melville penned *White Jacket* and *Moby Dick.* Henry David Thoreau wrote *Walden,* and Walt Whitman produced *Leaves of Grass.*[56] Of all these masterpieces, however, the work that reached more Americans and more readers throughout the world than the rest combined was Harriet Beecher Stowe's *Uncle Tom's Cabin*, written in 1852.

This book hit America like an earthquake. Written at the moment when the Fugitive Slave Act lacerated consciences throughout the North, Stowe's book created unforgettable characters—like poor Eliza, the young slave woman. Carrying her infant at her breast, she raced across the frozen

* "A second Moscow" referred to Tsar Alexander's decision to burn the city to the ground rather than let Napoleon occupy it. *Dagger John*'s nickname referred to his pointed homilies that went straight to the heart—not to any likelihood that he would actually use a dagger. (Online source: http://www.kevinbaker.info/c_tns.html.)

Ohio River. Stowe took care to depict Southern slave owners with charity. She showed them trapped in a system they did not devise. The worst villain of the book was the vicious Simon Legree, a transplanted Yankee. Even so, many Southerners reacted with hurt rage. The book was banned in many Southern communities.

"Uncle Tom" has become a term of abuse in our own time, referring to a black man who is obsequious toward whites. But Stowe's Uncle Tom was a messianic figure with whom millions of Americans—especially the evangelicals of the North—identified deeply. In England, Queen Victoria wept over the book. Her prime minister, Lord Palmerston, read it. For genereations thereafter, Americans repeated the legend that when Abraham Lincoln met Mrs. Stowe, he said, "So you are the little woman who wrote the book that started this great war."[57] *Uncle Tom's Cabin* has been translated into dozens of languages and has sold millions of copies. Since its first publication, it has never been out of print.

Frederick Douglass did not need to read *Uncle Tom's Cabin* to know the evils of slavery. As an escaped slave, he was asked to address an Independence Day crowd in Rochester, New York, in 1852. Douglass took care to *praise* the Founders. The signers of the Declaration, he said, "were brave men. They were great men, too—great enough to give fame to a great age . . . for the good they did, and the principles they contended for, I will unite with you to honor their memory."[58]

With penetrating insight, Douglass told his audience that Virginia had passed seventy-two laws mandating the death penalty if committed by a black man, compared to only two such laws that similarly punished a white man. What was this, he asked, but an official *concession* by Virginia that the black man was fully human, fully moral, fully capable of choosing between good and evil? Does anyone think it necessary to pass death penalty laws for their cattle and horses? Who could answer Douglass's piercing logic? Douglass defied anyone to say that the Constitution was a proslavery document. Instead, he believed it could be interpreted freely as an *antislavery* charter. Finally, he asked, "What to the Slave is the Fourth of July?"[59]

How thoroughly unlike William Lloyd Garrison. The outspoken white leader of American abolitionists publicly burned a copy of the Constitution.

Polar opposite of John C. Calhoun on the question of slavery, Garrison nonetheless shared with the Southern senator a vitriolic loathing of cherished American institutions. He denounced the Constitution in the pages of his newspaper, the *Liberator,* and damned it as "a covenant with death and hell."

Not only did Frederick Douglass break the chains by which white slaveholders bound him, he also had the courage to declare his independence from William Lloyd Garrison. Instead of calling for secession of the North from the South, Douglass stood for union. Douglass disputed the Garrisonian view that an abolitionist could never vote and could never even participate in the sinful American political system. Where Garrison condemned Washington and Jefferson to hell for the sin of owning slaves, Douglass spoke of the Founders with respect. Jesus Christ himself, Douglass pointedly reminded Garrison, ate with sinners and tax collectors.[60] Douglass made his break public with these bold words: "I would unite with anybody to do right; and with nobody to do wrong. And as the Union, under the Constitution, requires me to do nothing which is wrong, and gives me many facilities for doing good, I cannot go with the American Anti-Slavery Society in its doctrine of disunion."[61]

Garrison's blind intransigence had made the abolitionists hated throughout the North as well as the South. Garrison showed no prudence whatsoever. What if his insulting and degrading language *offended* more voters in the North than it won to the antislavery cause? Garrison did not care. He hated the Constitution. He hated the Union. At times, he seemed to hate America and his fellow Americans, too. This utterly humorless man would have been even more dangerous if he had commanded a large political following—as Calhoun did. But Garrison damned any of his followers who took any part in politics. Thus, he condemned his Anti-Slavery Society to the fringes of American politics.

Garrison responded to Douglass's manly show of independence with bitterness. He accused Douglass of selling out for money. Garrison had sacrificed much for the antislavery cause. He had been beaten and threatened. His family life had suffered. Now, here was the former slave whom he had hired as an orator, given place and prominence, but who had the temerity to challenge *his* authority.

Garrison was a man who brooked no opposition—and often showed no good sense. Once when his six-year-old son, Charley, fell ill, Garrison declined the aid of all physicians. Instead, he held Charley down in a steaming hot, medicated vapor bath. The little boy writhed and screamed piteously. But Garrison was unrelenting. Without intending it, Garrison had scalded his beloved boy. The child was delirious for days before dying in agony.[62] Even this horrible tragedy, however, brought no self-doubt or humility to the rigid, determined Garrison.

Harriet Beecher Stowe pleaded with Garrison to go easy on Douglass: "Where is this work of excommunication to end? Is there but one anti-slavery church and all others infidels?"[63]

Stowe recognized Douglass's superior abilities. Once, when lecturing in Britain, Douglass said that *he* had as much right to sell Thomas Auld, his former owner, as Auld had a right to sell him. Then, with a sparkle of wit, Douglass offered *to sell Auld to any and all comers!* The crowd whooped in delight.

III. "Bleeding Kansas"

The election of 1852 represented the Whig Party's last stand. Ironically, this anti-Jackson party noted for commanding intellects like John Quincy Adams, Henry Clay, and Daniel Webster never won the White House except with aged, infirm generals like William Henry Harrison and Zachary Taylor. Once again, they attempted to win the White House with a military hero.

This time, they chose the elderly General Winfield Scott. Scott had been a hero of the War of 1812, the Mexican War, and even the Nullification Crisis of 1832. A serious split between antislavery "Conscience" Whigs and Southern "Cotton" Whigs crippled Scott's campaign.

New Hampshire's former U.S. Senator Franklin Pierce had been a genuine "dark horse" candidate for the Democrats. When none of the serious candidates—Michigan's Lewis Cass, Illinois's Stephen A. Douglas, or Pennsylvania's James Buchanan—could muster the necessary two-thirds of delegates, the convention turned to the unobjectionable Pierce on the forty-ninth ballot. Significantly, the Democratic Party dropped any reference to the Declaration of Independence from its platform for the first time. Although the popular vote was closer (1,609,038 to 1,386,629), the Democrats swamped the Whigs in the electoral college (254 to 42).

Within just two years of the passage of the Compromise of 1850, both Clay and Webster joined Calhoun in death. Clay's black-draped funeral train wound through the major cities of the North on its way west to Kentucky. Abraham Lincoln captured the heart of feeling for Clay when he said: "With other men, to be defeated was to be forgotten; but to him, defeat was but a trifling incident. The spell—the long-enduring spell—with which the souls of men were bound to him is a miracle." And, true to his convictions, Clay followed George Washington's example by providing for the gradual emancipation of his slaves.[64]

As Daniel Webster lay dying at Marshfield, his Massachusetts farm, he called out for his son to read Gray's *Elegy in a Country Churchyard* to him: "The curfew tolls the knell of parting day. . . ." And with it, the devout Webster asked for the Twenty-third Psalm. When he was gone, it was said of him that "every Union cannon was shotted with Webster's Reply to Hayne."[65] For more than a century after Webster's death, American schoolchildren memorized key passages of his famous answer to South Carolina's Senator Hayne—"Liberty and Union, now and forever, one and inseparable!"

Calhoun had preceded "Great Harry of the West" and "the Godlike Daniel" by just two years. Thus passed the three giants of the Senate, the men whom historian Merrill Peterson calls "the great triumvirate." None was ever elected to the presidency, but each one towered over all those in this era—excepting Andrew Jackson, of course.

Abraham Lincoln at this point was a successful lawyer in Springfield, Illinois, and a former one-term Whig congressman. He was invited by local Whigs to deliver a eulogy for Henry Clay on 6 July 1852. It clearly marked Lincoln as a rising figure, for it not only showed his oratorical skills, it also demonstrated his devotion to the Union:

> As a politician or statesman, no one was so habitually careful to avoid all sectional ground. Whatever he did, he did for the whole country. In the construction of his measures he ever carefully surveyed every part

> of the field, and duly weighed every conflicting interest. Feeling, as he did, and as the truth surely is, that the world's best hope depended on the continued Union of these States, he was ever jealous of, and watchful for, whatever might have the slightest tendency to separate them.
>
> Mr. Clay's predominant sentiment, from first to last, was a deep devotion to the cause of human liberty—a strong sympathy with the oppressed everywhere, and an ardent wish for their elevation. With him, this was a primary and all controlling passion. Subsidiary to this was the conduct of his whole life. He loved his country partly because it was his own country, but mostly because it was a free country; and he burned with a zeal for its advancement, prosperity and glory, because he saw in such, the advancement, prosperity and glory, of human liberty, human right and human nature. He desired the prosperity of his countrymen partly because they were his countrymen, but chiefly to show to the world that freemen could be prosperous.[66]

In this eventful year of 1852, the Big Man of the West was not Lincoln. It was Democrat Stephen Douglas. At thirty-nine—four years younger than Lincoln—Douglas had already been a U.S. senator for five years. Ambitious for the White House, Stephen A. Douglas led Senate Democrats to support his Kansas-Nebraska Bill of 1854. Under Douglas's bill, the Missouri Compromise that had preserved sectional peace for thirty years would be repealed. It made the spread of slavery possible, at least in theory, anywhere in the western territories if local citizens voted for it.

Douglas advanced his Kansas-Nebraska bill under the flag of *Popular Sovereignty*. Under this banner, Democrats argued that the "sacred principle" of democracy was that the people of any territory could decide whether or not to permit slavery. Douglas famously took a neutral position on the extension of slavery itself. "I don't care," he often said, "whether slavery is voted up or down."

Personally, his view was not so neutral. Although he represented the free state of Illinois in the Senate, Douglas was known to own land and slaves in Mississippi.[67] President Pierce included in his cabinet proslavery Southern men, such as his fellow Mexican War veteran, Jefferson Davis. Davis served as secretary of war. Pierce's proslavery stance earned him the sobriquet *dough-face*—as Northern men with Southern principles became known.

Douglas used his powerful position as chairman of the Senate Territories Committee to advance his bill. The law galvanized antislavery sentiment throughout the country. It meant that slavery could spread to the Pacific if local settlers voted for it. Denounced as "squatter sovereignty," Douglas's solution to the slavery issue offended not only abolitionists and Free Soil supporters, but also those Southern "fire-eaters" who considered *any* limitation on slavery to be intolerable.*

Who could answer Douglas? He seemed to be rolling over all opposition. His natural opponents, the Whigs, were themselves splitting apart over the slavery issue.

With the breakup of the Whig Party, men like former congressman Abraham Lincoln were left without a political home. Lincoln hesitated before joining the new political party that was formed in Ripon, Wisconsin, in 1854. *New York Tribune* editor Horace Greeley urged the new alliance of anti-Nebraska groups, giving it the name *Republican*. Choosing this name was a good public relations move. Jefferson's Democratic-Republicans had long since dropped *Republican* from their name. Here, Greeley's friends could claim roots for their new party that went back to the Founder's vision (even if, in truth, these new Republicans were probably closer to the nationalism, financial conservatism, and antislavery beliefs of Hamilton than they were to Mr. Jefferson's agrarian roots). It was not entirely clear what direction the Republicans would take. Would they align with the anti-immigrant Know-Nothings? In a number of states, just such an unholy alliance did occur.[68] Lincoln was having none of it. In a letter to Joshua Speed, the friend of his youth, he wrote:

> I am not a Know-Nothing. That is certain. How could I be? How can any one who abhors the oppression of Negroes, be in favor of degrading

* "Fire-eaters" were Southern proslavery speakers who liked their rhetoric, their arguments—and their threats of disunion—hot. They contrasted with "Barn burners"—Northern antislavery men who were willing to burn down their own barns to get rid of the rats—in this case, the institution of slavery.

> classes of white people? Our progress in degeneracy appears to me to be pretty rapid. As a nation, we began by declaring that "all men are created equal." We now practically read it "all men are created equal, except Negroes." When the Know-Nothings get control, it will read "all men are created equal, except Negroes, and foreigners, and Catholics." When it comes to this I should prefer emigrating to some country where they make no pretence of loving liberty—to Russia, for instance, where despotism can be taken pure, and without the base alloy of hypocracy [sic].[69]

Soon, as we shall see, Lincoln's dedication to liberty and the equality of man will prompt him to take up the challenge laid down by Illinois's Little Giant—Stephen Douglas. Stephen Douglas's Kansas-Nebraska Act was signed by President Pierce, but it did not bring an end to conflict over slavery. In fact, it inflamed it. "Border Ruffians" from Missouri swept across the border and brought violence to the prairie. Antislavery elements throughout the North urged their followers to strengthen the Free Soil factions in Kansas.

Abolitionist preacher Henry Ward Beecher (Harriett Beecher Stowe's brother) encouraged resistance by force. Packing crates full of "Beecher's Bibles"—rifles, actually—turned up in the territory that newspaperman Horace Greeley had labeled "Bleeding Kansas."

Following a Border Ruffian raid on Lawrence, Kansas, in May 1856, Massachusetts's Charles Sumner delivered a stinging speech on the Senate floor titled "The Crime Against Kansas." Sumner grievously insulted Andrew Butler, an elderly South Carolina senator. His rude and personal attack suggested the old man was drooling. South Carolina, Sumner cried, had sent to the Senate "a Don Quixote who had chosen a mistress who, though polluted in the sight of the world, is chaste in his sight—I mean the harlot, Slavery."[70]

This talk of drooling and prostitutes was too much. Talk of sexual connection between white Southerners and slaves was always explosive.* Butler's nephew, South Carolina Congressman Preston Brooks, did not bother to

* It was explosive because it might be true. Southerner Mary Chesnut would admit as much in her famous Civil War diary. Or, it might be false, in which case it was seen as defamatory. Even in our own time, the revelation of Strom Thurmond's natural daughter by a family maid shows the issue remains one of the most sensitive and controversial.

challenge Sumner to a duel. The Yankee would never "give satisfaction," he felt sure. Instead, Brooks strode into the Senate chamber and, finding the Massachusetts lawmaker alone, caned Sumner brutally, nearly killing him. The violence of the slavery issue could not be confined to Bleeding Kansas. Now, it had invaded the Senate floor. "The only men who don't have a revolver and a knife," said South Carolina Senator James Hammond, "are those who have two revolvers!"[71]

Following the raid on Lawrence, Kansas, New England abolitionist John Brown determined to claim "an eye for an eye." He and his sons and several followers staged their own attack on Pottawotamie, Kansas. There, on 23 May 1856, they hacked to death several proslavery men—even as the men's terrified wives pleaded for their lives.

Stunned by all this violence, the Democracy in 1856 turned against President Pierce and chose instead James Buchanan. An elderly bachelor, Buchanan had the good fortune to be out of Congress and serving as ambassador to England during the rancorous debates over the Compromise of 1850 and the Kansas-Nebraska Act. Also known as a doughface, Buchanan's diplomatic skills would enable him, it was hoped, to resolve the deepening divisions at home.

The new Republican Party was determined to field a candidate. John Charles Frémont, the famous "Pathfinder," was a young, dynamic choice. The slogan: "Free Soil, Free Labor, Free Speech, Free Men, and Frémont." The first Republican Party platform condemned both slavery *and* polygamy as "relics of barbarism." Republicans championed the cause of freedom, striving to defend the Founders' vision. They opposed Calhoun's ideas and the Democrats' "don't care" indifference to the survival of freedom in an expanded republic.

Hopes for a calm resolution of issues in reasoned debate were in vain. The election of 1856 was another very ugly one. It was further complicated when the Know-Nothings nominated former President Millard Fillmore.

Frémont was attacked because he had been born out of wedlock, the son of a French Catholic. He had married Senator Thomas Hart Benton's intelligent and vivacious daughter, Jessie—a decided plus—but the ceremony had been performed by a Catholic priest. This was an affront to the Nativists.

Buchanan, on the other hand, had no wife at all. Some Republican papers depicted him as a spinster—*in a dress!*

Southern politicians regularly called the new party the "Black Republicans." This was to distinguish them from the *Jeffersonian* Republican Party and to taint them with the black flag of anarchy. But most of all, it was to associate the Republicans with black people. In Indiana, Democrats organized young women to carry banners saying: "Fathers, save us from n—— husbands!" All reason fled when the emotional issues of sex and race entered the campaign. Had these young women never heard the word "no"? Could they have married black men without themselves having said yes?

Increasingly, Southern leaders followed the earlier tack of the High Federalists and current path of the Garrisonians and threatened disunion: "The election of Frémont would be the end of the Union, and ought to be," growled fire-eater Robert Toombs.[72] The Republicans were denounced as a sectional party, even though they were forcibly kept off the ballot in most of the slave states. Democrats secretly financed Fillmore's campaign in key Northern states to divide the anti-Buchanan vote.[73]

In the end, Buchanan was elected. He carried the entire South, his own Pennsylvania, and Illinois. His 1,838,169 votes (45.3 percent) translated into 174 electoral votes. Frémont swept the Upper North, a truly impressive showing for the candidate of a new national party. His popular vote—1,341,264 (33.1 percent)—yielded a respectable 114 electoral votes. The new Republican Party had firmly displaced the Whigs and was clearly the only serious rival to the Democracy. Frémont did not get the vote of his famous father-in-law, Senator Benton. Nor did he carry California, where he had risen to national prominence. (Perhaps that was because Thomas Hart Benton and the Californians actually *knew* him.) Fillmore won 874,534 votes (21.6 percent), but garnered the electoral votes of only one state. Poor Maryland has the dubious distinction of being the only state ever carried by the Know-Nothings in a national race. It was the last gasp of the Know-Nothings. Former Massachusetts Senator Rufus Choate, a Whig, wrote their epitaph: "Anything more low, obscene, feculent the manifold heavings of history have not cast up."[74] It's safe to say Choate would not weep their passing.

IV. Dred Scott

President-elect James Buchanan and many other national Democrats hoped that the U.S. Supreme Court would resolve the divisive issue of extending slavery into the territories for them. Buchanan wrote privately—and quite improperly—to friends on the Supreme Court's urging a broad ruling. Buchanan thus tried to influence the outcome of the Court's decision. When he mounted the inaugural stands on 4 March 1857, Buchanan was seen whispering animatedly with Chief Justice Roger B. Taney. Could they have been discussing the momentous case then before Taney's court?[75] The case of *Dred Scott v. John F. A. Sandford* had been wending its way through federal courts for nearly a decade. The case was brought by Dred Scott, a slave, who sued to seek his own freedom and that of his family because his master had taken the Scotts to the free state of Illinois.

After his whispered discussion with Taney, Buchanan delivered his inaugural address, telling the assembled crowd the ruling was coming. "[I]n common with all good citizens, I shall cheerfully submit" to the Supreme Court's ruling, "whatever it may be."[76] This was a singularly *dishonest* comment, since it appears now that he knew very well what it would be. Buchanan went on to express the hope that mere "geographical" parties would rapidly become extinct. Of course, he meant the Republicans. That is surely *one* way to dispense with your opponents. Thomas Jefferson, who actually embraced *his* opponents in his inaugural address and pronounced their dissent legitimate, would have marveled to see what had become of the Democratic Party he and Madison had founded.

Two days later, the eighty-year-old Taney* read his fifty-page opinion in a Supreme Court chamber jammed with spectators.[77] The ruling was truly breathtaking. First, Taney found that Dred Scott was not an American citizen and could never become so because of his race. Taney might have stopped his reading there. Case dismissed. Despite the patent absurdity of the claim, if Scott were not a U.S. citizen, he could not sue in a U.S. court.

---

* Taney is pronounced TAW-nee in his home state of Maryland. The famous Coast Guard cutter named for him when he served as Jackson's Treasury secretary is pronounced TAY-nee.

But Taney was determined to plow ahead. He next ruled the Missouri Compromise *unconstitutional*, saying Congress had no power to interfere with Sandford's "property" without due process, as spelled out in the Fifth Amendment. Of course, Congress is *granted* authority under Article IV, Section 3 to make "all needful regulations in territories."[78] In effect, Taney was ruling the ancient and revered Northwest Ordinance of 1787 unconstitutional, too. For that act of Congress under the Articles of Confederation had famously banned slavery north of the Ohio River.

Finally, Taney offered the outrageous *obiter dictum** that as a black man Scott was "so inferior [that he] had no rights which the white man is bound to respect."[79] His opinion—which rested on an obviously false misreading of the history of the American founding—adopted Calhoun's doctrines. Under Taney's ruling, America would be a slave nation and free states would be mere local exceptions to the general rule.[80] Now, Frederick Douglass mourned, every black man in America would have to sleep with a pistol by his pillow.

If the Supreme Court's *Dred Scott* opinion had been meekly accepted, America would truly have ended her experiment in ordered liberty. She would have "lost the bubble" in 1857.

Southerners welcomed Taney's opinion. Georgia's Robert Toombs bragged in a speech that he would one day "call the roll of his slaves under the shadow of the Bunker Hill monument."[81] If Sumner had mortally offended Southern *honor* with his "Crime against Kansas" speech, Toombs had equally offended Northern dedication to *liberty* in this wildly offensive speech.

Following the doctrines of John C. Calhoun, many in the South began to clamor for territorial expansion, not for greater human liberty at all. Instead, they wanted more land to be brought under cultivation by more slaves. Senator Jefferson Davis, a Mississippi Democrat, demanded annexation of Cuba and her half million slaves.[82] Davis's colleague, Albert Gallatin Brown, spoke for this contingent when he declared on the Senate floor: "I want Cuba and sooner or later we must have it. I want Tamalpais,

* *Obiter dictum*—something said by way of passing. In law, it is a superfluous comment not necessary to decide the case at hand.

Potosi, and one or two other Mexican States; and I want them for the same reason—for the planting and spreading of slavery."[83]

But as much as Southerners appreciated the *Dred Scott* ruling, Northerners condemned it. No ruling more inimical to the Founders' vision had ever been handed down. But it was an overreach—and a grave misstep for the defenders of slavery. In a stroke Taney the Marylander shocked millions of Northerners into a belated recognition of freedom's peril. Horace Greeley spoke of it with sneering contempt. The *Dred Scott* opinion, he wrote in the *New York Tribune,* was entitled to "just so much moral weight as would be the judgment of a majority of those congregated in any Washington barroom."[84] To the *Chicago Tribune,* Taney had set back the "current of progressive ideas and Christian humanity."[85]

Far from settling the slavery question, Taney's *Dred Scott* ruling inflamed opposition to the extension of slavery. It served as the greatest recruitment tool for the new Republican Party.

Following his single term in Congress, Abraham Lincoln had returned to the circuit as a lawyer. He now made a comfortable living, especially as an advocate for the rising force of railroads. He continued, however, to maintain his interest in politics. Now fully committed to the new Republican Party, Lincoln used temperate language to challenge the opinion. But challenge the *Dred Scott* ruling he did.

> While the opinion of the Court . . . expressly declare[s] that the Constitution of the United States neither permits Congress nor a Territorial legislature to exclude slavery from any United States territory, the [majority justices] all omit to declare whether or not the same Constitution permits a state . . . to exclude it.[86]

A shudder must have gone through Lincoln's hearers. Despite the careful, lawyerly language, Lincoln raised the most frightening specter imaginable—that the United States would cease to have any free states at all. If slaves were nothing but "property," if Congress and the territories could not deprive slaveholders of the full use of that "property," how logically could free states prevent slavery from flooding the Union from

Maine to California? Under the misrule of *Dred Scott,* the question was, *How indeed?*

V. Lincoln Meets Douglas

To New England abolitionists, *any* concession to Southern slaveholders was unthinkable. But to Lincoln, the peace of the Union required Northerners to make some allowances.

Unlike the abolitionists, he went out of his way to recognize the humanity of his opponents—Northern and Southern alike. In a speech in Peoria, Illinois, in 1854, Lincoln pointedly said: "Only a small percentage [of the people] are natural tyrants. That percentage is no larger in the slave states than in the free. The great majority, south as well as north, have human sympathies." But granting this, Lincoln powerfully argued that these very human sympathies "manifest in many ways their sense of the wrong of slavery and their consciousness that, after all, there is humanity in the Negro." He showed how Southerners had joined Northerners to impose the death penalty on African slave traders in 1820. "But you never thought of hanging men for catching and selling wild horses, wild buffaloes or wild bears."[87] Lincoln's mild manner combined with his powerful use of *logic* made him a star of the new Illinois Republican Party.

Meanwhile, the powerful and nationally known Stephen A. Douglas would have to win reelection to the Senate or fade from prominence. "A steam engine in britches," the energetic Douglas determined to win.[88] His task was complicated by his open feud with his fellow Democrat, President Buchanan. First, they clashed over patronage. But soon they fought over Bleeding Kansas. Senator Douglas thought the proslavery constitution written by a rump legislature in Lecompton, Kansas, was a fraudulent expression of the people's will. He was right. President Buchanan, however, endorsed the Lecompton constitution. Horace Greeley was so impressed with Douglas's stance that he publicly urged Illinois Republicans to back the Little Giant.[89]

Lincoln knew this would destroy the Republicans—in Illinois and nationally. Ignoring the meddling of a faraway New York editor like Greeley,

Lincoln challenged Douglas to a series of debates around the state. Douglas could have stiff-armed the tall and gangly Lincoln. The one-term former congressman had gained a fine reputation in Illinois courtrooms and a good income as a lawyer for the railroads, but he could not match Douglas's international fame. Still, despite his underdog status, Lincoln had his reasons for throwing down the gauntlet, just as Douglas had his for accepting. He wanted—perhaps even *needed*—to show the Illinois legislature that he still commanded a great following among the voters; it was, after all, the legislature that would select the United States senator.*

Douglas had great confidence in his own booming voice, his quick wit, his slashing debating style. He had sharpened his skills in the United States Senate for five years, sitting next to men like Webster, Clay, and Calhoun.

But beyond demonstrating that his rhetorical mastery merited a return trip to the Senate, there were serious ideological issues at stake. Douglas accepted Lincoln's challenge in part because he was eager to show that *his* argument for Popular Sovereignty was superior to Lincoln's case for limiting the extension of slavery. "Let the people decide" had a powerful appeal. Lincoln's case for the Founders' vision of liberty and the equality of man could be made to sound woefully impractical, Douglas felt sure.

Douglas traveled around the state in high style. He had his own private railroad car, well-stocked with whiskey and refreshments. It was provided to him by George B. McClellan. McClellan was a West Pointer who had risen to become president of the Illinois Central Railroad.[90] His arrival in each town was hailed by a booming cannon and brass bands. Lincoln rode in the public cars and brought no contingent of campaign aides with him. Even so, some young women greeted him with a banner: "Westward thy Star of Empire takes its way / Thy girls *Link-on* to Lincoln / Their Mothers were for Clay."[91]

Douglas immediately attacked Lincoln's "House Divided" speech. Lincoln had electrified the state's Republican convention with this speech earlier that summer (1858). Lincoln was a dangerous radical, Douglas maintained. And

* From 1789 until the passage of the Seventeenth Amendment in 1914, U.S. senators were chosen by their state legislatures.

he was for mixing the races. Slavery, he argued, was perfectly acceptable *if the people of each state desired it.*

Lincoln once again used logic to deflate his opponent. "Although volume upon volume has been written to prove slavery a very good thing, we never hear of the man who wishes to take the good of it *by being a slave himself.*"[92]

Douglas could not resist playing on racial prejudice. "Those of you," he told one crowd, who believe the Negro is your equal and ought to be on equality with you socially, politically, and legally, have a right to entertain those opinions, and of course will vote for Mr. Lincoln."[93]* He accused Lincoln of seeking to promote marriage between whites and blacks.

Lincoln responded by saying that because he did not want a black woman for a *slave* that did not mean he had to take her for a *wife.* He already *had* a wife, he said, and as to the black woman, he could "just leave her alone." Then Lincoln showed from the Census of 1850 that the vast majority of mixed-race persons lived in the South. Clearly, slavery and not freedom produced such results. He playfully jabbed at Douglas, saying if the senator and his friends *needed a law* to prevent them from marrying across racial lines, he would support that. The crowd laughed at the reference to Douglas's *friends,* since it was widely known that a leading Democrat kept a black mistress.[94]**

Once again, Lincoln used *logic* to trip up his debate opponent. While he did not favor complete social equality between blacks and whites, he said

> [T]here is no reason in the world why the Negro is not entitled to all the natural rights enumerated in the Declaration of Independence, the right to life, liberty, and the pursuit of happiness. I hold that he is as

---

* Douglas meant they should vote for candidates for the state legislature pledged to Lincoln.

** Professor Harry Jaffa has written affectingly about this "leading Democrat." He was Richard Mentor Johnson, Van Buren's vice president. And the only reason he did not marry his beloved black housekeeper is because the laws of the time prevented it. When his mixed-race daughter died, Johnson was disconsolate. He wrote: "She was a firm and great prop to my happiness here, but she is gone where sorrow and sighing can never disturb her peaceful and quiet blossom." Such depth of feeling, such tenderness strike Professor Jaffa as fully equal to King Lear caressing the dead body of his beloved Cordelia. While Chief Justice Taney cited the laws against racial intermarriage as proof of the inferiority of black people, Jaffa points out in *A New Birth of Freedom* that they prove exactly the opposite.

> much entitled to these as the white man. I agree with Judge Douglas he is not my equal in many respects—certainly not in color, perhaps not in moral or intellectual endowment. But in the right to eat the bread, without leave of anybody else, which his own hand earns, he is my equal, and the equal of Judge Douglas, and the equal of every other man.

Douglas attempted to show himself humane with a crude analogy. In the struggle between the crocodile and the Negro, he said, he favored the Negro. But in the struggle between the white man and the Negro, he favored the white. Thus, he tried to dehumanize the black man and place him outside the community of concern for which the white majority had responsibility. Under Douglas's definition of Popular Sovereignty, it was always the white majority that would make decisions about black men's freedom. And he thought that was just. Lincoln responded that for a man to rule himself was freedom. But for a man to rule another man *without his consent* was tyranny.

Lincoln succeeded in pressing Douglas on slavery in the territories *after* Taney's *Dred Scott* decision. What was left of Douglas's Popular Sovereignty, Lincoln wanted to know. How could the people of a territory vote slavery *down* if Taney said every American had a right to carry his "property" with him?

In response, Douglas introduced his so-called Freeport Doctrine. Named for the Illinois town where they met, the Freeport Doctrine said slavery could not exist without "friendly legislation" to support it. Anti-slavery voters could simply refuse to pass such laws and slavery would effectively be kept out of a territory, Douglas claimed. Thus, he said, Popular Sovereignty was entirely consistent with Taney's ruling.

Like the seasoned lawyer he was, Lincoln skillfully maneuvered Douglas into making a concession that would prove fatal—not only to Douglas, but also to his Democratic Party. Southern fire-eaters were outraged. Douglas would *never* get their support for president, they cried. But unless Douglas had devised *some* barrier to the spread of slavery in the territories, how could he ever claim election as a Northern man? Lincoln would later exploit Douglas's fatal misstep. He knew it was absurd to contend that "a thing may be lawfully driven away from where it has a lawful right to be."[95] *Checkmate.*

Lincoln's performance in the debates marked him as a leader. Lincoln was also a powerful wrestler, and wrestlers know how to use their opponents' strength against them. Lincoln used Douglas's worldwide fame to catapult himself into national prominence, though the positive results seemed slow in coming. Douglas, for instance, went on to win reelection by the Illinois legislature despite Lincoln's impressive showing. Lincoln admitted he felt like the little boy who stubbed his toe in the dark: he was too big to cry, but it hurt too much to laugh. Yet he would later recognize that his famous sparring match was "a stumble, not a fall." The senator won reelection on the strength of the holdovers in the legislature. Lincoln scored well among those elected in 1858.

Lincoln excelled in the use of logic *and* homely analogies. While most abolitionists morally indicted slavery *and* slaveholders, Lincoln compared slavery in the South to a rattlesnake coiled in the children's cradle. You cannot strike it there without endangering the children's lives. But slavery in the territories was a rattlesnake in the open fields. There, he said, you should strike it with a hoe *and kill it.* This gripping picture showed that he was *not* reading Southerners out of the family—out of the Union. He knew and appreciated their concerns about a slave uprising. He would not encourage an insurrection that might create another Haiti in the Southland. All that Lincoln asked is that we treat slavery as a wrong, treat it the way Washington and Jefferson and Madison treated it. Let us return slavery to "the path of ultimate extinction" where our Founders placed it.

When Douglas attacked Lincoln's "House Divided" speech, Lincoln was able to turn away that thrust. He said Douglas thought a house *could* exist permanently divided. The conflict was really not between himself and Douglas, but between Douglas and "a higher authority." Lincoln's listeners laughed because they recognized his metaphor. It was Jesus who had said a house divided against itself cannot stand.*

The Lincoln-Douglas debates were the most important since the ratification of the Constitution. Lincoln showed a mastery of law, philosophy, and history that raised him not only above Douglas, but above every other statesman of the age. After these debates, there would be no more Republicans

* "And if a house is divided against itself, that house cannot stand." (Mark 3:25 NKJV)

flirting with Douglas the Democrat. The future of the Republican Party was now bound up with the future of freedom in America. "The fight must go on," Lincoln said after the votes were counted. "The cause of civil liberty must not be surrendered at the end of *one*, or even, one *hundred* defeats."[96]

VI. John Brown and Harpers Ferry

Extreme abolitionists like John Brown were in no way willing to place slavery on the path of *ultimate* extinction. They demanded action and they demanded it *now*. Brown moved freely among the leaders of the abolition cause. He began to share, but not completely, his plans for a dramatic strike against slavery. A group of financial backers known as the Secret Six helped Brown rent a Maryland farmhouse across the Potomac River from the federal arsenal at Harpers Ferry, Virginia.* Brown assembled a small force of twenty-one impressionable young men—including his own sons and some former slaves. He planned to raise the banner of liberation in that strategic town and call on slaves to join in a bold bid for freedom.

Brown was an unlikely choice to organize a revolution—or anything else. Father of twenty, he had failed as farmer, as a merchant, and in every other line of work. Still, he was charismatic. Tall, straight as a ramrod, bedecked with blazing eyes and a bushy beard, Brown seemed the picture of an Old Testament prophet to many. Others saw in him the demon of *unreasoning* fanaticism. No one would ever meet John Brown and think of Lincoln's appeal to "mind, all-conquering mind." Brown had escaped capture for his murders of proslavery men in Kansas. This only emboldened him to greater exploits. He tried to enlist Frederick Douglass in his plot, but Frederick recoiled from his friend. He was "shocked" at the plot and thought it would immediately be stamped out.[97] Embittered, Brown determined to go ahead without Douglass's aid.

When he finally struck on 16 October 1859, John Brown seized the federal arsenal at Harpers Ferry and took several Virginians as hostages. The news alarmed the entire nation.

---

* Harpers Ferry today is part of *West* Virginia.

Colonel Robert E. Lee was home on leave in Virginia when the news of Harpers Ferry came. He immediately reported to the White House, taking Lieutenant J. E. B. Stuart with him.[98]

There, President Buchanan authorized Lee to take a detachment of U.S. Marines to Harpers Ferry to capture Brown and his cohorts. Lee raced to retake the federal arsenal. He sent Stuart under a white flag of truce to demand the immediate surrender of Brown and his fellow insurrectionists. From inside the arsenal, Lee and his Marines could hear cries coming from some of the hostages. They feared they would die in an assault on the building. One of the hostages, Lewis W. Washington, yelled out: "Never mind about us, *fire*!" Lee knew the voice well. It was the grandnephew of George Washington. Smiling amid the tension, Lee told his Marines: "The old revolutionary blood does tell!"[99]

As soon as Brown rejected the lieutenant's demand, J. E. B. Stuart touched his hat. He gave the signal to Lee and the Marines to storm the place. Instantly, the Marines charged forward, battering the heavy oaken doors in, using their bayonets instead of bullets to spare the hostages.[100] Within minutes, Brown and his remaining men were captured. Two of Brown's sons were among the dead. The raid had ended barely thirty-six hours after it had begun.

Brown's venture was a complete and bloody failure. Frederick Douglass had predicted that. But Brown was soon able to change the impression. When he was brought to trial, he rejected with scorn his lawyers' attempt to plead not guilty by reason of insanity. Brown impressed all who saw him with his calm composure, his ready willingness to die for the cause of abolition. Even Virginia's proslavery governor Henry A. Wise, who visited the abolitionist in prison, marveled at Brown's steadfastness.[101]

He was charged with "treason" against Virginia and tried in a state court. This was further evidence of President Buchanan's doughface policies, since Brown's target was the *federal* arsenal. The verdict was a foregone conclusion. Sentenced to be hanged, Brown addressed the court:

> I believe to have interfered as I have done . . . in behalf of His despised poor, was not wrong, but right. Now, if it be deemed necessary that I

> should forfeit my life for the furtherance of the ends of justice, and mingle my blood further with the blood of my children, and with the blood of millions in this slave country whose rights are disregarded by wicked, cruel, and unjust enactments, I submit: so let it be done.

Brown's pose as Christian martyr was almost perfect. Northern writers generally praised him. Emerson said the "gallows would be glorious like the cross."[102] Henry David Thoreau told the citizens of Concord, Massachusetts: "No man in America has ever stood up so persistently and effectively for the dignity of human nature. . . ."[103]

Unknown to the general public was the letter Brown received from Mahala Doyle. She reminded Brown how he had invaded her Kansas home three years earlier and taken her husband and sons out to butcher them. "My son John Doyle whose life I begged of you is now grown up and is very desirous to be at Charlestown on the day of your execution," the unforgiving widow wrote.[104]

John Brown was hanged on 2 December 1859. On his way to the gallows, he handed this message to one of the officials: "I, John Brown, am now quite certain that the crimes of this guilty land will never be purged away but with Blood."[105]

In the crowd that assembled at Charlestown that day, a professor from the Virginia Military Institute, Thomas J. Jackson, noted Brown's "unflinching firmness." Soon, Professor Jackson—*Stonewall* Jackson—would be giving lessons in unflinching firmness. Standing nearby, fire-eater Edmund Ruffin actually admired Brown's courage. But young John Wilkes Booth, already a famous actor, had only contempt for the old man. Abolitionists were "the *only* traitors in the land," Booth said.[106]

VII. The Election of 1860

The Republican Party was eager to avoid the brand of John Brown's dangerous radicalism. Although Democrats in Congress struggled to implicate the "Black Republicans," none of their charges could be proved. A congressional investigation of John Brown's activities yielded no evidence of

Republican support. The fury that was unleashed in the wake of John Brown's raid was enough, however, to convince Frederick Douglass he had better *accept* the longstanding offer of a British speaking tour. Frederick's friends feared he might be kidnapped and dragged southward in chains to face an enraged all-white jury on charges he conspired with Brown. For such an offense, Douglass could have been hanged. Hurriedly, Douglass departed for England through Canada.

As for Abraham Lincoln, he had always stood *against* just such extremism as John Brown represented. Reverence for law must be the "political religion" of this country, Lincoln had said in his address to the Young Men's Lyceum in Springfield as long ago as 1838. "Old John Brown is hanged," Lincoln told his fellow Republicans, "we cannot object." Lincoln acknowledged Brown's courage and his moral opposition to slavery, but he thought the raid demonstrated Brown's insanity.[107] Then he reminded his listeners that just as Brown had been hanged for treason, so would they have to treat *other* traitors if they tried to rebel against the lawful government.

Lincoln moved boldly in February 1860 to give an address in New York City. Many Republicans assumed that New York Senator William H. Seward would be the party's 1860 presidential nominee. By speaking at the Cooper Union, Lincoln offered a challenge to Seward in his very backyard.

His speech thrilled New Yorkers. He was one of the first to respond after the abortive John Brown raid. Lincoln's speech took up and demolished *every* argument against the Republicans, every charge that had been lodged against them. He carefully outlined the Founders' views on slavery and aligned the Republicans *with those views*. He presented the Republican cause as prudent, moderate, but *firm*. To Southerners, he was patient, almost pleading. He did not indulge in the abolitionists' demonizing of slaveholders. But neither would he give in to the Slave Power's damning of the "Black Republicans" as dangerous radicals. Lincoln concluded with a ringing affirmation of freedom in these words:

> All they ask, we could readily grant, if we thought slavery right; all we ask, they could as readily grant, if they thought it wrong. Their thinking it right, and our thinking it wrong, is the precise fact upon which

depends the whole controversy. Thinking it right, as they do, they are not to blame for desiring its full recognition, as being right; but, thinking it wrong, as we do, can we yield to them? Can we cast our votes with their view, and against our own? In view of our moral, social, and political responsibilities, can we do this?

Wrong as we think slavery is, we can yet afford to let it alone where it is, because that much is due to the necessity arising from its actual presence in the nation; but can we, while our votes will prevent it, allow it to spread into the National Territories, and to overrun us here in these Free States? If our sense of duty forbids this, then let us stand by our duty, fearlessly and effectively. Let us be diverted by none of those sophistical contrivances wherewith we are so industriously plied and belabored—contrivances such as groping for some middle ground between the right and the wrong, vain as the search for a man who should be neither a living man nor a dead man—such as a policy of "don't care" on a question about which all true men do care—such as Union appeals beseeching true Union men to yield to Disunionists, reversing the divine rule, and calling, not the sinners, but the righteous to repentance—such as invocations to Washington, imploring men to unsay what Washington said, and undo what Washington did.

Neither let us be slandered from our duty by false accusations against us, nor frightened from it by menaces of destruction to the Government nor of dungeons to ourselves.

Let us have faith that right makes might, and in that faith, let us to the end dare to do our duty as we understand it.[108]

William Seward lacked this fluency of expression. His previous speech on the "irrepressible conflict" between slavery and freedom had hung the title of *radical* around his neck. He frightened people. When Lincoln said essentially the same thing in his "House Divided" speech, he took care to take his text from the Bible. It was much harder to label him dangerous—as Stephen Douglas had learned.

More than this, Seward's prominence had made him powerful enemies. The Know-Nothings hated Seward because he tried to give state aid to

Catholic school students in New York State. In effect, Seward would have granted them *vouchers*. That would mean Seward at the top of the ticket would lose votes among the Nativists. We have already seen how *unsympathetic* Lincoln was to Know-Nothingism, but he had not been called upon to fight them during his single term in Congress. They hated Seward. That could mean another Republican loss in states like Maryland and Pennsylvania.

When the Republican Party convention met in Chicago in May, the leading candidates were William H. Seward of New York, Salmon P. Chase, the ex-Democrat, of Ohio, and Simon P. Cameron of Pennsylvania. Lincoln's campaign manager, Judge David Davis, had shrewdly worked to make Lincoln everyone's *second* choice. Judge Davis made sure to fill the visitors' galleries at the Wigwam with Illinois "leather lungs." These were burly young men hired to shout their lungs out for Lincoln. Judge Davis took pains to show all the delegates that Lincoln could carry the states of the lower North.

Lincoln was concerned by reports that Judge Davis was wheeling and dealing to get him the nomination. "I authorize no bargains and will be bound by none," Lincoln telegraphed Davis.[109] Davis reportedly replied when he read the note: "Lincoln ain't here and don't know what we have to meet."[110] When Seward was blocked, Lincoln was nominated on the third ballot. In Springfield, cannons were fired in celebration. All seemed exultant except Lincoln.

Democrats were deeply divided. Mississippi Senator Jefferson Davis had demanded a federal slave code for the territories. There would be no states' rights for the North. If the federal government protected slavery in the territories—as Davis and his supporters argued—then these territories were overwhelmingly likely to vote to become slave *states*.

This, Senator Stephen A. Douglas could not accept. Alabama fire-eater William L. Yancey was prepared to press for a flat statement in the party's platform that slavery was *right*. Nothing less, Yancey said, could answer the antislavery agitation of the Republicans. The Democratic Party had *never* made such a pronouncement. True, Senator Pettit, a doughface from Indiana, had said the Declaration of Independence's assertion that "all men are created equal" was not a self-evident truth, but "a self-evident lie."[111] But now Yancey was going too far. "Gentlemen of the South, you mistake us," warned Democratic Senator Pugh of Ohio, "you mistake us. *We will not do it.*"[112] Everyone sensed that an historic clash was coming.

When the Democratic Party's nominating convention gathered in Charleston, South Carolina, disunion was already in the air. Unable to agree on a nominee for president—their rules required two-thirds to nominate—the Democrats suffered a walkout by cotton-state delegates. They agreed dispiritedly to reconvene in Baltimore. Baltimore was only slightly less vehement on the slavery issue than Charleston had been.

It was there that the fatal split finally occurred. When the convention refused to approve a platform calling for a federal slave code for the territories, another walkout occurred. The Southern delegates reconvened in Richmond, Virginia, to nominate Vice President John C. Breckinridge. This faction actually wanted to reopen the African slave trade. Senator Stephen A. Douglas had finally achieved his long-sought prize, the nomination for president of the national Democratic Party. But by the time he won it, the prize was hardly worth having.

A small faction of Old Line Whigs and former Know-Nothings assembled as the Constitutional Union Party and nominated Kentucky's John C. Bell and Massachusetts's distinguished Edward Everett. Now, the national election would be a four-way split.

Many Democrats understood that the major party split could only elect Lincoln. Fire-eaters Yancey and Robert B. Rhett welcomed the result. They had been agitating for Southern secession, and they believed Lincoln's election would be the shock needed to bring it about.

Stephen Douglas defied tradition and took to the rails to campaign with vigor. He wore himself out with speeches from train platforms in the North and the South denouncing secession and calling for national unity. Lincoln did not even appear on the ballot in ten Southern states. His supporters carried rails in honor of his title, the rail-splitter. Republicans gloried in the fact that Lincoln had worked with his hands.

By this time, Lincoln was a wealthy and successful lawyer. This did not detract from the appeal of his hardscrabble youth. Actually, this was a great part of the Republicans' appeal. You, too, by hard work and honesty can become rich, Republicans told workers. His young supporters marched in all the Northern cities in a quasi-military company of "Wide Awakes."* Soon, all of America would be on the march.

When the votes were tallied in November, Lincoln swept the populous Northern states. He won 1,866,452 votes in a four-way contest (more than Buchanan four years earlier). He gained 180 electoral votes (152 were required to win). Douglas came in second in popular votes, 1,375,157, but because most of those votes were cast in the North, he won only 12 electoral votes. Breckinridge swept the South with 847,953 votes and 72 electoral votes. Bell prevailed only in the Border States, winning 590,631 votes and 39 electoral votes.

It was the most important election in American history. Immediately, preparations began in the South for secession. The legislature in South Carolina called for a secession convention to meet in Charleston in December. There was no time to lose, secessionists told reluctant fellow Southerners. Once Lincoln had entered the White House, they reasoned, it would be harder to break free.

President Buchanan was in thrall to his Southern cabinet members. Secretary of War John Floyd made no effort to prevent the seizure of federal forts and arsenals throughout the South. Buchanan frittered. When South Carolina voted for secession, Buchanan was paralyzed. Fire-eater Robert Barnwell confronted him, demanding he turn over Fort Sumter. Buchanan waved his hands in impotent frustration: "You are pressing me too importunately, Mr. Barnwell; you don't give me time to consider; you don't give me time to say my prayers. I always say my prayers when required to act upon any State affair."[113]

Loyal Unionists prayed for "just one hour of Andrew Jackson" instead of the invertebrate Buchanan.

Seven states had seceded by the time Lincoln prepared to take the oath. Lincoln had been informed of an assassination threat against his life while in Philadelphia. Refusing to cancel his speech on Washington's Birthday at Independence Hall, Lincoln told the anxious crowd he would give his life for

* Wide Awakes, a paramilitary group of young men, were so called because of their torchlit parades at nightfall. They supported the Republican Party, but were widely suspected of voter intimidation and anti-Catholicism.

> that sentiment in the Declaration of Independence which gave liberty, not alone to the people of this country, but, I hope, to the world, for all future time. It was that which gave promise that in due time the weight would be lifted from the shoulders of all men. This is a sentiment embodied in the Declaration of Independence. Now, my friends, can this country be saved upon that basis? If it can, I will consider myself one of the happiest men in the world, if I can help to save it. If it cannot be saved upon that principle, it will be truly awful. But if this country cannot be saved without giving up that principle, I was about to say I would rather be assassinated on this spot than surrender it.[114]

It was an *uncharacteristically* emotional moment for Lincoln. Against his better judgment, he was persuaded to change his plans and pass through secessionist Baltimore—where the plot was said to be thickening—in the middle of the night. When he arrived safely in Washington, he faced international ridicule. It was said he had come through Baltimore disguised as a Scotchman. Cartoonists lampooned him.

Washington was little better. Rumors of treasonous plots swirled through the muddy streets of the capital. Old General Winfield Scott, a Virginian and a staunch Unionist, pledged to defend the city's streets. There would be no violence, no armed disruption of the peaceful transfer of government. For the inauguration on 4 March 1861, Scott stationed sharpshooters on all the federal buildings. Breathing defiance of the rebels, Scott said he would stuff them into his artillery pieces positioned at the Capitol and "manure the Virginia hills" with their bodies.[115]

President Buchanan and the president-elect came on to the inaugural stands arm in arm.[116] Lincoln approached the podium to be sworn in as the sixteenth president of the United States. None other than Chief Justice Roger B. Taney would administer the oath. Senator Stephen A. Douglas, his defeated rival, held Lincoln's tall, black hat.[117]

His inaugural address was the most eloquent yet delivered in Washington City. He offered an olive branch to the states that had passed secession ordinances even as he denied the right of any state to secede. In a passage sometimes overlooked, he laid out his view of Fort Sumter. The federal installation in Charleston harbor was surrounded by a Confederate "ring of fire." "The power confided to me will be used to hold occupy and possess the property and places belonging to the government and to collect the duties and imposts," Lincoln said, trying not to provoke. He spoke to his dissatisfied fellow countrymen: "You have not oath registered in heaven to destroy the government, while I shall have the most solemn one to 'preserve, protect, and defend it.' "* He appealed to reason, to friendship, and to those "mystic chords of memory stretching from every battlefield and patriot grave to every living heart and hearthstone."

The future of freedom hung on those words. Not just American freedom, but *world* freedom was at stake. If a dissatisfied minority could break up the government whenever it lost an election, popular government was indeed impossible. If the failure to gain sufficient ballots led dissenters to resort to bullets, this grand experiment in ordered freedom would fail.

The next four years would be the years of freedom's fiery trial. Before Abraham Lincoln looked out on another inaugural assembly, the sacred fire of liberty was nearly extinguished. The American republic would come close to death and would be reborn. The new president knew what was at stake. He believed our sacred Union was "the last, best hope of Earth." To save this precious experiment in ordered liberty, Lincoln in this inaugural address appealed to sweet reason and to "the better angels of our nature."[118]

* It sounds as if he had not yet taken the oath of office. He hadn't. At this time in our history, presidents delivered their inaugural addresses *before* taking the oath.

Nine

Freedom's Fiery Trial (1860–1863)

The events of 1860–1865 not only determined the fate of freedom in the United States, but they also set for years to come the terms of the struggle for freedom around the world. If human bondage is to be an inextricable part of the American heritage, extending into the limitless future, then democracy will have a hollow ring here, and it will be discredited around the world. The British constitution provides for a great measure of personal liberty even while the British ruling class firmly denies that all men were created equal. Just as firmly, they reject democracy as a political system. France, Prussia, and Russia are despotic regimes. Only in America is democracy embraced as a governing philosophy on a broad scale. The great Democrat Andrew Jackson creates a popular republic that extended voting rights far beyond any other nation on earth; he has welcomed millions of European immigrants and included them readily in the political community. As citizens, these new Americans enjoy full equality. Even as he powerfully stamps out the sparks of rebellion in South Carolina, Jackson still gives no hope to the slaves. Jackson never speaks even of the eventual liberation of the slaves. On his deathbed, he bids farewell to his family, including his slaves. He assures them they will all meet in heaven. But on earth, Jackson's slaves are still slaves. As long as Jackson's Democratic Party governs, this will be true. When Andrew Jackson's Democratic Party splits over slavery, the Union itself is torn.

I. Secession Winter (1860–61)

"South Carolina is too small for a republic and too large for an insane asylum,"[1] responded James L. Petigru to fire-eater Robert Barnwell Rhett during Christmas week 1860. Following Lincoln's election, Petigru was one of a small number of Charleston Unionists who found themselves outgunned and outvoted that fateful winter. South Carolina's secession convention voted to take the state out of the Union on 20 December 1860.

The mood was festive in Charleston. Fireworks greeted the Ordinance of Secession and revelers placed blue cockades on the bust of John C. Calhoun. Bands played France's revolutionary anthem, the *Marseillaise*.[2] Convention delegates drew up a declaration in which they gave their reasons for leaving the Union. The delegates condemned the Northern people for "denouncing as sinful the institution of Slavery."[3] They condemned abolition societies in the North. Governor William H. Gist ordered a state militia officer to carry the news to other Southern states. The officer chosen was named—jesting aside—States Rights Gist.[4]

Many fire-eaters in the South not only expected Lincoln's election, they *welcomed* it. They intended to use the election of an antislavery president to shock their fellow Southerners into seceding from the old Union. It did not matter to them that Lincoln and the Republicans had repeatedly assured them there would be no interference with the institution of slavery *in the South*. The Republican platform of 1860 was decidedly less radical than that of 1856. There was now no talk of slavery as "a relic of barbarism." Lincoln was widely viewed in the North as much more moderate than John Charles Frémont, the party's first presidential nominee, had been.

Lincoln was still in Springfield, dealing with the endless demands of office-seekers. He felt, he said, "like a man renting rooms at one end of his house while the other end is on fire." Still, he had to form a cabinet and staff a new administration. "We must run the machine as we find it," he told nervous questioners.[5]

While Lincoln struggled to balance all factions of the very factious new Republican Party, secessionists moved quickly to take more states out of the Union before Lincoln took the oath of office on 4 March 1861. Mississippi seceded and sent "commissioners" to other slave states to persuade them to join the new Southern Confederacy. Judge Alexander Hamilton Handy was Mississippi's man in Maryland. He got nowhere when he carried his message to Annapolis. Governor Thomas Hicks was a Union man. Fearing what the Maryland legislature might do, Hicks refused to summon it into special session. So Handy spoke instead to a large and sympathetic audience in Baltimore.[6] Slavery was not a sin before God and man, he said, but had been *ordained* by God. He added:

> The first act of the black republican party will be to exclude slavery from all the Territories, the District [of Columbia], the arsenals and the forts, by action of the general government. That would be a recognition that slavery is a sin, and confine the institution to its present limits. The moment that slavery is pronounced a moral evil—a sin—by the general government, that moment the safety of the rights of the South will be entirely gone.[7]

Andrew Calhoun, son of the great South Carolinian, was his state's commissioner to Alabama. He wasn't singing the *Marseillaise*. Instead, he offered a chilling parallel between the radicalism of the French Revolution with all its heady rhetoric about "liberty, equality, fraternity" and the bloody slave uprising on Santo Domingo (Haiti). The Republicans' belief in equality would produce the same result in the South, he charged. He spoke heatedly of "skull-built" walls and "white fiends" of the North inciting insurrection among the slaves.[8]

Georgia seceded and sent its young Supreme Court justice, Henry Benning, as commissioner to Virginia. Speaking to delegates at the Old Dominion's secession convention, Benning told them Georgia's decision to leave the Union was based on one idea: "It was a conviction, a deep conviction on the part of Georgia, that a separation from the North was the only thing that could prevent the abolition of her slavery."[9]

To these extreme advocates of slavery, it did not matter that Lincoln and the Republicans were bound not to interfere with slavery in the states where it *already* existed. It did not matter that he even pledged to enforce the Fugitive Slave Act. He would enforce it because the Constitution commanded it (although, as he wrote his friend Joshua Speed, it would "crucify our feelings"). It did not matter that Lincoln's moderation had earned him the contempt of all-out abolitionists like William Garrison and Wendell Phillips. Phillips sneeringly dismissed Lincoln as "that slave-hound from Illinois."[10] None of this mattered as the South was dragooned and Calhouned into secession. What mattered was that Lincoln had said "if slavery is not wrong, then nothing is wrong."

President-elect Lincoln saw a ray of hope when he read the speech of Georgia's Alexander Hamilton Stephens, his old friend from Congress. Stephens had spoken out strongly *against* disunion at his state's secession convention.[11] "What reason can you give to the nations of the earth to justify [secession]?" he asked. "What right has the North assailed? What interest of the South has been invaded? What justice has been denied? And what claim founded in justice and right has been withheld?"[12]

Lincoln wrote to Stephens, assuring him of his friendly intentions toward the South. The South, he said, would be no more threatened by him than it was by George Washington.[13] "You think slavery is *right*, and ought to be extended; while we think it is *wrong* and ought to be restricted," Lincoln wrote plaintively. Stephens did not dispute his old friend's description of the conflict. But he said the mere fact that the majority in the North had voted to put "the institutions of half the states under the ban of public opinion and national condemnation" would be enough to spark a revolt in the slave states.[14]

When seven states had seceded, they sent delegates to Montgomery, Alabama, in February 1861 to write a constitution for their new government. The Confederate States of America, as they would call their new nation, would have a president eligible for a single six-year term. He would have a line-item veto.* Members of the cabinet could sit in the Confederate

* Some wags have said the line-item veto, long sought by President Reagan, was the only thing in the Confederate constitution worth fighting for. That was before Bill Clinton showed everyone how the line-item veto could be used creatively to bid *up* federal spending. President Clinton threatened to veto public works bills favored by congressmen unless they voted *for* his social spending bills.

Congress, thus opening the way for the development over time of cabinet government like that in Britain.

The most important aspects of the Confederate constitution were, however, less obvious. For a movement that claimed states' rights, their constitution allowed *no state* the right to emancipate slaves. *No state* could even be admitted to the Confederacy from the old Union unless it agreed to maintain slavery always. And, a stunning development: the drafters of this constitution debated and emphatically *rejected* a passage that would have recognized a right of a state to secede from this Confederacy.[15]

When the delegates moved to choose a president and vice president, they shunned fire-eaters like Robert Barnwell Rhett and Robert Toombs. The able Toombs might have fared better had he never gone to Montgomery. His friend Alexander Stephens reported that he was drinking heavily there. "He was *tighter* than I ever saw him, too tight for his character and reputation."[16] Delegates instead chose the sober Mississippian Jefferson Davis. Davis, a West Pointer, hero of the Mexican war, a former secretary of war and U.S. senator, seemed admirably qualified. As Davis's vice president, the secessionists chose none other than Lincoln's old friend, Alexander Hamilton Stephens. A slight, short man, Stephens was chosen precisely because he was no fire-eater. His very moderation would appeal to many other Southerners who were still not sure about secession.[17] Once Georgia acted, however, little Aleck Stephens threw in his lot wholeheartedly with the Confederacy.

He expressed his beliefs in another speech a month after his election. Stephens's Cornerstone Speech emphasized that the Founders were *wrong* when they asserted all men are created equal. Just as Lincoln had chosen to base his famous "House Divided" speech on the words of Jesus, now Stephens also cited Scripture.*

> Our new [Confederate] government is founded upon exactly the opposite idea [to the idea of equality in the Declaration]; its foundations are laid, its cornerstone rests upon the great truth that the negro

* "The stone which the builders rejected has become the chief cornerstone" (Psalm 118:22). The *cornerstone,* as listeners to a thousand Christian sermons knew, was Jesus himself.

> is not equal to the white man. That slavery—subordination to the superior race, is his natural and normal condition. This, our new Government, is the first, in the history of the world, based upon this great physical and moral truth.[18]

Unlike Chief Justice Taney and Senator Stephen A. Douglas, Stephens confirmed what Lincoln had said about the Founders. They *did* believe what they wrote in the Declaration. Stephens simply contended that the Founders were wrong. In this speech, Stephens goes beyond John C. Calhoun, who seemed to think the "created equal" doctrine of the Declaration of Independence was an idea *peculiar* to Thomas Jefferson. Stephens here admits that Lincoln was right when he claimed to believe and defend no more than the principle the Founders gave us. The reason the Confederacy had come into being was to assert racial *inequality* and to defend Negro slavery.[19]

No one in the South contradicted Vice President Stephens when he delivered this Cornerstone Speech. It was a clear defense of the Confederates' reasons for secession and going to war.

Mindful of the need for European intervention in behalf of the Confederacy, President Jefferson Davis avoided any direct mention of slavery in his inaugural address, which he delivered in Montgomery on 18 February 1861. That is because slavery was widely condemned in Europe. Instead, he stressed the right of self-determination for the states. "Thus the sovereign States, here represented, proceeded to form this Confederacy, and it is by abuse of language that their act has been denominated a revolution," said Davis. "They formed a new alliance, but within each State its government has remained, and the rights of person and property have not been disturbed."[20]

Two important things stand out. First, Jefferson Davis specifically and explicitly rejects the idea that the Confederacy is based on the natural right of revolution. This makes tactical if not philosophical sense: had he cited the right of revolution, he would have justified the right of his slaves to revolt against *him*. His namesake Thomas Jefferson had explicitly invoked Americans' natural right to revolution in the Declaration of Independence. Jefferson Davis was having none of it.

Second, he speaks *in code* about property rights. For slaveholders who regarded their slaves as *chattels* and who followed Chief Justice Roger B. Taney's reasoning in the *Dred Scott* ruling, this language was confirmation that slavery would exist as long as the right to property existed—that is, forever.

II. Fort Sumter: The Circle of Fire

The broad respect that President Jefferson Davis enjoyed throughout the South was not shared by Texas Governor Sam Houston. Formerly governor of Tennessee and the victor at the Battle of San Jacinto that gained Texas's independence from Mexico, this old friend of Andrew Jackson had served in the Senate with Davis and found him "as ambitious as Lucifer and cold as a lizard."[21]

The secession crisis found Houston increasingly isolated in the Lone Star State. At seventy, he had taken to the hustings to warn against secession. In Galveston, he spoke like an Old Testament prophet. In truth, Houston *always* spoke like an Old Testament prophet, but his words are nonetheless worth recalling here:

> Some of you laugh to scorn the idea of bloodshed as the result of secession, but let me tell you what is coming. You may, after the sacrifice of countless millions of treasures and hundreds of thousands of precious lives, as a bare possibility, win Southern independence, if God be not against you. But I doubt it. The North is determined to preserve this Union.[22]

Once, when he was speaking in the small Texas town of Belton, an armed man advanced toward him menacingly. "It is nothing but a fice [a small dog] barking at the lion in his den," Houston responded, staring the man down.[23] Houston would not be so successful in staring down the state's secession convention, however. When the delegates voted to take Texas out of the Union, they demanded that Governor Houston take an oath of loyalty to the Confederacy. Houston paced the floor of the Executive

Mansion all night before giving his answer. He prayed with his family into the night. The next morning, he told his worried wife: "Margaret, I will never do it."[24] On 16 March 1861, he faced the convention. "In the name of the Constitution of Texas, which has been trampled upon, I refuse to take this oath," he said in bold defiance. "In the name of my own conscience and manhood . . . I refuse to take this oath. . . . I protest in the name of the people of Texas against all the acts and doings of this convention and I declare them null and void."[25]

But Houston would not go so far as to initiate civil war in his beloved Texas by clinging to the office to which he was freely elected. He turned down the offer of troops from the new Lincoln administration. A group of armed men came to him, offering to help him fight for the governor's office. One of the crowd was Noah Smithwick, the blacksmith who had forged the first cannon fired in the Texas War of Independence. Houston would not let these men keep him in power by force. "My God, is it possible that all the people have gone mad?" he asked as he thanked them and sent them away.[26] He refused to fight against his fellow Texans. But he saw clearly what was coming: "Our people are going to war to perpetuate slavery, and the first gun fired in the war will be the knell of slavery."[27] His dire warnings went unheeded. It was for this last episode of his political life that John F. Kennedy would later make Sam Houston an American "profile in courage."

Colonel Robert E. Lee was departing Texas even as secession was being voted. Lee had turned over his command to the brave General David Twiggs. Twiggs had won honors in the Mexican War. He was, however, a Georgia native. When Georgia and Texas seceded, Twiggs turned over his entire U.S. Army command to the Texas secessionists. Lee was appalled. Twiggs had surrendered a tenth of the U.S. Army's weapons and supplies without firing a shot.[28] Leaving San Antonio, Lee bade farewell to his many friends, saying: "When I get to Virginia, I think the world will have one less soldier. I shall resign and go to planting corn."[29] But, as he would soon discover, the world had other plans for Robert E. Lee.

One of President Lincoln's first acts was to sign a commission for Lee's promotion to full colonel.[30] Lee accepted this, giving hope to General Scott that Lee might stay with the Union in any clash. The aged, infirm Scott was a Virginian, yes, but he was also the hero of many battles. For him the Union was his life. But Lee's friend Jefferson Davis now led the Confederacy and his Mexican War comrade, Pierre Gustave Toutant Beauregard, was ringing Fort Sumter with a "circle of fire."[31]

Soon, Lee was invited to meet with Francis P. Blair Sr., a powerful member of Washington's political establishment. Blair had been a member of President Jackson's "Kitchen Cabinet," and he now wanted to sound out Lee's plans.[32] Blair told Lee he had been authorized by President Lincoln to offer him command of all Union forces—a vast army of seventy-five to one hundred thousand—a greater force than had ever been seen on the continent.

Lee heard Blair out, but refused in his famously courteous manner. "Though opposed to secession and deprecating war," he said, "I could take no part in an invasion of the Southern States."[33] General Scott was heartbroken. Lee was his favorite. Scott and most others thought Lee the ablest man in the U.S. Army. Deeply moved, Scott told Lee: "You have made the greatest mistake of your life; but I feared it would be so."[34] It was, as Lee's illustrious biographer Douglas Southall Freeman wrote, "the answer he was born to make." Like Sam Houston, Lee would spend a long, wakeful night in prayer. He stayed at Arlington House, his stately home overlooking the City of Washington. There, he penned his letter of resignation to Secretary of War Simon P. Cameron.

The die was cast.

Meanwhile, in Charleston, General Beauregard had taken command of the forces surrounding Fort Sumter on behalf of the Confederate States on the third of March. He tactfully but forcefully rearranged the guns and repaired the slap-dash breastworks that had been thrown up by South Carolina state militiamen more eager than able. Beauregard knew his task well. He had been trained for it at West Point. There, his instructor was Robert Anderson. Anderson was so highly impressed with the young Beauregard that he had held the Louisiana cadet back in order to train incoming plebes in artillery.[35] Like Lee, Beauregard had been a West Point superintendent. But Beauregard had resigned when Louisiana seceded.[36]

Major Robert Anderson now faced his pupil across the water. Anderson, a military professional from a slaveholding Kentucky family,

Harriet Beecher Stowe. *Her novel,* Uncle Tom's Cabin, *touched the hearts of millions of readers. Although the major villain in the book was the transplanted Yankee, Simon Legree, many slaveholders moved to ban the book. Queen Victoria wept over it. Lincoln greeted Mrs. Stowe in the White House: "So you are the little woman who wrote the book that started this great war." It has never been out of print.*

Frederick Douglass. *When he fought Edward Covey, who tried to break him, Frederick Douglass experienced his "resurrection" as a man. So he wrote in his powerful autobiography. Douglass escaped slavery in Maryland and went on to become a leading orator, writer, and editor. He recruited volunteers for all-black Union regiments in the Civil War. "[L]et the black man get upon his person the brass letters, U.S.; let him get an eagle on his button . . ." and there is no power on earth that can deny him citizenship in the United States, Douglass wrote. He was right. He fought for emancipation and then for full civil rights for half a century, never backing down. "Agitate, agitate, agitate," he told a young follower. And he did.*

The Lincoln-Douglas debates, Illinois 1858. *This unprecedented series of face-to-face encounters around Illinois pitted the powerful Senator Stephen Douglas—"a steam engine in britches"—against an obscure one-term former congressman. Lincoln's great skill in putting "the Little Giant" on the defensive marked him as a national leader for the new Republican Party. Although holdover Democrats in the Illinois legislature returned Douglas to the Senate, Lincoln the wrestler recognized his loss as "a stumble, not a fall."*

Firing on Fort Sumter. *If you surrender Fort Sumter, "Bluff" Ben Wade told the newly inaugurated President Lincoln, "Jeff Davis will have you a prisoner of war in less than thirty days." Lincoln lived up to his inaugural promise to "hold, occupy, and possess" this federal fort in Charleston's harbor—but it took four long years of civil war to do it.*

Monitor* and *Merrimack. *The CSS* Virginia*—as* Merrimack *was renamed—rammed and sank the wooden ships of the Union blockade. It was the U.S. Navy's worst day prior to Pearl Harbor. This clash of the ironclads off Hampton Roads, Virginia, on 9 March 1862 rendered obsolete every other navy on earth. The USS* Monitor, *that little "cheesebox on a raft," fought the larger Confederate warship to a fateful draw. Battered, the* Merrimack *withdrew, giving the Union a strategic victory.*

The dead at Antietam. *Matthew Brady's gritty photographs of the Confederate dead at Antietam showed Americans the tragic toll of the bloodiest single day in American history—17 September 1862. General George McClellan found a copy of General Lee's Order No. 191. With it, he fought Lee to a standstill. Lee withdrew from Maryland. Now, Lincoln had the victory he needed to issue his preliminary Emancipation Proclamation.*

commanded the federal garrison at Fort Sumter. With a small force and dwindling supplies, Anderson continued to fly the flag of the United States and to resist Confederate demands that he surrender.

President Buchanan had held on to the fort through the secession winter, just barely. After a financial scandal had forced his prosecession secretary of war out of office, Buchanan's reshuffled cabinet demanded he continue to hang on. Edwin M. Stanton, Buchanan's new attorney general, bluntly told the dithering old man: "No administration much less this one can afford to lose a million [dollars] and a fort in the same week."[37] But Buchanan was now out and Lincoln in, and the new president was receiving contradictory advice on whether Fort Sumter should or even *could* be held. Secretary of State William H. Seward was telling Southerners Lincoln would withdraw from the fort. But Senator Ben Wade of Ohio—*Bluff Ben Wade* as he was known—lived up to his name. If you surrender Fort Sumter, he told Lincoln, "Jeff Davis will have you as a prisoner of war in less than thirty days."[38] It was little wonder that Charles Francis Adams, the son and grandson of presidents, confided to his diary that Lincoln was "not equal to the hour."[39] But Seward, Wade, Adams—everyone, actually—misjudged Lincoln.

Lincoln ordered a naval flotilla to resupply Fort Sumter. He sent word to South Carolina's new governor that the federal installation would be provisioned but the garrison would not be strengthened. War, if it came, would be the Confederates' decision.[40]

Too late, Robert Toombs awoke to the South's danger. "The firing upon that fort will inaugurate a civil war greater than any the world has yet seen. . . . [It] is suicide, murder." He warned President Davis that attacking Fort Sumter would be like striking a hornets' nest. Legions would swarm from that hornets' nest and "sting us to death."[41] The timing couldn't have been worse. Toombs's ardor had cooled, just as President Davis's heated up.

Davis disregarded Toombs's words. He ordered Beauregard to open fire on Fort Sumter if any relief squadron approached. When a delegation of Southerners delivered an ultimatum to Major Anderson to surrender Fort Sumter, he politely refused. Escorting them back to their boat, the major said: "If we never meet in this world again, God grant that we may meet in the next."[42]

Before dawn on the morning of 12 April 1861, General Beauregard signaled for his batteries to open fire on the fort out in the middle of the harbor. Edmund Ruffin of Virginia, his long, white hair flowing down over his shoulders, was given the honor of firing the first shot. Ruffin, actually a transplanted New Yorker, thirsted for action. "The shedding of blood" he wrote, "will . . . change many voters from the hesitating states, [and make them] zealous for immediate secession."[43] The aged fire-eater was quick to pull the lanyard and plunge his country into war.

Beauregard's batteries lit up the predawn darkness in Charleston harbor. Major Anderson had only a token force of brave federal troops, but he held out as long as he could. Finally, after thirty hours of furious bombardment, and with flames creeping toward his powder magazines, Anderson was forced to surrender. The still incomplete Fort Sumter—built from sturdy New Hampshire granite—was turned over to the triumphant Confederate forces. Anderson and his men were treated with all the "honors of war," but all over the North, men rushed to enlist.

III. "A People's Contest": The Civil War Begins

The attack on Fort Sumter electrified the North. Senator Stephen Douglas spoke for the Northern Democratic Party in pledging his full support to the new administration in putting down the rebellion. President Lincoln issued a proclamation calling for seventy-five thousand volunteers to put down "combinations too powerful to resist" to ensure that federal law would be enforced. It would be four long years before the flag of the United States would fly once again over Sumter's broken battlements. After Sumter's fall, Lincoln called Congress into a special Fourth of July session. The outbreak of hostilities ended Virginia's hesitation. The Old Dominion's secession convention voted to leave the Union. Delegates now forgotten voted to break their ties with the American Republic that Virginia's greatest sons—Washington, Jefferson, Madison, Marshall, Mason, and Henry—had risked their lives to bring forth. They voted, too, to invite the Confederate government to relocate to Richmond.

With Virginia's secession and Maryland on the verge, Washington, D.C., might have been encircled. Lincoln could see Confederate batteries from his Executive Mansion window. As Massachusetts and New York troops hurried south to relieve the capital, they encountered a secessionist mob in Baltimore. A riot broke out as some of the civilians heaved paving stones at the federal troops. Massachusetts soldiers fired on the crowd, killing twelve of the civilians and suffering four dead. It was April 19, the eighty-sixth anniversary of Lexington and Concord. That was a fight for liberty. Not all Americans agreed during the Revolution on the meaning of liberty. Some, especially the Tories, fought *against* independence. Especially in the South, this struggle turned bloody and bitter. Now, because Americans could not agree on the meaning of liberty, they were once again killing each other.

Lincoln told skittish Maryland Unionists he would not bring more troops through bleeding Baltimore, but he could not promise to avoid the Old Line State altogether. He told Maryland's governor the troops were not birds who could fly into Washington, nor were they moles to burrow underground. Wisely, though, he ordered General Ben Butler to ferry his forces by water to Annapolis and bring them into Washington by rail. Butler was a political general, one of many promoted not for any military ability but to cement the loyalties of their considerable following among the people. A Massachusetts Democrat, Butler only the year before had been scheming to make Senator Jefferson Davis his party's presidential candidate!

Lincoln would take no chances with strategic Maryland. He authorized the temporary imprisonment of prosecession state legislators and the suppression of disloyal newspapers in the state. He also suspended the writ of habeas corpus. That meant more arrests could follow, without recourse to the courts. Lincoln's suspension of habeas corpus was the first such action on such a broad scale. Still, the Constitution specifically allows for such a suspension in time of rebellion. ("The privilege of the Writ of Habeas Corpus shall not be suspended, unless when in Cases of Rebellion or Invasion the public Safety may require it." Article I, Section 9) His quick and effective actions in Maryland are debated to this day. The Old Line State's official song, "Maryland, My Maryland," which speaks of spurning the "Northern scum," still contains these anti-Lincoln lyrics:

The despot's heel is on thy shore, Maryland!
His torch is at thy temple door, Maryland!
Avenge the patriotic gore
That flecked the streets of Baltimore,
And be the battle queen of yore,
*Maryland! My Maryland!**

The despot referred to in the first stanza is President Lincoln.

Surely rebellion was afoot. If a vote of the white citizens of Maryland had been taken, the state would very likely have seceded. Western Maryland was loyal to the Union, just as mountainous western Virginia was. But crowded Baltimore and Maryland's Eastern Shore were "secesh." Lincoln was determined to save Maryland and the nation's capital for the Union.

He had little choice. Secession was in the air. Disloyalty, real and suspected, was everywhere. The situation was critical. The Confederate secretary of war boasted that the rebel flag would "float over the old Capitol dome before the first of May."[44]

When the creaking Chief Justice Taney ordered the release of a rebel sympathizer, a civilian, Lincoln ignored him.[45] Taney's opinion in *Ex Parte Merryman* was actually a carefully reasoned analysis of history and constitutional law. Taney scolded Lincoln for suspending habeas corpus, a power which Taney argued the Constitution *implicitly* gave to Congress, not to the president. Taney quoted the great John Marshall to good effect.[46]

John Merryman had been arrested by military authorities acting under Lincoln's expansive orders. They charged Merryman with helping to blow up railroad bridges leading to the endangered capital of Washington.[47] Taney seemed not to be concerned with this mortal threat to the life of the republic. Could a rebel blow up the bridges over which returning congressmen must pass in order to reassemble and vote a suspension of habeas corpus—and then point to Congress's failure to convene as a justification for court orders against the president?

* "Maryland, My Maryland" was adopted as the state song in 1939 (Chapter 451, Acts of 1939; Code State Government Article, sec. 13–307).

Lincoln could well have quoted the great John Marshall to the recalcitrant old Taney. Marshall had written for a unanimous Supreme Court in the famous case of *McCullough v. Maryland* in 1819: "Let the end be legitimate, let it be within the scope of the constitution, and all means which are appropriate, which are plainly adapted to that end, which are not prohibited, but consist with the letter and spirit of the constitution, are constitutional."[48]

What could be *more* legitimate for the embattled President Lincoln than to keep disloyal elements from seizing control of the nation's capital, preventing the Congress from meeting, and thereby breaking up the government? It is a good thing the widely rumored arrest of the aged Chief Justice never went forward. But it must be recorded that in heat of civil war, Maryland's Roger Brooke Taney did nothing to protect the nation he had sworn to serve. It is also true that it was Taney's disastrous *Dred Scott* opinion that, as much as anything else, had put the nation's young men at bayonet point with one another.

Many high-ranking military officers—but no enlisted men—"went with their states." The superintendent of the U.S. Naval Academy in Annapolis, Maryland, sensed the spirit of his neighbors. Captain Franklin Buchanan joined the Southern forces.*

Even many in the North were willing to let the Union be sundered. *New York Tribune* editor Horace Greeley wrote of the seceding states: "Wayward sisters, depart in peace." Many abolitionists—but *not* Frederick Douglass—similarly saw secession as a means to rid the United States of slaveholding states. Many Northern whites hated the abolitionists and blamed them for the war. When he tried to address a public meeting in Boston, the heart of antislavery sentiment, Douglass was thrown down a staircase by hired thugs. But he gave as good as he got, fighting them off "like a trained pugilist."[49]

As he reported in his first Message to Congress, Lincoln acted to preserve the Union. That was the first duty of the president. The chief executive also has a constitutional duty to "take care that the laws be faithfully executed" (Article II, Section 3). Pointing out that the laws were being

* Despite this, the superintendent's spacious thirty-seven-room mansion at the Naval Academy is called *Buchanan House*—named for Franklin Buchanan, the academy's first "supe."

flouted in all the seceding states, Lincoln asked: "Are all the laws *but one* to go unexecuted and the Government itself go to pieces lest that one be violated?"[50] Despite arguments at the time (and those that continue to this day) that Lincoln was acting as a *dictator,* the president reminded Congress that it *shared* responsibility for saving the Union and that it had the ultimate power to remove him from office if Congress found he had violated his oath of office. His Fourth of July message spoke powerfully of the stakes involved in the war:

> This is essentially a People's contest. On the side of the Union, it is a struggle for maintaining in the world that form and substance of government whose leading object is to elevate the condition of men—to lift artificial weights from all shoulders—to clear the paths of laudable pursuit for all—to afford all an unfettered start and a fair chance in the race of life. . . . I am most happy to believe that the plain people understand and appreciate this . . . [for] not one common soldier or common sailor is known to have deserted his flag. . . . It is now for [Americans] to demonstrate to the world that those who can fairly carry an election can also suppress a rebellion—that ballots are the rightful and peaceful successors of bullets; and that when ballots have fairly and constitutionally decided, there can be no successful appeal back to bullets.[51]

Lincoln hoped that pro-Union sentiment in other border states would assert itself. There was plenty of evidence that secession was not being accepted across the South. In East Tennessee, a mountainous region where few farmers held slaves, men like Andrew Johnson and William G. Brownlow fought *against* the rebellion. Johnson was a staunch Jackson Democrat. Brownlow, a former Whig newspaper editor, vowed to fight "the Secession leaders till Hell freezes over—*and then fight them on the ice!*"[52] Men like Johnson and Brownlow had no aristocratic pretensions. They were feisty commoners and proud of it.

In Virginia, the western counties that had voted *against* secession, refused to follow Richmond's lead. With the help of federal troops under

General George B. McClellan, they withdrew from the state of Virginia. (In time, West Virginia would be admitted as a separate state of the Union.)

Lincoln treated Kentucky with kid gloves. Unwilling to challenge for the time being Kentucky's dubious claim of "neutrality," Lincoln hoped through patience and mild measures to retain its loyalty. Kentucky was not only Lincoln's birthplace, it was also the birthplace of Jefferson Davis and the home state of John Bell, a minor party candidate for president in 1860. His critics laughed at the president's caution: "Lincoln would like to have God on his side, but he *must* have Kentucky."[53] That was very nearly true, for without Kentucky, the entire heartland of the Union—states like Ohio, Indiana, and Illinois—would have been exposed to Confederate attack.

Missouri was another slaveholding border state whose loyalty came hard. Lincoln backed the military efforts of General Nathaniel Lyon—who hastened to disarm pro-Confederate militia in St. Louis. Following Lyon's death in battle, however, Lincoln had to support General John Charles Frémont. Frémont, the Republicans' 1856 presidential nominee, still had considerable support among congressional party members. Frémont caused Lincoln grave political embarrassment when he issued on his own authority an emancipation order for Missouri. Lincoln and the Republicans had pledged *no interference* with slavery in the states where it existed. Missouri had remained loyal to the Union. Lincoln had to publicly demand that Frémont revoke his order. Frémont sent his bright, beautiful wife, the politically savvy daughter of Missouri's famous Senator Thomas Hart Benton, to argue his case with the president.

Jessie Frémont arrived in Washington late on a September night. She was summoned immediately to the Executive Mansion, though she was tired and dusty from long, hot days of travel. The president received her coldly. He didn't offer her a chair. When she lectured him on the need for emancipating the slaves to gain support from Britain, Lincoln interrupted her, saying: "You are quite the female politician." Then he lectured *her*: "This is a war for a great national idea: the Union, and . . . General Frémont should not have dragged the Negro into it."[54]

Abolitionists and their allies in Congress were outraged. Frederick Douglass thought John Charles Frémont was being unjustly treated by

Lincoln. The president was too willing to appease proslavery elements in the "loyal border," Douglass charged. They are not *loyal* at all, he wrote. They are "a millstone about the neck of the Government . . . their so-called loyalty [is] the very best shield to the treason of the cotton states."[55]

But Lincoln was determined not to allow military commanders in the field to make policy—especially on so sensitive an issue as emancipation. He responded to a thirteen-page letter of protest from his good friend from Illinois, Senator Orville Browning. "Can it be pretended," the president wrote, "that it is any longer the government of the U.S.—any government of Constitution and laws—wherein a general or a president may make permanent rules of property by proclamation?"[56] Lincoln was unwilling to delegate this momentous question to *any* subordinate, especially not the erratic Frémont.

Not only was Lincoln determined to keep in his own hands the reins of so powerful a movement as emancipation, but he knew he could not act on slavery in the wake of the Union military disaster at Bull Run. Spirits were depressed throughout the North that July when General Irwin McDowell—prodded by Lincoln and an impatient Congress—had marched out to meet the Confederate force near Manassas Junction, a day's march from Washington. The fickle Greeley now joined the general cry of "On to Richmond!" Green federal troops broke and ran in panic before the victorious rebels. "Skedaddled" was the humiliating description of the federal rout. General Beauregard added the victory's laurels at Manassas to his win at Fort Sumter. (But in so doing, the "Napoleon in gray" earned the jealous mistrust of his chief, President Davis.) At this battle, General Thomas Jonathan Jackson commanded his line of Virginians, ignoring cannon and rifle fire. "There stands Jackson, *like a stone wall*," cried General Bernard Bee.*

Mrs. Frémont was not the only politically important lady to cause Lincoln trouble in 1861. His own wife, Mary Todd Lincoln, embarrassed Lincoln greatly by overspending a $20,000 congressional appropriation for

* Whether General Bee was *admiring* Jackson's brave stand or *annoyed* that Jackson was not moving up to support him—as Civil War writer Shelby Foote suggests may have been the case—will never be known. General Bee was killed by a federal bullet moments after giving Jackson his immortal nickname.

refurbishing the badly dilapidated Executive Mansion. It had seemed important—like the plan to go ahead with the construction of the half-completed Capitol dome—to underscore the continuity of the Union and its institutions. But while a distracted president cast about for a winning general with a winning plan, "the first lady of the land" went on a shopping spree in New York and Philadelphia.

She innocently wanted to make the Executive Mansion a showplace (the better to answer her catty critics among the capital's pro-Southern society matrons). But Mrs. Lincoln's sense of style exceeded her sense of propriety. Merchants saw in her an easy mark. When a Philadelphia decorator demanded payment for some $7,000 worth of elegant Parisian wallpaper, Mrs. Lincoln's extravagance was exposed. Lincoln was infuriated. How could Mary so thoughtlessly overspend on "*flubdubs* for this damned old house," he demanded to know. Lincoln was acutely aware that some Union soldiers were going without blankets.[57] Mortified, the president said he would pay the difference out of his own salary of $25,000 a year.* Congress, belatedly, would quietly decide to cover for Mrs. Lincoln's spendthrift ways, but the damage done to her reputation was irreparable.

IV. "One War at a Time": The Trent Affair

General Winfield Scott had to have help mounting his horse, a gentle mare. Aged, overweight, and frequently ill, General Scott nonetheless had a keen mind. And the Virginia-born hero of many wars was a staunch Unionist. When this most senior U.S. Army officer presented his plan for the *gradual* crushing of the rebellion that relied on imposing a naval blockade around the Southern states, his plan was derisively called "the Anaconda." Even so, it was a variant of this same Anaconda Plan that President Lincoln employed in bottling up the Confederacy.

Union control of the seas and the Mississippi River would be essential to weaken the Confederacy so that federal armies could advance against a

* President Lincoln's salary would be worth approximately $550,000 today. Presidents today receive $400,000 a year. (Online source: http://www.eh.net/hmit/compare/.)

Southern nation starved for imports and, especially, munitions.[58] Lincoln issued a proclamation closing off Southern ports to international trade. The Union navy—with ships far-flung throughout the world—was still incapable of enforcing the president's policy against daring and resourceful Southern "blockade runners."

The potential for a clash with Britain or France was great. In order for a blockade to be accepted under international law, it had to be *real* and not just a *paper* blockade. There was a further problem, for in international law, blockades were declared against *belligerents*. In the very act of imposing his blockade, Lincoln took a serious risk that foreign nations would recognize the Confederacy as a legitimate government. If they did so, they might use Lincoln's own proclamation against him.

Also, it would take time for Union ships to return to American waters. Some of them were still patrolling off the shores of Africa in an ineffectual effort to stop the slave trade. Other ships were accompanying American whalers as far away as Alaska. In these days before the Panama Canal, it would take months to make the return voyage around the tip of South America.

Lincoln's plans for the blockade were aided, improbably enough, by the Southerners themselves. Confederates who rejected Thomas Jefferson's principles of human equality in the Declaration of Independence were only too eager to embrace Jefferson's *disastrous* embargo concept. As a result, they deliberately withheld cotton from European markets. They thought that since "cotton is king," Britain and France would be forced to break the Union blockade in order to get it. Other than secession itself, this may have been the Southern leaders' worst miscalculation.[59] There had been a glut on the textile markets in 1859 and 1860. By the time the cotton famine began really to be felt in Britain and France—that is, in 1862 and 1863—Confederate military reverses would make intervention unlikely. Confederate leaders also failed to take account of the potential for Egypt and India to supply the cotton the American South could no longer export.

President Lincoln might have been grateful that he did not have to appoint politicians as admirals in the navy.[60] But this fact did not save him from one of the severest crises of the war—a crisis born at sea. The commanding officer of the USS *San Jacinto* was a tough, fearless, gung-ho career sailor. On 8 November 1861, Captain Charles Wilkes intercepted a British mail steamer, the *Trent*. Instead of hauling the ship, passengers, and crew before a federal magistrate for adjudication, Wilkes took it upon himself to arrest two Confederate diplomats—former U.S. Senators James Mason and John Slidell—and their secretaries. Then he allowed the *Trent* to proceed. Wilkes clapped the men into prison in Boston and was hailed throughout the North as a hero. After the humiliation of Manassas, the Northern public yearned for a victory. Congress even struck a medal to commend Captain Wilkes for his timely snatch.

The British Parliament and public were outraged. Wilkes's bold action was an insult to the British flag. All the *jingoes* of the British popular press (those "penny dreadfuls") were beating the drums for war with the impudent Yankees.* Henry John Temple, Lord Palmerston, the aggressive prime minister, was infuriated. He told his cabinet: "*You* may stand for this, but *damned* if I will."[61] Richard Cobden, a British friend of America, wrote that "three fourths of the House [of Commons] will be glad to find an excuse for voting for the dismemberment of the Great Republic."[62] The British upper classes hardly needed an excuse to vent their hostility to democracy. The *Times* of London spoke for the ruling aristocracy when it yearned openly for the downfall of the Union: "[It would be] good riddance of a nightmare. . . . Excepting a few gentlemen of Republican tendencies, we all expect, we nearly all wish, success to the Confederate cause."[63]

Fortunately for the United States, the newly laid transatlantic cable had gone dead. Thus, there were necessary delays in communication across the ocean.[64] Even so, the British cabinet increased the size of their Canadian garrison, adding another 14,000 redcoats to their force of just 6,400.[65] The British even beefed up their North American naval squadron. War with the United States loomed.

Secretary of State Seward had just a few months earlier recommended to Lincoln a war against *all* the major European powers as a way to unite

* The word *jingo* actually comes from a slightly later period in British history. In 1878, the British government resorted to the press to whip up anti-Russian sentiment. They gave the world a new word: "jingoism" (*"If they need our help, by jingo we will go. . ."*). (Online source: http://www.loyno.edu/~seduffy/eveWWI.html.)

the bitterly divided Americans against a common foe. Lincoln had politely dismissed Seward's plan to "wrap the world in flames" then. And now, he cautioned Seward: "One war at a time."

At this moment of grave tension and maximum danger for the American republic, a *royal* intervention saved the day. Prince Albert, Queen Victoria's respected consort, offered an amended draft of Foreign Minister Lord John Russell's warlike demand for satisfaction. Under Albert's draft: "Her Majesty's Government are unwilling to believe that the United States Government intended wantonly to put an insult upon this country and to add to their many distressing complications by forcing a question of dispute upon us. . . ."[66] Thus toned down, Prince Albert's generous interpretation of U.S. actions was accepted by the Palmerston ministry. Britain asked only for an apology and the restoration of the interned Confederate envoys. It was to be Albert's last official act. Within days, the poor prince was dead, the victim of typhoid fever. He had labored for peace between the United States and Britain almost literally with his last breath.

Meanwhile, Massachusetts Senator Sumner lectured Lincoln's cabinet for four hours on Christmas Day. Sumner, an Anglophile with many well-connected friends among Britain's elite, spelled out terrible consequences if the United States was drawn into war with Britain at this critical hour.[67] Not only would Southern independence likely be achieved, but the continued existence of the United States itself would be in jeopardy, Sumner warned at a somber meeting.

Seward was proving a liability in the middle of the unfolding crisis. The previous year, 1860, when the Prince of Wales had visited the United States, the heir to the British throne and the Colonial secretary, Lord Newcastle, had met then Senator Seward. A leading presidential candidate at the time, Seward informed Lord Newcastle that if he won the office it would be his duty to "insult" Great Britain. Worse, Seward supposedly told Newcastle that the United States planned to annex Canada to compensate for the loss of the slave states should Southerners go ahead with plans for secession.[68]

The story of this astonishingly foolish encounter is recorded in the letters of the United States's very able minister to Great Britain, Charles Francis Adams. It may well have been exaggerated in Lord Newcastle's retelling, but it sounds so like the swaggering Seward it is hard to discount it completely. This was, after all, the same man who recommended war with the entire continent of Europe to avoid conflict at home. Influential Britons saw the story as confirmation "that Mr. Seward is an ogre fully resolved to eat all Englishmen raw."[69] Adams was a rare exception to the general rule in the Lincoln administration of using diplomatic postings to pay off party hacks. Lincoln allowed Seward to play party politics in filling the embassies.[70] But, since Britain was the most important of *all* posts, and since Lincoln approved Seward's choice of highly capable Adams for the London post, no real harm was done to the Union war effort.

Lincoln determined to do everything possible to keep peace with Britain. The Confederate agents would be released. The United States would acknowledge that Captain Wilkes acted without authority. And Lincoln would apologize. Seward could not resist giving the British lion's tail one last jerk. He pointed out that the violation of neutral rights of which Britain now complained was exactly the grounds upon which the United States had gone to war with Britain in 1812![71] Such tact.

The crisis eased as Mason and Slidell were released. The Union turnabout produced an astonished reaction in Britain. Henry Adams, son of the U.S. minister, wrote that the "current which ran against us with such extreme violence six weeks ago now seems to be going with equal fury in our favor."[72] And, for friends of the Union, the best part is that Mason and Slidell proved to be terrible choices for the Confederacy as diplomats. Both men were so lacking in tact and so intimately associated with the fire-eaters and slavery expanders that their influence in Britain and France can be said to have been *zero*.

V. 1862: "Year of Jubilee"

When Lincoln had to replace General McDowell following the embarrassing Union defeat at Manassas, General Scott recommended the brilliant young George Brinton McClellan. It was a natural choice. McClellan had been the star of his West Point class of 1846. Following exemplary service in the Mexican War, he was sent by the army as an observer of the Anglo-French effort in the Crimean War. When he left the army, McClellan rose quickly to become president of the Illinois Central Railroad.

The charismatic thirty-four-year-old wore a neat mustache and French-style goatee to conceal his boyish features. In uniform, he wore a French hat, a *kepi*, and was happy to accept the nickname "the young Napoleon" that journalists had given him.*

Son of a socially prominent Philadelphia family, the dashing "little Mac" cut an impressive figure in the saddle. (He had, in fact, designed the saddle used throughout the U.S. Army.) And McClellan was a Democrat. Following Senator Stephen A. Douglas's untimely death from cirrhosis, McClellan was probably the country's most prominent pro-Union Democrat.

McClellan's politics meant trouble for him in Congress. Increasingly, *radical* Republicans sought a hard war. When McClellan gathered up the broken elements of the army following Manassas, he was grudgingly accepted on Capitol Hill. McClellan loved his men and they returned his affection. He trained them, equipped them with the best uniforms, boots, and weaponry. He made sure that food and medical care were always the best for his army. He held regular, impressive military parades. He excelled in the ceremonial and celebratory side of military life. His men called out "Little Mac" wherever he went and cheered him lustily. He succeeded in restoring the morale of his men, grandly renaming the federal force the Army of the Potomac. An organizational genius, McClellan built the greatest fighting force ever seen on this continent. He did everything with his army—except fight.

Determined not to push McClellan as he had pushed McDowell, Lincoln nonetheless offered Little Mac fatherly advice. "You must act," he wrote his commanding general when Congress and the press began to complain of McClellan's too frequent reports of "all quiet on the Potomac." But action was not soon coming. As the first year of the war ended, McClellan came down with typhoid fever. Lincoln was discouraged. Turning to the Union quarter-

* Despite the Emperor Napoleon's defeat at Waterloo, French military thinking, engineering, and fashion continued to dominate in the United States. Both Northern and Southern armies fielded colorful *Zouave* regiments outfitted in French North African uniforms. Their baggy, red pantaloons were soon discarded, however, when they proved to have a fatal attraction for sharpshooters on the battlefield.

master, Montgomery Meigs, Lincoln opened his heart: "General, what shall I do? The people are impatient; [Secretary] Chase has no money and tells me he can raise no more; the General of the Army has typhoid fever. The bottom is out of the tub. What shall I do?"[73] Lincoln's new secretary of war, Edwin M. Stanton, resolved to put an end to McClellan's inactivity. No more elegant staff dinners of "champagne and oysters," Stanton said.[74]

The power was truly going to McClellan's head—all the more after he forced the aged General Scott out of office and claimed his title of general in chief. He even treated the president with contempt. Privately, he referred to Lincoln as "the original gorilla" and "a well-meaning baboon." Once, he even returned home from a wedding celebration and left the president and Secretary Seward sitting in his front parlor. After an hour, a servant told the president his general had retired for the night! Lincoln bore this rudeness with patient humility: "Never mind, I will hold McClellan's horse if he will only bring us success."[75]

And what of that success?

McClellan finally decided on a bold move in which he would transport a huge portion of the Army of the Potomac to the Virginia Peninsula, near the city of Norfolk, to attack the Confederate capital at Richmond. McClellan's force of more than one hundred thousand men, twenty-five thousand horses and mules, and some three hundred artillery pieces was transported by four hundred ships.[76] This entire force was assembled by General Montgomery Meigs, the Union's brilliant, determined, loyal quartermaster.[77] In the spring of 1862, Meigs's logistical miracle was the largest amphibious assault in history.

And the success?

When Lincoln visited McClellan and the Army of the Potomac on the Virginia Peninsula, the headstrong general proceeded to lecture the president on the need to avoid "an abolition war." The army, he told Lincoln menacingly, would not support any action on emancipation of the slaves. Clearly, he intruded on civilian authority. In February, he boasted he would be in Richmond "in ten days."[78] A month later, he was no closer to the rebel capital. Always, always, McClellan complained that he had too few troops and inflated the enemy's strength. Relying on *unreliable* reports from private detective Allan Pinkerton, McClellan's estimate actually *tripled* the size of the Confederate army he faced. He put its numbers at 200,000. In truth, it was McClellan's Army of the Potomac that vastly outnumbered the defending rebels.[79] McClellan had every Napoleonic quality save two: speed and the willingness to fight.

So much for success.

In frustration, Lincoln finally said, "If General McClellan does not want to use the army, I would like to *borrow* it."[80]

McClellan lost his nerve on the peninsula. He began sending hysterical telegrams to the War Department, blaming Secretary Stanton, blaming everyone in Washington for his army's failure to take Richmond. Lincoln, who had *never* favored McClellan's waterborne invasion but who had indulged his high-strung young general, telegraphed him: "I give you all I can, and act on the presumption that you will do the best you can with what you have, while you continue, ungenerously I think, to assume that I could give you more if I would."[81]

The truth about McClellan was emerging. Lincoln grimly concluded that the Army of the Potomac may have a grand title, but in reality "it is only McClellan's bodyguard."[82]

The peninsula campaign was as inconclusive as it was preposterous. Richmond was never taken, McClellan spent his energies blaming everyone else for the failure, and—most troublesome for the Union—wounded Confederate General Joseph Johnston was replaced by the more capable Robert E. Lee.

Lincoln was finally forced to remove McClellan from command. Typical of Union luck in those months, his replacement proved no better. General John Pope had all the soldierly bearing, but proved to be a blowhard. On assuming command, he told the Army of the Potomac he had just come from the West, "where we have always seen the backs of our enemies."[83] He reported to Lincoln from his "headquarters in the saddle," leading the president memorably to observe it might be "a better place for his *hind*quarters."[84] When Pope led the army into a second humiliating defeat at Manassas, Lincoln had no choice but to restore McClellan.

It wasn't all bad news and embarrassment, however. While McClellan and the star-crossed Army of the Potomac were busy bolstering Confederate morale in the East, the Union enjoyed several important victories in the West. General Ulysses S. Grant demanded and got *unconditional surrender* from the defenders of Fort Donelson on the Cumberland River between Kentucky and Tennessee—thereby becoming an instant hero throughout the North and earning him the nickname "Unconditional Surrender Grant."

The war on the water was roiling. In the Chesapeake Bay, the Confederate Navy launched a new warship, the CSS *Virginia,* formerly the USS *Merrimack.* This ironclad, propeller-driven vessel rammed and sank two of the blockading Union wooden warships. The *Merrimack* was skippered by Captain Franklin Buchanan, the former superintendent of the U.S. Naval Academy at Annapolis. Buchanan later reported to Stephen R. Mallory, the able Confederate secretary of the navy, that the *Cumberland* "commenced sinking, gallantly fighting her guns as long as they were above water. She went down with her colors flying."[85] He had trained those midshipmen well. Next, Captain Buchanan trained the *Merrimack*'s guns on the USS *Congress*—where his own brother was serving.[86]

The USS *Congress* and the USS *Cumberland* were lost. The *Merrimack* next ran the USS *Minnesota* aground, its direct cannon fire bouncing off the sloping armor-plating of the *Merrimack.* The Union blockade—in fact the entire U.S. Navy—was in the gravest danger. The worst day in the U.S. Navy's history prior to Pearl Harbor was 8 March 1862.[87] But on March 9 an improbable little craft chugged into action against the Southern monster.

The USS *Monitor* looked like "a cheesebox on a raft." She was also an ironclad. She rode low in the water and had but a single turret with two powerful Dahlgren guns to face the *Merrimack*'s ten guns. For three hours, the *Monitor* and the *Merrimack* were locked in a deadly embrace off Hampton Roads, Virginia. When both damaged vessels broke off the action, it appeared to be a tie. But, because the Confederates had a greater need of a naval breakthrough, *Monitor*'s action actually represented a Union victory. The Union fleet—and hence, the strategically indispensable blockade of the South—was saved. Control of the sea, a critical advantage to the Union, was maintained.[88]

The world took notice. Even the *London Times*, normally so contemptuous of the Yankees, said the British fleet could not be risked against such a warship as the USS *Monitor*.[89] This stunning example of "Yankee ingenuity" had actually been designed by Swedish immigrant John Ericsson. An engineering genius, the irascible Ericsson would live to see his designs incorporated into every modern navy in the world.

The navy also provided the Union's first great victory in 1862 when a fleet under Flag Officer David Glasgow Farragut sailed past menacing shore batteries and seized the greatest Confederate port—New Orleans. Farragut, a Southerner, had rejected pleas from other Southerners in the fleet that he join the Confederates. "You fellows will catch the *devil* before you get through with this business," the sixty-year-old salty sailor told them.[90] When the irrepressible General Ben Butler came ashore with his fifteen thousand bluecoats, he established firm control of the Crescent City.

High-spirited Southern ladies showed their contempt for Butler and his troops by throwing slops and chamber pots on them as they passed beneath elegant balconied windows in the city's fabled French Quarter. Butler earned international condemnation with his notorious "woman order." He said that any woman who insulted U.S. forces would be treated as "a woman of the town plying her trade"—by which he meant a prostitute. Butler's order earned him the nickname "The Beast," but it stopped outrages against the uniform of the United States.

In New Orleans Butler continued his controversial "contraband" policy. Since Southerners boasted that slave labor enabled them to keep more white men in the front lines for combat, Butler seized slaves as "contraband of war." Previously, the term *contraband* had been applied only to war materiel, not to human beings. But if Southerners were going to claim that slaves were mere *chattels*, then Ben Butler was only too happy to oblige them. Slaves caught on as well. Soon, thousands of slaves were liberating themselves, coming into Union army lines crying, "Contraband!"

By the summer of 1862, the "friction of war" that Lincoln spoke of was bringing the slavery issue more sharply into focus. Lincoln was disappointed that congressmen from the loyal slave states would not embrace his *compensated* emancipation plan.*

---

* These loyal states that maintained slavery were Delaware, Maryland, Kentucky, and Missouri.

If they did not respond to the government's generous offer, he warned them in an Executive Mansion meeting, they were likely to lose all in "the friction of war." How could the Union continue to fight with one hand tied behind its back, Frederick Douglass demanded to know. How was it that the "Colored men were good enough to fight under Washington, [but] they are not good enough to fight under McClellan?" Douglass asked pointedly.[91]

President Lincoln invited a delegation of free men of color to the Executive Mansion on 14 August 1862. It was the first official meeting between a president and black Americans. But Lincoln was inviting the gentlemen *in* only in order to invite them *out*. He told his visitors that irreducible white prejudice had condemned black people to suffer injustice throughout the United States. Nowhere, he said, was the black man regarded as the equal of the white. He deplored white prejudice but said he was powerless to change it. "But for your race among us there could not be war," he told them. Therefore, it was better that the two races should part. He encouraged his listeners to consider his plan for colonization of black Americans in Central America. They would have the full support of his administration, he assured them.[92]

Frederick Douglass spoke for nearly all black Americans when he *denounced* Lincoln's colonization bid. He charged that Lincoln's address to the free men of color "showed all his inconsistencies, his pride of race, his contempt for Negroes and his canting hypocrisy."[93] "We live here—have lived here—have a right to live here, *and mean to live here*," Douglass wrote.[94]

Douglass threw himself into the fight *against* the "bugbear of colonization" with a fury. Passionately, he lashed out at those who continued to deny the human rights of black Americans. "We are *Americans* by birth and education, and have a preference for *American* institutions as against those of any other country."[95] It's an astonishing statement! Black Americans were regularly denied education in the land of their birth, forced, even in the North, to attend *segregated* schools. As for American institutions, the highest Court in the land had declared black people noncitizens, bearing *no rights* which the white man was bound to respect. Nonetheless, Frederick Douglass demanded justice: "That we should wish

Lincoln as president. *Lincoln was known as the rail splitter, a westerner and a lawyer with no executive experience. Fire-eaters spurned his mild talk of "the better angels of our nature." Lincoln told Congress that when ballots had spoken, there must be no appeal to bullets. The plain people called Lincoln Old Abe and Uncle Abe. Following his decision to issue the Emancipation Proclamation, however, he was known widely as Father Abraham.*

General Robert E. Lee. *Marse Robert was known as the Marble Model in his days as a West Point cadet. He was the son of Lighthorse Harry Lee. His wife's grandmother was Martha Washington. He deplored slavery and secession, but when Virginia left the Union, he went with the Old Dominion. "I wish he were ours," a young Pennsylvania girl said of him. Millions of Northerners agreed.*

General George B. McClellan. *The Young Napoleon lacked only two Napoleonic qualities: speed and decision. Lincoln bore with him for a year until he finally fired him. McClellan had the slows. As Lincoln's Democratic opponent for the presidency in 1864, McClellan dithered about whether to accept or reject a peace plank that effectively meant surrender. "He's intrenching," Lincoln joked. In the end, McClellan could not even carry the soldier vote of his beloved Army of the Potomac.*

General "Stonewall" Jackson. *Old Blue Light, his men called him when his blood was up. Thomas Jonathan Jackson was a fierce warrior and a general of real tactical genius. His Shenandoah Valley campaign of 1862 gave him world fame. He was wounded by friendly fire following his total victory at Chancellorsville. "He has lost his left arm," said Robert E. Lee, "but I have lost my right." Jackson's death a week after the battle plunged the South into mourning.*

to remain here is natural to us and creditable to you."[96] With unassaila logic, Douglass pierced the heart of the case for colonization: "The argu ment that makes it necessary for the black man to go away when he is fre equally makes it necessary for him to be a slave while he remains here."[97]

When Lincoln had first raised the question of colonization for emancipated slaves, it was to have been completely voluntary—and under the benevolent protection of the U.S. Navy. Colonization in Africa or Central America for black Americans had been the position espoused by such "enlightened" Americans as James Monroe and Henry Clay. None of them had consulted black men's feelings on the subject. No one asked Frederick Douglass, either, but the outspoken Douglass would not go quietly. In fact, he wouldn't go at all. Lincoln may well have been persuaded by the force of Frederick Douglass's passionate opposition to colonization.

Next, Lincoln turned to white Americans. He answered Horace Greeley's shrill editorial, "The Prayer of Twenty Million," that had demanded immediate emancipation. (This is the same Greeley who, just a year before, had been eager to let the Southern states "depart in peace.")

> My paramount object in this struggle is to save the Union, and it is not either to save or to destroy slavery. If I could save the Union without freeing any slave I would do it, and if I could save it by freeing all the slaves I would do it; and if I could save it by freeing some and leaving others alone I would also do that. What I do about slavery and the colored race I do because I believe it helps to save the Union; and what I forbear, I forbear because I do not believe it would help to save the Union.[98]

This letter is often cited by critics who think Lincoln an insincere friend of freedom and a man of callous indifference to the plight of black Americans. But we must remember that this was the Lincoln who said a house divided could not stand, that it would become all slave or all free. It was the Lincoln who firmly believed that slavery confined to the Southern states would be put on the "path to ultimate extinction." It was the same Lincoln who had advised the Republicans to hold fast against the extension

General Ulysses S. Grant. *Grant was the son of a tanner, a failed farmer, and store clerk. A West Pointer and combat hero of the Mexican War, he washed out of the peacetime army. But in battle, he had "four o'clock in the morning" courage. Grant demanded nothing but unconditional surrender of his old friend at Fort Donelson—and the United States had a new hero. Lincoln rebuffed demands for his dismissal: "I can't spare the man. He fights." Coming east in 1864, Grant alone could "face the arithmetic." He endured high casualties to grind down Robert E. Lee's starving Army of Northern Virginia.*

General William Tecumseh Sherman. *Sherman was almost dismissed as a madman early in the war when he predicted a long, bloody struggle. Red-haired, brilliant, and garrulous, he hated reporters and politicians. Sherman gladly served under the steadier, quieter Grant. "Grant stood by me when I was crazy and I stood by him when he was drunk. Now we stand by each other always," Sherman said. "War is hell," he told those who objected to his destruction of civilian farms and towns—and he did his best to make it so. His March to the Sea saved Lincoln's presidency in the election of 1864.*

The surrender at Appomattox. *General Lee met General Grant in Wilmer McLean's front parlor in this quiet southside Virginia town on Palm Sunday, 9 April 1865. Lee was resplendent in his best uniform, astride his famous horse, Traveler. Hastening from the field, Grant's rumpled uniform and boots were specked with mud. Grant paroled Lee and all his men. Grant later defied a vindictive President Andrew Johnson, who wanted to prosecute Lee for treason.*

of slavery into the Territories "as with a chain of steel." And it was this very Lincoln who, even as he wrote this famous letter to Greeley, had a draft of the Emancipation Proclamation in his desk drawer. He waited only for a Union victory to issue it.

The trouble was that in any conflict there are too many competing visions, agendas, hopes, and opinions to easily appease or reconcile. In these trying years, Lincoln was barely afloat in the middle trying to coordinate the mess to the best advantage of the Union.

As if the domestic issues were not enough, Lincoln continued to suffer frustration in his relations with his reluctant general in chief. "If by magic," he said, he could "reinforce McClellan with 100,000 men," Lincoln told Senator Browning, "[the general] would be in ecstasy over it, thank [me] for it and tell [me] he would go to Richmond tomorrow, but when tomorrow came [McClellan] would telegraph that he had certain information that the enemy had *400,000* men and that he could not advance without reinforcements."[99] Besides, Lincoln noted in exasperation, every time he did send reinforcements, only a fraction of the number actually arrived. It was, he noted, "like shoveling fleas."

In September, General Robert E. Lee boldly took his Army of Northern Virginia into Maryland. He was joined by Stonewall Jackson, who had spent the spring making fools of Union Generals McDowell, Frémont, and Banks. Nathaniel Banks, another political general, had been a Democratic speaker of the House of Representatives. Banks not only was routed, but he left behind so many supplies for the hungry Confederates that they cheerfully nicknamed him "Commissary Banks." Jackson's "Valley Campaign" in the Shenandoah in the spring of 1862 was so daring, so brilliant that military colleges the world over study it to this day.

With their bands playing "Maryland, My Maryland," the rebels spread panic through Northern cities. Lee hoped to influence the fall elections for Congress and to gain British and French recognition of the Confederacy by winning a signal victory in the North. But Lee reckoned without one "accident" of history. A copy of Lee's "General Order No. 191" to his subordinate commanders, wrapped around three cigars, was picked up by a Union soldier. Immediately, General McClellan knew Lee's plans.

Near the town of Sharpsburg, Maryland, on the banks of Antietam Creek,* ragged, hungry but determined Confederates met a superior Union army. All day on 17 September 1862, the two armies clashed.

McClellan fed his men into the meat-grinder of Southern fire piecemeal, never committing enough to win the battle, never risking enough to lose. Typical of the day was this eyewitness account left by a young Georgia soldier of Lee's army:

> Five bullets struck down the 34th New York's color bearer. "You could hear laughing, cursing, yelling and the groans of the wounded and dying, while the awful roar of musketry was appalling," Sergeant William Andrews of the 1st Georgia recalled. "Where the line stood the ground was covered in blue, and I believe I could have walked on them without putting my feet on the ground."[100]

The First Minnesota Volunteers reported how "hot" the rebel artillery made it for them. A young Virginia artilleryman was helping to make it hot for the Minnesotans that bloody day. He was seventeen-year-old Private Robert E. Lee Jr., whose father was in command of the Army of Northern Virginia.[101]

Another survivor of the Battle of Antietam was Colonel John Bell Gordon of the Sixth Alabama.[102] He had been hit five times at the Sunken Road. When his wife was ushered into his sickroom, he yelled out: "Here's your handsome husband; been to an Irish wedding!"[103] He recovered from the bullet in his face, and with his wife's skillful nursing, even his shattered arm was saved.[104]

America had never experienced anything like this. Matthew Brady, the famous New York photographer, sent his assistant Alexander Gardner to record the horror at Sharpsburg. Brady displayed the photos of the battle's carnage to a stunned society audience as "The Dead of Antietam." "There is one side of the picture that has escaped the photographer's skill," wrote a *New York Times* reporter: "It is the background of widows and orphans.... Homes

* Confederate records call this Battle Sharpsburg; the Union forces styled it Antietam.

have been made desolate, and the light of life in thousands of hearts has been quenched forever. All of this desolation imagination must paint—broken hearts cannot be photographed."[105]

Although McClellan had fresh troops in reserve at Antietam, he never committed them to the battle. Instead, both armies fought to a bloody stalemate. Lee was forced to retreat. McClellan claimed it as a great victory. In anguish, Lincoln pressed McClellan to pursue Lee and destroy the Army of Northern Virginia. McClellan held back.

The Union casualties of Antietam were reckoned at 2,108 dead, 9,540 wounded, and 753 missing—one-quarter of all those engaged.[106] Confederate losses were fewer, but Lee could afford them less. Because he was operating on Northern soil, there would never be a full account of Lee's "butcher's bill." Estimates suggest the Confederates suffered 1,546 dead, 7,752 wounded, and 1,018 missing.[107] Combined losses are counted as 22,719, making the Battle of Antietam the bloodiest single day in American history.

The Civil War has been called "the brothers' war." That was especially the case in many a Maryland and Kentucky regiment whose members had brothers on the opposite side. But it was also a father-and-son war, as this letter makes clear:

> A soldier in the 21st Connecticut . . . got leave to search out the grave of his eighteen-year-old son, killed in the attack on Burnside Bridge, but he could not find it. "Oh how dreadful was that place to me, where my dear boy had been buried like a beast in the field!" he wrote. He had sworn vengeance, he added bitterly, on "this uncalled for, and worse than hellish, wicked rebellion."[108]

Newly enlisted soldiers would speak of this first experience of battle ever after as having "seen the elephant." It was the half humorous way they described the shocking brutality of combat.

The North rejoiced as a battered Southern army withdrew. Lincoln accepted this bloodiest day in American history as a sign from the Almighty. He issued his Preliminary Emancipation Proclamation. Unless they rejoined the Union by 1 January 1863, Lincoln warned the seceded states, *all* their slaves would be freed. Reaction in the North initially was *not* favorable. The Republicans lost some key state races and several seats in Congress. Even abolitionists did not welcome this preliminary Emancipation Proclamation. What if the rebellious states *did* return to the Union? Then the slaves would remain in bondage. Lincoln was taking an enormous risk.

McClellan continued to stall. He complained that his *horses* were tired. Finally, Lincoln's patience snapped. Confederate horses weren't tired. He telegraphed the Young Napoleon: "Will you pardon me for asking what the horses of your army have done since the battle of Antietam that fatigues *anything?*"[109] The powerful Frank Blair tried to intercede with the president, to prevent the blow he knew was coming. He had tried long enough to "bore with an auger too dull to take hold," Lincoln told Blair. "I said I would remove him if he let Lee's army get away from him, and I must do so. He's got the 'slows,' Mr. Blair."[110]

When Senator Ben Wade earlier that summer had demanded McClellan's ouster, Lincoln replied, "Whom shall I replace him with?" *Anybody,* replied Bluff Ben, exasperated. "Anybody will do for *you*, Wade, but I must have *somebody,*" Lincoln responded wearily.[111] Now the lack of *somebody* came home to haunt Lincoln's deliberations. He decided to name General Ambrose Burnside, one of Little Mac's closest subordinates, to succeed McClellan. He sent one of McClellan's good friends, General Catharinus Buckingham, through a blinding snowstorm with orders for McClellan to turn over his command.

This was a moment of grave danger for the republic. Freedom hung in the balance. There had been ugly talk at McClellan's headquarters of turning the Army of the Potomac *against* the politicians of Washington. McClellan made little secret of his opposition to emancipation. And he was still adored by his troops, who cheered him at every opportunity. If McClellan could not fight like Napoleon, might he have Napoleon's skill for political intrigue—and for a coup d'état?

Fortunately, McClellan's relations with the Democratic Party were excellent. He saw his future not as a military dictator, but as the standard bearer for the opposition party. This he was to become. And the country was spared the specter of the army's turning its guns on civilian authority.

Lincoln knew his place in history would be determined by forces beyond his control. He said he had made a "covenant with his Maker." If Lee was driven out of Maryland, he would hit slavery, and hit it hard. "The moment came when I felt that slavery must die that the nation might live," Lincoln said, when he hearkened to "the groaning of the children of Israel whom the Egyptians kept in bondage."[112]* The American people also seemed to sense a change had come over him. Up to this time, Lincoln was popularly known as "Old Abe" or "Uncle Abe." Following his issuance of the Preliminary Emancipation Proclamation, however, the common people began to refer to their president as "Father Abraham."[113]

As the year 1862 closed, General Burnside took the Army of the Potomac deep into Virginia. At Fredericksburg on December 13, Burnside proved to all what he had modestly said of himself: that although he was a competent corps commander, he was *not* capable of commanding an entire army. Ordering one futile frontal assault after another against the terrible stone wall, Burnside saw his men mowed down like wheat before a scythe. Burnside had to be restrained from leading a suicidal charge himself. Viewing the carnage from Marye's Heights above the battlefield, General Lee said: "It is well that war is so terrible, lest we should grow too fond of it."[114] That night, soldiers marveled at seeing the aurora borealis, a rare occurrence at such southerly latitudes. It was as if the heavens themselves were draped in iridescent waves of purple mourning crepe.

In the Executive Mansion, Lincoln was nearly in despair. Not only had this terrible year seen the death of his beloved son, Willy, it had closed out with the loss of some 12,600 young men killed and wounded at Fredericksburg. "We are on the brink of destruction," Lincoln told his friend, Illinois Senator Orville Browning. "It appears to me the Almighty is against us. . . ."[115]

Rebel editors taunted Lincoln as the winter gloom deepened:

---

* Exodus 6:5.

The days are growing shorter,
The sun has crossed the line,
And the people are all asking
Will Abraham resign?[116]

VI. Emancipation: "Forever Free"

Abraham would not resign; instead, he would *sign*. On 1 January 1863, Secretary of State William H. Seward and his son, Frederick, came early to the Executive Mansion with a copy of the engrossed Emancipation Proclamation, ready for the president's signature.* Quickly reading it over, Lincoln noted an error in the text. It had to be sent back to the State Department for correction.[117] Lincoln could not afford to have a single syllable wrong. He knew this proclamation would be picked apart by a hostile judiciary. No one was more hostile to emancipation than was Chief Justice Roger B. Taney.

The president then proceeded to receive hundreds of visitors at the annual New Year's Day reception. He shook their hands vigorously. Only at 2 p.m. were the doors closed, and Lincoln could turn once again to the corrected text of the Emancipation Proclamation.[118]

"I never, in my life, felt more certain that I was doing right than I do in signing this paper," Lincoln told the dozen or so witnesses.[119] He then took up the gold pen that had been given to him for the occasion by Massachusetts Senator Charles Sumner. But then his right hand began to tremble. He had difficulty holding the pen. At first, he had a superstitious feeling: was this a sign that he had made a fatal error?[120] Then he recalled that he had been shaking hands for three hours and that that was not a way to improve one's penmanship.

Lincoln was concerned because he knew his signature would be examined. "They will say, 'he had some compunctions,'" he explained to the witnesses.[121] Flexing his arm, he set about resolutely to sign the historic document. He wrote out his full name—*Abraham Lincoln*—then looked up, smiling, and said: "That will do."[122] He handed the gold pen back to Sumner.

* To *engross* is to prepare a "fair copy" of a state document for a high official's signature.

Some modern scholars have disparaged the proclamation. Historian Richard Hofstadter spoke to several generations when he sneered that the proclamation had "all the moral grandeur of a bill of lading."[123] But could Hofstadter be serious about any document that so eloquently concludes,

> And upon this act, sincerely believed to be an act of justice, warranted by the Constitution, upon military necessity, I invoke the considerate judgment of mankind, and the gracious favor of Almighty God.[124]

What more could we ask of Lincoln? Today, the proclamation is rarely displayed. When it is, the text, which those State Department clerks labored so diligently on a holiday to correct, is faded and indistinct. But the signature of Abraham Lincoln stands forth bold and bright and clear.

When President Jefferson Davis was inaugurated for a full six-year term in Richmond on 22 February 1862, Washington's birthday, Davis and his Negro footmen wore formal black suits. When his black coachman was asked why, he replied with sly humor: "This, ma'am, is the way we always does in Richmond at funerals and sichlike."[125]

This new year of 1863 was not the funeral of the Confederacy, not yet, but Lincoln's Emancipation Proclamation, issued on the first of January, surely forestalled any possibility that Great Britain would intervene on the side of the South. Britain had led the world in abolishing first the African slave trade (1807), then slavery itself (1831). British evangelical William Wilberforce had agitated the issue for nearly half a century. Britons were decidedly antislavery.

France's Emperor Napoleon III, always more eager for intervention than the British, was equally unwilling to act on his own. He had no navy capable of tangling with the U.S. fleet. British recognition was always "the glittering illusion" of Southern politicians. By late 1862, the cotton embargo was causing widespread unemployment among the textile workers of England and France. Despite their suffering, however, these workers held mass rallies to *commend* President Lincoln for his Emancipation Proclamation. One group of six thousand workingmen in Manchester sent Lincoln this plain-spoken message: "The erasure of that foul blot upon civilization and Christianity—

chattel slavery—during your Presidency will cause the name of Abraham Lincoln to be honoured and revered by posterity. Accept our high admiration in upholding the proclamation of freedom."[126]

Lincoln was especially touched by these warm words from cloth-capped workingmen. Just a year earlier, the United States was on the brink of war with Britain. He took time from his domestic cares to express his thanks to these common people. The president took note of the hardships the war had imposed on the poor people of Europe, saying their message was "an instance of sublime Christian heroism which has not been surpassed in any age or in any country."[127] In France, writers Jules and Edmond de Goncourt deplored the fact that "cotton weavers of Rouen now eat grass, mothers register their daughters as prostitutes!"[128] But ask these workers their opinion of the American Civil War and they would answer: "We would rather go on suffering poverty and hunger than see four million human beings continue to live in bondage."[129]

When Lincoln declared the slaves in rebel hands "shall be, then, thenceforward, and forever free," he had carefully *exempted* from his proclamation vast territories then under Union control. These included not only the four loyal border states—Missouri, Kentucky, Maryland, and Delaware—but also occupied areas of Tennessee, Louisiana, Florida, Virginia, and North Carolina. The *London Spectator* sneered that the only *principle* in the proclamation was that a man may not own another *unless* he is loyal to Lincoln's government.[130] But the *Spectator* then (and cynical Lincoln critics ever since) misunderstood the basis of Lincoln's action. Because he was a *constitutional* leader and not a despot, Lincoln could only free the slaves as a war measure to suppress rebellion. The confiscation of enemy property during wartime is recognized as legitimate under the rules of war.

Thus, it is not true to say he freed the slaves where he had no power and left in bondage those over whom he exercised control. Lincoln had no constitutional authority to free the slaves in the loyal border states. And he knew he could not emancipate slaves in those areas where Union arms had quelled the rebellion. The practical effect of the Emancipation Proclamation was that the Union army became an army of liberation.

Wherever it moved, thousands of slaves swarmed into its ranks, because the soldiers of the United States carried *freedom* in their haversacks.

Some British observers were more perceptive than the ruling aristocracy. Philosopher John Stuart Mill showed an acute understanding of what Lincoln had achieved:

> The present government of the United States is not an Abolitionist government. Abolitionists, in America, mean those who do not keep within the constitution; who demand the destruction (as far as slavery is concerned) of as much of it as protects the internal legislation of each State from the control of Congress; who aim at abolishing slavery wherever it exists, by force if need be, but certainly by some other power than the constituted authorities of the Slave States. The Republican party neither aim nor profess to aim at this object. And when we consider the flood of wrath which would have been poured out against them if they did, by the very writers who now taunt them with not doing it, we shall be apt to think the taunt a little misplaced. But though not an Abolitionist party, they are a Free-soil party. If they have not taken arms against slavery, they have against its extension. And they know, as we may know if we please, that this amounts to the same thing. The day when slavery can no longer extend itself, is the day of its doom. The slave-owners know this, and it is the cause of their fury. They know, as all know who have attended to the subject, that confinement within existing limits is its death-warrant.[131]

"I expect to maintain this contest until successful, or till I die, or am conquered, or my term expires, or Congress or the country forsakes me," Lincoln had written at a time of discouragement. It must be admitted that Jefferson Davis was no less committed to fight on till the end. Lincoln's task was greater. He had to win the war and to win the peace—for both North and South. Davis merely had to avoid *losing.*

Jefferson Davis reacted to the Emancipation Proclamation with predictable fury: it was, he told the Confederate Congress "the most execrable measure in the history of guilty man." Lincoln wanted "to incite servile insurrection and light the fires of incendiarism," charged Davis. He made this charge even though Lincoln had specifically urged freed slaves to engage in no violence—*except in necessary self-defense.* Frederick Douglass had written that the fear expressed by so many slaveholders "as to the danger of having their throats cut is because they *deserve* to have them cut."[132] Lincoln was becoming converted to the hard war theory that meant great destruction of rebel *property.* But he gave no support whatever to a slave uprising. The fact that there are no reported cases of murder or rape on Southern plantations speaks volumes of the character of Lincoln and the character of the freed slaves. The "wolf by the ears" so feared by Thomas Jefferson and hundreds of other Southern slaveholders for sixty years did not howl.

Following that "Day of Jubilee"—1 January 1863—there was no more talk of colonizing black Americans. Instead, all attention shifted to determining how quickly and how thoroughly black men might be recruited for the Union armies. Lincoln's administration now was fully committed to employing what Douglass picturesquely referred to as its "Sable Arm" against the rebellion. It was not an easy decision. There had been widespread resistance to black recruitment—even in the army itself. In July of 1862, Union cavalryman Charles Francis Adams Jr. had written to his father in London: "The idea of arming the blacks as soldiers must be abandoned." But just one year later, young Adams could tell his famous father: "The negro regiment question is our greatest victory of the war so far, and I can assure that in the army these [black soldiers] are so much a success that they soon will be the fashion."[133]

One thing that made Northern leaders hesitate was the threat by Confederates to treat black soldiers not as prisoners if they were captured, but as *insurrectionists* meriting only hanging. Their white officers, too, were threatened with death if taken. General Beauregard, with a grisly French flair, called for their execution by *garrote.* Only after Lincoln issued stern orders for retaliation were the bloodthirsty threats from the South quietly shelved. Following Douglass's impassioned appeals, Lincoln decreed that any black Union soldier who was re-enslaved would be matched by a white Confederate prisoner of war put to hard labor. And any Union prisoner in Southern hands who was put to death would be answered by a Southern

POW chosen by lot—*and shot*. Mercifully, Lincoln never had to enforce this grim order.

Still, freedom for black *and* white Americans depended ultimately on the success of Union arms. In the West, General Grant was laying siege to the great Confederate bastion on the Mississippi at Vicksburg. Grant worked in close harmony with Union naval gunboats. But it was a long, drawn-out affair. Grant had won a bloody victory at Shiloh the previous April. There, the Union lost thirteen thousand men (of fifty-five thousand) and the Confederates lost eleven thousand (of forty-two thousand).[134] Confederate General Albert Sidney Johnston—a favorite of President Davis—bled to death from a leg wound covered by his boot. The battle at Shiloh resulted in more casualties in two days than the United States had suffered in its *entire existence* as a nation! When Grant's critics complained to Lincoln, claiming that the general was drinking once again, Lincoln dismissed them, saying: "I can't spare this man; he fights."[135]

In the East, Lincoln had little choice but to confer command of the Army of the Potomac on "Fighting Joe" Hooker. Lincoln was critical of Hooker for the way he had undermined the honorable but incapable Burnside. Lincoln also had heard of Hooker's loose talk about the need for a military dictatorship in the country. Even so, Lincoln gave Hooker the command with these memorable words: "I have heard in such way as to believe it of your recently saying that both the Army and the Government needed a Dictator. Of course it was not for this, but in spite of it, that I have given you the command. Only those generals who gain successes can set up dictators. What I now ask of you is military success, and I will risk the dictatorship."[136]

Hooker ably reorganized the army, improving rations, medical care, and the troops' morale. He energetically moved the army deeper into Virginia. But he could not resist boastfulness. "May God have mercy on General Lee, for I shall have none," he told the press. Then he took his army into another federal disaster on 3 May 1863 at Chancellorsville.

Robert E. Lee's greatest triumph—Chancellorsville—was also the scene of his worst loss. Southern victory was assured when Stonewall Jackson's "foot cavalry" rushed out of the woods hallooing and giving the terrifying rebel yell. They put the Union troops to panicked flight. Hooker himself was stunned by a Confederate artillery shell that shattered the column upon which he was leaning. But after the day's action, General Jackson rode out on Little Sorrel to inspect his lines and prepare for the next day's fight. Only his aides accompanied him. Confederate pickets thought he was a Union officer and opened fire, wounding Jackson severely. Jackson soon had to have his arm amputated—the standard procedure for almost any serious wound. "He has lost his left arm," a grieving Robert E. Lee said, "but I have lost my right." Within the week, Jackson developed pneumonia and died. In these days before penicillin, almost any infection could prove fatal. The entire South was plunged into deepest mourning. Even in the North, Jackson was honored as the brave and resourceful opponent he was.

Hooker's defeat—he confessed he had "lost confidence in Joe Hooker"—meant Lincoln would have to find another commander in the vital eastern theater. McClellan, Pope, McClellan again, Burnside, Hooker—each had been tried and found wanting in less than a year.

Planning a second invasion of the North, Lee needed to conceal his movements from the Federal forces. Union cavalry under Major General Alfred Pleasanton searched for Lee's army and, instead, surprised the bold J. E. B. Stuart's mounted troopers at Brandy Station, about twenty-five miles from Fredericksburg, Virginia. This clash on 9 June 1863 proved to be the largest cavalry battle ever fought in the Western Hemisphere. Nearly 1,100 of the 22,000 troopers engaged became casualties.[137]

Pleasanton did not find Lee, but the all-day fight with Stuart proved that Union cavalry could face the world-famous Confederate cavalry without fear. After this saber-slashing, bloody encounter on horseback—fought to a draw—Stuart and "his puffed up cavalry" were widely criticized in the Southern press.[138] From this point on, Union cavalry would fight with increased skill and spirit.[139]

Now Lee was on the move and heading north. The fate of a nation once again hung in the balance.

Ten

A New Birth of Freedom

(1863–1865)

President Lincoln comes to Gettysburg, just four months after the climactic battle of 1–3 July 1863. There, in the chill November air, he pronounces the words that have been regarded ever after as immortal. But Lincoln's words in the Gettysburg Address and even his deeds will come to naught if the Union army fails. After two full years of war, the Union armies have not yet succeeded in putting down the rebellion. All depends on the success of federal arms. Gettysburg will be the high-water mark of the Confederacy. There, the gray tide surges, surges again, and then breaks on the rock of Union valor. There, Robert E. Lee begins the long, slow path that ends almost two years later at a little courthouse in Southside Virginia called Appomattox. Lincoln will live to see that moment, but not a week longer. His assassination in 1865 will leave the United States in unsteady hands—at the very moment we most need his mind and heart.

I. Gettysburg: The Confederacy's High-Water Mark

Lee moved north once again in late June 1863, pushing hard into Pennsylvania. With crisis looming, Lincoln accepted the petulant resignation of General Joe Hooker. He turned to General George G. Meade, a native of the Keystone State. Lincoln hoped that Meade could be relied upon to "fight well on his own dunghill."[1]

When Lee encountered the federal main force at Gettysburg, he resolved "to whip them." Lee was hampered by the absence of his great cavalry commander, General James Ewell Brown (J. E. B.) Stuart. Stuart had once humiliated the federals by riding completely around them. Now, he was ranging too far away, capturing badly needed Union supply wagons, but leaving Lee "blind" as to his enemy's movements. Confederate Generals Stuart and George Pickett had long since captured hearts throughout the South as dashing Cavaliers; the former sported a full red beard, an ostrich plume in his hat, and a brilliant red sash around his middle, while the latter wore his hair shoulder-length in perfumed ringlets. Pickett was the last man in the West Point class of 1846 (an appointment about which he was advised, ironically, by Illinois state Representative Abraham Lincoln), but he made up for his dismal academic standing by his bravery and energy.

A Union officer, Colonel Joshua Lawrence Chamberlain at thirty-four was tall and lean with a flowing mustache. He was a professor of classics in civilian life. He could speak eight languages—English, Greek, Latin, Arabic, Syriac, Hebrew, French, and German.[2] It is doubtful any other man on the field that day was so learned. But many fine minds and brave hearts threw their bodies into the breach on those disputed grounds. Commanding the Twentieth Maine, Chamberlain knew he had to hold Little Round Top on the field at Gettysburg. If the Confederates gained that high point, they could pour artillery fire down onto Union troops below and very likely win the battle—maybe the war.

Chamberlain summoned his Maine farm boys and fishermen to hold off the rebel attack. His company had already lost a third of its men, and he had already been slightly wounded twice during the battle.[3] Facing yet another attack, Chamberlain would later recall, "[M]y thought was running deep. . . . Five minutes more of such a defensive, and the last roll-call would sound for us. Desperate as the chances were, there was nothing for it but to take the offensive. I stepped to the colors. The men turned toward me. One word was enough—'BAYONET!' It caught like fire and swept through the ranks."[4]

When his soldiers ran out of ammunition, Chamberlain could honorably have surrendered. Instead, he led his yelling men down from the heights of the Little Round Top, swinging about like a great gate on a hinge. Chamberlain drove the startled Alabamians before him. For his actions that day, the young Mainer was awarded the Congressional Medal of Honor.

Union lines wavered as General Meade's forces were being hard-pressed on the Rose family farm. Places with prosaic names like The Wheatfield and the Peach Orchard there gained immortality in the annals of warfare. Meade was determined to hold. He ordered Major General Winfield Scott Hancock to support the Third Corps. Among General Hancock's seasoned troops were the soldiers of the famous Irish Brigade. Under their brilliant green flags with their distinctive harps, these Fighting Irish prepared to go into action. Before turning to meet their foe, they turned to their priest for absolution. Standing on a boulder overlooking the earnest, upturned faces, Father William Corby gave the men his blessing. Then he warned them: "The Catholic Church refuses Christian burial to the soldier who turns his back upon the foe or deserts the flag."[5] Today, a monument to Father Corby stands on the boulder where he pronounced those words.

One Irish officer who missed Father Corby's blessing was Colonel Patrick H. O'Rourke. He had graduated first in his class at West Point, just two years earlier. Paddy O'Rourke had bounded off his horse and was leading his Sixteenth Michigan with a hearty shout of "Down this way, boys!" as he was struck in the neck by a rebel bullet and killed. A New York soldier who came upon the pitiful scene said that "that was Johnny's last shot." Companies A and G vied with each other to take down the beloved Paddy's killer. That "Johnny Reb" was hit *seventeen times*.[6]

After two days of fierce fighting (July 1 and 2) in the stifling heat of a Gettysburg summer, Lee determined to attack the main body of the Union line. General James Longstreet opposed the move, recalling perhaps the devastation of the Union forces at Maryes' Heights at Fredericksburg. But such was *Marse Robert's** prestige that no one had the courage to challenge his judgment. Seeing a startled rabbit run off the road, a "Southron" responded with grim good humor. "Run, ol' hare," the soldier yelled to his

* "Marse" was the Virginia slaves' pronunciation for master. It was eagerly adopted by Lee's adoring men.

brothers lined up in a clump of trees awaiting the order to advance. "If ah was a ol' hare, ah'd run, too."*

When Pickett led his now-famous charge, rank upon rank of Confederates in gray and butternut brown marched straight into the teeth of the Union artillery. And they were cut to pieces. Thousands of men died in mere minutes. Union riflemen behind stone walls were completely protected. They marveled at the magnificent sight of the advancing Confederates. As Pickett's charge failed, it broke like a great wave ebbing against the rocks. The cry went up from the Union lines that had held fast: "Fredericksburg! Fredericksburg!" Then the sky was rent with a deep, satisfied roar from the Union ranks. They had saved their country, and they knew it. For the rest of their lives, these Union veterans would pay tribute to the sheer courage and unquestioned dedication of the soldiers in gray.

"Too bad, oh, too bad," cried Robert E. Lee in anguish as the tattered remnants of Pickett's division staggered back to their lines. He rode out to tell his men, "It's all *my* fault."

Instantly, he wired President Davis his resignation. Just as quickly, it was rejected. Lee was that rare figure in war—loved, even *worshipped*, by his soldiers, revered by the people of the South and deeply admired by nearly all his adversaries in the North. "I wish he were *ours*," said a young Pennsylvania girl who saw him on his ride to Gettysburg. She spoke for millions in the North. Lee had denounced slavery as "a moral and political evil."[7] He had even spoken *against* secession: "The framers of our Constitution never exhausted so much labor, wisdom, and forbearance in its formation if it was intended to be broken by every member of the [Union] at will. . . ."[8] Still, when Virginia seceded, Lee could see no other course than to support his state. Hundreds of thousands of brave and honorable Southerners reasoned the same way.

The First Minnesota Volunteers had been in every major battle of the Union Army. They played a conspicuous part at Gettysburg, too. They tried, but failed, to capture a rebel flag, following the orders of General

* This poignant tale was related by the late Shelby Foote, with a sad chuckle, in Ken Burns's magnificent *Civil War* series on PBS.

Winfield Scott Hancock. In just fifteen minutes of intense action, they suffered 68 percent casualties.[9]

After the battle, Minnesotan Sergeant Henry Taylor recorded how he learned of his brother Isaac's fate:

> About 8:30, Mr. Snow of Company B tells me thinks he saw my brother, and I accompany him to the spot, and I find my dear brother dead! A shell struck him on the top of his head and passed out through his back, cutting his belt in two. The poor fellow did not know what hit him. I secured his pocketbook, watch, diary, knife, etc., and with Wm. E. Cundy and J.S. Brown buried him at 10 o'clock a.m., 350 paces west of a road that passes north and sought by the house of Jacob Hummelbaugh and John Swisher (colored) and equi-distant from each, and by a stone wall where he fell, about a mile south of Gettysburg. I placed a board at his head on which I inscribed:
>
> No useless coffin enclosed his breast,
> Nor in sheet nor in shroud we bound him,
> But he lay like a warrior taking his rest
> With his shelter tent around him.[10]

Henry filled in the last entry in his brother's diary: "The owner of this diary was killed by a shell about sunset July 2, 1863—his face was toward the enemy."[11] The entry was dated—4 July 1863—*fourscore and seven years* after the birth of the nation for which young Isaac laid down his life.

For the defeated Confederates, this was a most mournful Independence Day, especially since some of them had come to speak of the war as the *Second War for Independence.*[12] On the blood-soaked roads of Pennsylvania, in a drenching rain, Lee's beaten army limped away. Dispirited and expecting a federal attack at any moment, the Army of Northern Virginia rushed to cross the rain-swollen Potomac. Lincoln was desperate for Meade to close with Lee and put an end to the rebellion. When Meade issued an order congratulating his men for driving "the invader" from our soil, Lincoln cried out: "Will our generals never get that idea out of their heads? The *whole* country is our soil."[13]

On this same July 4 came an electrifying message from the West. General Ulysses S. Grant accepted the surrender of the city of Vicksburg. Grant conducted a smart, hard-driving campaign against indecisive and divided Confederate defenders. Vicksburg commanded the heights over the Mississippi River. It was a strategic outpost. One of the Confederate leaders was General John C. Pemberton, actually a Philadelphian who had joined the Southern ranks because he married a Virginia lady.[14] This was a war, after all, in which brother fought against brother, father against son. Dashing Confederate cavalryman J. E. B. Stuart scorned his Virginia father-in-law's decision to remain on duty with the "old Army"—the *U.S. Army*. "He will regret it only once," Stuart said, "but that will be forever."

Grant had begun his drive with some hesitation. Rebel hero Nathan Bedford Forrest had bedeviled the Union forces. Forrest had been a slave trader and rich plantation owner before the war. He rose from private to general, the only Civil War soldier on either side to do so. And he did it without important connections in Richmond.

"That devil, Forrest," as Sherman called him, was a major obstacle to Union army movements in Tennessee. Once surrounded, Forrest ordered an attack *in both directions* and succeeded in breaking out. Another time, Forrest grabbed a Union soldier, pulled him up on his horse, behind his saddle, and used the unfortunate man as a human shield to protect himself from Yankee bullets. Forrest had thirty horses shot out from under him during the war—and killed thirty-one men. After the war, he boasted, "I was a horse ahead at the end."[15]

Grant had distinguished himself for bravery in the Mexican War. But then, he did not have responsibility for an army. Now, he was a general. He would later describe his feelings in his first taste of real combat while in command:

> As we approached the brow of the hill from which it was expected we could see [the Confederate] Harris' camp, and possibly find his men ready formed to meet us, my heart kept getting higher and higher until it felt to me as though it was in my throat. I would have given anything to have been back in Illinois, but I had not the moral courage

> to halt and consider what to do; I kept right on. When we reached a point from which the valley below was in full view I halted. The place where Harris had been encamped a few days before was still there and the marks of a recent encampment were plainly visible, but the [Southern] troops were gone. My heart resumed its place. It occurred to me at once that Harris had been as much afraid of me as I had been of him. This was a view of the question I had never taken before; but it was one I never forgot afterwards. From that event to the close of the war, I never experienced trepidation upon confronting an enemy.[16]

Here we may see the secret of Grant's success: his unadorned style, so clear, so candid, his deadpan humor, his *realistic* view of himself and others. Above all, we see Grant's self-deprecating wit and his bulldog determination: "*I kept right on.*"

After months of Grant's siege, the starving Mississippians gave up. (Vicksburg would not celebrate the Fourth of July again until 1942!) The city's fall gave control of the Mississippi River to the Union—splitting the Confederacy in two. *U. S. Grant!* Could anyone have had more symbolic initials? And to have *united* the upper and lower Mississippi River on the nation's birthday made an indelible impression on the American people. President Lincoln wrote, "The Father of Waters again goes unvexed to the sea."

Back East, the mood was not so celebratory. President Lincoln had hoped for, prayed for General Meade to take the unconditional surrender of Lee's army in Pennsylvania just as Grant had totally conquered Vicksburg in the West. It was not to be so.

Robert Todd Lincoln had never seen his father cry. But Abraham Lincoln wept bitter tears in the aftermath of the battle of Gettysburg. He could not believe Meade was allowing Lee to escape. Lee's retreat was even blocked by the rain-swollen river and still Meade did not descend upon him to crush the rebellion once and for all. Porter Alexander, the Confederate artillery chief, described Meade's desultory pursuit: "As a mule goes on the chase of a grizzly bear—as if catching up with us was the last thing he wanted to do."[17]

Lee did escape and Lincoln did not remove Meade. Meade—called "a goggle-eyed old snapping turtle" by his men—thought himself ill-used by an ungrateful commander in chief after so great a victory. He submitted his resignation. Lincoln immediately wrote a reply which, although he never sent it, reveals so much of his anguish:

> Again, my dear general, I do not believe you appreciate the magnitude of the misfortune involved in Lee's escape. He was within your easy grasp, and to have closed upon him would, in connection with our other late successes, have ended the war. As it is, the war will be prolonged indefinitely. If you could not safely attack Lee last Monday, how can you possibly do so South of the river, when you can take with you very few more than two thirds of the force you then had in hand? It would be unreasonable to expect, and I do not expect you can now effect much. Your golden opportunity is gone, and I am distressed immeasurably because of it.[18]

Not only does this unsent letter show Lincoln's deepest yearning to put an end to the bloodletting, but it also reveals his keen strategic sense. Lincoln had become the best strategist either side produced during the Civil War. He alone understood from the earliest days that the destruction of Lee's army—and *not* the capture of Richmond—was the primary objective of Union arms. Where others panicked as Lee invaded the North in 1862 and 1863, Lincoln saw it as a heaven-sent opportunity to cut Lee off from his base of supply and to capture his ragged army of barefoot warriors. "If I had gone up there, I could have whipped them myself," Lincoln told his young secretaries John Hay and John Nicolay.[19]

In this instance, however, Lincoln may have been wrong. The task of pursuing and crushing Lee's defeated army surely looked easier from Washington than it did to General Meade on the ground at Gettysburg.[20]

If Meade had launched a counterattack to finish off Lee's retreating ranks, he might have been the one surprised. Confederate General James Longstreet rode out after Pickett's failed charge to inspect. "Old Peter," as he was called, was taking a big chance. This was exactly what Stonewall Jackson had done after his great victory at Chancellorsville two months before—and paid for it with his life.

Old Peter was surprised to find an artillery battery in place, after he had ordered all his guns pulled back. "Whose are these guns?" he demanded to know, scowling. A pipe-smoking rebel officer came up to the general and answered mildly, "I am the captain. I am out here to have a little skirmishing on my own account, if the Yanks come out of their holes."[21]

Lee had taken great care—as he did in most things—to prepare his line of retreat. But he could not compensate for the terrible losses to his officer corps. In the three days of Gettysburg alone, Lee had lost seventeen of fifty-two generals—nearly a third of his finest officers.[22] This could not last. And Lee knew it.

So did others.

Lieutenant Colonel Arthur James Lyon Fremantle, a British officer of Queen Victoria's Coldstream Guards, was an observer with the Army of Northern Virginia. Watching Pickett's men stream back from their failed charge, he said: "They will never do it again."[23] He asked his Confederate friends: "Don't you see your system feeds upon itself? You cannot fill the places of these men. Your troops do wonders, but every time at a cost you cannot afford."[24]

Robert E. Lee understood this. But he was also an avid reader of Northern newspapers. He was well aware of the war-weariness of the Northern people. He knew, too, of the outright opposition of many Northern politicians to the war. If only, Lee reasoned, if only he could win some striking victory—especially one deep in Northern territory—the people of the North might cry out for peace. Some of the Democratic politicians in high offices did exactly that.

Lee was George Washington's stepgrandson-in-law. He knew as well as any man in America how Washington had fought many a losing battle only to triumph in the end. Yorktown had been that decisive victory that convinced a war-weary British public they could never subdue America. Lee constantly hoped that he could keep his ragged army going and make the cost of putting down the rebellion too high for the people of the North to bear.

This may explain his determination to win a major battle on Northern soil. He had won spectacular victories in Virginia. Fredericksburg was a triumph. Chancellorsville is still studied in military colleges as a textbook example of courage and skill.[25]*

Lincoln in these days began to appreciate what General Meade had accomplished. The people of the North rejoiced in the Gettysburg and Vicksburg victories, and the president seemed to share in their mood. After days of distress, Lincoln sent a dispatch intended for Meade's eyes. This time, he said: "A few days having passed, I am now profoundly grateful for what was done, without criticism for what was not done. General Meade has my confidence as a brave and skillful officer, and a true man." George Gordon Meade would command the Army of the Potomac until the last day of the war.

Lincoln contacted Grant in the same days. Noting that he'd never even met his western commander, Lincoln telegraphed: "I thought you should go down the river and join Gen. Banks; and when you turned Northward East of the Big Black, I feared it was a mistake. I now wish to make the personal acknowledgement that you were right and I was wrong." Presidents are not always known for such grace, such affecting humility. Not only was Grant a man he'd never met, he was also very possibly a rival for the presidency in 1864!

Despite the victories, Lincoln's immeasurable distress would soon deepen. Within days of winning the ground at Vicksburg and Gettysburg, New York City erupted into the worst riots in U.S. history. The draft—*conscription*—was widely hated in this city of immigrants. Poor Irish

* Recent scholarship by U.S. Army historian Tom Carhart sheds light on Robert E. Lee's actions that fateful day of 3 July 1863. Delving deeply into the records of both the Army of Northern Virginia and the Army of the Potomac, Carhart maintains that Lee planned a renewed assault on Culp's Hill by General Richard Ewell's Corp. Ewell was to have crushed the Union right flank while Pickett charged the Union center. The death blow was to have been delivered by that dashing General J. E. B. Stuart's six thousand cavalry. That plan was foiled by the bravery of the Union soldiers who pushed Ewell back and those who had scythed down Pickett's men. But most of all, Tom Carhart believes that General George Armstrong Custer's repulse of Stuart's previously unbeaten cavalry may have saved the day, the battle, and thus the Union. Carhart shows how Custer's incredible assaults on Stuart's "invincibles" was the previously undiscovered key to victory. Custer had graduated *last* in the same West Point class in which Paddy O'Rourke graduated *first.* Yet this July afternoon, General Custer was all brilliance and dash. Custer's spirited call to his First and Seventh Michigan troopers—"Come on you Wolverines"—could have been the battle cry of freedom. Tom Carhart's challenging thesis has yet to be fully accepted, but it will spark a debate at many a Civil War roundtable around the country.

laborers had no way to pay the $300 that exempted a man from service in the Union army.*

They lived in crowded, ill-lit tenements. Even their low wages and low-skilled jobs were threatened when Yankee Protestants employed free black stevedores as strikebreakers. The promises of American freedom seemed hollow to these struggling immigrants. New York Governor Horatio Seymour had attacked the Lincoln administration's emancipation and conscription policies in a demagogic Fourth of July speech to city Democrats. When conscription officers began drawing names for the draft on July 11, it was the spark that kindled the flames of rebellion. Mobs attacked black people, lynching six black men and burning a colored orphanage. The editor of the *New York Times* had to defend his offices by installing three newly invented Gatling guns.[26]**

Archbishop John Hughes had loyally traveled to Europe to stave off recognition of the Confederacy by Catholic powers even as he warned against making the war an "abolition war." Now, as rioting began, the archbishop and his Irish priests appealed to their flocks for order. And New York's Finest—its fearless police force (also largely Irish)—battled the rioters. The police were overwhelmed as hundreds died.

Only when troops from Pennsylvania's battlefield arrived in the city was the worst race riot in American history finally put down.[27] Unfair as it was, the draft proceeded because the government could not afford to let the opposition prevail. It is a tribute to Lincoln that he did *not* clap Governor Seymour in prison for inciting the riot.

When the civic leaders of Pennsylvania decided to dedicate a military cemetery at Gettysburg, they sought America's greatest orator as their leading speaker. Edward Everett, former president of Harvard, former U.S. secretary of state, was the natural choice. Republican Governor Andrew Curtin was then in a tough reelection race and a major event commemorating the battle could only help him. The battlefield, though, was still a scene of horror three

---

* Among those prominent New Yorkers who paid the $300 for a substitute were Grover Cleveland and Theodore Roosevelt Sr., TR's father.

** Who could resist contrasting this bit of history with the boundless enthusiasm of today's *Timesmen* for every form of gun control?

weeks after the battle. The young Gettysburg banker, David Wills, who was to chair the event, reported to the governor: "In many instances arms and legs and sometimes heads protrude and my attention has been directed in several places where the hogs were actually rooting out the bodies and devouring them."[28] Simply to bury the dead among the 22,807 Union and 28,000 Confederate casualties was an overwhelming task. Once Everett had confirmed as the day's primary orator, President Lincoln was asked to make "a few appropriate remarks."[29] The event was viewed primarily as a *state* occasion. Since Washington was only ninety miles away, the president was asked, almost as an afterthought, to attend.[30]

Everett had been the vice presidential running mate on the Constitutional Union ticket in 1860 with John Bell. In effect, event organizers had invited one of the president's *opponents* and had given him star billing. They also invited New York's Democratic Governor Horatio Seymour, whose state had contributed so much to the victory. Lincoln's "remarks" were never thought of as an *address* before he delivered them. Now, when it is recognized as one of the greatest speeches ever delivered in the English language, it is the *Gettysburg Address* that comes to mind whenever the word *address* is used:

> Fourscore and seven years ago, our fathers brought forth upon this continent a new nation, conceived in liberty and dedicated to the proposition that all men are created equal.
>
> Now we are engaged in a great civil war, testing whether that nation, or any nation so conceived and so dedicated, can long endure. We are met on a great battlefield of that war. We have come to dedicate a portion of that field as a final resting-place for those who here gave their lives that that nation might live. It is altogether fitting and proper that we should do this.
>
> But in a larger sense, we cannot dedicate, we cannot consecrate, we cannot hallow this ground. The brave men, living and dead, who struggled here have consecrated it, far above our poor power to add or detract. The world will little note nor long remember what we say here, but it can never forget what they did here. It is for us, the living, rather, to be dedicated here to the unfinished work which they who

> fought here have thus far so nobly advanced. It is rather for us to be here dedicated to the great task remaining before us—that from these honored dead we take increased devotion to that cause for which they gave the last full measure of devotion—that we here highly resolve that these dead shall not have died in vain, that this nation, under God, shall have a new birth of freedom, and that government of the people, by the people, for the people, shall not perish from the earth.

Here, Lincoln speaks of no North, no South, impugns no man's motives, makes no charges, sounds no note of triumph. But he explains in 266 spare words the meaning of the war. And his words will live as long as the *idea* of America lives.

Nor did Lincoln "refound" the nation. He did not *remake* America. He would have rejected such a notion. Every act of his was simply an effort to defend "the proposition" that had been central to the Founders' vision. If all men are *not* created equal, then they have no God-given right to freedom and no claim to self-government. For Lincoln, this was *axiomatic*.

Happily, the very *Honorable* Edward Everett recognized the genius of Lincoln's speech. He sent the president this gracious note shortly afterward: "I should be glad if I could flatter myself that I came as near to the central idea of the occasion in two hours as you did in two minutes."[31]

II. The Agony of Abraham Lincoln

We have only to see Lincoln's photographs from 1860 and compare them with those taken at the end of the war to see the effects of those five years on him. He was fifty-one when he was elected. During the war years, he seems to have aged a quarter of a century. Lincoln described himself as "old" in his farewell address to his neighbors in Springfield, Illinois, as he departed on the special train for Washington, D.C.

The ravages of war took their toll on him. The loss of his beloved son Willy in 1862 was a cruel blow. After that, Lincoln's relationship with his wife, Mary, suffered. She was driven nearly mad with grief. She even invited *spiritists* into the Executive Mansion who claimed to be able to communicate with her dead son. Lincoln attended at least one of these séances. He appears to have placed little stock in necromancy. Avid student of Shakespeare that he was, Lincoln would have read the line in which "the sheeted dead did squeak and gibber in the Roman streets" (*Hamlet*, act 1, scene 1). Burdened as he was by the cares of the war, it is most likely that Lincoln indulged his emotional, extravagant, and unsteady wife.

They could not be as close as they had once been because Mary could not be trusted. It was not that she ever intended to harm her husband. She adored him and sought his political advancement from the day that she married him. But Mary was cruelly shunned by Washington society. She shared too many confidences with the senator from Massachusetts, Charles Sumner. Sumner aligned himself with radical Republicans in Congress. And these radicals were increasingly out of sorts with Lincoln's mild reconstruction plans for the South.

Lincoln and his family spent their summers during the Civil War at the Soldiers Home in northeast Washington. Three miles from the President's House, this refuge was cooler and less hectic than the Executive Mansion. There, few office-seekers could pursue the overworked president. Overworked he surely was. Lincoln usually breakfasted on coffee and toast and often skipped lunch. He visibly wasted during his presidency. His clothes, always ill-fitting, now seemed to hang on his six-feet-four-inch frame. Often, Lincoln would ride alone the three miles to his office. Ominously, his movements did not go unobserved. He risked death by assassination every day he served as president.

Lincoln faced death with a fatalistic resolve. He believed that anyone could kill him if he was willing to give up his own life.* Despite the violent emotions that had been unleashed by the war, and by the inflamed political rhetoric that had led to it, many Americans discounted the possibility of assassination. It had never happened in America, after all.

Lincoln was savaged in the press—Northern, Southern, and foreign. Openly racist articles and cartoons were published. A London paper famously

* In a famous passage in one of Plato's *Dialogues*, Socrates reminds us that the lowliest citizen of a *polis* can kill the king if he's willing to give up his own life.

cartooned him as a disheveled, uncouth card player about to throw into a losing game the ace of spades. The face on the card was, not surprisingly, that of a young black man. Lincoln's winning opponent in that continental card game was an elegant, confidently smiling Jefferson Davis. It may have been the origin of our term—*playing the race card*. If some hostile newspapers did not show Lincoln as black, he was nonetheless mockingly depicted in the company of black people, dancing and socializing with them. Lincoln was painfully awkward in formal situations. He didn't dance and sing with white people, much less a mixed-race grouping. The cartoons were used to stir up racial animosities against the president.

"That giraffe," was the dismissive way the prosperous Pennsylvania railroad lawyer Edwin M. Stanton had referred to the Illinoisan before the war. But when he needed him, Lincoln did not hesitate to bring that able War Democrat into his cabinet. And so he was with most people. He had lived with their condescension all his life—and had used it to master them in the slippery game of politics. Stephen Douglas, William Seward, Roger B. Taney, Charles Sumner, Salmon P. Chase, George B. McClellan—these were but a few of the powerful men who underestimated Abraham Lincoln.

Lincoln sought some relief from his sorrows in humor, his own and that of others. He would always share a funny story or amusing anecdote with visitors to his office. Often, they would come expecting an office or some other favor, then be escorted to the door by the president, pumping their hand, and sharing some old "chestnut." Lincoln's penchant for humorous stories was viciously caricatured by the cartoonist who showed the president standing among the Union dead at Antietam with the caption: "This reminds me of a little story."

The day he assembled his cabinet to hear the Emancipation Proclamation, he tried to break the ice with a clever story from Artemis Ward, his favorite humorist.* Significantly, he told them, "With the fearful strain that is upon me night and day, if I did not laugh, I should die, and you need this medicine as much as I do."[32] There is little indication they appreciated his ministrations that day. Except for the cigar-chomping Seward,

* It was Ward's "Outrage at Utica" that Lincoln enjoyed.

with whom Lincoln came to enjoy funny stories and a genuine camaraderie, Lincoln's cabinet consisted mostly of solemn asses. He used their talents. There's not much indication he enjoyed their company. Or they his.

Lincoln searched with mounting desperation for a fighting general. McDowell had failed him early. McClellan stayed with Lincoln for more than a year, but failed him. So did Pope and Burnside. And Hooker. Meade proved more successful, at least on the defensive. But he, too, complained. He never enjoyed Lincoln's full confidence.

Grant was different. Lincoln liked him from the start. Grant was an Illinoisan. He was quiet—and businesslike. Lincoln hoped that Grant shared his ideas for political reconstruction of the Union, but it was far more important that Grant should be "on the same page" on military matters. Grant had one advantage over all his fellow Union generals: he didn't complain. He took the resources he was given and he fought. How he fought.

Lincoln had waited so long for a military hero, for someone he could brag about. Even before the fall of Vicksburg, Lincoln was ecstatic about his fellow Illinoisan: "Whether Gen. Grant shall or shall not consummate the capture of Vicksburg, his campaign from the beginning of this month [May, 1863] up to the twenty-second day of it, is one of the most brilliant in the world."[33] It wasn't—but it wasn't bad, either. And when compared with the handiwork of Lincoln's other generals, it certainly *looked* brilliant.

Lincoln was dismayed to hear renewed complaints about Grant's drinking. Discreetly, he sent Assistant Secretary of War Charles Dana to visit Grant. Ostensibly, Dana was there to inspect Grant's army. Grant soon figured out that Dana was there to look *him* over.[34] Shrewdly, Grant opened up his headquarters to Lincoln's "spy." It proved a smart move. Dana wrote back glowing reports about Grant's intelligence, skill, and devotion to the Union cause.[35]

Only once did Lincoln find it necessary to overrule his commander in the West. Grant's father had come into his son's camp. He had come not to congratulate his son, but to profit from his command. Several of the unscrupulous Jesse Grant's cohorts, in a scheme to profiteer from cotton in the occupied territories, were speculators. Making the matter even more prickly, some of them were Jewish. Instead of banning Jesse Grant and the friends of Jesse Grant from the Union camp, General Grant issued an order banning "the Jews as a class."[36]

Horrified, Jewish leaders rushed to the president's office for relief.[37] Lincoln was not fully briefed on the issues. He greeted the Jews with a biblical jest: "And so the children of Israel were driven from the happy land of Canaan?" Just as quickly, the Jewish leader shot back: "And that is why we have come unto Father Abraham's bosom, asking protection."[38] Beset with troubles, Lincoln must have delighted in this witty rejoinder. "And this protection they shall have at once," the president said before writing out an order countermanding Grant's ban.[39]

After the fall of Vicksburg, Lincoln wanted Grant to attend to the situation in Tennessee. After a promising start, Union General William S. Rosecrans had been hit hard by the rebels at the Battle of Chickamauga. To Lincoln, Rosecrans seemed "like a duck hit on the head." Grant quickly dispatched Rosecrans and replaced him with General George Thomas.[40] It was a smart move that would pay off for the Union cause. Thomas, a Virginian, had stood firm during the battle—earning him the title "the Rock of Chickamauga." But his men fondly referred to him as "Pap." Advancing toward Chattanooga, Tennessee, Grant ordered General Joe Hooker to take Lookout Mountain. And Hooker did it.[41] Then he directed Thomas to seize the Confederate positions at the base of Missionary Ridge and hold up. Thomas's high-spirited troops took those works—and pressed on. They took Missionary Ridge in a hard-fought "battle above the clouds."[42] Grant—and Lincoln—rejoiced.

Always, Lincoln searched desperately for a military commander who could, in his words, "face the arithmetic." By this, Lincoln meant a general who could face the heavy casualties that would be suffered by Union forces as they closed in on Lee's army. The president understood what Lee and some of the Confederate leaders understood: given the vastly superior resources of the North in men and materiel, it would be only a matter of time before the North would grind the South down. Grant was by far the most savvy, the most resourceful, the most courageous of his generals. Surely he could face the arithmetic. Lincoln brought Grant back East and gave him command over all the Union armies. Grant was promoted to lieutenant general, a rank Congress had last bestowed on George Washington.

Grant's manner of taking command of the armies of the United States was typical of him. He came back to Washington and immediately checked in to the famed Willard Hotel—just a few blocks from the Executive Mansion. A bored hotel clerk told him that there was only one small room—on the top floor under the eaves—for the general and his fourteen-year-old son. Grant said he'd take it. Only when he signed the hotel register simply as "U. S. Grant and son, Galena, Illinois" did the clerk realize who his powerful guest was. Sputtering, he quickly assigned the new lieutenant general the best room in the house.[43] The other guests in the lobby began to applaud.*

In short order, Grant locked horns with Lee in Virginia. It was a rolling, horrific engagement, with wounded men screaming as the woods caught fire and they were consumed. Around Spotsylvania Court House, Grant tenaciously pursued Lee, taking terrible casualties and inflicting many more. "If you see the president," Grant told a colleague, "tell him there will be no turning back."[44] And there was no turning back.

Not for Grant.

Or Lincoln.

Or the United States of America.

Initially, the North thrilled to hear this man of few words say: "I propose to fight it out on this line if it takes all summer."[45] But soon, as the long lists of dead and wounded appeared in Northern newspapers, the horror of close engagement in the Virginia woodlands sank in. Hooker and Burnside had traveled this road before him. They had always turned back. True to Lincoln's assumption, Grant faced the arithmetic and pressed on. But at what cost! Doomed Union soldiers sewed their names inside their coats the night before Cold Harbor.**

They wanted their bodies identified after the battle.[46]

"I regret this assault more than any I have ever ordered," Grant would

---

* It was to be Grant's first introduction to the lobby of the Willard. Later, as president, Grant would come to refer to those who hung out there hoping to buttonhole high government officials as "lobbyists," thus coining the word. (Online source: http://www.c-span.org/questions/week175.asphttp://www.c-span.org/questions/week1.)

** Cold Harbor is barely ten miles northeast of Richmond.

say of his orders to attack at Cold Harbor.[47] Well he might. Grant lost seven thousand Union soldiers killed or wounded *in just thirty minutes* on the morning of 3 June 1864.[48]

Soon, the word *butcher* began to be thrown at Grant. Even Mrs. Lincoln called him that. No one called Robert E. Lee a butcher. And yet it was Lee's strategy of defense that yielded these terrible numbers. Lee knew he was killing two Federals for every man he lost in the defense of Richmond.[49] Lee's reputation as the stainless Christian knight was real, but it should not blind us to the fact that Lee was a *lethal* opponent. Lee consumed Northern newspapers. He knew that *political* opposition to Lincoln was increasing. He also knew that the South's only chance in 1864 was to inflict so many battle casualties on the North that anguished Union voters would defeat Lincoln and the Republicans.

Lincoln stood by his general. Grant did his job, efficiently and with focused resolve. He did not meddle in politics. He did not demand more support than Lincoln could give him. He even found a new way to handle the pressures—trading his bottle for a knife and whittling stick.

Grant's cool confidence, his lack of dramatic flair impressed many. George S. Boutwell, a leading Massachusetts Republican, said, "It is difficult to comprehend the qualities of a man who could be moved by a narrative of individual suffering, and yet could sleep surrounded by the horrors of the battles of the Wilderness."[50]

Horrors they surely were. What must have been the thoughts of young Union soldiers marching, fighting, then bedding down in "ghoul-haunted woodlands" that their older brothers had fought over and many had died in the previous two years? Herman Melville captured the eerie feeling in a poem, "The Armies of the Wilderness":

In glades they meet skull after skull
Where pine-cones lay—the rusted gun,
Green shoes full of bones, the mouldering coat
And cuddled-up skeleton;
And scores of such. Some start as in dreams,
And comrades lost bemoan:

By the edge of those wilds Stonewall had charged—
But the Year and the Man were gone.

Lincoln grieved at the toll the grinding trench warfare was taking on the Union forces—and the entire Union. For Lincoln did not simply mourn Northern losses. He believed the entire country was one, North and South. As reports came back of the trenches around Petersburg, Virginia, the whole country understood what it meant. Southern boys as young as thirteen were found dead there, lying next to fallen white-bearded grandfathers. Whose heart could remain untouched at such a loss?

Few families North or South were untouched by the hand of death. The Lincoln family was no different. When Lincoln's favorite sister-in-law, Emilie Helm, was detained at Fort Monroe, Virginia, she refused to take an oath of allegiance to the United States. Emilie had married Mary Lincoln's younger half-brother, Ben Helm. Ben Helm had been killed at Atlanta. "Send her to me," Lincoln telegraphed the Union officers who had stopped the young widow whom Lincoln and his wife thought of as the daughter they never had.[51] When she arrived at the Executive Mansion, Emilie was embraced by the president and the first lady. "'You know, Little Sister,'" Emilie Helms later reported his saying to her, "'I tried to have Ben come with me.' Mr. Lincoln put his arms around me and we both wept."[52] In a sense, Lincoln wrapped his arms around the entire country.

III. "Long Abraham a Little Longer"

Despite the great Union victories of 1863, a growing war-weariness among the people of the North was the last remaining hope of the Confederacy. The Emancipation Proclamation had broken the unity of the Northern public. The Democratic Party loudly denounced it. When Democrats captured the legislatures of Illinois and Indiana, they passed resolutions *demanding* the revocation of the proclamation as a condition for their states' continued support of the Union war effort. Clement Vallandigham, an Ohio Democrat, gave a speech on 1 May 1863 in which he denounced the war as an attempt to free black men while enslaving whites.[53] He demanded the Union accept the French offer of mediation—an offer that assumed Southern independence. General Ambrose Burnside—recently dismissed from command of the Army of the Potomac—acted with dispatch to haul Vallandigham before a military tribunal in Ohio. Convicted of disloyalty, Vallandigham was imprisoned. He was lucky not to be shot. But even this merited prison sentence proved too severe for Lincoln. The president ordered Vallandigham *banished* behind Confederate lines. From the South, the cagey Vallandigham slipped away to Canada, where he ran for governor of Ohio from his frosty exile.[54] Vallandigham was just one of a growing number of "Copperheads" who sought to obstruct the Union war effort.* When antiwar Democrats denounced Lincoln as a tyrant for his treatment of Vallandigham, he memorably replied: "Must I shoot a simple soldier boy who deserts while I must not touch a hair of the wily agitator who *induces* him to desert?"[55]

After issuing the Emancipation Proclamation, Lincoln opened the ranks of the U.S. military to black soldiers and sailors. Frederick Douglass responded enthusiastically, traveling throughout the North to encourage enlistments. His perennial speech topic: "Why should the colored man enlist?" "You will stand more erect, walk more assured, feel more at ease, and be less liable to insult than you ever were before," Douglass said. "He who fights the battles of America may claim America as his country—and have that claim respected," he told his avid listeners.[56]

Not just self-respect was at stake. Douglass wanted nothing less than full civil and political equality for black people. "Once let the black man get upon his person the brass letters, U.S.; let him get an eagle on his button, and a musket on his shoulder, and bullets in his pocket," he told a Philadelphia crowd, "and there is no power on earth or under the earth that can deny he has earned the right of citizenship in the United States." With his own massive dignity, with the moral force he brought to his cause, he challenged his hearers: "I say again, this is our chance, and woe betide us if we fail to embrace it."[57] Black Americans would heed the abolitionist's call; by war's end, more than two hundred thousand of them would "rally 'round the flag."

---

* Antiwar Copperheads got their name from the copper pennies with the Liberty head figure that they filed down and wore as lapel pins. Loyal Northerners relished the double meaning of the word, comparing Copperheads to the poisonous snake of the same name.

Eighteen sixty-four was an election year. Most blacks could not vote, but sullen and resentful whites could. Lincoln had to respond to the rising antiblack sentiment expressed by many Democrats. He did so in a widely circulated letter:

> You say you will not fight to free Negroes. Some of them seem willing to fight for you; but, no matter. Fight you, then exclusively to save the Union. I issued the proclamation on purpose to aid you in saving the Union. Whenever you shall have conquered all resistence to the Union, if I shall urge you to continue fighting, it will be an apt time, then, for you to declare you will not fight to free Negroes.
>
> I thought that in your struggle for the Union, to whatever extent the Negroes should cease helping the enemy, to that extent it weakened the enemy in his resistence to you. Do you think differently? I thought that whatever Negroes can be got to do as soldiers, leaves just so much less for white soldiers to do, in saving the Union. Does it appear otherwise to you?
>
> But Negroes, like other people, act upon motives. Why should they do any thing for us, if we will do nothing for them? If they stake their lives for us, they must be prompted by the strongest motive—even the promise of freedom. And the promise being made, must be kept. . . .
>
> Peace does not seem so distant as it did. I hope it will come soon. . . . [Then] there will be some black men who can remember that, with silent tongue, and clenched teeth, and steady eye, and well-poised bayonnet, they have helped mankind on to this great consummation; while, I fear, there will be some white ones, unable to forget that, with malignant heart, and deceitful speech, they strove to hinder it.[58]

Once again, we see Lincoln's use of overpowering logic to deflate his opponents. How could they claim to be loyal to the Union while being willing to leave black Southerners in bondage to harvest the crops that would feed rebel armies?

When Lincoln brought Grant east and gave him overall command of the Union armies, great things were expected. In a strategy conference, Lincoln saw the force of Grant's plan for simultaneous army assaults on the stricken South. The anaconda of the Union blockade was taking its toll by this third winter of war. Lincoln exclaimed at Grant's plan: "I see it. Those not skinning can hold a leg." This frontier metaphor was not lost on Grant, the tanner's son. It meant that even if one or more Union armies were not on the move, they could still help the main thrust by "holding a leg" to prevent the Confederacy from reinforcing using internal lines of communication.

Some Republicans' dissatisfaction with Lincoln's direction of the war was expressed by the radical wing. They wanted a harder, more punitive prosecution of the war. They toyed with running former Secretary of the Treasury Salmon P. Chase against Mr. Lincoln. Lincoln did not worry about Chase's machinations. He let Chase know he had him in mind as a replacement for the rapidly failing Chief Justice Roger B. Taney. Chase took the bait and announced his support for Lincoln's reelection.

Lincoln was renominated by the Republicans in June 1864. The radicals in Congress were unenthusiastic. Desperate to gain support from prowar Democrats, the party nominated for vice president Tennessee's military governor, Andrew Johnson, a Jackson Democrat.

Grant was seemingly stalemated in the trenches before Petersburg. His assault on Lee's ragged remnant at Cold Harbor had been thrown back with terrible Union casualties.

General William Tecumseh Sherman was a tall, red-haired, cigar-chomping West Pointer who brooked no nonsense. Early in the war, he had suffered a nervous breakdown. Many still thought him crazy. He was one of the few who had predicted a long, bloody, very destructive war. Sherman looked like an unmade bed. Although he was older than Grant, and had outranked Grant in the Old Army, he was fully willing to put himself wholly under Grant's command. "Grant stood by me when I was crazy," Sherman said, "and I stood by him when he was drunk. Now we stand by each other always."[59]

When Grant was bogged down in a muddy and bloody siege before Petersburg while Sherman was moving briskly up the Atlantic Seaboard, there were rumors that Sherman might be placed in command over Grant. If anyone thought they could sow the seeds of dissension in the Union high command by circulating such rumors, they underestimated both Grant and Sherman. Grant wrote his loyal friend: "No one would be more pleased at your advancement than I, and if you should be placed in my position and I subordinate it would not change our personal relations in the least."[60] It is hard to imagine any other Civil War generals—except perhaps Lee and Jackson—who could have penned those lines.

Even though his brother was an influential U.S. senator, "Cump" Sherman hated politicians and the press. That did not, ironically, make him any friend to the black man. The plan Sherman now offered must have seemed very risky. His plan was to expose the weakness of the Confederacy for the world to see. He would sweep into Georgia from Tennessee. "My aim [is] to whip the rebels, to humble their pride, to follow them to their inmost recesses, and to make them fear and dread us."[61]

Sherman is credited with being the first "modern" warrior in America, the first practitioner of "total war." Destructive he was. "I can make Georgia howl," he said—and did. But while he left a trail of burned out, blackened plantation houses sixty miles wide, there is no record of civilians shot, hanged, or raped by Sherman's army. He burned public buildings. His "bummers" often killed or ran off all the livestock they could find. Sherman's army was steeled in its determination to wield a "terrible swift sword" by its discovery of starving Union prisoners just escaped from the notorious Confederate prison at Andersonville.

Sherman was informed that his Confederate opponent, the Gettysburg hero General John Bell Hood, was headed for the Ohio River. He knew that Hood was hoping thereby to divert Sherman's Army of the Tennessee from its objective. Sherman growled: "If he will go to the Ohio, I'll send him rations." Sherman's conquering horde was the first example in America of "shock and awe." He cut himself loose from cumbersome baggage trains so he could move faster. He lived off the land.

Dissatisfied Republican radicals joined with abolitionists, rejected applicants for patronage jobs, and even some Copperheads to nominate Union General John Charles Frémont at a Cleveland, Ohio, third-party convention. This move could have assured a Democratic victory in 1864.

Lincoln was not moved. He received word of the Frémont challenge while in the telegraph office. It was where he spent much of his time during his presidency. The telegrapher informed the president that some four hundred delegates had come together in Cleveland. Convention organizers had promised thousands. Lincoln took his Bible and read from 1 Samuel 22:2: "And everyone who was in distress, everyone who was in debt, and every one who was discontented gathered to him. So he became captain over them. And there were about four hundred men with him."[62] Soon, the famed "Pathfinder" would beat a path to the exit. Frémont withdrew from the race as the autumn leaves and Lincoln's military fortunes turned.

Lincoln's main opponent, George B. McClellan, marched to an easy nomination by Democrats who met in the same Chicago convention center—the Wigwam—where Lincoln had himself been nominated in 1860. McClellan had his own problems of party unity. The same Democratic convention that had enthusiastically chosen him also adopted a platform plank proposed by the Copperhead Vallandigham. The Vallandigham "peace" plank called the Union war effort "a failure" and proposed a truce and peace negotiation with the Confederates. Once stopped, of course, the federal war machine could not be restarted. Acceptance of the Vallandigham Plank essentially meant the Democratic Party was calling for surrender in the Civil War.

McClellan was troubled. (Lincoln joked: "He's intrenching."[63]) At last, he spoke out *against* the Vallandigham Plank. "I could not look in the face of my gallant comrades of the army and navy who have survived so many bloody battles," he said, if he accepted the Copperheads' ideas.[64]

Military victories changed the political picture. First, U.S. Navy Admiral David Glasgow Farragut steamed through mine-infested waters to seize Mobile, Alabama. "Damn the torpedoes," he said, "full speed ahead."[65] Then General Phil Sheridan, the Union's greatest cavalry chieftain, put Virginia's bountiful Shenandoah Valley to the torch. The valley was the "breadbasket of the Confederacy." No longer could the Confederates look to the Shenandoah for their cornmeal and hardtack. Now, said, Sheridan: "A crow flying over it would have to carry its own provender."

Finally, on September 2 came the news that would reelect Lincoln. Sherman telegraphed: "Atlanta is ours, and fairly won."[66] Sherman then proceeded on his storied "March to the Sea." He tore up all railroad lines. His men heated, then twisted the iron rails around telegraph poles—they called them "Sherman bowties." Sherman wanted to make war so terrible that generations would pass before Southerners would resort to it again.*

If ever a president was tempted to delay or cancel an election, it was Lincoln. He thought he would surely lose. And to lose was to give up the struggle for the Union. He said, "We cannot have free government without elections, and if the rebellion should force us to forego or postpone a national election, it might fairly claim to have already conquered and ruined us."[67]

Lincoln trusted the people. And they, ultimately, trusted him. It must have been especially gratifying to Lincoln that he carried the "soldier vote" against that darling of the Army of the Potomac, General McClellan. Lincoln won 212 electoral votes and 2,213,635 popular votes (55.1 percent). McClellan garnered only 21 electoral votes from Delaware, Kentucky, and New Jersey, and 1,805,237 popular votes (44.9 percent). Eighty electoral votes not cast—representing the states still in rebellion—would not have elected McClellan. Cartoonists had a field day. One showed an elongated president holding a sheet of paper labeled "four more years."

"Long Abraham a Little Longer" was the caption.

General Sherman wired the president. He presented him with the seaport of Savannah, Georgia, as a Christmas gift. Thankfully, beautiful Savannah had surrendered and was spared the torch. Also spared was elegant Charleston, which had jubilantly greeted the Ordinance of Secession. Columbia, South Carolina's capital, was not so fortunate. There, for thirty years, fire-eating politicians had plotted to break up the Union. When he learned that Columbia had burned, Lincoln's reply was grave and biblical, taken from the gospel of Matthew: "The people who sat in darkness have seen a great light."

He was seeing many things in spiritual terms as this most terrible of all wars ground on. To a friend he wrote in this fateful year of 1864: "I claim not to have controlled events, but confess plainly that events have controlled me."[68] This is an astonishing statement from a man who placed such store in human reason, in "all conquering *mind*." Lincoln was a driven man. His Springfield, Illinois, law partner, Billy Herndon, said his ambition was a little engine that

* Presidential candidate Jimmy Carter often winced in 1976 as he was greeted by Iowa high school bands playing "Marching through Georgia," a song celebrating Sherman's March. That's how long these painful memories lasted.

knew no rest. Lincoln had to know his intellect greatly surpassed that of other men. He was physically strong, too. He had been a champion wrestler in his youth. Even as an older man he could still hold a double-blade axe at arms length. And keep it there. Try it sometime. Lincoln was accused of being a dictator. Even his staunchest defenders concede that no other president ever exercised such great power. Yet here was Lincoln confessing to a friend his own sense of being controlled by events. It was as if an angel rode in the whirlwind.

IV. The Union Victorious

Lincoln's landslide reelection doomed the Confederacy. Now, there was no hope of foreign intervention. The anaconda squeeze of the U.S. Navy blockade was strangling the Southern war effort. The guns of the USS *Kearsarge* remorselessly pounded the great Confederate commerce raider CSS *Alabama*, sending her to the bottom off Cherbourg, France. Everywhere Jefferson Davis looked, the Confederacy was crumbling. By the beginning of 1865, there were more black men serving in the federal armies and the navy than there were whites in all Confederate forces.

Davis even had to swallow the bitterest pill of all: Robert E. Lee's suggestion that slaves be recruited for the army with the promise of freedom if the South gained her independence. "If slaves will make good soldiers our whole theory of slavery is wrong," responded Georgia's Howell Cobb.[69]

The famed Massachusetts Fifty-fourth Regiment had proved itself at Fort Wagner in South Carolina. This "colored" regiment—the U.S. Army would remain segregated until 1948—had been led into battle by the brave young Colonel Robert Gould Shaw, scion of a Boston Brahmin family. When Colonel Shaw fell in the assault, his body was contemptuously thrown into a ditch with those of his dead black troops. Shaw's father was a leading lawyer in Massachusetts. He *declined* an offer to have his son's body disinterred, saying Robert was *honored* to be buried with his men. Stories like this worked a profound change in Northern opinion.*

* The story of Massachusetts's famed Fifty-fourth is admirably told in the Hollywood movie *Glory*. It is accurate in most respects except one: Governor Andrew would never have permitted his brave troops to leave the Bay State without good boots.

President Lincoln had been disappointed in many of his generals, as we have seen, until he found the winning team of Grant and Sherman. But he never had occasion to complain of one staunchly loyal Georgian. Montgomery Cunningham Meigs was the Union Quartermaster General. Winfield Scott the Virginian had insisted on Meigs's appointment early in 1861 to compensate for the chaos and corruption of Secretary of War Simon Cameron. General Meigs soon brought order to the Union army's procurement of nearly everything from horses to "pup" tents. He constructed massive numbers of hospitals for the wounded.[70] Rigorously honest, tireless, and a brilliant organizer, Meigs had supervised the construction of the Capitol before the war. Then, his boss was Jefferson Davis. Now, it was Abraham Lincoln. Because of Meigs's unstinting efforts, the Union Army was better supplied, better clothed, and better sheltered than any army in history. Everything except food and arms were Meigs's responsibility; among his other acheivements, Meigs began the *sizing* of boots and clothing—thus giving a powerful boost to the U.S. civilian economy as soon as the fighting ended.[71]

Because he had to send out the ambulances to tend the hundreds of thousands of Union *and* Confederate wounded, General Meigs understandably became bitter toward his fellow West Pointers who, he believed, had betrayed their oaths as officers. He had once served under Robert E. Lee. Now, when called upon to select a site for a huge new Union cemetery, General Meigs unhesitatingly chose the front lawn of the Custis-Lee Mansion. By putting the Union dead in Lee's front yard, Meigs knew, the Confederate commander's family could never return to their historic home.[72] But in October 1864, General Meigs would face his own family tragedy. Union Major John Rodgers Meigs was killed, and General Meigs saw his own son's body buried in Mrs. Lee's rose garden.[73] Robert E. Lee's magnificent home thus became the site of Arlington National Cemetery. It is hallowed ground.*

* After the war, Robert E. Lee's son, George Washington Custis Lee, sued the U.S. government for the return of his parents' home. The U.S. Supreme Court in 1882 ruled 5–4 that the Lee home had been improperly seized and ordered it returned to the Lees. The heirs of Robert E. Lee then sold the property to the United States for $150,000. Ten years later, General Meigs himself was buried at Arlington National Cemetery—*where valor sleeps.* (Arlington National Cemetery Source: http://www.arlingtoncemetery.net/arlhouse.htm.)

Lincoln approached the inaugural stands for the second time on 4 March 1865. Symbolizing the Union, the Capitol dome now stood completed. This time he would be sworn in by Chief Justice Salmon P. Chase, a man who just the year before had been conspiring to take the presidency from him. Vice President Johnson, suffering the effects of a long train ride from Tennessee and a bout of typhoid fever, had taken too much to drink before being sworn in. He launched into a long—embarrassingly long—mawkish address inside the Capitol. "Do not let Johnson speak outside," Lincoln told a parade marshal.[74] Andrew Johnson would never recover from this disgrace.

The day was wet and windy. As Lincoln arose amid waves of applause, the sun broke through the clouds. Sunbeams shone down on the newly completed dome of the U.S. Capitol. Lincoln had pressed Congress to finish the work of decades, making the Capitol itself a symbol of the completed Union. The Statue of Freedom that topped the dome had originally been brought by wagon to the city of Washington. Many of the teamsters and laborers who hauled the great female figure were, ironically, slaves. By the time she was put in place atop the building where she stands today, they were free.

He then delivered the greatest inaugural address in American history. Describing the war, he noted that slavery had been the cause of it. Lincoln urged his listeners *not* to claim all righteousness for themselves. He offered then perhaps the most terrible, most thought-provoking idea ever uttered in American public life.[75]

> Fondly do we hope, fervently do we pray, that this mighty scourge of war may speedily pass away. Yet, if God wills that it continue until all the wealth piled by the bondsman's two hundred and fifty years of unrequited toil shall be sunk, and until every drop of blood drawn with the lash shall be paid by another drawn with the sword, as was said three thousand years ago, so still it must be said "the judgments of the Lord are true and righteous altogether."*

* "The judgments of the LORD are true and righteous altogether." (Psalm 19:9 NKJV)

Lincoln ended with these immortal words:

> With malice toward none, with charity for all, with firmness in the right as God gives us to see the right, let us strive on to finish the work we are in, to bind up the nation's wounds, to care for him who shall have borne the battle and for his widow and his orphan, to do all which may achieve and cherish a just and lasting peace among ourselves and with all nations.

Lincoln's words were carried in a fine tenor voice—not the baritone so often portrayed by Hollywood. Everyone in the vast crowd could hear him distinctly. Including Frederick Douglass.

And John Wilkes Booth.

Later, at the Executive Mansion, Lincoln would greet the celebratory crowd. Frederick Douglass, denied entrance by an usher, climbed through a window and joined the receiving line. Seeing him, Lincoln cried out: "Ah, Douglass!" He told the great abolitionist he wanted to know his opinion of the address. "Mr. President, it was a *sacred* effort," Douglass answered. Later, he would say of his relationship with Lincoln that he was the only white man he ever knew who did not instantly make him aware he was a black man.

On 2 April 1865, Richmond fell. General Lee sent a message to President Davis telling him he must abandon the lines. The messenger reached Davis while he was in church. The congregation noted the Southern president's ashen face as he left his pew. The Confederate government frantically packed up and left the city. An attempt to fire key military installations to deny them to the Yankees got out of hand and the city was soon in flames. Two days later, President Lincoln visited the city. He had his young son, Tad, in tow as he walked to the Confederate White House. Outside, crowds of soldiers and free Negroes cheered as he sat at Jefferson Davis's desk. White Virginians generally looked out glumly from behind shuttered windows. U.S. Army authorities established a quick, firm, but mild control of the old city. And when the invalid Mrs. Robert E. Lee complained of having a black soldier posted as a guard outside her house, he was quickly replaced with a white one. The Stars and Stripes once again flew over the Capitol that Thomas Jefferson had designed.

A week after Richmond's fall, General Lee agreed to meet General Grant at Appomattox Courthouse. Because of a bureaucratic snarl, his hungry soldiers had been sent several boxcars of *ammunition*, not rations. The Southside Virginia countryside could barely feed itself. Lee *rejected* calls by some of his junior officers to take the army into the mountains and fight a guerilla war. Lee had seen how guerilla war degenerated in Missouri. He wanted no part of a merciless, decades-long bloodletting.

Grant had been suffering from a debilitating headache before he received Lee's surrender note. But as soon as he read the welcome news, his headache was gone.[76] General Lee rode Traveler to the Wilbur McLean home in Appomattox Court House, Virginia, where the meeting would take place on 9 April 1865. Attired in his finest uniform, his engraved sword at his side, Lee cut a magnificent figure. When he rode up, General Grant apologized for being late. He was dressed in a private's rumpled jacket, the stars of a lieutenant general* incongruously attached to his shoulders. His boots were muddy.

Grant did everything he could to ease Lee's agony. He spoke pleasantly of their Mexican War days. He remembered Lee. Lee could not recall him. When it came to writing out terms for the surrender, Grant asked Colonel Ely Parker, a full-blooded Seneca Indian, to copy out the terms in his beautiful handwriting. Lee froze. He initially thought Colonel Parker was a black man, that his presence might be a way of humbling him. Catching himself, Lee maintained his dignity and military bearing. He asked Grant to amend the terms to allow his men to keep their horses, which most of them owned. Grant declined to change the terms, but said it would be understood that any man claiming a horse as his own could keep it. They would be needed for spring planting for "their little farms."

Grant treated Lee with complete tenderness and respect. And when Union troops began to cheer the news of the surrender, Grant immediately ordered it to stop. Nothing should be done to humiliate the rebels who

* Grant was the first American since George Washington to hold this rank.

were once again "our countrymen." Grant also ordered tens of thousands of Union rations to feed the "famished rebel horde."* General Lee and all of his twenty-eight thousand soldiers of the Army of Northern Virginia were paroled by Grant—allowed simply to go home to live under the laws of their once again *United* States.

Grant would record his thoughts about that day at Appomattox in his memoirs:

> What General Lee's feelings were I do not know. As he was a man of much dignity, with an impassible face, it was impossible to tell whether he felt inwardly glad that the end had finally come, or felt sad over the result, and was too manly to show it. Whatever his feelings, they were entirely concealed from my observation; but my own feelings, which had been jubilant on the receipt of his letter, were sad and depressed. I felt like anything rather than rejoicing at the downfall of a foe who had fought so long and valiantly, and had suffered so much for a cause, though that cause was, I believe, one of the worst for which a people ever fought, and one for which there was the least excuse. I do not question, however, the sincerity of the great mass of those who were opposed to us.[77]

Grant then selected the twice-wounded Union hero, General Joshua Lawrence Chamberlain, to receive the formal surrender of Southern arms. Chamberlain matched in every way the gallantry and chivalry so long associated with fallen Southerners like J. E. B. Stuart and Stonewall Jackson. As the barefoot, ragged Confederates marched in two days later to lay down their arms and their beloved flags, Chamberlain ordered a smart salute. All along the Union lines, battle-hardened veterans snapped to the call: "Carry Arms!" Confederate General John Bell Gordon wheeled his horse around and executed an elegant response, his horse almost bowing as Gordon touched his saber to his toe: "Honor answering Honor."[78]

---

* "Fair as the Garden of the Lord / To the eyes of the famished rebel horde," wrote Poet John Greenleaf Whittier of the Southern invasion of Maryland in 1862 in *Barbara Freitchie*. Lee's army had been hungry for years.

Chamberlain would later describe the scene:

> On they came with the old swinging route step and swaying battle flags . . . crowded so thick, by thinning out of men, that the whole column seemed crowned with red. . . . In the van, the proud Confederate ensign. . . . Before us in proud humiliation stood the embodiment of manhood; men whom neither toils and sufferings, nor the fact of death nor disaster nor hopelessness . . . could bend from their resolve; standing before us now, thin, worn, and famished, but erect, and with eyes looking level into ours, waking memories that bound us together as no other bond. . . . On our part not a sound of trumpet more, nor roll of drum; not a cheer, nor word, nor whisper or vaingloryng, nor motion of man . . . but an awed stillness rather, and breath-holding, as if it were the passing of the dead. . . . How could we help falling on our knees, all of us together, and praying God to pity and forgive us all![79]

Too little credit goes to U. S. Grant for this sublime moment in the history of our wounded world. We need only compare how rebellions in Mexico and Canada had ended just thirty years before. Santa Anna put all the Alamo rebels—both "Anglos" from the North and local Hispanic *tejanos*—to the sword in 1836. The British in Canada in 1837 had hanged dozens of rebel leaders who demanded nothing more than the same representative government enjoyed by millions of their neighbors in the United States.[80]

In treating his defeated foe with such high regard and compassion, Grant was faithfully reflecting the policies of his commander in chief. Lincoln had vowed to "let 'em up easy." He would have "no bloody work." When asked what he planned to do with Confederate leaders, Lincoln made a "shooing" motion with his hands, as if he were driving geese from the kitchen garden.

Back in Washington, hundreds of Union cannon boomed a joyous salute to the news from Appomattox. President Lincoln appeared at a window of his official residence to acknowledge the cheers of an enthusiastic crowd. His little boy, Tad, excitedly waved a captured Confederate flag to the delight of the spectators. Lincoln requested the band play "Dixie." He said it was always a favorite tune of his and now, according to the attorney general, it was federal property. When he made some serious remarks about returning Louisiana to the Union on moderate terms, actor John Wilkes Booth bitterly told a fellow conspirator, "That means n—— citizenship!" He vowed it would be Lincoln's *last* speech. It was.

On Friday night, April 14, President and Mrs. Lincoln went to Ford's Theatre to attend a comedy, *Our American Cousin*. The Lincolns were late, but the play was stopped as they arrived and entered the presidential box. The orchestra played "Hail to the Chief," and Lincoln acknowledged the applause of the audience. Then, shortly after 10:00 p.m., a shot rang out and smoke wafted out of the box. A man brandishing a large dagger jumped down to the stage, catching his spur on the bunting that decorated the box. "*Sic semper tyrannis!*"* he cried as he limped toward the stage door exit. Many in the audience immediately recognized him as John Wilkes Booth, one of the most famous actors in America.

The unconscious president was carried through the cold, foggy night to the Peterson house, across from the theater on Tenth Street. There, the six-foot-four-inch giant of a man was placed *diagonally* on a bed in the rear of the house. And the long deathwatch began. Mrs. Lincoln, haunted by the death of their son Willy, in 1862, gave way to hysteria. She could not be consoled by son Robert Todd Lincoln, or even by her good friend, Senator Charles Sumner. Finally, the brusque, autocratic secretary of war, Edwin M. Stanton, ordered soldiers to "get that woman out of here and keep her out."

All through the night, terrible reports came in to the front parlor where Stanton had set up a command post. Vice President Johnson had also been targeted, but George Atzerodt, a German immigrant, got drunk and failed to go through with the attack. At 7:22 on the morning of April 15, doctors confirmed that the president had breathed his last. Stanton, in tears, arose and said: "Now he belongs to the Ages."[81]

Booth escaped from Washington, riding through Prince George's County into Southern Maryland. There, he hid out at the home of Dr. Samuel Mudd.

---

* "Thus ever to tyrants" is Virginia's state motto.

Dr. Mudd knew Booth well. He set the assassin's broken leg. But Booth and fellow plotter Davey Herold set off at dawn for Virginia. Booth had expected a hero's welcome. Instead, he was shunned.

The North was plunged into deepest mourning. No president had ever been assassinated before. Many people believed that Jefferson Davis—now a refugee in full flight—was behind the foul deed. (There would never be any link found between Davis's government and Booth's conspirators.*) Vice President Johnson was sworn in, but he was an unsteady, inadequate replacement for the slain Emancipator.

Grief was nearly universal. "I never before or since have been with such a large body of men overwhelmed by a single emotion; the whole division was sobbing together," wrote a Union officer in North Carolina.[82] Fearing that the freedmen might take vengeance on fellow Southerners they might hold responsible, Colonel John Eaton was amazed to find not one word of revenge in the black churches he visited in Memphis. "They were in despair . . . but there was no whisper against those who sympathized with all that he opposed," wrote Eaton.[83] General Lee was widely and approvingly quoted when he said the assassination was a calamity for the South and "a crime previously unknown in this country, and one that must be deprecated by every American."[84] One Southern woman told General Sherman she was *glad* Lincoln had been shot. Sherman replied: "Madam, the South has lost the best friend it had."[85]

Around the world, messages of condolence poured in to America. Defying their malevolent emperor, forty thousand Frenchmen contributed to a special commemorative medallion. A delegation presented it to the U.S. ambassador in Paris. "Tell Mrs. Lincoln," they said, that "in this little box is the heart of France."[86] Queen Victoria wrote an affecting personal letter to Mrs. Lincoln as one widow to another.** The *London Times* repented

* Booth was shot April 26 by federal troops inside a burning barn near Bowling Green, Virginia. The other conspirators were tried and hanged. Dr. Mudd was imprisoned. No one else was put to death in the plot.

** No doubt sincere, the queen's letter was also a shrewd act of statesmanship. The British had reason to fear for the safety of Canada if the now all-powerful Union were in a vengeful mood. Britain eventually agreed to international arbitration on U.S. claims for damages caused by the CSS *Alabama* and several other British-built Southern commerce raiders.

of its vicious attacks on Lincoln. And *Punch*, which had skewered Lincoln throughout the war, published this contrite, moving poem:

Yes, he lived to shame me for my sneer,
To lame my pencil, and confute my pen—
To make me own this kind of prince's peer,
The rail-splitter a true-born king of men.[87]

The staunchly *republican* Alice Cary, however, was having none of it. She wrote this withering response to *Punch*:

What need hath he now of a tardy crown,
His name from mocking jest and sneer to save
When every ploughman turns his furrow down
As soft as if it fell upon his grave.[88]

Lincoln's funeral train retraced much of the same route that had brought him to Washington just four years earlier. Comparing photographs of Lincoln taken in 1860 with those taken the week before his death showed a man who had aged at least twenty-five years in five. Now, many of the same plain people who had gathered trackside in 1861 to cheer the elected leader along his route to power returned. They bore witness in 1865 to the passing of the funeral train as it carried him to glory.

Lincoln's legacy is liberty and union. That which Webster had immortalized in words, Lincoln achieved in word *and* deed. America's poet of the heart, Henry Wadsworth Longfellow, had offered his tribute to the Union Lincoln labored so long to save in "The Building of the Ship":

Thou, too, sail on, O Ship of State!
Sail on, O Union, strong and great!
Humanity with all its fears
With all its hopes of future years,
Is hanging breathless on thy fate![89]

Eleven

To Bind Up the Nation's Wounds (1865–1877)

The United States in 1865 has the largest army and the second largest navy in the world.[1] *With this great power, the United States pressures France to leave Mexico and prompts Canadians to form a Confederation in self-defense. Following Lee's surrender and the collapse of the Confederacy, Generals Grant and Sherman successfully resist President Andrew Johnson's vengeful plans for trials of rebel leaders. After a brief period of cooperation, Johnson the War Democrat and the radical Republicans in Congress fight over Reconstruction, seriously impeding efforts to bring the defeated Southern states back into the Union with the rights of all—including four million freedmen—fully guaranteed. Radicals in Congress will eventually seek to remove Johnson from office, but they wait too long, botch the charges, and offer no acceptable alternative to Johnson's failed leadership. Ulysses S. Grant sweeps into office as president pledging, "Let us have peace." He pursues, in the main, wise and humane policies, especially toward the Indians. Grant's diplomacy prevents war with Britain over U.S. Civil War claims. Grant himself is honest and sincere, but his administration is nonetheless tainted by the corruption of some of his closest associates. In the dangerous disputed election of 1876, Ulysses S. Grant's leadership helps avert civil war. But with the removal of federal troops from the South in 1877, Reconstruction is over. Without support from the national*

Democratic Party, black Americans will wait another ninety years for their rights to be vindicated in the South.

I. Pass in Review

Out of regard for Robert E. Lee, General Grant had issued strict orders at Appomattox against cheering by victorious Union troops. Nothing but respect to those gallant men in ragged gray was allowed. They were countrymen once more. But six weeks later, the people of the North and the armies of the Great Republic were determined to celebrate their victory.

The little southern city of Washington, D.C., would be the scene of the greatest triumphal parade ever seen in this hemisphere. The armed forces of the Union now numbered nine hundred thousand men—white and black.[2] A full two-thirds of that great host, six hundred thousand men of Meade's Army of the Potomac and Sherman's Army of the Tennessee, would pass in review—united as the Grand Army of the Republic. It was not easy bringing these high-spirited young men together, even for a parade.*

Riots broke out when the spit-and-polish Army of the Potomac encountered the rangy, rough, almost slovenly veterans of Sherman's "March to the Sea." General Grant soon had to step in and order the two rival Union armies to bivouac on *opposite* sides of the Potomac.[3]

Down Pennsylvania Avenue they marched—sixty abreast—these strong, determined young men in blue. They marched past the reviewing stands in front of the Executive Mansion, the president, the cabinet, the leaders of Congress, and the foreign diplomatic corps. It took all day May 23 for the Army of the Potomac to pass in review. It took all the next day for Sherman's lean, tough, battle-hardened men to march past the assembled notables. Sherman had apologized to his fellow West Pointer, General Meade, for his men's unmilitary bearing. He needn't have. On this day of days, the Army of the Tennessee stepped off smartly and marched in step with drill parade precision. Hard-bitten, hard-boiled, and sometimes

---

* Winston Churchill would have understood their exuberance. He would write of his own brush with death: "Nothing is so exhilarating as to be shot at without result."

hard-drinking, William Tecumseh Sherman admitted it was one of the happiest days of his life.[4]

That night, a clear and still evening, the men in their camps on a whim put candles in their rifles and began to march on and on.[5] Soon bands joined in. The men cheered and cheered and cheered themselves hoarse. A *New York Herald* reporter wrote that the procession looked "as though the gaslights of a great city had suddenly become animated and had taken to dancing."[6] It had all happened spontaneously. No orders were given.

They would not forget this moment for the rest of their lives. They felt that this time of testing and trial would mark them forever. For many of them, it *was* their life and they would spend their remaining decades reliving it. Oliver Wendell Holmes—later a great justice of the Supreme Court—spoke to this sense:

> The generation that carried on the war has been set apart by its experience. Through our great good fortune, in our youth our hearts were touched with fire. It was given to us to learn at the outset that life is a profound and passionate thing. While we are permitted to scorn nothing but indifference, and do not pretend to undervalue the worldly rewards of ambition, we have seen with our own eyes, beyond and above the gold fields, the snowy heights of honor, and it is for us to bear the report to those who come after us.[7]

And sometimes, Holmes knew, just sometimes, they felt they had more in common with their fallen comrades than with their own unblooded kith and kin: "The army of the dead sweep before us, wearing their wounds like stars."[8]

II. Thunder on the Borders: South and North

"I'm mad! I'm mad!" screamed the huge, powerfully built young man as he ran into the darkened streets of Washington, covered with blood. He was brandishing a long, bloodstained knife. Lewis Powell was one of the Booth conspirators. He had been assigned the task of murdering Secretary of State Seward that fateful night of 14 April 1865. Seward was laid up in bed in his house, the victim of a carriage accident. Powell brushed past a servant claiming to bring medications for the ailing Seward.[9] Charging upstairs, Powell was stopped by Seward's son Frederick. He pistol whipped the younger Seward, knocking him out. Then he set upon the secretary, who was immobilized by a large neck brace. Powell stabbed Seward repeatedly, lunging for his jugular and nearly cutting off the older man's cheek.[10] Seward's younger son, Augustus, was stabbed seven times as Powell sought to escape. In front of the Seward house, Powell sank his Bowie knife into the chest of a State Department messenger. Blocks away, on this fog-shrouded night of horror, the president of the United States lay dying of an assassin's bullet.

William H. Seward was tall, stoop-shouldered, with a receding chin and a large, bird-like nose. He had first been Abraham Lincoln's rival. Nearly everyone expected the Republicans to nominate this cigar-chomping New Yorker for president in 1860. Then he sought to run the government as a kind of prime minister to the inexperienced rail splitter president. Finally, however, harnessed by Lincoln's tact and skill, Seward settled into the role of Lincoln's genuinely trusted friend and advisor. By all rights, Seward should have died that haunted night. But, miraculously, he recovered and rallied back to health. His greatest achievement in foreign policy for the United States lay before him. We would need all of Seward's experience.

Americans did not like Napoleon III, as the emperor of the French styled himself. As Louis Napoleon, this nephew of the military genius Napoleon Bonaparte had come to power under France's Second Republic. He had promised the French democracy and reform. But he was no Andrew Jackson.

Louis Napoleon soon staged a coup d'état, overthrowing republican institutions and imposing a "Second Empire." Napoleon III was almost too ridiculous to be menacing. He was done up in elaborate uniforms with medals he bestowed on himself. He sported long, waxed mustaches that stood out six inches from his too-prominent nose. And the only battles he won were those fought in his mistresses' boudoirs. He was a walking absurdity.

This destroyer of French liberty used the occasion of America's Civil War to plot against freedom in this hemisphere. He persuaded the dimwitted Archduke Maximilian of Austria-Hungary to take part in a French-backed effort to set up an "Empire" in Mexico.

This was a flagrant violation of the Monroe Doctrine, which had said the United States would not permit any European power to form new colonies in the Americas. But with the United States fighting for its very existence, from Manassas to Appomattox, Secretary of State William Seward could do no more than growl at the French emperor.

With the war's end, however, the situation changed, dramatically. The Union army that had been the butt of ridicule and scorn when it "skedaddled" from First Manassas in 1861, now shook the buildings and filled the dusty streets of the nation's capital with their unending tread. The diplomats in those stands for the Grand Review had to report to their governments across the seas that America's armed might was not to be trifled with.

General Grant ordered General Phil Sheridan to the Mexico-U.S. border in Texas with fifty thousand seasoned troops.[11] This was a pointed reminder to Napoleon III that he had worn out his welcome in Mexico.

Secretary Seward sent General Schofield on a secret mission to France. "Get your legs under Napoleon's mahogany [desk] and tell him he must get out of Mexico," Seward told the general.[12]

Seward did not want to humiliate the French people. So publicly he spoke with great tact: "We shall be gratified," he wrote in a communiqué that was published, "when the Emperor shall give to us definitive information . . . when French military operations may be expected to cease in Mexico."[13]

Napoleon's waxed mustaches must have drooped when he got that message. In a diplomatic manner, Seward was saying, *Get out!*

This he quickly did. Within a year of Seward's note, Napoleon withdrew the French troops that alone propped up the "archdupe" Maximilian and his bogus empire.[14] Without French military aid, Mexico's President Juarez soon trapped poor Maximilian. He went before a Mexican firing squad, a victim of Napoleon's harebrained plotting. The *Portland (Maine) Transcript* spoke for most Americans when it wrote: "If anybody deserves to be shot it is Louis Napoleon."[15] For Secretary Seward, this was a bloodless triumph. American honor had been vindicated, and American purposes had been achieved without firing a shot.

As Americans looked northward to their other border, they saw a tempting target in Canada. On American maps, Canada had always loomed large—and a royal British Red. People in the North were especially angry with Britain for the fact that the ruling elite there had openly sided with the Confederacy. And they didn't just root for the rebels. British rifles, British bullets, and British cannon were sold to the Confederates to kill Union soldiers. Not only that, but Confederate commerce raiders, the famous CSS *Alabama*, CSS *Florida*, and CSS *Shenandoah*, had been built and outfitted in British shipyards. Then, too, there was the case of the Laird rams.*

These powerful warships were ready to be launched and handed over to Confederate agents in England.** Only U.S. Minister Charles Francis Adams's vehement last minute protests—and blunt threats of war—prevented them from adding to the Union's troubles.

Many Americans seemed to forget Lincoln's eloquent call for "malice toward none." They itched to settle scores with Mother England. Union soldiers caught the mood when they sang a new verse of "Yankee Doodle":

Secession first he would put down
Wholly and forever,
And afterwards from Britain's crown
He Canada would sever.[16]

The situation was complicated, too, by Irish Americans organized as Fenians. They wanted to take Canada and hold her hostage for independence of their homeland from England. They had staged raids into the royal realm north of the forty-ninth parallel for decades. Now, many battle-hardened

---

* A *ram* was a warship that mounted a seven-foot solid iron probe on her bow. With it, she could splinter the wooden ships of the American merchant fleet. The U.S. merchant fleet never fully recovered from the Civil War.

** The chief Confederate agent in Liverpool was Naval Captain James Dunwood Bulloch. After the war, he would regale his New York-born nephew with stirring tales of intrigue on the high seas. The nephew, young Theodore Roosevelt, never forgot Uncle James's stories. (Online source: http://civilwartalk.com/cwt_alt/resources/articles/acws/laird_rams.htm.)

Irish American veterans of the Union army were ready for action. With typical Irish wit, they had their own marching song:

We are the Fenian Brotherhood, skilled in the art of war,
And we're fighting for Ireland, the land that we adore.
Many battles we've won along with the boys in blue,
And we'll go and capture Canada, for we've nothing else to do.[17]

Faced with this dangerous situation, the British and Canadians were not found wanting. *Finesse* may be a French word, but it was the British and Canadians, not Napoleon III, who showed it. Americans were touched by the letter Queen Victoria had sent to the grieving Mrs. Lincoln. The queen wrote, "As one widow to another." It was a shrewd reminder that her late, beloved Prince Albert had intervened to prevent war between Britain and America in 1861.

Secretary Seward was in the midst of another diplomatic triumph, the purchase of Alaska from Russia, when the British and Canadians concluded they must unite the provinces of Canada under one Confederation government. Senator Charles Sumner of Massachusetts urged the Senate to ratify Seward's Alaska purchase as "a visible step in the occupation of the whole North American continent."[18]

In Canada, Sir John A. MacDonald led the drive toward confederation. The beloved "Sir John A." warned Canadians that their sparsely populated domains could not resist the expansive Yankees unless they united under the British Crown. The Americans "coveted Florida, and seized it; they coveted Louisiana, and purchased it; they coveted Texas, and stole it, and they picked a quarrel with Mexico, which ended by their getting California," Canadian nationalist D'Arcy McGee summed up the dangers for his hesitant listeners. Without "the strong arm of England over us, we should not now have a separate existence."[19]

Americans did *not* welcome Canadian confederation. They resented a strengthened *monarchical* presence on this continent. Union war hero Joshua Lawrence Chamberlain, now the popular governor of Maine, spoke for many when he said, "If [Confederation] is successful, the result cannot but be injurious to us. The friends of this country in the Provinces [of Canada] are earnestly opposing the scheme."[20]

There were not enough such "friends" of America in Canada. The queen signed the British North America Act on 29 March 1867. Signed less than twenty-four hours before Seward inked the deal to buy Alaska, it granted *Dominion* status to the Canadian Confederation. Unity and a considerable measure of self-government for the Canadians were thus achieved—in the face of, and in a sense, *because of* American saber rattling. As for that word *Dominion*, British Foreign Secretary Lord Stanley had pressed the name change from kingdom of Canada and skillfully avoided provoking the Yankees.[21] The British and Canadians showed calm courage and gritty resolution.

Secretary Seward smilingly pocketed Alaska. This huge region boxed in the Royal Canadians on the West. He laughed off the shrill complaints about "Seward's Ice Box" and "Seward's Folly." He had achieved the one goal that had eluded the Democrats under President James Knox Polk. Seward the Republican had gotten for America "Fifty-four Forty"—without a fight. And, as was typical of the wily Seward, he approached that border line *coming south*, down from the Alaskan panhandle!

III. Reconstruction and Renewal

The assassination of Lincoln had also wrought a profound change in Northern sentiment. Many were now less willing to follow Lincoln's mild policy of reconciliation between the North and South. Massachusetts writer Herman Melville captured the dark mood of Northern public with his poem, "The Martyr":

Good Friday was the day
Of the prodigy and crime,
When they killed him in his pity,
When they killed him in his prime
Of clemency and calm—
When with yearning he was filled

To redeem the evil-willed,
And, though conqueror, be kind;
But they killed him in his kindness,
In their madness and their blindness,
And they killed him from behind.
There is sobbing of the strong,
And a pall upon the land;
But the People in their weeping
Bare the iron hand:
Beware the People weeping
When they bare the iron hand.
He lieth in his blood—
The father in his face;
They have killed him, the Forgiver—
The Avenger takes his place,
The Avenger wisely stern,
Who in righteousness shall do
What the heavens call him to,
And the parricides remand;
For they killed him in his kindness,
In their madness and their blindness,
And his blood is on their hand.
There is sobbing of the strong,
And a pall upon the land;
But the People in their weeping
Bare the iron hand:
Beware the People weeping
When they bare the iron hand.[22]

General and Mrs. Grant had turned down a theater invitation from the Lincolns that fateful night. They offered a polite excuse about having to take the train to New Jersey, but the truth was Julia Dent Grant could not stand the often outrageous behavior of Mrs. Lincoln.[23] Mrs. Grant heard a scuffle on the train platform at Havre de Grace, Maryland. The train's brakeman, unlike the Lincolns' police guard that night, was alert to danger. He fought off an assailant who tried to get into the Grants' private car.[24] Only when their train stopped in Philadelphia did General Grant tell his wife the terrible news that Lincoln had been assassinated. Mrs. Grant asked her husband if Vice President Johnson would now assume the presidency. Yes, the general replied, "and for some reason, *I dread the change*."[25]

No sooner had Andrew Johnson entered the Executive Mansion than he prepared to prosecute General Lee and the Southern leaders. "Treason must be made odious," the new president declared, "and traitors must be impoverished."[26] "Bluff" Ben Wade, the radical Republican Senator from Ohio, advocated punishing the leading rebels. Wade suggested trials for a small number of worst cases—perhaps "thirteen, just a baker's dozen."[27] Johnson replied that he couldn't justify hanging so few, reported James Gillespie Blaine, a congressman from Maine.[28] Perhaps remembering Lincoln's words about "no bloody work," even Ben Wade began to worry that perhaps Johnson would go too far.[29]

When a federal grand jury sitting at Norfolk, Virginia, indicted Lee, Longstreet, and the Confederate high command for treason, Lee immediately wrote to General Grant. How could this indictment be squared with the *parole* Lee and his army had received at Appomattox, Lee inquired with his customary courtesy. It couldn't. And Grant had no hesitation saying so. Grant immediately wrote to Secretary of War Stanton saying, "The officers and men paroled at Appomattox and since . . . cannot be tried for treason as long as they observe the terms of their parole."[30]*

But Johnson was stubborn. He was determined to exercise his sudden new powers. Grant visited Johnson in the Executive Mansion to press his case. What right, Johnson truculently asked, did a *subordinate* have to "interfere to protect an arch-traitor from the laws?"[31]

Grant was a man famously in control of his emotions. Not now. He was enraged. Lee never would have surrendered if he thought he and his men would be subject to criminal proceedings, Grant told Johnson. And

* Following Lee's surrender, other Confederate armies surrendered within six weeks on similar terms. Jefferson Davis was captured in Georgia and imprisoned at Virginia's Fortress Monroe.

if they hadn't surrendered, the war would have dragged on indefinitely, with far more loss of life to Union and Confederate forces. Then Grant leveled *his* verbal artillery at the stunned Johnson: "I will *resign* rather than execute any order to arrest Lee or any of his commanders so long as they obey the law!"[32] Grant had also secured a similar pledge from his loyal friend, Sherman.

Frustrated, Johnson asked Grant: "When *can* these men be tried?"

"Never," answered Grant. "Never, unless they violate their parole."[33]

As willful and bigoted as he was, Andrew Johnson knew when he was outgunned. As a Southern, prowar Democrat, he knew he had little support among the Republicans who dominated Congress. He also knew that in any contest between himself and Grant, the country would back its beloved war hero. Johnson's attorney general instructed the U.S. attorneys in Norfolk to quash the indictments.[34]

Grant's trust in Robert E. Lee was well placed. Lee's character was completely unlike that of the arch-secessionist, Edmund Ruffin. Ruffin, so eager for bloodshed that he fired the first shot at Fort Sumter, fired his last shot into his own brain.[35] Once he was free from the threat of federal prosecution, Lee moved quickly to assume the presidency of struggling Washington College. He dedicated the remaining five years of his life to education.*

Johnson claimed to be following Lincoln's mild reconstruction policies, but it soon became clear his motives were entirely different. Johnson had been openly hostile to the aristocratic slaveholders. But this was more a matter of class envy—he could not *afford* slaves—than a matter of justice to the slave. Johnson granted clemency to many former Confederate leaders *provided that they appeal personally to him.* He soon made his attitudes known. He had no concern for the civil rights of the freedmen. "This country is for the white men," he told the Democratic governor of Missouri, "and by God as long as I am President, it shall be governed by white men."[36]

Johnson was eager to accept reconstituted Southern state governments as soon as possible. But Republicans in Congress—not just the radicals—

* When Robert E. Lee died in 1870, he was widely mourned in the South *and* the North. Washington College today is thriving as Washington & Lee University.

were scandalized when elections in the South returned sixteen high ranking Confederate officeholders, four Southern generals and five colonels to Washington.[37] A young French reporter, Georges Clemenceau, put his finger on the trouble: "When anyone has for four successive years joined in a struggle as that which the United States has seen, [he desires] not to lose the dearly bought fruits of so many painful sacrifices."[38]*

Congress had set up a new organization, the Freedmen's Bureau, to help the newly freed black Southerners. General Oliver O. Howard, a brave one-armed hero of the Union army, was named its head.**

Many freedmen erroneously thought each family would be given "forty acres and a mule" to begin new lives as independent farmers.[39] Instead, the Freedmen's Bureau tried with varying success to persuade black agricultural workers to return to the fields in return for reasonable wages. In trying to help the freedmen, the bureau often found itself also trying to aid cash-strapped white Southern farmers.

This *might have been* the formula for a Southern renaissance. A federal government plan to help both white and black Southerners *might have been* an earlier Marshall Plan. But it was tragically not to be.

For the plan to succeed, Democrats would have to support the Republicans in Reconstruction, and the national Democratic Party was not willing to do so.

When the Republicans who controlled Congress returned to Washington, they were alarmed by what they saw.***

They knew that if Northern Democrats combined with those Democrats from the defeated South, Republicans would be in the minority. Worse, they feared the loss of all they had struggled for. Congress had passed the Thirteenth Amendment to the Constitution early in 1865. This amendment abolished slavery throughout the United States. The Lincoln

* Clemenceau's words were prophetic. This is *precisely* the view he would take half a century later when, as France's World War I premier, he would strive to retain the fruits of a hard-won victory against the Germans.

** It was to honor General Howard that one of America's great historically black institutions of higher learning was named—Washington's Howard University.

*** Congress did not meet year-round in this era. The old Congress adjourned in March 1865. The Congress elected in 1864—a much more strongly Republican Congress—did not convene until December 1865.

administration supported it fully. Thus, the *exemptions* that were necessary to issue the Emancipation Proclamation as a war measure were corrected when the amendment was speedily ratified.

Congress overrode Johnson's vetoes of legislation reauthorizing the Freedmen's Bureau and new civil rights laws. Democratic Party newspapers had headlined Johnson's vetoes: "ALL HAIL! GREAT AND GLORIOUS! VICTORY FOR THE WHITE MAN!"[40] Moderate Republicans were deeply disappointed.[41] They had hoped to work with Johnson. They wanted nothing of the radicals' vengeful plans for Reconstruction. But Johnson's intransigence united Republicans against him. The unified votes on overrides were just tokens of an increasing hostility between the new president and Congress.

Meanwhile, throughout the South, racial tensions were rising. Black Southerners had gone on no postliberation sprees of violence, but they quickly became the targets of violence.[42]

In Memphis, Tennessee, in May 1866, two horse-drawn wagons collided on a city street, a common event for any city in America. But in this case, one of the wagoneers was white, the other black. White Memphis police arrested the black man, but black veterans of the Union army intervened, charging that he was the victim of prejudice. White mobs quickly formed. Riots broke out across the city.[43] Following were three days of rioting by off-duty white policemen that left forty-six dead in black sections of the city. Hundreds of homes, schools, and churches were burned.[44] City officials did nothing.

That summer in New Orleans, a convention organized to support black suffrage was attacked and subsequent riots killed forty people. Federal troops had to restore order.[45] President Johnson's policies were seriously discredited by this and other such incidents. Northerners were beginning to see that a firmer hand was required with the defeated South.[46]

Infamous "black codes" were passed in a number of Southern states. These laws severely limited the rights of black workers to contract, to engage in many occupations, to sue, to serve on juries (unless a black person was on trial), even to travel seeking new work. It seemed that the results of the Emancipation Proclamation itself were at risk.

Republicans in Congress struggled to frame an appropriate response.

They quickly realized reconstruction would be impossible with the Democrat Johnson wielding presidential powers against them.[47] Initially, defeated Southerners were willing to do what they had to do to regain their full status. But Johnson loudly proclaimed his support for "white man's government," and this encouraged former rebels to resist federal authority.[48]

Soon, congressional Republicans settled on another constitutional amendment to require all states to give freedmen citizenship and to provide "equal protection of the laws" to all citizens. Representative John Bingham (Ohio) and Senator Jacob M. Howard (Michigan), two leading Republicans in Congress, sponsored Amendment XIV. The Fourteenth Amendment also provided that states' representation in Congress could be limited if it did not comply with this amendment. Republicans made *ratification* of the Fourteenth Amendment a condition of allowing Southern representatives to be readmitted to the Congress.[49]

The danger was law with no teeth; means to enforce the laws were quickly disappearing. Before the year 1865 was out, the great armies and navy of the Union were demobilized. The numbers in uniform declined from more than *one million* (a tenth of whom were black) to just 152,000.[50]

Relations between the Executive Mansion and Congress continued to worsen throughout 1866. "Jefferson Davis is in the casemate [prison cell] at Fortress Monroe," complained Massachusetts Senator Charles Sumner, "but Andrew Johnson is doing his work."[51] Johnson received a delegation of black leaders headed by Frederick Douglass. The black leaders were pleading for Johnson's support for Negro suffrage as a part of reconstruction. Johnson remained civil and noncommittal. Afterward, he snarled to his secretary: "Those damned sons of bitches thought they had me in a trap. I know that damned Douglass; he's just like any n———, and he would sooner cut a white man's throat than not!"[52]

Johnson determined to challenge the Republicans in Congress. He set out on a far-flung train trip. He would "swing around the circle" to explain his policies to the people. He persuaded Ulysses S. Grant, then commanding general of the Army, to accompany him. Grant, trying to get along with his commander in chief, agreed to go. At first, the trip went well. There was even an amusing high-speed carriage race through Central Park in New York

City. Taking hold of the reins, Grant took off at breakneck speed in friendly competition with a carriage bearing the president. Johnson's elegant coach was owned and driven by wealthy industrialist Abram Hewitt. In addition to the president of the United States, it contained Secretary of State Seward, New York's mayor, and local dignitaries. Grant was a famously good horseman and, not surprisingly, he won. His carriage contained General Meade, General George A. Custer, and Admiral Farragut. Grant had taken over the reins from the swift carriage's owner, New York's powerful financier Leonard Jerome.[53]*

As it was, the crowds that came out to see Johnson cried out for Grant. And Grant was increasingly disgusted by Johnson's vulgar, vituperative attacks on Congress.

Completely lacking in dignity, Johnson responded to taunts from the crowd by getting into the gutter with his hecklers. He even bawled out that he would hang Congressman Thaddeus Stevens, a leader of the radicals, as well as the famous abolitionist Wendell Phillips.[54] As Grant wrote his wife, he looked upon Johnson's tirades as "a National disgrace."[55] Grant was especially offended by Johnson's fierce hatred of black Americans.[56] Johnson had never been a member of Lincoln's Republican Party; he was put on the ticket as a War Democrat in 1864 only in an effort to bring about greater national unity during the Civil War.

As soon as he could, Grant pleaded illness and left the train. Johnson's speechifying was turning into a disaster, personal and political, for the president. Rejecting Johnson's strident appeals for support, voters in November returned an overwhelmingly Republican Congress.[57]

Republican leaders of Congress now had the bit between their teeth. They were determined to reconstruct the South according to their own plan. They passed a Reconstruction Act that divided the defeated South into military districts. Military governors were appointed who would take their orders from General Grant, not the president. Seeing how Johnson had made clever use of his appointment powers, Congress passed the

* Jerome's beautiful daughter would soon marry England's Lord Randolph Churchill and make him the *grandfather* of Winston *Leonard* Spencer Churchill. Leonard Jerome owned the *New York Times*.

Tenure of Office Act. Under this clearly *unconstitutional* measure, the president could not remove an official who had been confirmed by the Senate until his successor was likewise confirmed.

The Reconstruction Act was used to remove from office governors of six Southern states and thousands of state and local officials on grounds of "loyalty." An army of occupation suppressed many manifestations of Southern patriotism, including veterans groups, memorial parades, and historical societies.[58] Radicals in Congress were determined to suppress rebellious sentiment in the conquered South.

Even Lincoln had had trouble with some of the more radical Republicans. When he saw Senator Sumner, Ohio's Bluff Ben Wade, and grizzled old Thad Stevens headed in a grim procession for the Executive Mansion, Lincoln told the story of the little boy in his Indiana "blab school" who burst into tears every time he had to read the Bible verses of the three young Israelites in the fiery furnace. The strange-sounding names of *Shadrach, Meshach*, and *Abednego* were too much for the little Hoosier lad. All he could manage between sobs was "here come them damned three fellers again!" With humor and wisdom, Lincoln managed the radicals and rarely clashed openly with them. Johnson never even tried.

White Southerners bitterly resisted what they termed Northern despotism. They denounced Northerners who came south to help with the work of reconstruction as "carpetbaggers"—no-accounts and opportunists who had packed everything they owned into a cheap, shoddy carpetbag. Those few Southerners—like former Confederate General James Longstreet—who were willing to cooperate with Union authorities were slammed as scalawags.[59] Able, literate black politicians were denounced as readily as unprepared, illiterate ex-slaves who suddenly found themselves in legislative arenas.

President Johnson tried to obstruct the Fifteenth Amendment to the Constitution. It would give the vote to adult black males. Even his military aide, Colonel William G. Moore, noted in his diary that "the president has at times exhibited morbid distress and feeling against the Negroes."[60] Once, seeing a number of black men working in the Executive Mansion, Johnson angrily asked if all the white men had been laid off.[61]

Johnson deliberately determined to stick his head in the lion's mouth over the power of appointment. Johnson removed Edwin M. Stanton as secretary of war. Stanton had been reporting all cabinet discussions to the radicals. But when the order to vacate his position came to Stanton, the irascible ex-Democrat, whom Lincoln called *Mars*,* barricaded himself in his office and refused to leave![62]

IV. Impeachment

The radicals were outraged. Representative Thaddeus Stevens even introduced a bill to suspend President Johnson pending the outcome of an impeachment and trial. This was too much for General Grant. He recognized Stevens's move as clearly unconstitutional. He assured Johnson, whom he despised, that he would *resist* any attempt to arrest the commander in chief prior to a properly conducted impeachment and trial.[63] When Grant told Congress he would not participate in anything so unprecedented, Stevens's plans for an arrest fizzled.[64]

Thad Stevens was hardly a reassuring figure for leadership. He had some estimable qualities, to be sure. He had been an early and ardent opponent of racial discrimination. He even refused to sign Pennsylvania's new constitution in 1838 because it failed to extend the vote to black Pennsylvanians.[65] He was one of the first members of Congress to advocate full emancipation and civil and political equality for the four million slaves in the South. But Stevens's postwar plan to confiscate Southern planters' lands and resettle them with Northern migrants and freed slaves was too extreme even for his own fellow radicals![66]** His plan to arrest President Johnson only added to Stevens's reputation as an unforgiving and intemperate man.

Grant's intervention barely slowed the rush to impeachment. The House

---

* *Mars* was the Roman god of war. Lincoln had a sense of humor, even if Stanton did not.

** Stevens, though driven and humorless, had the virtue of sincerity. When he died, his will provided that he be buried in one of Pennsylvania's few racially integrated cemeteries. His epitaph proclaims, "the Equality of Man before his Creator." (Foner and Mahoney, *America's Reconstruction*, p. 91.)

of Representatives brought eleven charges against the president. Ten of these related to the willful violation of the Tenure of Office Act.

When the trial before the Senate took place in March 1868, the country held its breath. In just three years, the people of the United States had endured the bloody end of the nation's most devastating war, the assassination of its president, a tumultuous reconstruction era, and now *this*—the first presidential impeachment proceeding.

From the beginning of the trial before the Senate, the House managers were "shrill and unfocused and too careless with fine points of law," reported *The Nation* magazine.[67] Chief Justice Salmon P. Chase presided, as the Constitution provides. He set a high standard of proof.* Frederick Douglass's German friend, Ottilia Assing, thought Chase was a "traitor"; she wrote bitterly for her Berlin newspaper that Chase "burns with desire" for the presidency.[68] (If Johnson remained in office, some reasoned, Chase's chances of getting the Democratic Party's presidential nomination in 1868 would be improved.)

Seven Republican senators saved Johnson from conviction and removal from office. Three of these were well-respected moderate Republicans who did not fear the radicals' wrath: William Pitt Fessenden (Maine), James Grimes (Iowa), and Lyman Trumbull (Illinois).[69] Fessenden spoke for many when he said, "The president is on trial for specific offences charged, and for none other. It would be contrary to every principle of justice . . . to try and condemn any man, however guilty he may be thought, for an offense not charged. . . ."[70]

Grant favored Johnson's impeachment "because he is such an infernal liar," but Grant's supporters in the Senate, not surprisingly, did not.[71] The reason for this can be seen in the calendar. The next presidential election was scheduled for just eight months away. Those senators who wanted Grant for president did not want to replace Johnson with Senator Ben Wade.** They

* Chase had good precedents. Chief Justice Marshall had done this during Aaron Burr's 1805 trial for treason (and Vice President Burr himself had done this during the impeachment of Justice Chase in 1804).

** The vice presidency had been vacant since Johnson succeeded President Lincoln in 1865. Senate President Wade was next in line of succession under the laws then in effect.

were afraid a President Wade might decide to make a bid to stay in the Executive Mansion.[72]

Johnson avoided conviction by one vote in the Senate. He escaped, as Winston Churchill would later write of an opponent, "unsung and unhung." But our bleeding country did not escape Andrew Johnson's vindictive rule.

Senator John F. Kennedy named Kansas Senator Edmund Ross as one of his *Profiles in Courage* for voting *against* the Johnson impeachment. Young Jack Kennedy had presidential ambitions and naturally wanted to leave unimpaired the powers of the office. But a successful impeachment process would have demonstrated that the presidency is too important an office to bestow on such an unworthy man as Andrew Johnson.

The radicals can be blamed in three ways for this debacle. First, they should have taken care to elect a more confidence-inspiring figure than Bluff Ben Wade as their Senate president. Second, they should have moved *sooner* to impeach the odious Johnson to avoid entanglement with the presidential election of 1868. Third, they should have impeached Johnson on more substantial grounds. Johnson was doing everything possible to *obstruct* the laws of Congress. The president is constitutionally bound to "take care that the laws be *faithfully* executed." This, and not the flagrantly unconstitutional Tenure of Office Act, might have constituted valid grounds for impeachment.

The Andrew Johnson presidency—just six weeks short of four dreadful years—was a national tragedy.

V. "Let Us Have Peace"

The Republican Party assembled in Chicago in May 1868 for its fourth national nominating convention. The convention opened just four days after Johnson's acquittal. Grant's selection for president was a foregone conclusion. Above the speakers' platform at the convention was a great portrait of General Grant. "Match him!" the banner dared unhappy Democrats.[73]

"Let us have peace," said Ulysses S. Grant when informed he had been unanimously nominated by Republican delegates. The phrase became a byword for the campaign, the Grant presidency, and his life.

When the Democrats assembled in Tammany Hall in New York City on the Fourth of July, they had little choice but to nominate New York's governor, Horatio Seymour. Seymour had "skated close to copperheadism" during the war.[74] Governor Seymour had greeted draft rioters in New York City in 1863 as "my friends" and had publicly compared President Lincoln to England's King Charles I.[75]*

Cartoonist Thomas Nast drew Seymour with New York City in flames behind him. Seymour was literally depicted as the devil. "Matched!" said the cartoon's caption.[76]

The campaign of 1868 was marred by ugly racism on *both* sides. Democrats and the gutter press appealed to antiblack sentiment of voters in the South and the North. But the "respectable" *Harper's Weekly* employed the politically lethal skills of Thomas Nast to dubious ends. Nast was one of America's great cartoonists. He was, however, rabidly anti-Catholic, and he hated Irish immigrants. One of his cartoons showed the Democratic nominee Seymour clasping hands with a dagger-brandishing Nathan Bedford Forest. The former Confederate general was the Grand Dragon of the Ku Klux Klan. That was bad enough, but these two were joined by an ape-like Irishman, and all three have their feet on the prostrate body of a brave black Union soldier.[77]

One of the few serious issues raised against Grant was his wartime Order No. 11. Grant had lashed out at the *sutlers* who frequented Union army camps. They were notorious for overcharging for inferior foodstuffs and other goods the homesick young soldiers desperately craved. But instead of focusing on wrongdoers and their specific actions, Grant had banned Jewish peddlers from his camp. The reaction during the war was swift. President Lincoln immediately *countermanded* Grant's order, the only time he did so.

During the campaign, Grant expressed his regret for having drafted the order. "Please give Mr. Moses [a Jewish ex-Confederate] assurances that I have no prejudice against sect or race but want each individual to be judged

* At four feet eleven inches tall, England's shortest monarch was made *shorter* still when Oliver Cromwell cut off his head in 1649.

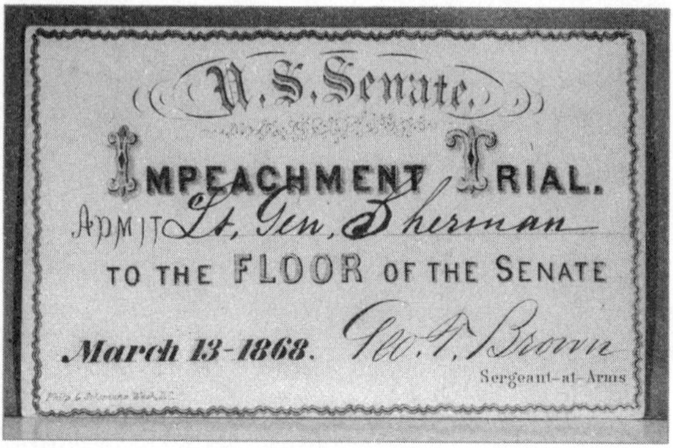

The impeachment of Andrew Johnson. *Grant as commanding general would not go along with radical Republicans' plan to arrest or suspend Andrew Johnson before impeaching him. Grant would tolerate no unconstitutional measures, even though he favored impeachment. Johnson was impeached by the House, but saved from conviction in the Senate.*

"Long Abraham Lincoln a Little Longer."
Harper's Weekly *1864 cartoon of the newly reelected Lincoln.*

The Transcontinental Railroad (driving the Golden Spike, 1869). *President Lincoln signed legislation passed by the Republican-controlled Congress to build a transcontinental railroad. Finally, on 10 May 1869, they drove a Golden Spike at Promontory Point, Utah, as the Central Pacific and the Union Pacific railroad construction crews met.*

Grant as president. *"Let us have peace," Grant said to the nominating committee. His goal was to reconcile North and South. As president, he advocated humane policies toward the Indians and supported the civil rights of black Americans. He vigorously enforced the Ku Klux Klan Act. Some questionable appointments brought corrupt practices perilously close to Grant's office, tarnishing his record of genuine achievement. His steadiness during the disputed election of 1876 averted a constitutional crisis.*

Plains Indians hunting buffalo. *Brave and skilled, the Plains Indians felt their way of life was threatened by the Iron Horse (as they called the railroad) and a flood of new immigrants. Settlers were determined to break the prairies to modern agriculture. The Indians rode mounts descended from those brought to the New World by Spanish conquistadores. After the Sioux wiped out Col. George Armstrong Custer and his 7th Cavalry Regiment at the Battle of Little Big Horn in 1876, the Indians of the Plains fought a long and hopeless battle to preserve their endangered way of life.*

by his own merit," he wrote. But then he went further. "Order No. 11 does not sustain this statement, I admit, but then I do not sustain that order. It would never have been issued if it had not been telegraphed the moment penned, without one moment's reflection."[78] Grant's candid admission of his wrongdoing gained him great credit in the country.

While Grant's election promised an end to the bitter rivalry between both ends of Pennsylvania Avenue, the renewal of united government under the Republicans would not prove an easy task. In the South, resistance was digging in. The Ku Klux Klan arose to terrorize black freedmen and those whites who sympathized with them. Former Confederate General Nathan Bedford Forrest was recognized as one of the greatest military geniuses of the Civil War. Fearless and fierce, he was all of that. He was also a former slave trader and a commander whose men could cold-bloodedly shoot black prisoners at Fort Pillow. ("The river was dyed with blood for 200 yards," he said. "It is hoped that these facts will demonstrate to the northern people that Negro soldiers cannot cope with southerners."[79]) Now, Forrest was the "Grand Dragon" of the Klan. In one county alone in 1871, 163 black Southerners were murdered. Fully 300 were murdered in parishes near New Orleans.[80]* The Fifteenth Amendment had given the right to vote only to those brave enough to exercise it.

Republicans' efforts to focus attention on conditions in the South were frustrated by the very *success* of some of their wartime policies. The Republican-controlled Congress had passed a Homestead Act, opening up vast tracts of western lands to farmers. Agitation over the extension of slavery had limited the westward expansion prior to the Civil War.

Soon after Grant took the oath of office as president, Americans thrilled to the driving of the Golden Spike at Promontory Point, Utah, on 10 May 1869. Here, again, the Transcontinental Railroad was the result of Republican policies. Prior to the war, Jefferson Davis had served as President Pierce's secretary of war and later as a U.S. senator from Mississippi. He led his Southern colleagues in refusing to approve federal aid for the construction of the railroad unless it followed a *southerly* route. The completion of

* In Louisiana, counties are referred to as *parishes*, a holdover from the days of French rule.

the railroad knitted the country together, to be sure, but it also emphasized the opening of the West and naturally distracted attention from conditions in the South.

Labor unions began to agitate for higher wages and better working conditions in the North. The sacrifices demanded by the war could no longer justify failure to pay attention to the concerns of the workingman. Typical was this appeal of a labor activist: "The workingmen of America will in future claim a more equal share in the wealth their industry creates in peace and a more equal participation in the privileges and blessings of those free institutions defended by their manhood on many a bloody field of battle."[81]

In fact, it was in the same period as Reconstruction (1865–77) that America saw the highest percentage of workers joining unions of any period in the nineteenth century.[82]

Workers, many of them Union war veterans, were increasingly put off by the antics of some Republican politicians who constantly "waved the bloody shirt" to gain their votes.[83]* The Democratic Party descended to blatant racism in many of its election appeals. But that did not change the party's historic appeal to workers.

Republicans were hampered, too, by all-too-credible charges of corruption. Too many of Grant's appointees and close associates had shown themselves eager to dip their spoons in the gravy of corporate largesse. Grant had unwisely given his grasping father, Jesse, an important postmaster job in Kentucky. Dubious characters included even his brother-in-law, Abel Corbin, his appointments secretary, and a few cabinet members. Although Grant was personally honest and profited in no way from the shenanigans, he was too naïve about *appearances*.

Early in his presidency, Grant had spent time socially with Wall Street financiers Jay Gould and Jim Fisk. They tried to get the president to hold off on government purchases of greenbacks for gold. Grant did not realize that they wanted to corner the gold market.

---

* Congressman Ben Butler had waved a bloody shirt—allegedly from an Ohio "carpetbagger" beaten by the Klan—to support the impeachment of Johnson. It was another *innovation* from the man who invented the term *contraband* for escaped slaves. Ironically, Butler was an ex-Democrat.

While vacationing, President Grant received a long letter from Corbin. His brother-in-law listed all the reasons why the president should *suspend* government sales of gold.[84] When Grant learned that his brother-in-law was in cahoots with the slippery pair, he was furious. He refused even to reply. But the local telegraph office sent back a message that would be widely misinterpreted. "Letter received all right," wrote the courier. But the message was sent as: "Letter delivered. All right."[85] There's a cruel irony here. As a winning general, U. S. Grant was famous for the crisp clarity of his written orders. No one ever misunderstood a Grant order. But Grant did not write this garbled message.

Quickly, Grant ordered Treasury Secretary George Boutwell to *increase* the sales of gold to $4 million.[86] Fisk and Gould escaped unscathed from the collapse of their scheme, but thousands of gullible investors in their scam were ruined. It was known as *Black Friday* on Wall Street, and it stained Grant's reputation. Jim Fisk brazened it all out, telling his cronies "nothing lost, boys, save *honor*." The results of this misguided attempt to corner the gold market were to cast a shadow over the Grant presidency.

This was shameless corruption, shabby influence peddling. It served no higher goal than greed. It was the theme of the successful novel, *The Gilded Age*, written by Mark Twain and Charles Dudley Warner. Commander Alfred Thayer Mahan testified before Congress that a *million* board feet of lumber bound for the Boston Navy Yard had simply disappeared. And the radical Republican Ben Butler was caught refurbishing the famed yacht *America* for his own use—at taxpayer expense.[87]

The Republicans were further embarrassed by the money liberally spread around by those railroads that had benefited so much from the national craze for laying track.* Vice President Schuyler Colfax's career was quietly sidetracked in 1872. It was revealed that he, Maine's Congressman James Gillespie Blaine, and even the normally upright Congressman James Abram Garfield

* Only Alexander Hamilton among the Founders would not have been embarrassed by the rich and powerful using government connections to advance their interests. Hamilton would have pointed to the great national *good* of a modern railroad system and would have dismissed widespread bribery as a small price to pay. Indeed, had Republicans not promised California a Transcontinental Railroad, the Golden State's vast resources of gold might have gone to help the Confederacy.

had received *gifts* of stock from the Crédit Mobilier. Crédit Mobilier was a front group organized by promoters of the Union Pacific Railroad.[88]

Massachusetts Senator Charles Sumner was not content with his radical plans for the South. In 1869, with an eye to the Northern border, he boldly put forth a fantastic charge. He claimed that Britain's construction of the commerce raider CSS *Alabama* had not only caused the United States to lose $15 million directly, but had *indirectly* prolonged the Civil War for two full years! The cost of this was reckoned in billions. Many vengeful people thought *Canada* would be an appropriate payback for Britain's *unneutral* acts in the Civil War. Young Henry Adams was the son of the great wartime minister to England, Charles Francis Adams. Young Adams thought Sumner's claim was *insane*.[89]

Only someone with Grant's enormous prestige could have successfully resisted the *jingo* sentiment Sumner aroused. Grant was the first American to attain four-star rank. This gave him an authority on war and peace that no other American could challenge. He worked closely with his very able secretary of state, New Yorker Hamilton Fish. Grant signed the Treaty of Washington in 1871. Under the terms of this treaty, Britain agreed to submit the America's *Alabama* claims to arbitration.

The Geneva tribunal that considered the case endured stormy sessions, and there were fears of war on both sides of the Atlantic. Finally, though, respected international judges found Britain liable. Charles Francis Adams was America's representative on the tribunal. The body called upon Great Britain to pay the United States $15.5 million in damages. This she promptly did. British diplomats even posted the cancelled check on the wall of the Foreign Office as a warning to future ministries.[90] Ever since, the Treaty of Washington of 1871 has been considered a diplomatic triumph of the Grant administration.[91]

President Grant sincerely sought reconciliation of the sections while upholding the threatened rights of the freedmen. Grant pressed Congress to pass the Ku Klux Klan Act. This act gave the federal government new powers to suppress the "invisible empire." Grant quickly signed the bill and used it to great effect against the white-sheet-wearing nightriders of the KKK. Grant's election and reelection were enthusiastically supported by

Frederick Douglass. He complained to dissatisfied freedmen that while the Republicans too often "ignore us, the Democrats kill us!"

Many institutions for higher learning—Fisk, Tuskegee, Atlanta, and Howard—testify to the sincerity of Northern efforts to help educate and uplift the freedmen. Some of the best men in the South encouraged these efforts.

Eventually, the North was worn down by the resistance of a determined few in the South. The formal, constitutional safeguards for equality under the law had been put in place by the Thirteenth, Fourteenth, and Fifteenth Amendments. But these would prove hollow assurances for nearly a century. Reconstruction failed. Americans yearned for an end to ceaseless agitation and recurrent troubles in the South. Exhausted by civil strife and controversy, most Northerners wanted to get on with their lives. They longed to *ignore* politics and to seek the means of happiness in their private pursuits.[92]

While the people of the North turned their attention to economic pursuits, black and white Southerners suffered immeasurably. For the rest of the century, the South was "an economic basket case."[93] It might all have been avoided. Had Northern politicians followed Lincoln's enlightened principles, had they guaranteed equal rights and suppressed terrorists like the KKK, they might have helped restore their prostrate fellow countrymen. It was a failure of imagination not to see the opportunities for renewal in a Union restored with liberty for all; for as Frederick Douglass wrote: "The abolition of slavery has not only emancipated the Negro, but liberated the whites" as well.[94]

As the depression following the Panic of 1873 deepened, President Grant came under extreme pressure to inflate the currency. Debtors, especially in the western states, cried out for relief from Washington.[95]

Republican Party campaign officials panicked, too. They pleaded with Grant to sign a measure demanded by farmers and ranchers to print up to $100 million in greenbacks. Grant's cabinet also favored the inflation bill.[96] The president later reflected on the pressures—and his final action:

> The only time I ever deliberately resolved to do an expedient thing for party reasons, against my own judgment, was on the occasion of the inflation bill. I was never so pressed in my life to do anything as to sign

> that bill—never. It was represented to me that a veto would destroy the Republican Party in the west. . . . I resolved to write a message that the bill need not mean inflation. . . . I wrote the message with great care and put in every argument I could call up to show that the bill was harmless. When I finished my wonderful message, I read it over and said to myself, "What is the good of all this? You do not believe it. I know it is not true." . . . I resolved to do what I believed to be right [and] veto the bill.[97]

Veto the inflation bill he did. And those Republican Party leaders were not wrong about the political consequences of such an act. The party suffered its worst defeat in its history that fall. The House of Representatives went from a Republican majority of 194–92 to a Democratic majority of 181–107.[98] It was a net loss of *eighty-seven seats* for the Republicans.

After this, Grant's honest efforts to help freedmen in the South were hampered by divided government.

The elections of 1874, while disastrous for Republicans, proved a boon for political cartoonists ever after. The irrepressible Thomas Nast produced a cartoon for *Harper's Weekly* that explained the results—at least to the satisfaction of Republican Party loyalists. He showed a frightened elephant—meant to represent the Republican *voters*, not the party, and a jackass happily cavorting in a lion's skin. The literary Nast was drawing on Aesop's fable, where the ass dressed in a lion skin to scare all the animals of the jungle. Democrats had scared many Republican voters with talk of "Caesarism"—the idea that President Grant was preparing to run for an unprecedented *third* term. Here, Nast was having fun with a stunt that had been pulled by the leading Democratic paper of the day, James Gordon Bennett's *New York Herald*. The *Herald* had published a hoax that said the animals in the zoo had escaped and had headed to Central Park to prey upon unwary walkers. Thus, Nast gave us—in an unforgettable way—the symbols for *both* parties—Republican elephants and Democratic donkeys.[99]

One obvious and important development in these years after the Civil War: Americans ceased to concentrate their gaze on the South. The South had dominated the nation's politics from 1800 to 1860. After the Civil War, New York and Ohio were the most important states. Whether the focus of attention was on the teeming cities of the North and Midwest, the farm belt of the Great Plains, the embattled frontier regions, or the coalfields, iron ranges, and railroad yards, the South mattered less.

This was a tragedy for black Americans, most of whom continued to live in the states of their birth. It was also a tragedy for white Southerners. While the nation recovered and moved on to greater heights, the South languished. Jim Crow laws that separated the races held *all* of its talented and devoted people down.

VI. A Tragic Divorce in Freedom's Ranks

Until the Civil War, many reformers worked together to end slavery and to enfranchise women. The leading suffragettes were all antislavery advocates. And abolitionists nearly all favored votes for women. It seemed the two causes were bound together. But the debate over the Fifteenth Amendment would cause a split in the two movements that would have consequences that extend even to our own day. Susan B. Anthony spoke for most of her movement when she dramatically said she would "sooner cut off my right hand than ask the ballot for the black man and not for woman."[100]

When Frederick Douglass left an early women's convention, Miss Anthony scolded him: "Not one word from you since you suddenly and mysteriously disappeared at Albany. . . ."[101] He declined even to show up at another conference.

The reason for the split was simple. Republicans were preparing to extend the vote to black men North and South, but they were unwilling to give votes to women. They thought the move would be too radical for the time. Democrats in Congress were opposed to enfranchising either women *or* black men. In a letter he wrote to a friendly woman reformer, Douglass explained his motives. As usual, his considerations were not only principled but practical:

> The right of woman to vote is as sacred in my judgment as that of a man, and I am quite willing at any time to hold up both my hands in favor of this right. . . . [But] I am now devoting myself to a cause [if]

> not more sacred, certainly more urgent, because it is one of life and death to the long enslaved people of this country. While the Negro is stabbed, hanged, burnt and is the target of all that is malignant in the north and all that is murderous in the south, his claims may be preferred by me. . . . [Susan B. Anthony and Elizabeth Cady Stanton oppose the Fifteenth Amendment if it fails to include women.] Their principle is that no Negro shall be enfranchised while woman is not.[102]

It was a cruel dilemma. Millions of women throughout the North and the South were fully literate. Unlike Douglass, most of the freedmen were not. In a number of slave states, it had even been against the law to teach a black man to read. Women had contributed substantially to the political debates of the nation. They had sacrificed greatly in the Civil War for the nation's sake. How *could* their just claims be cast aside? At the same time, the chance to give votes to black men seemed to Republicans the only way to ensure that the hard-won gains of the Civil War could be maintained. With their right to vote protected by federal troops, Southern black leaders were sitting in Congress for the first time. Senators Blanche K. Bruce and Hiram R. Revels and Representatives Benjamin S. Turner, Josiah T. Walls, Joseph H. Rainey, Robert Brown Elliot, Robert D. De Large, and Jefferson H. Long represented Southern constituencies. It was very unlikely they could survive in office if the Fifteenth Amendment was not passed.

Few could have known at the time that the long struggle for women's suffrage would take fully half a century to achieve its goal—or that the period of black male enfranchisement, even *with* the ratification of the Fifteenth Amendment, would prove pathetically brief. Still, the adoption of the Fifteenth Amendment in 1870 provided a logical basis for the eventual passage of the Nineteenth Amendment in 1920. And many states preceded the federal amendment in recognizing women's right to vote.

VII. The Spirit of *1876*

Americans had many reasons to congratulate themselves as they approached their great centennial celebration. They had declared their independence and made it stick in a long but ultimately successful revolution against the British monarchy. They had accepted a French alliance but had been relieved to see the large and powerful French army peacefully sail away.* They had drafted and ratified a Constitution unprecedented in the world that established a "new order of the ages." Their new federal republic in 1789 stretched from the Maine woods to the Florida border and west to the Mississippi River. They negotiated the greatest land deal in history—the Louisiana Purchase. Americans fought the War of 1812. They had repulsed the British invasion from Canada, withstood the enemy burning their capital city, and finally they had triumphed over the most serious British threat at New Orleans. Following an extraordinary period of national expansion, Americans carried their democratic institutions across the continent, as far as the Pacific Ocean. And they had saved their Union, with liberty, after a harrowing four years of civil war. They freed four million slaves. By constitutional amendment, Americans abolished slavery, pronounced equal protection of the laws, and proposed votes for men newly freed from bondage. America, it seemed, had truly seen "a new birth of freedom." Following the Civil War, Americans referred to their united *nation* as a singular noun: the United States *is*, not the United States *are*.[103]

And the nation *avoided* a military dictatorship. Grant and Sherman were as daring and inventive on the battlefield as Napoleon had been. They were as single-minded for national unity as Bismarck was. Sherman's opponent, Confederate General Joseph Johnston, said no army since Caesar's had moved with such an irresistible force. But Grant and Sherman both deferred always to the people's *elected* representatives.**

Americans also avoided a war of revenge on this continent. We chased the French out of Mexico without resort to war. Despite indignation with Britain's favored treatment of the rebels in the war, the nation refrained from invading British Canada.

---

* One of General Washington's serious concerns in the War of Independence was that the French would not send enough troops. A second, equally serious worry was that the French would send so many troops that Americans would find themselves colonists all over. It was a very delicate balancing act.

** So had Lee and Jackson in the South. The willing subordination of these great generals to civilian authority was doubtless a result of their West Point training, another tribute to "the long gray line" of distinguished graduates of the U.S. military academy.

In material terms, America's wealth and power would have astonished even such visionaries as Franklin and Jefferson. Everywhere, sail gave way to steam. Canal building—which had so strongly appealed to future-oriented leaders like Washington—was rapidly eclipsed by railroad construction. Americans followed up the Golden Spike of the Transcontinental Railroad with a rush of tributary lines to bind the country together with rails of steel. Immigrants flocked to the country. Even with 540,000 deaths in the Civil War, America in the 1860s showed a robust *26 percent increase* in population. The population in 1860 was 31,443,321, one-seventh of whom were slaves and 13 percent of whom were immigrants. By 1870, with slavery abolished, the U.S. population was 39,818,449. Immigrants accounted for 14.2 percent of these.[104]

For all the criticisms of a materialistic age, the material changes in American life were stunning. Civil War veterans said that it seemed they had grown up in a different *country* than the one to which they returned from the battlefield. For Americans who lived after the Civil War and through the remainder of the nineteenth century, the country they saw must have seemed part of a different *world.*

Breakthroughs in agriculture and industry made it possible to feed more people than at any time in history. America became an important *exporter* of foodstuffs throughout the world. Refrigeration and canning created a continental market for meats and vegetables. Most Americans wanted a greater share of the material abundance that freedom made possible. They didn't turn their noses up at a land of plenty. They agreed with Samuel Gompers when he said his very *American* workers simply wanted "more."

President Ulysses S. Grant looked forward to opening the International Centennial Exhibition at Philadelphia in 1876. He yearned to finish out his two presidential terms with such an honorable and dignified event. The presidency had not been kind to the Victor of Appomattox. Corruption tarnished his administration's reputation.

Following its 10 May 1876 opening, nearly ten million people flocked to Philadelphia for the International Centennial Exhibition.[105] President Grant joined Brazil's Emperor Dom Pedro at the opening ceremonies. German composer Richard Wagner pocketed a fee of $5,000 for his heavy, pompous original work, the "Centennial March."[106]* America's Centennial followed the great 1851 London exhibition in the Crystal Palace. That event had been brilliantly organized by Queen Victoria's consort, Prince Albert. Since then, such demonstrations of science, technology, and commerce were the hallmarks of an Age of Progress. The United States's entry into this competition was a signal of the rising power and prestige of the Great Republic. Americans took great satisfaction that their democracy stood on a par with the imperial powers of Europe.

One of the attractions that caused a great stir at the Centennial Exhibition was the huge extended female arm, its hand holding a giant torch. This was just the first section of a monumental statue, a gift from the people of France. Sent over in advance to spark interest, the statue would be known formally as *Liberty Enlightening the World*. The Statue of Liberty, as we know it, was originally conceived by the noted French friend of freedom, Edouard de Laboulaye. He had courageously opposed the proslavery policy of the tyrannical Emperor Napoleon III. Following President Lincoln's assassination, Laboulaye wanted to pay tribute to the Great Emancipator's vision. He shared his idea with the young Alsatian sculptor, Frédéric-Auguste Bartholdi. Soon, the people of France caught the spirit. They enthusiastically subscribed to a lottery to raise the funds needed to construct the massive monument. Bartholdi brought the arm and the torch to fire Americans' imaginations—and he did. Bartholdi's arrival in New York's majestic harbor gave him the inspiration for the site of Lady Liberty.**

A second marvel at the Centennial Exhibition was a demonstration by Alexander Graham Bell. The young Scottish immigrant brought a working model of his new invention—the telephone. Few were even interested in the telephone until the Brazilian emperor hailed Bell. Dom Pedro had met him at his school for the deaf. Now, he asked to see the young inventor's new

* Mark Twain may have captured the essence of the great composer's *Sturm und Drang* (storm and upheaval) when he said: "I'm told that Wagner's music is better than it sounds."

** Bartholdi's passion for *liberty* was an intensely personal commitment. By the time he arrived in America, his own beloved province of Alsace-Lorraine had been wrenched from France by Germany following the Franco-Prussian War of 1870–71.

device. As the crowd gathered, they heard passages from Hamlet's soliloquy: "To be or not to be?"

Bell had to borrow lunch money from his assistant, Watson. He was finally recognized months later by the exhibition's judges for "the greatest marvel hitherto achieved by the telegraph."[107] Bell's telephone was clearly superior to the telegraph. The telegraph never had the capacity for a mass audience, but the telephone would soon spread to thousands of businesses, government agencies, and millions of American homes.

Not everyone was awed by the Centennial Exhibition. With some wit and much candor, Japan's commissioner to the event recorded the opening day:

> The first day crowds come like sheep, run here, run there, run everywhere. One man start, one thousand follow. Nobody can see anything, nobody can do anything. All rush, push, tear, shout, make plenty noise, say damn great many times, get very tired, and go home.[108]

VIII. A Dangerous Dispute

Ulysses S. Grant doubtless could have won a third term in 1876 had he seriously wanted to contest for his party's nomination. He was only fifty-four years old, still younger than most presidents had been on first entering the office. But he had given his word that he would not seek reelection in 1876, and he resolved to keep it. Not even the Battle of the Little Big Horn shook Grant's determination to leave office. Colonel George Armstrong Custer and 265 men of the Seventh Cavalry were killed on 25 June 1876.* Custer's death led to many cries for retribution against the Sioux. There had been some two hundred clashes between Indians and the bluecoats during Grant's two terms.[109] Grant was particularly concerned to deal fairly with the Indians. In this, he did not hesitate to stand *against* public opinion, especially the views of settlers on the frontier.

* No, Custer was not busted from general's rank to colonel. With the vast downsizing of the post-Civil War army and navy, many who wished to remain on active duty had to be willing to serve at a lower rank.

Thomas Nast: Boss Tweed. *Nast's caricature of Tweed was accurate—and so devastating that Spanish authorities used a cartoon to identify the fleeing Boss Tweed.*

Thomas Nast: Donkey and Elephant. *The symbols of our two national political parties—from the incomparably talented but occasionally acid-dipped pen of Thomas Nast.*

Thomas Nast: St. Nicholas. *Nast gave us this indelible portrait of good old Saint Nick. (But I have to wonder if the Pope-bashing Nast knew of Nicholas's Roman origins.)*

Booker T. Washington. *Dr. Washington was one of the most respected educators in America. His Tuskegee Institute in Alabama gained a world reputation. In his highly acclaimed autobiography,* Up from Slavery, *he advocated self-help for black Americans. He resolved not to challenge segregation laws directly, but to work for change from within his own community. Invited to the White House for dinner by President Theodore Roosevelt in 1901, both Dr. Washington and his host endured a torrent of abuse. Washington's moderate views clashed with those of W. E. B. DuBois and the more confrontational strategy of the newly-formed National Association for the Advancement of Colored People (NAACP).*

William Jennings Bryan. *Bryan electrified the 1896 Democratic National Convention with his "Cross of Gold" speech. He opposed the sound money policies of Democratic President Grover Cleveland. Bryan, 36, conducted an extensive whistle-stop campaign by railroad. His prairie populism frightened eastern banking and manufacturing interests. He ran three times for the White House, finally serving as Woodrow Wilson's hapless secretary of state. He died in 1925, shortly after his personal huniliation in the famous Scopes trial in Tennessee.*

The Statue of Liberty. *"Liberty Enlightening the World" was the title given to this gift of the French people to the United States. Sculptor Auguste Bartholdi and his sponsors hoped it would inspire liberal and republican ideals at home in Europe, but Emma Goldman's poem—"The New Colossus"—turned the Lady in the Harbor into a symbol for immigrants.* New York World *publisher Joseph Pulitzer's appeal to schoolchildren to give their pennies to build the statue's base was a stroke of marketing genius.*

Democrats had been out of power since 1861. They sensed that 1876 would be their year. The Panic of 1873 is a misnomer, since the effects of this economic depression were felt for much of the decade of the 1870s. Democrats chose as their 1876 presidential nominee Governor Samuel J. Tilden of New York. For Tilden's running mate, Democrats chose U.S. Senator Thomas Hendricks of Indiana. Hendricks had vigorously *opposed* both the Thirteenth Amendment abolishing slavery and the Fourteenth Amendment, which granted U.S. citizenship and required *equal protection of the laws* for newly freed slaves.[110]

Democratic Governor Samuel J. Tilden had risen to national prominence when he cleaned up the notoriously corrupt Tweed Ring of New York City. William Marcy Tweed was the Democratic honcho of the city—"Boss Tweed," as he was known. He stole millions. When cartoonist Thomas Nast took up a campaign to expose Tweed's wrongdoing, he portrayed the political organizer as a huge moneybag. Nast invented the tiger to depict Tammany Hall, the headquarters of the city's Democratic political machine. In one cartoon, Nast showed members of the Tweed Ring in a circle, each one pointing to his left under the caption "Who stole the people's money?" Legend has it that Tweed wanted someone to stop Nast's "damned pictures."[111] He didn't care what the lordly *New York Times* wrote about him in its editorials because so many of his voters were immigrants who could not read English. But they can see the pictures, he complained. So accurate was Nast in portraying Tweed that Spanish authorities in 1876 used his cartoons to identify the "Boss" as he attempted to flee to Spain to avoid prosecution for fraud![112]

With credit for bringing down his fellow Democrat, Tilden's credentials as a reformer could hardly be higher. He hammered away at the corruption of the Grant administration. Tilden had been a sickly youth. He sat out the war—as did many prominent New Yorkers, including Grover Cleveland and Theodore Roosevelt Sr.—and he was unmarried.[113] These were hardly the traits of a popular candidate. Tilden did not impress with his intellect, either. Kate Sprague, the lively daughter of Chief Justice Salmon P. Chase, was heard to observe: "I fear that when the South seceded, the brains of the [Democratic] Party went with it."[114]

To face him, Republicans chose Ohio Governor Rutherford Birchard Hayes. In Hayes, they had a Civil War hero with a clean if colorless record.

A Democratic victory in 1876 seemed inevitable. The party had not won a presidential election since 1856. Many party speakers advised Union army veterans to "vote as you shot." Republican Robert Ingersoll whipped up crowds by claiming "every man that shot Union soldiers was a *Democrat*" and even that "the man that shot Lincoln was a *Democrat*."[115] (Ingersoll, a famous atheist, must never have read Lincoln's words "with malice toward none.") Such illogic, such frenzy led many thoughtful Americans nearly to despair of the prospects for freedom in a *reasoned* debate of serious issues—at least, during an election year.

The 1876 campaign saw the return of an ugly element that had been submerged since the collapse of the Know-Nothings: anti-Catholicism. President Grant had warned in 1875 of a threat to the nation's public schools. He told a reunion of the Army of the Tennessee that "not one dollar" of public funds should be appropriated to the support of any sectarian schools. Thomas Nast showed real genius in defending the civil rights of black Americans and attacking civic corruption. But he was shamelessly anti-Catholic. Nast drew Grant "hitting the nail on the head." He was shown nailing down a Republican platform plank that advocated support for public schools only. Lest anyone should miss the point, Nast showed the pope's triple crown cast off next to the hammering Grant.[116] Worse, Nast's human sympathy for poor and threatened black people did not extend to the downtrodden Irish. He depicted them with an inhuman, sinister, and even *simian* cast to their features.[117] Grant went so far as to recommend a federal constitutional amendment to bar vouchers even *indirectly* helping Catholic schools. When Senator James G. Blaine introduced the amendment, *every Republican Senator supported it.*[118] Although the amendment failed, Republicans made it a part of many western state constitutions.

When the votes came in, a dangerous dispute arose. Tilden's victory seemed clear. He had won 4,288,546 popular votes (51 percent). Hayes trailed with 4,034,311 popular votes (48.0 percent). But then, as now, it is the *electoral vote* that determines who wins the presidency. What was especially perilous in 1876 was the multiple sets of electors vying for acceptance. In the states of South Carolina, Louisiana, Oregon, and Florida, rival slates had been chosen. The issue was further complicated by the fact that the former Confederate states were still under Reconstruction. Federal troops were stationed throughout the South. Despite this, there were widespread accusations of voter intimidation in the South: that white "Redeemer" organizations had combined to terrorize black men and prevent them from exercising their *constitutional* right to vote. In South Carolina, former Confederate General Wade Hampton led a campaign of intimidation against freedmen. Reacting to the murder of five black militiamen and the killing of the marshal in Hamburg, a former slave warned Republicans that Democrats "would wade in blood knee-deep" to return to power.[119]

To make matters more dangerous, the House of Representatives was controlled by Democrats; the Senate was controlled by the Republicans. Worse, there was even talk of armed conflict.[120] Could a new civil war break out? Even many high-minded Republicans were willing to bend the rules because they feared what a Democratic administration might mean.

They had seen disloyal Copperheads join the party of Jefferson and Jackson during the Civil War. These Republicans were appalled when Democrats put forward the name of Fernando Wood for a proposed electoral commission.[121] Wood had been mayor of New York when Fort Sumter was fired on. And he then urged the city to secede and join the Confederacy!

Republicans knew that Democrats were bitterly opposed to Negro suffrage and to the three constitutional amendments passed to secure the black man's freedom. Could such a party really be trusted to lead a Union saved only at such incredible cost? But if election outcomes were not respected, what kind of Union *was* it that they had saved?

Governor Hayes was prepared to accept his defeat—at least initially. "Your mother and I have not been disappointed in the result, however much we would have preferred it to be otherwise," he wrote his son. "We escape a heavy responsibility, severe labors, great anxiety and care, and a world of obliging by defeat."[122]

President Grant was a pillar of strength during the entire election crisis of 1876. He gave strict orders to his great friend, General Sherman, to guard the election returns and to keep order throughout the disputed states. Grant wrote to Sherman: "No man worthy of the office of President would be willing to hold the office if counted in, placed there by fraud; either Party can afford to be disappointed in the result, but the country cannot afford to have the result tainted by the suspicion of illegal or false returns."[123]

Those were high-minded words—sincerely meant. But not all on the Republican side were so scrupulous. Charles Farwell, Chicago businessman, probably greased the palms of members of Louisiana's Returning Board—to assure a result favorable to Hayes.[124] Democrats, on the other hand, were more subtle. Tilden agents in Florida telegraphed the Democratic nominee's nephew—*in a cleverly coded message*. Colonel W. T. Pelton—who lived in his uncle's Gramercy Park home—was asked to approve $200,000 in a telegram that spoke of "Bolivia," "London," "Glasgow," "France," and "Russia." All these were code words for canvassing boards and their members who had to be paid off. Pelton, who worked for the Democratic National Committee, replied: "Too High."[125]

Congress created an electoral commission to decide which slates of electors to accept as valid. The Democrat Tilden had undisputed claim to 184 electoral votes. Only 185 were required for election. It was hard to see how the Republican Hayes could prevail on *all* the disputed electors.

But that is exactly what happened. The electoral commission included such Southern Democrats as Congressman Lucius Q. Lamar (Mississippi) and Senator John B. Gordon (Georgia). Lamar had served as Robert E. Lee's judge advocate general. Gordon had chivalrously returned General Joshua Lawrence Chamberlain's salute at Appomattox. Less chivalrously, he sought Ku Klux Klan backing to win his election to the U.S. Senate from Georgia. Among the Republicans on the commission were Ohio Representative James A. Garfield, a Civil War hero, and Senator John Sherman, brother of the great Union general. Not until 2 March 1877—just three days before inauguration day—did the electoral commission award *every* disputed electoral vote to Hayes. He was elected by 185–184 electoral votes. In return cially perilous in 1876 was the multiple sets of electors vying for acceptance. In the states of South Carolina, Louisiana, Oregon, and Florida, rival slates had been chosen. The issue was further complicated by the fact that the former Confederate states were still under Reconstruction. Federal troops were stationed throughout the South. Despite this, there were widespread accusations of voter intimidation in the South: that white "Redeemer" organizations had combined to terrorize black men and prevent them from exercising their *constitutional* right to vote. In South Carolina, former Confederate General Wade Hampton led a campaign of intimidation against freedmen. Reacting to the murder of five black militiamen and the killing of the marshal in Hamburg, a former slave warned Republicans that Democrats "would wade in blood knee-deep" to return to power.[119]

To make matters more dangerous, the House of Representatives was controlled by Democrats; the Senate was controlled by the Republicans. Worse, there was even talk of armed conflict.[120] Could a new civil war break out? Even many high-minded Republicans were willing to bend the rules because they feared what a Democratic administration might mean.

They had seen disloyal Copperheads join the party of Jefferson and Jackson during the Civil War. These Republicans were appalled when Democrats put forward the name of Fernando Wood for a proposed electoral commission.[121] Wood had been mayor of New York when Fort Sumter was fired on. And he then urged the city to secede and join the Confederacy!

Republicans knew that Democrats were bitterly opposed to Negro suffrage and to the three constitutional amendments passed to secure the black man's freedom. Could such a party really be trusted to lead a Union saved only at such incredible cost? But if election outcomes were not respected, what kind of Union *was* it that they had saved?

Governor Hayes was prepared to accept his defeat—at least initially. "Your mother and I have not been disappointed in the result, however much we would have preferred it to be otherwise," he wrote his son. "We escape a heavy responsibility, severe labors, great anxiety and care, and a world of obliging by defeat."[122]

President Grant was a pillar of strength during t
of 1876. He gave strict orders to his great friend, Ger
the election returns and to keep order throughout th
wrote to Sherman: "No man worthy of the office of I
ing to hold the office if counted in, placed there by
afford to be disappointed in the result, but the count
the result tainted by the suspicion of illegal or false

Those were high-minded words—sincerely me
Republican side were so scrupulous. Charles Farwell
probably greased the palms of members of Louisia
to assure a result favorable to Hayes.[124] Democrats, c
more subtle. Tilden agents in Florida telegraphed th
nephew—*in a cleverly coded message*. Colonel W. T. I
uncle's Gramercy Park home—was asked to approv
that spoke of "Bolivia," "London," "Glasgow," "Fr
these were code words for canvassing boards and th
be paid off. Pelton, who worked for the Democrat
replied: "Too High."[125]

Congress created an electoral commission to
electors to accept as valid. The Democrat Tilden h
184 electoral votes. Only 185 were required for ele
how the Republican Hayes could prevail on *all* the

But that is exactly what happened. The elector
such Southern Democrats as Congressman Lucius
and Senator John B. Gordon (Georgia). Lamar had
judge advocate general. Gordon had chivalrously r
Lawrence Chamberlain's salute at Appomattox. Les
Ku Klux Klan backing to win his election to the U.
Among the Republicans on the commission we
James A. Garfield, a Civil War hero, and Senator Jo
the great Union general. Not until 2 March 1877-
inauguration day—did the electoral commissio
electoral vote to Hayes. He was elected by 185–184

for t
Unio
F
right
barga
ical p
free a
face.
South
balan
M
and "
He co
the fi
T
would
was o
pictu
P
black
puted
would
days,
five h
1878,
patch
invol
with
mach
attack
A
one w
Appo

To Grant more than any other man the Negro owes his enfranchisement and the Indian a humane policy. In the matter of the protection of the freedman from violence, his moral courage surpassed that of his party.[129]

Twelve

An Age More Golden than Gilded? (1877–1897)

Why Great Men Are Not Chosen President. *That was an important theme of Lord Bryce's two-volume study,* The American Commonwealth. *Many Americans then and since have uncritically accepted the British nobleman's dismissive commentary on the Great Republic. Today, we can take up Lord Bryce's challenge and suggest that Britain's rulers at that time were certainly no greater than our elected presidents. One thing should be clear from this study of our nation's experience: we Americans chose honorable, intelligent, and decent men. In the Executive Mansion in this era, we had Hayes, Garfield, Arthur, Cleveland, Harrison, and McKinley. All these presidents have been denigrated by historians. "Great" they may not have been, but most countries in the world today would consider themselves blessed to have been governed by such men. Why should we Americans not appreciate them more?*

I. A Gilded Age?

"The King of Frauds!" screamed the headlines that broke the story of the Crédit Mobilier story in 1872. "Colossal Bribery," the popular press howled. The scandal that ensued helped to tarnish the monumental achievement of the Transcontinental Railroad. For many Americans, the foreign name for the financing company made the whole thing even more fishy. For generations, American students have been taught that the "driving of the Golden Spike" was only accomplished at the cost of lining the pockets of compromised politicians with cash. Clearly, there was corruption involved in the building of the Transcontinental Railroad. Still, the project that Abraham Lincoln embraced and promoted achieved its goal in just seven years. In Canada, corruption abounded, too, and it took their government-run rail construction twenty years to complete. Russia's Trans-Siberian Railroad took forty years and was also awash in corruption.

Government grants to the railroads for construction were not gifts. They were loans intended to be paid back. And paid back they were—with interest. By 1898, the U.S. government was repaid $63,023,512 in principal and $104,722,978 in interest.[1] To Harvard Professor Hugo Meyer, the U.S. taxpayer did not get bilked in the building of the Transcontinental Railroad: "For the government, the whole outcome has been financially not less than brilliant."[2] If the government's interest had only been the investment, it would have been a great success. But we got a great national institution that helped immeasurably to bind up the nation's wounds from the Civil War. Those trains not only carried freight further and cheaper, reducing the price of goods, and not only carried immigrants "yearning to breathe" free, those trains also carried newspapers whose headlines deplored the very rails that made them truly national journals.

Railroads profoundly changed America. Until 1883, there were no time zones as we know them today. "Noon" occurred in each locality when the sun reached its zenith. Railroad schedules forced Congress to act to create "standard time zones."[3] This is one of the measures for which railroads "lobbied" Congress. Should we consider this corruption? Hardly.

We have been taught that the last part of the nineteenth century was, in Mark Twain's inimitable phrase, a "Gilded Age." Its glitter, Twain winked, was only on the surface, only a thin veneer of shininess. The *New York Times* slammed the captains of industry who built great corporations as "robber barons." The title stuck. But *Harper's Weekly* saw through the propaganda: "Wherever [Commodore Vanderbilt] 'laid on' an opposition line, the fares were instantly reduced, and however he bought out his opponents . . . or they bought him out, the fares were never again raised to the old standard."[4] It was the American people who benefited from those lower fares. "Barons" had never before stooped to so perfectly serve the needs of the little guy.

Railroads were tying the country together. From 1870 to 1900, miles of rail increased from 52,922 to 193,346.[5] Railroads dominated American life for one hundred years. Steel production went from a mere 1,643 tons in 1867 to a phenomenal 7,156,957 tons in 1897.[6] The United States, by the end of the century, outstripped both Germany and Great Britain in steel production[7]—a fact of far-reaching political and military significance. American inventiveness in this period—telephones, light bulbs, phonographs, sewing machines, typewriters, and automobiles—was not only a marvel in itself and not only changed Americans' lives forever, but it helped transform the *world* economy.

In saying all this, we must not lose sight of the fact that all the growth was not equally distributed throughout the country. It never is. The South, devastated by war, suffered from economic backwardness and from unjust Jim Crow laws that kept the races legally separated. They barred the way to progress for black and white Southerners alike. Immigrants piled into slums in the cities of the North. These blighted neighborhoods appalled reformers. The average immigrant family got out of the slums in less than fifteen years,[8] and even these eyesores were often better than the grinding poverty they had known in the "Old Country." There is no denying there was corruption of our political system in the late nineteenth century. But, then as now, free government and a free press unleash the vast engines of reform.

II. Reform, Roosevelts, and Reaction

President Rutherford B. Hayes was scorned as *Rutherfraud* when an electoral commission handed him the presidency just two days before inauguration day in 1877. Hayes helped his own case with the American people. Nothing about his conduct of his office justified the word *fraud*. Upright, intelligent, dignified, he formed a distinguished cabinet. He included such reformers as German immigrant Carl Schurz and William Evarts. Evarts's legal skill had saved Andrew Johnson from removal during the impeachment. Republican Party regulars, known as *Stalwarts*, were horrified. They were even more upset when Hayes named a former Confederate to his cabinet. He chose David M. Key of Tennessee as postmaster general. Hayes also elevated Kentucky's John Marshall Harlan to the U.S. Supreme Court. An ex-slaveholder, Harlan began a long and distinguished career committed to equal rights for *all* Americans. Of great symbolic importance was Hayes's nomination of Frederick Douglass to be U.S. Marshal for the District of Columbia.[9] It was the highest and most prominent appointive position yet attained by a black American.

Hayes's clean government record led some of the more cynical believers in the "spoils" system to sneer at him as "Granny Hayes." And these hardened party politicos were even more put off when the beautiful and intelligent first lady declined to serve alcohol at the Executive Mansion.[10] "Lemonade Lucy" was a gracious and accomplished hostess. Her performance of her official duties was as well respected by Americans as that of Mrs. Julia Dent Grant. During Mrs. Hayes's years in the Executive Mansion, the "water flowed like champagne."

Because he had committed to serving only one term, Hayes did not flinch from fighting with Stalwarts in his own party over patronage positions. Civil service reform was a rising issue in the nation. Not all the Stalwarts were dull party hacks. With parliamentary skill and devilish wit, regulars like New York Senator Roscoe Conkling punctured what they saw as moralistic posturing for "snivel service reform." Conkling opposed his own president's efforts to appoint more public officials on the basis of merit and fewer in return for service to the party. "When Dr. Johnson defined patriotism as the last refuge of a scoundrel, he was unconscious of the then underdeveloped capabilities and uses of the word 'reform.'"[11]

Conkling's opposition to Hayes succeeded in delaying the "reform" effort. New York State was in the 1880s as big an electoral prize as California is today. Powerful bosses like Conkling were not to be trifled with. Even so, Hayes removed Chester Alan Arthur as collector of the Port of New York. Despite the unimportant-sounding title, this position was actually *the* premium patronage "plum" in the country. Tall and distinguished looking, with great, bushy side whiskers, Arthur was a capable public official. But the important thing was he was *Conkling's* man.

To replace Conkling's ally, Hayes nominated Theodore Roosevelt Sr. (father of TR). He sent Roosevelt's name to the Senate in October 1878. Conkling appealed to his fellow lawmakers to support the tradition of "senatorial courtesy." (This tradition means that a president will not appoint an official in a state if he does not have the support of the U.S. senator from that state, if they are of the same party. It continues to our day.) Conkling knew he was in the fight of his life. He snarled at the reformers, branding them "man milliners"—a not-too-veiled reference to homosexuals.[12]*

Theodore Roosevelt Sr. was not a career politician. He was a scion of one of New York's great Dutch families. A dedicated husband, father, and community leader, the senior Roosevelt hated the rough-and-tumble of politics. He was completely unprepared to be in the middle of a national battle royal, especially an ugly political row over presidential patronage. The senior Roosevelt's reaction to political and personal attack was to draw inward. His nomination was voted down by Conkling's friends in the Senate, 31–25. The man called "Greatheart" by his wide circle of admiring family and friends kept the hurt inside. Young Theodore wrote to his sister Bamie after their father's rejection: "We have been very fortunate in having a father whom we can love and respect more than any man in the world."[13] When his father died of stomach cancer just four months later, young Theodore was stunned and almost broken. It would have been hard for TR *not* to believe that the brutal confirmation fight his revered father had been through had killed him.** For the rest of his life, Theodore Roosevelt would battle "the vested interests" with a passion and a force that defied logical analysis.[14]

Hayes's last years in office were stormy. Despite anti-Chinese riots in San Francisco and heavy pressure to sign the bill, he vetoed a Chinese Exclusion Act passed by Democrats in 1879. He also vetoed Democrats' attempts to roll back black voters' rights in the South. Hayes's Ohio friend, Congressman James A. Garfield, called this veto message by far the ablest

* A *milliner* makes women's hats.

** Having been through three *successful* confirmations of my own, I can testify that even the most routine can be a strenuous experience.

he had ever produced.[15] Hayes also expressed increasing concern for the status of *marriage* in the United States. He went so far as to ask Congress to bar *polygamists* from holding office or serving on juries.[16]

By committing himself in advance to only one term, Hayes limited his political clout. Nonetheless, he took quiet satisfaction in the 1880 nomination of his close friend to succeed him. James A. Garfield was selected by Republican delegates following the collapse of a third-term boom for ex-President Grant. Hayes was even philosophical when the pro-Grant Stalwart faction of the Republican Party put the ousted Chester Alan Arthur on the ticket as the vice presidential nominee. Ohio and New York had become the keys to the election of a president, and the Republicans had balanced their ticket with care.

Garfield was elected over a lackluster Democrat, Winfield Scott Hancock. Like old General Winfield Scott, Hancock had been a great general but a poor candidate. The Garfield-Arthur ticket won by a mere 9,500 votes. But at least they had won. The Garfield campaign stressed his stellar war record. They recirculated the dramatic story of Garfield's ride into a panicked crowd on Wall Street. It was the day news came of Lincoln's assassination. Bravely, Garfield had charged into the crowd, calming them with these words: "Fellow citizens! God reigns and the government at Washington lives!" His timely action probably averted a riot or financial collapse. Garfield was a multitalented man. Among large immigrant audiences, he spoke German. He would entertain his friends by having them call out Shakespeare quotations. He would then simultaneously translate them into Latin and Greek, writing them out with both hands.

The country had little chance to embrace this gifted man. On 2 July 1881, barely four months after he was inaugurated, a disgruntled office seeker shot Garfield. Charles A. Guiteau stalked the young president into Washington's Union Station. Crying "I'm a Stalwart and now *Arthur* is president," he shot Garfield in the back. The president lingered throughout the brutally hot Washington summer. Various doctors came to the Executive Mansion to try their skills. Still, the president weakened. Urgently, they called Alexander Graham Bell to come and use his telephone equipment to locate the bullet. "The whole world watched and hopes and fears filled every passing hour. No one could venture to predict the end so long as the position of the bullet remained unknown," Bell recalled.[17] Bell was frustrated when he could hear nothing but static. Bell even went so far as to buy a slab of meat and fire a bullet into it. His equipment performed flawlessly. But what the president's doctors had *neglected* to tell Bell was that the stricken Garfield lay on a steel-spring mattress. This caused static on the line. Some of those who had put their unwashed fingers into the president's wound now leaked word of Bell's failure to the press. Some in the press even accused Bell of being a faker.[18] Poor Bell was to learn that he had greater freedom in America than in his native Scotland, but he also lacked the protections of Britain's stringent libel laws.

America had survived her second presidential assassination in just sixteen years. Guiteau was soon tried, convicted, and hanged. There were lingering questions about whether President Arthur would align himself with Conkling and the Stalwarts, or whether he would follow the path of reform laid out in Garfield's all-too-brief tenure. Arthur was an urbane New Yorker, known to his friends as "Our Chet." Fashionable and suave of manner, he soon returned champagne and whiskey to presidential receptions. That's all the Stalwarts got.[19] Arthur stunned them by signing the Pendleton Civil Service Reform Act in 1883. Arthur also committed the nation to a naval rebuilding program. Surely, he had seen the need when he served as collector of the Port of New York. He followed Hayes's precedent in vetoing a second Chinese Exclusion Act.

Arthur had burned too many bridges with the movers and shakers of the Republican Party, however, to be considered for a second term. We now know that he was secretly suffering from Bright's disease, a kidney malfunction. He died soon after leaving the White House. A contemporary put it well: "I am only one in fifty-five million, still in the opinion of this one fifty-five *millionth*, it would be hard to better President Arthur's administration."[20] Actually, Mark Twain spoke for far more than his one voice. As a publisher generously said of Arthur: "No man ever entered the presidency so profoundly and widely distrusted, and no one ever retired . . . more generally respected."[21]

III. Grover Cleveland: "Tell the Truth!"

The election of 1884 produced another raucous contest. Many Republicans hoped to draft another Civil War hero, General William Tecumseh Sherman. He had recently retired from active service. But Sherman "stonewalled" them with this memorable refusal: "If nominated, I will not run. If elected, I will not serve." So the Republicans chose as their standard bearer James Gillespie Blaine, of Maine. Blaine had been speaker of the House, U.S. senator, and secretary of state. A brilliant speaker, Blaine had a dedicated following among Republican Party moderates. Leader of the "Half-Breed" faction of Republicans that produced Hayes and Garfield, Blaine supported a measure of civil service reform and sought reconciliation with the South. Twice before, he had failed to win his party's presidential nomination. Once he was sidetracked when accused of prostituting the speaker's office in a railroad deal. He had been cleared on a party-line vote. Now, the way seemed clear for the man his followers called "the Plumed Knight" to win the presidency.

The Democratic candidate was Governor Grover Cleveland of New York. Cleveland was a large bear of a man, a bachelor with a drooping walrus mustache. He had not served in the Civil War. Neither had Blaine served, so the "Bloody Shirt" issue was taken off the table. Unlike Blaine, Cleveland had a reputation for fighting for reform, even if that meant crossing his own party's leaders. In Cleveland's case, battling the bosses of Tammany Hall made him a national figure. "We love him for the enemies he made," said Cleveland's admirers. Cleveland advocated lower tariffs against the Republicans' "protectionism," but agreed with them on the need for "sound money." By that, he meant the currency had to be backed by gold.

Had the campaign stayed on this high plane, Cleveland probably would have won easily. But 1884 was to prove another brutal contest. When the German American immigrant leader Carl Schurz came out for Cleveland, he led a number of other influential Republican reformers in support of the burly New Yorker. These reformers were known as "Mugwumps." The Indian word meant *chieftain*,[22] but humorists immediately said it meant they had their *mugs* on one side of the fence and their *wumps* on the other.

Republican regulars were desperate. It seemed they were saved when a tawdry story leaked out of Cleveland's hometown of Buffalo, New York. Cleveland had fathered a son out of wedlock. He was also forced to have the boy's mother committed to an insane asylum. Horrified Democratic leaders pleaded with Cleveland to deny the story. A local Buffalo editor suggested Cleveland name his late law partner, John Folsom, as the child's real father. Folsom had been intimate with the woman, too. "Is this man crazy," asked an exasperated Cleveland, "is he fool enough to suppose for a moment . . . that I would permit my dead friend's memory to suffer for my sake?"[23] Cleveland stoutly refused to do any such thing. He immediately admitted to fathering the child. Memorably, he instructed his campaign aides to "*tell the truth*." When Democrats brought him evidence that Mrs. Blaine had been pregnant before the Blaines' marriage, Cleveland grabbed the papers, ripped them up, and threw them into the fire: "The other side can have the monopoly on *all* the dirt in this campaign," he told them.[24]

Republicans were delighted. "Ma! Ma! Where's my Pa?" went up the chant from coast to coast. Even in England, the humor magazine *Puck* skewered Cleveland. It cartooned him outside the White House holding his ears as a lady with a crying baby hid her face for shame.

Republicans would soon have cause to join that crying baby, however. The charges of corruption that Blaine thought he had overcome were renewed by Carl Schurz and the Mugwumps. They produced a letter from Blaine in which he addressed the Little Rock and Fort Smith Railroad issue. Blaine had made a tidy $100,000 for his role in this affair. Devastating to his cause, though, was a note in Blaine's own handwriting that said: "Burn this letter."[25] Younger members of the *Grand Old Party** like delegates Theodore Roosevelt (New York) and Henry Cabot Lodge (Massachusetts) had to hold their noses when they continued to support their party's nominee.[26] But the Republicans were now the ones holding their ears as Democrats throughout the country took up their *own* chant:

---

* The Democratic Party of today traces its origins to the famous "Botanizing Expedition" taken by Virginians James Madison and Thomas Jefferson to New York State in 1791. Thus, it is older than the Republican Party, founded in Ripon, Wisconsin, in 1854. By the mid-1880s, however, it *seemed* the Grand Old Party (GOP) had been in office forever.

Blaine, Blaine, You oughtta be ashamed
A continental liar from the State of Maine.[27]

Republican campaign leaders hoped that the candidacy of Ben Butler on the Greenback Party ticket might drain enough votes from Cleveland to elect their somewhat wilted Plumed Knight. Butler had been nicknamed "Spoons" for his supposed eagerness to steal the silver from Southern plantations during the war. Now, Republican leaders secretly paid for Spoons to take a private railway car across the country, campaigning against the "sound money" Democratic candidate.[28]

Republican chances in 1884 were ruined by one of their own most *zealous* supporters. A Presbyterian minister, Samuel Burchard, gave a speech to a New York Republican gathering. With Blaine seated next to him on the platform, Reverend Burchard sneered at the Mugwumps. Then he lambasted the Democrats as the party of "Rum, Romanism, and Rebellion!" Blaine had little chance of carrying any states in the Solid South anyway, but Burchard's ill-considered attack on alcohol alienated the beer-drinking Germans of the North. His bigoted anti-Catholic slam on "Romanism" offended immigrants nationwide.

Blaine failed to disavow the *irreverent* reverend's speech. This *intemperate* Temperance advocate gave Blaine's opponents all the ammunition they needed for victory. New York was the key to the election. "Wait till you hear from the slums," Blaine's managers said ruefully as they watched the votes in the Empire State.[29] Publisher Joseph Pulitzer, an immigrant from Hungary, provided Cleveland's strongest appeal when he editorialized in his *New York World*: "There are four reasons for electing Cleveland: 1. He is an honest man. 2. He is an honest man. 3. He is an honest man. 4. He is an honest man."[30] Who could deny that? And who could seriously claim that Blaine was *not* crooked?

The national totals were very close. "Grover the Good" won with 4,874,986 popular votes and 219 electoral votes. Blaine trailed with 4,851,981 popular votes and 182 electoral votes. New York's 36 electoral votes had done it. Cleveland carried his home state by just 1,149 votes.[31] After twenty-four years in the political wilderness, gleeful Democrats answered that "Where's my Pa?" taunt: "Gone to the White House, Ha! Ha! Ha!"

Cleveland's election was a monument to freedom. The Civil War had demonstrated what Lincoln said: there could be no appeal "from ballots to bullets." But in order for America to make good her claims to liberty, there had to be elections that gave the peoples' ballots a fair chance to "throw the bums out." By 1884, the Republicans' Circus Big Tent covered a lot of bums—and not a few clowns.

The country over which Grover Cleveland presided was troubled. The Republicans' ideal of free land, free labor, and free enterprise was a compelling one. But a world agricultural depression that began in the 1870s hit the U.S. farm belt hard. Wheat sank from $1.19 a bushel in 1881 to just 49 cents in 1894. Corn slid from 63 cents a bushel to 18 cents during those years.[32] In order to increase their yields, farmers invested heavily in expensive new equipment. When credit contracted, though, farmers were left in perilous straits. That is why they increasingly demanded free coinage of silver, greenbacks, lower tariffs, *anything* to give them some relief. It was called Prairie Populism. It would express itself in the Granger Movement. At one point, as many as eight hundred thousand farmers signed on. Grangers tried "co-ops," schemes for *cooperative* action on storage and marketing of grains.[33] The Grange was a social and intellectual organization whose charter forbade it to engage in political activity. It was a simple matter, though, to gather farmers for a regular Grange meeting and then vote to "adjourn." Organizers would then harangue the assembled crowd on economics and politics. As the farm belt sank deeper into depression, Mary Lease ("the Kansas pythoness") exhorted farmers to "raise less corn and more *hell!*"[34]

The face of urban America was changing rapidly. From his first demonstration of his telephone in 1876 to 1885, Alexander Graham Bell had seen his Bell Telephone Company gain 134,000 subscribers, mostly in cities and towns. This was ten times as many subscribers as Britain recorded.[35] Thomas A. Edison invented the electric light in 1879 and created a sensation throughout the world. William H. Vanderbilt, one of the great shipping and railroad Vanderbilts, was an early financial backer of the incredible invention. So was banker J. Pierpont Morgan, who wrote about it to his brother-in-law in Paris: "Secrecy at the moment is so essential that I do not dare put it on paper. Subject is Edison's Electric light—importance can be realized from editorials in London Times . . . and the effect upon gas stocks which have declined 25-50% since rumors of Edison's success. . . ."[36]

What we see here is the support given by men of great wealth to the brilliant inventor in order to bring his new product to market in a timely manner. We also see the *dynamism* of free enterprise: even a rumor of an electric light depresses gas stocks overnight. They didn't attempt to stifle the electric light in order to "protect" the gas industry. Today, we know that gas suffers not at all from the competition of electricity. Americans now heat their homes with gas. But this episode teaches us that market vitality brings more and better products to more people at lower prices. It offers better lives for millions. Today's General Electric Company was brought into being by the creative genius of Thomas A. Edison.

America was in the middle of a second industrial revolution. U.S. steel production of twenty thousand tons right after the Civil War outstripped Great Britain by 1895, with six million tons.[37] And steel was used in new ways. Not only was it essential for railroad locomotives and, now, passenger and freight cars, steel was increasingly being used for major construction. The magnificent new Brooklyn Bridge that connected Manhattan, a part of New York City, to the independent city of Brooklyn was the creation of engineers John and Washington Roebling. Opened in 1883, the Brooklyn Bridge is still in daily use. Frenchman Gustave Eiffel provided a steel "skeleton" for the Statue of Liberty that would soon grace New York Harbor.* Andrew Carnegie, like Bell a Scots immigrant, led the way in organizing the steel industry. (An expert *telegrapher* during the Civil War, Carnegie might have been thrown out of work, had he stayed put, by Bell's invention of the telephone.) John D. Rockefeller organized the Standard Oil Trust in 1879. The word *trust* came to describe the new form of industrial organization. But Rockefeller's methods—though they made possible a world transportation

* French writers denounced the engineer's famous Eiffel Tower when it opened in Paris in 1889. They called it too "American." In a real sense, it was. The steel undercarriage provided the basis for such modern "skyscrapers" as the Chrysler Building, the Empire State Building, and the now-destroyed World Trade Center.

revolution that started in America—would arouse a nation against the growing power of trusts. The power the trusts exerted over the U.S. government was a matter of mounting concern in the late nineteenth century. Humorist Mark Twain captured this sentiment when he said, "It is the foreign element that commits our crime. There is no native American criminal class—except Congress."

President Cleveland made no pretense of "running the country." Who could *run* such a vast nation? But he worked away diligently at the elegant *Resolute* desk given to the American people by Queen Victoria.* He braved the enmity of the powerful veterans lobby when he vetoed hundreds of private pension bills for Civil War soldiers. This was particularly *resolute* for one who had himself hired a substitute rather than serve in combat in the war. Yet Cleveland firmly believed that Congress was trying to give "shirkers and skedaddlers" a place at the public trough.[38]

Grover Cleveland was not all work and no play, however. The forty-eight-year-old bachelor found time to court the daughter of the very friend whose reputation he had so nobly guarded—the lovely Miss Frances Folsom. Although a wag might say she was half his age and not quite half his weight,[39] it is a known fact that election as president notably *improves* a man's marital prospects. He and Frances were married in the Executive Mansion on 2 June 1886. "The March King" John Philip Sousa—the son of Portuguese immigrants—led the Marine Band for the ceremony. It was the first such wedding there, but Cleveland thought it an inappropriate place to call a home. So he bought and refurbished a comfortable country house for his new bride and himself. Called Red Top, the house was located in what is today the quiet, pleasant Washington neighborhood known as Cleveland Park.

According to a well-circulated story of the day, the new Mrs. Cleveland rousted her snoring husband to tell him there were *burglars* in the house. Sleepily, he reassured her: "No, no, my dear. In the *Senate* maybe, but not in the House."[40]

* The double pedestal desk made from the timbers of the HMS *Resolute* remained in the family quarters of the White House until President Kennedy had it moved to the Oval Office. There it remains to this day.

IV. The Golden Door

To the mournful skirl of bagpipes, the Seventy-ninth New York Cameron Highlanders Regiment marched through the black shrouded streets of Manhattan. The unit had been formed of Scottish immigrants from New York City. They sported full highland regalia, including kilts, Scottish military caps called *glengarries*, and coats of the highland cut. In July 1885, they marched in the funeral procession for General Ulysses S. Grant. Grieving Americans had waited in line for two days and two nights to file past the bier of the sixty-three-year-old Victor of Appomattox. Grant was sincerely mourned throughout the country. General Winfield Scott Hancock led the mile-long procession. President Cleveland led the nation in mourning the departed hero. Luxurious private trains had been ordered up to bring the nation's new industrial elite to the fashionable event. The flashy display of wealth struck many people as tasteless. To them, it was a showy example of excesses of the Gilded Age. But America's new class of entrepreneurs were proud of the free enterprise system. Grant's military exploits had saved it for them. Just as firmly, they believed that *their* industrial might had given Grant the sinews of victory. In the harbor, ironclad warships boomed a twenty-one-gun salute. Former Presidents Hayes and Arthur stood guard at the general's tomb. Union Generals Sherman and Sheridan were joined by ex-Confederate heroes Simon Bolivar Buckner and Fitzhugh Lee.[41]

Grant won his last campaign. He ran a race against death to complete his *Personal Memoirs*. Less than a year before his death, Grant was diagnosed with cancer of the throat. It soon spread to the tongue. For much of the year, Grant was either groggy from pain medication or suffering so that even water felt like fire. Every quality that had made Grant a great general made him a great writer—courage, personal integrity, intense concentration, and a clear and compelling message. No one in war ever misunderstood a Grant order. Not even his enemies. Day after day, while the nation watched the drama, he doggedly wrote on.[42]

He had to. Grant was nearly destitute. In these days before generous pensions for ex-presidents, Grant sank all his money in the Wall Street investment firm of Grant & Ward. Ferdinand Ward, his younger partner, defaulted and defrauded him. As Ward headed off to prison, Grant and his family were ruined.[43]

Samuel Langhorne Clemens, better known to us as Mark Twain, came to Grant's rescue. His new publishing house offered Grant a most generous contract for his memoirs. A year later, Twain was able to hand Julia Grant a check for $200,000. At that time it was the largest royalty check ever written.[44]

In time, the *Personal Memoirs* of Ulysses S. Grant in two volumes sold three hundred thousand sets and earned $450,000 for Grant's heirs.[45] Grant had produced a literary masterpiece. Civil War historian James McPherson has said of them: "To read the *Personal Memoirs* with a knowledge of the circumstances under which Grant wrote them is to gain insight into the reasons for his military success."[46] Robert E. Lee would have been a great man in any country, but U. S. Grant's story showed the unique possibilities of freedom in America.

Americans' attention focused once again on New York City in 1886. President Cleveland returned to lead the dedication ceremonies for the Statue of Liberty. Thousands crowded the shores to witness. As Frédéric-Auguste Bartholdi pulled away the giant French tricolor flag that had shrouded the great statue, the harbor scene erupted with noise and celebration. Naval vessels, passenger ships, and innumerable small boats in the harbor were decked with flags and bunting. Guns boomed, bands played, and horns blared. The president maintained his dignified repose even as the event chairman, New York Senator William Evarts, struggled in vain to make himself heard.

The event almost didn't come off. When the French donors completed the colossal figure, American fund-raising had failed to pay for construction of the solid pedestal on which the Lady would stand. Publisher Joseph Pulitzer did not turn cap-in-hand to the nation's new-rich titans to pay for the pedestal. In a stroke of marketing genius, his *New York World* appealed instead to the *children* of America to donate their pennies to the cause. While denouncing the provincialism of some Americans who had refused to donate to a monument to be sited in New York, Pulitzer also spurred New Yorkers to action by warning them that other American cities—Philadelphia, Boston, even Minneapolis—were bidding for the statue.[47]

Pulitzer's campaign sparked an art auction to raise funds "in aid of the

Bartholdi pedestal." For this auction, the thirty-three-year-old poet Emma Lazarus wrote the words that would completely change the way the Statue of Liberty would be understood by succeeding generations. They are worth reading in full:

"The New Colossus"

Not like the brazen giant of Greek fame,
With conquering limbs astride from land to land;
Here at our sea-washed, sunset gates shall stand
A mighty woman with a torch, whose flame
Is the imprisoned lightning, and her name
Mother of Exiles. From her beacon-hand
Glows world-wide welcome; her mild eyes command
*The air-bridged harbor that twin cities frame.**
"Keep ancient lands, your storied pomp!" cries she
with silent lips. "Give me your tired, your poor,
Your huddled masses yearning to breathe free,
The wretched refuse of your teeming shore.
Send these, the homeless, tempest-tost to me,
I lift my lamp beside the golden door!"

Our French benefactors had three objectives in mind. First, they wanted to commemorate the centennial of the alliance between France and America. Second, they sought to inspire their fellow citizens of the *Third* French Republic to *emulate* America's republican ideals of *liberty and union*. Finally, they wanted to encourage *other* Europeans to cast off the outmoded idea of hereditary monarchy.

Artfully, Emma Lazarus's poem substituted her own powerful vision. "The New Colossus" made the Statue of Liberty a symbol for immigrants departing from Europe's "teeming shore" to enter America's "golden door."

* The "twin cities" referred to here are New York and Brooklyn, then two separate municipalities. Lazarus's words would eventually be inscribed in the Statue's base.

Lazarus's writing was an unparalleled example of what happens under freedom. The power of *words* to express new and different ideas could change what years of effort, hundreds of thousands of dollars of investment, 225 tons of steel, and a 305 foot-and-one-inch high statue represented.[48] In this, too, America was an extraordinary place. Freedom of speech and of the press, freedom of religion—all this was opening new doors—actual doors *and* symbolic doors.

America has had lapses in her attempts to realize the ideals that Emma Lazarus raised on high with her awesome words. Think of the Chinese Exclusion Act that Grover Cleveland signed. Think of the turn-of-the-twentieth century debates over "desirable" and "undesirable" immigrants. These arguments drew on a vulgarized Social Darwinism. Unjust and restrictive immigration laws were approved in the 1920s. These were followed in 1939 by the shame of turning away the SS *St. Louis*. Hundreds of desperate Jews were thereby doomed to face Hitler's wrath. In our own time, Vietnamese "boat people" have been welcomed. Even as we acknowledge the failure of Americans always to act on our own highest ideals, we must also point out that this nation has welcomed millions of people "yearning to breathe free." No other nation on earth has accorded to so many the blessings of liberty and opportunity. In the same decade during which America accepted the Statue of Liberty, our population soared a full 25 percent. In 1880, official census figures put U.S. population at 50,155,783. Of these, 13.1 percent were foreign-born. These numbers rose by 1890 to comprise 62,947,714 Americans, of whom 14.5 percent were immigrants.[49] By any account, it is an astonishing record. No other country can match it.

The prominence of Joseph Pulitzer and Emma Lazarus in this story of the Statue of Liberty points to another important change in America's story of freedom. Pulitzer was a recent immigrant. Lazarus hailed from an old and distinguished New York family. Both were Jewish. America had had Jewish immigrants as early as 1654, when twenty-four Sephardic Jewish immigrants came to New Amsterdam.* It was in the latter part of the nineteenth century, however, that the numbers of European Jews would begin

* *Sephardic* Jews came to the New World from Spain and Portugal.

to increase significantly. As with so many other groups, Jews were drawn to freedom and opportunity in America and they were repelled by militarism, political tyranny, and the lack of religious liberty in the old country.

In the case of Jewish immigrants, the spur of increasingly vicious anti-Semitism in Europe made America especially attractive. America was not just the "golden door" of Emma Lazarus's poem. In the Yiddish language of so many European Jews, America was *die goldeneh medina*—the golden land.

V. Winning the West

The only good Indian is a dead Indian.

—Philip H. Sheridan, 1869[50]

Phil Sheridan was not a brutal man. He was a tough, battle-hardened Union cavalry commander who had laid waste the Shenandoah Valley. But we tend to remember men by such ill-considered and ugly sentiments. As Shakespeare's Marc Antony says in *Julius Caesar*: "The evil that men do lives after them; the good is oft interred with their bones." We are less likely to recall this more humane and, we might hope, more considered statement by General Sheridan: "We took away their country and their means of support, broke up their mode of living, their habits of life, introduced disease and decay among them, and it was for this and against this they made war. Could anyone expect less?"[51]

With the nation distracted by the Civil War in 1862, the frontier exploded. When Sioux from the Dakotas carried fire to Minnesota that year, they killed nearly a thousand settlers before being put down by the U.S. Army. Stories of murder, rape, and mutilation chilled the reading public. President Lincoln was beset by Union defeats and the death of his own son. Still, he took time carefully to review the trial records of every one of 303 condemned Sioux warriors. He pared down the list to 38. Even so, his clemency was attacked by Minnesota's Governor Ramsey. When Ramsey later came to Washington as a senator, he berated Lincoln. He blamed his merciful actions for Republican losses in the fall elections. "I could not afford to hang men for votes," Lincoln mildly replied.[52]

Lincoln's moderation was not untypical of presidents in the latter part of the nineteenth century. No president endorsed harsh policies toward the Indians. All presidents called for justice and mercy. But none of the presidents of this period pursued a peace policy with the single-minded determination that Jackson had pursued Indian removal in the 1830s.

With a sudden strike in the Black Hills in Dakota Territory ("There's gold in them thar hills!"), efforts to preserve lands for the Sioux collapsed.[53] When Sitting Bull and Crazy Horse surrounded and wiped out Colonel George Armstrong Custer and hundreds of his Seventh Cavalry troopers at the Battle of Little Big Horn in 1876, many Americans thirsted for revenge.

President Grant hoped that by recruiting religious leaders to help as Indian agents, he might pacify the Plains Indians with mild treatment—a "conquest by kindness." He told a visiting group of the Society of Friends, "If you can make Quakers out of the Indians, it will take the fight out of them." Then he applied his signature line: "Let us have peace."[54] Grant's appointment of Lawrie Tatum was characteristic of his attempt to find capable and honest Indian agents. Even the mild-mannered Tatum, however, eventually came to believe that force was needed. Neither President Grant's peace policy nor even Christian evangelism was the answer to the stubborn ferocity of the Plains Indians, Tatum thought.[55] No one in American history showed greater goodwill toward the Indians than U. S. Grant. Yet his policy was not notably more successful.

Indians were forced off tribal reserves in Montana territory (Crow and Blackfeet) and the new state of Colorado (Utes).[56] Chief Joseph of the Nez Percé Indians struck back when gold-hungry prospectors invaded his lands in the Idaho Territory. He led U.S. Army troops on a long, exhausting chase as he fled toward the Canadian border. His tactics continue to be studied at military staff colleges to this day, but he was eventually brought to ground less than thirty miles from his refuge. Eloquently, he told his disheartened people he would surrender (5 October 1877): "Hear me, my chiefs. I am tired; my heart is sick and sad. From where the sun now stands I will fight no more forever."[57]

The right path eluded leaders of both parties and all segments of society. Railroad men and hunters used the new mobility made possible by the trains to shoot hundreds of thousands of buffalo. They killed far more than they needed to feed construction crews and settlers. It was a shocking spectacle to see hundreds of magnificent bison left to rot in the sun. The buffalo slaughter was *not* unprecedented, however. The Indians themselves sometimes drove whole herds off cliffs, taking only their tongues—a prized delicacy.

An old Sioux spoke for all the tribes when he said: "They made us many promises, more than I can remember. But they never kept but one; they promised to take our land and they took it."[58] Fitfully, the government tried to mend its ways. In 1887, spurred by the protests of such reformers as Carl Schurz, Bishop Henry Whipple, and authors like Helen Hunt Jackson, Congress passed the Dawes Act.[59] President Cleveland signed it. Under this act, the government gave incentives to Indians to become individual homesteaders. But even with title to their lands, Indians were inexperienced in agriculture. They could not afford the increasingly heavy investment required to put land in crops. Thus, they remained prey for unscrupulous land speculators.[60]

In this instance, some of the institutions of American freedom could frustrate justice. Most Americans wanted justice for the Indians. These Americans lived in the burgeoning cities and populous states of the East and Midwest. They were far away from the frontier. Frontier juries were composed of men who could remember horrible Indian raids. In many cases, members of their own families had been slaughtered. It was exceedingly difficult to get such juries to convict settlers accused of crimes against the Indians.

Helen Hunt Jackson's 1881 book *A Century of Dishonor* continues to trouble us to this day:

> President after president has appointed commission after commission to inquire into and report upon Indian affairs, and to make suggestions as to the best methods of managing them. The[se] reports are filled with eloquent statements of wrongs done to the Indians, of perfidies on the part of Government; they counsel, as earnestly as words can, a trial of the simple and unperplexing expedients of telling truth, keeping promises, making fair bargains, dealing justly in all ways and all things. These reports are bound up with the Government's Annual Reports, and that is the end of them. It would probably be no exaggeration to say that not one American citizen out of ten thousand ever

> sees them or knows that they exist, and yet any one of them, circulated throughout the country, read by the right-thinking, right-feeling men and women of this land, would be of itself a "campaign document" that would initiate a revolution which would not subside until the Indians wrongs were, so are as is now left possible, righted.[61]

Sitting Bull, the great Sioux chieftain who had defeated Custer, joined "Buffalo Bill" Cody's traveling Wild West Show. Thousands in the United States and Europe delighted to see the famous warrior, but he was finally killed in an altercation with tribal police.[62]

In 1890, ironically, almost at the moment the Census Bureau announced the closing of the American frontier, a tragic clash occurred at Wounded Knee in the Dakota Territory. Five hundred U.S. soldiers attempted to disarm a small band of Sioux led by Chief Big Foot. They ran into resistance. The phenomenon of "Ghost Dancing" had raised apprehension on all sides. Suddenly, a tribal medicine man threw dirt into the air, a signal for warriors to shoot.[63] They would not die, he assured them, because they were dressed in "ghost shirts." Fierce hand-to-hand fighting ensued. A Sioux warrior, firing a Winchester rifle, took off Captain George C. Wallace's head.[64] When the troopers withdrew, other soldiers opened up with deadly Hotchkiss guns. The rapid fire killed at least 150, and wounded 50. Many of the dead included women and children caught in the crossfire.[65] It was a terrible and discreditable episode, but it was not the unprovoked and willful massacre that has been portrayed by Hollywood. The military force in the West was always one-sided, but that did not mean the violence was one-sided. Before he was subdued, the Apache leader Geronimo eluded capture for fifteen years. In that time, he managed to kill 2,500 U.S. citizens.[66]

The Dakota country also beckoned a young New Yorker. Theodore Roosevelt Jr. had barely begun his political career as an assemblyman in the Empire State when a double tragedy struck. On a single day—14 February 1884—his mother and his beautiful young wife died in the same Manhattan brownstone house. Valentine's Day would never again be mentioned in the Roosevelt family. Overwhelmed by grief, TR "lit out for the territories." He invested a major portion of his inheritance in a ranch in the Dakota

Territory. There, the spindly young aristocrat would become hardened by the challenges that made frontier life always a danger. He faced cattle stampedes, floods, and blizzards.

Once, he had himself deputized by the sheriff so he could pursue some shiftless men who had stolen his worthless boat. The wealthy easterner didn't *need* the boat. But the code of the Badlands said that a man was not a man if he let the riffraff trifle with him. TR captured his outlaws and dragged them back to face justice.* Later, he walked into a saloon. There, an armed, drunken bully drew his sixguns and announced that "Four-eyes" would be buying the house a round of drinks. "Four-eyes" was a reference to TR's milk-bottle-thick pince-nez eyeglasses. TR records what happened next:

> He stood leaning over me, a gun in each hand, using very foul language. He was foolish to stand so near, and, moreover, his heels were close together so that his position was unstable. Accordingly, in response to his reiterated command that I should set up the drinks, I said: "Well, if I've got to, I've got to," and rose, looking past him. As I rose, I struck quick and hard with my right just to one side of the point of his jaw, hitting with my left as I straightened out, and then again with my right. He fired his guns, but I do not know whether this was merely a convulsive action of his hands or whether he was trying to shoot at me. When he went down, he struck the corner of the bar with his head. It was not a case in which one could afford to take chances, and if he had moved I was about to drop on his ribs with my knees; but he was senseless.[67]

TR's vivid experiences in the West would change his life and the life of his country. His colorful writing would fire the imagination of an entire generation. He never forgot the Badlands. Nor did he let anyone *else* forget. In this, he was part of the unique American tradition of westward pioneers

---

* Significantly, he did *not* exact his own punishment. Many a horse thief and cattle rustler would be lynched in the West. The institutions of justice were sometimes slow to keep up with the pace of settlement. In Canada, the Dominion government kept a stricter rein on settlement and, hence, the "Wild West" never really applied where the Royal Canadian Mounted Police ("Mounties") held sway.

that stretched from George Washington and Daniel Boone through Lewis and Clark and the Mountain Men.

More than this, TR's experiences in the West made him a lifelong conservationist. Thoughtful Americans read TR as they read the writings of John Muir on "The Treasures of the Yosemite"* and John Wesley Powell on the Grand Canyon** and resolved to save the vanishing wilderness. From this era of rampant development and often heedless exploitation of natural resources, we can also date the first of America's great national parks.*** In this, America's Indians may have had their influence. In their native religion, the "purple mountains' majesty" was not simply awe-inspiring, it was *sacred*. TR helped all Americans appreciate the priceless treasure that is the West.

VI. A Social Gospel

At the same time the West was being won, many powerful men thought *they* were God's instruments to modernize their country and bring more goods and services to more people at cheaper prices. That this vital process also involved child labor and mothers' toiling away in "sweatshops" did not trouble these new captains of industry. For industrial workers who worked for ten hours a day, the titans' protestations of God's benevolence soon wore thin. "You'll have pie in the sky when you die" was a bitter and biting commentary on the consolations of religion.

As it always has, the reforming spirit in America called out for *action* to correct abuses. Jane Addams was determined to do something about the conditions she saw in the crowded immigrant slums of Chicago. So she opened Hull House in 1889. Her description of it gives us a unique glimpse into conditions in the teeming tenements:

> Hull House is an ample old residence, well built and somewhat ornately decorated after the manner of its time, 1856. It has been used for many

* "The Treasures of the Yosemite," *Century Magazine*, Vol. XL, August 1890, No. 4.

** Powell, J. W. (1875) *Exploration of the Colorado River of the West and Its Tributaries.*

*** President Grant signed legislation as early as 1872 creating Yellowstone National Park, another of his great and too little appreciated achievements.

> purposes, and although battered by its vicissitudes, is essentially sound and has responded kindly to repairs and careful furnishing. Its wide hall and open fires always insure it a gracious aspect. It once stood in the suburbs, but the city has steadily grown up around it and its site now has corners on three or four more or less distinct foreign colonies. Between Halstead Street and the river live ten thousand Italians: Neapolitans, Sicilians, and Calabrians with an occasional Lombard or Venetian. To the south on Twelfth Street are many Germans, and side streets are given over almost entirely to Polish and Russian Jews. Still further south, these Jewish colonies merge into a huge Bohemian colony, so vast that Chicago ranks as the third Bohemian city in the world. To the northwest are many Canadian-French, clannish in spite of their long residence in America, and to the north are many Irish and first-generation Americans. On the streets directly west and farther north are well-to-do English-speaking families, many of whom own their houses and have lived in the neighborhood for years. I know one man who is still living in his old farm-house. This corner of Polk and Halsted Streets is in the fourteenth precinct of the nineteenth ward. This ward has a population of about fifty thousand, and at the last presidential election registered 7,072 voters. It has had no unusual political scandal connected with it, but its aldermen are generally saloon-keepers and its political manipulations are those to be found in the crowded wards where the activities of the petty politician are unchecked.... The streets are inexpressibly dirty, the number of schools inadequate, factory legislation unenforced, and the stables defy all laws of sanitation. Hundreds of houses are unconnected with the street sewer. . . . An unscrupulous contractor regards no basement as too dark, no stable loft too foul, no rear shanty too provisional, no tenement room too small for his workroom, as these conditions imply low rental.[68]

Jane Addams's settlement house work would provide shelter and affection for thousands. Everything from maternal care and education to concerts and lessons in citizenship and philosophy could be found at Hull House. Americans complained that the immigrants smelled bad. Jane

Addams provided bathtubs—and recorded the eagerness with which they were used. Miss Addams struck to the heart of Americans' profession of Christian principles when she pointed out that we gave the immigrant man the vote, but "dub him with epithets deriding his past or present occupation, and feel no duty to invite him into our homes."[69] She called for a democracy that opened doors.

Decades before child psychologists noted a "failure-to-thrive" syndrome, Jane Addams had it pegged. "We are told that the 'will to live' is aroused in each baby by his mother's irresistible love for him, the physiological value of joy that a child is born, and that the high death rate in institutions is increased by 'the discontented babies' whom no one 'persuades into living.'"[70] Boys' clubs, girls' clubs, meeting places for working mothers to organize—a union! This was Hull House's daily fare. Seeing in her efforts to give practical help to the poor the "spirit of Christ," Jane Addams said: "If you don't take charge of a child at night, you can't feel a scared trembling little hand grow confiding and quiet as soon as it lies within your own. If you don't take little children out in the yard to spend the morning you can't see their unbounded delight and extravagant joy when they see a robin taking his bath."[71]

The meat-packing trust, the railroad trust, the oil trust, the steel trust. It was an age dominated by the *trusts*. Still an older kind of trust was shown by the knot of weary, smoke-stained firemen who crowded into the parlor of Hull House one cold midnight. There had been a fire in the stables. The horses were not all dead. Many were just horribly burned. It took a court order to discharge a firearm within city limits, and the courts were closed until the morning. Meanwhile, the horses were in agony. Could *Miss Addams* authorize these hardened men to shoot the poor horses? "I have no *legal* authority but I will take the responsibility," she said. She didn't go back to bed, but rode with the firemen to stand watch while they put the horses out of their misery.[72]

We tend today to think of such saintliness as very remote, almost unbelievable. Mother Teresa is believable. The Calcutta streets where she ministered to untouchables who were dying in the ditch are half a world away. But such grace was seen here, too, with an American accent, in Chicago.

VII. "A Cross of Gold"

Cleveland's commitment to lower tariffs cost him reelection in 1888. Republicans chose Benjamin Harrison of Indiana. Harrison was the grandson of William Henry Harrison and also a war hero. Skillfully, Republican campaign operatives worked among the Irish Americans in New York. They showed Cleveland doing the bidding of the British Empire in lowering the "protective" tariff. Their campaign literature showed Cleveland wrapped in the Union Jack while Harrison waved the Stars and Stripes. Cleveland, they charged, was "employed by Ireland's cruel enemy to aid her work of enslavement."[73] It worked.

Cleveland actually won *more* popular votes nationally than Harrison did. Harrison had carried New York State by 14,363 votes—a mere 1.1 percent. With New York's 36 electoral votes, Harrison was elected. Only twice since Lincoln in 1860 had New York failed to go with the winner. Often, New York provided the winning margin in the electoral college. The need to carry New York's large contingent of black voters and immigrants, including many Catholics and Jews, gave increased attention to minority concerns. Thus, the Founders' wisdom in creating an electoral college was confirmed once again. The electoral college has usually operated to protect minorities from majority tyranny. And minority rights are essential to freedom.

Cleveland never questioned the result. He did not complain that the election had been stolen from him. Nor he did not disavow his views on the tariff. "I would rather have my name [on] that tariff measure," he said of the bill he signed to lower import duties, "than be president."[74]

Republicans sincerely believed that high tariffs were necessary not only to protect young American industries but also to protect the working man. They rejected the arguments of free traders that competition would cause every boat to be lifted by a rising tide of prosperity.

In addition to battles over the tariff, politics came to be dominated by arguments over the currency. Grover Cleveland agreed with many easterners, including most Republicans, that the nation needed to stand squarely on the gold standard. These "goldbugs," however, were opposed by advocates for free coinage of silver and by those who wanted to inflate the currency by printing "greenbacks." "Why should this Grand and Glorious Country be stunted and dwarfed—its activities chilled and its very life blood curdled by these miserable 'hard coin' theories, the musty theories of a bygone age?" asked Jay Cooke, an opponent of the gold standard.[75]

President Harrison presided over three critically important pieces of legislation, two of which were sponsored by Ohio Republican Senator John Sherman (General Sherman's brother).

The Sherman Anti-Trust Act of 1890 was the first attempt to control "every contract, combination in the form of trust or otherwise, or conspiracy, in restraint of trade or commerce among the several States or with foreign nations." A certain vagueness in the definition of the law's terms would give the U.S. Supreme Court an opportunity to apply its provisions to *labor* unions.[76]

President Benjamin Harrison also signed in 1890 the Sherman Silver Purchase Act. This bill represented some "logrolling" by western state Congressmen who favored *bi-metallism*, i.e., regarding both gold *and* silver as the basis for the currency.[77] In return for easterners backing them on silver, these westerners supported the McKinley Tariff Act that reversed Cleveland's lowering of duties.

The McKinley Tariff of 1890 raised rates to the highest levels in history. It also raised prices sharply even as it raised *havoc* with the Republicans' election prospects that year.[78] Only 88 members of the GOP were returned to the House of Representatives as opposed to 235 Democrats![79]

These sharp fluctuations in tariffs created a mood of uncertainty in the nation's financial institutions. This instability was felt—*painfully*—in the nation's farm belt. There, the new Populist (People's) Party appealed for votes from desperate farmers. Once again, Mary Lease spoke for many:

> We were told two years ago to go to work and raise a big crop, that was all we needed. We went to work and plowed and planted; the rains fell, the sun shone, nature smiled, and we raised the big crop they told us to and what came of it? Eight-cent corn, ten-cent oats, two-cent beef, and

> no price at all for butter and eggs—that's what came of it. Then the politicians said that we suffered from over-production![80]*

Over-production would hardly have been possible for most farming communities before the nineteenth century. Cyrus Hall McCormick's reaper helped make America an agricultural force in world markets by the 1880s.[81]

Cultivation of the rich, loamy soil of the Midwest might not have been possible at all had it not been for "the plough that broke the plains." John Deere was a young Vermont blacksmith who took Horace Greeley's advice to "Go west, young man." Deere settled in Illinois. There, his highly polished steel hay forks and shovels made his reputation. Soon, farmers were coming to him with a serious problem. The cast iron plows they had brought from home were adequate for New England's sandy soil. But here, the rich, fertile soil of the Midwest clung to the moldboard, requiring farmers to stop every few feet to clear it. Deere imported high-grade polished steel from England and developed a "self-scouring" plow that revolutionized agriculture around the world. One hundred fifty years later, the company slogan—"Nothing runs like a Deere"—could be traced to that first John Deere plow.[82]

Plows, combines, reapers—all these required far more cash investment than subsistence farming. It explains why so many immigrants and so many newly enfranchised black Southerners were unable to take advantage of the generous Homestead Act passed during Lincoln's term. Two-thirds of the four hundred thousand who accepted the government's 160-acre land grant eventually gave up on farming.[83] Frederick Douglass knew these daunting odds. He appealed to black Southerners *not* to join the "Exodusters" who fled discrimination for the open prairies. He called on them, instead, to stand and fight for their rights in their home states.[84]

"The Communist is here!" That was the caption on another brilliant Thomas Nast cartoon. As early as 1874, Nast depicted a workingman and his poor family's being lured into a parade by a beckoning skeleton. The

---

* Mary Lease spoke in a verbal shorthand that farmers readily understood. She meant eight cents and ten cents for a *bushel* of corn and oats, respectively, and two cents for a *pound* of beef.

cartoon is clear evidence of the fear and loathing Communism spread among millions of Americans. That Communism could bring death could hardly be doubted. The world had been shocked and horrified by the bloody uprising of the Paris Commune in 1871 (and the even bloodier suppression of the *communards* by the military forces of the Third French Republic). Nast's dramatic rendering of the workman, pulled away from his weeping wife and child, included a typically nasty libel: Nast showed the Communist skeleton in the characteristic garb of the Ancient Order of Hibernians—an Irish Catholic fraternal group—decked out for a St. Patrick's Day parade.*

Nast doubtless thought the violence practiced by such unorganized groups as the Molly Maguires in the Pennsylvania coalfields was a trait of all the Irish Americans in labor. Those groups gained sympathy in America with such legitimate tactics as the boycott. When their opposition to brutal conditions in the mines extended to intimidation of other workers and allegedly to murder of mine company officials, however, they lost public support.[85]

In truth, Irish Americans in particular and Catholics in general were to prove themselves tireless advocates for organized labor and against Communism. The history of American organized labor is replete with such Irish names as Terence Vincent Powderly of the Knights of Labor, John Mitchell of the United Mine Workers, and more recently, George Meaney, longtime president of the AFL-CIO. All resisted the siren song of Karl Marx's *Communist Manifesto.*

To make the case for workers' right to organize, Cardinal Gibbons of Baltimore traveled to Rome in 1887 to persuade Pope Leo XIII not to denounce the labor movement. James Gibbons was America's first cardinal. He had been born in Baltimore to poor Irish immigrants. His visit achieved its purposed in 1891 when the pope issued *Rerum Novarum*, an encyclical letter "On the Condition of Workers." In it, the pope showed how Communism's attack on all private property denied the workingman's

---

* The gifted Nast gave us our modern benign image of Santa Claus—*Saint Nicholas.* Apparently, Nast was blithely unaware of the good saint's very *Catholic* antecedents.

right to the fruit of his own labor—an inherent contradiction. But the pope also upheld the workingman's right to organize to achieve "a living wage."

Samuel Gompers was backed strongly as leader of the rising labor movement by the Irish in the American Federation of Labor (A. F. of L.). Gompers was a Jewish immigrant from England. He fiercely resisted Communist and Socialist influence in the labor movement.[86] He wanted *economic* action only. He rejected any wholesale plan for political action to remake America's democratic form of government. When asked what the workingman wanted, Gompers answered succinctly, "More." More pay, more time off, more protection from dangerous accidents on the job. More benefits for old age. *More.*

Gompers's only interest in politics was to "reward our friends and punish our enemies."[87] His influence is a major reason why the United States never developed a Labor Party as England and so many European states did. Gompers's natural sympathy for the workingman also rejected trade unionism for whites only. Gompers never sought to run the government; he simply wanted *more* for his members.

Henry Clay Frick was an avowed enemy of labor unions. When his boss, Andrew Carnegie, set sail for a sentimental return to Scotland in 1892, Frick used the occasion to slash wages for the Amalgamated Iron and Steel Workers Union.[88] Frick wanted to break the union. He refused even to talk to the union leaders. When the workers went out on strike, he hired Pinkerton Company agents as a private police force to take over the Carnegie Company's steel plant at Homestead, Pennsylvania.[89] The *New York Tribune* reported that the Pinkertons fired first from their boat as it approached the plant's riverside entrance.[90] In the clash that followed, thirteen died and a hundred were wounded. From Scotland, an agitated Carnegie called for federal troops to be called out.[91] He wanted them to break the strike. Frick overcame an anarchist's bullet, so determined was he to teach Carnegie's employees "a lesson they will never forget."[92] Carnegie valued his image as a progressive employer. He was appalled when London newspapers condemned him while he was making his Scottish homecoming tour. Those press accounts of the strike soured what he'd long looked forward to as a triumphal return to the land of his birth.

The Homestead Strike was not the most violent clash of the Gilded Age. But it still echoed throughout the world. It was a problem for Carnegie, who had written of his paternal responsibility in his widely read book *The Gospel of Wealth*. With his many charitable activities—endowing libraries, concert halls, colleges—he claimed to be exercising an enlightened stewardship of the resources God had given him. He was a world figure. He entertained Russian composer Pyotr Illyich Tchaikovsky. The maestro conducted the opening performance at New York's Carnegie Hall.[93] The capitalist system, Carnegie wrote,

> is best calculated to produce the most beneficial result for the community—the man of wealth thus becoming the sole agent and trustee for his poorer brethren, bringing to their service his superior wisdom, experience, and ability to administer—doing for them better than they would or could do for themselves.[94]

On the other hand, his workers put in twelve-hour days with only Sundays, Christmas, and the Fourth of July off.[95] A skilled worker might make $280 a month, but unskilled laborers worked for fourteen cents an hour, less than $50 a month. There were rivalries to be exploited between older stock workers—Irish, Welsh, English, and Germans—and newer, less skilled, immigrant workers. These hailed from Hungary, Bohemia, Italy, and Poland.[96] Steelworker Andrew Keppler died in one of the terrible industrial accidents. Molten metal had spilled out of a ladle. His friends tried frantically to pry his body loose, but he had to be buried in the slab of steel.[97] There were three hundred such deaths each year in Carnegie's mills.[98]

The irrepressible Mary Lease had this sharp response to Carnegie's *Gospel of Wealth*: "You may call me an anarchist, a socialist or a communist, I care not, but I hold to the theory that if one man has not enough to eat three meals a day and another man has $25,000,000, that last man has something that belongs to the first."[99]

Republican leaders appealed to Carnegie not to slash wages—at least not in an election year.[100] But Henry Clay Frick—acting on Carnegie's orders—won his battle with the union. The steel industry would not be organized for another fifty years. One of Andrew Keppler's friends said later it was the anarchist's bullet that had pierced the heart of the strike.[101]

Grover Cleveland, running for a second term, denounced Henry Clay Frick for "the exactions wrung from [labor] to build up and increase the fortunes" of the very rich.[102] Workers, he said, "have the right to insist on the permanency of their employment."[103]

Benjamin Harrison was intelligent, honest, and hard working. He was also aloof and colorless. Few Americans were strongly attracted to him. His two most outstanding appointments were rather low-ranking ones: Frederick Douglass as U.S. minister to Haiti and Theodore Roosevelt as a civil service commissioner.

When Frances Folsom Cleveland left the White House on 4 March 1889, she told the head usher to take good care of the place because she expected to return. Asked when that would be, she gave him a charming smile and said: "Four years from today."[104]

And so she did.

Carnegie himself said that the Homestead Strike had elected Cleveland in 1892.[105] Grover Cleveland's two nonconsecutive terms make him unique among American presidents.* The Populist Party nominee, James Baird Weaver, polled more than one million votes. He carried several western states that previously had backed the Republicans.

President Cleveland looked forward to the opening ceremonies for the World's Columbian Exposition in Chicago. This world's fair would commemorate the four-hundredth anniversary of Columbus's voyages to the New World. The exposition featured the first Ferris Wheel, an Edison prototype of the motion picture projector, and many other wonders. Exhibitors from across the world vied for space to reach the millions of visitors. One of the exposition's most popular attractions was the White City. It was the promising beginning of the "city beautiful" movement among architects, landscape designers, and city planners.

But there was also a *downside* to the White City—it seemed to offer no

* It's a record unlikely to be repeated, since parties today shun one-term presidents who fail in their reelection bids. Imagine Jimmy Carter running in 1984 or George H. W. Bush making a second bid in 1996.

place for black Americans. The country was even then undergoing some of the worst outbreaks of lawless violence against black people. More than two-thirds of the victims of the 226 *lynchings* that occurred in 1892 were of black men.[106] Outstanding young writers like Ida B. Wells protested the exclusion of black influence from the Exposition. But when organizers offered a "Colored People's Day" as a concession, it seemed even more patronizing. Miss Wells publicly pleaded with Frederick Douglass *not* to demean himself by delivering a speech on the *designated* day.[107]

Wells's foreboding seemed to have been proven correct when the great orator rose to speak. He was heckled and insulted by some fairgoers on the fringe of the crowd. The old abolitionist's voice "faltered," but then he cast aside his text and roared back at his tormentors: "Men talk of the Negro problem, but there is no Negro problem. The problem is whether the American people have loyalty enough, honor enough, patriotism enough, to live up to their own Constitution!"[108] For an hour, without notes, the old lion roared. His hecklers were reduced to silence. Soon, Ida Wells apologized and said his speech had done more to bring the plight of black Americans to the attention of the world than anything else that had happened.[109]

Frederick Douglass's presence at the World Columbian Exposition was due to his role as representative of the *Haitian* government. Both as U.S. ambassador to Haiti and afterward, Douglass was desperate to help the black republic succeed. However laudable this impulse, Douglass turned a blind eye to the murderous misrule of Florvil Hyppolite, the Haitian dictator. It was perhaps the most deplorable episode in his long and honorable public life.*

Grover Cleveland would soon have reason to wish he had lost the 1892 election. A series of bank failures resulted in the Panic of 1893 and the country slid into a severe depression.[110] Hard times would shadow Cleveland's unhappy second term. When a wealthy New Yorker brought his son to the Executive Mansion to meet the president, Cleveland patted the boy on the head. "My little man," he told young Franklin Delano Roosevelt, "I am making a strange wish for you. It is that you may never be President

* Even today, it is exceedingly difficult for Americans to find Haitian leaders with whom to cooperate for the sake of the long-suffering Haitian people.

of the United States."[111] Faithful to his convictions, he persuaded Congress to *repeal* the Silver Purchase Act of 1890. Farmers felt betrayed.

Worse, Cleveland received a devastating doctor's report: he had cancer of the jaw. In these days before radiation or chemotherapy, surgery was the only hope. But the president's condition had to be kept secret. With the panic at its height, the thought of the president's going under the knife could have wrecked the nation's economy. This was especially the case since Vice President Adlai E. Stevenson was a committed *silver* advocate.*

Casually, the president went onboard a yacht owned by one of his wealthy friends. The *Oneida*, anchored in New York's East River, became a floating operating room. He told the yacht's skipper: "If you hit a rock, hit it good and hard so that we all go to the bottom."[112] With part of his jaw removed, the president emerged to an unsuspecting public.

Cleveland would seriously alienate labor by his conduct in the 1894 Pullman Strike. George Pullman had invented the railway "sleeper" car. Pullman envisioned an ideal of industrial paternalism. His company town outside Chicago was a model. The Pullman Company provided rental housing for factory workers. Company literature boasted, "All that is ugly and discordant and demoralizing is eliminated, and all that inspires to self-respect is generously provided."[113] Reality was not quite up to this ideal. High rents forced families to accept lodgers.[114] Pullman's policy of giving hiring preference to residents of company housing meant that a worker who moved out risked losing his job. Rents remained high as wages were slashed during the deepening depression. Families were left with mere pennies after their rent was deducted from pay envelopes.[115]

Eugene Victor Debs's American Railway Union (ARU) went out on strike. With workers' refusing to handle Pullman cars, the federal government claimed the U.S. mails were not getting through. Even though the union tried to make an exception for mail cars, President Cleveland ordered in federal troops to assure delivery of the mails. Debs appealed to the American Federation of Labor's leader for support. Samuel Gompers turned

* Vice President Stevenson was the grandfather of Governor Adlai E. Stevenson, who twice ran unsuccessfully for president against Dwight D. Eisenhower in the 1950s.

him down. He thought it was a bad time to risk a strike. If Debs persisted, Gompers and the A. F. of L. leadership feared the ARU would be broken.[116]

Republican leaders pleaded in vain for Pullman to be reasonable. Ohio's Mark Hanna was already trying to get William McKinley elected in 1896. To his friends, Hanna burst out against Pullman: "A man who won't meet his men halfway is a G—damned fool!"[117]

Cleveland brushed aside protests from the governor of Illinois, John Peter Altgeld. Altgeld was a German immigrant and also a Democrat. He spoke out against Cleveland's use of federal troops, saying it violated the Constitution. Who was this immigrant to be lecturing the president about the Constitution, hostile newspapers demanded to know. The *Philadelphia Telegraph* denounced Altgeld. This "sausage maker from Wurttemburg . . . permitted by the strange folly of the people of Illinois to be made governor of that State, has the insolence to offer a gross and outrageous affront to the President of the United States."[118] Stubbornly, Cleveland said: "If it takes every soldier in the United States to deliver a postal card in Chicago, that postal card should be delivered."[119] The Pullman Strike was broken, and Debs was jailed for violating a court injunction. While in prison, Debs read Karl Marx and became a Socialist.

Gompers was proven right about the strike, but he took little comfort from it. He wrote a strong letter to President Cleveland protesting against his calling out the troops. "[T]he people have answered at the polls your . . . use of the military power to crush labor," Gompers wrote after Democrats suffered heavy losses in the 1894 congressional elections. "Though the change may benefit us little, the rebuke will nevertheless be appreciated and remembered."[120]

The Pullman Strike was just one of 1,300 strikes in 1894.[121] It was a dramatic example of the use of court *injunctions* against labor. And Gompers's A. F. of L. would continue trying to "reward our friends and punish our enemies."

As in all depressions, black Americans suffered greatly. Added to economic misfortune was the rising power of segregation. Ida Wells had exposed the national shame of lynchings in her writings. Early in her career, Frederick Douglass inspired her. Now, *she* inspired *him*.[122]

In 1894, he rose to the challenge in a speech entitled "The Lessons of the Hour."

In it, he denounced the charge of *rape*. Why is it that no one charged rape when white women were alone on Southern plantations during the Civil War? he asked pointedly.

The real purpose of the spurious charge, he said, was to disenfranchise the black man. The hateful cry of rape was raised, he said, "simultaneously with well-known efforts now being . . . made to degrade the Negro by legislative enactments, and by repealing all laws for the protection of the ballot, and by drawing the color line in all railroad cars and stations and in all other public places in the south."[123]

Frederick Douglass then turned on some in his own community who had sought relief from injustice through emigration to Africa. Douglass didn't even want his fellow black Americans to *identify* with Africa: "All of this native land talk is nonsense. The native land of the American Negro is America. His bones, his muscles, his sinews are all American. His ancestors for two hundred and seventy years have lived, and labored, and died on American soil. . . ."[124]

It was to be his last, great effort. Even as the shadow of Jim Crow stalked the land, he never gave in. Asked by a young follower what he should do with his life, Frederick answered fiercely: "Agitate. Agitate. Agitate." In 1895, he collapsed and died at his stately Cedar Hill mansion in Washington, D.C. He was mourned throughout the world. Elizabeth Cady Stanton, the great leader for women's suffrage, recalled her first meeting with him: "All the other speakers seemed tame after Frederick Douglass. He stood there like an African prince, majestic in his wrath."[125]

Poet Vachel Lindsay wrote of *another* American majestic in his wrath. The election of 1896 presented a fundamental challenge to American democracy. The depression had made men desperate. William Jennings Bryan spoke to that desperation:

Prairie avenger, mountain lion,
Bryan, Bryan, Bryan, Bryan,
Gigantic troubadour, speaking like a siege gun,
Smashing Plymouth Rock with his boulders from the West.

The thirty-six-year-old Nebraska delegate to the 1896 Democratic National Convention had a chance to reach a great crowd with his address on the party platform. That platform was a direct repudiation of Grover Cleveland, the Democrat then sitting in the Executive Mansion. No matter, all over the country people blamed the gold standard for the worst depression in living memory. As Bryan concluded his speech, the delegates were swept away with emotion. His fiery ending captured their hearts:

> Having behind us the producing masses of this nation and the world, supported by the commercial interests, the laboring interests, and the toilers everywhere, we will answer their demand for a gold standard by saying to them: You shall not press down upon the brow of labor this crown of thorns, you shall not crucify mankind upon a cross of gold.

It was hard to defend a gold standard during times of "tight money"—that is, during a depression or during times of high interest rates. Essentially, what a gold standard means is that the federal government will use gold as the currency, or issue "notes" that can be exchanged for gold. To go "off the gold standard" creates inflation. Inflation is always favored by people in debt because it means they can pay back what they owe in depreciated dollars.

Barrel-chested and balding, Bryan was fully capable of making the rafters ring with the power of his voice. His "Cross of Gold" speech swept him to the party's nomination for president. (His achievement is not *quite* as impressive as it seems. Many of the party's senior leaders knew that defeat was the usual fate of a political party that holds the presidency in times of great economic hardship.*)

Undeterred by the daunting task of mounting a campaign in opposition to the Republicans *and* the Cleveland Democrats, Bryan won the endorsement of the Populist Party. He then undertook an unprecedented "whistle stop" tour of thirteen thousand miles by train to reach the voters.[126] He spoke to hundreds of thousands.

---

* If Democratic Party leaders thought they could give Bryan a worthless nomination and thereby be rid of him, they miscalculated. Bryan would be their party's standard bearer in *three* national contests and a major figure in the party until his death in 1925!

The prairies seemed on fire with Bryan's hot rhetoric. He told the farmers how important they were to the nation's well-being: "Burn down your cities and leave our farms, and your cities will spring up again as if by magic; but destroy our farms and the grass will grow in the streets of every city in the country."

Against Bryan the Republicans had nominated William McKinley, author of the McKinley Tariff. McKinley had served in Congress from Ohio and now served as governor of the Buckeye State. His campaign presented the perfect contrast to Bryan's frenetic stumping around the country. The Republican Party brought thousands of citizens *to their candidate*. Staging a "front porch campaign," McKinley addressed these polite, orderly crowds, offering them staid homilies and comfortable platitudes. He may have been put down as "a bronze in search of a pedestal," but he presented Americans with a figure of dignity and solidity to compare with Bryan's impassioned rabble-rousing.[127] And given a choice, Americans usually prefer dull to dangerous.

Senator Mark Hanna ran McKinley's campaign for him. Hanna stressed McKinley's respectable Civil War record, always a plus for presidential candidates.* Hanna was a wily political boss who "assessed" Big Business for campaign contributions. Voters were told that McKinley was "the advance agent of prosperity." Some workers got the hint when employers said if Bryan was elected on Tuesday, don't bother showing up for work on Wednesday.[128]

When the votes were tallied, McKinley swept the Northwest and the industrial Midwest. He was elected with 7,104,779 popular votes (50.2 percent) and 271 electoral votes. Bryan got 6,502,925 popular votes (46 percent) and 176 electoral votes. It was a very respectable showing for a young Democrat who had held no significant office. This race would make Bryan a national figure for a generation.

While Bryan was setting the prairies afire, Theodore Roosevelt remained *incombustible*:

* McKinley had served as a young sergeant in the same Ohio unit in which Rutherford B. Hayes had been a general.

> Mr. Bryan is appealing more and more openly to the base malignancy and hatred of those demagogues who strive to lead laboring men to ruin, in order to wreak their vengeance on the thrifty and well-to-do. He advocates principles sufficiently silly and wicked to make them fit well in the mouth of the anarchist leader. For the government of Washington and Lincoln, for the system of orderly liberty bequeathed to us by our forefathers, he would substitute a welter of lawlessness as fantastic and as vicious as the dream of a European communist. . . . Instead of a government of the people, by the people, for the people, which we now have, Mr. Bryan would substitute a government of the mob.[129]

VIII. "From the New World"

For four hundred years, America had been known to Europe as the New World. America in the late nineteenth century still held a fascination for Old Europe. When Czech composer Antonín Dvorák came to New York in 1892, he was inspired by the legend of Hiawatha. While in New York, he would compose his Symphony No. 9—*From the New World*—for a debut at Carnegie Hall. Jeannette Thurber had engaged Dvorák to make the journey from Prague to New York to lead the National Conservatory of Music. Mrs. Thurber was the wife of a wealthy merchant.[130] The very practical son of Bohemian peasants, Dvorák jumped at the opportunity to make *twenty times* what he had been earning under the Austro-Hungarian Empire. Dvorák was quite taken with what were then called Negro spirituals. Henry Burleigh often sang them for the great composer in his home. He said Dvorák "saturated himself in the spirit of these old tunes."[131] Dvorák appreciated Mrs. Thurber's concern for a distinctively *American* music. "I am convinced that the future music of this country must be founded on what are called Negro melodies," he told her. "These can be the foundation of a serious and original school of composition, to be developed in the United States. These beautiful and varied themes are the product of the soil. They are the folk songs of America and your composers must turn to them."[132]

When he became homesick, Dvorák left New York for Iowa for a working vacation. Dvorák would take a bucket of beer down to the Mississippi

River to take in the songs and spirit of manual laborers. There, in the Bohemian immigrant colony of Spillville, he completed the Ninth Symphony. He especially enjoyed seeing Indians perform the music and dance of their people. Conductor Leonard Bernstein would later trace the major themes in Dvorák's *From the New World*. Dvorák had drawn on Czech, French, Scottish, German, and even Chinese sources.[133] In this one powerful work, we see the theme of the American "melting pot."

The new rich elites of America's Gilded Age have many critics, both then and now. It cannot be forgotten, however, that they contributed mightily to the power and dynamism of the great and free republic. They also outdid themselves in acts of charity and high culture. Not only did they seek to preserve the best of European civilization, but in patronizing an artist like Antonín Dvorák, they fostered new and beautiful contributions to world culture.

We can make much of the political corruption of the Gilded Age because American poets and writers and journalists of the time made much of them. They were shocked by slippery dealing. And they demanded reform. People seeking honest government were horrified by the Tweed Ring and the Whiskey Ring. They embarrassed Americans who were taught to think of republican government as inherently more responsive to the people and less inclined to corruption than European monarchies. James Russell Lowell spoke for many when he wrote:

> *Show your State Legislatures; show your Rings;*
> *And challenge Europe to produce such things.*[134]

Actually, Europe could hardly afford to scorn America. Power exercised by the rich alone and for the rich alone was the rule there. This is why only a few American *émigré* artists and writers like James McNeill Whistler and Henry James and hardly any common people went there, while millions of Europeans came *here*. That Statue of Liberty beckoned them.

We can be proud of those called to the highest office in America during this era. Garfield and Arthur rose above questionable conduct in their pasts to set a fine example in the White House. America's other presidents in this period—Hayes, Harrison, and Cleveland—were honorable, diligent, and serious-minded. Given this era of revolutionary change, and comparing America's development to other countries, this is an estimable record, more glittering than gilded.

Thirteen

The American Dynamo—Shadowed by War

(1897–1914)

In 1896, William Jennings Bryan unites old biblical ideas with very contemporary issues. He decries a "Cross of Gold" and a "Crown of Thorns." Bryan's whirlwind campaign tours capture the imagination of tens of thousands, and Bryan is quite a show. William McKinley is solid, reliable, and not a little dull. But he presides over an expanding economy and, rather against his wishes, over an expanding overseas empire. Theodore Roosevelt is the Republicans' answer—almost their antidote—to Bryan and Bryanism. When an anarchist's bullet propels Teddy into the presidency, the White House truly becomes what he called it: a Bully Pulpit. Roosevelt shapes the modern presidency as none of his predecessors has done. When William H. Taft proves to be an incapable successor, his failure is more a matter of style than of substance. The great Republican smashup of 1912 pitts TR and Taft, these two longtime friends and political allies, against one another in one of the most tragic and consequential political feuds in our history. Woodrow Wilson, son of a Southern pastor, revels in the presidency as a place of moral leadership. Wilson's first term is marked by major legislation on labor and banking. Wilson's dissent from the Founders' vision of checks and balances will bring a fatal clash, but not until later. When European states careen into the abyss of The Great War, Wilson maneuvers successfully to keep the United States out. Things will change as America enters history's bloodiest century. Reformers are especially keen to stay out of Europe's internecine conflict, believing that wartime restrictions will mean the end of their fondest hopes for change. Change comes, to be sure, but not the changes they have sought.

I. "A Splendid Little War"

Commissioner Theodore Roosevelt stalked the streets of New York City at night. As the most visible member of the city's Police Board, he had gained a reputation for surprising members of "New York's Finest" who were not exactly fulfilling their duties. To make sure that his night patrols would not go unnoticed by the press, TR took along his friend Jacob Riis, a Jewish immigrant from Denmark. Riis was a journalist who was making a name for himself as a reformer.

Outside a restaurant late one night, Roosevelt and Riis saw the owner impatiently rapping on the street with his stick. "Where *does* that copper sleep?" the owner barked with irritation. He was not aware that the man he was addressing was in fact the president of the city's Police Board.[1]

The public loved reading the adventures of their night-stalking "commish." TR was called "Haroun al Rashid Roosevelt," after the famous vizier of Baghdad who moved in disguise among his people.[2] But he wasn't always loved by his men. Some of the sleeping constables, shown up by TR's antics, tried to get even. One night, they raided a society dinner at which "Little Egypt," an exotic-dancing sensation of the Chicago Columbian Exposition, planned to do her thing. Roosevelt was said to be present, and they hoped to nail him. For once, however, Commissioner Roosevelt was asleep in his New York mansion. TR laughed when told of the renegade policemen's attempt to embarrass him. He had been at home all night with his wife Edith and their growing young family.

Jake Riis must have been puzzled when his friend announced that a German pastor—a notorious anti-Semite—would indeed be allowed to give a speech in New York City. Teddy was, after all, a firm advocate of free speech. But to underscore his own feelings about the speaker's hate-filled message, TR took care to provide an escort of large, muscular patrolmen from NYPD—every one of them Jewish.

When William McKinley returned Republicans to power in Washington in 1897—after the dignified rule of Grover Cleveland—even the rising skyline of Manhattan would prove too confining for Theodore Roosevelt. His friend John Burroughs, the famous naturalist, captured Roosevelt's essence when he said TR was a many-sided man and "every side was like an electric battery."[3] Henry Adams, the grandson and great-grandson of presidents, hit the mark when he called TR "pure act."[4]

TR's friend Massachusetts Senator Henry Cabot Lodge lobbied hard to get an important appointment with the new McKinley administration for the energetic cowboy from the Dakotas. TR was especially interested in naval matters. When barely out of Harvard, he penned *The Naval History of the War of 1812*. The book was, and is, considered a classic. Roosevelt was convinced early that the United States needed a modern, powerful navy. He and Lodge worked closely with Navy Captain Alfred Thayer Mahan. Mahan argued in his great book, *The Influence of Sea Power Upon History*, that the ability of a nation to master the seas in order to "project force" was the key to its world power. TR wrote Mahan that he had "devoured" the massive work in just two nights.[5] Mahan's work was persuasive not only to important American thinkers, but also to influential figures in Britain, Japan, and, most ominously, Germany. Kaiser Wilhelm II read the book avidly and had a copy placed on *every* German ship.[6]

President McKinley was not eager to bring the rambunctious Roosevelt into his cabinet. He had already promised the post of navy secretary to the easygoing John Long—a New England politician, who wouldn't "rock the boat." McKinley told one of TR's many advocates that he worried about the young dynamo. "I want peace," the president said, "and I'm told that your friend Theodore—whom I know only slightly—is always getting into rows with everybody. I'm afraid he's too *pugnacious*."[7]

If McKinley could have peeked at Theodore's private correspondence, he would have had good reason to fear. "Teddy" was even then writing to a friend that he wanted to conquer Canada and drive the Spaniards out of Cuba![8] And to his sister, Bamie, Teddy wrote of his own feelings toward the president: McKinley "is an upright and honorable man, of very considerable ability and good record as a soldier . . . he is not a strong man, however, and unless he is well backed I should feel rather uneasy about him in a serious crisis."[9]

Assured that TR was a faithful party man, the president relented and named the New Yorker *assistant* secretary of the navy. It was to be a fateful move. Teddy the battery soon gave the navy a jolt.

The United States had been viewing developments in nearby Cuba with mounting concern for nearly fifty years. Prior to the Civil War, various proslavery "filibusters" wanted to seize this "Pearl of the Antilles" from the weakening grasp of royal Spain. After the Civil War, the persistence of slavery in Cuba presented a bar to annexation by the United States. But when Cuban rebels seeking independence from Spain began their agitation, American sympathies were all with these freedom-seeking *insurrectos.* When a full-scale revolt broke out in 1895, millions of Americans cried, "*Cuba libre!*" ("Free Cuba!").

Spain sent General Valeriano Weyler to put down the rebellion. The American press went wild. General Weyler reacted to the insurrectos' "scorched earth" tactics by rounding up Cuban peasants in rebel areas and confining them to concentration camps. This *reconcentrado* policy resulted in thousands dead from hunger and disease. Weyler was vilified in the "Yellow Press" (so called because of the cheap newsprint on which the penny-a-sheet sensationalist newspapers were printed). Atrocity stories from Cuba daily filled the pages of Joseph Pulitzer's *New York World* and the rival *New York Journal.* The bumptious young millionaire, William Randolph Hearst, owned the *Journal.* Hearst and Pulitzer were in a circulation war, and they used Cuban horrors to gain readership. As the old journalistic saw has it: *if it bleeds, it leads.*

Hearst sent the great American artist, Frederic Remington, to Cuba during a lull in the fighting. "There is no trouble here," Remington cabled Hearst, "There will be no war. I wish to return." Hearst quickly responded by telegram. "Please remain. You furnish the pictures and I'll furnish the war."[10] Pulitzer's *World* fanned anti-Spanish sentiment with paragraphs like this: "Blood on the roadsides, blood in the fields, blood on the doorsteps, blood, blood, blood! The old, the young, the weak, the crippled—all are butchered without mercy. . . . Is there no nation wise enough, brave enough, and strong enough to restore peace in this bloodsmitten land?"[11]

All of these horrors, the reader was led to believe, were committed on the direct orders of General Weyler. When a new ministry came to office in Madrid, it attempted to quiet the storm in Cuba. Weyler was recalled. His *reconcentrado* policy was eased. Soon, it appeared, order and peace would be restored to Cuba.

Just at this moment, the United States sent the battleship *Maine* to Havana, Cuba. We wanted to "show the flag" and let pro-Weyler Cubans know that the *Yanquis* would not tolerate abuse of Americans or their property in Cuba. President McKinley's closest friend, Senator Mark Hanna, opposed the move. He saw it as a needless provocation. It was, he said, "like waving a match in an oil well [just] for fun."[12]

The Hearst press intercepted and published a letter from Dupuy de Lôme, the Spanish minister in Washington. A most *undiplomatic* row soon broke out. De Lôme's very negative assessment of McKinley's Message to Congress was spread out for all America to read. The hapless envoy said the message showed "what McKinley is, weak and a bidder for the admiration of the crowd."[13] It was no more than what many American critics had been saying about the mild-mannered president, but it was intolerable for Americans to hear it from an outsider. Soon, the unfortunate Señor de Lôme was packing his bags for home.

President McKinley did not want to be rushed into war. He even joked about it with his White House physician. Army Colonel Leonard Wood was a close friend of TR. "Well, have you and Theodore declared war yet?" said McKinley. "No Mr. President, but we think *you* should."[14]

No sooner had de Lôme left for Spain than terrible news came from Havana. The USS *Maine* had exploded in the harbor with heavy loss of American life. More than 250 sailors died instantly, more still would die from burns and wounds. The Yellow Press went wild. "*Maine Destroyed by Treachery!*" screamed Hearst's nationwide chain of papers.[15]

Without waiting for the navy's official investigation, TR resolved to act. When Secretary Long, feeling ill, took a Friday afternoon off, *acting* Secretary Roosevelt immediately cabled to Commodore George Dewey, commanding the navy's Asiatic Squadron:

> Dewey, Hong Kong: ORDER THE SQUADRON . . . TO HONG KONG. KEEP FULL OF COAL. IN THE EVENT OF DECLARATION OF WAR WITH SPAIN, YOUR DUTY WILL BE TO SEE THAT THE SPANISH SQUADRON DOES NOT LEAVE THE ASIATIC COAST, AND THEN OFFENSIVE OPERATIONS IN THE PHILIPPINE ISLANDS. KEEP OLYMPIA UNTIL FURTHER ORDERS.
>
> ROOSEVELT[16]

Members of Congress hounded McKinley for war with Spain. "Don't your President know where the war-making power is lodged?" growled one senator at the secretary of state.[17] This presented the McKinley administration with a dangerous prospect, that Congress would declare war *whether or not* the president asked for it. Nothing would make the president look more feeble. Worse, the president's defeated 1896 rival, William Jennings Bryan, was speaking out for "Free Cuba and Free Silver." If McKinley failed to act, might the Democrats take up the cause of Cuban independence, if only for political gain?[18] A cartoon published in Hearst's *New York World* showed McKinley as a determined old lady, futilely trying to sweep back a hurricane with her broom. The winds were labeled "the people" and the waves were labeled "Congress."[19]

Theodore Roosevelt was disgusted by the president's failure to call openly for war. "McKinley has no more backbone than a chocolate éclair!" Teddy cried.[20] When the official navy board of inquiry reported an external submarine mine had caused the explosion of the *Maine*, it did *not* place the blame on Spain. It didn't have to. Around the country, the cry went up:

Remember the Maine
To Hell with Spain![21]*

Wall Street did not want war. Most Europeans thought America would lose. Business leaders worried what would become of Americans' major

---

* A 1976 investigation by Admiral Hyman G. Rickover concluded that the Battleship *Maine* was destroyed by coal dust's igniting *within* the ship.

investments in Cuba. Roosevelt confronted Senator Hanna bluntly. Hanna, Wall Street's man in the Capitol, dug in his heels against war. "We will have this war for the freedom of Cuba," TR said in a Washington speech. "The interests of the business world and of financiers may be paramount in the Senate," but the American people cared about morality. "Now, Senator," Theodore said, appealing directly to Hanna, "may we please have war?"[22]

Teddy's boss, Secretary Long, may have hoped to restrain him by letting him attend meetings of the president's cabinet. But TR lectured the cabinet graybeards on the need to fight Spain. Still, the humane McKinley hesitated. "I have been through one war," the heroic Civil War veteran said. "I have seen the dead piled up, and I do not want to see another."[23]

Trying to avoid war, the Spanish government in Madrid made belated concessions. The Spanish people, however, were hostile to any compromise with the Yanqui "pigs."

McKinley wasn't alone in opposition. An influential group of Americans spoke out eloquently against imperialism. Mark Twain skewered the pretensions of the *jingoes* with wit, as did the Irish American humorist Finley Peter Dunne. Industrialist Andrew Carnegie and the respected ex-Mugwump Carl Schurz criticized the rush to war. The powerful Republican speaker of the House, Thomas B. Reed of Maine, opposed war with Spain. TR derided these men as "goo goos," an unflattering reference to these high-minded supporters of "good government."

Teddy admitted to his sister, Bamie, that he was "something of a jingo." Actually, there was no one in America *jingoer*. What decided the fate of the nation, however, was a speech by Vermont Senator Redfield Proctor. No jingo, the seasoned and highly respected Proctor had actually gone to Cuba. His speech to the Senate, delivered in a calm and deliberative tone, changed minds. He confirmed the atrocity stories. The people there were "living like pigs and dying like flies." "To me, the strongest appeal is not the barbarity practiced by Weyler, nor the loss of the *Maine* . . . but the spectacle of a million and a half people [of Cuba] struggling for freedom and deliverance from the worst misgovernment of which I ever had knowledge."[24]

Speaker Reed cynically observed that Proctor's stance for war would at least be good for the family's business (the Proctors owned a Vermont marble company, from which tombstones would be made).[25] But neither Reed nor the president could hold out longer. Congress soon voted for war.

Assistant Secretary of the Navy Roosevelt promptly resigned. Henry Adams was stunned. "Is his wife dead? Has he quarreled with everybody? Is he quite mad?"[26] Theodore was determined to join the fight. TR said he had to "act up to my preachings."[27] Although vigorous and strong, TR could never have been accepted in today's military. Not only had he suffered from asthma as a child, but his vision was so poor that he was virtually blind without his spectacles. And he was nearly forty. No matter. Teddy immediately joined with his friend Leonard Wood to recruit a company of volunteers.

Teddy accepted a commission as a *lieutenant* colonel, modestly taking second in command of the regiment he and Colonel Wood raised. Teddy called on all his Ivy League friends, his fellow cowboys from the Dakotas, and Indian fighters from the prairies. Soon, the regiment was nicknamed the "Rough Riders." TR would later describe them as "Indian and cowboy, miner, packer and college athlete, the man of unknown ancestry from the Western plains, and the man who carried on his watch the crest of the Stuyvesants and the Fishes."[28]

Before the Rough Riders could get to Cuba, however, the navy went into action against Spain in the Philippines. No one expected the Americans to beat the Spaniards. When the U.S. ships weighed anchor in Hong Kong, their British hosts said of them: "A fine set of fellows, but unhappily we shall never see them again."[29] Commodore Dewey struck hard at Manila Bay. Taking the Spanish fleet by surprise on 1 May 1898, Dewey gave the order to Captain Charles V. Gridley of the USS *Olympia*: "You may fire when ready, Gridley." Gridley *was* ready, and the Spanish fleet that had spanned the globe for four centuries was destroyed in a matter of minutes.* Below decks on the *Olympia*, the temperatures rose to 150 degrees! Still, the sailors were in high spirits. They stripped down to nothing but shoes and sang a popular rag tune of the day: "There'll be a hot time in the old town tonight."[30]*

* Captain Gridley had little chance to enjoy his worldwide fame. He died of illness in Kobe, Japan, less than a month after his great victory. His name is remembered in a succession of naval vessels. Lieutenant John Kerry served on USS *Gridley*, a destroyer, off Vietnam.

When the Rough Riders landed in Cuba, they soon found that the war was no lark. The Spanish soldiers who faced them were well trained, highly disciplined, and excellent shots. They were well equipped with 7x57 mm-caliber German Mausers, the best rifle in the world. TR said the sound of a Mauser—*a-z-z-z-eu*—was like "ripping silk."[31] Most dangerous was the fact Mausers used smokeless powder. Those firing from the dense jungle undergrowth could not be easily located. On 1 July 1898, the Rough Riders went into action at San Juan Hill. When retreating Spaniards broke into a run, Army General "Fighting Joe" Wheeler, an old veteran of the *Confederate* army, excitedly cried out: "We've got the damn Yankees on the run!"[32]

One of the first Rough Riders killed was New Yorker Hamilton Fish Jr. The nephew and namesake of U. S. Grant's distinguished secretary of state, Sergeant Fish was one of the glamorous "Fifth Avenue boys" TR had recruited.[33] (B. F. Goodrich and the jeweler's son, Bill Tiffany, were other famous names who survived the war. Frank Knox would live to serve as secretary of the navy under TR's cousin, Franklin.)

Another famous Rough Rider was Bucky O'Neill. O'Neill had fought Indians and chased outlaws as sheriff of Prescott, Arizona. As he exhaled smoke from his ever-present cigarette, Bucky boasted that the Spanish bullet hadn't been made that could kill him. At that moment, a German-made Mauser bullet hit him in the mouth and took off the back of his head.[34]

For all the comic opera aspect of this war, once the Americans got to Cuba they found it all too real. Huge land crabs attacked corpses, as did vultures.[35] In the assault on San Juan Hill, Lieutenant Colonel Roosevelt scolded some of the regulars who were hunkered down. "Are you afraid to stand up when I am on horseback?" he asked. Even as one of the crouching soldiers rose, though, the poor man was cut down by a well-aimed Spanish shot.[36] Soon, TR found it more prudent to *dismount* from Little Texas and proceed on foot.

---

* The American victory at Manila Bay would begin the long association of the U.S. Navy with the Philippines. Many an American sailor would head for the wild liberty port of Alongopo City. It was the location of some of the most notorious saloons and brothels in Asia. To be fair, "Po Town" was also hometown to some of the most enduring marriages in American service life.

Coming upon a company of black regulars who were headed for the rear, Roosevelt pulled out his service revolver and threatened to shoot them. If they doubted him, he said, they could ask his men if he kept his word. "My cow-punchers, hunters and miners solemnly nodded their heads. . . . 'He always does; he always does,'" TR wrote in his best-selling book, *The Rough Riders.*[37]

TR did not know that the black soldiers were actually moving *under orders.* These hardened veterans had gained fame on the plains as "Buffalo Soldiers." They good naturedly joined Roosevelt's assault on San Juan Hill—and shared in the immortal glory of his triumph. Teddy's "crowded hour" at San Juan Hill catapulted him into international fame. For the rest of his life, TR would be known as the Rough Rider. The middle-aged husband and father, the desk-bound bureaucrat had proven himself in the white heat of combat.

The war quickly wound down. American victories on land were equaled by more at sea. When "Fighting Bob" Evans's ship, USS *Iowa,* met and destroyed the Spanish fleet at Santiago, Cuba, his men cheered. "Don't cheer boys," Captain Evans ordered, "those poor devils are dying!"[38] Spanish Admiral Cervera's fleet was magnificently turned out. With decks polished and brass gleaming, they sailed into the *Iowa's* deadly line of fire. Despite all the foolish talk about Spanish cowardice, the Americans gained great respect for the courage of the doomed men in the antiquated Spanish vessels.

Half a world away, Americans gratefully accepted British intervention. When Commodore Dewey shelled Spanish shore positions at Manila on August 13, a Royal Navy squadron put itself between the Americans and a German naval flotilla that had attempted to interfere with the American attack. The German battleships actually *trained* their guns on the Americans! Unwilling to risk war with *both* the British and the Americans, the German commander backed down.

Britain was the only European power openly to back the Americans in the Spanish-American War. Young Winston Churchill was a war correspondent. He spoke for many Englishmen when he said: "The Americans should be admired for their action in Cuba . . . though as a nation . . . they always contrive to disgust polite people. Yet their heart is honest."[39] Britain had its own *goo goos*. America's minister in London, John Hay, had worked hard to gain British support for the U.S. position. As a young man, Hay had served as Lincoln's secretary. Then, he saw what horrors war could bring. Now, he called TR's project "a splendid little war."[40] For Spain, which lost 50,000 men—2,000 in combat, the rest to disease—it was a painful experience. For America, the 385 battle deaths and 2,000 lost to disease were the cost of the country's emergence as a world power.[41]

To President McKinley now came the difficult task of deciding what to do about America's conquests. Cuba would be granted independence. That much was sure. But what about Guam, Puerto Rico, and the Philippines? McKinley struggled over the Philippines, especially. He told a delegation of Methodists he had prayerfully decided it was his duty "to take them all and to educate the Filipinos, and uplift and civilize and *Christianize* them."[42] The Filipinos, under Spanish guidance for three centuries, were mostly Christian.[43] And soon, Americans would have their own *insurrectos* to contend with there. McKinley's decision was widely criticized as an imperialist power grab. The truth is the Philippines cast adrift would have been snapped up by either Germany or Japan in 1898. Under American rule, at least, they would have the *promise* of independence. For good measure, McKinley took the occasion to annex the Hawaiian Islands.

"Japan has her eye on them," he told an aide.[44] Senator Lodge and Captain Mahan, among others, had convinced the president that in the modern world of great ironclad fleets, Hawaii was necessary for the defense of California.

II. Rough Rider Politics

Colonel Roosevelt and the Rough Riders came to Montauk, on Long Island's East End, to be "mustered out." After a brief and glorious tour of duty, they were honorably discharged from active service. There, President McKinley came to greet the returning heroes. TR jumped off his horse and struggled to get his glove off to shake hands with the commander in chief. Finally, frustrated at not being able to pull the glove off, he took it in his teeth and yanked it off so he could pump the chief executive's hand. Those prominent teeth, the pince-nez eyeglasses, the slouch hat—all had become the stuff of legend and the delight of cartoonists. Though he hated the nickname, Roosevelt was "Teddy" to the whole country.[45] The Rough Riders gave him a Frederic Remington sculpture, *The Bronco Buster*, and wept as they bade him good-bye.[46]

TR could not have returned at a more politically advantageous time. Senator Thomas Platt was known as New York's Easy Boss for his soft-spoken manner. He saw sure defeat for New York Republicans if they renominated their scandal-tainted governor, Frank Black. Black's administration couldn't explain how a million dollars intended for repairs on the Erie Canal got misdirected.[47] Platt hated to dump a loyal Republican, but he hated losing even more. Respectfully, Theodore went to Platt's headquarters in Manhattan's Fifth Avenue Hotel. There, Platt held court with his group of hangers-on. They were known as the Amen Corner. By going to *him,* Teddy was showing that he could cooperate. Platt insisted that Teddy reject the pleas of enthusiastic reformers that he run for governor as an *independent.* In return, the senator would throw the Republican nomination for governor to the Rough Rider.

Teddy, smelling victory, agreed.[48] The fall campaign was a whirlwind. Teddy appeared at the back of his train, the Roosevelt Special. He waved his uniform hat and surrounded himself with Rough Riders who announced his speeches with a bugle. One of his sergeants, Southerner Buck Taylor, happily told one crowd: "He kept ev'y promise he made to us and he will to you. . . . He led us up San Juan Hill like sheep to the slaughter—and so he will lead you!"[49]

Despite this *dubious* endorsement, Teddy went on to win the governorship—but narrowly. The corruption of the state's Republicans had not been forgotten. TR won by less than 18,000 votes out of more than 1,300,000.[50] But he had won, and in winning he had kept the critical Empire State in the hands of the Republicans. This was vitally important. President McKinley was surely relieved as he extended his congratulations to "the Colonel." He would need the Empire State's electoral votes when he ran for reelection in 1900.

The president's reelection prospects at midterm did not look so promising. The acquisition of an overseas empire was proving difficult—the Filipino *insurrectos* were no fonder of American rule than they had been of Spanish rule. American soldiers were dying in the fight to put down Emilio Aguinaldo's nationalist forces. The little war had shown the complete lack of preparedness of the American army. Criticism mounted of McKinley's inept war secretary, Russell Alger. When TR had to go to Alger personally to get a requisition signed for weapons, one of the secretary's aides sighed: "Oh dear! I had this office running in such good shape—and along came the war and upset *everything*!"[51]

The McKinley administration had a hard time getting the Senate to approve the Treaty of Paris ending the short war. McKinley had taken care to send a mixed delegation of Democrats and Republicans to Paris to negotiate the peace. But it was clear that if the acquisition of the Philippines had been voted upon separately from the conclusion of the war, it would have failed. Senator Henry Cabot Lodge wrote to TR: "It was the closest, hardest fight I have ever known."[52]

On one critical vote, the administration even had to enlist the tie-breaking vote of Vice President Garrett A. Hobart. It would be one of the vice president's last official acts. He died in November 1899, leaving a critical vacancy to be filled.*

The fight over the peace treaty would have been lost had it not been for the endorsement of William Jennings Bryan. Bryan had been the Democrats' presidential nominee in 1896. Now, because of Bryan's backing, ten Senate Democrats voted to ratify the peace treaty.[53] Massachusetts Republican Senator George Hoar tried to blame the treaty's approval on Bryan. Hoar wrote to his fellow Bay Stater, George Boutwell, president of the Anti-Imperialist League, to complain that *Bryan* was "the most thoroughly guilty man in the United States of this whole Philippine business."[54] That two old Republican "stalwarts" like Boutwell and Hoar were so vocally anti-imperialist shows how both major parties were split by America's new world role.

It is easy to poke fun at the pretensions of the imperialists. British

* The vice president votes only when there is a tie in the Senate. Prior to the Twenty-fifth Amendment, when a vice president died or resigned, there was a vacancy in the number two position.

poet Rudyard Kipling urged us to "take up the white man's burden." Uninformed people spoke of "civilizing the Filipino." These ideas sound absurd to us today. Yet American intervention made a great difference in the lives of Cubans in one important respect. The dreaded Yellow Fever took thousands of lives there. American troops, Spanish troops, Cuban nationals, all suffered. When U.S. Army doctor Walter Reed investigated the causes, he learned of Cuban physician Carlos Finlay's work. Dr. Finlay's research showed that mosquitoes carried the disease. Dr. Reed advised General Leonard Wood, TR's old commanding officer, to attack the carrier. General Wood took up the challenge and waged "war" on the insect. By 1901, Havana was free of the killer disease.[55]

In the case of the Philippines, American rule would prove brief. Four hundred years of Spanish colonial rule had not equipped Filipinos for self-government. In light of later events in the Pacific, especially three long, brutal years of Japanese occupation during World War II, America's role in protecting and guiding the Filipinos formed the basis for our continuing friendship with that country.

In another way, America's newfound prestige benefited others. McKinley had summoned John Hay home from Britain to become U.S. secretary of state. Hay examined the growing turmoil in China and saw the imperial powers of Europe—and Japan—eager to carve up the ancient Celestial Empire. In 1899, Hay circulated a letter to the Powers, calling on them to prevent the further disintegration of the country and to treat all of China's trading partners equally. This became known as the "Open Door Policy," for which Hay is justly famous.

Hay's generous sentiments were misinterpreted by one small group of Chinese, however. Young martial arts students called the Fists of Righteous Harmony rose up. They wanted to drive out the "foreign devils" entirely. Called *boxers* by the Europeans, their bloody action in 1900 is known as the Boxer Rebellion. Thousands of Christian missionaries and Chinese Christian converts were slaughtered as the Boxers laid siege to the foreign legations in Peking. When an international force finally rescued the diplomats and other westerners, the Boxer Rebellion was ruthlessly put down. All over the world, readers of the Yellow Press gawked in horror to see photographs of *Chinese* pyramids. But these pyramids were made of the severed heads of the Boxers. The world shuddered as well when Kaiser Wilhelm II ordered his troops—part of the multinational force—to suppress the Boxers with all the ferocity of the "Huns" of old. German soldiers would never shake that sobriquet.

Facing the election of 1900, Republicans sought to shift the public's attention to the prosperity of "the full dinner pail." To fill the vacancy in the vice presidency, they nominated Governor Theodore Roosevelt. The Easy Boss, Tom Platt, had quickly tired of Theodore in Albany and hoped to get rid of him by "kicking him upstairs."

The Democrats again chose William Jennings Bryan. This time, Bryan shifted ground once more and campaigned *against* imperialism. Charles Francis Adams Jr., another member of the famous Adams family, thought little of McKinley, but he liked Bryan even less: "He is in one sense scripturally formidable, for he is unquestionably armed with the jaw-bone of an ass. He can talk longer and say less than any man in Christendom."[56]

Bryan once again conducted a whistle stop campaign, barnstorming the country by rail.

This time, however, Republicans sent TR to combat the man who was called the Great Commoner. Teddy's popular appeal proved more than a match for Bryan's. Teddy campaigned in his Rough Rider hat to enthusiastic whoops from his audiences. Bryan's free silver issue commanded less voter attention this time around because gold had been discovered in the Yukon and South Africa. Those "strikes" had created vastly more wealth, something silver advocates had hoped to do with their precious metal. When the votes were finally counted, the Republicans won in a landslide. McKinley *improved* on his 1896 performance, winning with 7.2 million votes (292 electoral votes) to Bryan's 6.3 million votes (155 electoral votes).

At the inauguration on 4 March 1901, New York's Boss Platt joked that he had come to watch "Theodore take the veil."[57] It was no convent that TR was entering, however. Six months later, the kind-hearted president visited the Pan American Exposition in Buffalo, New York. He was greeting well-wishers. He extended the hand of friendship to a young man whose own hand was wrapped in a large bandage. Leon Czolgosz, an anarchist, fired two shots that struck the president in the chest and abdomen.* "Be easy with him, boys," the stricken president called out as Secret Service agents pummeled the assassin with their fists. For a time, the president seemed to rally. Medical reports were so encouraging that his vigorous vice president thought it safe to take some time off for recreation. He set out to scale New York's highest peak, Mount Marcy. Mount Marcy is near Lake Tear of the Clouds, in Essex County, close to the border with Vermont. Suddenly, below him, TR saw a ranger running toward him waving a yellow telegram. Teddy knew what it meant.[58] He jumped in a buckboard for the mad dash to the train station. A special train sped him nearly four hundred miles westward to Buffalo, to the stately home of the Roosevelts' wealthy friends, the Wilcoxes, where Theodore Roosevelt was sworn in as president. He was just a few weeks shy of his forty-third birthday, the youngest man ever to take the oath as president.

Riding in the presidential funeral train, Senator Mark Hanna ruefully reflected on his conversation with his dearest friend: "I told William McKinley it was a mistake to nominate that wild man at [the Republican National Convention in Philadelphia the previous summer]. I asked him if he realized what would happen if he should die. Now look, that damned cowboy is President of the United States!"[59]

III. TR in the White House

We are so used to identifying the presidency with the White House that it's hard to believe that the *official* title of the president's residence for more than a century was the Executive Mansion. But that would not last long with TR. By proclamation, he renamed the building the White House. This was but one of the whirlwinds of change that Roosevelt brought to the office. He of course presided over the nation's period of deep and sincere mourning for the slain McKinley. But he did not let this tragedy slow him down:

* Czolgosz was quickly tried, convicted, and sentenced to die in New York State's new electric chair. He was executed on 20 October 1901, barely five weeks after the president died. The electric chair was one of Thomas Edison's less salubrious inventions.

> It is a dreadful thing to come into the Presidency in this way; but it would be far worse to be morbid about it. Here is the task, and I have got to do it to the best of my ability; and that is all there is to it.[60]

Shortly after moving into the White House, the president heard that Booker T. Washington was in the capital. Dr. Washington was the president of the Tuskegee Institute, the leading black college in America. Without hesitation, TR invited the distinguished educator to dinner. Teddy liked to boast of his Southern ancestry. His mother was from Georgia and his two dashing uncles served on the CSS *Alabama*. But he was completely unprepared for the storm of protest in the South that greeted this first White House dinner given to a black man.* Southern newspapers denounced the president for this "most damnable outrage." Even worse was the reaction of a Democratic senator from South Carolina. "Pitchfork Ben" Tillman said: "The action of President Roosevelt in entertaining that n——— will necessitate our killing a thousand n———s in the South before they will learn their place again."[61] Tillman was not exaggerating. Each year hundreds of black Southerners died at the hands of lynch mobs. To the everlasting shame of the U.S. Senate, Tillman was *not* expelled at that instant!

What made the reaction even more astonishing was that Dr. Washington had gone out of his way to *avoid* challenging the white Democrats who ruled the one-party South. He was an advocate of reconciliation, and he accepted the burden of segregation. The U.S. Supreme Court had even approved racial segregation in its appalling *Plessy v. Ferguson* ruling of 1896. Bowing to this reality, Booker T. Washington advocated black self-help. His best-selling autobiography, *Up from Slavery*, urged black Americans to improve themselves through education and training *before* demanding their constitutional right to vote and social equality.

This very "moderate" position led young black intellectuals like W. E. B. DuBois to criticize Booker T. Washington:

---

* President Lincoln had famously invited Frederick Douglass to confer man-to-man with him in the White House, and to attend the reception following his second inaugural, but this was the first dinner invitation extended to a black man. Ironically, the White House head waiter, who was black, seemed to disapprove.

> But so far as Mr. Washington apologizes for injustice, North or South, does not rightly value the privilege and duty of voting, belittles the emasculating effects of caste distinctions, and opposes the higher training and ambition of our brighter minds,—so far as he, the South, or the Nation, does this,—we must unceasingly and firmly oppose them. By every civilized and peaceful method we must strive for the rights which the world accords to men, clinging unwaveringly to those great words which the sons of the Fathers would fain forget: "We hold these truths to be self-evident: That all men are created equal; that they are endowed by their Creator with certain unalienable rights; that among these are life, liberty, and the pursuit of happiness."

Stressing "continuity of government," TR asked a number of McKinley's cabinet members to stay on. He particularly wanted Secretary of State John Hay to remain. TR's father had known Hay in the Lincoln White House. When Theodore Senior got the idea of *allotments* for Union soldiers, Hay whisked *Greatheart* in to see President Lincoln. Lincoln instantly approved the idea.* Now, the slender young man of the Lincoln White House was a portly, witty, and wise senior statesman. TR turned to him as to a trusted old family friend. He wanted John Hay to use his excellent contacts with the British to negotiate a better U.S. treaty for a Central American canal. Hay succeeded brilliantly. By the terms of the Hay-Pauncefote Treaty of 1901, the United States now had a free hand to negotiate, build, *and fortify* a canal across the isthmus.[62] (Hay refused to pay any attention to what he called the *hyphenated* Americans. This was a not-too-veiled reference to anti-British German and Irish Americans.[63]) And TR fully intended to use that free hand in constructing an *American* canal to link the Atlantic and Pacific Oceans.

Another great test of TR's presidency came in 1902 as the United Mine

---

* Prior to Lincoln's adoption of the Roosevelt *allotment* system, thousands of Northern families were left destitute. Their young men frittered away their military pay in camp on high-priced snacks, whiskey, gambling, and prostitutes. The Roosevelt system—still in use today—permitted these men to send cash *allotments* home to their needful families before the money was ever paid out to them.

Workers union called a national strike against the anthracite coal owners. The nation was completely dependent upon coal. Homes, factories, and public buildings were heated by coal. Railroad trains and steamships were fueled by it. Without coal, the nation would be crippled.

TR summoned the mine owners to the White House to meet with John Mitchell and other union leaders. "Are you asking us to meet with a set of *outlaws*?" asked John Markle of the owners' group.[64] Infuriated, Teddy said of Markle's arrogance: "If it wasn't for the high office I held, I would have taken him by the seat of the breeches and the nape of the neck and chucked him out of that window!"[65] The attitude of the owners was exemplified by a private letter from George Baer that soon leaked out: "The rights and interests of the laboring man will be protected and cared for—not by labor agitators, but by the Christian men to whom God in His infinite wisdom has given the control of the property interests of the country."[66] Such a cocksure notion of what the Almighty intended made the owners seem ridiculous to the public at large.

The miners were striking against deplorable working conditions. As Irving Stone would write in his biography of radical lawyer Clarence Darrow: "Six men of a thousand [miners] were killed every year; hundreds were maimed by explosions and cave-ins; few escaped the ravages of asthma, bronchitis, chronic rheumatism, consumption, heart trouble. By the age of fifty the miners were worn out and broken, good for little but the human slag heap."[67]

One of the most frightening hazards miners faced occurred when a bootlace or shirtsleeve became entangled in the gears of a coal-crushing machine and the miner was dragged to a slow and agonizing death. Owner representative George Baer denied that the miners suffered at all: "Why, they can't even speak English!"[68] Perhaps Teddy could identify with United Mine Worker President John Mitchell because he could remember fighting for breath when he was a sickly boy, stricken with asthma.

TR rattled his saber (something he *loved* doing). He let it be known he was contemplating taking over the coal mines and having the army operate them.

Worried that he might do something rash like that, the owners soon agreed to an arbitration panel. TR quickly named Catholic Bishop John

Spalding to the panel. The largely Catholic miners trusted their bishop. In addition, Teddy recruited a willing former president, Democrat Grover Cleveland. Soon, the miners and owners came to a compromise agreement, and the nation was saved from paralysis. It was the first instance of "jawboning" by a president, and it was a great success for Roosevelt.

Mindful of the fierce reaction from the South over his invitation to Dr. Washington, TR decided to visit his mother's homeland for a hunting trip. He wanted to mend political fences. Because of the many death threats TR had received and the recent McKinley assassination, the Secret Service nervously watched the New Yorker president as he descended on Dixie "loaded for bear."* The trip, however, was an embarrassing failure as TR repeatedly failed to bag a catch. Finally, TR's Mississippi hosts cornered a small black bear, wounded it, and called eagerly for the president to come and shoot it. Teddy the sportsman resolutely refused. He had eagerly shot grizzly bears, but he could not bring himself to take unfair advantage of the terrified, trapped animal. *Washington Post* cartoonist Clifford Berry immediately offered a picture he called "Drawing the line in Mississippi." Berry intended it as a commentary on "drawing the line" on *race* in the South. But the country missed the barbed point entirely. Instead, the whole nation thrilled to their Teddy's nobly sparing the poor little bear. In no time, it became the story of "Teddy's bear." That Christmas, New York's posh F.A.O. Schwarz store offered an elegant bear crafted by Germany's Steiff toy company. In Brooklyn's much less swankier precincts, Morris Michtom offered a stuffed toy bear for just $1.50.[69] Instantly, a worldwide craze began that shows no sign of ebbing a century later. The teddy bear captured the hearts of children everywhere.

When TR turned his attention to the powerful railroad trusts, he next decided to go after the new Northern Securities Company. Banker J. Pierpont Morgan had brought together controlling shares in the Northern Pacific, Union Pacific, and Burlington Railroads. The board was composed of such

* Following the assassination of President William McKinley in 1901, the *third* chief executive assassinated in just thirty-five years, Congress voted to provide Secret Service agents to protect the president and his family. The irrepressible Roosevelt clan gave their Secret Service detail quite a workout.

titans of industry as Morgan himself, James J. Hill, and E. H. Harriman. Morgan was called *Jupiter* on Wall Street. "The boldest man was likely to become timid under his piercing gaze," men said of him.[70] Wall Street was therefore shocked when TR instructed his attorney general, Philander Knox, to file suit in federal court *against* the Northern Securities Company. TR said they were violating the Sherman Anti-Trust Act of 1890. But what was *this?* The magnates were used to the federal government using the Sherman Act against *unions*. How dare the president wield this club against *them*?

Exhaling clouds of cigar smoke—like an active volcano—Jupiter came to the White House to put the new president in his place. "If we have done anything wrong, [just] send your man [Attorney General Knox] to see my man and they can fix it up."[71] TR did not think he was settling on the sale of a private yacht or arranging the swap of thoroughbred racehorses. He marveled at the way the Wall Street baron talked down to him. "That can't be done," TR responded.

When the Roosevelt administration finally won its case in the Supreme Court in 1904, TR was elated. The Court ruled that the Northern Securities Company had indeed violated the Sherman Act and ordered that the giant trust be broken up.

Roosevelt's reputation as a "trust buster" was well earned. The only downside of the Court's decision was the fact that TR's own appointee, Justice Oliver Wendell Holmes, had voted with the minority. TR was furious with Holmes. He would not be the last president to find disappointment in one of his nominees to the High Court, but few presidents expressed their displeasure more colorfully: "I could carve out of a *banana* a judge with more backbone than that!"[72]

Teddy's acts as president had made him wildly popular with the American people, if not with leaders of his party and their friends on Wall Street. Still, Teddy was something of a force of nature. He preached the *strenuous* life—and practiced it. He loved to lead foreign diplomats, military officers, and panting civil servants on his soon-famous "point-to-point" walks through Washington's Rock Creek Park. "Over, under or through," Teddy called out to sweating hikers clambering over boulders and through muddy streams, "*never* around!" It would be a watchword for Roosevelt's style of governance. Commenting on the president's boundless enthusiasm, the British minister reportedly said: "You must remember that Theodore is really a six-year-old boy." Not many six-year-old boys read *Anna Karenina* as they bed down on a saddle under the Dakota stars, or headed off in hot pursuit of outlaws. Nor are many six-year-olds conversant with Icelandic *sagas*. TR was the most widely read and genuinely scholarly president to occupy the White House since Thomas Jefferson. (Despite this, TR vocally denounced the Sage of Monticello for his neglect of the navy.) Still, the British minister did capture TR's exuberance, his boyish *love* of action and adventure.

The Roosevelt family, too, made a great splash in TR's White House years. Theodore Jr., Archie, Kermit, and Quentin were always getting in scrapes. One time, Archie and Kermit brought their pony, Algonquin, upstairs in the White House elevator. They wanted to charm their sick brother, Quentin. Another time they loosed a four-foot king snake on a cabinet meeting. The country watched with wonder as the Roosevelts sent their children to Washington, D.C.'s public schools. There, the children of a president sat next to the children of milk wagon drivers, seamstresses, and postal workers. The capital's public schools were then segregated, a fact that TR deplored in a Message to Congress:

> It is out of the question for our people as a whole permanently to rise by treading down any of their own number. The free public school, the chance for each boy or girl to get a good elementary education, lies at the foundation of our whole political situation. . . . It is as true for the Negro as for the white man.[73]

TR's daughter by his first wife was known throughout the country as *Princess* Alice. Headstrong and spoiled, she defiantly quit school and took up smoking. When friends pleaded with him to rein her in, Theodore, exasperated, responded: "I can govern the country or I can govern Alice. I cannot possibly do both." Over it all, First Lady Edith Kermit Carow Roosevelt presided with intelligence, grace, and patience. A friend once remarked to Mrs. Roosevelt how surprised she was to see all the tusks, heads, and hides TR had proudly displayed at Sagamore Hill, the family's Oyster Bay, New York, home. Mrs. Roosevelt tolerantly showed her friend the only stuffed animal she allowed in the dining room. It was *behind* the chair of the lady of the house, where she would never have to look at it. Mrs. Roosevelt made sure the White House was a genuine cultural center. In the days before Washington, D.C. had any but vaudeville theaters, this was an important achievement.

IV. TR and the Square Deal

Few of America's leaders in 1901 could claim to know *How the Other Half Lives.* That was the title of an 1890 book of photos and text by Roosevelt's friend Jacob Riis. It catalogued the truly deplorable conditions in which hundreds of thousands of slum dwellers lived. Especially poignant were Riis's pictures of homeless little boys. Theodore Roosevelt, almost alone among Republicans, knew. He had investigated slum conditions on excursions through Brooklyn with Riis when he was a police commissioner. His father had founded the Children's Aid Society. The elder Roosevelt had spent Sunday evenings for many years reading stories to the impoverished newsboys. He made sure they had at least one hot, nourishing meal that day.

What TR already knew, the country was soon to learn, when *McClure's Magazine* began the series called "The Shame of the Cities." Writer Lincoln Steffens appealed for reform of the municipal corruption that rested on a rotting foundation of slums. TR called many of the progressive writers who constantly dug up stories of want and wrongdoing "muckrakers," and warned against a fixed focus on what was wrong in society. Nonetheless, he also spearheaded reform.

Teddy was well-born. His family had made millions in glass and real estate. He could "ride to hounds" in the fox hunts the social elite of Long Island thoroughly enjoyed, but then Teddy would ride the fourteen miles back to Oyster Bay to avoid spending the night in the "intolerable companionship" of the *Four Hundred.** He criticized vain rich people whom he accused of living "lives of ignoble ease."[74]

* The Four Hundred was shorthand for the number of prominent names that appeared in the Social Register, a listing of the best-connected, usually wealthiest New Yorkers of TR's day.

Rough Rider Theodore Roosevelt. *As assistant secretary of the Navy, Theodore Roosevelt prepared the fleet for war with Spain. Then, he volunteered for duty in Cuba. He raised a regiment of his friends. It was an eclectic group of Ivy League athletes, society swells, and rough-hewn cowboys he had befriended in the Dakota Territory. TR's "crowded hour" at San Juan Hill made his reputation and provided the launching pad for his national political career.*

Jane Addams. *She was "beautiful with virtue." Miss Addams dedicated her life to serving the poor at Hull House, amid the slums of Chicago. Once, when distraught firemen begged her to authorize them to shoot horses badly burned in a fire, Jane Addams gave the order. She rode with them to the stables, bearing only the moral authority of the community's respect. She lent her great prestige to Theodore Roosevelt's Bull Moose candidacy for the White House in 1912, but she broke with TR over U.S. entry into World War I.*

TR as president. *Roosevelt was the youngest man ever to serve as president. He dominated the political landscape, reveling in the White House as his Bully Pulpit. He was a trustbuster who nonetheless warned against too much muckraking. He "made the dirt fly" in Panama, wielded the big stick in diplomacy, and won the Nobel Peace Prize for settling the Russo-Japanese War. The antics of Roosevelt's large and lively family thrilled American newspaper readers. With the return of his Great White Fleet from its round-the-world voyage in 1909, TR voluntarily turned over the keys to the White House to his friend, William Howard Taft. It was a move he, Taft, and the country would soon regret.*

Taft and Wilson at the 1913 inauguration. *"Vote for Roosevelt, pray for Taft, but bet on Wilson." That was the sound advice given to the young Harvard professor, Samuel Eliot Morison. The bitter split of TR and Taft, once the dearest of friends, splintered the Republican majority and guaranteed the election of New Jersey's Democratic governor, Woodrow Wilson. Wilson's first term saw many progressive measures passed through Congress, eliciting strong approval from many reformers. In foreign policy, however, Wilson was frustrated in Mexico. He labored tirelessly but ultimately without success to keep America out of the Great War in Europe.*

TR fearlessly took on the all-powerful railroads. With the Elkins Act (1903), rebates to favored customers were outlawed. This was the very technique that John D. Rockefeller of Standard Oil had exploited so effectively. Rockefeller would demand and receive from railroads great rebates based on the huge volume of business he gave them. This comparative advantage over other independent oil producers helped Rockefeller drive them into bankruptcy. Rockefeller excelled at this "cutthroat competition." When Congress balked at passage of the reform bill, TR let it be known that Rockefeller was using his vast wealth to "influence" wavering senators. Congress had little choice but to give the president his reform.[75]

Around this time Upton Sinclair, another muckraking journalist, published *The Jungle.* He hoped it would lead Americans to embrace Marxism. It didn't. But it did lead readers to demand reform of the meatpacking industry Sinclair so vividly exposed. Sinclair wrote of the rats, filth, diseased cattle, and swine that went into the canning process. He even described workers who fell into the open vats: "Sometimes they would be overlooked for days, till all but the bones of them had gone out to the world as Durham's Pure Leaf Lard."[76]

Humorist Finley Peter Dunne's Irish character, *Mr. Dooley*, commented on the wild success of Sinclair's novel. "It was a sweetly sintimintal little volume to be r-read durin' Lent."[77] And Mr. Dooley's description of the president at his breakfast table had the country rollicking. "There was Tiddy, readin' the book and, whoop, all iv a sudden, he jumps up an' flings his sausages outer the winder, yellin' 'I'm p'isoned, I'm p'isoned!'"

The result of all this agitation was the Pure Food and Drug Act, which Teddy signed with relish. Now, clearly, TR had broken away from the philosophy of Senator Mark Hanna. Hanna told his fellow Ohioans they could do no better than to "stand pat" with the GOP.[78] Theodore, Rough Rider, cowboy, big game hunter, was not about to *stand pat* for anything he thought was morally wrong.

Stand-patters in the Republican Party hoped someone would rescue them from their cowboy president. Referring to his accession through assassination, they called him *His Accidency* and pleaded with Senator Mark Hanna to fight TR for the 1904 Republican nomination for president.

Senator Hanna seemed willing enough, but his untimely death left the Stand-patters without a horse in the race.

Hoping to attract support among disaffected business leaders in 1904, Democrats turned their backs on Bryan and radicalism and nominated Wall Street lawyer Alton B. Parker. Without public opinion polling, TR could not be sure how he stood with the American people. He worried that the Democrats might beat him by clever politicking. "They are trying to carry New York by putting Cleveland on the stump and keeping out Bryan; and Indiana by putting Bryan on the stump and keeping out Cleveland. . . ."[79] For his part, Teddy steered a steady course between the extremes of both parties. He explained his viewpoint: "My action on labor should always be considered with my action as regards capital, and both are reducible to my favorite formula—a square deal for every man."[80]

Americans obviously approved of the Square Deal. They returned TR to the White House by a landslide. Roosevelt won 7,623,486 popular votes (56.4 percent) and 336 electoral votes to Parker's 5,077,911 popular votes (37.6 percent) and only 140 electoral votes. Parker won only the states of the old Confederacy plus Kentucky and Maryland. Of particular significance in this race was the strong vote pulled by Eugene V. Debs, the Socialist candidate, who polled 402,283 popular votes (3 percent).

Theodore Roosevelt had just turned forty-six when he was elected overwhelmingly to a full term in his own right. He had every reason to feel that his leadership was vindicated. Then, at the height of his power, he committed a grave error: he announced "under no circumstances" would he be a candidate for reelection in 1908. It was a decision he and millions of his countrymen would come to regret bitterly.

Surely one of TR's most enduring achievements was his passion for conservation. No American president since Washington had spent as much time in the wilderness. Even as a young man, TR had written authoritatively on American birds. Hunting, hiking, rowing, riding: these were all second nature to this intrepid adventurer. He worked closely with his friend, Gifford Pinchot, the U.S. chief forester, to set aside vast tracts of woodlands as national parks.

At the time, most other politicians formed an Amen Corner for the blinkered views of the speaker of the House. Joe Cannon growled "not one cent for scenery!"[81]* Theodore personally intervened with Speaker Cannon to save his National Reclamation Bill for irrigating arid western lands.[82] He appointed an Inland Waterways Commission in 1907 to study the complex interrelation of rivers, soil, waterpower, and transportation. The same year, he convened a White House conference on conservation, an unprecedented act that gave the subject a big boost in publicity.[83]

Where he could not get the desired legislation from a grudging Congress, Teddy would act by Executive Order—as he did in creating national wildlife sanctuaries. And when neither route was possible, Teddy could *preach* conservation. For this, especially, he regarded the White House as his "Bully Pulpit." Teddy's vigor, his enthusiasm, his integrity, and his powerful intellect helped keep Americans excited about the Bully Pulpit concept. Later in the twentieth century, as we shall see, Americans became less eager to be "preached to" from presidents mounting the Bully Pulpit.

As president, Roosevelt used the bully pulpit to raise public concerns about what we today call family values.[84] Studying government reports and census statistics, President Roosevelt noted that the birthrate of Americans was dropping for the first time since independence.[85] He comprehended the challenges to family life that were presented by the new industrial order. He viewed economic issues in terms of their impact on the family. As he would later say: "I do not wish to see this country a country of selfish prosperity where those who enjoy the material prosperity think only of the selfish gratification of their own desires, and are content to import from abroad not only their art, not only their literature, but even their babies."[86]

Roosevelt practiced what he preached. Not only did he have a large and boisterous family, but his and Edith's family was a "blended family," combining his daughter from his first marriage with *five* children from his second. Even in the White House, the president always made time to romp with his lively brood. More important, he obviously took joy in their life together.

* This is the Republican speaker for whom the Cannon House Office Building in Washington, D.C., is named.

V. Wielding the Big Stick

"I have always been fond of the West African proverb: 'Speak softly and carry a big stick, you will go far,'" TR had said.[87] He proved it again and again during his White House years.

No sooner had he inherited the office, however, than President Roosevelt faced a great moral crisis over U.S. policy in the Philippines. Anti-imperialists got hold of an army report of U.S. atrocities toward Filipino guerillas. What kind of "civilizing" and "Christianizing" was this, they demanded to know. TR had tried to keep the reports from coming out—always a mistake in Washington. But when the country was sufficiently horrified by the lurid stories, TR counterattacked.

He gave his close friend, Senator Henry Cabot Lodge, the army files that documented what the Filipino *insurrectos* had done to captured Americans. Our soldiers suffered greatly. They had their eyes gouged. They had been disemboweled, slow-roasted, some even castrated and gagged with their own testicles. Lodge's cool, dispassionate cataloguing of these horrors created a sensation: "Perhaps the action of the American soldier is not entirely without provocation."[88]

Fortunately for the United States, the Philippine insurrection was even then collapsing. More fortunate, still, was the dispatch of the able Ohio lawyer, William Howard Taft, to Manila as governor of the Philippines. Brimming with genuine goodwill, the 350-pound Taft brought intelligence and humanity to his task. He referred to the Filipinos as his "little brown brothers." Although rudely condescending to our ears, that sentiment reassured Americans and Filipinos that our rule in the island territory would be humane and temporary. Soon, major land reform in the islands created a rising middle class. U.S. soldiers still griped, "He may be a brother of Big Bill Taft / But he ain't even a [cousin] of mine!"[89] Taft's success in the Philippines opened up wider vistas to his considerable talents. Americans chuckled at the story of a supposed exchange of telegrams between Taft and TR.

Hearing reports that the indispensable governor was seriously ill, TR was said to have cabled Manila:

TR: Alarmed you're unwell. Report.

TAFT: Am Fine. Rode 25 miles horseback.

TR: How is horse?

Soon, Teddy's gaze shifted north. Gold strikes in Alaska's Klondike region and Canada's Yukon Territory made a boundary dispute between the United States and Canada especially contentious. Canadian claims to a greater portion of the Alaskan panhandle were something utterly novel, and TR was having none of it. "This Canadian claim is entirely modern," he complained in March 1902. He showed friends Canadian maps that twenty years before had marked the boundary just where he now said it was. "If we suddenly claimed part of Nova Scotia you would not arbitrate," he said to a British friend.[90] He felt so strongly about it that he threatened to send in U.S. troops to reinforce the border. Instead, he sent Supreme Court Justice Oliver Wendell Holmes to Britain with an emphatic personal letter to underscore his determination not to yield.

Sir Wilfred Laurier, Canada's first prime minister from Quebec, sought a way out through mediation. Sir Wilfred admitted he needed "to save his face."[91] The British, worried about the rising naval power of Germany, made sure their representative on the boundary commission ruled in favor of the Americans. The Canadians howled, but TR won an important victory.

France's West Indian colony of Martinique was considered by some to be a veritable paradise. St. Pierre, the island's capital, was called the "Paris of the Caribbean." Americans and Europeans therefore reacted with horror when, on 8 May 1902, Mount Pélée erupted, covering the beautiful town with lava and ash and killing twenty-nine thousand people. Only two survivors were rescued.

Philippe Jean Bunau-Varilla was an engineer for the French company that had gone bankrupt trying to dig a canal through the Isthmus of Panama. He kept an eye out for volcanoes. He had come to Washington to try to persuade the Americans to select the Panamanian route for a canal and to *reject* the Nicaraguan route preferred by many. If the Americans chose the Panama district of Colombia, the canal would be further *away* from the mainland United States, true, but it would also bail out Bunau-

Varilla's French investors. Nicaragua was eager to have the Americans build their canal through that impoverished country.

But Nicaragua also had a volcano. When Bunau-Varilla saw a picture of Mount Momotombo on a Nicaraguan postage stamp, he made sure every member of Congress got a *personal* copy. Even Nature cooperated when Mount Momotombo sent up a fiery jet of lava—just in time for the Panama-Nicaragua Senate debate.[92]

Everything seemed ready when Secretary of State John Hay successfully negotiated a treaty with Colombia's foreign minister, Tomás Herrán. Under the Hay-Herrán Treaty, quickly ratified by the U.S. Senate in early 1903, the United States would pay Colombia $10 million outright and $250,000 annually to lease the canal. Herrán was a cultured, honorable advocate. But when the Hay-Herrán Treaty was rejected by the Colombian senate, TR was outraged. He suspected the Colombians were squeezing the *Yanquis* for more money. Colombia's dictator José Marroquín might be trying to wait out the Americans until October 1904, when the French lease would run out. Then, he could gain a major share of the $40 million the United States was prepared to pay French stockholders for their rights.[93] Privately, Teddy fumed that the "blackmailers of Bogotá" should not be permitted to block the progress of the world.

Panamanians were also upset. They had revolted fifty-three times in fifty-seven years against Colombian rule. Now, it seemed, the faraway dictator in Bogotá and his corrupt senate were about to derail their best opportunity in years. In the White House, TR met with Bunau-Varilla. TR probably did *not* encourage Bunau-Varilla to incite a Panamanian revolt against Colombia, but he doubtless did nothing to *discourage* such a revolt. Bunau-Varilla soon cabled his friends in Panama City that the USS *Nashville* would conveniently arrive off Colón on 2 November 1903. That was assurance enough for the small band of Panamanian rebels. Roosevelt instructed Hay to grant official U.S. diplomatic recognition to the new Panamanian Republic on 6 November 1903, just three days after the not wholly spontaneous revolt took place.[94]

Bunau-Varilla was authorized to act *for* the new republic in quickly renegotiating a canal treaty. Panamanians later claimed that the French citizen had conceded far too much and gained too little in his rush to claim the $40 million prize for his French stockholders. Panamanians would ever after complain that the ten-mile "Canal Zone" over which the United States would exercise sovereignty "in perpetuity" was an intolerable infringement on their national dignity. They would charge that John Hay had so hurried the negotiations that Bunau-Varilla even had to use the Hay family signet ring to "seal" the document. Europeans sneered at Teddy's "cowboy diplomacy." Many in the United States denounced the "indecent haste" with which Teddy had acted.

"Piracy."

"Scandal."

"The most discreditable incident in our history."

These were just some of the criticisms lodged against TR's highhanded action.[95] But Teddy was having none of it. He had resolved to "make the dirt fly" in Panama. He later reflected on it as one of his greatest achievements: "If I had followed the traditional, conservative methods, I would have submitted a dignified State paper of probably 200 pages to Congress and the debates on it would have been going on yet [in 1911]; but I took the Canal Zone and let Congress debate: and while the debate goes on the Canal does also."[96]

Later, when Woodrow Wilson's administration expressed regrets and agreed to pay Colombia $25 million in damages, opponents called the payment *canalimony*.[97]

As loud as TR was over Panama, he exercised *quiet* diplomacy with Germany over Venezuela. When the British and Germans threatened a joint occupation of the South American republic because of a chronic failure to pay just debts, TR let the German ambassador know that any European occupation of an independent nation in the Western Hemisphere would be a violation of the Monroe Doctrine. Any such violation, TR said, would *surely* mean war with the United States. When the British backed away, the Kaiser felt exposed. Roosevelt was careful *not* to let the confrontation leak out. He would give the Kaiser "the satisfaction of feeling that his dignity and reputation in the face of the world were safe," TR later wrote.[98] Thus, Roosevelt showed his subtle understanding of the many uses of diplomacy. The frequent indebtedness of Latin American nations led to a constant threat of foreign intervention. To forestall such assaults on the Monroe Doctrine, Theodore Roosevelt asserted his own belief that the United States might, from time to time, be called upon to intervene in order to defend the hemisphere. This "Roosevelt Corollary" to the Monroe Doctrine was highly controversial in its own day and has since been abandoned by the United States But it did ensure no foreign interventions in this continent during the Roosevelt presidency.

Roosevelt faced another foreign crisis when a North African desert chieftain called the *Raisuli* took hostage the U.S. consul, Ion Perdicaris. The Raisuli was trying thereby to exert pressure against a rival Arab ruler. TR instructed Secretary of State John Hay to send this terse message: "We want Perdicaris alive or Raisuli dead." He got Perdicaris alive.

Roosevelt's reputation for wielding the big stick strengthened his hand as a peacemaker. When Japan smashed the Russian fleet in a sudden, overwhelming attack in 1904, a major war broke out. TR called both parties to New Hampshire in 1905 and hammered out the Treaty of Portsmouth to end the Russo-Japanese War. His efforts made him the first American to win the Nobel Peace Prize.[99]

Roosevelt's last years in power were stained by one ineradicable act of injustice on his part. Black troopers from the army were assigned to Brownsville, Texas, at the height of racial tension. When a riot broke out in 1906 and some civilians were killed, accused troopers refused to step forward, and their brothers refused to point them out. TR thought the soldiers were showing a loyalty to race over their duty to the country and the army. He ordered the dishonorable discharge of the entire company of 167 black soldiers. As someone who knew the ugly truth of race relations at the time, who even loudly condemned lynchings, how could TR have expected the black troopers to have confidence in the military or civilian justice systems of the day? Teddy is justly famous as an advocate of civil rights. In fact, he had sent his own children to an integrated public school on Long Island. Still, his Brownsville judgment was a cruel and unjust act.*

President Roosevelt constantly sought ways to dramatize American

---

* President Richard Nixon in 1972 signed legislation to restore the discharged troopers to pay status, and President Bill Clinton expunged the dishonorable discharges. Both worthy measures were long overdue.

naval power. In 1905, he sent a squadron to France to bring back the body of naval hero John Paul Jones. Jones's body had been interred in a Paris cemetery since his death in 1792. With a flair for the historic, Roosevelt presided over an impressive ceremony at the Naval Academy in April 1906. There, before a glittering international audience, he marked the return of Jones's remains to America. France sent a large portion of their fleet to the Chesapeake Bay to honor the Revolutionary War captain.[100]

Approaching the end of his presidency, TR resolved to brandish his big stick one last time. He sent the large, modern fleet of U.S. battleships on an unprecedented round the world cruise. The Great White Fleet—so called because the ships' hulls were painted white—showed the flag in dozens of foreign ports.*

Congress balked at the distance and the expense of the voyage. So Teddy used his allotted funds to send the fleet to Yokahama, Japan. Then he forced Congress to pay to bring the Great White Fleet home!

The trip was a public relations bonanza for the United States, while demonstrating to the crowned heads of Europe and Japan all the muscle of the brash young republic. At a time of growing Anglo-German naval rivalry, TR forcefully demonstrated that the United States was not a country to be trifled with on the high seas.

Roosevelt was determined to choose his own successor. Throughout his second term, he had come increasingly to rely on his loyal and efficient secretary of war, William Howard Taft. Taft would have preferred to be chief justice, but TR and Mrs. Taft had other ideas. The Republican Party was happy to have the popular, jovial Ohioan at the head of its ticket. Democrats again chose the Great Commoner, William Jennings Bryan. Older, now, but not notably wiser, Bryan mounted a *third* vigorous campaign for the White House.

Taft benefited from the great popularity of TR and the progressive record of his administration. When the votes were counted in 1908, Taft bested the

* "Unlike the Army, the Navy had a long tradition of accepting blacks as crew members. Moreover the very nature of naval service militated against any effort to segregate blacks and whites." –from *The Navy,* edited by Rear Admiral W. J. Holland, Jr., USN (Ret.), p. 47. While true enough, many black sailors were restricted to ratings like steward and mess cook for too long.

Democrat Bryan by 7,678,908 votes (321 electoral votes) to 6,409,104 for the Prairie populist. Perennial Socialist candidate Eugene Victor Debs remained strong, with 420,793 votes. Most of Debs votes, it was agreed, came from the Democratic ranks, while the Prohibition candidate took 253,840 votes, mostly from the Republicans. Bryan responded to his loss with good humor. He compared himself to the town drunk who was tossed out of the saloon not once, or twice, but three times. "I'm beginning to get the idea," called the disheveled man from a mud puddle, "that you all don't want me *in* there!"

As Taft prepared his smooth transition, TR insisted on one more headline grabber as president. When he issued new fitness regulations for the army, some of the desk-bound brass loudly complained that they were too demanding. Nobody can be expected to ride ninety miles in three days, they said. "Nonsense," TR said, taking up the challenge. He assured skeptics he could ride ninety miles *in one day*! With just weeks remaining in office, the fifty-year-old Teddy mounted a succession of horses and took off in the dead of winter for Warrenton, Virginia. His faithful military aide, Major Archie Butt, and a small contingent of hardy souls joined him. He stopped at Warrenton, shook hands all around, and addressed the schoolchildren there. Then he remounted and galloped back to Washington. The presidential party returned to the capital after dark. The ice-covered roads made riding treacherous. Rejecting calls to dismount, TR charged on. When they reached the White House, Edith Roosevelt greeted the ice-covered party and brought them in for a hot meal and warm hospitality.[101]

Reporters who asked the outgoing—very *outgoing*—president to speculate on the role of former presidents of the United States got no detached and philosophical comment from TR. ". . . [So] far as it is concerned with *this* president, you can say that the United States need do nothing with the ex-president. I will do all the doing that is going to be done myself."[102] Roosevelt exulted in his nearly eight-year stand at the helm of the ship of state: "While president, I have *been* president—emphatically."[103]

Wistfully, Henry Adams looked across Lafayette Park from his Victorian mansion. He scanned the White House that Theodore Roosevelt had transformed. "This old house will seem dull and sad when my Theodore has gone," he said.[104] Taft was inaugurated 4 March 1909, with all pomp and circumstance in the middle of a blinding snowstorm. Theodore wanted to give his man some time to put his own stamp on the presidency. He cooperatively announced he was heading to Africa for a hunting safari.

Not everyone was sorry to see him go. One critic wrote: "Mr. Roosevelt is to leave us for awhile, and certainly the manner of his going is appropriate. Shots will sound and blood will flow and his knife will find its living hilt. The . . . skins of the kings of the jungle will dry upon his tent pegs." But when he came back, TR would resume his role as America's "Dominant Note and Big Noise," this acerbic observer said.[105] Teddy's old Wall Street adversary, J. Pierpont Morgan, is said to have offered this toast to the departing president's trip: "America expects every lion to do his duty."*

VI. The Taft Interlude

America was ready for a breather. William Howard Taft's 1908 election victory was even stronger than TR's vote of 1904 had been. Americans embraced their genial new president with respect and affection. A favorite story of the time said the president stood up on a streetcar to give *three* ladies his seat.[106] But Taft was highly intelligent, loyal, and able. As with any period of revolutionary activity, there is the trailblazer who marks out the new course to be followed. Then there is the necessary period of consolidation. Taft was a consolidator. He enacted *more* of the Roosevelt program than TR had been able to do.[107] During his four years in office, Taft's administration would prosecute *twice* as many antitrust cases as Roosevelt had done in seven and a half years.[108] This was no easy task, since the power of the trusts was daunting. At this time, U.S. Steel *alone* had a greater budget than the entire U.S. government![109] Taft got little credit for this among reformers. They saw him leisurely swinging a golf club in the company of wealthy friends. It was hard to see him as a trust-buster.

An early conflict caused a serious rift between the Taft administration and TR's conservationist supporters. While Teddy was slaying wild beasts in Africa, his great friend, Gifford Pinchot, leveled a serious charge against

* The witty "Jupiter" of Wall Street was referring, of course, to the famous signal sent by Lord Nelson before the Battle of Trafalgar in 1805: "England expects every man will do his duty."

his boss, Richard Ballinger. Ballinger was Taft's secretary of the interior. Pinchot, America's chief forester, charged the secretary with corruption. Worse, he suggested the secretary had given away federal lands to a syndicate controlled by Benjamin Guggenheim and TR's old nemesis, J. Pierpont Morgan. Congress cleared Ballinger of wrongdoing, but the reformers sided with Pinchot.[110] Nonetheless, Taft dismissed Pinchot, creating a rift between himself and TR's partisans.

Teddy's return from Africa was delayed by his appointment as President Taft's personal representative to the funeral of Britain's King Edward VII. As a *former* head of state, TR was placed behind all the crowned heads of Europe as they marched through London streets. Many Americans thought it ridiculous to have their Teddy give place to the grand dukes of what Winston Churchill called "pumpernickel principalities." But that was royal protocol. No matter. Teddy stole the show just by showing up. He was the bride at every wedding, goes the saying, and the corpse at every wake. He met many of the crowned heads, but he *avoided* Churchill, then Britain's first lord of the admiralty.* In an incredible example of pot-and-kettling, TR thought Churchill a questionable self-promoter![111]

Following the brilliant diplomatic success of Roosevelt's Great White Fleet steaming around the globe, President Taft sent a squadron of battleships on a goodwill tour of England in 1910. There, U.S. Admiral Sims got carried away in a speech in London's Guildhall, pledging that if Britain were ever threatened, the British could "count upon every man, every dollar, every ship, and every drop of blood of their kinsmen across the ocean."[112] The Germans were outraged (but were they *planning* to threaten Britain?); Irish Americans and German Americans certainly did not consider themselves *kinsmen* to the British. The president, faultless in his intent, had to issue a stern rebuke of his admiral.** In America, president and Congress make foreign policy, not admirals.

---

* Churchill's title made him responsible for the Royal Navy, the greatest fleet on earth. TR and Churchill should have had many things to talk about.

** Despite this *contretemps,* Admiral William S. Sims was destined for great leadership in WWI. He had a quick mind and a fine sense of humor. He once suggested an improvement on the French use of carrier pigeons for military communications: crossbreed the pigeons with parrots so we wouldn't have to write the messages!

To put his own mark on the presidency, Taft tried to lower tariffs with Canada. It was a generous, wise move (and the precursor to Ronald Reagan's North American Free Trade Agreement—NAFTA). Seven million Canadians would gain access to a market of ninety-two million Americans.[113] Poor Taft's good deed did not go unpunished, however. Canadians were still bruised from TR's big sticking over the Alaskan boundary dispute of 1902. When the Democratic speaker of the House, Missouri's Champ Clark, spoke in favor of the treaty, he said he was for it because he wanted to see the Stars and Stripes flying over "every foot of North America."[114] This incredibly oafish statement caused a furor across the border. Canadian conservatives raised a war cry of "No Truck or Trade with the Yankees!" They trounced the great French-Canadian prime minister, Sir Wilfred Laurier, in a special election in 1911.[115] Worse, TR had campaigned vigorously *against* the treaty as a sellout to the trusts.[116] It was shabby treatment for America's great Canadian friend.

Taft suffered another diplomatic setback when a dispute broke out between the United States and czarist Russia. American Jews who had come to the United States from Russia often prospered under American freedom. Now, as American citizens, they returned to their little *shtetls* and shared their new-earned wealth with impoverished relatives in the Old Country. Russia, bitterly anti-Semitic, tried to require that these naturalized American citizens apply all over again to leave the country. Americans were indignant at this insult to our sovereignty. Congress cancelled a U.S.-Russian trade agreement. The Russian *Duma* retaliated by banning all U.S. Jews from visiting their benighted country.[117] It was an ugly controversy. Taft was, again, faultless. But it was also true that U.S.-Russian relations, which had been so good for so long, collapsed on his watch.

VII. Unsinkable, Unthinkable

It's not surprising that pressures should have risen at the White House during Taft's term. America was undergoing rapid change. Following the Wright Brothers' historic flight in 1903, an aviation industry was born. Henry Ford was putting ever-more Americans on the roads with his *Model T*. (Ford was a pioneer in cutting costs by mass production, putting thousands of cars on

America's poorly paved roads. Critics said you could have any color you want, so long as its black. Ford soon provided consumer choice on color, too.) Along with this increased mobility came danger. Highway fatalities for 1911 rose to 1,291.[118]

Theodore Roosevelt thought he had the answer to this quickening pace of change. He delivered a far-ranging speech in Osawatomie, Kansas, in August 1910, in which he called for more regulation of corporations and railroads, a graduated income tax, reform of banks, labor legislation, and direct primaries. He called his program the New Nationalism.[119] It marked a sharp departure from Taft administration policies, and it split the GOP. Democrats, not surprisingly, took over Congress that November.

Taft felt the burden greatly. So did Major Archie Butt of Georgia, Taft's loyal military aide. When he saw TR upon his return from Europe, the gallant Southerner remarked how the old Rough Rider had changed: "He is bigger, broader, capable of greater good or greater evil, than when he left."[120] Major Butt was deeply devoted to *both* Theodore Roosevelt and William Howard Taft. To give Archie Butt a much-needed break, President Taft sent him on a diplomatic mission to the Vatican. He could relax in Europe afterward and enjoy a homeward cruise on the maiden voyage of the White Star Line's luxurious new liner, the Royal Mail Steamer *Titanic*.

The *Titanic* represented the latest in marine technology. Her steel compartments and watertight doors led many in the press to label her "unsinkable."[121] Her passenger list for her first voyage from Southampton to New York read like the Social Register. Some of the first-class suites went for as much as $4,000–$50,000 in today's dollars.

The magnificent ship struck an iceberg on the moonless night of 14 April 1912. The collision occurred at 11:40 p.m. She sank in less than three hours, at 2:20 a.m. At the end, the ship's orchestra played "Nearer My God to Thee" to keep doomed passengers from panicking. It was not the greatest maritime disaster in history, but it was surely the most sensational.* John Jacob Astor

* For example, 9,343 people died on 30 January 1945, when the German liner *Wilhelm Gustloff* was sunk in the Baltic Sea by a Soviet submarine. The liner was carrying wounded sailors, soldiers, and civilians. They were fleeing from Soviet troops advancing into what was then East Prussia. (Online source: http://in.rediff.com/news/2005/may/09spec1.htm.)

and Benjamin Guggenheim, Mr. and Mrs. Isidore Strauss, and many other very wealthy British and American passengers died. Despite this, the heavy loss of life among third-class passengers—mostly immigrants crammed into the steerage compartments—led to widespread denunciations of privilege in the Yellow Press. In all, more than 1,500 passengers died. A Canadian newspaper estimated at $191 million the net worth of just twelve of the leading first class passengers who were lost.[122] (That's $2.3 billion in today's dollars.) Owners of the *Titanic* were rightly criticized for the wholly inadequate number of lifeboats provided. J. Pierpont Morgan's holding company owned the White Star Line and was thus ultimately responsible.[123]

Instead, most press criticism at the time focused on Bruce Ismay, managing director of the White Star Line. Ismay had quietly stepped into a lifeboat at the instruction of a crew member. Many thought Ismay, like Captain Smith, should have "gone down with his ship."[124]

By all accounts, Major Archie Butt faced death in the icy waters with heroic resolution. He and others of the men of the *Titanic* brought credit to themselves by the stoic way in which they gave preference to women and children. Captain Arthur Henry Rostron, master of the SS *Carpathia*, steamed at a top speed of seventeen and one-half knots through treacherous waters to arrive at the disaster scene. Without Captain Rostron's heroic rescue dash, few of the 712 survivors would have lived in the freezing temperatures. Winston Churchill reflected that "the strict observance of the great traditions of the sea towards women & children reflects nothing but honor on our civilization."[125]

Not entirely. The testimony of Sir Cosmo Duff Gordon at a London inquest revealed he had gotten into a boat designed for forty but which held only twelve. Worse, Sir Cosmo offered each of the seamen in the boat a promissory note for £5 (approximately $312 in today's money). On the witness stand, he maintained that the payment was only offered to reimburse poor seamen who had lost everything when the great ship went down. But critics charged that Sir Cosmo's payment was a bribe to keep the seamen from going back to pull dying passengers out of the frigid waters.

---

* *Lady* Duff Gordon—Lucille—suffered no lasting damage to her reputation. She opened a stylish dress shop in Paris that thrived. The French love a little *soupcon* of scandal.

Sir Cosmo's reputation, like Ismay's, never recovered. And they seemed a symbol of the callous indifference of the rich to the plight of the poor.[126]*

President and Mrs. Taft were devastated by brave Archie's loss. They had loved him as a son. The president immediately ordered an ice patrol. Soon, U.S. Coast Guard cutters took on the responsibility for safety of life at sea. Mrs. Taft appealed to the women of America to contribute to a *Titanic* memorial dedicated to the men who gave up their lives so that women and children might live. The handsome monument was erected on the banks of the Potomac.*

VIII. A Bull Moose on the Loose: The Election of 1912

Taft tried hard to avoid a break with his dear friend, Theodore. "I have had a hard time," he wrote the former president. "I have been conscientiously trying to carry out *your* policies."[127] Indeed he had. By early 1912, however, many in the Republican Party were convinced they had to have new leadership if they were to win the White House. The loss of Congress to the Democrats had been a terrible shock to the GOP. Many blamed Taft, even though their party had had an abnormally long run in control of the legislative branch.

"My hat is in the ring, the fight is on and I am stripped to the buff," TR finally told supporters in February 1912.[128] He would challenge the president of his own choice for the Republican presidential nomination. Teddy's insurgent campaign picked up some important endorsements. TR gained support from Jim Garfield, son of the slain president, and Dan Hanna, the late Senator Mark Hanna's son. Most significant was the fact that these two men hailed from the president's home state of Ohio.[129] Taft supporters were called Republican regulars or the Old Guard. Roosevelt's backers—*progressives*—heaped scorn on them. (But hadn't young Roosevelt and Lodge declined to join the "Mugwumps" in 1884, aligning themselves with the *regulars* of the day?) In the middle of one pro-Roosevelt rally, some Old Guard Republicans became dispirited. "Oh hell, what's the use?" they said. "Even babies cry for

* The *Titanic* memorial still stands in Washington, D.C., although it was moved to make way for the Kennedy Center.

Roosevelt. He is the whole three rings, ringmaster and elephant. Maybe he will let us into the show if we carry water for the elephant."[130]

Most despondent of all was William Howard Taft. He had not wanted to run for president. He did so only out of loyalty to his beloved friend, Theodore. He never relished political combat the way Teddy did. Now Teddy was attacking him most cruelly. "Roosevelt was my closest friend," Taft told a reporter on the presidential train. With that, he dissolved into tears.[131] But fight he would when TR attacked the independent judiciary. Taft became convinced that Teddy was a menace to the system of checks and balances at the heart of the American system. Taft's supporters went much further, denouncing Teddy as a demagogue and *his* supporters as snake-oil salesmen.[132]

TR won most of the direct primaries held that spring. He piled up 278 delegates to Taft's 78. Wisconsin's "Fighting Bob" LaFollette, another progressive Republican, had 36 delegates. Realizing that a split in the party would only elect a Democrat, Taft's forces generously offered to withdraw in favor of a *compromise* candidate who might unite the GOP. "I'll name the compromise candidate," TR shot back: "He'll be *me*."[133]

When the regulars closed ranks behind Taft, they outmaneuvered Teddy's backers. LaFollette might have aligned with TR and carried the day, but he refused.

Mr. Dooley looked forward to the coming crackup. It will be a "combination of the Chicago fire, the Saint Bartholomew's massacre, the battle iv th' Boyne, th' life iv Jesse James, an' the night iv th' big wind."[134] When delegates whose credentials were in dispute were not allowed to vote, Teddy's forces cried *foul*. But Taft's people were using no technique TR himself had not used to secure the nomination he wanted for Taft in 1908.

Despite all that, TR's "Dutch" was up. He bitterly attacked Taft in the most personal terms. And he whipped up his troops with this appeal: we are "fearless of the future, unheeding of our individual fates; with unflinching hearts and undimmed eyes, we stand at Armageddon, and we battle for the Lord!"[135]

Armageddon? It's a little hard to believe the rhetoric nearly a century later, yet this is a classic example of how people—even highly intelligent people of undeniable integrity—can work themselves into a lather in the heat of political combat. It gets worse. TR called Taft "a fathead" with "the intellect of a guinea pig." Taft shot back: TR was a "dangerous egotist" and a "demagogue."[136]

Charging bad faith and foul play, Teddy led his delegates in a walkout from the Republican National Convention in Chicago. Several weeks later, they reconvened in the same rented hall, now calling themselves the Progressive Party. When the Progressives took the bunting off the speakers' platform, they were amazed to find that Taft's Republican floor managers had placed *barbed wire* underneath! The Republican regulars had been ready for an assault by Teddy's delegates.

TR gave the new party its name when he said he felt as fit "as a bull moose."[137] Suffragettes—as advocates of women's suffrage were known—embraced the Progressive Party's call for equal voting rights. Jane Addams of Hull House pitched in. She said: "To keep aloof from [politics] must be to lose one opportunity of sharing the life of the community."[138] So did Oscar Strauss, a leading reformer and a Jew, who outsang other Progressive delegates in a spirited version of "Onward Christian Soldiers."[139] TR's soldiers, Christian or not, marched for direct election of U.S. senators, a federal income tax (both soon to be enacted as constitutional amendments), direct primaries and initiative, referendum, and recall (several western states, notably California, would soon enact these reforms). Along with all the earnest social do-gooders, the high-minded intellectuals, and the veterans of grassroots organizing, even TR had to admit the Progressives attracted more than their share of the "lunatic fringe."[140]

Experienced pols knew what the split in the GOP meant: Democrats would win. TR knew it, too.[141]

The only question: *Which* Democrat? Incredibly, William Jennings Bryan was making his *fourth* try for the White House. Speaker of the House James Beauchamps "Champ" Clark, fresh from wrecking U.S.-Canadian relations, was a strong contender. Irish and German Americans loved anyone who gave the British lion's tail a yank. William Randolph Hearst, millionaire publisher of Yellow Journals, had spent the last decade trying to incite a war with Japan. After his unsavory role in Cuba, Hearst's newspapers ceaselessly prated on about a so-called "yellow peril" from immigration and Japanese imperialism.* Now, Hearst actually thought he might be nominated for president.

Finally, the Democrats considered Governor Woodrow Wilson of New Jersey. Wilson had been in Trenton little more than a year, but he had built a national reputation as a scholar and reforming president of Princeton University. Theodore Roosevelt respected Wilson and had actually conferred with him in Buffalo in the dark hours following McKinley's assassination. After forty-six ballots in sweltering Baltimore, the tall, angular "schoolmaster in politics" was nominated.

The fall campaign rolled on to its predetermined end. In October, TR's train pulled into Milwaukee, LaFollette's base and a hotbed of Progressive agitation. While proceeding to the auditorium where he would give another stemwinder of a speech, Teddy was shot once by a would-be assassin. Fortunately, the bullet was slowed by the thick sheaf of papers—Teddy's speech—and an eyeglass case that he carried in his vest pocket. Rejecting medical attention, Teddy mounted the podium and delivered the speech to an audience amazed at his courage and blown away by his endurance.[142]

Harvard's Samuel Eliot Morison, the great historian, cast his first vote that year. He asked a colleague how he should vote: "Vote for Roosevelt, pray for Taft, but *bet* on Wilson."[143]

That proved to be shrewd advice. Although he won only 41.9 percent of the popular vote (6,293,152), Wilson won a huge majority in the electoral college, 435. TR did something never done before or since: He came in *second* running on a third-party ticket. He garnered 4,119,207 popular votes (27.4 percent) and 88 electoral votes. Taft came in third with 3,486,333 popular votes (23.2 percent) and only 8 electoral votes. Eugene V. Debs ran again on the Socialist ticket. He campaigned vigorously in a train called "the red special." Debs won over one million votes, but carried no state. In effect, TR and Taft had knocked each other out. Wilson was elected with 110,952 *fewer* popular votes than Bryan had won in his disastrous third run for president in 1908.

* Germany's Kaiser Wilhelm II had invented the racist phrase. He had it incorporated into a painting which he showed off to every statesman who visited his palace in Berlin.

The Bull Moose Party effort of 1912 is convincing proof, if ever it was needed, that the *only* thing a third-party campaign can do is to break up the ruling coalition and elect a minority president. William Howard Taft might well have lost to Wilson anyway. His administration had been "a series of political explosions," true.[144] But most of them were not of his making. He deserved better of his country. He surely deserved better of his friend, Theodore Roosevelt.

IX. Woodrow Wilson and the New Freedom

The new president, tall and dignified, mounted the speaker's rostrum in the House of Representatives. There, on 7 April 1913, Woodrow Wilson delivered an address to a joint meeting of Congress.[145] The practice of delivering State of the Union Messages and other important speeches *in person* before the assembled lawmakers had been dropped by Thomas Jefferson more than a century earlier. Jefferson said it smacked too much of the English monarch's Speech from the Throne, but it was also the case that Jefferson was a poor public speaker, and he knew it. Wilson was a great public speaker and he knew it.

Not only did it provide a dramatic setting for the president's messages, but it ensured that the president would thenceforth take the initiative in proposing important legislation. Wilson was the first Ph.D. to win the presidency. His specialty was political science. He was determined to bring major change to the institutions of government that he had studied, taught, and written about.*

Wilson was determined as well to bring about major economic reforms. President Wilson was the first leader since Lincoln to go up to the Capitol to confer in person with members of his party.[146] Democrats now controlled both houses of Congress, but even so, success for Wilson's economic program would take hard work. Wilson succeeded in his objectives, achieving a major overhaul of the nation's banking system. The Federal

* Wilson received a *doctorate* in political science in 1886 from Johns Hopkins University in Baltimore, Md. He was the first, and to date the last, Ph.D. in the White House.

Reserve Act of 1913 divided the country into twelve districts, each with a federal reserve bank to regulate the currency and provide a modern banking system. This measure, authored by Virginia's courtly Senator Carter Glass, remains essentially unchanged to this day and counts as one of Wilson's major achievements.[147]

Wilson plowed ahead with reforms. The Underwood Tariff, sponsored by Senator Oscar Underwood of Alabama, lowered import duties by 10 percent across the board. Wilson took on the manufacturers and lobbyists and prevailed with hard bargaining. It stands as his second major achievement.[148]*

The Clayton Anti-Trust Act of 1914 was another major piece of legislation Wilson strongly backed. The act was sponsored by Alabama Congressman Henry de Lamar Clayton. Samuel Gompers, president of the American Federation of Labor, called the Clayton Act "labor's charter of freedom." Under this act, labor unions would no longer be considered "combinations in restraint of trade," as they had often been under the Sherman Anti-Trust Act of 1890. Labor was specifically allowed to engage in strikes, boycotts, and picketing, although violence against persons and property continued to be against the law. Court injunctions had been a major weapon used *against* unions in labor disputes. The Clayton Act required federal courts to use more restraint in issuing such injunctions.[149]

All did not run completely smoothly in Wilson's first term, however. It never does. Wilson had felt obliged to appoint the three times defeated Democratic presidential nominee, William Jennings Bryan, as his secretary of state. This had secured Wilson his party's nomination at Baltimore. Bryan, of course, had no qualifications to be secretary of state. (He had no qualifications to be president, either, but that is another matter.)

Bryan used the State Department as a stable for party donkeys. Even Colonel Edward M. House, President Wilson's closest advisor, admitted Bryan was "a spoilsman."[150] Bryan filled embassies and consulates with time

* Tariff issues have always loomed large in American politics. In the years before the 1913 ratification of Amendment XVI that allowed a federal income tax, the tariff was the primary means of financing the federal government.

servers and hangers-on, seriously undermining the professionalism of America's diplomatic corps at a critical time.*

Bryan horrified foreign ambassadors by banning wine at diplomatic receptions. The secretary "not only suffers for his principles and mortifies the flesh, but insists that *others* should suffer and be mortified," complained an English newspaper.[151] Worse, the secretary signed a contract to give lectures on the popular Chautauqua circuit.

The world was treated to the spectacle of an American secretary of state appearing on stage on the same bill with magicians, jugglers, and Alpine yodelers. Bryan's enthusiasm, his lack of pretense, his hearty good fellowship—these qualities had endeared him to millions. The fact that he was an outspoken evangelical Christian was significant, too. This important group of Americans often took eastern snobbery toward Bryan as condescension toward *them.*

Bryan's pacifism was sincere and constituted a major *disqualification* for high office in a time of rising international tension. Bryan believed intensely in *conciliation* treaties as instruments of statecraft. He threw himself into negotiating such treaties with as many foreign states as he could. Although there was little chance of war with either Britain or France at this stage, Bryan proceeded without hesitation to ink new agreements that required signatories to "wait a year" before even considering the use of force. Many editors found Bryan's eagerness naïve. The *Memphis Commercial-Appeal* derided Bryan's "cooling off" treaties with Switzerland, Denmark, and Uruguay: that "takes a great load off our minds. The thought of war with them was terrible."[152] Former President Theodore Roosevelt was scathing; he called Bryan "that yodeler, that human trombone."[153] Even the even-tempered former President Taft was exasperated with Bryan's simplistic approach to foreign policy. Taft wrote a friend that Bryan was showing "greater sublimity as an ass."[154]

In one important way, Woodrow Wilson distinguished himself during

* In fairness, Lincoln had allowed *his* secretary of state, William Seward, to do the same thing. Seward chose Charles Francis Adams as minister to London, an inspired choice, but many other critical postings were filled with party hacks. Lincoln, of course, had a Civil War to command his attention.

his first term. He boldly challenged the nation to live up to its founding creed when he nominated Louis D. Brandeis to the Supreme Court. Brandeis was a highly respected reformer, beloved of the Progressives. Labor loved him for his "Brandeis briefs," sociological studies that showed the often terrible impact of management decisions on the lives of workers, especially women and child laborers. Although Wilson had passed over Brandeis for a cabinet post, he had looked to him as architect of the New Freedom legislation. Now, Wilson was determined to name the first Jew ever to sit on the High Court.[155] In the face of fierce opposition, some of it anti-Semitic, Wilson backed his man and secured a signal victory for America as an open society. Indeed, this was a New Freedom.

For one group of Americans, however, Woodrow Wilson's New Freedom rang hollow. Although black Americans certainly were helped by Wilson's labor and social legislation, they found no interest among the Democrats in civil rights. As the names of the sponsors of Wilson's landmark reform legislation show, Wilson was highly dependent upon white Southern Democrats to get his program through Congress. Since most black Americans at the time were firm supporters of the party of Lincoln, the Democratic victories in Congress and the presidency meant that hundreds of black federal officeholders would be swept out.[156] One of Wilson's Georgia appointees said it bluntly: "A Negro's place is in the cornfield."[157] The president did not rebuke him.

Segregation in federal government offices was only partially reversed by Wilson, despite his personal claim of sympathy for the plight of black Americans.[158] His speech at the fiftieth anniversary of the Battle of Gettysburg made no mention of the fact that black Americans were still denied their rights as citizens of the United States. If, as the Declaration of Independence said and Lincoln reaffirmed at Gettysburg in 1863, "all men are created equal," no one listening to Wilson's forgotten Gettysburg Address of 1913 would have thought so.[159]

Worse, Wilson gave a platform to one of the worst examples of racial intolerance in American history. The movie *The Birth of a Nation* may have been a silent film, but it shouted its contempt for black people from the housetops. The epic silent movie depicted the Ku Klux Klan not as terrorists and murderers, but as freedom fighters. The movie was the first film ever screened at the White House. Wilson watched it and praised it extravagantly. "It is like writing history with lightning. My only regret is that it is all so terribly true," he enthused.[160]*

Frustrated by the slow pace of change, even by backsliding in Washington, W. E. B. Du Bois and other dedicated black and white reformers (including Jane Addams) had banded together to form the National Association for the Advancement of Colored People (NAACP). They resolved to challenge the "go along to get along" attitude they saw in Booker T. Washington's Tuskegee Machine.[161] The NAACP began its half-century fight for full equal rights for black Americans.

X. "The Lights Are Going Out . . ."

As Ellen Axson Wilson lay dying of cancer in the White House in the summer of 1914, the president was bowed down with grief. He and the first lady had been married for twenty-nine years. She was the center of his close-knit and supportive family. Aside from Mrs. Wilson, his faithful aide Joseph Tumulty, and his intimate friend and adviser, Texas "Colonel" Edward M. House, Woodrow Wilson had few people upon whom he could rely.** Wilson was described as one who loved humanity—in the abstract.[162] Wilson was aware of this trait: "I have a sense of power in dealing with men collectively which I do not feel in dealing with them singly."[163] His own very able secretary of the interior, Franklin K. Lane, said he was "clean, strong, high-minded and cold-blooded."[164] Now, with Mrs. Wilson's untimely death, there would be a terrible void in his life.

Meanwhile, in Europe death stalked the corridors of power in a very different way. In late June, Archduke Franz Ferdinand, the heir to the throne of the unsteady Austro-Hungarian Empire, paid a "goodwill" trip to

* President Ronald Reagan spoke to a Catholic men's group about *The Birth of a Nation.* The Knights of Columbus were meeting in New Haven, Conn. in 1982. The KKK's hatred encompassed not only black Americans, but also Catholics, Jews, and foreigners. Reagan told the knights that he was proud of his Hollywood movie career. "But," he said, "I have never seen that film . . . *and I never will!*" The knights erupted in loud, sustained applause.

** House was given an honorary title as colonel as an adviser to the governor of Texas.

the beautiful medieval city of Sarajevo, in the province of Bosnia-Herzegovina. Young Slavic nationalists in the province resented being ruled from distant Vienna by the Teutonic and mostly Catholic Austrians. Aided by a shadowy Serbian terrorist underground group called the Black Hand, some of these students resolved to kill the archduke.

As Franz Ferdinand and his wife, Sophie, were being driven through the narrow streets of Sarajevo on 28 June 1914, a band of young terrorists prepared their bombs. "One was so jammed in the crowd that he could not pull the bomb out of his pocket. A second saw a policeman standing near him and decided that any movement was too risky. A third felt sorry for the Archduke's wife and did nothing. A fourth lost his nerve and slipped off home."[165] But twenty-year-old Gavrilo Princip did not flinch. When a first bomb exploded but failed to injure the imperial couple, Princip thought the plot had failed. Minutes later, he was astounded to see the archduke and archduchess in their official car, just five feet from him. (The car had taken a wrong turn down a narrow side street.) Princip knew he could not throw his bomb; there was no room. So he pulled out his Browning pistol and fired two shots, point blank. He hit Franz Ferdinand in the throat, severing his carotid artery. His second shot hit Sophie in the abdomen. Both were dead within the hour.[166]

In Vienna, the humorless and harsh Franz Ferdinand had been unloved. Still, the assassination of the heir to the imperial throne had to be avenged. Austria-Hungary decided to use the "outrage" as a pretext to destroy Serbia. For this, though, the Austrians needed the backing of their powerful ally, Germany. The Austrians feared that if they went to war against Serbia, Russia would hasten to protect their Slavic brothers.

At this critical moment, when the life of Europe teetered in the balance, Germany's Kaiser Wilhelm II gave Austria-Hungary a "blank check." Germany would back Austria-Hungary in whatever she decided to do about Serbia, the Kaiser said.[167]

Europe was quite literally sitting on a powder keg. If Austria-Hungary moved against Serbia, Russia would come to Serbia's aid. If Russia came in Germany would declare war against Russia. If Germany attacked Russia, France was bound by treaty to race to Russia's defense. And if France was attacked, Great Britain would feel honor bound to stand by her. If Britain joined the war, so, too, would Canada, Australia, New Zealand, South Africa, and India. In a matter of days, what began as a localized conflict would become a *world war.*

Worse, Germany's ruler was Europe's "powder monkey." That is, he was running around the continent with explosives in hand. One of Wilhelm II's early acts was to "drop the pilot," to get rid of "the Iron Chancellor" Otto von Bismarck in 1890. Bismarck would never have risked his German Empire on a conflict in the Balkans. "The whole of the Balkans is not worth the bones of a single Pomeranian grenadier," he had said contemptuously. But Bismarck also had played the prophet: "If there is another war in the future," he had said, "it will come out of some damned foolish thing in the Balkans."

Now, even as the president was attending the Georgia funeral for Mrs. Wilson, Europe was sliding into war. Nor would it be a localized, limited war. Europe had seen a score of these in the hundred years since the defeat of Napoleon at Waterloo in 1815. This would be a war more terrible, more total than anything previously seen.

Several hundred years earlier, America was fresh on the world horizon, a land infinite with opportunity and electric with optimism. Now an ocean away, despair gripped the Old World, and the only opportunities seemed for destruction. Britain's foreign secretary, Sir Edward Grey, spoke of the hushed sense of anticipation all truly knowledgeable people felt in August 1914:

> "The lights are going out all over Europe. We shall not see them lit again in our lifetime."

Notes

Chapter One: Westward the Course (1492–1607)

1. Boorstin, Daniel J., *The Discoverers: A History of Man's Search to Know His World and Himself,* Random House, New York: 1983, p. 173.
2. Boorstin, p. 164.
3. Boorstin, p. 167.
4. Boorstin, p. 167.
5. Boorstin, p. 167.
6. Thomas, Hugh, *The Slave Trade: The Story of the Atlantic Slave Trade, 1440-1870,* Simon & Schuster, New York: 1997, p. 21.
7. Thomas, p. 23.
8. Thomas, p. 43.
9. Thomas, p. 44.
10. Thomas, p. 46.
11. Morison, Samuel Eliot, Commager, Henry Steele, and Leuchtenburg, William E., *A Concise History of the American Republic,* Oxford University Press, New York: 1977, p. 9.
12. Morison, Samuel Eliot, *The Great Explorers: The European Discovery of America,* Oxford University Press, New York: 1978, p. 431.
13. Morison, p. 399.
14. Morison, p. 400.
15. Morison, p. 401.
16. Gately, Iain, *Tobacco,* Grove Press, New York: 2002.
17. Morison, p. 403.
18. Morison, p. 432.
19. Morison, p. 415.
20. Morison, p. 421.
21. Morison, p. 422.
22. Morison, p. 422.
23. Morison, p. 425.
24. Morison, p. 427.
25. Morison, p. 430.
26. Royal, Robert, *1492 and All That: Political Manipulations of History,* Ethics and Public Policy Center, Washington, D.C.: 1992, p. 121.
27. Royal, p. 73.

28. Ibeji, Dr. Mike, *Black Death: The Disease,* "Origins," BBCi (online), 1 January 2001, p. 3.
29. Royal, p. 61.
30. Royal, p. 66.
31. Royal, p. 75.
32. Royal, p. 73.
33. Royal, p. 77.
34. Royal, p. 78.
35. Morison, p. 434.
36. Morison, p. 253.
37. Thomas, Hugh, *Conquest: Montezuma, Cortes, and the Fall of Old Mexico,* Simon & Schuster, New York: 1993, p. 70.
38. Boorstin, p. 177.
39. Morison, Commager, p. 11.
40. Morison, Samuel Eliot, *The European Discovery of America: The Southern Voyages,* Oxford University Press, New York: 1974, p. 280.
41. Morison, *The Southern Voyages,* p. 281.
42. Morison, *The Southern Voyages,* p. 284.
43. Morison, *The Southern Voyages,* p. 289.
44. Morison, pp. 129–168.
45. Morison, pp. 177, 179.
46. Morison, p. 174.
47. Morison, p. 174.
48. Morison, p. 273.
49. Morison, p. 549.
50. Morison, p. 567.
51. Boorstin, p. 260.
52. Boorstin, p. 261.
53. Morison, pp. 594–595.
54. Morison, p. 597.
55. Morison, p. 598.
56. Boorstin, p. 261.
57. Boorstin, p. 265.
58. Boorstin, p. 265.
59. Boorstin, p. 266.
60. Morison, p. 644.
61. Boorstin, p. 266.
62. Morison, Commager, p. 13.
63. Online source: www.royal.gov.uk.
64. Morison, p. 683.
65. Morison, p. 691.
66. Morison, p. 694.
67. Morison, p. 696.

Chapter Two: A City Upon a Hill (1607–1765)

1. Secretary of State's Office, Commonwealth of Massachusetts, online source: http://www.sec.state.ma.us/pre/presea/sealhis.htm.
2. Fischer, David Hackett, *Albion's Seed: Four British Folkways in America,* Oxford University Press, New York: 1989, p. 355.
3. Brinkley, Douglas, *American Heritage History of the United States,* Viking Penguin, New York: 1998, p. 30.
4. Mann, Charles C., *1491,* Knopf, New York: 2005, p. 58.

5. Brinkley, p. 30.
6. Brinkley, p. 30.
7. Online source: http://www.apva/org/history/pocahont.html.
8. Online source: http://www.apva/org/history/pocahont.html.
9. Online source: http://www.apva/org/history/pocahont.html.
10. Schlesinger, Arthur M. Jr., gen. ed., *The Almanac of American History,* G.P. Putnam's Sons, New York: 1983, p. 34.
11. Morison, Samuel Eliot, Commager, Henry Steele, and Leuchtenberg, William E., *A Concise History of the American Republic,* Oxford University Press, New York: 1977, p. 19.
12. Brinkley, p. 31.
13. Carnes, Mark C., gen. ed., *A History of American Life: Revised and Abridged,* Simon & Schuster, Inc., New York: 1996, p. 107.
14. Schlesinger, p. 36.
15. Boorstin, Daniel J., *The Americans: The Colonial Experience,* Vintage Books, New York: 1958, p. 56.
16. Morison, Commager, p. 21.
17. Morison, Commager, p. 22.
18. Online source: http://pilgrims.net/plymouth/history.
19. Morison, Commager, p. 25.
20. Morison, Commager, p. 25.
21. Online source: http//pilgrims.net/native_americans/massasoit.html.
22. Mansfield, Harvey C. and Winthrop, Delba, eds., *Alexis de Tocqueville: Democracy in America,* University of Chicago Press, Chicago: 2000, p. 34.
23. Dreuillette, Gabriel, *The Narrative of the Journey made in behalf of the Mission of the Abnaquiois, 1651,* Pilgrim Hall Museum, Plymouth, Mass., www.pilgrimhall.org.
24. Morison, Commager, p. 26.
25. Brinkley, p. 34.
26. Fischer, p. 18.
27. McDougall, Walter A., *Meditations on a High Holy Day: The Fourth of July,* online source: http://anglicanpck.org/resources/acu/July4McDougall.htm.
28. Fischer, p. 14.
29. Fischer, p. 13.
30. Niebuhr, Reinhold, *The Irony of American History,* Scribner Library of Contemporary Classics, reprinted ed., New York: 1952.
31. Online source: http://media.wiley.com/product_data/excerpt/53/04711516/0471151653.pdf.
32. Online source: http://www.nd.edu/~rbarger/www7/neprimer.html.
33. Online source: http://www.nd.edu/~rbarger/www7/neprimer.html.
34. Morison, Commager, p. 28.
35. Morison, Commager, p. 23.
36. Morison, Commager, p. 30.
37. Brinkley, p. 40.
38. Morison, Commager, p. 36.
39. Brinkley, p. 34.
40. Morison, Commager, p. 37.
41. Keegan, John, *Fields of Battle: The Wars for North America,* Random House, New York: 1995, p. 83.
42. Morison, Commager, p. 43.
43. *Catholic Encyclopedia,* www.newadvent.org/cathen/08420b.htm.
44. *Catholic Encyclopedia,* www.newadvent.org/cathen/08420b.htm.
45. Morison, Commager, p. 43.
46. Morison, Commager, p. 43.
47. Keegan, p. 103.

48. Keegan, p. 103.
49. Keegan, p. 105.
50. Morison, Commager, p. 51.
51. Morison, Commager, p. 51.
52. Online source: www.geocities.com/js_source/adframe04.html.
53. Isaacson, Walter, *Benjamin Franklin: An American Life,* Simon & Schuster, New York: 2003, p. 110.
54. Online source: www.geocities.com/js_source/adframe04.html.
55. Clark, Ronald, *Benjamin Franklin: A Biography,* Random House, New York: 1983, p. 18.
56. Clark, p. 20.
57. Morison, Commager, p. 56.
58. Ferling, John, *A Leap in the Dark: The Struggle to Create the American Republic,* Oxford University Press, New York: 2003, p. 4.
59. Ferling, p. 6.
60. Ferling, p. 7.
61. Flexner, James Thomas, *Washington: The Indispensable Man,* Little, Brown and Company, Boston: 1974, p. 16.
62. Flexner, p. 17.
63. Flexner, p. 17.
64. Flexner, p. 17.
65. Keegan, p. 109.
66. Flexner, p. 26.
67. Flexner, p. 26.
68. Keegan, p.110.
69. Keegan, p. 114.
70. Keegan, p. 116.
71. Keegan, p. 122.
72. Keegan, p. 120.
73. Keegan, p. 130.
74. Online source: http://www.britannia.com/gov/primes/prime5.html.
75. Online source: http://www.number10.gov.uk/output/Page 167.asp.
76. Online source: http://www.britannia.com/gov/primes/prime5.html.
77. Clark, p. 157.
78. Online source: http://www.britannia.com/gov/primes/prime5.html.
79. Clark, p. 157.
80. Clark, p. 159.

Chapter Three: The Greatest Revolution (1765–1783)

1. Isaacson, Walter, *Benjamin Franklin: An American Life,* Simon & Schuster, New York: 2003, p. 224.
2. Isaacson, p. 224.
3. Bobrick, Benson, *Angel in the Whirlwind: The Triumph of the American Revolution,* Penguin Books, New York: 1997, p. 72.
4. Morgan, Edmund S., *Benjamin Franklin,* Yale Nota Bene, New Haven, Conn.: 2003, p. 152-153.
5. Morgan, Edmund S., and Helen M. Morgan, *The Stamp Act Crisis,* Collier, New York: 1967, p. 311.
6. Morison, Samuel Eliot, Steele, Henry Commager, and Leuchtenburg, William E. *A Concise History of the American Republic,* Oxford University Press, New York: 1977, p. 68.
7. Morgan, Edmund S., *The Birth of the Republic: 1763-1789,* University of Chicago Press, Chicago: 1956, p. 19. Ferling, John, *A Leap in the Dark: The Struggle to Create the American Republic,* Oxford University Press, New York: 2003, p. 31.

8. Mayer, Henry, *A Son of Thunder: Patrick Henry and the American Republic,* University Press of Virginia, Charlottesville: 1991, p. 93.
9. Freeman, Douglas Southall, *George Washington: A Biography, Vol. III,* Charles Scribner's Sons, New York: 1951, p. 129.
10. Bobrick, p. 72.
11. Freeman, p. 136.
12. Freeman, p. 136.
13. Morgan, *Birth of the Republic,* p. 21.
14. Morgan, *Birth of the Republic,* p. 22.
15. Ferling, p. 35.
16. Morison, Commager, p. 69.
17. Ferling, p. 35.
18. Ferling, p. 35.
19. Morgan, *Birth of the Republic,* p. 17.
20. Robson, Eric, *The American Revolution in Its Political and Military Aspects, 1763–1783,* Norton Library, W.W. Norton & Co., Inc., New York: 1966.
21. Brinkley, Douglas, *The American Heritage History of the United States,* Viking Penguin, New York: 1998, p. 54.
22. Ferling, p. 40.
23. Ferling, p. 40.
24. Ferling, p. 38.
25. Maier, Pauline, *From Resistance to Revolution: Colonial Radicals and the Development of Opposition to Britain, 1765-1776,* W.W. Norton & Company, New York: 1991, p. 81.
26. McCullough, David, *John Adams,* Simon & Schuster, New York: 2001, p. 62.
27. Catton, Bruce and Catton, William B., *The Bold and Magnificent Dream: America's Founding Years: 1492-1815,* Gramercy Books, New York: 1978, p. 255.
28. Robson, p. 45.
29. Ferling, p. 40.
30. Catton and Catton, p. 264.
31. Ferling, p. 83.
32. Ferling, p. 83.
33. Catton and Catton, p. 259.
34. Robson, p. 63.
35. Robson, p. 64.
36. Robson, p. 65.
37. Robson, p. 64.
38. Maier, p. 114–115.
39. Maier, p. 114.
40. Robson, p. 65.
41. Ferling, p. 84.
42. Ferling, p. 71.
43. Clark, Ronald W., *Benjamin Franklin: A Biography,* Random House, New York: 1983, p. 58.
44. Bobrick, p. 86.
45. Bobrick, p. 86.
46. Robson, p. 66.
47. Catton and Catton, p. 267.
48. Robson, p. 67.
49. Catton and Catton, p. 268.
50. Catton and Catton, p. 268.
51. Ferling, p. 86.
52. Churchill, Winston S., *The Great Republic: A History of America,* Random House, New York: 1999, p. 62.
53. Ferling, p. 106.

54. Ferling, p. 106.
55. Bobrick, p. 90.
56. Churchill, p. 62.
57. Bobrick, p. 91.
58. Catton and Catton, p. 269.
59. Middlekauff, Robert, *The Glorious Cause: The American Revolution, 1763-1789,* Oxford University Press, New York: 1982, p. 207.
60. Flexner, James Thomas, *Washington: The Indispensable Man,* Little, Brown, Co., Boston: 1969, p. 58.
61. Ferling, p. 108.
62. Brands, H. W., *Franklin: The First American,* Doubleday, New York: 2000, pp. 464–490.
63. Catton and Catton, p. 272.
64. Brands, p. 488.
65. Brands, p. 488.
66. Fischer, David Hackett, *Paul Revere's Ride,* Oxford University Press, New York: 1994, p. 96.
67. Fischer, p. 104.
68. Fischer, p. 109.
69. Leckie, Robert, *George Washington's War: The Saga of the American Revolution,* HarperCollins: New York: 1993, p. 110.
70. Leckie, p. 110.
71. Leckie, p. 110.
72. Leckie, p. 115.
73. Catton and Catton, p. 279.
74. Churchill, p. 65.
75. Brands, p. 502.
76. Catton and Catton, p. 276.
77. Catton and Catton, p. 277.
78. Brands, p. 507.
79. Maier, Pauline, *American Scripture: Making the Declaration of Independence,* Alfred A. Knopf, New York: 1997, p. 33.
80. Maier, *American Scripture,* p. 33.
81. Maier, *American Scripture,* p. 33.
82. Paine, Thomas, *Common Sense,* Barnes & Noble Books, New York: 1995, pp. 19–20.
83. Paine, p. 42.
84. Morison, Commager, p. 80.
85. Morison, Commager, p. 80.
86. Maier, *American Scripture,* p. 98.
87. Maier, *American Scripture,* p. 135.
88. Spalding, Matthew, ed., *The Founders' Almanac,* The Heritage Foundation, Washington, D.C.: 2001.
89. Brands, p. 512.
90. Spalding, p. 230.
91. Leckie, p. 265.
92. McCullough, David, *1776,* Simon & Schuster, New York: 2005, p. 170.
93. McCullough, p. 175.
94. McCullough, p. 190.
95. McCullough, p. 191.
96. Flexner, James Thomas, *Washington: The Indispensable Man,* Little, Brown, and Company, Boston: 1974, p. 84.
97. Fischer, David Hackett, *Washington's Crossing,* Oxford University Press, New York: 2004, p. 108.
98. Brands, p. 527.
99. Churchill, p. 67.

100. Leckie, p. 329.
101. Leckie, p. 343.
102. Leckie, p. 401.
103. Catton and Catton, p. 307.
104. Leckie, p. 417.
105. Leckie, p. 419.
106. Royster, Charles, *A Revolutionary People at War: The Continental Army and American Character, 1775-1783,* The University of North Carolina Press, Chapel Hill, N.C.: 1986, p. 76.
107. Royster, p. 76.
108. Leckie, p. 492.
109. Leckie, p. 499.
110. Bobrick, p. 378.
111. McCullough, p. 304.
112. Leckie, p. 499.
113. Thomas, Evan, *John Paul Jones, Sailor, Hero, Father of the American Navy,* Simon & Schuster, New York: 2003, p. 182.
114. Morison, Samuel Eliot, *John Paul Jones: A Sailor's Biography,* Northeastern University Press, Boston, 1959, p. 233.
115. Morison, *John Paul Jones,* p. 233.
116. Morison, *John Paul Jones,* p. 233.
117. Thomas, p. 188.
118. Thomas, p. 197.
119. Leckie, p. 546.
120. Leckie, p. 565.
121. Churchill, p. 74.
122. Bobrick, p. 416.
123. Bobrick, p. 419.
124. Churchill, p. 82.
125. Churchill, p. 82.
126. Bobrick, p. 402.
127. Bobrick, p. 402.
128. Bass, Robert D., *Swamp Fox: The Life and Campaigns of General Francis Marion,* Sandlapper Publishing Co, Inc., Orangeburg, S.C.: 1974, p. 175.
129. Bass, p. 175.
130. Bobrick, p. 426.
131. National Park Service, Web site, www.nps.gov/cowpens.
132. National Park Service, Web site, www.nps.gov./cowpens.
133. Keegan, John, *Fields of Battle: The Wars for North America,* Vintage Books, New York: 1997, p. 178.
134. Keegan, p. 178.
135. Catton and Catton, p. 319.
136. Bobrick, p. 448.
137. Bobrick, p. 452.
138. Keegan, p. 184.
139. Bobrick, p. 453.
140. Bobrick, p. 459.
141. Bobrick, p. 462.
142. Bobrick, p. 464.
143. Bobrick, p. 464.
144. Leckie, p. 658.
145. Leckie, p. 660.
146. Flexner, p. 170.
147. Flexner, p. 174.

148. Flexner, p. 174.
149. Clark, Harrison, *All Cloudless Glory: Vol. II,* Regnery Publishing, Washington, D.C.: 1996, p. 62.
150. Bobrick, p. 479.
151. Bobrick, p. 480.

Chapter Four: Reflection and Choice: Framing the Constitution (1783–1789)

1. Isaacson, Walter, *Benjamin Franklin: An American Life,* Simon & Schuster, New York: 2003, p. 420.
2. Isaacson, p. 421.
3. Brookhiser, Richard, *Alexander Hamilton, American,* The Free Press, New York: 1999, p. 78.
4. Bailyn, Bernard, David, Brion Davis, David, Herbert Donald, Thomas, John L., Wiebe, Robert H., and Wood, Gordon S., *The Great Republic: A History of the American People,* Little, Brown and Company, Boston: 1977, p. 302.
5. Bailyn et al., p. 302.
6. Morison, Samuel Eliot, Commager, Henry Steele, and Leuchtenburg, William S., *A Concise History of the American Republic,* Oxford University Press, New York: 1977, p. 108.
7. Morison, Commager, p. 109.
8. Morison, Commager, p. 109.
9. Hitchens, Christopher, *Thomas Jefferson: Author of America,* HarperCollins, New York: 2005, p. 51.
10. Morris, Richard B., *Witnesses at the Creation: Hamilton, Madison, Jay and the Constitution,* Holt, Rinehart and Winston, New York: 1985, p. 219.
11. Koch, Adrienne, *Jefferson & Madison: The Great Collaboration,* Oxford University Press, New York: 1976, p. 15.
12. Koch, p. 30.
13. Koch, p. 30.
14. Morison, Commager, p. 111.
15. Rossiter, Clinton, *1787:The Grand Convention,* The Macmillan Company, New York: 1966, p. 47.
16. Bailey, Thomas A., *A Diplomatic History of the United States,* Prentice-Hall, Inc., Englewood Cliffs, N. J.: 1980, p. 61.
17. Bailey, p. 61.
18. Bailey, p. 62.
19. Kukla, Jon, *A Wilderness So Immense: The Louisiana Purchase and the Destiny of America,* Alfred A. Knopf, New York: 2003, p. 91.
20. Kukla, p. 90.
21. Morison, Commager, p. 113.
22. Morison, Commager, p. 113.
23. Rossiter, p. 56.
24. Mayer, Henry, *A Son of Thunder: Patrick Henry and the American Republic,* The University Press of Virginia, New York: 1991, p. 375.
25. Peterson, Merrill D., ed., *Thomas Jefferson: Writings,* Literary Classics of America, New York: 1984, p. 882.
26. Ketchum, Ralph, *James Madison: A Biography,* University Press of Virginia, New York: 1990, p. 186.
27. Van Doren, Carl, *The Great Rehearsal,* The Viking Press, New York: 1948, p. 7.

28. Mayer, p. 375.
29. Van Doren, p. 6.
30. Rossiter, p. 41.
31. Ketcham, p. 183.
32. Van Doren, p. 5.
33. Bowen, Catherine Drinker, *Miracle at Philadelphia: The Story of the Constitutional Convention, May to September, 1787,* The American Past/Book-of-the-Month Club, Inc., New York: 1986, p. 20.
34. Van Doren, p. 5.
35. Bowen, p. 20.
36. Flexner, p. 203.
37. Peterson, p. 908.
38. Ketcham, p. 195.
39. Bowen, p. 24.
40. Bowen, p. 106.
41. Bowen, p. 131.
42. Morison, Commager, p. 114.
43. Koch, p. 53.
44. Koch, p. 53.
45. Brands, H. W., *The First American: The Life and Times of Benjamin Franklin,* Doubleday, New York: 2000, p. 678.
46. Bowen, p. 83.
47. Bowen, p. 32.
48. Bowen, p. 187.
49. West, Thomas G., *Vindicating the Founders: Race, Sex, Class, and Justice in the Origin of America,* Rowman & Littlefield Publishers, Inc., Lanham, Maryland: 1997, p. 17.
50. Rossiter, pp. 32–33.
51. Rossiter, p. 32.
52. Bowen, p. 201.
53. Bowen, p. 201.
54. Morris, p. 215.
55. Bowen, p. 201.
56. Bowen, p. 202.
57. Morris, p. 216.
58. Morris, p. 216.
59. Jaffa, Harry V., *A New Birth of Freedom: Abraham Lincoln and the Coming of the Civil War,* Rowman & Littlefield Publishers, Inc., New York: 2000, p. 265.
60. Brands, p. 690.
61. Brands, p. 689.
62. Ketcham, p. 202.
63. Bowen, pp. 98–99.
64. Morgan, Edmund S., *The Meaning of Independence: John Adams, George Washington and Thomas Jefferson,* W.W. Norton & Company, New York: 1976, p. 29.
65. Van Doren, p. 15.
66. Brands, p. 691.
67. Bowen, p. 29.
68. Brookhiser, p. 72.
69. Brookhiser, p. 72.
70. Brookhiser, p. 162.
71. Morison, Commager, p. 121.
72. Morison, Commager, p. 121.
73. Ketcham, p. 266.
74. Noonan, John, *The Lustre of Our Country: The American Experience of Religious Freedom,* University of California Press, Berkeley, Calif.: 1998, p. 2.

75. Noonan, p. 4.
76. Morison, Commager, p. 121.
77. Mayer, pp. 436-437.
78. Brookhiser, p. 74.
79. Morison, Commager, p. 121.
80. Morison, Commager, p. 121.
81. Brookhiser, p. 74.

Chapter Five: The New Republic (1789–1801)

1. Flexner, James Thomas, *Washington: The Indispensable Man,* Little, Brown and Company, Boston: 1974, p. 215.
2. Flexner, p. 215.
3. Hunt, John Gabriel, ed., *The Inaugural Addresses of the Presidents,* Gramercy Books, New York: 1995, p. 6.
4. Catton, Bruce and Catton, William B., *The Bold and Magnificent Dream: America's Founding Years, 1492–1815,* Gramercy Books, New York, p. 393.
5. McCullough, David, *John Adams,* Simon & Schuster, New York: 2001, pp. 405–406.
6. McCullough, p. 406.
7. McCullough, p. 408.
8. Bailyn, Bernard, Davis, David Brion, David, Herbert Donald, Thomas, John L., Wiebe, Robert H., and Wood, Gordon S., *The Great Republic: A History of the American People,* Little, Brown & Co., Boston: 1977, p. 344.
9. Morison, Samuel Eliot, Commager, Henry Steele, and Leuchtenburg, William S., *A Concise History of the American Republic,* Oxford University Press, New York: 1977, p. 128.
10. McCullough, pp. 406-407.
11. Jaffa, Harry V., *A New Birth of Freedom: Abraham Lincoln and the Coming of the Civil War,* Rowman & Littlefield Publishers, Inc., Lanham, Md.: 2000, p. 491.
12. Rhodehamel, John, ed., *George Washington: Writings,* The Library of America, New York: 1997, p. 767.
13. Ketcham, Ralph, *James Madison: A Biography,* University Press of Virginia, New York: 1990, p. 290.
14. Ketcham, p. 290.
15. Koch, Adrienne, *Jefferson & Madison: The Great Collaboration,* Oxford University Press, New York: 1976, p. 41.
16. Online source: http://www.jmu.edu/madison/center/main_pages/madison_archives/era/parties/power/partnership.htm.
17. Ferling, John, *A Leap in the Dark: The Struggle to Create the American Republic,* Oxford University Press, New York: 2003, p. 324.
18. Flexner, p. 386.
19. Flexner, p. 386.
20. Flexner, p. 258.
21. Flexner, p. 258.
22. Flexner, p. 259.
23. Ferling, p. 346.
24. Flexner, p. 268.
25. McDonald, Forrest, *The American Presidency: An Intellectual History,* University Press of Kansas, Lawrence, Kan.: 1994, p. 230.
26. McDonald, p. 230.
27. McDonald, p. 230.
28. Brookhiser, Richard, *Alexander Hamilton: American,* The Free Press, New York: 1999, p. 104.

29. Brookhiser, p. 104.
30. Jefferson letter to Lafayette, 2 April 1790.
31. Stanlis, Peter J., ed., *Edmund Burke: Selected Speeches and Writings,* Regnery Publishing, Washington, D.C.: 1997, p. 515.
32. Elkins, Stanley and McKitrick, Eric, *The Age of Federalism: The Early American Republic, 1788-1800,* Oxford University Press, New York: 1993, p. 332.
33. Catton and Catton, p. 421.
34. Elkins and McKitrick, p. 342.
35. Elkins and McKitrick, p. 336.
36. Elkins and McKitrick, p. 340.
37. Elkins and McKitrick, p. 340.
38. Peterson, Merrill D., *Thomas Jefferson: Writings,* Library of America, New York: 1984, p. 1004.
39. Bailey, Thomas, *A Diplomatic History of the American People,* Prentice-Hall, Inc., Englewood Cliffs, N.J.: 1980, p. 72.
40. Elkins and McKitrick, p. 346.
41. Elkins and McKitrick, p. 356.
42. Elkins and McKitrick., p. 358.
43. Bailey, p. 87.
44. Bailey, p. 88.
45. Bailey, p. 88.
46. Bailey, p. 87.
47. Morison, Commager, p. 137.
48. BBC Web site, http://www.bbc.co.uk/dna/h2g2/alabaster/A481682, General "Mad Anthony" Wayne.
49. Morison, Commager, p. 138.
50. Morison, Commager, p. 138.
51. Catton and Catton, p. 426.
52. McDonald, p. 240.
53. Elkins and McKitrick, p. 481.
54. Morison, Commager, p. 139.
55. McDonald, p. 241.
56. Catton and Catton, p. 427.
57. Bailey, Thomas A., *A Diplomatic History of the American People,* Prentice-Hall, Inc., Englewood Cliffs, N.J.: 1980, p. 78.
58. Ferling, John, *A Leap in the Dark: The Struggle to Create the American Republic,* Oxford University Press, New York: 2003, p. 380.
59. Ferling, p. 380.
60. Ferling, p. 380.
61. Bailey, p. 79.
62. Bailey, p. 79.
63. Elkins and McKitrick, p. 483.
64. Bailey, p. 80.
65. Rodehamel, p. 971.
66. McCullough, p. 469.
67. McCullough, p. 469.
68. Furet, Francois and Ozouf, Mona, eds., trans. by Arthur Goldhammer, *A Critical Dictionary of the French Revolution,* The Belknap Press of Harvard University Press, Cambridge Mass.: 1989, p. 143.
69. Furet and Ozouf, p. 145.
70. Morison, Commager, p. 143.
71. Zvesper, John, *From Bullets to Ballots: The Election of 1800 and the First Peaceful Transfer of Political Power,* The Claremont Institute, Claremont, Calif.: 2003, p. 100.
72. Elkins and McKitrick, p. 694.

73. Churchill, Winston S., *The Great Republic: A History of America,* Random House, New York: 1999, p. 103.
74. Ferling, p. 422.
75. Elkins and McKitrick, p. 729.
76. Peterson, Merrill D., *Thomas Jefferson: Writings,* The Library of America, New York: 1984, p. 455.
77. Elkins and McKitrick, p. 721.
78. Elkins and McKitrick, p. 723.
79. Jaffa, p. 59.
80. Bailey, p. 95.
81. Bailey, p. 98.
82. Bailey, p. 98.
83. McCullough, David, *John Adams,* Simon & Schuster, New York: 2001, p. 586.
84. McCullough, p. 567.
85. Elkins and McKitrick, p. 744.
86. Elkins and McKitrick, p. 242.
87. Koch, p. 212.
88. Elkins and McKitrick, p. 736.
89. McCullough, p. 549.
90. McCullough, p. 550.
91. McCullough, p. 548.
92. Catton and Catton, p. 443.
93. Elkins and McKitrick, p. 747.
94. Elkins and McKitrick, p. 744.
95. McCullough, p. 562.
96. Hunt, John Gabriel, ed., *The Inaugural Addresses of the Presidents,* Gramercy Books, New York: 1995, p. 25.
97. Koch, p. 217.
98. Jaffa, p. 61.

Chapter Six: The Jeffersonians (1801–1829)

1. Conversation with Stephen Breyer, John F. Kennedy School of Government, 21 September 2003, online source: http://www.jfklibrary.org/forum_breyer.html.
2. Roosevelt, Theodore, *The Naval War of 1812,* Naval Institute Press, Annapolis, Md.: 1987, p. 405.
3. Dreisbach, Daniel, L., *Thomas Jefferson and the Wall of Separation,* New York University Press, New York: 2002, p. 10.
4. Dreisbach, p. 12.
5. Dreisbach, p. 12.
6. Dreisbach, p. 45.
7. Dreisbach, p. 48.
8. Dreisbach, p. 19.
9. Dreisbach, p. 19.
10. Dreisbach, p. 18.
11. Peterson, Merrill D., ed., *Thomas Jefferson: Writings,* The Library of America, New York: 1984, p. 1082.
12. Peterson, p. 1082.
13. Peterson, *The New Nation,* p. 704.
14. Peterson, *The New Nation,* p. 704.
15. McCullough, David, *John Adams,* Simon & Schuster, New York: 2001, p. 583.
16. Peterson, *The New Nation,* p. 708.

17. Whipple, A. B. C., *To the Shores of Tripoli: The Birth of the U.S. Navy and Marines*, William Morrow and Company, Inc., New York: 1991, p. 20.
18. Hitchens, Christopher, *Thomas Jefferson: Author of America*, HarperCollins Publishers, New York: 2005, p. 126.
19. Hitchens, p. 128.
20. Hitchens, p. 129.
21. Whipple, p. 27.
22. Morison, Samuel Eliot, *The Oxford History of the American People*, Vol. 2, Penguin Books, New York: 1994, p. 89.
23. McDonald, Forrest, *The Presidency of Thomas Jefferson*, University of Kansas Press, Lawrence, Kan.: 1976, p. 77.
24. Peterson, *The New Nation*, p. 799.
25. Morison, p. 89.
26. Whipple, p. 282.
27. Wheelan, Joseph, *Jefferson's War: America's First War on Terror, 1801-1805*, Carroll & Graf Publishers, New York: 2003, p. 363.
28. Wheelan, p. 368.
29. Ambrose, Stephen E. and Abell, Sam, *Lewis & Clark: Voyage of Discovery*, National Geographic Society, Washington, D.C.: 1998, p. 28.
30. Morison, p. 90.
31. Fleming, Thomas, *The Louisiana Purchase*, John Wiley & Sons, Inc., Hoboken, N.J.: 2003, p. 110.
32. Fleming, p. 117.
33. Fleming, p. 117.
34. Fleming, p. 80.
35. Fleming, p. 86.
36. Ketcham, Ralph, *James Madison: A Biography*, University of Virginia Press, Charlottesville, Va.: 1990, p. 417.
37. Fleming, p. 120.
38. Fleming, p. 134.
39. Kukla, Jon, *A Wilderness So Immense: The Louisiana Purchase and the Destiny of America*, Alfred A. Knopf, New York: 2003, p. 286.
40. Kukla, p. 286.
41. Morison, p. 92.
42. Fleming, p. 135.
43. Fleming, p. 162.
44. Kukla, p. 294.
45. Ketcham, p. 421.
46. Fleming, p. 141.
47. Kukla, p. 274.
48. Ketcham, p. 421.
49. Bailey, Thomas A., *A Diplomatic History of the American People*, Prentice-Hall, Inc., Englewood Cliffs, N.J.: 1980, p. 112.
50. Ambrose and Abell, p. 40.
51. Kukla, p. 296.
52. Cerami, Charles A., *Jefferson's Great Gamble*, Sourcebooks, Inc., Napierville, Ill.: 2003, p. 205.
53. Ambrose and Abell, p. 28.
54. Ambrose and Abell, p. 37.
55. Ambrose and Abell, p. 37.
56. Ambrose, Stephen E., *Undaunted Courage: Meriwether Lewis, Thomas Jefferson, and the Opening of the American West*, Simon & Schuster, New York: 1996, p. 99.
57. Ambrose and Abell, p. 36.
58. Morison, p. 92.

59. Ambrose and Abell, p. 143.
60. Ambrose, p. 154.
61. Ambrose, p. 171.
62. Morison, p. 93.
63. Ambrose, p. 89.
64. Morison, p. 94.
65. Brookhiser, p. 211.
66. Holland, Barbara, *Gentlemen's Blood,* Bloomsbury, New York: 2003, pp. 113–115.
67. Brookhiser, Richard, *Alexander Hamilton, American,* The Free Press, New York: 1999, p. 211.
68. Brookhiser, p. 213.
69. Brookhiser, p. 213.
70. Brookhiser, p. 214.
71. McDonald, p. 87.
72. Koch, Adrienne, *Jefferson & Madison: The Great Collaboration,* Oxford University Press, New York: 1976, p. 228.
73. Jefferson, Thomas, *Autobiography,* Capricorn, New York: 1959, p. 92.
74. McDonald, p. 90.
75. McDonald, p. 91.
76. Peterson, *The New Nation*, p. 796.
77. McDonald, p. 93.
78. Morison, p. 95.
79. Fleming, Thomas, *Duel: Alexander Hamilton, Aaron Burr, and the Future of America,* Basic Books, New York: 1999, p. 383.
80. Morison, p. 95.
81. Morison, p. 96.
82. Fleming, *Duel,* p. 385.
83. Fleming, *Duel,* p. 392.
84. Morison, p. 96.
85. Fleming, *Duel,* p. 392.
86. Fleming, *Duel,* p. 392.
87. Morison, p. 99.
88. Morison, p. 98.
89. McDonald, p. 106.
90. McDonald, p. 106.
91. Peterson, p. 528.
92. Peterson, *The New Nation,* p. 920.
93. Ketcham, p. 482.
94. Morison, p. 105.
95. Morison, p. 105.
96. Utley, Robert M. and Washburn, Wilcomb E., *Indian Wars,* Houghton Mifflin Company, Boston: 1977, p. 117.
97. Morison, p. 109.
98. Utley and Washburn, p. 121.
99. Leckie, Robert, *The Wars of America,* Harper & Row, Publishers, New York: 1981, p. 233.
100. Leckie, p. 232.
101. Morison, p. 109.
102. Morison, p. 111.
103. Morison, p. 113.
104. Berton, Pierre, *The Invasion of Canada: 1812–1813,* Penguin Books Canada, Ltd., Toronto: 1980, p. 254.
105. Berton, p. 256.
106. Berton, pp. 257–259.

107. Berton, Pierre, *Flames Across the Border: 1813-1814,* Penguin Books Canada, Ltd., Toronto: 1981, pp. 85–87.
108. Morison, p. 121.
109. Morison, p. 121.
110. Leckie, p. 288.
111. Lord, Walter, *The Dawn's Early Light,* Johns Hopkins University Press, Baltimore, Md.: 1972, pp. 72–73.
112. Lord, p. 176.
113. Lord, p. 176.
114. Lord, p. 182.
115. Leckie, p. 296.
116. Leckie, p. 296.
117. Leckie, p. 298.
118. Remini, Robert V., *The Life of Andrew Jackson,* Penguin Books, New York: 1988, pp. 72–72.
119. Morison, p. 124.
120. Remini, p. 84.
121. Morison, p. 129.
122. Morison, p. 125.
123. Remini, Robert V., *The Battle of New Orleans: Andrew Jackson and America's First Military Victory,* Penguin Books, New York: 1999, pp. 66–68.
124. Remini, *Battle,* p. 189.
125. Leckie, p. 310.
126. Remini, Robert V., *The Battle of New Orleans,* Penguin Books, New York: 1999, p. 88.
127. Remini, *Battle,* p. 88.
128. Remini, *Battle,* p. 88.
129. Remini, *Battle,* p. 88.
130. Remini, *Life,* p. 99.
131. Morison, p. 126.
132. Remini, *Life,* p. 104.
133. Remini, *Battle,* p. 152.
134. Remini, *Battle,* p. 142.
135. Remini, *Battle,* p. 142.
136. Remini, *Battle,* p. 157.
137. Remini, *Life,* p. 105.
138. Remini, *Battle,* p. 192.
139. Remini, *Battle,* p. 199.
140. Morison, p. 128.
141. Remini, *Life,* p. 121.
142. Remini, *Life,* p. 122.
143. Morison, p. 145.
144. Remini, Robert V., *Henry Clay: Statesman for the Union,* W.W. Norton & Company, New York: 1991, p. 165.
145. Remini, *Henry Clay: Statesman for the Union,* p. 165.
146. Morison, p. 139.
147. Peterson, *Writings,* p. 1434.
148. Peterson, *Writings,* p. 1434.
149. Bailey, p. 181.
150. Bailey, p. 182.
151. Bailey, p. 185.
152. Morison, p. 157.
153. Morison, p. 156.
154. Bennett, William J., ed., *Our Sacred Honor,* Simon & Schuster, New York: 1997, p. 413.

155. Young, Daniel, *The Cavalier Daily,* 13 April 2005, online source: http://www.cavalierdaily.com/CVArticle.asp?ID=23175&pid=1288.
156. Young, online source: http://www.cavalierdaily.com/CVArticle.asp?ID=23175&pid=1288.
157. Koch, Adrienne, *Jefferson and Madison: The Great Collaboration,* Koneckey & Konecky, Old Saybrook, Conn., p. 260.
158. McCullough, David, *John Adams,* Simon & Schuster, New York: 2001, p. 603.
159. Peterson, *Writings,* p. 1517.
160. McCullough, p. 646.

Chapter Seven: Jackson and Democracy (1829–1849)

1. Remini, Robert V., *The Life of Andrew Jackson,* Penguin Books, New York: 1988, p. 44.
2. Remini, Robert V., *Henry Clay: Statesman for the Union,* W.W. Norton & Company, New York: 1991, p. 271.
3. Remini, *Clay,* p. 266.
4. Morison, Samuel Eliot, *The Oxford History of the American People, Volume 2: 1789-Reconstruction,* Penguin Books, New York: 1994, p. 159.
5. Remini, Robert V., *John Quincy Adams,* Henry Holt & Company, New York: 2002, p. 123.
6. Remini, Robert V., *The Jacksonian Era,* Harlan Davidson, Inc., Arlington Heights, Ill.: 1989, p. 13.
7. Holland, Barbara, *Gentlemen's Blood,* Bloomsbury, New York: 2003, pp. 51.
8. Remini, pp. 53–54.
9. Remini, *John Quincy Adams,* p. 127.
10. McDonald, Forrest, *The American Presidency: An Intellectual History,* University Press of Kansas, Lawrence, Kan.: 1994, p. 317.
11. Remini, *Era,* p. 20.
12. Morison, p. 163.
13. Online source: http://college.hmco.com/history/readerscomp/gahff/html/ff_108500_kitchencabin.htm.
14. Remini, *Life,* p. 190.
15. Remini, *Life,* p. 191.
16. Remini, *Life,* p. 11.
17. Morison, p. 167.
18. Burstein, Andrew, *The Passions of Andrew Jackson,* Alfred A. Knopf, New York: 2003, p. 175.
19. Peterson, Merrill D., *The Great Triumvirate: Webster, Clay, and Calhoun,* Oxford University Press, New York: 1987, p. 19.
20. Peterson, p. 19.
21. Coit, Margaret L., *John C. Calhoun: American Portrait,* Houghton Mifflin Company, Boston, Mass., 1950, p. 35.
22. Coit, p. 24.
23. Coit, p. 28.
24. Peterson, p. 23.
25. Coit, p. 44.
26. Coit, p. 45.
27. Peterson, p. 18.
28. Hofstadter, Richard, *The American Political Tradition: And the Men Who Made It,* Vintage Books, New York: 1948, p. 74.
29. Peterson, p. 236.
30. Peterson, p. 236.

31. Hofstadter, p. 74.
32. Peterson, p. 27.
33. Hofstadter, p. 75.
34. Hofstadter, p. 78.
35. Coit, p. 397.
36. Hofstadter, p. 79.
37. Remini, *Life*, p. 195.
38. Ketcham, p. 641.
39. Freehling, William W., *Prelude to Civil War: The Nullification Controversy in South Carolina, 1816-1836*, Harper & Row, Publishers, New York: 1966, p. 192.
40. Ketcham, Ralph, *James Madison: A Biography*, University Press of Virginia, Charlottesville, Va.: 1990, pp. 640-641.
41. Farber, Daniel, *Lincoln's Constitution*, University of Chicago Press, Chicago: 2003, p. 67.
42. Freehling, p. 193.
43. Remini, *Era*, p. 66.
44. Remini, *Life*, p. 239.
45. Remini, *Life*, p. 239.
46. Remini, *Era*, p. 66.
47. Morison, p. 177.
48. Remini, *Era*, p. 68.
49. Freehling, p. 53.
50. Freehling, p. 11.
51. Freehling, p. 53.
52. Remini, *Life*, p. 235.
53. Remini, *Life*, p. 236.
54. Freehling, p. 157.
55. Remini, *Era*, p. 68.
56. Remini, *Era*, p. 69.
57. Morison, p. 254.
58. Remini, *Era*, p. 41.
59. Morison, p. 188.
60. Remini, *Life*, p. 219.
61. Morison, p. 192.
62. Remini, *Era*, p. 45.
63. Bailyn, Bernard, Davis, David Brion, David, Herbert Donald, Thomas, John L., Wiebe, Robert H., and Wood, Gordon S., *The Great Republic: A History of the American People*, Little, Brown and Company, Boston: 1977, p. 439.
64. Utley, Robert M. and Washburn, Wilcomb E., *Indian Wars*, Houghton Mifflin Company, Boston: 1977, p. 137.
65. Utley and Washburn, p. 138.
66. Morison, p. 189.
67. Remini, *Era*, p. 51.
68. Utley and Washburn, p. 139.
69. Morison, p. 192.
70. Morison, p. 193.
71. Remini, *Life*, p. 218.
72. Morison, p. 193.
73. Tocqueville, Alexis de, *Democracy in America*, trans., ed., with an introduction by Harvey Mansfield, The University of Chicago Press, Chicago and London: 2000, p. 309.
74. Tocqueville, pp. 310–311.
75. Peterson, p. 208.
76. Remini, *Life*, p. 229.
77. Schlesinger, Arthur M. Jr., *The Age of Jackson*, Little, Brown and Company, Boston: 1945, p. 113.

78. Morison, p. 180.
79. Remini, *Life*, p. 229.
80. Peterson, p. 239.
81. Remini, *Life*, p. 272.
82. Freehling, p. 84.
83. Remini, *John Quincy Adams*, p. 143.
84. Remini, *John Quincy Adams*, p. 140.
85. Remini, *John Quincy Adams*, p. 134.
86. Morison, p. 276.
87. Remini, *John Quincy Adams*, p. 147.
88. Remini, *John Quincy Adams*, p. 148.
89. Online source: http://www.law.umkc.edu/faculty/projects/ftrials/amistad/AMI_SCT2.HTM.
90. Morison, p. 276.
91. Morison, p. 209.
92. Morison, p. 211.
93. Bailyn et al., p. 598.
94. Morison, p. 318.
95. Bailyn et al., p. 599.
96. Bailyn et al., p. 599.
97. Peterson, p. 353.
98. Peterson, p. 373.
99. Peterson, p. 352.
100. Peterson, p. 352.
101. Morison, p. 319.
102. Morison, p. 303.
103. DeVoto, Bernard, *The Year of Decision: 1846*, Houghton Mifflin Company, Boston: 1942, p. 55.
104. DeVoto, p. 65.
105. Morison, p. 308.
106. Leckie, Robert, *The Wars of America*, Harper & Row, Publishers, New York: 1981, p. 325.
107. Bailey, Thomas A., *A Diplomatic History of the American People*, Prentice-Hall, Inc., Englewood Cliffs, N.J.: 1980, p. 228.
108. Bailey, p. 229.
109. Bailey, p. 235.
110. Leckie, p. 325.
111. Bailey, p. 254.
112. Leckie, p. 326.
113. Morison, p. 323.
114. Morison, p. 321.
115. Leckie, p. 326.
116. Leckie, p. 327.
117. Leckie, p. 327.
118. Bailey, p. 259.
119. Bailey, p. 259.
120. Morison, p. 325.
121. Morison, p. 325.
122. Morison, p. 325.
123. Cain, William E., ed., *William Lloyd Garrison and the Fight Against Slavery*, Bedford Books of St. Martin's Press, Boston: 1995, p. 115.
124. Morison, p. 327.
125. Leckie, p. 374.
126. Leckie, p. 375.

127. Online source: http://www.infoplease.com/ipa/A0004615.html.
128. DeVoto, pp. 472–476.
129. Morison, p. 325.
130. Morison, p. 330.
131. Remini, *John Quincy Adams,* p. 155.
132. Cain, p. 121.

Chapter Eight: The Rising Storm (1849–1861)

1. Graebner, Norman A., *Empire on the Pacific: A Study in Continental Expansion,* Regina Books, Claremont, Calif.: 1983, pp. 224–225.
2. McPherson, James M., *The Illustrated Battle Cry of Freedom: The Civil War Era,* Oxford University Press, New York: 2003, p. 51.
3. Boritt, Gabor S., ed., *The Historian's Lincoln,* University of Illinois Press, Urbana and Chicago, Ill.: 1988, p. 6.
4. Boritt, p. 6.
5. Cooper, John S., "The Free Soil Campaign of 1848," online article: http://www.suite101.com/article.cfm/presidents_and_first_ladies/59853.
6. Cooper.
7. Morison, Samuel Eliot, *The Oxford History of the American People: Volume Two,* Penguin Books, New York: 1994, p. 334.
8. Brands, H. W., *The Age of Gold: The California Gold Rush and the New American Dream,* Doubleday, New York: 2002, p. 63.
9. Brands, p. 48.
10. Brands, p. 46.
11. Peterson, Merrill D., *The Great Triumvirate: Webster, Clay, and Calhoun,* Oxford University Press, New York: 1987, p. 452.
12. Peterson, p. 461.
13. McPherson, p. 60.
14. McPherson, p. 53.
15. Peterson, p. 460.
16. Peterson, p. 456.
17. Peterson, p. 455.
18. Peterson, p. 456.
19. Bartlett's Familiar Quotations, online edition, http://www.bartleby.com/100/348.4.html.
20. Bartleby's online quotations, http://www.bartleby.com/66/17/37317.html.
21. Online Source: http://www.dartmouth.edu/~dwebster/speeches/seventh-march.html.
22. Peterson, p. 463.
23. Morison, p. 332.
24. Morison, p. 334.
25. Jaffa, Harry V., *A New Birth of Freedom: Abraham Lincoln and the Coming of the Civil War,* Roman & Littlefield Publishers, Inc., Lanham, Md.: 2000, p. 212.
26. Jaffa, p. 213.
27. Peterson, p. 466.
28. Morison, p. 339.
29. McPherson, p. 74.
30. McPherson, p. 74.
31. Morison, p. 336.
32. McPherson, p. 57.
33. Peterson, p. 472.
34. Morison, pp. 338–339.

35. Peterson, p. 467.
36. Peterson, p. 496.
37. Vance, James E. Jr., *The North American Railroad: Its Origin, Evolution, and Geography,* The Johns Hopkins University Press, Baltimore, Md.: 1995, p. 32.
38. Vance, p. 95.
39. Vance, p. 107.
40. Morison, p. 342.
41. Carnes, Mark C., gen. ed., *A History of American Life,* revised and abridged, Simon & Schuster, Inc., New York: 1996, p. 530.
42. Carnes, p. 532.
43. Carnes, pp. 530–532.
44. McFeely, William S., *Frederick Douglass,* Simon & Schuster, New York: 1991, p. 93.
45. Stampp, Kenneth M., *America in 1857: A Nation on the Brink,* Oxford University Press, New York: 1990, p. 215.
46. Faust, Patricia L., ed., *Historical Times Illustrated Encyclopedia of the Civil War,* Harper and Row, New York: 1986, p. 609.
47. Carnes, p. 537.
48. Carnes, p. 537.
49. Morison, p. 217.
50. Morison, p. 340.
51. Morison, p. 340.
52. Carnes, p. 536.
53. Morison, p. 272.
54. Carnes, p. 646.
55. Morison, p. 359.
56. Morison, p. 341.
57. Online source: http://americancivilwar.com/women/hbs.html.
58. Andrews, William L., *The Oxford Frederick Douglass Reader,* Oxford University Press, New York: 1996, p. 113.
59. Andrews, p. 129.
60. George M. Frederickson, *William Lloyd Garrison: Great Lives Observed,* Prentice-Hall, Inc., Englewood Cliffs, N.J.: 1968, p. 92.
61. Andrews, p. 93.
62. Oates, Stephen B., *The Approaching Fury Voices of the Storm, 1820-1861,* HarperCollins, New York: 1997, p. 75.
63. McFeely, p. 178.
64. Peterson, p. 488.
65. Peterson, p. 498.
66. Basler, Roy P. , ed., *The Collected Works of Abraham Lincoln,* Vol. II, Rutgers University Press, New Brunswick, N.J.: 1953, p. 126.
67. Oates, p. 295.
68. Stampp, p. 54.
69. Basler, p. 323.
70. McPherson, p. 117.
71. Oates, p. 300.
72. McPherson, p. 124.
73. McPherson, p. 124.
74. Morison, p. 360.
75. Stampp, p. 92.
76. Hunt, John Gabriel, ed., *The Inaugural Addresses of the Presidents,* Gramercy Books, New York: 1995, p. 177.
77. Stampp, p. 93.
78. Stampp, p. 95.

79. Jaffa, Harry V., *Crisis of the House Divided,* University of Chicago Press, Chicago: 1982, p. 310.
80. Morison, p. 363.
81. Stampp, p. 105.
82. Hummel, Jeffrey Rogers, *Emancipating Slaves, Enslaving Free Men: A History of the Civil War,* Open Court Publishing Company, Chicago, Ill.: 1996, p. 96.
83. McPherson, p. 84.
84. Stampp, p. 104.
85. Stampp, p. 104.
86. Basler, Volume II, p. 466.
87. Jaffa, *Crisis,* p. 311.
88. McPherson, p. 63.
89. Donald, p. 204.
90. Morison, p. 365.
91. Oates, p. 262.
92. Jaffa, *Crisis,* p. 337.
93. Oates, p. 256.
94. Jaffa, pp. 332–333.
95. Jaffa, *Crisis*, p. 356.
96. Donald, p. 229.
97. Oates, Stephen B., *To Purge This Land with Blood: A Biography of John Brown,* University of Massachusetts Press, Amherst, Mass.: 1984, p. 282.
98. Freeman, Douglas Southall, *R.E. Lee: A Biography,* Charles Scribner's Sons, New York: 1936, p. 395.
99. Freeman, p. 399.
100. McPherson, p. 162.
101. Oates, *Purge,* p. 337.
102. Oates, *Purge,* p. 318.
103. Oates, *Purge,* p. 318.
104. Oates, *Purge,* p. 345.
105. Oates, *Purge,* p. 351.
106. Oates, *Purge,* pp. 351–352.
107. Donald, David Herbert, *Lincoln,* Simon & Schuster, New York: 1995, p. 239.
108. Basler, Volume III, p. 550.
109. Catton, Bruce, *The Coming Fury,* Doubleday & Co., Garden City, N.Y.: 1961, p. 61.
110. Catton, p. 61.
111. Cong. Globe, 33rd Cong. 1st Sess. p. 214 (20 February 1854).
112. Morison, p. 375.
113. Catton, p. 161.
114. Donald, p. 277.
115. Catton, p. 224.
116. Catton, p. 264.
117. Catton, p. 264.
118. Hunt, John Gabriel, ed., *The Inaugural Addresses of the Presidents,* Gramercy Books, New York: 1995, pp. 187–197.

Chapter Nine: Freedom's Fiery Trial (1860–1863)

1. Online source, http://www.bartleby.com/73/1969.html.
2. Catton, Bruce, *The Coming Fury,* Doubleday & Company, Garden City, N.Y.: 1961, p. 138.
3. Catton, p. 137.

4. Catton, p. 106.
5. Porter, Bruce D., "The Warfare State," *American Heritage Magazine,* Jul./Aug. 1994, Vol. 45, Issue 4, online source: http://www.americanheritage.com/articles/magazine/ah/1994/4/1994_4_56.shtml.
6. Dew, Charles B., *Apostles of Disunion: Southern Secession Commissioners and the Causes of the Civil War,* University Press of Virginia, Charlottesville, Va.: 2001, p. 33.
7. Dew, p. 33.
8. Dew, p. 40.
9. Dew, pp. 64–65.
10. Donald, David Herbert, *Lincoln,* Simon & Schuster, New York: 1995, p. 137.
11. Catton, p. 113.
12. Jaffa, Harry V., *A New Birth of Freedom: Abraham Lincoln and the Coming of the Civil War,* Rowman & Littlefield, Lanham, Md.: 2000, p. 215.
13. Catton, p. 113.
14. Catton, pp. 113–114.
15. Davis, William C., *Look Away! A History of the Confederate States of America,* The Free Press, New York: 2002, pp. 97–98.
16. Davis, p. 66.
17. Davis, p. 66.
18. Jaffa, p. 222.
19. Jaffa, p. 222.
20. Online source: Jefferson Davis Inaugural Address, 18 February 1861, http://www.pointsouth.com/csanet/greatmen/davis/pres-ad1.htm.
21. Kennedy, John F., *Profiles in Courage,* Harper & Brothers Publishers, New York: 1956, p. 107.
22. Kennedy, p. 115.
23. Kennedy, p. 114.
24. Haley, James L., *Sam Houston,* University of Oklahoma Press, Norman, Okla.: 2002, p. 390.
25. Haley, pp. 390–391.
26. Haley, p. 394.
27. Haley, p. 386.
28. Haley, p. 388.
29. Freeman, Douglas Southall, *R.E. Lee: A Biography,* Charles Scribner's Sons, New York: 1934, p. 429.
30. Freeman, p. 433.
31. Freeman, p. 435.
32. Freeman, p. 436.
33. Freeman, p. 437.
34. Freeman, p. 437.
35. Catton, p. 253.
36. Catton, p. 252.
37. Catton, p. 173.
38. Catton, p. 278.
39. Catton, p. 286.
40. Catton, p. 297.
41. Catton, p. 302.
42. Catton, p. 311.
43. McPherson, James M., *The Illustrated Battle Cry of Freedom,* Oxford University Press, New York: 2003, p. 215.
44. Farber, Daniel, *Lincoln's Constitution,* University fo Chicago Press, Chicago: 2003, p. 16.
45. McPherson, p. 228.
46. Farber, p. 17.
47. Farber, p. 17.

48. *McCullough v. Maryland* (1819), Online source: http://www.answers.com/topic/mcculloch-v-maryland.
49. Blight, David W., *Frederick Douglass' Civil War,* Louisiana State University Press, Baton Rouge, La.: 1989, p. 64.
50. McDonald, Forrest, *The American Presidency: An Intellectual History,* University Press of Kansas, Lawrence, Kan.: 1994, pp. 400–401.
51. Basler, Roy P., ed., *The Collected Works of Abraham Lincoln,* Vol. IV, Rutgers University Press, New Brunswick, N.J.: 1953, pp. 438–439.
52. McPherson, p. 244.
53. Morison, Samuel Eliot, *The Oxford History of the American People, Volume Two,* The Penguin Group, New York: 1972, p. 394.
54. Donald, David Herbert, *Lincoln,* Simon & Schuster, New York: 1995, p. 315.
55. Blight, p. 151.
56. Donald, David Herbert, *We Are Lincoln Men,* Simon & Schuster, New York: 2003, p. 127.
57. Donald, *Lincoln Men*, p. 197.
58. Morison, p. 402.
59. Morison, p. 405.
60. Morison, p. 421.
61. McPherson, p. 322.
62. McPherson, James M., ed., *We Cannot Escape History: Lincoln and the Last Best Hope of Earth,* University of Illinois Press, Urbana and Chicago: 1995, p. 5.
63. McPherson, *We Cannot Escape History,* p. 5.
64. Gordon, John Steele, *A Thread Across the Ocean,* Harper, New York: 2003.
65. Morison, p. 412.
66. Mahin, Dean B., *One War at a Time,* Brassey's, Washington, D.C.: 1999, p. 69.
67. Mahin, p. 77.
68. Mahin, p. 71.
69. Mahin, p. 71.
70. Bellow, Adam, *In Praise of Nepotism,* Doubleday, New York: 2003, p. 357.
71. Mahin, p. 78.
72. McPherson, p. 323.
73. Borritt, Gabor S., ed., *Lincoln's Generals,* Oxford University Press, New York: 1994, p. 22.
74. Borritt, p. 25.
75. Morison, p. 414.
76. McPherson, p. 358.
77. McPherson, p. 358.
78. Morison, p. 425.
79. Borritt, p. 15.
80. Morison, p. 414.
81. Williams, T. Harry, *Lincoln and His Generals,* Vintage Books, New York: 1952, p. 114.
82. Borritt, p. 46.
83. Morison, p. 430.
84. Morison, p. 430.
85. Tucker, Spencer C., *A Short History of the Civil War at Sea,* SR Books, Wilmington, Del.: 2002, p. 40.
86. Tucker, p. 40.
87. McPherson, p. 311.
88. Morison, p. 421.
89. McPherson, p. 313.
90. McPherson, p. 353.
91. Blight, p. 154.
92. Donald, *Lincoln,* p. 367.

93. Blight, p. 139.
94. Blight, p. 125.
95. Blight, p. 145.
96. Blight, p. 145.
97. Blight, p. 145.
98. Donald, *Lincoln,* p. 368.
99. Donald, *Lincoln,* p. 369.
100. Sears, Stephen W., *Landscape Turned Red: The Battle of Antietam,* Ticknor & Fields, New York: 1983, p. 225.
101. Moe, p. 187.
102. Sears, p. 316.
103. Sears, p. 316.
104. Sears, p. 316.
105. McPherson, p. 466.
106. Sears, pp. 294, 296.
107. Sears, p. 296.
108. Sears, p. 317.
109. Williams, p. 176.
110. Williams, p. 177.
111. Waugh, John C., *The Class of 1846,* Warner Books, Inc., New York: 1994, p. 365. The reference in Lincoln's statement is to Exodus 6:5.
112. Morison, p. 435.
113. Lord Charnwood, *Lincoln: A Biography,* Madison Books, Lanham, Md.: 1996, p. 236.
114. Morison, p. 438.
115. Guelzo, Allen C., *Lincoln's Emancipation Proclamation: The End of Slavery in America,* Simon & Schuster, New York: 2004, p. 354.
116. Guelzo, p. 354.
117. Guelzo, p. 181.
118. Guelzo, p. 182.
119. Klingaman, William K., *Abraham Lincoln and the Road to Emancipation: 1861-1865,* Viking, New York: 2001, p. 227.
120. Guelzo, p. 182.
121. Guelzo, p. 183.
122. Klingaman, p. 228.
123. Guelzo, p. 2.
124. Online source: http://www.archives.gov/exhibit_hall/featured_documents/emancipation_proclamation/transcript.html.
125. McPherson, p. 336.
126. Morison, p. 436.
127. Basler, Vol. VI, pp. 64–65.
128. Sideman, Belle Becker and Friedman, Lillian, eds., *Europe Looks at the Civil War,* Collier Books, New York: 1960, pp. 176–177.
129. Sideman and Friedman, pp. 176–177.
130. McPherson, *We Cannot Escape History,* p. 9.
131. Mill, J. S., *The Contest in America,* Online source: http://www.gutenberg.org/dirs/etext04/conam10h.htm.
132. Blight, p. 96.
133. Cornish, Dudley Taylor, *The Sable Arm,* University Press of Kansas, Lawrence, Kan.: 1987, p. 132.
134. Morison, p. 419.
135. Morison, p. 419.
136. McPherson, p. 507.
137. National Park Service, online source: www.cr.nps..gov/hps/abpp/battles/va035.htm

138. McPherson, p. 561.
139. National Park Service, online source: www.cr.nps.gov/hps/abpp/battles/va035.htm.

Chapter Ten: A New Birth of Freedom (1863–1865)

1. Borritt, Gabor S., ed., *Lincoln's Generals,* Oxford University Press, New York: 1994, p. 85.
2. McPherson, James M., *Hallowed Ground: A Walk at Gettysburg,* Crown Publishers, New York: 2003, p. 80.
3. McPherson, p. 81.
4. McPherson, pp. 81–82.
5. McPherson, p. 85.
6. Sears, Stephen W., *Gettysburg,* Houghton Mifflin Company, Boston: 2003, p. 294.
7. McPherson, James M., *The Illustrated Battle Cry of Freedom,* Oxford University Press, New York: 2003, p. 222.
8. McPherson, *Battle Cry,* p. 222.
9. Sears, p. 321.
10. Moe, Richard, *The Last Full Measure: The Life and Death of the First Minnesota Volunteers:* Henry Holt and Company, New York: 1993, p. 277.
11. Moe, p. 277.
12. McPherson, James M., *For Cause and Comrades: Why Men Fought in the Civil War,* Oxford Univeristy Press, New York: 1997, p. 21.
13. Borritt, p. 89.
14. McPherson, *Battle Cry,* p. 498.
15. Ward, Geoffrey C., *The Civil War: An Illustrated History,* Alfred A. Knopf, New York: 1990, pp. 270–271.
16. Bunting, Josiah III, *Ulysses S. Grant,* Henry Holt and Company, LLC, New York: 2004, p. 39.
17. Borritt, p. 98.
18. Basler Roy, ed., *The Collected Works of Abraham Lincoln*, Vol. VI, Rutgers University Press, New Brunswick, N.J.: 1953, p. 328.
19. Basler, Vol. VI, p. 329.
20. Sears, p. 495.
21. Foote, Shelby, *Stars in Their Courses: The Gettysburg Campaign,* The Modern Library, New York: 1994, pp. 258–59.
22. Foote, p. 259.
23. Foote, p. 260.
24. Foote, p. 260.
25. Carhart, Tom, *Lost Triumph: Lee's Real Plan at Gettysburg—And Why It Failed,* Penguin Group, New York: 2005, p. xiii.
26. McPherson, pp. 526–527.
27. Morison, Samuel Eliot, *Oxford History of the American People,* Vol. Two, The Penguin Group, New York: 1972, p. 451.
28. Wills, Garry, *Lincoln at Gettysburg,* Simon & Schuster, New York: 1992, p. 21.
29. Wills, p. 25.
30. Wills, p. 25.
31. Basler, Vol. VII, p. 25.
32. Anastaplo, George, *Abraham Lincoln: A Constitutional Biography,* Rowman & Littlefield, Lanham, Md.: 1999, p. 226.
33. Goodwin, Doris Kearns, *Team of Rivals: The Political Genius of Abraham Lincoln,* Simon & Schuster, New York: 2005.
34. Bunting, Josiah III, *Ulysses S. Grant,* Times Books, New York: 2004, p. 51.

35. Bunting, p. 51.
36. Goodwin, p. 529.
37. Goodwin, p. 529.
38. Goodwin, p. 529.
39. Goodwin, p. 529.
40. Bunting, p. 53.
41. Bunting, p. 53.
42. Bunting, p. 53.
43. McFeely, William S., *Grant: A Biography,* W.W. Norton & Co., New York: 1981, p. 153.
44. Bunting, p. 58.
45. Bunting, p. 58.
46. Bunting, p. 58.
47. Bunting, p. 58.
48. Bunting, p. 59.
49. McPherson, *Battle Cry,* p. 643.
50. McFeely, p. 152.
51. Turner, Justin G. and Turner, Linda Levitt, *Mary Todd Lincoln: Her Life and Letters,* Alfred A. Knopf, New York: 1972, p. 155.
52. Turner and Turner, p. 156.
53. Donald, David Herbert, Baker, Jean H., and Holt, Michael F., *The Civil War and Reconstruction,* WW. Norton & Company, Inc., New York: 2001, p. 291.
54. Donald, Baker, and Holt, p. 291.
55. McPherson, p. 517.
56. Goodwin, p. 549.
57. Goodwin, p. 550.
58. Basler, Vol. VI, pp. 406–410.
59. Online source: http://www.mycivilwar.com/leaders/sherman_william.htm.
60. McFeely, p. 210.
61. Borritt, p. 152.
62. Goodwin, p. 624.
63. Waugh, John C., *Re-Electing Lincoln,* Crown Publishing, New York: 1997, p. 300.
64. Waugh, p. 301.
65. Waugh, p. 295.
66. Waugh, p. 297.
67. Morison, p. 483.
68. Basler, Vol. VII, p. 282.
69. McPherson, p. 734.
70. Nevins, Allan, *The War for the Union, Vol. III, The Organized War,* Charles Scribner's Sons, New York: 1971, p. 293.
71. McPherson, *Battle Cry of Freedom,* p. 264.
72. Arlington National Cemetery, online source: http://www.arlingtoncemetery.net/meigs.htm.
73. Ward, p. 316
74. Donald, David Herbert, *Lincoln,* Simon & Schuster, New York: 1995, p. 565.
75. Donald, p. 567.
76. Grant, U. S., *Personal Memoirs of U. S. Grant,* Vol. II, Charles L. Webster & Company, New York: 1885, p. 485.
77. Grant, pp. 489–490.
78. Winik, Jay, *April 1865: The Month That Saved America,* HarperCollins, New York: 2001, p. 197.
79. Winik, pp. 197–198.
80. Morison, p. 499.
81. Peterson, Merrill D., *Lincoln in American Memory,* Oxford University Press, New York: 1994, p. 4.

82. Peterson, p. 4.
83. Peterson, p. 7.
84. Crocker, H. W. III, *Robert E. Lee on Leadership,* Prima Publishing, Roseville, Calif.: 2000, p. 164.
85. Flood, Charles Bracelyn, *Grant and Sherman: The Friendship that Won the Civil War,* Farrar, Stauss and Giroux, New York: 2005, pp. 332–333.
86. Peterson, p. 25.
87. Peterson, p. 25.
88. Peterson, p. 25.
89. Morison, p. 286.

Chapter Eleven: To Bind Up the Nation's Wounds (1865–1877)

1. Tucker, Spencer C., *A Short History of the Civil War at Sea,* SR Books, Wilmington, Del.: 2002, p. 174.
2. Bailey, Thomas A., *A Diplomatic History of the American People,* Prentice-Hall, Inc., Englewood Cliffs, N.J.: 1980, p. 353.
3. Catton, Bruce, *This Hallowed Ground: The Story of the Union Side of the Civil War,* Castle Books, Edison, N.J.: 2002, p. 398.
4. Catton, p. 399.
5. Catton, p. 400.
6. Catton, p. 400.
7. Online source: http://www.people.virginia.edu/~mmd5f/memorial.htm.
8. Online source: http://www.people.virginia.edu/~mmd5f/memorial.htm.
9. Winik, Jay, *April 1865: The Month That Saved America*, Harper Collins, New York: 2001, p. 225.
10. Winik, p. 225.
11. Bailey, p. 353.
12. Bailey, p. 354.
13. Bailey, p. 354.
14. Bailey, p. 356.
15. Bailey, p. 357.
16. Bailey, p. 374.
17. Bailey, p. 375.
18. Waite, P. B., *The Life and Times of Confederation, 1864-1867,* University of Toronto Press, Toronto: 1962, p. 305.
19. Moore, Christopher, *1867: How the Fathers Made a Deal,* McClelland & Stewart, Inc., Toronto: 1997, p. 240.
20. Waite, p. 304.
21. Waite, p. 304.
22. "The Martyr" was originally published in *Battle Pieces and Aspects of the War,* Herman Melville, Harper & Brothers, New York: 1866.
23. Bunting, Josiah III, *Ulysses S. Grant,* Henry Holt and Company, New York: 2004, p. 71.
24. Bunting, p. 71, emphasis added.
25. Bunting, p. 71.
26. Bunting, p. 72.
27. Trefousse, Hans L., *Andrew Johnson: A Biography,* W.W. Norton & Company, New York: 1989, p. 198.
28. Trefousse, p. 198.

29. Trefousse, p. 198.
30. Smith, Jean Edward, *Grant*, Simon & Schuster, New York: 2001, p. 417.
31. Smith, p. 418.
32. Smith, p. 418.
33. Smith, p. 418.
34. Smith, p. 418.
35. Ward, Geoffrey C., *The Civil War: An Illustrated History,* Alfred A. Knopf, New York: 1990, p. 382.
36. Smith, p. 422.
37. Smith, p. 422.
38. Donald, David Herbert, Baker, Jean H., and Holt, Michael F., *The Civil War and Reconstruction,* W.W. Norton & Company, New York: 2001, p. 479.
39. Morison, Samuel Eliot, *Oxford History of the American People,* Vol. Two, The Penguin Group, N.Y.: 1972, p. 515.
40. Trefousse, p. 243.
41. Trefousse, p. 243.
42. Morison, p. 514.
43. Foner, Eric and Mahoney, Olivia, *America's Reconstruction: People and Politics after the Civil War,* HarperCollins, New York: 1995, p. 82.
44. Smith, p. 424.
45. Smith, p. 425.
46. Foner and Mahoney, p. 82.
47. Trefousse, p. 233.
48. Trefousse, p. 233.
49. Morison, p. 510.
50. Donald, Baker, and Holt, p. 481.
51. Morison, p. 511.
52. Smith, p. 426.
53. Smith, p. 426.
54. Bunting, p. 78.
55. Smith, p. 427.
56. Bunting, p. 78.
57. Smith, p. 426.
58. Morison, p. 512.
59. Morison, p. 513.
60. Trefousse, p. 341.
61. Trefousse, p. 341.
62. Morison, p. 516.
63. Smith, p. 444.
64. Smith, p. 444.
65. Foner and Mahoney, p. 91.
66. Foner and Mahoney, p. 91.
67. Smith, p. 455.
68. McFeely, William S., *Frederick Douglass,* Simon & Schuster, New York: 1991, p. 262.
69. Rehnquist, William H., *Grand Inquests: The Historic Impeachments of Justice Samuel Chase and President Andrew Johnson,* William Morrow, New York: 1992, p. 240.
70. Rehnquist, p. 241.
71. Smith, p. 454.
72. Smith, p. 454.
73. Bunting, p. 82.
74. Morison, p. 518.
75. Rehnquist, William H., *Centennial Crisis: The Disputed Election of 1876,* Alfred A. Knopf, New York: 2004, p. 75.
76. Bunting, p. 83.

77. Foner and Mahoney, p. 89.
78. Smith, p. 460.
79. Ward, p. 335.
80. Morison, p. 519.
81. Donald, Baker, and Holt, p. 490.
82. Donald, Baker, and Holt, p. 490.
83. Morison, p. 517.
84. Bunting, p. 20.
85. Bunting, p. 20.
86. Smith, Jean Edward, *Grant,* Simon & Schuster, New York: 2001, p. 489.
87. Morison, Samuel Eliot, *The Oxford History of the American People,* Vol. 2, The Penguin Group, New York: 1994, p. 35.
88. Morison, p. 35.
89. Bailey, Thomas A., *A Diplomatic History of the American People,* Prentice-Hall, Inc., Englewood Cliffs, N.J.: 1980, p. 378.
90. Bailey, p. 388.
91. Rehnquist, *Crisis,* p. 16.
92. Donald, Baker, and Holt, p. 479.
93. Donald, Baker, and Holt, p. 500.
94. Gates, Henry Louis Jr., ed., *Douglass,* Library of America, New York: 1994, p. 885.
95. Bunting, p. 141.
96. Bunting, p. 141.
97. Bunting, p. 141.
98. Bunting, p. 142.
99. Safire, William, *The New Language of Politics,* revised ed., Collier Books, New York: 1972, cited online at: http://www.gop.com/About/AboutRead.aspx?AboutType=6.
100. McFeely, William S., *Frederick Douglass,* Simon & Schuster, New York: 1991, p. 266.
101. McFeely, p. 267.
102. McFeely, p. 269.
103. Bailyn, Bernard, Davis, David Brion, Donald, David Herbert, Thomas, John L., Wiebe, Robert H., and Wood, Gordon S., *The Great Republic: A History of the American People,* Little, Brown and Company, Boston: 1977, p. 769.
104. *TIME* Almanac, 2004, Pearson Education, Inc., Needham, Mass.: 2003, pp. 175, 179.
105. Grosvenor, Edwin S. and Wesson, Morgan, *Alexander Graham Bell,* Harry N. Abrams, Inc., New York: 1997, p. 69.
106. Grosvenor and Wesson, p. 69.
107. Grosvenor and Wesson, p. 73.
108. Rehnquist, *Crisis,* p. 8.
109. Morison, p. 59.
110. Rehnquist, *Crisis,* p. 79.
111. Bailyn, p. 804.
112. Zwick, Jim. "Political Cartoons of Thomas Nast," http://www.boondocksnet.com/gallery/nast_intro.html In Jim Zwick, ed., *Political Cartoons and Cartoonists.* http://www.boondocksnet.com/gallery/pc_intro.html (25 February 2004).
113. Rehnquist, *Crisis,* p. 76.
114. Rehnquist, *Crisis,* p. 76.
115. Morison, p. 38.
116. Donald, Baker, and Holt, p. 630.
117. Donald, Baker, and Holt, p. 618.
118. Donald, Baker, and Holt, p. 632.
119. Bunting, p. 143.
120. Trefousse, Hans L., *Rutherford B. Hayes,* Times Books, New York: 2002, p. 79.
121. Rehnquist, *Crisis,* p. 114.

122. Trefousse, *Hayes,* p. 75.
123. Rehnquist, *Crisis,* p. 101.
124. Rehnquist, *Crisis,* p. 103.
125. Rehnquist, *Crisis,* p. 103.
126. Trefousse, *Hayes,* p. 105.
127. Trefousse, *Hayes,* p. 98.
128. Trefousse, *Hayes,* p. 104.
129. Bunting, p. 116.

Chapter Twelve: An Age More Golden than Gilded? (1877–1897)

1. Ambrose, Stephen E., *Nothing Like It in the World: The Men Who Built the Transcontinental Railroad: 1863–1869,* Simon & Schuster, New York: 2000, p. 377.
2. Ambrose, p. 377.
3. Rehnquist, William H., *Centennial Crisis: The Disputed Election of 1876,* Alfred A. Knopf, New York: 2004, p. 95.
4. Gordon, John Steele, *An Empire of Wealth: The Epic History of American Economic Power,* HarperCollins, New York: 2004, p. 211.
5. Gordon, p. 235.
6. Gordon, p. 248.
7. Gordon, p. 248.
8. Gordon, p. 244.
9. Trefousse, Hans L., *Rutherford B. Hayes,* Times Books, New York: 2002, p. 89.
10. Morison, Samuel Eliot, *Oxford History of the American People,* Vol. 3, The Penguin Group, New York: 1972, p. 40.
11. Trefousse, p. 96.
12. Brands, H. W., *T.R.: The Last Romantic,* Basic Books, New York: 1997, p. 78.
13. Brands, p. 79.
14. Brands, p. 80.
15. Trefousse, p. 113.
16. Trefousse, p. 125.
17. Grosvenor, Edwin and Wesson, Morgan, *Alexander Graham Bell,* Harry N. Abrams, Inc., New York: 1997, p. 105.
18. Grosvenor and Wesson, p. 107.
19. Morison, p. 40.
20. Jeffers, H. Paul, *An Honest President,* HarperCollins, New York: 2000, p. 192.
21. Online source: http://www.whitehouse.gov/history/presidents/ca21.html.
22. Graff, Henry F., *Grover Cleveland,* Times Books, New York: 2002, p. 55.
23. Jeffers, p. 110.
24. Jeffers, p. 110.
25. Morison, p. 44.
26. Morison, p. 44.
27. Jeffers, p. 111.
28. Morison, p. 44.
29. Jeffers, p. 118.
30. Jeffers, p. 117.
31. Morison, p. 45.
32. Bailyn, Bernard, Davis, David Brion, Donald, David Herbert, Thomas, John L., Wiebe, Robert H., and Wood, Gordon S., *The Great Republic: A History of the American People,* Little, Brown and Company, Boston: 1977, p. 850.

33. Bailyn et al., p. 851.
34. Morison, p. 105.
35. Morison, p. 69.
36. Israel, Paul, *Edison: A Life of Invention,* John Wiley & Sons, Inc., New York: 1998, p. 174.
37. Morison, p. 72.
38. Morison, p. 46.
39. Morison, p. 45.
40. Jeffers, p. 186.
41. Schlesinger, Arthur, M. Jr., ed., *The Almanac of American History,* G.P. Putnam's Sons, New York: 1983, pp. 357-358.
42. Smith, p. 626.
43. Smith, p. 609.
44. Smith, p. 627.
45. Smith, p. 627.
46. Smith, p. 627.
47. Online source: http://www.libertystatepark.org/statueofliberty/sol3.shtml.
48. Jeffers, p. 187.
49. *TIME (Magazine) Almanac,* 2004, New York, pp. 175, 179.
50. Smith, p. 516.
51. Smith, p. 516.
52. Donald, David Herbert, *Lincoln,* Simon & Schuster, New Ork: 1995, pp. 393–395.
53. Morison, p. 60.
54. Utley, Robert M. and Washburn, Wilcomb E., *Indian Wars,* Houghton Mifflin Company, Boston: 1977, p. 227.
55. Utley and Washburn, p. 227.
56. Morison, p. 61.
57. Morison, p. 61.
58. Utley and Washburn, p. 294.
59. Morison, p. 63.
60. Morison, p. 63.
61. Ravitch, Diane, ed., *The American Reader: Words That Moved a Nation,* HarperCollins, New York: 2000, pp. 291–292.
62. Utley and Washburn, p. 298.
63. Utley and Washburn, p. 299.
64. Utley and Washburn, p. 299.
65. Utley and Washburn, p. 300.
66. Jeffers, p. 207.
67. Brands, H. W., *TR: The Last Romantic,* Basic Books, New York: 1997, p. 184.
68. Elshstain, Jean Bethke, *Jane Addams and the Dream of American Democracy,* Basic Books, New York: 2002, p. 98.
69. Elshtain, p. 95.
70. Elshtain, p. 83.
71. Elshtain, p. 97.
72. Elshtain, p. 94.
73. Jeffers, p. 220.
74. Jeffers, p. 222.
75. Bailyn et al., p. 790.
76. Schlesinger, p. 370.
77. Schlesinger, p. 370.
78. Morison, p. 48.
79. Morison, p. 48.
80. Bailyn et al., p. 878.
81. Bailyn et al., p. 786.
82. Online source: www.deere.com.

83. Bailyn et al., p. 778.
84. McFeely, p. 300.
85. Bailyn et al., p. 796.
86. Harvey, Rowland Hill, *Samuel Gompers: Champion of the Toiling Masses,* Stanford University Press, New York: 1935, p. 101.
87. Harvey, p. 101.
88. Bailyn et al., p. 881.
89. Bailyn et al., p. 881.
90. Krass, Peter, *Carnegie,* John Wiley & Sons, Inc., Hoboken, N.J.: 2002, p. 285.
91. Morison, p. 85.
92. Krass, p. 294.
93. Krass, p. 272.
94. Carnegie, Andrew, "Wealth," *North American Review,* 148, no. 391 (June 1889): 653, 657–62.
95. Krass, p. 295.
96. Krass, p. 277.
97. Krass, p. 268.
98. Krass, p. 295.
99. Krass, p. 295.
100. Krass, p. 288.
101. Krass, p. 290.
102. Jeffers, p. 248.
103. Jeffers, p. 248.
104. Jeffers, pp. 227–228.
105. Krass, p. 296.
106. Morison, p. 110.
107. McFeely, William S., *Frederick Douglass,* Simon & Schuster, New York: 1991, p. 371.
108. McFeely, p. 371.
109. McFeely, p. 371.
110. Morison, p. 111.
111. Meacham, Jon, *Franklin and Winston: An Intimate Portrait of an Epic Friendship,* Random House, New York: 2003, p. 150.
112. Jeffers, p. 272.
113. Brands, H. W., *The Reckless Decade: America in the 1890s,* St. Martin's Press, New York, 1995, p. 147.
114. Brands, *Reckless,* p. 147.
115. Morison, p. 112.
116. Morison, p. 113.
117. Brands, *Reckless,* p. 149.
118. Brands, *Reckless,* p. 153.
119. Graff, Henry F., *Grover Cleveland,* Times Books, New York: 2002, p. 119.
120. Harvey, p. 78.
121. Bailyn et al. p. 883.
122. McFeely, p. 377.
123. McFeely, p. 380.
124. McFeely, p. 380.
125. McFeely, p. 383.
126. Morison, p. 116.
127. O'Toole, Patricia, *When Trumpets Call: Theodore Roosevelt After the White House,* Simon & Schuster, New York: 2005, p. 15.
128. Morison, p. 116.
129. Brands, p. 299.
130. Gutmann, Peter, online source: http://www.classicalnotes.net/classics/newworld.html.

131. Gutmann.
132. Gutmann.
133. Gutmann.
134. Morison, p. 37.

Chapter Thirteen: The American Dynamo— Shadowed by War (1897–1914)

1. Morris, Edmund, *The Rise of Theodore Roosevelt,* Ballantine Books, New York: 1979, p. 493.
2. Brands, H. W., *TR: The Last Romantic,* Basic Books, New York: 1997, p. 280.
3. Zimmermann, Warren, *First Great Triumph,* Farrar, Giroux and Strauss, New York: 2002, p. 229.
4. Zimmermann, p. 213.
5. Zimmermann, p. 100.
6. Zimmermann, p. 117.
7. Zimmermann, p. 228.
8. Morris, p. 513.
9. Zimmermann, p. 228.
10. Roosevelt, Theodore, with additional text by Richard Bak, *The Rough Riders,* Taylor Publishing, Dallas, Tx. 1997, p. 113.
11. Bailey, Thomas A., *A Diplomatic History of the American People,* Prentice-Hall, Inc., Englewood Cliffs, N.J.: 1980, p. 454.
12. Bailey, p. 455.
13. Bailey, p. 456.
14. Morris, p. 606.
15. Bailey, p. 456.
16. Morris, p. 602.
17. Morris, p. 602.
18. Bailey, p. 461.
19. Bailey, p. 461.
20. Morris, p. 610.
21. Morris, p. 608.
22. Morris, p. 608.
23. Morris, p. 600.
24. Morris, p. 607.
25. Zimmermann, p. 257.
26. Traxel, David, *1898: The Birth of the American Century,* Alfred A. Knopf, New York: 1998, p. 143.
27. Traxel, p. 144.
28. Morris, p. 647.
29. Traxel, p. 135.
30. Traxel, p. 137.
31. Traxel, p. 179.
32. Traxel, p. 181.
33. Roosevelt, p. 121.
34. Morris, p. 634.
35. Morris, p. 646.
36. Traxel, p. 193.
37. Traxel, p. 197.
38. Traxel, p. 206.

39. Gilbert, Martin, *Churchill: A Life*, Henry Holt and Company, New York: 1991, p. 80.
40. Morison, Samuel Eliot, *The Oxford History of the American People, Vol. Three*, Penguin Books, New York: 1972, p. 118.
41. Zimmermann, p. 250.
42. Morison, p. 123.
43. Morison, p. 124.
44. Traxel, p. 215.
45. Morris, pp. 673–674.
46. Morris, p. 673.
47. Brands, p. 363.
48. Morris, p. 675.
49. Morris, p. 685.
50. Brands, p. 368.
51. Traxel, p. 143.
52. Beisner, Robert L., *Twelve Against Empire: The Anti-Imperialists, 1898-1900,* McGraw-Hill Book Company, New York: 1968, p. 157.
53. Beisner, p. 158.
54. Beisner, p. 158.
55. Morison, p. 127.
56. Beisner, p. 125.
57. Morison, p. 129.
58. Morris, p. 741.
59. Morison, Samuel Eliot, Commager, Henry Steele, and Leuchtenburg, William E., *A Concise History of the American Republic,* Oxford University Press, New York: 1977, p. 514.
60. *Theodore Roosevelt Inaugural* pamphlet, National Historic Site, New York, National Park Service, U.S. Department of the Interior.
61. Morris, Edmund, *Theodore Rex,* Random House, New York: 2001, p. 54.
62. Bailey, p. 488.
63. Bailey, p. 487.
64. Brands, p. 455.
65. Brands, p. 455.
66. Brands, p. 457.
67. Harbaugh, William Henry, *Power and Responsibility: The Life and Times of Theodore Roosevelt,* Farrar, Straus and Cudahy, New York: 1961, p. 169.
68. Harbaugh, p. 169.
69. Morris, *Rex,* p. 174.
70. Harbaugh, p. 158.
71. Harbaugh, p. 160.
72. Harbaugh, p. 162.
73. Harbaugh, p. 307.
74. Morison, p. 136.
75. Harbaugh, p. 164.
76. Morison, Commager, p. 518.
77. Morison, Commager, p. 518.
78. Harbaugh, p. 215.
79. Brands, p. 509.
80. Brands, p. 509.
81. Morris, *Rex,* p. 114.
82. Morris, *Rex,* p. 114.
83. Morison, Commager, p. 520.
84. Carlson, Allan, *The "American Way": Family, and Community in the Shaping of the American Identity,* ISI Books, Wilmington, Del.: 2003, p. 1.
85. Carlson, p. 2.
86. Carlson, p. 1.

87. Bailey, p. 499.
88. Morris, *Rex,* p. 104.
89. Morris, *Rex,* p. 102.
90. Harbaugh, p. 188.
91. Harbaugh, p. 188.
92. Harbaugh, p. 202.
93. Bailey, p. 491.
94. Bailey, p. 493.
95. Bailey, p. 495.
96. Bailey, p. 497.
97. Bailey, p. 497.
98. Brands, p. 469.
99. Morison, Commager, p. 498.
100. Online source: http://eorr.home.netcom.com/JPJ/jpj.html.
101. Brands, p. 634.
102. O'Toole, Patricia, *When Trumpets Call: Theodore Roosevelt after the White House,* Simon & Schuster, New York: 2005, p. 21.
103. O'Toole, p. 22.
104. Morris, *Rex,* p. 526.
105. O'Toole, pp. 15–16.
106. Morison, Commager, p. 522.
107. Morison, p. 155.
108. Morison, p. 157.
109. Bailyn, Bernard, David, Brion Davis, Donald, Herbert David, Thomas, John L., Wiebe, Robert H., and Wood, Gordon S., *The Great Republic: A History of the American People,* Little, Brown and Company, Boston: 1977, p. 840.
110. Morison, p. 156.
111. Brands, p. 663.
112. Gilbert, Martin, *A History of the Twentieth Century, Vol. I (1900-1933),* William Morrow and Company, New York: 1997, p. 208.
113. Morison, p. 159.
114. Morison, p. 159.
115. *The Canadian Encyclopedia, Year 2000 Edition,* McClelland & Stewart, Inc., Toronto: 2000, p. 1302.
116. Morison, p. 160.
117. Gilbert, p. 236.
118. Gilbert, p. 243.
119. Bailyn et al, p. 943.
120. Brands, p. 670.
121. Online source: http://www.uscg.mil/lantarea/iip/General/history.shtml.
122. "Estimated Wealth of 12 Men Lost in Titanic Disaster is $191 Million," *Truro Daily News,* St. John, New Brunswick, 27 April 1912, p. 3.
123. Lynch, Don and Marschall, Ken, *Titanic: An Illustrated History,* The Madison Press Limited, New York: 1992, p. 19.
124. Lynch and Marschall, p. 192.
125. Gilbert, p. 265.
126. Lynch and Marschall, pp. 184–185.
127. Morison, p. 162.
128. Gould, Lewis L., *Grand Old Party: A History of the Republicans,* Random House, New York: 2003, p. 181.
129. Brands, p. 697.
130. Brands, p. 679.
131. Brands, p. 707.
132. Brands, p. 708.

133. Gould, p. 187.
134. Gould, p. 188.
135. Gould, p. 188.
136. Brands, p. 712.
137. Morison, p. 164.
138. Bailyn, p. 963.
139. Brands, p. 719.
140. Bailyn, et al, p. 924.
141. Brands, p. 717.
142. Brands, p. 721.
143. Morison, p. 166.
144. Bailyn et al, p. 942.
145. Morison, p. 168.
146. Heckscher, August, *Woodrow Wilson: A Biography,* Charles Scribner's Sons, New York: 1991, p. 306.
147. Morison, p. 169.
148. Bailyn et al, p. 974.
149. Morison, p. 169.
150. Heckscher, p. 288.
151. Heckscher, p. 295.
152. Bailey, pp. 545–546.
153. Black, Conrad, *Franklin Delano Roosevelt: Champion of Freedom*, Public Affairs Press, New York: 2003, p. 73.
154. Heckscher, p. 295.
155. Heckscher, p. 396.
156. Heckscher, p. 290.
157. Morison, p. 173.
158. Heckscher, p. 292.
159. Heckscher, p. 309.
160. Peterson, Merrill D., *Lincoln in American Memory,* Oxford University Press, New York: 1994, p. 170.
161. Bailyn et al. p. 958.
162. Morison, p. 167.
163. Bailyn et al., p. 946.
164. Morison, p. 167.
165. Fromkin, David, *Europe's Last Summer: Who Started the Great War in 1914?* Alfred A. Knopf, New York: 2004, pp. 134–135.
166. Fromkin, pp. 135–136.
167. Fromkin, p. 157.

Index